D0129567

Advanced Programming in the UNIX® Environment

Addison-Wesley Professional Computing Series

Brian W. Kernighan, Consulting Editor

Ken Arnold/John Peyton, *A C User's Guide to ANSI C*

Tom Cargill, *C++ Programming Style*

William R. Cheswick/Steven M. Bellovin, *Firewalls and Internet Security: Repelling the Wily Hacker*

David A. Curry, *UNIX® System Security: A Guide for Users and System Administrators*

Erich Gamma/Richard Helm/Ralph Johnson/John Vlissides, *Design Patterns: Elements of Reusable Object-Oriented Software*

David R. Hanson, *C Interfaces and Implementations: Techniques for Creating Reusable Software*

John Lakos, *Large-Scale C++ Software Design*

Scott Meyers, *Effective C++: 50 Specific Ways to Improve Your Programs and Designs*

Scott Meyers, *More Effective C++: 35 New Ways to Improve Your Programs and Designs*

Robert B. Murray, *C++ Strategies and Tactics*

David R. Musser/Atul Saini, *STL Tutorial and Reference Guide: C++ Programming with the Standard Template Library*

John K. Ousterhout, *Tcl and the Tk Toolkit*

Craig Partridge, *Gigabit Networking*

J. Stephen Pendergrast Jr., *Desktop KornShell Graphical Programming*

Radia Perlman, *Interconnections: Bridges and Routers*

David M. Piscitello/A. Lyman Chapin, *Open Systems Networking: TCP/IP and OSI*

Stephen A. Rago, *UNIX® System V Network Programming*

Curt Schimmel, *UNIX® Systems for Modern Architectures: Symmetric Multiprocessing and Caching for Kernel Programmers*

W. Richard Stevens, *Advanced Programming in the UNIX® Environment*

W. Richard Stevens, *TCP/IP Illustrated, Volume 1: The Protocols*

W. Richard Stevens, *TCP/IP Illustrated, Volume 3: TCP for Transactions, HTTP, NNTP, and the UNIX Domain Protocols*

Gary R. Wright/W. Richard Stevens, *TCP/IP Illustrated, Volume 2: The Implementation*

Advanced Programming in the UNIX ® Environment

W. Richard Stevens

Many of the designations used by manufacturers and sellers to distinguish their products are claimed as trademarks. Where those designations appear in this book, and Pearson Education was aware of a trademark claim, the designations have been printed with initial capital letters or in all capitals.

The programs and applications presented in this book have been included for their instructional value. They have been tested with care, but are not guaranteed for any particular purpose. The publisher does not offer any warranties oe representations, nor does it accept any liabilities with respect to the programs or applications.

Copyright © 1993 by Pearson Education, Inc.
This edition is published by arrangement with Pearson Education, Inc.

All rights reserved. No part of this publication may be reproduced, stored in a database or retrieval system, or transmitted in any form or by any means, electronic, mechanical, photocopying, recording, or otherwise, without the prior written permission of the publisher.

ISBN 81-7808-096-6

First ISE Reprint, 1998
Second ISE Reprint, 1999
Third Indian Reprint, 2000
Fourth Indian Reprint, 2000
Fifth Indian Reprint, 2001
Sixth Indian Reprint, 2001
Seventh Indian Reprint, 2001
Eighth Indian Reprint, 2001
Ninth Indian Reprint, 2002
Tenth Indian Reprint, 2002
Eleventh Indian Reprint, 2003

This edition is manufactured in India and is authorized for sale only in India, Bangladesh, Pakistan, Nepal, Sri Lanka and the Maldives.

Published by Pearson Education (Singapore) Pte. Ltd., Indian Branch, 482 F.I.E. Patparganj, Delhi 110 092, India

Printed in India by Saurabh Print O Pack.

*To MTS, the Michigan Terminal System,
and the 360/67.*

Contents

Preface

Introduction

This book describes the programming interface to the Unix system—the system call interface and many of the functions provided in the standard C library. It is intended for anyone writing programs that run under Unix.

Like most operating systems, Unix provides numerous services to the programs that are running—open a file, read a file, start a new program, allocate a region of memory, get the current time-of-day, and so on. This has been termed the *system call interface*. Additionally, the standard C library provides numerous functions that are used by almost every C program (format a variable's value for output, compare two strings, etc.).

The system call interface and the library routines have traditionally been described in Sections 2 and 3 of the *Unix Programmer's Manual*. This book is not a duplication of these sections. Examples and rationale are missing from the *Unix Programmer's Manual*, and that's what this book provides.

Unix Standards

The proliferation of different versions of Unix during the 1980s has been tempered by the various international standards that were started during the late 1980s. These include the ANSI standard for the C programming language, the IEEE POSIX family (still being developed), and the X/Open portability guide.

This book also describes these standards. But instead of just describing the standards by themselves, we describe them in relation to popular implementations of the standards—System V Release 4 and the forthcoming 4.4BSD. This provides a real-world description, which is often lacking from the standard itself and from books that describe only the standard.

Organization of the Book

This book is divided into six parts:

1. An overview and introduction to basic Unix programming concepts and terminology (Chapter 1), with a discussion of the various Unix standardization efforts
   and different Unix implementations (Chapter 2).

2. I/O—unbuffered I/O (Chapter 3), properties of files and directories
   (Chapter 4), the standard I/O library (Chapter 5), and the standard system data
   files (Chapter 6).

3. Processes—the environment of a Unix process (Chapter 7), process control
   (Chapter 8), the relationships between different processes (Chapter 9), and signals (Chapter 10).

4. More I/O—terminal I/O (Chapter 11), advanced I/O (Chapter 12), and daemon
   processes (Chapter 13).

5. IPC—Interprocess communication (Chapters 14 and 15).

6. Examples—a database library (Chapter 16), communicating with a PostScript
   printer (Chapter 17), a modem dialing program (Chapter 18), and using pseudo
   terminals (Chapter 19).

A reading familiarity with C would be beneficial as would some experience using
Unix. No prior programming experience with Unix is assumed. This text is intended
for programmers familiar with Unix and programmers familiar with some other operating system who wish to learn the details of the services provided by most Unix systems.

Examples in the Text

This book contains many examples—approximately 10,000 lines of source code. All the
examples are in the C programming language. Furthermore, these examples are in
ANSI C. You should have a copy of the *Unix Programmer's Manual* for your system
handy while reading this book, since reference is made to it for some of the more eso-
teric and implementation-dependent features.

Almost every function and system call is demonstrated with a small, complete program. This lets us see the arguments and return values and is often easier to compre-
hend than the use of the function in a much larger program. But since some of the small
programs are contrived examples, a few bigger examples are also included (Chapters
16, 17, 18, and 19). These larger examples demonstrate the programming techniques in
larger, real-world examples.

All the examples have been included in the text directly from their source files. A
machine-readable copy of all the examples is available via anonymous FTP from the
Internet host ftp.uu.net in the file published/books/stevens.advprog.tar.Z.
Obtaining the source code allows you to modify the programs from this text and experiment with them on your system.

Systems Used to Test the Examples

Unfortunately all operating systems are moving targets. Unix is no exception. The following diagram shows the recent evolution of the various versions of System V and 4.xBSD.

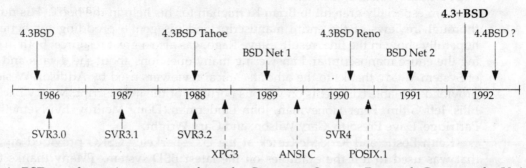

4.xBSD are the various systems from the Computer Systems Research Group at the University of California at Berkeley. This group also distributes the BSD Net 1 and BSD Net 2 releases—publicly available source code from the 4.xBSD systems. SVRx refers to System V Release x from AT&T. XPG3 is the X/Open Portability Guide, Issue 3, and ANSI C is the ANSI standard for the C programming language. POSIX.1 is the IEEE and ISO standard for the interface to a Unix-like system. We'll have more to say about these different standards and the various versions of Unix in Sections 2.2 and 2.3.

> **In this text we use the term *4.3+BSD* to refer to the Unix system from Berkeley that is somewhere between the BSD Net 2 release and 4.4BSD.**
>
> At the time of this writing, 4.4BSD was not released, so the system could not be called 4.4BSD. Nevertheless a simple name was needed to refer to this system and *4.3+BSD* is used throughout the text.

Most of the examples in this text have been run on four different versions of Unix:

1. Unix System V/386 Release 4.0 Version 2.0 ("vanilla SVR4") from U.H. Corp. (UHC), on an Intel 80386 processor.

2. 4.3+BSD at the Computer Systems Research Group, Computer Science Division, University of California at Berkeley, on a Hewlett Packard workstation.

3. BSD/386 (a derivative of the BSD Net 2 release) from Berkeley Software Design, Inc., on an Intel 80386 processor. This system is almost identical to what we call 4.3+BSD.

4. SunOS 4.1.1 and 4.1.2 (systems with a strong Berkeley heritage but many System V features) from Sun Microsystems, on a SPARCstation SLC.

Numerous timing tests are provided in the text and the systems used for the test are identified.

Acknowledgments

Once again I am indebted to my family for their love, support, and many lost weekends over the past year and a half. Writing a book is, in many ways, a family affair. Thank you Sally, Bill, Ellen, and David.

I am especially grateful to Brian Kernighan for his help in the book. His numerous thorough reviews of the entire manuscript and his gentle prodding for better prose hopefully show in the final result. Steve Rago was also a great resource, both in reviewing the entire manuscript and answering many questions about the details and history of System V. My thanks to the other technical reviewers used by Addison-Wesley, who provided valuable comments on various portions of the manuscript: Maury Bach, Mark Ellis, Jeff Gitlin, Peter Honeyman, John Linderman, Doug McIlroy, Evi Nemeth, Craig Partridge, Dave Presotto, Gary Wilson, and Gary Wright.

Keith Bostic and Kirk McKusick at the U.C. Berkeley CSRG provided an account that was used to test the examples on the latest BSD system. (Many thanks to Peter Salus too.) Sam Nataros and Joachim Sacksen at UHC provided the copy of SVR4 used to test the examples. Trent Hein helped obtain the alpha and beta copies of BSD/386.

Other friends have helped in many small, but significant ways over the past few years: Paul Lucchina, Joe Godsil, Jim Hogue, Ed Tankus, and Gary Wright. My editor at Addison-Wesley, John Wait, has been a great friend through it all. He never complained when the due date slipped and the page count kept increasing. A special thanks to the National Optical Astronomy Observatories (NOAO), especially Sidney Wolff, Richard Wolff, and Steve Grandi, for providing computer time.

Real Unix books are written using troff and this book follows that time-honored tradition. Camera-ready copy of the book was produced by the author using the groff package written by James Clark. Many thanks to James Clark for providing this excellent system and for his rapid response to bug fixes. Perhaps someday I will really understand troff footer traps.

I welcome electronic mail from any readers with comments, suggestions, or bug fixes.

Tucson, Arizona   W. Richard Stevens
April 1992   rstevens@noao.edu
                                                       http://www.noao.edu/~rstevens

1

Introduction

1.1   Introduction

All operating systems provide services for programs they run. Typical services are execute a new program, open a file, read a file, allocate a region of memory, get the current time-of-day, and so on. The focus of this text is to describe the services provided by various versions of the Unix operating system.

Describing Unix in a strictly stepwise fashion, without any forward references to terms that haven't been described yet, is nearly impossible (and would probably be boring). This chapter is a whirlwind tour of Unix from a programmer's perspective. We'll give some brief descriptions and examples of terms and concepts that will be encountered throughout the text. We describe these features in much more detail in later chapters. This chapter also provides an introduction and overview of the services provided by Unix, for programmers new to Unix.

1.2   Logging In

Login Name

When we log in to a Unix system we enter our login name, followed by our password. Our login name is then looked up in the system's password file, usually the file /etc/passwd. If we look at our entry in the password file we see that it's composed of seven colon-separated fields: our login name, encrypted password, numeric user ID (224), numeric group ID (20), a comment field, home directory (/home/stevens), and shell program (/bin/ksh).

Many newer systems have moved the encrypted password to a different file. In Chapter 6 we'll look at these files and some functions to access them.

Shells

Once we log in, some system information messages are typically displayed, and then we are able to enter commands to the shell program. A *shell* is a command line interpreter that reads user input and executes commands. The user input to a shell is normally from the terminal (an interactive shell) or sometimes from a file (called a *shell script*). The common shells in use are

- the Bourne shell, /bin/sh
- the C shell, /bin/csh
- the KornShell, /bin/ksh

The system knows which shell to execute for us from the final field in our entry in the password file.

The Bourne shell has been in use since Version 7 and is provided with almost every Unix system in existence. The C shell was developed at Berkeley and is provided with all the BSD releases. Additionally the C shell was provided by AT&T with System V/386 Release 3.2 and is also in System V Release 4 (SVR4). (We'll have more to say about these different versions of Unix in the next chapter.) The KornShell is considered to be a successor to the Bourne shell and is provided in SVR4. The KornShell runs on most Unix systems, but before SVR4 it was usually an extra cost add-on, so it is not as widespread as the other two shells.

> The Bourne shell was developed by Steve Bourne at Bell Labs. Its control flow constructs are reminiscent of Algol 68. The C shell was done at Berkeley by Bill Joy. It was built on the 6th Edition shell (not the Bourne shell). Its control flow looks more like the C language, and it supports additional features that weren't provided by the Bourne shell—job control, a history mechanism, and command-line editing. We return to Bell Labs with the KornShell, where it was developed by David Korn. It is upward-compatible from the Bourne shell and includes those features that made the C shell popular—job control, command line editing, etc.
>
> Throughout the text we will use parenthetical notes such as this to describe historical notes and comparisons between different Unix implementations. Often the reason for a particular implementation technique becomes clear when the historical reasons are described.

Throughout this text we'll show shell examples to execute a program that we've developed. This interactive use will use features common to both the Bourne shell and the KornShell.

1.3   Files and Directories

Filesystem

The Unix filesystem is a hierarchical arrangement of directories and files. Everything starts in the directory called *root* whose name is the single character /.

A *directory* is a file that contains directory entries. Logically we can think of each directory entry as containing a filename along with a structure of information describing the attributes of the file. The attributes of a file are things such as: type of file, size of the file, owner of the file, permissions for the file (e.g., can other users access this file?), time of last modification of the file, and the like. The stat and fstat functions return a structure of information containing all the attributes of a file. In Chapter 4 we'll examine all the attributes of a file in great detail.

Filename

The names in a directory are called *filenames*. The only two characters that cannot appear in a filename are the slash character (/) and the null character. The slash separates the filenames that form a pathname (described next) and the null character terminates a pathname. Nevertheless, it's good practice to restrict the characters in a filename to a subset of the normal printing characters. (The reason we restrict it to a subset is because if we use some of the shell's special characters in the filename, we have to use the shell's quoting mechanism to reference the filename.)

Two filenames are automatically created whenever a new directory is created: . (called *dot*) and .. (called *dot-dot*). Dot refers to the current directory and dot-dot refers to the parent directory. In the ultimate parent directory, the root, dot-dot is the same as dot.

Some Unix filesystems restrict a filename to 14 characters. BSD versions extended this limit to 255 characters.

Pathname

A sequence of zero or more filenames, separated by slashes, and optionally starting with a slash, forms a *pathname*. A pathname that begins with a slash is called an *absolute pathname*, otherwise it's called a *relative pathname*.

Example

Listing the names of all the files in a directory is not hard. Program 1.1 is a bare bones implementation of the ls(1) command.

```
#include      <sys/types.h>
#include      <dirent.h>
#include      "ourhdr.h"

int
main(int argc, char *argv[])
{
    DIR           *dp;
    struct dirent *dirp;

    if (argc != 2)
        err_quit("a single argument (the directory name) is required");

    if ( (dp = opendir(argv[1])) == NULL)
        err_sys("can't open %s", argv[1]);

    while ( (dirp = readdir(dp)) != NULL)
        printf("%s\n", dirp->d_name);

    closedir(dp);
    exit(0);
}
```

Program 1.1 List all the files in a directory.

The notation ls(1) is the normal way to reference a particular entry in the Unix manual set. It refers to the entry for ls in Section 1. The sections are normally numbered 1 through 8, and all the entries within each section are arranged alphabetically. We assume throughout this text that you have a copy of the Unix manuals for your system.

Older Unix systems lumped all eight sections together into what was called the *Unix Programmer's Manual*. The trend today is to distribute the sections among separate manuals: one for the users, one for the programmers, and one for the system administrators, for example.

Some Unix systems further divide the manual pages within a given section using an uppercase letter. For example, all the standard I/O functions in AT&T [1990e] are indicated as being in Section 3S, as in fopen(3S).

Some Unix systems, notably Xenix-based systems, don't number the manual sections numerically. Instead they use the notation C for commands (Section 1), S for services (normally Sections 2 and 3), and so on.

If your manuals are on-line, the way to see the manual pages for the ls command would be something like

```
man 1 ls
```

Program 1.1 just prints the name of every file in a directory, and nothing else. If the source file is named myls.c, we compile it into the default a.out executable file by

```
cc myls.c
```

Some sample output is

```
$ a.out /dev
.
..
MAKEDEV
console
tty
mem
kmem
null
```
many more lines that aren't shown
```
printer
$ a.out /var/spool/mqueue
can't open /var/spool/mqueue: Permission denied
$ a.out /dev/tty
can't open /dev/tty: Not a directory
```

Throughout this text we'll show commands that we enter and the resulting output in this fashion: characters that we enter are shown in **this font** while output from programs is shown like this. If we need to add comments to this output we'll show the comments in *italics*. The dollar sign that precedes our input is the prompt that is printed by the shell. We'll always show the shell prompt as a dollar sign.

Note that the directory listing is not in alphabetical order. The ordering that we are familiar with is done by the ls command itself.

There are many details to consider in this 20-line program:

- First, we include a header of our own, ourhdr.h. We include this header in almost every program in this text. It includes some standard system headers and defines numerous constants and function prototypes that we use throughout the examples in the text. A listing of this header is in Appendix B.

- The declaration of the main function uses the new style supported by the ANSI C standard. (We'll have more to say about the ANSI C standard in the next chapter.)

- We take an argument from the command line, argv[1], as the name of the directory to list. In Chapter 7 we'll look at how the main function is called, and how the command-line arguments and environment variables are accessible to the program.

- Since the actual format of directory entries varies from one Unix system to another, we use the functions opendir, readdir, and closedir to manipulate the directory.

- The opendir function returns a pointer to a DIR structure, and we pass this pointer to the readdir function. We don't care what's in the DIR structure. We then call readdir in a loop, to read each directory entry. It returns a pointer to a dirent structure, or a null pointer when it's finished with the directory. All we examine in the `dirent` structure is the name of each directory entry (d_name). Using this name we could then call the `stat` function (Section 4.2) to determine all the attributes of the file.

- We call two functions of our own to handle the errors: `err_sys` and `err_quit`. We can see from the output above that the `err_sys` function prints an informative message describing what type of error was encountered ("Permission denied" or "Not a directory"). These two error functions are shown and described in Appendix B. We also talk more about error handling in Section 1.7.

- When the program is done it calls the function `exit` with an argument of 0. The function `exit` terminates a program. By convention an argument of 0 means OK, and an argument between 1 and 255 means an error occurred. In Section 8.5 we show how any program (such as a shell or a program that we write) can obtain the exit status of a program that it executes.   □

Working Directory

Every process has a *working directory* (sometimes called the *current working directory*). This is the directory from which all relative pathnames are interpreted. A process can change its working directory with the `chdir` function.

For example, the relative pathname `doc/memo/joe` refers to the file (or directory) `joe`, in the directory `memo`, in the directory `doc`, which must be a directory within the working directory. From looking just at this pathname we know that both `doc` and `memo` have to be directories, but we can't tell if `joe` is a file or directory. The pathname `/usr/lib/lint` is an absolute pathname that refers to the file (or directory) `lint` in the directory `lib`, in the directory `usr`, which is in the root directory.

Home Directory

When we log in, the working directory is set to our *home directory*. Our home directory is obtained from our entry in the password file (recall Section 1.2).

1.4   Input and Output

File Descriptors

File descriptors are small nonnegative integers that the kernel uses to identify the files being accessed by a particular process. Whenever the kernel opens an existing file, or creates a new file, it returns a file descriptor that we use when we want to read or write the file.

Standard Input, Standard Output, and Standard Error

By convention, all shells open three descriptors whenever a new program is run: the standard input, standard output, and standard error. If nothing special is done, as in the simple command

```
ls
```

then all three are connected to our terminal. Most shells provide a way to redirect any or all of these three descriptors to any file. For example,

```
ls > file.list
```

executes the `ls` command with its standard output redirected to the file named `file.list`.

Unbuffered I/O

Unbuffered I/O is provided by the functions `open`, `read`, `write`, `lseek`, and `close`. These functions all work with file descriptors.

Example

If we're willing to read from the standard input and write to the standard output, then Program 1.2 copies any Unix file.

```
#include        "ourhdr.h"

#define BUFFSIZE    8192

int
main(void)
{
    int     n;
    char    buf[BUFFSIZE];

    while ( (n = read(STDIN_FILENO, buf, BUFFSIZE)) > 0)
        if (write(STDOUT_FILENO, buf, n) != n)
            err_sys("write error");

    if (n < 0)
        err_sys("read error");

    exit(0);
}
```

Program 1.2 Copy standard input to standard output.

The <unistd.h> header (that's included by ourhdr.h) and the two constants STDIN_FILENO and STDOUT_FILENO are part of the POSIX standard (about which we'll have a lot more to say in the next chapter). In this header are function prototypes for many of the Unix system services, such as the read and write functions that we call. Function prototypes are part of the ANSI C standard, and we talk more about them later in this chapter.

The two constants STDIN_FILENO and STDOUT_FILENO are defined in the <unistd.h> header, and specify the file descriptors for standard input and standard output. These values are typically 0 and 1, respectively, but we'll use the new names for portability.

In Section 3.9 we'll examine the BUFFSIZE constant in detail, seeing how various values affect the efficiency of the program. Regardless of the value of this constant, however, this program still copies any Unix file.

The read function returns the number of bytes that are read, and this value is used as the number of bytes to write. When the end of the input file is encountered, read returns 0 and the program stops. If a read error occurs, read returns −1. Most of the system functions return −1 when an error occurs.

If we compile the program into the standard a.out file and execute it as

```
a.out > data
```

standard input is the terminal, standard output is redirected to the file data, and standard error is also the terminal. If this output file doesn't exist, the shell creates it by default.   □

In Chapter 3 we describe the unbuffered I/O functions in more detail.

Standard I/O

The standard I/O functions provide a buffered interface to the unbuffered I/O functions. Using standard I/O prevents us from having to worry about choosing optimal buffer sizes, such as the BUFFSIZE constant in Program 1.2. Another advantage of using the standard I/O functions is when we're dealing with lines of input (a common occurrence in Unix applications). The fgets function, for example, reads an entire line. The read function, on the other hand, reads a specified number of bytes.

The standard I/O function that we're most familiar with is printf. In the programs that call printf, we'll always include <stdio.h> (normally by including ourhdr.h), since this header contains the function prototypes for all the standard I/O functions.

Example

Program 1.3, which we'll examine in more detail in Section 5.8, is like the previous program that called read and write. It copies standard input to standard output and can copy any Unix file.

```
#include     "ourhdr.h"

int
main(void)
{
    int     c;

    while ( (c = getc(stdin)) != EOF)
        if (putc(c, stdout) == EOF)
            err_sys("output error");

    if (ferror(stdin))
        err_sys("input error");

    exit(0);
}
```

Program 1.3 Copy standard input to standard output using standard I/O.

The function getc reads one character at a time, and this character is written by putc. After the last byte of input has been read, getc returns the constant EOF. The standard I/O constants stdin and stdout are defined in the <stdio.h> header and refer to the standard input and standard output.   □

1.5   Programs and Processes

Program

A *program* is an executable file residing in a disk file. A program is read into memory and executed by the kernel as a result of one of the six exec functions. .We'll cover these functions in Section 8.9.

Processes and Process ID

An executing instance of a program is called a *process*. We'll encounter this term on almost every page of the text. Some operating systems use the term task to refer to a program that is being executed.

Every Unix process is guaranteed to have a unique numeric identifier called the *process ID*. The process ID is always a nonnegative integer.

Example

Program 1.4 prints its process ID.

```
#include     "ourhdr.h"

int
main(void)
{
    printf("hello world from process ID %d\n", getpid());
    exit(0);
}
```

Program 1.4 Print the process ID.

If we compile this program into the file a.out and execute it, we have

```
$ a.out
hello world from process ID 851
$ a.out
hello world from process ID 854
```

When this program runs it calls the function getpid to obtain its process ID.   □

Process Control

There are three primary functions used for process control: fork, exec, and waitpid.
(There are six variants of the exec function, but we often refer to them collectively as
just the exec function.)

Example

The process control features of Unix can be demonstrated using a simple program
(Program 1.5) that reads commands from standard input and executes the commands.
This is a bare bones implementation of a shell-like program. There are several features
to consider in this 30-line program.

- We use the standard I/O function fgets to read one line at a time from the
  standard input. When we type the end of file character (often Control-D) as the
  first character of a line, fgets returns a null pointer, the loop stops, and the process terminates. In Chapter 11 we describe all the special terminal characters
  (end of file, backspace one character, erase entire line, etc.) and how to change
  them.

- Since each line returned by fgets is terminated with a newline character, followed by a null byte, we use the standard C function strlen to calculate the
  length of the string, and then replace the newline with a null byte. We do this
  because the execlp function wants a null terminated argument, not a newline
  terminated argument.

- We call fork to create a new process. The new process is a copy of the caller,
  and we say the caller is the parent and the newly created process is the child.
  Then fork returns the nonnegative process ID of the new child process to the

```
#include     <sys/types.h>
#include     <sys/wait.h>
#include     "ourhdr.h"

int
main(void)
{
    char     buf[MAXLINE];
    pid_t    pid;
    int      status;

    printf("%% ");   /* print prompt (printf requires %% to print %) */
    while (fgets(buf, MAXLINE, stdin) != NULL) {
        buf[strlen(buf) - 1] = 0;    /* replace newline with null */

        if ( (pid = fork()) < 0)
            err_sys("fork error");

        else if (pid == 0) {          /* child */
            execlp(buf, buf, (char *) 0);
            err_ret("couldn't execute: %s", buf);
            exit(127);
        }

        /* parent */
        if ( (pid = waitpid(pid, &status, 0)) < 0)
            err_sys("waitpid error");
        printf("%% ");
    }
    exit(0);
}
```

Program 1.5 Read commands from standard input and execute them.

parent, and it returns 0 to the child. Since fork creates a new process, we say that it is called once (by the parent) but returns twice (in the parent and in the child).

- In the child we call execlp to execute the command that was read from the standard input. This replaces the child process with the new program file. The combination of a fork, followed by an exec, is what some operating systems call spawning a new process. In Unix the two parts are separated into individual functions. We'll have a lot more to say about these functions in Chapter 8.

- Since the child calls execlp to execute the new program file, the parent wants to wait for the child to terminate. This is done by calling waitpid, specifying which process we want to wait for (the pid argument, which is the process ID of the child). The waitpid function also returns the termination status of the child (the status variable), but in this simple program we don't do anything with this value. We could examine it to determine exactly how the child terminated.

- The most fundamental limitation of this program is that we can't pass arguments to the command that we execute. We can't, for example, specify the name of a directory to list. We can only execute `ls` on the working directory. To allow arguments would require that we parse the input line, separating the arguments by some convention (probably spaces or tabs) and then pass each argument as a separate argument to the `execlp` function. Nevertheless, this program is still a useful demonstration of the process control functions of Unix.

If we run this program we get the following results. Notice that our program has a different prompt (the percent sign).

```
$ a.out
% date
Fri Jun  7 15:50:36 MST 1991
% who
stevens   console Jun  5 06:01
stevens   ttyp0   Jun  5 06:02
% pwd
/home/stevens/doc/apue/proc
% ls
Makefile
a.out
shell1.c
% ^D                          type our end-of-file character
$                             the regular shell prompt is output
```

1.6 ANSI C Features

All the examples in this text are written in the version of the C programming language that is called ANSI C.

Function Prototypes

The header `<unistd.h>` includes function prototypes for many of the Unix system services, such as the `read`, `write`, and `getpid` functions that we've called. Function prototypes are part of the ANSI C standard. These function prototypes probably look like

```
ssize_t   read(int, void *, size_t);
ssize_t   write(int, const void *, size_t);
pid_t     getpid(void);
```

The final one says that `getpid` takes no arguments (`void`) and returns a value that has the data type `pid_t`. By providing these function prototypes we are able to let the compiler do additional checking at compile time, to verify that we are calling functions with the correct arguments. In Program 1.4, if we had called `getpid` with an argument, as in `getpid(1)`, we would get an error message of the form

```
line 8: too many arguments to function "getpid"
```

from an ANSI C compiler. Also, since the compiler knows the data types of the arguments, it is able to cast the arguments to their required data types, if possible.

Generic Pointers

Another difference that we'll note in the function prototypes shown previously is that the second argument for read and write is now of type void *. All earlier Unix systems used char * for this pointer. This change is because ANSI C uses void * as the generic pointer, instead of char *.

Combining function prototypes and generic pointers lets us remove many of the explicit type casts that are needed with non-ANSI C compilers. For example, given the prototype for write earlier, we can write

```
float  data[100];

write(fd, data, sizeof(data));
```

With a non-ANSI compiler, or without the function prototype, we need to write

```
write(fd, (void *) data, sizeof(data));
```

We'll also use this feature of void * pointers with the malloc function (Section 7.8). The prototype for malloc is now

```
void *malloc(size_t);
```

This lets us write

```
int  *ptr;

ptr = malloc(1000 * sizeof(int));
```

without explicitly casting the returned pointer to an int *.

Primitive System Data Types

The prototype for the getpid function shown earlier defines its return value as being of type pid_t. This is also new with POSIX. Earlier versions of Unix defined this function as returning an integer. Similarly both read and write return a value of type ssize_t and require a third argument of type size_t.

These data types that end in _t are called the primitive system data types. They are usually defined in the header <sys/types.h> (which the header <unistd.h> must have included). They are usually defined with the C typedef declaration, which has been in C for over 15 years (so it doesn't require ANSI C). Their purpose is to prevent programs from using specific data types (such as int, short, or long, for example) to allow each implementation to choose which data type is required for a particular system. Everywhere we need to store a process ID, we'll allocate a variable of type pid_t.

(Notice that we did this for the variable named `pid` in Program 1.5.) While the definition of this data type might differ from one implementation to another, the differences are restricted to one header. All we have to do is recompile the application on another system.

1.7   Error Handling

When an error occurs in one of the Unix functions, a negative value is often returned, and the integer `errno` is usually set to a value that gives additional information. For example, the open function returns either a nonnegative file descriptor if all is OK, or –1 if an error occurs. In the case of an error from open, there are about 15 different `errno` values (file doesn't exist, permission problem, etc.). Some functions use a convention other than returning a negative value. For example, most functions that return a pointer to an object return a null pointer to indicate an error.

The file `<errno.h>` defines the variable `errno` and constants for each value that `errno` can assume. Each of these constants begins with the character E. Also, the first page of Section 2 of the Unix manuals, named `intro(2)`, usually lists all these error constants. For example, if `errno` is equal to the constant EACCES, this indicates a permission problem (we don't have permission to open the requested file, for example). POSIX defines `errno` as

```
extern int errno;
```

> This POSIX.1 definition of `errno` is stricter than the definition in the C standard. The C standard allows `errno` to be a macro that expands into a modifiable lvalue of type integer (such as a function that returns a pointer to the error number).

There are two rules to be aware of with respect to `errno`. First, its value is never cleared by a routine if an error does not occur. Therefore, we should examine its value only when the return value from a function indicates that an error occurred. Second, the value of `errno` is never set to 0 by any of the functions, and none of the constants defined in `<errno.h>` have a value of 0.

Two functions are defined by the C standard to help with the printing of error messages.

```
#include <string.h>

char *strerror(int errnum);
```
                                                             Returns: pointer to message string

This function maps *errnum* (which is typically the `errno` value) into an error message string and returns a pointer to the string.

The perror function produces an error message on the standard error (based on the current value of errno) and returns.

```
#include <stdio.h>

void perror(const char *msg);
```

It first outputs the string pointed to by *msg*, followed by a colon and a space, followed by the error message corresponding to the value of errno, followed by a newline.

Example

Program 1.6 shows the use of these two error functions.

```
#include        <errno.h>
#include        "ourhdr.h"

int
main(int argc, char *argv[])
{
    fprintf(stderr, "EACCES: %s\n", strerror(EACCES));

    errno = ENOENT;
    perror(argv[0]);

    exit(0);
}
```

Program 1.6 Demonstrate strerror and perror.

If this program is compiled into the file a.out, we have

```
$ a.out
EACCES: Permission denied
a.out: No such file or directory
```

Note that we pass the name of the program (argv[0], whose value is a.out) as the argument to perror. This is a standard Unix convention. By doing this, if the program is executed as part of a pipeline, as in

```
prog1 < inputfile | prog2 | prog3 > outputfile
```

we are able to tell which of the three programs generated a particular error message. □

Instead of calling either strerror or perror directly, all the examples in this text use the error functions shown in Appendix B. The error functions in this appendix let us use the variable argument list facility of ANSI C to handle error conditions with a single C statement.

1.8   User Identification

User ID

The *user ID* from our entry in the password file is a numeric value that identifies us to the system. This user ID is assigned by the system administrator when our login name is assigned and we cannot change it. It is normally assigned so that every user has a unique user ID. We'll see how the user ID is utilized by the kernel to check if we have the appropriate permissions to perform certain operations.

We call the user whose user ID is 0 either *root* or the *superuser*. The entry in the password file normally has a login name of root and we refer to the special privileges of this user as superuser privileges. As we'll see in Chapter 4, if a process has superuser privileges, most file permission checks are bypassed. Some operating system functions are restricted to only the superuser. The superuser has free reign over the system.

Example

Program 1.7 prints the user ID and the group ID (described next).

```
#include     "ourhdr.h"

int
main(void)
{
    printf("uid = %d, gid = %d\n", getuid(), getgid());
    exit(0);
}
```

Program 1.7   Print user ID and group ID.

We call the functions getuid and getgid to return the user ID and group ID. Running the program yields

```
$ a.out
uid = 224, gid = 20
```

□

Group ID

Our entry in the password file also specifies our numeric *group ID*. This group ID is also assigned by the system administrator when our login name is assigned. Typically there are multiple entries in the password file that specify the same group ID. Groups are normally used under Unix to collect users together into projects or departments. This allows the sharing of resources (such as files) between members of the same group. We'll see in Section 4.5 that we can set the permissions on a file so that all members of a group can access the file, while others outside the group cannot.

There is also a group file that maps group names into numeric group IDs. The group file is usually /etc/group.

The use of numeric user IDs and numeric group IDs for permissions is historical. The directory entry for every file on the system contains both the user ID and the group ID of the owner of the file. Storing both of these values in the directory entry requires only four bytes, assuming each is stored as a two-byte integer. If the full eight-byte login name and eight-byte group name were used instead, additional disk space would be required. Users, however, work better with names instead of numbers, so the password file maintains the mapping between login names and user IDs, and the group file provides the mapping between group names and group IDs. The Unix ls -l command, for example, prints the login name of the owner of a file, using the password file to map the numeric user ID into the corresponding login name.

Supplementary Group IDs

In addition to the group ID specified in the password file for a login name, some versions of Unix allow a user to belong to additional groups. This started with 4.2BSD, which allowed a user to belong to up to 16 additional groups. These *supplementary group IDs* are obtained at login time by reading the file /etc/group and finding the first 16 entries that list the user as a member.

1.9 Signals

Signals are a technique used to notify a process that some condition has occurred. For example, if a process divides by zero, the signal whose name is SIGFPE is sent to the process. The process has three choices for dealing with the signal:

1. Ignore the signal. This isn't recommended for signals that denote a hardware exception, such as dividing by zero, or referencing memory outside the address space of the process, since the results are undefined.

2. Let the default action occur. For a divide by zero the default is to terminate the process.

3. Provide a function that is called when the signal occurs. By providing a function of our own, we'll know when the signal occurs and we can handle it as we wish.

Many conditions generate signals. There are two terminal keys, called the *interrupt key* (often the DELETE key or Control-C) and the *quit key* (often Control-backslash). These are used to interrupt the currently running process. Another way to generate a signal is by calling the function named kill. We can call this function from a process to send a signal to another process. Naturally there are limitations: we have to be the owner of the other process to be able to send it a signal.

Example

Recall the bare bones shell example (Program 1.5). If we invoke this program and type the interrupt key, the process terminates. The reason is that the default action for this signal (named SIGINT) is to terminate the process. The process hasn't told the kernel to do anything other than the default with this signal, so the process terminates.

To change this program so that it catches this signal, it needs to call the signal function, specifying the name of the function to call when the SIGINT signal is generated. The function is named sig_int and when it's called it just prints a message and a new prompt. Adding 12 lines to Program 1.5 gives us the version in Program 1.8. (The 12 new lines are indicated with a plus sign at the beginning of the line.)

```
  #include      <sys/types.h>
  #include      <sys/wait.h>
+ #include      <signal.h>
  #include      "ourhdr.h"

+ static void sig_int(int);          /* our signal-catching function */
+
  int
  main(void)
  {
      char    buf[MAXLINE];
      pid_t   pid;
      int     status;

+     if (signal(SIGINT, sig_int) == SIG_ERR)
+         err_sys("signal error");
+
      printf("%% ");  /* print prompt (printf requires %% to print %) */
      while (fgets(buf, MAXLINE, stdin) != NULL) {
          buf[strlen(buf) - 1] = 0;    /* replace newline with null */

          if ( (pid = fork()) < 0)
              err_sys("fork error");

          else if (pid == 0) {         /* child */
              execlp(buf, buf, (char *) 0);
              err_ret("couldn't execute: %s", buf);
              exit(127);
          }

          /* parent */
          if ( (pid = waitpid(pid, &status, 0)) < 0)
              err_sys("waitpid error");
          printf("%% ");
      }
      exit(0);
  }
```

```
+ void
+ sig_int(int signo)
+ {
+       printf("interrupt\n%% ");
  }
```

Program 1.8 Read commands from standard input and execute them.

In Chapter 10 we'll take a long look at signals, since most nontrivial applications deal with them.   □

1.10 Unix Time Values

Historically, two different time values have been maintained by Unix systems.

1. *Calendar time.* This value counts the number of seconds since the Epoch, which is 00:00:00 January 1, 1970, Coordinated Universal Time (UTC). (Older manuals refer to UTC as Greenwich Mean Time.) These time values are used to record the time that a file was last modified, for example.

   The primitive system data type `time_t` holds these time values.

2. *Process time.* This is also called CPU time and measures the central processor resources used by a process. Process time is measured in clock ticks, which have historically been 50, 60, or 100 ticks per second.

   The primitive system data type `clock_t` holds these time values. Further, POSIX defines the constant `CLK_TCK` to specify the number of ticks per second. (The constant `CLK_TCK` is now obsolete. We'll show how to obtain the number of clock ticks per second with the `sysconf` function in Section 2.5.4.)

When we measure the execution time of a process, as in Section 3.9, we'll see that Unix maintains three values for a process:

- clock time
- user CPU time
- system CPU time

The clock time is sometimes called *wall clock time*. It is the amount of time the process takes to run, and its value depends on the number of other processes being run on the system. Whenever we report the clock time, the measurements are made with no other activities on the system.

The user CPU time is the CPU time that is attributed to user instructions. The system CPU time is the CPU time that can be attributed to the kernel, when it executes on behalf of the process. For example, whenever a process executes a system service, such as `read` or `write`, the time spent within the kernel performing that system service is charged to the process. The sum of the user CPU time and system CPU time is often called the *CPU time*.

It is easy to measure the clock time, user time, and system time of any process—just execute the `time`(1) command with the argument to the `time` command being the command we want to measure. For example,

```
$ cd /usr/include
$ time grep _POSIX_SOURCE */*.h > /dev/null

real    0m19.81s
user    0m0.43s
sys     0m4.53s
```

The output format from the `time` command depends on the shell being used.

In Section 8.15 we see how to obtain these three times from a running process. The general topic of times and dates is covered in Section 6.9.

1.11 System Calls and Library Functions

All operating systems provide service points through which programs request services from the kernel. All variants of Unix provide a well-defined, limited number of entry points directly into the kernel called *system calls*. The system calls are one feature of Unix that we cannot change. Unix Version 7 provided about 50 system calls, 4.3+BSD provides about 110, and SVR4 has around 120.

The system call interface has always been documented in Section 2 of the *Unix Programmer's Manual*. Its definition is in the C language, regardless of the actual implementation technique used on any given system to invoke a system call. This differs from many older operating systems, which traditionally defined the kernel entry points in the assembler language of the machine.

The technique used on Unix systems is for each system call to have a function of the same name in the standard C library. The user process calls this function, using the standard C calling sequence. This function then invokes the appropriate kernel service, using whatever technique is required on the system. For example, the function may put one or more of the C arguments into general registers and then execute some machine instruction that generates a software interrupt in the kernel. For our purposes, we can consider the system calls as being C functions.

Section 3 of the *Unix Programmer's Manual* defines the general purpose functions available to programmers. These functions are not entry points into the kernel, although they may invoke one or more of the kernel's system calls. For example, the `printf` function may invoke the `write` system call to perform the output, but the functions `strcpy` (copy a string) and `atoi` (convert ASCII to integer) don't involve the operating system at all.

From an implementor's point of view, the distinction between a system call and a library function is fundamental. But from a user's perspective, the difference is not as critical. From our perspective in this text, both system calls and library functions appear as normal C functions. Both exist to provide services for application programs. We should realize, however, that we can replace the library functions if desired, whereas the system calls usually cannot be replaced.

Consider the memory allocation function `malloc` as an example. There are many ways to do memory allocation and its associated garbage collection (best fit, first fit, etc.). No single technique is optimal for all programs. The Unix system call that handles memory allocation, `sbrk(2)`, is not a general purpose memory manager. It increases or decreases the address space of the process by a specified number of bytes. How that space is managed is up to the process. The memory allocation function, `malloc(3)`, implements one particular type of allocation. If we don't like its operation we can define our own `malloc` function, which will probably use the `sbrk` system call. There are, in fact, numerous software packages that implement their own memory allocation algorithms, with the `sbrk` system call. Figure 1.1 shows the relationship between the application, the `malloc` function, and the `sbrk` system call.

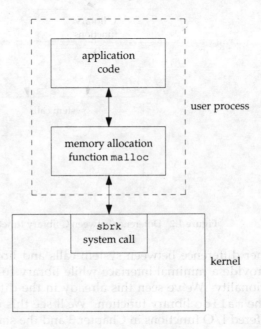

Figure 1.1 Separation of `malloc` function and `sbrk` system call.

Here we have a clean separation of duties—the system call in the kernel allocates an additional chunk of space to the process. The library function `malloc` manages this space.

Another example to illustrate the difference between a system call and a library function is the interface provided by Unix to determine the current time and date. Some operating systems provide one system call to return the time and another to return the date. Any special handling, such as the switch to or from daylight savings time, is handled by the kernel or requires human intervention. Unix, on the other hand, provides a single system call that returns the number of seconds since the Epoch: midnight, January 1, 1970, Coordinated Universal Time. Any interpretation of this value, such as converting it to a human-readable time and date using the local time zone, is left to the user process. Routines are provided in the standard C library to handle most cases. These library routines handle details such as the various daylight savings time algorithms.

An application can call either a system call or a library routine. Also realize that many library routines invoke a system call. This is shown in Figure 1.2.

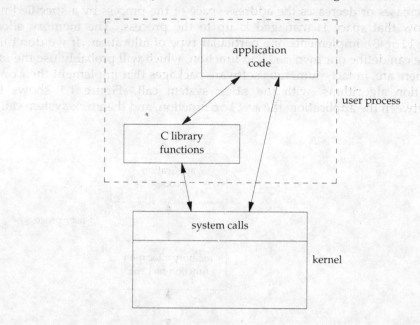

Figure 1.2   Difference between C library functions and system calls.

Another difference between system calls and library functions is that system calls usually provide a minimal interface while library functions often provide more elaborate functionality. We've seen this already in the difference between the sbrk system call and the malloc library function. We'll see this difference later when we compare the unbuffered I/O functions in Chapter 3 and the standard I/O functions in Chapter 5.

The process control system calls (fork, exec, and wait) are usually invoked by the user's application code directly. (Recall the bare bones shell in Program 1.5.) But some library routines exist to simplify certain common cases: the system and popen library routines, for example. In Section 8.12 we'll show an implementation of the system function that invokes the basic process control system calls. We'll enhance this example in Section 10.18 to handle signals correctly.

To define the interface to the Unix system that most programmers utilize, we have to describe both the system calls and some of the library functions. If we described only the sbrk system call, for example, we would skip the malloc library function that many applications utilize.

In this text we'll use the term *function* to refer to both system calls and library functions, except when the distinction is necessary.

1.12 Summary

This chapter has been a whirlwind tour of Unix. We've described some of the fundamental terms that we'll encounter over and over again. We've seen numerous small examples of Unix programs to give us a feel for what the remainder of the text talks about.

The next chapter is about Unix standardization and the effect of recent work in this area on current systems. Standards, particularly the ANSI C standard and the POSIX.1 standard, will affect the rest of the text.

Exercises

1.1 Verify on your system that the directories dot and dot-dot are not the same, except in the root directory.

1.2 In the output from Program 1.4, what happened to the processes with process IDs 852 and 853?

1.3 In Section 1.7 the argument to perror is defined with the ANSI C attribute const, while the integer argument to strerror isn't defined with this attribute. Why?

1.4 In the error handling function err_sys in Appendix B, why is the value of errno saved when the function is called?

1.5 If the calendar time is stored as a signed 32-bit integer, in what year will it overflow?

1.6 If the process time is stored as a signed 32-bit integer, and if the system counts 100 ticks per second, after how many days will the value overflow?

2

Unix Standardization and Implementations

2.1 Introduction

Much work has gone into standardizing the various flavors of Unix and the C programming language. Although Unix applications have always been quite portable between different versions of Unix, the proliferation of versions and differences during the 1980s led many large users (such as the U.S. government) to lead the call for standardization.

In this chapter we first look at the various standardization efforts that are underway. We then discuss the effects of these standards on the actual Unix implementations that are described in this book. An important part of all the standardization efforts is the specification of various limits that each implementation must define, so we look at these limits and the various ways to determine their values.

2.2 Unix Standardization

2.2.1 ANSI C

In late 1989 the ANSI Standard X3.159–1989 for the C programming language was approved [ANSI 1989]. This standard has also been adopted as international standard ISO/IEC 9899:1990. ANSI is the American National Standards Institute. It is a non-profit organization composed of vendors and users. It is the national clearinghouse for voluntary standards in the United States and is the U.S. member in the International Organization for Standardization (ISO).

The intent of the ANSI C standard is to provide portability of conforming C programs to a wide variety of operating systems, not just Unix. This standard defines not only the syntax and semantics of the programming language but also a standard library [Chapter 4 of ANSI 1989; Plauger 1992; Appendix B of Kernighan and Ritchie 1988]. This library is important to us because many newer Unix systems (such as the ones described in this book) provide the library routines that are specified in the C standard.

This library can be divided into 15 areas based on the headers defined by the standard. Figure 2.1 lists the headers defined by the C standard, along with the headers defined by the other two standards that we describe in the following sections (POSIX.1 and XPG3). We also list which of these headers are supported by the two implementations (SVR4 and 4.3+BSD) that are described later in this chapter.

2.2.2 IEEE POSIX

POSIX is a family of standards developed by the IEEE (Institute of Electrical and Electronics Engineers). POSIX stands for Portable Operating System Interface. It originally referred only to the IEEE Standard 1003.1–1988 (the operating system interface), but the IEEE is currently working on other related standards in the POSIX family. For example, 1003.2 will be a standard for shells and utilities, and 1003.7 will be a standard for system administration. There are over 15 other subcommittees in the 1003 working group.

Of specific interest to this book is the 1003.1 operating system interface standard. This standard defines the services that must be provided by an operating system if it is to be "POSIX compliant" and is being adopted by most computer vendors. Although the 1003.1 standard is based on the Unix operating system, the standard is not restricted to Unix and Unix-like systems. Indeed, there are vendors that supply proprietary operating systems who claim that these systems will be made POSIX compliant (while still leaving all their proprietary features in place).

Because the 1003.1 standard specifies an *interface* and not an *implementation*, no distinction is made between system calls and library functions. All the routines in the standard are called *functions*.

Standards are continually evolving, and the 1003.1 standard is no exception. The 1988 version of this standard, IEEE Standard 1003.1–1988, was modified and submitted to the International Organization for Standardization. No new interfaces or features were added but the text was revised. The resulting document was published as IEEE Std 1003.1–1990 [IEEE 1990]. This is also the international standard ISO/IEC 9945–1:1990. This standard is commonly referred to as *POSIX.1*, which we'll use in this text.

The IEEE 1003.1 working group then made more changes, which should be approved by 1993. These changes (currently called 1003.1a) should be published by the IEEE as a supplement to IEEE Standard 1003.1–1990. These changes affect this text, primarily because Berkeley-style symbolic links will probably be added as a required feature. The changes will probably become an addendum to ISO/IEC 9945–1:1990. In this text we describe the 1003.1a version of POSIX.1 with notes specifying which features will probably be added with 1003.1a.

POSIX.1 does not include the notion of a superuser. Instead, certain operations require "appropriate privileges," although POSIX.1 leaves the definition of this term up

Header	Standards			Implementations		Description
	ANSI C	POSIX.1	XPG3	SVR4	4.3+BSD	
`<assert.h>`	•			•	•	verify program assertion
`<cpio.h>`			•	•		cpio archive values
`<ctype.h>`	•		•	•	•	character types
`<dirent.h>`		•	•	•	•	directory entries (Section 4.21)
`<errno.h>`	•	•	•	•	•	error codes (Section 1.7)
`<fcntl.h>`		•	•	•	•	file control (Section 3.13)
`<float.h>`	•		•	•	•	floating point constants
`<ftw.h>`			•	•	•	file tree walking (Section 4.21)
`<grp.h>`		•	•	•	•	group file (Section 6.4)
`<langinfo.h>`			•	•		language information constants
`<limits.h>`	•	•	•	•	•	implementation constants (Section 2.5)
`<locale.h>`	•		•	•	•	locale categories
`<math.h>`	•		•	•	•	mathematical constants
`<nl_types.h>`			•	•		message catalogs
`<pwd.h>`		•	•	•	•	password file (Section 6.2)
`<regex.h>`			•	•		regular expressions
`<search.h>`			•	•		search tables
`<setjmp.h>`	•		•	•	•	nonlocal goto (Section 7.10)
`<signal.h>`	•	•	•	•	•	signals (Chapter 10)
`<stdarg.h>`	•		•	•	•	variable argument lists
`<stddef.h>`	•		•	•	•	standard definitions
`<stdio.h>`	•		•	•	•	standard I/O library (Chapter 5)
`<stdlib.h>`	•		•	•	•	utility functions
`<string.h>`	•		•	•	•	string operations
`<tar.h>`			•	•		tar archive values
`<termios.h>`		•	•	•	•	terminal I/O (Chapter 11)
`<time.h>`	•	•	•	•	•	time and date (Section 6.9)
`<ulimit.h>`			•	•		user limits
`<unistd.h>`		•	•	•	•	symbolic constants
`<utime.h>`		•	•	•	•	file times (Section 4.19)
`<sys/ipc.h>`			•	•	•	IPC (Section 14.6)
`<sys/msg.h>`			•	•		message queues (Section 14.7)
`<sys/sem.h>`			•	•		semaphores (Section 14.8)
`<sys/shm.h>`			•	•		shared memory (Section 14.9)
`<sys/stat.h>`		•	•	•	•	file status (Chapter 4)
`<sys/times.h>`		•	•	•	•	process times (Section 8.15)
`<sys/types.h>`		•	•	•	•	primitive system data types (Section 2.7)
`<sys/utsname.h>`		•	•	•	•	system name (Section 6.8)
`<sys/wait.h>`		•	•	•	•	process control (Section 8.6)

Figure 2.1 Headers defined by the various standards and implementations.

to the implementation. Some newer Unix systems, which conform to the Department of Defense security guidelines, have many different levels of security. In this text, however, we use the traditional Unix terminology and refer to operations that require super-user privilege.

2.2.3 X/Open XPG3

X/Open is an international group of computer vendors. They have produced a seven-volume portability guide called the *X/Open Portability Guide*, Issue 3 [X/Open 1989]. We'll call this *XPG3*. Volume 2 of XPG3 (*XSI System Interface and Headers*) defines an interface to a Unix-like system that is built on the IEEE Std. 1003.1–1988 interface. But XPG3 contains additional features that are not in POSIX.1.

For example, one feature that is in XPG3 but not in POSIX.1 is the X/Open messaging facility. This facility can be used by applications to display text messages in different languages.

One thing to be aware of is that the XPG3 interface was built on the draft ANSI C standard, not the final standard. For this reason a few features in the XPG3 interface specification are out of date. These will probably be fixed in a future release of the XPG specification. (Work is underway on XPG4, and it will probably be completed by 1993.)

2.2.4 FIPS

FIPS stands for Federal Information Processing Standard, and these standards are published by the U.S. government. They are used for procurement of computer systems by the U.S. government. FIPS 151-1 (April 1989) is based on the IEEE Std. 1003.1–1988 and a draft of the ANSI C standard. FIPS 151-1 requires some features that POSIX.1 lists as optional. This FIPS is sometimes called the POSIX.1 FIPS. Section 2.5.5 lists the POSIX.1 options required by the FIPS.

The effect of the POSIX.1 FIPS is to require any vendor who wishes to sell POSIX.1-compliant computer systems to the U.S. government to support some of the optional features of POSIX.1. We won't consider the POSIX.1 FIPS as another standard since practically it is just a tightening of the POSIX.1 standard.

2.3   Unix Implementations

The previous section described three standards done by independent organizations: ANSI C, IEEE POSIX, and the X/Open XPG3. Standards, however, are interface specifications. How do these standards relate to the real world? These standards are taken by vendors and turned into actual implementations. In this book we are interested in both these standards and their actual implementation.

Section 1.1 of Leffler et al. [1989] gives a detailed history (and a nice picture) of the Unix family tree. Everything starts from the Sixth Edition (1976) and Seventh Edition (1979) of the Unix Time-Sharing System on the PDP-11 (usually called Version 6 and Version 7). These were the first releases widely distributed outside of Bell Labs. Three branches of the tree evolved: (a) one at AT&T that led to System III and System V (the so-called commercial versions of Unix), (b) one at the University of California at Berkeley that led to the 4.xBSD implementations, (c) the research version of Unix, under continuing development at the Computing Science Research Center of AT&T Bell Laboratories, that led to the 8th, 9th, and 10th Editions.

2.3.1 System V Release 4

System V Release 4 (SVR4) is a product of AT&T's Unix System Laboratories. It is a merging of AT&T Unix System V Release 3.2 (SVR3.2), Sun Microsystem's SunOS system, the 4.3BSD release from the University of California, and the Xenix system from Microsoft. (Xenix was originally developed from Version 7, with many features later taken from System V.) The source code was released in late 1989 with the first end-user copies being available during 1990. SVR4 conforms to both the POSIX 1003.1 standard and the X/Open XPG3 standard.

AT&T also publishes the System V Interface Definition (SVID) [AT&T 1989]. Issue 3 of the SVID specifies the functionality that a Unix system must offer to qualify as Unix System V Release 4. As with POSIX.1, the SVID specifies an interface and not an implementation. No distinction is made in the SVID between system calls and library functions. The reference manual for an actual implementation of SVR4 must be consulted to see this distinction [AT&T 1990e].

SVR4 contains a Berkeley compatibility library [AT&T 1990c] that provides functions and commands that operate like their 4.3BSD counterparts. Some of these functions, however, differ from their POSIX counterparts. None of the SVR4 examples in this text use this compatibility library. This library should be used only if you have an older application that you do not want to convert. New applications should not use it.

2.3.2 4.3+BSD

The Berkeley Software Distributions (BSD) are produced and distributed by the Computer Systems Research Group at the University of California at Berkeley. 4.2BSD was released in 1983 and 4.3BSD in 1986. Both of these releases ran on the VAX minicomputer. The next release, 4.3BSD Tahoe in 1988, also ran on a particular minicomputer called the Tahoe. (The book by Leffler et al. [1989] describes the 4.3BSD Tahoe release.) This was followed in 1990 with the 4.3BSD Reno release. 4.3BSD Reno supported many of the POSIX.1 features. The next major release, 4.4BSD, should be released in 1992.

The original BSD systems contained proprietary AT&T source code and were covered by AT&T licenses. To obtain the source code to the BSD system you had to have an AT&T source license for Unix. This has been changing as more and more of the AT&T source code has been replaced over the years with non-AT&T source code, and many of the new features added to the Berkeley system were derived from non-AT&T sources.

In 1989 Berkeley identified much of the non-AT&T source code in the 4.3BSD Tahoe release and made it publicly available as the BSD Networking Software, Release 1.0. This was followed in 1991 with Release 2.0 of the BSD Networking Software, which was derived from the 4.3BSD Reno release. The intent is that most, if not all, of the 4.4BSD system will be free of any AT&T license restrictions. This will make the source code available to all.

> As we mentioned in the preface, throughout the text we use the term 4.3+BSD to refer to the BSD system being described. This system is between the BSD Networking Software Release 2.0 and the forthcoming 4.4BSD.

The Unix development done at Berkeley started with PDP-11s, then moved to the VAX minicomputer, and has since moved to other so-called workstations. During the early 1990s support was provided to Berkeley for the popular 80386-based personal computers, leading to what is called 386BSD. This was done by Bill Jolitz and is documented in a series of monthly articles in *Dr. Dobb's Journal* throughout 1991. Much of this code appears in the BSD Networking Software, Release 2.0.

2.4   Relationship of Standards and Implementations

The standards that we've mentioned define a subset of any actual system. Although the IEEE POSIX efforts plan to define standards in other required areas (such as the networking interface, communication between different processes, and system administration), these additional standards don't exist at the time of this writing.

The focus of this book is to describe two real Unix systems: SVR4 and 4.3+BSD. Since both claim to be POSIX compliant we will also concentrate on the features that are required by the POSIX.1 standard, noting any differences between POSIX and the actual implementations of these two systems. Those features and routines that are specific only to SVR4 or 4.3+BSD are clearly marked. Since XPG3 is a superset of POSIX.1, we'll also note any features that are part of XPG3 but not part of POSIX.1.

Be aware that both of the implementations (SVR4 and 4.3+BSD) provide backward compatibility for features in earlier releases (such as SVR3.2 and 4.3BSD). For example, SVR4 supports both the POSIX.1 specification for nonblocking I/O (O_NONBLOCK) and the traditional System V method (O_NDELAY). In this text we'll use only the POSIX.1 feature, although we'll mention the nonstandard feature that it replaces. Similarly, both SVR3.2 and 4.3BSD provided reliable signals in a way that differs from the POSIX.1 standard. In Chapter 10 we describe only the POSIX.1 signal mechanism.

2.5   Limits

There are many magic numbers and constants that are defined by the implementation. Many of these have been hard coded into programs or were determined using ad hoc techniques. With the various standardization efforts that we've described, more portable methods are now provided to determine these magic numbers and implementation-defined limits. This can greatly aid the portability of our software.

Three types of features are needed:

- compile-time options (does the system support job control?)
- compile-time limits (what's the largest value of a short integer?)
- run-time limits (how many characters in a filename?)

The first two features, compile-time options and compile-time limits, can be defined in headers that any program can include at compile time. But run-time limits require the process to call a function to obtain the value of the limit.

Additionally, some limits can be fixed on a given implementation (and could therefore be defined statically in a header) yet vary on another implementation (and would require a run-time function call). An example of this type of limit is the maximum number of characters in a filename. System V has historically allowed only 14 characters in a filename while Berkeley-derived systems increased this to 255. SVR4 allows us to specify, for each filesystem that we create, whether it is a System V filesystem or a BSD filesystem, and each has a different limit. This is the case of a run-time limit that depends where in the filesystem the file in question is located. A filename in the root filesystem, for example, could have a 14-character limit, while a filename in some other filesystem could have a 255-character limit.

To solve these problems, three types of limits are provided:

1. compile-time options and limits (headers);

2. run-time limits that are not associated with a file or directory (the sysconf function);

3. run-time limits that are associated with a file or directory (the pathconf and fpathconf functions).

To further confuse things, if a particular run-time limit does not vary on a given system, it can be defined statically in a header. If it is not defined in a header, however, the application must call one of the three conf functions (which we describe shortly) to determine its value at run time.

2.5.1 ANSI C Limits

All the limits defined by ANSI C are compile-time limits. Figure 2.2 shows the limits from the C standard that are defined in the file <limits.h>. These constants are always defined in the header and don't change in a given system. The third column shows the minimum acceptable values from the ANSI C standard. This allows for a system with 16-bit integers using 1's-complement arithmetic. The fourth column shows the values from a current system with 32-bit integers using 2's-complement arithmetic. Note that none of the unsigned data types has a minimum value, as this value must be 0 for an unsigned data type.

One difference that we will encounter is whether a system provides signed or unsigned character values. From the fourth column in Figure 2.2 we see that this particular system uses signed characters. We see that CHAR_MIN equals SCHAR_MIN and CHAR_MAX equals SCHAR_MAX. If the system uses unsigned characters we would have CHAR_MIN equal to 0 and CHAR_MAX equal to UCHAR_MAX.

There is a similar set of definitions for the floating point data types in the header <float.h>. Anyone doing serious floating point work should examine this file.

Another constant from ANSI C that we'll encounter is FOPEN_MAX, the minimum number of standard I/O streams that the implementation guarantees can be open at once. This value is in the <stdio.h> header, and its minimum value is 8. The POSIX.1 value STREAM_MAX, if defined, must have the same value as FOPEN_MAX.

Name	Description	Minimum acceptable value	Typical value
CHAR_BIT	bits in a char	8	8
CHAR_MAX	max value of char	(see later)	127
CHAR_MIN	min value of char	(see later)	-128
SCHAR_MAX	max value of signed char	127	127
SCHAR_MIN	min value of signed char	-127	-128
UCHAR_MAX	max value of unsigned char	255	255
INT_MAX	max value of int	32,767	2,147,483,647
INT_MIN	min value of int	-32,767	-2,147,483,648
UINT_MAX	max value of unsigned int	65,535	4,294,967,295
SHRT_MIN	min value of short	-32,767	-32,768
SHRT_MAX	max value of short	32,767	32,767
USHRT_MAX	max value of unsigned short	65,535	65,535
LONG_MAX	max value of long	2,147,483,647	2,147,483,647
LONG_MIN	min value of long	-2,147,483,647	-2,147,483,648
ULONG_MAX	max value of unsigned long	4,294,967,295	4,294,967,295
MB_LEN_MAX	max number of bytes in a multibyte character constant	1	1

Figure 2.2 Sizes of integral values from <limits.h>.

ANSI C also defines the constant TMP_MAX in <stdio.h>. It is the maximum number of unique filenames generated by the tmpnam function. We'll have more to say about this constant in Section 5.13.

2.5.2 POSIX Limits

POSIX.1 defines numerous constants that deal with implementation limits of the operating system. Unfortunately, this is one of the more confusing aspects of POSIX.1. (Reading and comprehending Sections 2.8 and 2.9 of the POSIX.1 standard are an exercise in deciphering "standardese.")

There are 33 different limits and constants. These are divided into the following eight categories:

1. Invariant minimum values (the 13 constants in Figure 2.3).

2. Invariant value: SSIZE_MAX.

3. Run-time increasable value: NGROUPS_MAX.

4. Run-time invariant values (possibly indeterminate): ARG_MAX, CHILD_MAX, OPEN_MAX, STREAM_MAX, and TZNAME_MAX.

5. Pathname variable values (possibly indeterminate): LINK_MAX, MAX_CANON, MAX_INPUT, NAME_MAX, PATH_MAX, and PIPE_BUF.

6. Compile-time symbolic constants: _POSIX_SAVED_IDS, _POSIX_VERSION, and _POSIX_JOB_CONTROL.

7. Execution-time symbolic constants: _POSIX_NO_TRUNC, _POSIX_VDISABLE, and _POSIX_CHOWN_RESTRICTED.

8. Obsolete constant: CLK_TCK.

Of these 33 limits and constants, 15 are always defined and others may or may not be defined, depending on certain conditions. We describe the limits and constants that may or may not be defined (items 4–8) in Section 2.5.4, when we describe the sysconf, pathconf, and fpathconf functions. We summarize all the limits and constants in Figure 2.7. The 13 invariant minimum values are shown in Figure 2.3.

Name	Description: minimum acceptable value for	Value
_POSIX_ARG_MAX	length of arguments to exec functions	4096
_POSIX_CHILD_MAX	number of child processes per real user ID	6
_POSIX_LINK_MAX	number of links to a file	8
_POSIX_MAX_CANON	number of bytes on a terminal's canonical input queue	255
_POSIX_MAX_INPUT	space available on a terminal's input queue	255
_POSIX_NAME_MAX	number of bytes in a filename	14
_POSIX_NGROUPS_MAX	number of simultaneous supplementary group IDs per process	0
_POSIX_OPEN_MAX	number of open files per process	16
_POSIX_PATH_MAX	number of bytes in a pathname	255
_POSIX_PIPE_BUF	number of bytes that can be written atomically to a pipe	512
_POSIX_SSIZE_MAX	value that can be stored in ssize_t object	32767
_POSIX_STREAM_MAX	number of standard I/O streams a process can have open at once	8
_POSIX_TZNAME_MAX	number of bytes for the name of a time zone	3

Figure 2.3 POSIX.1 invariant minimum values from <limits.h>.

These values are invariant—they do not change from one system to another. They specify the most restrictive values for these features. A conforming POSIX.1 implementation must provide values that are at least this large. This is why they are called minimums, although their names all contain MAX. Also, a portable application must not require a larger value. We describe what each of these constants refers to as we proceed through the text.

Unfortunately, some of these invariant minimum values are too small to be of practical use. For example, most Unix systems today provide far more than 16 open files per process. Even Version 7 in 1978 provided 20 open files per process! Also, the minimum limit of 255 for _POSIX_PATH_MAX is too small. Pathnames can exceed this limit. This means that we can't use the two constants _POSIX_OPEN_MAX and _POSIX_PATH_MAX as array sizes at compile time, for example.

Each of the 13 invariant minimum values in Figure 2.3 has an associated implementation value whose name is formed by removing the _POSIX_ prefix from the name in Figure 2.3. The names without the leading _POSIX_ were intended to be the actual values that a given implementation supports. (These 13 implementation values are items 2–5 from our list earlier in this section: the invariant value, the run-time increasable value, the run-time invariant values, and the pathname variable values.) The problem is that not all of the 13 implementation values are guaranteed to be defined in the <limits.h> header. The reason a particular value may not be defined in the header is because its actual value for a given process may depend on the amount of memory on the system, for example. If they're not defined in the header, we can't use them as array bounds at compile time. So, POSIX.1 decided to provide three run-time functions for us to call, sysconf, pathconf, and fpathconf, to determine the actual implementation value at run time. There is still a problem, however, because some of the values are defined by POSIX.1 as being possibly "indeterminate" (logically infinite). This means that the value has no practical upper bound. For example, the limit on the number of open files per process in SVR4 is virtually unlimited, so OPEN_MAX is considered indeterminate under SVR4. We'll return to this problem of indeterminate run-time limits in Section 2.5.7.

2.5.3 XPG3 Limits

XPG3 defines seven constants that always appear in the <limits.h> header. POSIX.1 would call these invariant minimum values. They are listed in Figure 2.4. Most of these values deal with message catalogs.

Name	Description	Minimum acceptable value	Typical value
NL_ARGMAX	maximum value of digit in calls to printf and scanf	9	9
NL_LANGMAX	maximum number of bytes in LANG environment variable	14	14
NL_MSGMAX	maximum message number	32,767	32,767
NL_NMAX	maximum number of bytes in N-to-1 mapping characters		1
NL_SETMAX	maximum set number	255	255
NL_TEXTMAX	maximum number of bytes in a message string	255	255
NZERO	default process priority	20	20

Figure 2.4 XPG3 invariant minimum values from <limits.h>.

XPG3 also defines the value PASS_MAX, which can appear in <limits.h> as the maximum number of significant characters in a password (not including the terminating null byte). POSIX.1 would call this value a run-time invariant value (possibly indeterminate). The minimum acceptable value is 8. The value of PASS_MAX can also be obtained at run time with the sysconf function, as described in Section 2.5.4.

2.5.4 sysconf, pathconf, and fpathconf Functions

We've listed various minimum values that an implementation must support, but how do we find out the limits that a particular system actually supports? As we mentioned earlier, some of these limits might be available at compile time and others must be determined at run time. We've also mentioned that some don't change in a given system, while others are associated with a file or directory. The run-time limits are obtained by calling one of the following three functions.

```
#include <unistd.h>

long sysconf(int name);

long pathconf(const char *pathname, int name);

long fpathconf(int filedes, int name);
```
                    All three return: corresponding value if OK, −1 on error (see later)

The difference between the last two functions is that one takes a pathname as its argument and the other takes a file descriptor argument.

Figure 2.5 lists the *name* arguments that are used by these three functions. Constants beginning with _SC_ are used as arguments to sysconf and arguments beginning with _PC_ are used as arguments to either pathconf or fpathconf.

There are some restrictions for the *pathname* argument to pathconf and the *filedes* argument to fpathconf. If any of these restrictions aren't met, the results are undefined.

1. The referenced file for _PC_MAX_CANON, _PC_MAX_INPUT, and _PC_VDISABLE must be a terminal file.

2. The referenced file for _PC_LINK_MAX can be either a file or directory. If it is a directory, the return value applies to the directory itself (not the filename entries within the directory).

3. The referenced file for _PC_NAME_MAX and _PC_NO_TRUNC must be a directory. The return value applies to filenames within the directory.

4. The referenced file for _PC_PATH_MAX must be a directory. The value returned is the maximum length of a relative pathname when the specified directory is the working directory. (Unfortunately this isn't the real maximum length of an absolute pathname, which is what we want to know. We'll return to this problem in Section 2.5.7.)

5. The referenced file for _PC_PIPE_BUF must be a pipe, FIFO, or directory. In the first two cases (pipe or FIFO) the return value is the limit for the referenced pipe or FIFO. For the other case (a directory) the return value is the limit for any FIFO created in that directory.

6. The referenced file for _PC_CHOWN_RESTRICTED must be either a file or directory. If it is a directory, the return value indicates whether this option applies to files within that directory.

We need to specify in more detail the different return values from these three functions.

1. All three functions return −1 and set errno to EINVAL if the *name* isn't one of the appropriate constants from the third column of Figure 2.5.

Name of limit	Description	*name* argument
ARG_MAX	maximum length of arguments to the exec functions (in bytes)	_SC_ARG_MAX
CHILD_MAX	maximum number of processes per real user ID	_SC_CHILD_MAX
clock ticks/second	number of clock ticks per second	_SC_CLK_TCK
NGROUPS_MAX	maximum number of simultaneous supplementary process group IDs per process	_SC_NGROUPS_MAX
OPEN_MAX	maximum number of open files per process	_SC_OPEN_MAX
PASS_MAX	maximum number of significant characters in a password (XPG3 and SVR4, not POSIX.1)	_SC_PASS_MAX
STREAM_MAX	maximum number of standard I/O streams per process at any given time—if defined, it must have the same value as FOPEN_MAX	_SC_STREAM_MAX
TZNAME_MAX	maximum number of bytes for the name of a time zone	_SC_TZNAME_MAX
_POSIX_JOB_CONTROL	indicates if the implementation supports job control	_SC_JOB_CONTROL
_POSIX_SAVED_IDS	indicates if the implementation supports the saved set-user-ID and the saved set-group-ID	_SC_SAVED_IDS
_POSIX_VERSION	indicates the POSIX.1 version	_SC_VERSION
_XOPEN_VERSION	indicates the XPG version (not POSIX.1)	_SC_XOPEN_VERSION
LINK_MAX	maximum value of a file's link count	_PC_LINK_MAX
MAX_CANON	maximum number of bytes on a terminal's canonical input queue	_PC_MAX_CANON
MAX_INPUT	number of bytes for which space is available on terminal's input queue	_PC_MAX_INPUT
NAME_MAX	maximum number of bytes in a filename (does not include a null at end)	_PC_NAME_MAX
PATH_MAX	maximum number of bytes in a relative pathname (does not include a null at end)	_PC_PATH_MAX
PIPE_BUF	maximum number of bytes that can be written atomically to a pipe	_PC_PIPE_BUF
_POSIX_CHOWN_RESTRICTED	indicates if use of chown is restricted	_PC_CHOWN_RESTRICTED
_POSIX_NO_TRUNC	indicates if pathnames longer than NAME_MAX generate an error	_PC_NO_TRUNC
_POSIX_VDISABLE	if defined, terminal special characters can be disabled with this value	_PC_VDISABLE

Figure 2.5 Limits and *name* arguments to sysconf, pathconf, and fpathconf.

2. The 12 *name*s that contain MAX and the *name* _PC_PIPE_BUF can return either the value of the variable (a return value ≥ 0) or an indication that the value is indeterminate. An indeterminate value is indicated by returning –1 and not changing the value of errno.

3. The value returned for _SC_CLK_TCK is the number of clock ticks per second, for use with the return values from the times function (Section 8.15).

4. The value returned for _SC_VERSION indicates the four-digit year and two-digit month of the standard. This can be either 198808L or 199009L, or some other value for a later version of the standard.

5. The value returned for _SC_XOPEN_VERSION indicates the version of the XPG that the system complies with. Its current value is 3.

6. The two values _SC_JOB_CONTROL and _SC_SAVED_IDS represent optional features. If sysconf returns −1 without changing errno for either of these, the feature isn't supported. Both of these features can also be determined at compile time from the <unistd.h> header.

7. _PC_CHOWN_RESTRICTED and _PC_NO_TRUNC, return −1 without changing errno if the feature is not supported for the specified *pathname* or *filedes*.

8. _PC_VDISABLE returns −1 without changing errno if the feature is not supported for the specified *pathname* or *filedes*. If the feature is supported, the return value is the character value to be used to disable the special terminal input characters (Figure 11.6).

Example

Program 2.1 prints all these limits, handling the case where a limit is not defined.

```
#include     <errno.h>
#include     "ourhdr.h"

static void pr_sysconf(char *, int);
static void pr_pathconf(char *, char *, int);

int
main(int argc, char *argv[])
{
    if (argc != 2)
        err_quit("usage: a.out <dirname>");

    pr_sysconf("ARG_MAX            =", _SC_ARG_MAX);
    pr_sysconf("CHILD_MAX          =", _SC_CHILD_MAX);
    pr_sysconf("clock ticks/second =", _SC_CLK_TCK);
    pr_sysconf("NGROUPS_MAX        =", _SC_NGROUPS_MAX);
    pr_sysconf("OPEN_MAX           =", _SC_OPEN_MAX);
#ifdef _SC_STREAM_MAX
    pr_sysconf("STREAM_MAX         =", _SC_STREAM_MAX);
#endif
#ifdef _SC_TZNAME_MAX
    pr_sysconf("TZNAME_MAX         =", _SC_TZNAME_MAX);
#endif
    pr_sysconf("_POSIX_JOB_CONTROL =", _SC_JOB_CONTROL);
    pr_sysconf("_POSIX_SAVED_IDS   =", _SC_SAVED_IDS);
    pr_sysconf("_POSIX_VERSION     =", _SC_VERSION);
```

```
        pr_pathconf("MAX_CANON      =", "/dev/tty", _PC_MAX_CANON);
        pr_pathconf("MAX_INPUT      =", "/dev/tty", _PC_MAX_INPUT);
        pr_pathconf("_POSIX_VDISABLE =", "/dev/tty", _PC_VDISABLE);
        pr_pathconf("LINK_MAX       =", argv[1], _PC_LINK_MAX);
        pr_pathconf("NAME_MAX       =", argv[1], _PC_NAME_MAX);
        pr_pathconf("PATH_MAX       =", argv[1], _PC_PATH_MAX);
        pr_pathconf("PIPE_BUF       =", argv[1], _PC_PIPE_BUF);
        pr_pathconf("_POSIX_NO_TRUNC =", argv[1], _PC_NO_TRUNC);
        pr_pathconf("_POSIX_CHOWN_RESTRICTED =",
                                argv[1], _PC_CHOWN_RESTRICTED);
        exit(0);
}

static void
pr_sysconf(char *mesg, int name)
{
        long    val;

        fputs(mesg, stdout);
        errno = 0;
        if ( (val = sysconf(name)) < 0) {
            if (errno != 0)
                err_sys("sysconf error");
            fputs(" (not defined)\n", stdout);
        } else
            printf(" %ld\n", val);
}

static void
pr_pathconf(char *mesg, char *path, int name)
{
        long    val;

        fputs(mesg, stdout);
        errno = 0;
        if ( (val = pathconf(path, name)) < 0) {
            if (errno != 0)
                err_sys("pathconf error, path = %s", path);
            fputs(" (no limit)\n", stdout);
        } else
            printf(" %ld\n", val);
}
```

Program 2.1 Print all possible sysconf and pathconf values.

We have conditionally included two constants that were added to POSIX.1 but were not part of the IEEE Std 1003.1–1988 version of the standard. Figure 2.6 shows sample output from Program 2.1 for some different systems. The entries "not def" mean the constant is not defined. We'll see in Section 4.14 that the SVR4 S5 filesystem is the

Limit	SunOS 4.1.1	SVR4		4.3+BSD
		S5 filesys	UFS filesys	
ARG_MAX	1048576	5120	5120	20480
CHILD_MAX	133	30	30	40
clock ticks/second	60	100	100	60
NGROUPS_MAX	16	16	16	16
OPEN_MAX	64	64	64	64
_POSIX_JOB_CONTROL	1	1	1	1
_POSIX_SAVED_IDS	1	1	1	not def
_POSIX_VERSION	198808	198808	198808	198808
MAX_CANON	256	256	256	255
MAX_INPUT	256	512	512	255
_POSIX_VDISABLE	0	0	0	255
LINK_MAX	32767	1000	1000	32767
NAME_MAX	255	14	255	255
PATH_MAX	1024	1024	1024	1024
PIPE_BUF	4096	5120	5120	512
_POSIX_NO_TRUNC	1	not def	1	1
_POSIX_CHOWN_RESTRICTED	1	not def	not def	1

Figure 2.6 Examples of configuration limits.

traditional System V filesystem, that dates back to Version 7. UFS is the SVR4 implementation of the Berkeley fast filesystem. ☐

2.5.5 FIPS 151–1 Requirements

The FIPS 151–1 standard that we mentioned in Section 2.2.4 tightens the POSIX.1 standard by requiring the following features.

- The following POSIX.1 optional features are required: _POSIX_JOB_CONTROL, _POSIX_SAVED_IDS, _POSIX_NO_TRUNC, _POSIX_CHOWN_RESTRICTED, and _POSIX_VDISABLE.

- The minimum value of NGROUPS_MAX is 8.

- The group ID of a newly created file or directory must be set to the group ID of the directory in which the file is created. (We describe this feature in Section 4.6.)

- If a read or write is interrupted by a signal that is caught after some data has been transferred, the function must return the number of bytes that have been transferred. (We discuss interrupted system calls in Section 10.5.)

- A login shell must define the environment variables HOME and LOGNAME.

Since the U.S. government purchases many computer systems, most vendors of POSIX systems will support these added FIPS requirements.

Constant name	Compile-time		Run-time name	Minimum value
	Header	Required?		
ARG_MAX	`<limits.h>`	*optional*	_SC_ARG_MAX	_POSIX_ARG_MAX = 4096
CHAR_BIT	`<limits.h>`	required		8
CHAR_MAX	`<limits.h>`	required		127
CHAR_MIN	`<limits.h>`	required		0
CHILD_MAX	`<limits.h>`	*optional*	_SC_CHILD_MAX	_POSIX_CHILD_MAX = 6
clock ticks/second			_SC_CLK_TCK	
FOPEN_MAX	`<stdio.h>`	required		8
INT_MAX	`<limits.h>`	required		32,767
INT_MIN	`<limits.h>`	required		−32,767
LINK_MAX	`<limits.h>`	*optional*	_PC_LINK_MAX	_POSIX_LINK_MAX = 8
LONG_MAX	`<limits.h>`	required		2,147,483,647
LONG_MIN	`<limits.h>`	required		−2,147,483,647
MAX_CANON	`<limits.h>`	*optional*	_PC_MAX_CANON	_POSIX_MAX_CANON = 255
MAX_INPUT	`<limits.h>`	*optional*	_PC_MAX_INPUT	_POSIX_MAX_INPUT = 255
MB_LEN_MAX	`<limits.h>`	required		
NAME_MAX	`<limits.h>`	*optional*	_PC_NAME_MAX	_POSIX_NAME_MAX = 14
NGROUPS_MAX	`<limits.h>`	required	_SC_NGROUPS_MAX	_POSIX_NGROUPS_MAX = 0
NL_ARGMAX	`<limits.h>`	required		9
NL_LANGMAX	`<limits.h>`	required		14
NL_MSGMAX	`<limits.h>`	required		32,767
NL_NMAX	`<limits.h>`	required		
NL_SETMAX	`<limits.h>`	required		255
NL_TEXTMAX	`<limits.h>`	required		255
NZERO	`<limits.h>`	required		20
OPEN_MAX	`<limits.h>`	*optional*	_SC_OPEN_MAX	_POSIX_OPEN_MAX = 16
PASS_MAX	`<limits.h>`	*optional*	_SC_PASS_MAX	8
PATH_MAX	`<limits.h>`	*optional*	_PC_PATH_MAX	_POSIX_PATH_MAX = 255
PIPE_BUF	`<limits.h>`	*optional*	_PC_PIPE_BUF	_POSIX_PIPE_BUF = 512
SCHAR_MAX	`<limits.h>`	required		127
SCHAR_MIN	`<limits.h>`	required		−127
SHRT_MAX	`<limits.h>`	required		32,767
SHRT_MIN	`<limits.h>`	required		−32,767
SSIZE_MAX	`<limits.h>`	required		_POSIX_SSIZE_MAX = 32,767
STREAM_MAX	`<limits.h>`	*optional*	_SC_STREAM_MAX	_POSIX_STREAM_MAX = 8
TMP_MAX	`<stdio.h>`	required		10,000
TZNAME_MAX	`<limits.h>`	*optional*	_SC_TZNAME_MAX	_POSIX_TZNAME_MAX = 3
UCHAR_MAX	`<limits.h>`	required		255
UINT_MAX	`<limits.h>`	required		65,535
ULONG_MAX	`<limits.h>`	required		4,294,967,295
USHRT_MAX	`<limits.h>`	required		65,535
_POSIX_CHOWN_RESTRICTED	`<unistd.h>`	*optional*	_PC_CHOWN_RESTRICTED	
_POSIX_JOB_CONTROL	`<unistd.h>`	*optional*	_SC_JOB_CONTROL	
_POSIX_NO_TRUNC	`<unistd.h>`	*optional*	_PC_NO_TRUNC	
_POSIX_SAVED_IDS	`<unistd.h>`	*optional*	_SC_SAVED_IDS	
_POSIX_VDISABLE	`<unistd.h>`	*optional*	_PC_VDISABLE	
_POSIX_VERSION	`<unistd.h>`	required	_SC_VERSION	
_XOPEN_VERSION	`<unistd.h>`	required	_SC_XOPEN_VERSION	

Figure 2.7 Summary of compile-time and run-time limits.

2.5.6 Summary of Limits

We've described various limits and magic constants, some of which always appear in a header, some of which may optionally appear in a header, and others that can be determined at run time. Figure 2.7 summarizes all these constants alphabetically and the various ways to obtain their values. A run-time name that begins with _SC_ is an argument to the sysconf function, and a name that begins with _PC_ is an argument to the pathconf and fpathconf functions. If the constant has a minimum value, it is listed. Note that the 13 POSIX.1 invariant minimum values from Figure 2.3 appear in the rightmost column of Figure 2.7.

2.5.7 Indeterminate Run-Time Limits

We mentioned that some of the values from Figure 2.7 can be indeterminate. These values are the ones with a third column of *optional*, whose names contain MAX, and the value PIPE_BUF. The problem we encounter is that if these aren't defined in the <limits.h> header we can't use them at compile time. But they might not be defined at run time if their value is indeterminate! Let's look at two specific cases—allocating storage for a pathname and determining the number of file descriptors.

Pathnames

Lots of programs need to allocate storage for a pathname. Typically the storage has been allocated at compile time and various magic numbers (few of which are the correct value) have been used by different programs as the array size: 256, 512, 1024, or the standard I/O constant BUFSIZ. The 4.3BSD constant MAXPATHLEN in the header <sys/param.h> is the correct value, but many 4.3BSD applications didn't use it.

POSIX.1 tries to help with the PATH_MAX value, but if this value is indeterminate, we're still out of luck. Program 2.2 is a function that we'll use throughout this text to allocate storage dynamically for a pathname.

If the constant PATH_MAX is defined in <limits.h> then we're all set. If it's not, we need to call pathconf. Since the value returned by pathconf is the maximum size of a relative pathname when the first argument is the working directory, we specify the root as the first argument and add 1 to the result. If pathconf indicates that PATH_MAX is indeterminate, we have to punt and just guess some value. The +1 in the call to malloc is for the null byte at the end (which PATH_MAX doesn't account for).

The correct way to handle the case of an indeterminate result depends on how the allocated space is being used. If we were allocating space for a call to getcwd, for example (to return the absolute pathname of the current working directory, see Section 4.22) and if the allocated space is too small, an error is returned and errno is set to ERANGE. We could then increase the allocated space by calling realloc (see Section 7.8 and Exercise 4.18) and try again. We could keep doing this until the call to getcwd succeeded.

```
#include    <errno.h>
#include    <limits.h>
#include    "ourhdr.h"

#ifdef  PATH_MAX
static int  pathmax = PATH_MAX;
#else
static int  pathmax = 0;
#endif

#define PATH_MAX_GUESS  1024    /* if PATH_MAX is indeterminate */
                        /* we're not guaranteed this is adequate */
char *
path_alloc(int *size)
                /* also return allocated size, if nonnull */
{
    char    *ptr;

    if (pathmax == 0) {      /* first time through */
        errno = 0;
        if ( (pathmax = pathconf("/", _PC_PATH_MAX)) < 0) {
            if (errno == 0)
                pathmax = PATH_MAX_GUESS;   /* it's indeterminate */
            else
                err_sys("pathconf error for _PC_PATH_MAX");
        } else
            pathmax++;          /* add one since it's relative to root */
    }

    if ( (ptr = malloc(pathmax + 1)) == NULL)
        err_sys("malloc error for pathname");

    if (size != NULL)
        *size = pathmax + 1;
    return(ptr);
}
```

Program 2.2 Dynamically allocate space for a pathname.

Maximum Number of Open Files

A common sequence of code in a daemon process (a process that runs in the background, not connected to a terminal) is one that closes all open files. Some programs have the code sequence

```
#include  <sys/param.h>

for (i = 0; i < NOFILE; i++)
    close(i);
```

assuming the constant NOFILE was defined in the <sys/param.h> header. Other programs use the constant _NFILE that some versions of <stdio.h> provide as the upper limit. Some hard code the upper limit as 20.

We would hope to use the POSIX.1 value OPEN_MAX to determine this value portably, but if the value is indeterminate we still have a problem. If we wrote

```
#include   <unistd.h>

for (i = 0; i < sysconf(_SC_OPEN_MAX); i++)
    close(i);
```

and if OPEN_MAX was indeterminate, the loop would never execute, since sysconf would return −1. Our best option in this case is just to close all descriptors up to some arbitrary limit (say 256). As with our pathname example, this is not guaranteed to work for all cases, but it's the best we can do. We show this technique in Program 2.3.

```
#include     <errno.h>
#include     <limits.h>
#include     "ourhdr.h"

#ifdef  OPEN_MAX
static int   openmax = OPEN_MAX;
#else
static int   openmax = 0;
#endif

#define OPEN_MAX_GUESS  256     /* if OPEN_MAX is indeterminate */
                                /* we're not guaranteed this is adequate */
int
open_max(void)
{
    if (openmax == 0) {        /* first time through */
        errno = 0;
        if ( (openmax = sysconf(_SC_OPEN_MAX)) < 0) {
            if (errno == 0)
                openmax = OPEN_MAX_GUESS;   /* it's indeterminate */
            else
                err_sys("sysconf error for _SC_OPEN_MAX");
        }
    }
    return(openmax);
}
```

Program 2.3 Determine the number of file descriptors.

We might be tempted to call close until we get an error return, but the error return from close (EBADF) doesn't distinguish between an invalid descriptor and a descriptor that wasn't open. If we tried this technique and descriptor 9 was not open but descriptor 10 was, we would stop on 9 and never close 10. The dup function (Section 3.12) does return a specific error when OPEN_MAX is exceeded, but duplicating a descriptor a couple of hundred times is an extreme way to determine this value.

The SVR4 and 4.3+BSD `getrlimit(2)` function (Section 7.11) and the 4.3+BSD function `getdtablesize(2)` return the maximum number of descriptors that a process can have open. Calling these two functions, however, isn't portable.

The `OPEN_MAX` value is called run-time invariant by POSIX, meaning its value should not change during the lifetime of a process. But under SVR4 and 4.3+BSD we can call the `setrlimit(2)` function (Section 7.11) to change this value from a running process. (This value can also be changed from the C Shell with the `limit` command, and from the Bourne shell and KornShell with the `ulimit` command.) If our system supports this functionality we could change Program 2.3 to call `sysconf` every time it is called, not just the first time.

2.6   Feature Test Macros

The headers define numerous POSIX.1 and XPG3 symbols, as we've described. But most implementations can add their own definitions to these headers, in addition to the POSIX.1 and XPG3 definitions. If we want to compile a program so that it depends only on the POSIX definitions and doesn't use any implementation-defined limits, we need to define the constant `_POSIX_SOURCE`. All the POSIX.1 headers use this constant to exclude any implementation-defined definitions when `_POSIX_SOURCE` is defined.

The constant `_POSIX_SOURCE`, and its corresponding constant `_XOPEN_SOURCE`, are called *feature test macros*. All feature test macros begin with an underscore. When used, they are typically defined in the `cc` command as in

```
cc -D_POSIX_SOURCE file.c
```

This causes the feature test macro to be defined before any header files are included by the C program. We can also set the first line of a source file to

```
#define _POSIX_SOURCE  1
```

if we want to use only the POSIX.1 definitions.

Another feature test macro is `__STDC__`, which is automatically defined by the C compiler if the compiler conforms to the ANSI C standard. This allows us to write C programs that compile under both ANSI C compilers and non-ANSI C compilers. For example, a header could look like

```
#ifdef __STDC__
void  *myfunc(const char *, int);
#else
void  *myfunc();
#endif
```

to take advantage of the ANSI C prototype feature, if supported. Be aware that the two consecutive underscores at the beginning and end of the name `__STDC__`, often print as one long underscore (as in the preceding sample source code).

2.7   Primitive System Data Types

Historically certain C data types have been associated with certain Unix variables. For example, the major and minor device numbers have historically been stored in a 16-bit short integer, with 8 bits for the major device number and 8 bits for the minor device number. But many larger systems need more than 256 values for these device numbers, so a different technique is needed. (Indeed, SVR4 uses 32 bits for the device number: 14 bits for the major and 18 bits for the minor.)

The header <sys/types.h> defines some implementation-dependent data types, called the *primitive system data types*. More of these data types are defined in other headers also. These data types are defined in the headers with the C typedef facility. Most end in _t. Figure 2.8 lists the primitive system data types that we'll encounter in this text.

Type	Description
caddr_t	core address (Section 12.9)
clock_t	counter of clock ticks (process time) (Section 1.10)
comp_t	compressed clock ticks (Section 8.13)
dev_t	device numbers (major and minor) (Section 4.23)
fd_set	file descriptor sets (Section 12.5.1)
fpos_t	file position (Section 5.10)
gid_t	numeric group IDs
ino_t	i-node numbers (Section 4.14)
mode_t	file type, file creation mode (Section 4.5)
nlink_t	link counts for directory entries (Section 4.14)
off_t	file sizes and offsets (signed) (lseek, Section 3.6)
pid_t	process IDs and process group IDs (signed) (Sections 8.2 and 9.4)
ptrdiff_t	result of subtracting two pointers (signed)
rlim_t	resource limits (Section 7.11)
sig_atomic_t	data type that can be accessed atomically (Section 10.15)
sigset_t	signal set (Section 10.11)
size_t	sizes of objects (such as strings) (unsigned) (Section 3.7)
ssize_t	functions that return a count of bytes (signed) (read, write, Section 3.7)
time_t	counter of seconds of calendar time (Section 1.10)
uid_t	numeric user IDs
wchar_t	can represent all distinct character codes

Figure 2.8 Primitive system data types.

By defining these data types this way, we do not build into our programs implementation details that can change from one system to another. We describe what each of these data types is used for when we encounter them later in the text.

2.8 Conflicts Between Standards

All in all these different standards fit together nicely. Our main concern is any differences between the ANSI C standard and POSIX.1, since XPG3 is an older standard (and is being revised) and FIPS is a tightening of POSIX.1. There are some differences.

ANSI C defines the function clock to return the amount of CPU time used by the process. The value returned is a clock_t value. To convert this value to seconds we divide it by CLOCKS_PER_SEC, which is defined in the <time.h> header. POSIX.1 defines the function times that returns both the CPU time (for the caller and all its terminated children) and the clock time. All these time values are `clock_t` values. The IEEE Std. 1003.1–1988 defined the symbol `CLK_TCK` as the number of ticks per second that these `clock_t` values were measured in. With the 1990 POSIX.1 standard the symbol `CLK_TCK` is declared obsolete and we should use the `sysconf` function instead, to obtain the number of clock ticks per second for use with the return values from the `times` function. What we have is the same term, clock ticks per second, defined differently by ANSI C and POSIX.1. Both standards also use the same data type (`clock_t`) to hold these different values. The difference can be seen in SVR4, where `clock` returns microseconds (hence `CLOCKS_PER_SEC` is 1 million) while `CLK_TCK` is usually 50, 60, or 100, depending on the CPU type.

Another area of potential conflict is when the ANSI C standard specifies a function, but doesn't specify it as strongly as POSIX.1. This is the case for functions that require a different implementation in a POSIX environment (with multiple processes) than an ANSI C environment (where very little can be assumed about the host operating system). Nevertheless, many POSIX-compliant systems implement the ANSI C function, for compatibility. The `signal` function is an example. If we unknowingly use the `signal` function provided by SVR4 (hoping to write portable code that can be run in ANSI C environments and under older Unix systems), it'll provide different semantics than the POSIX.1 `sigaction` function. We'll have more to say about the `signal` function in Chapter 10.

2.9 Summary

Much has been happening over the past few years with the standardization of the different versions of Unix. We've described the three dominant standards—ANSI C, POSIX, and XPG3—and the effect of these standards on the two implementations that we'll examine in this text: SVR4 and 4.3+BSD. These standards try to define certain parameters that can change with each implementation, but we've seen that these limits are imperfect. We'll encounter all these limits and magic constants as we proceed through the text.

The bibliography lists how one can order copies of these standards that we've discussed.

Exercises

2.1 We mentioned in Section 2.7 that some of the primitive system data types are defined in more than one header. For example, `size_t` is defined in six different headers. Since a program could `#include` all six of these different headers and since ANSI C does not allow multiple `typedef`s for the same name, how must the headers be written?

2.2 Examine your system's headers and list the actual data types used to implement the primitive system data types.

3

File I/O

3.1 Introduction

We'll start our discussion of the Unix system by describing the functions available for file I/O—open a file, read a file, write a file, and so on. Most Unix file I/O can be performed using only five functions: open, read, write, lseek, and close. We then examine the effect of different buffer sizes on the read and write functions.

The functions described in this chapter are often referred to as *unbuffered I/O* (in contrast to the standard I/O routines, which we describe in Chapter 5). The term unbuffered refers to the fact that each read or write invokes a system call in the kernel. These unbuffered I/O functions are not part of ANSI C, but are part of POSIX.1 and XPG3.

Whenever we describe the sharing of resources between multiple processes, the concept of an atomic operation becomes important. We examine this concept with regard to file I/O and the arguments to the open function. This leads to a discussion of how files are shared between multiple processes and the kernel data structures involved. Once we've described these features, we describe the dup, fcntl, and ioctl functions.

3.2 File Descriptors

To the kernel all open files are referred to by file descriptors. A file descriptor is a nonnegative integer. When we open an existing file or create a new file, the kernel returns a file descriptor to the process. When we want to read or write a file, we identify the file with the file descriptor that was returned by open or creat as an argument to either read or write.

By convention the Unix shells associate file descriptor 0 with the standard input of a process, file descriptor 1 with the standard output, and file descriptor 2 with the standard error. This is a convention employed by the Unix shells and many Unix applications—it is not a feature of the kernel. Nevertheless, many Unix applications would break if these associations weren't followed.

The magic numbers 0, 1, and 2 should be replaced in POSIX.1 applications with the symbolic constants STDIN_FILENO, STDOUT_FILENO, and STDERR_FILENO. These are defined in the <unistd.h> header.

File descriptors range from 0 through OPEN_MAX. (Recall Figure 2.7.) Older versions of Unix had an upper limit of 19 (allowing a maximum of 20 open files per process) but this was increased to 63 by many systems.

> With SVR4 and 4.3+BSD the limit is essentially infinite, bounded by the amount of memory on the system, the size of an integer, and any hard and soft limits configured by the system administrator.

3.3 open Function

A file is opened or created by calling the open function.

```
#include <sys/types.h>
#include <sys/stat.h>
#include <fcntl.h>

int open(const char *pathname, int oflag, ... /* , mode_t mode */ );
```
Returns: file descriptor if OK, –1 on error

We show the third argument as ..., which is the ANSI C way to specify that the number and types of the remaining arguments may vary. For this function the third argument is only used when a new file is being created, as we describe later. We show this argument as a comment in the prototype.

The *pathname* is the name of the file to open or create. There are a multitude of options for this function, which are specified by the *oflag* argument. This argument is formed by OR'ing together one or more of the following constants (from the <fcntl.h> header).

O_RDONLY   Open for reading only.

O_WRONLY   Open for writing only.

O_RDWR   Open for reading and writing.

> Most implementations define O_RDONLY as 0, O_WRONLY as 1, and O_RDWR as 2, for compatibility with older programs.

One and only one of these three constants must be specified. The following constants are optional:

O_APPEND   Append to the end of file on each write. We describe this option in detail in Section 3.11.

O_CREAT   Create the file if it doesn't exist. This option requires a third argument to the open function, the *mode*, which specifies the access permission bits of the new file. (When we describe a file's access permission bits in Section 4.5, we'll see how to specify the *mode*, and how it can be modified by the umask value of a process.)

O_EXCL   Generate an error if O_CREAT is also specified and the file already exists. This test for whether the file already exists and the creation of the file if it doesn't exist is an atomic operation. We describe atomic operations in more detail in Section 3.11.

O_TRUNC   If the file exists, and if the file is successfully opened for either write-only or read write, truncate its length to 0.

O_NOCTTY   If the *pathname* refers to a terminal device, do not allocate the device as the controlling terminal for this process. We talk about controlling terminals in Section 9.6.

O_NONBLOCK   If the *pathname* refers to a FIFO, a block special file, or a character special file, this option sets the nonblocking mode for both the opening of the file and for subsequent I/O. We describe this mode in Section 12.2.

> In earlier releases of System V the O_NDELAY (no delay) flag was introduced. This option is similar to the O_NONBLOCK (nonblocking) option, but an ambiguity was introduced in the return value from a read operation. The no-delay option causes a read to return 0 if there is no data to be read from a pipe, FIFO, or device, but this conflicts with a return value of 0 indicating an end of file. SVR4 still supports the no-delay option, with the old semantics, but new applications should use the nonblocking option instead.

O_SYNC   Have each write wait for physical I/O to complete. We use this option in Section 3.13.

> The O_SYNC option is not part of POSIX.1. It is supported by SVR4.

The file descriptor returned by open is guaranteed to be the lowest numbered unused descriptor. This is used by some applications to open a new file on standard input, standard output, or standard error. For example, an application might close standard output (normally file descriptor 1) and then open some other file, knowing that it will be opened on file descriptor 1. We'll see a better way to guarantee that a file is open on a given descriptor in Section 3.12 with the dup2 function.

Filename and Pathname Truncation

What happens if NAME_MAX is 14 and we try to create a new file in the current directory with a filename containing 15 characters? Traditionally, earlier releases of System V allowed this to happen, silently truncating the filename beyond the 14th character, while Berkeley-derived systems return the error ENAMETOOLONG. This problem does not apply just to the creation of new files. If NAME_MAX is 14 and a file exists whose name is exactly 14 characters, then any function that accepts a *pathname* argument (open, stat, etc.) has to deal with this problem.

With POSIX.1 the constant _POSIX_NO_TRUNC determines whether long filenames and long pathnames are truncated or whether an error is returned. As we saw in Chapter 2, this value can vary on a per-filesystem basis.

> FIPS 151−1 requires that an error be returned.
>
> SVR4 does not generate an error for a traditional System V filesystem (S5). (See Figure 2.6.) For a Berkeley-style filesystem (UFS), however, SVR4 does generate an error.
>
> 4.3+BSD always returns an error.

If _POSIX_NO_TRUNC is in effect, then the error ENAMETOOLONG is returned if either the entire pathname exceeds PATH_MAX, or if any filename component of the pathname exceeds NAME_MAX.

3.4   creat Function

A new file can also be created by

```
#include <sys/types.h>
#include <sys/stat.h>
#include <fcntl.h>

int creat(const char *pathname, mode_t mode);
```
                                    Returns: file descriptor opened for write-only if OK, −1 on error

Note that this function is equivalent to

    open(*pathname*, O_WRONLY | O_CREAT | O_TRUNC, *mode*);

> In earlier versions of Unix the second argument to open could only be 0, 1, or 2. There was no way to open a file that didn't already exist. Therefore a separate system call, creat, was needed to create new files. With the O_CREAT and O_TRUNC options now provided by open, a separate creat function is no longer needed.

We'll show how to specify *mode* in Section 4.5 when we describe a file's access permissions in detail.

One deficiency with creat is that the file is opened only for writing. Before the new version of open was provided, if we were creating a temporary file that we wanted to write and then read back, we had to call creat, close, and then open. A better way is to use the new open function, as in

    open(*pathname*, O_RDWR | O_CREAT | O_TRUNC, *mode*);

3.5   close **Function**

An open file is closed by

```
#include <unistd.h>

int close(int filedes);
```
Returns: 0 if OK, −1 on error

Closing a file also releases any record locks that the process may have on the file. We'll discuss this in Section 12.3.

When a process terminates, all open files are automatically closed by the kernel. Many programs take advantage of this fact and don't explicitly close open files. See Program 1.2, for example.

3.6   lseek **Function**

Every open file has an associated "current file offset." This is a nonnegative integer that measures the number of bytes from the beginning of the file. (We describe some exceptions to the "nonnegative" qualifier later in this section.) Read and write operations normally start at the current file offset and cause the offset to be incremented by the number of bytes read or written. By default, this offset is initialized to 0 when a file is opened, unless the O_APPEND option is specified.

An open file can be explicitly positioned by calling lseek.

```
#include <sys/types.h>
#include <unistd.h>

off_t lseek(int filedes, off_t offset, int whence);
```
Returns: new file offset if OK, −1 on error

The interpretation of the *offset* depends on the value of the *whence* argument.

- If *whence* is SEEK_SET, the file's offset is set to *offset* bytes from the beginning of the file.

- If *whence* is SEEK_CUR, the file's offset is set to its current value plus the *offset*. The *offset* can be positive or negative.

- If *whence* is SEEK_END, the file's offset is set to the size of the file plus the *offset*. The *offset* can be positive or negative.

Since a successful call to lseek returns the new file offset, we can seek zero bytes from the current position to determine the current offset.

```
off_t     currpos;

currpos = lseek(fd, 0, SEEK_CUR);
```

This technique can also be used to determine if the referenced file is capable of seeking: if the file descriptor refers to a pipe or FIFO, lseek returns −1 and sets errno to EPIPE.

The three symbolic constants, SEEK_SET, SEEK_CUR, and SEEK_END, were introduced with System V. Before System V *whence* was specified as 0 (absolute), 1 (relative to current offset), or 2 (relative to end of file). Much software still exists with these numbers hard coded.

The character l in the name lseek means "long integer." Before the introduction of the off_t data type, the *offset* argument and the return value were long integers. lseek was introduced with Version 7 when long integers were added to C. (Similar functionality was provided in Version 6 by the functions seek and tell.)

Example

Program 3.1 tests its standard input to see if it is capable of seeking.

```
#include     <sys/types.h>
#include     "ourhdr.h"

int
main(void)
{
    if (lseek(STDIN_FILENO, 0, SEEK_CUR) == -1)
        printf("cannot seek\n");
    else
        printf("seek OK\n");
    exit(0);
}
```

Program 3.1 Test if standard input is capable of seeking.

If we invoke this program interactively, we get

```
$ a.out < /etc/motd
seek OK
$ cat < /etc/motd | a.out
cannot seek
$ a.out < /var/spool/cron/FIFO
cannot seek
```

□

Normally a file's current offset must be a nonnegative integer. It is possible, however, that certain devices could allow negative offsets. But for regular files the offset must be nonnegative. Since negative offsets are possible, we should be careful to compare the return value from lseek as being equal to or not equal to −1 and not test if it's less than 0.

> The /dev/kmem device on SVR4 for the 80386 supports negative offsets.

> Since the offset (off_t) is a signed data type (Figure 2.8), we lose a factor of 2 in the maximum file size. For example, if off_t is a 32-bit integer, the maximum file size is 2^{31} bytes.

lseek only records the current file offset within the kernel—it does not cause any I/O to take place. This offset is then used by the next read or write operation.

The file's offset can be greater than the file's current size, in which case the next write to the file will extend the file. This is referred to as creating a hole in a file and is allowed. Any bytes in a file that have not been written are read back as 0.

Example

Program 3.2 creates a file with a hole in it.

```
#include        <sys/types.h>
#include        <sys/stat.h>
#include        <fcntl.h>
#include        "ourhdr.h"

char    buf1[] = "abcdefghij";
char    buf2[] = "ABCDEFGHIJ";

int
main(void)
{
    int     fd;

    if ( (fd = creat("file.hole", FILE_MODE)) < 0)
        err_sys("creat error");

    if (write(fd, buf1, 10) != 10)
        err_sys("buf1 write error");
    /* offset now = 10 */

    if (lseek(fd, 40, SEEK_SET) == -1)
        err_sys("lseek error");
    /* offset now = 40 */

    if (write(fd, buf2, 10) != 10)
        err_sys("buf2 write error");
    /* offset now = 50 */

    exit(0);
}
```

Program 3.2 Create a file with a hole in it.

Running this program gives us

```
$ a.out
$ ls -l file.hole                              check its size
-rw-r--r--   1 stevens      50 Jul 31 05:50 file.hole
$ od -c file.hole                              let's look at the actual contents
0000000    a   b   c   d   e   f   g   h   i   j  \0  \0  \0  \0  \0  \0
0000020   \0  \0  \0  \0  \0  \0  \0  \0  \0  \0  \0  \0  \0  \0  \0  \0
0000040   \0  \0  \0  \0  \0  \0  \0  \0   A   B   C   D   E   F   G   H
0000060    I   J
0000062
```

We use the od(1) command to look at the actual contents of the file. The -c flag tells it to print the contents as characters. We can see that the 30 unwritten bytes in the middle are read back as zero. The seven-digit number at the beginning of each line is the byte offset in octal. In this example we call the `write` function (Section 3.8). We'll have more to say about files with holes in Section 4.12.   □

3.7   `read` Function

Data is read from an open file with the `read` function.

```
#include <unistd.h>

ssize_t read(int filedes, void *buff, size_t nbytes);
```

                        Returns: number of bytes read, 0 if end of file, –1 on error

If the `read` is successful, the number of bytes read is returned. If the end of file is encountered, 0 is returned.

There are several cases in which the number of bytes actually read is less than the amount requested:

- When reading from a regular file, if the end of file is reached before the requested number of bytes has been read. For example, if there are 30 bytes remaining until the end of file and we try to read 100 bytes, `read` returns 30. The next time we call `read` it will return 0 (end of file).

- When reading from a terminal device, normally up to one line is read at a time (we'll see how to change this in Chapter 11).

- When reading from a network, buffering within the network may cause less than the requested amount to be returned.

- Some record-oriented devices, such as a magnetic tape, return up to a single record at a time.

The read operation starts at the file's current offset. Before a successful return, the offset is incremented by the number of bytes actually read.

POSIX.1 changed the prototype for this function in several ways. The classic definition is

```
int read(int filedes, char *buff, unsigned nbytes);
```

First, the second argument was changed from a char * to a void * to be consistent with ANSI C: the type void * is used for generic pointers. Next, the return value must be a signed integer (ssize_t) to return either a positive byte count, 0 (for end of file), or −1 (for an error). Finally, the third argument historically has been an unsigned integer, to allow a 16-bit implementation to read or write up to 65534 bytes at a time. With the 1990 POSIX.1 standard the new primitive system data type ssize_t was introduced to provide the signed return value, and the unsigned size_t was used for the third argument. (Recall the SSIZE_MAX constant from Figure 2.7.)

3.8   write Function

Data is written to an open file with the write function.

```
#include <unistd.h>

ssize_t write(int filedes, const void *buff, size_t nbytes);
```
Returns: number of bytes written if OK, −1 on error

The return value is usually equal to the *nbytes* argument, otherwise an error has occurred. A common cause for a write error is either filling up a disk or exceeding the file size limit for a given process (Section 7.11 and Exercise 10.11).

For a regular file, the write starts at the file's current offset. If the O_APPEND option was specified in the open, the file's offset is set to the current end of file before each write operation. After a successful write, the file's offset is incremented by the number of bytes actually written.

3.9   I/O Efficiency

Using only the read and write functions, Program 3.3 copies a file. The following caveats apply to Program 3.3:

- It reads from standard input and writes to standard output. This assumes that these have been set up by the shell before this program is executed. Indeed, all normal Unix shells provide a way to open a file for reading on standard input and to create (or rewrite) a file on standard output. This prevents the program from having to open the input and output files.

- Many applications assume that standard input is file descriptor 0 and standard output is file descriptor 1. In this example we use the two defined names STDIN_FILENO and STDOUT_FILENO from <unistd.h>.

```
#include    "ourhdr.h"

#define BUFFSIZE    8192

int
main(void)
{
    int     n;
    char    buf[BUFFSIZE];

    while ( (n = read(STDIN_FILENO, buf, BUFFSIZE)) > 0)
        if (write(STDOUT_FILENO, buf, n) != n)
            err_sys("write error");

    if (n < 0)
        err_sys("read error");

    exit(0);
}
```

Program 3.3 Copy standard input to standard output.

- The program doesn't close the input file or output file. Instead it uses the fact that whenever a process terminates, Unix closes all open file descriptors.

- This example works for both text file and binary files, since there is no difference between the two to the Unix kernel.

One question we haven't answered, however, is how we chose the BUFFSIZE value. Before answering that, let's run the program using different values for BUFFSIZE. In Figure 3.1 we show the results for reading a 1,468,802 byte file, using 18 different buffer sizes.

The file was read using Program 3.3 with standard output redirected to /dev/null. The filesystem used for this test was a Berkeley fast filesystem with 8192-byte blocks. (The st_blksize, which we describe in Section 4.12, is 8192.) This accounts for the minimum in the system time occurring at a BUFFSIZE of 8192. Increasing the buffer size beyond this has no effect.

We'll return to this timing example later in the text. In Section 3.13 we show the effect of synchronous writes, and in Section 5.8 we compare these unbuffered I/O times with the standard I/O library.

3.10 File Sharing

Unix supports the sharing of open files between different processes. Before describing the dup function, we need to describe this sharing. To do this we'll examine the data structures used by the kernel for all I/O.

BUFFSIZE	User CPU (seconds)	System CPU (seconds)	Clock time (seconds)	#loops
1	23.8	397.9	423.4	1468802
2	12.3	202.0	215.2	734401
4	6.1	100.6	107.2	367201
8	3.0	50.7	54.0	183601
16	1.5	25.3	27.0	91801
32	0.7	12.8	13.7	45901
64	0.3	6.6	7.0	22951
128	0.2	3.3	3.6	11476
256	0.1	1.8	1.9	5738
512	0.0	1.0	1.1	2869
1024	0.0	0.6	0.6	1435
2048	0.0	0.4	0.4	718
4096	0.0	0.4	0.4	359
8192	0.0	0.3	0.3	180
16384	0.0	0.3	0.3	90
32768	0.0	0.3	0.3	45
65536	0.0	0.3	0.3	23
131072	0.0	0.3	0.3	12

Figure 3.1 Timing results for reading with different buffer sizes.

Three data structures are used by the kernel, and the relationships among them determines the effect one process has on another with regard to file sharing.

1. Every process has an entry in the process table. Within each process table entry is a table of open file descriptors, which we can think of as a vector, with one entry per descriptor. Associated with each file descriptor are

   (a) the file descriptor flags,

   (b) a pointer to a file table entry.

2. The kernel maintains a file table for all open files. Each file table entry contains

   (a) the file status flags for the file (read, write, append, sync, nonblocking, etc.),

   (b) the current file offset,

   (c) a pointer to the v-node table entry for the file.

3. Each open file (or device) has a v-node structure. The v-node contains information about the type of file and pointers to functions that operate on the file. For most files the v-node also contains the i-node for the file. This information is read from disk when the file is opened, so that all the pertinent information about the file is readily available. For example, the i-node contains the owner of the file, the size of the file, the device the file is located on, pointers to where the actual data blocks for the file are located on disk, and so on. (We talk more about i-nodes in Section 4.14 when we describe the typical Unix filesystem in more detail.)

We're ignoring some implementation details that don't affect our discussion. For example, the table of open file descriptors is usually in the user area and not the process table. In SVR4 this data structure is a linked list of structures. The file table can be implemented in numerous ways—it need not be an array of file table entries. In 4.3+BSD the v-node contains the actual i-node, as we've shown. SVR4 stores the v-node in the i-node for most of its filesystem types. These implementation details don't affect our discussion of file sharing.

Figure 3.2 shows a pictorial arrangement of these three tables for a single process that has two different files open—one file is open on standard input (file descriptor 0) and the other is open on standard output (file descriptor 1).

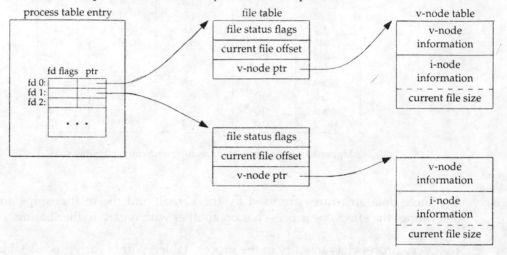

Figure 3.2 Kernel data structures for open files.

The arrangement of these three tables has existed since the early versions of Unix [Thompson 1978], and this arrangement is critical to the way files are shared between different processes. We'll return to this figure in later chapters, as we describe additional ways that files are shared.

> The v-node structure is a recent addition. It evolved when support was provided for multiple filesystem types on a given system. This work was done independently by Peter Weinberger (Bell Laboratories) and Bill Joy (Sun Microsystems). Sun called this the Virtual File System and called the filesystem independent portion of the i-node the v-node [Kleiman 1986]. The v-node propagated through various vendor implementations as support for Sun's Network File System (NFS) was added. The first release from Berkeley to provide v-nodes was the 4.3BSD Reno release, when NFS was added.

> In SVR4 the v-node replaced the filesystem independent i-node of SVR3.

If two independent processes have the same file open we could have the arrangement shown in Figure 3.3. We assume here that the first process has the file open on descriptor 3, and the second process has that same file open on descriptor 4. Each process that opens the file gets its own file table entry, but only a single v-node table entry

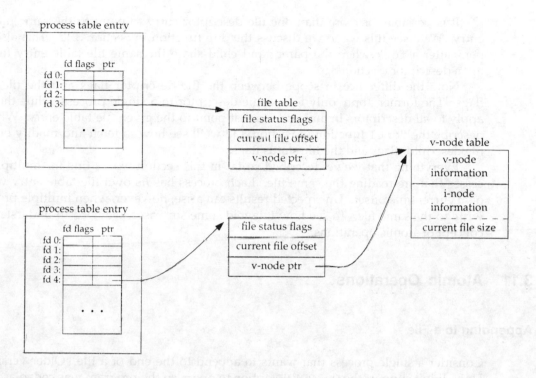

Figure 3.3 Two independent processes with the same file open.

is required for a given file. One reason each process gets its own file table entry is so that each process has its own current offset for the file.

Given these data structures we now need to be more specific about what happens with certain operations that we've already described.

- After each write is complete, the current file offset in the file table entry is incremented by the number of bytes written. If this causes the current file offset to exceed the current file size, the current file size in the i-node table entry is set to the current file offset (e.g., the file is extended).

- If a file is opened with the O_APPEND flag, a corresponding flag is set in the file status flags of the file table entry. Each time a write is performed for a file with this append flag set, the current file offset in the file table entry is first set to the current file size from the i-node table entry. This forces every write to be appended to the current end of file.

- The lseek function only modifies the current file offset in the file table entry. No I/O takes place.

- If a file is positioned to its current end of file using lseek, all that happens is the current file offset in the file table entry is set to the current file size from the i-node table entry.

It is possible for more than one file descriptor entry to point to the same file table entry. We'll see this when we discuss the dup function in Section 3.12. This also happens after a fork when the parent and child share the same file table entry for each open descriptor (Section 8.3).

Note the difference in scope between the file descriptor flags and the file status flags. The former apply only to a single descriptor in a single process, while the latter apply to all descriptors in any process that point to the given file table entry. When we describe the fcntl function in Section 3.13 we'll see how to fetch and modify both the file descriptor flags and the file status flags.

Everything that we've described so far in this section works fine for multiple processes that are reading the same file. Each process has its own file table entry with its own current file offset. Unexpected results can arise, however, when multiple processes write to the same file. To see how to avoid some surprises, we need to understand the concept of atomic operations.

3.11 Atomic Operations

Appending to a File

Consider a single process that wants to append to the end of a file. Older versions of Unix didn't support the O_APPEND option to open, so the program was coded as

```
if (lseek(fd, 0L, 2) < 0)              /* position to EOF */
    err_sys("lseek error");
if (write(fd, buff, 100) != 100)       /* and write */
    err_sys("write error");
```

This works fine for a single process, but problems arise if multiple processes use this technique to append to the same file. (This scenario can arise if multiple instances of the same program are appending messages to a log file, for example.)

Assume two independent processes, A and B, are appending to the same file. Each have opened the file but *without* the O_APPEND flag. This gives us the same picture as Figure 3.3. Each process has its own file table entry, but they share a single v-node table entry. Assume process A does the lseek and this sets the current offset for the file for process A to byte offset 1500 (the current end of file). Then the kernel switches processes and B continues running. It then does the lseek, which sets the current offset for the file for process B to byte offset 1500 also (the current end of file). Then B calls write, which increments B's current file offset for the file to 1600. Since the file's size has been extended, the kernel also updates the current file size in the v-node to 1600. Then the kernel switches processes and A resumes. When A calls write, the data is written starting at the current file offset for A, which is byte offset 1500. This overwrites the data that B wrote to the file.

The problem here is that our logical operation of "position to the end of file and write" requires two separate function calls (as we've shown it). The solution is to have the positioning to the current end of file and the write be an atomic operation with regard to other processes. Any operation that requires more than one function call cannot be atomic, as there is always the possibility that the kernel can temporarily suspend the process between the two function calls (as we assumed previously).

Unix provides an atomic way to do this operation if we set the O_APPEND flag when a file is opened. As we described in the previous section, this causes the kernel to position the file to its current end of file before each write. We no longer have to call lseek before each write.

Creating a File

We saw another example of an atomic operation when we described the O_CREAT and O_EXCL options for the open function. When both of these options are specified, the open will fail if the file already exists. We also said that the check for the existence of the file and the creation of the file was performed as an atomic operation. If we didn't have this atomic operation we might try

```
if ( (fd = open(pathname, O_WRONLY)) < 0)
    if (errno == ENOENT) {
        if ( (fd = creat(pathname, mode)) < 0)
            err_sys("creat error");
    } else
        err_sys("open error");
```

The problem occurs if the file is created by another process between the open and the creat. If the file is created by another process between these two function calls, and if that other process writes something to the file, that data is erased when this creat is executed. By making the test for existence and the creation an atomic operation, this problem is avoided.

In general, the term *atomic operation* refers to an operation that is composed of multiple steps. If the operation is performed atomically, either all the steps are performed, or none is performed. It must not be possible for a subset of the steps to be performed. We'll return to the topic of atomic operations when we describe the link function in Section 4.15 and record locking in Section 12.3.

3.12 dup and dup2 Functions

An existing file descriptor is duplicated by either of the following functions:

```
#include <unistd.h>

int dup(int filedes);

int dup2(int filedes, int filedes2);
```

Both return: new file descriptor if OK, −1 on error

The new file descriptor returned by dup is guaranteed to be the lowest numbered available file descriptor. With dup2 we specify the value of the new descriptor with the *filedes2* argument. If *filedes2* is already open, it is first closed. If *filedes* equals *filedes2*, then dup2 returns *filedes2* without closing it.

The new file descriptor that is returned as the value of the functions shares the same file table entry as the *filedes* argument. We show this in Figure 3.4.

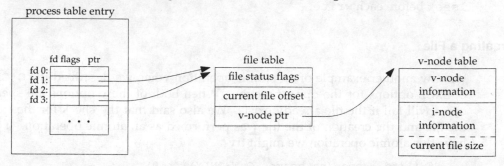

Figure 3.4 Kernel data structures after dup(1).

In this figure we're assuming that the process executes

```
newfd = dup(1);
```

when it's started. We assume the next available descriptor is 3 (which it probably is, since 0, 1, and 2 are opened by the shell). Since both descriptors point to the same file table entry they share the same file status flags (read, write, append, etc.) and the same current file offset.

Each descriptor has its own set of file descriptor flags. As we describe in the next section, the close-on-exec file descriptor flag for the new descriptor is always cleared by the dup functions.

Another way to duplicate a descriptor is with the fcntl function, which we describe in the next section. Indeed, the call

```
dup(filedes);
```

is equivalent to

```
fcntl(filedes, F_DUPFD, 0);
```

and the call

```
dup2(filedes, filedes2);
```

is equivalent to

```
close(filedes2);
fcntl(filedes, F_DUPFD, filedes2);
```

In this last case, the dup2 is not exactly the same as a close followed by an fcntl.

The differences are

1. dup2 is an atomic operation, while the alternate form involves two function calls. It is possible in the latter case to have a signal catcher called between the close and fcntl that could modify the file descriptors. (We describe signals in Chapter 10.)

2. There are some errno differences between dup2 and fcntl.

> The dup2 system call originated with Version 7 and propagated through the BSD releases. The fcntl method for duplicating file descriptors appeared with System III and continued with System V. SVR3.2 picked up the dup2 function and 4.2BSD picked up the fcntl function and the F_DUPFD functionality. POSIX.1 requires both dup2 and the F_DUPFD feature of fcntl.

3.13 fcntl Function

The fcntl function can change the properties of a file that is already open.

```
#include <sys/types.h>
#include <unistd.h>
#include <fcntl.h>

int fcntl(int filedes, int cmd, ... /* int arg */ );
```
                                 Returns: depends on *cmd* if OK (see following), −1 on error

In the examples we show in this section, the third argument is always an integer, corresponding to the comment in the function prototype just shown. But when we describe record locking in Section 12.3, the third argument becomes a pointer to a structure.

The fcntl function is used for five different purposes:

- duplicate an existing descriptor (*cmd* = F_DUPFD),
- get/set file descriptor flags (*cmd* = F_GETFD or F_SETFD),
- get/set file status flags (*cmd* = F_GETFL or F_SETFL),
- get/set asynchronous I/O ownership (*cmd* = F_GETOWN or F_SETOWN),
- get/set record locks (*cmd* = F_GETLK, F_SETLK, or F_SETLKW).

We'll now describe the first seven of these 10 *cmd* values. (We'll wait until Section 12.3 to describe the last three, which deal with record locking.) Refer to Figure 3.2 since we'll be referring to both the file descriptor flags associated with each file descriptor in the process table entry and the file status flags associated with each file table entry.

F_DUPFD   Duplicate the file descriptor *filedes*. The new file descriptor is returned as the value of the function. It is the lowest numbered descriptor that is not already open, that is greater than or equal to the third argument (taken as an integer). The new descriptor shares the same file table entry as *filedes*. (Refer to Figure 3.4.) But the new descriptor has its own set of file descriptor flags and its FD_CLOEXEC file descriptor flag is cleared. (This means that the descriptor is left open across an exec, which we discuss in Chapter 8.)

F_GETFD   Return the file descriptor flags for *filedes* as the value of the function. Currently only one file descriptor flag is defined: the FD_CLOEXEC flag.

F_SETFD   Set the file descriptor flags for *filedes*. The new flag value is set from the third argument (taken as an integer).

> Be aware that many existing programs that deal with the file descriptor flags don't use the constant FD_CLOEXEC. Instead the programs set the flag to either 0 (don't close-on-exec, the default) or 1 (do close-on-exec).

F_GETFL   Return the file status flags for *filedes* as the value of the function. We described the file status flags when we described the open function. They are listed in Figure 3.5.

File status flag	Description
O_RDONLY	open for reading only
O_WRONLY	open for writing only
O_RDWR	open for reading and writing
O_APPEND	append on each write
O_NONBLOCK	nonblocking mode
O_SYNC	wait for writes to complete
O_ASYNC	asynchronous I/O (4.3+BSD only)

Figure 3.5 File status flags for fcntl.

Unfortunately, the three access mode flags (O_RDONLY, O_WRONLY, and O_RDWR) are not separate bits that can be tested. (As we mentioned earlier, these three often have the values 0, 1, and 2, respectively, for historical reasons; also these three values are mutually exclusive—a file can have only one of the three enabled.) Therefore we must first use the O_ACCMODE mask to obtain the access mode bits and then compare the result against any of the three values.

F_SETFL   Set the file status flags to the value of the third argument (taken as an integer). The only flags that can be changed are O_APPEND, O_NONBLOCK, O_SYNC, and O_ASYNC.

F_GETOWN   Get the process ID or process group ID currently receiving the SIGIO and SIGURG signals. We describe these 4.3+BSD asynchronous I/O signals in Section 12.6.2.

F_SETOWN   Set the process ID or process group ID to receive the SIGIO and SIGURG signals. A positive *arg* specifies a process ID. A negative *arg* implies a process group ID equal to the absolute value of *arg*.

The return value from fcntl depends on the command. All commands return –1 on an error or some other value if OK. The following four commands have special return values: F_DUPFD, F_GETFD, F_GETFL, and F_GETOWN. The first returns the new file descriptor, the next two return the corresponding flags, and the final one returns a positive process ID or a negative process group ID.

Example

Program 3.4 takes a single command-line argument that specifies a file descriptor and prints a description of the file flags for that descriptor.

```
#include     <sys/types.h>
#include     <fcntl.h>
#include     "ourhdr.h"

int
main(int argc, char *argv[])
{
    int     accmode, val;

    if (argc != 2)
        err_quit("usage: a.out <descriptor#>");

    if ( (val = fcntl(atoi(argv[1]), F_GETFL, 0)) < 0)
        err_sys("fcntl error for fd %d", atoi(argv[1]));

    accmode = val & O_ACCMODE;
    if      (accmode == O_RDONLY)    printf("read only");
    else if (accmode == O_WRONLY)    printf("write only");
    else if (accmode == O_RDWR)      printf("read write");
    else err_dump("unknown access mode");

    if (val & O_APPEND)          printf(", append");
    if (val & O_NONBLOCK)        printf(", nonblocking");
#if !defined(_POSIX_SOURCE) && defined(O_SYNC)
    if (val & O_SYNC)            printf(", synchronous writes");
#endif
    putchar('\n');
    exit(0);
}
```

Program 3.4 Print file flags for specified descriptor.

Notice that we use the feature test macro _POSIX_SOURCE and conditionally compile the file access flags that are not part of POSIX.1. The following script shows the operation of the program, when invoked from a KornShell.

```
$ a.out 0 < /dev/tty
read only
$ a.out 1 > temp.foo
$ cat temp.foo
write only
$ a.out 2 2>>temp.foo
write only, append
$ a.out 5 5<>temp.foo
read write
```

The KornShell clause 5<>temp.foo opens the file temp.foo for reading and writing on file descriptor 5.   □

Example

When we modify either the file descriptor flags or the file status flags we must be careful to fetch the existing flag value, modify it as desired, and then set the new flag value. We can't just do an F_SETFD or an F_SETFL, as this could turn off flag bits that were previously set.

Program 3.5 shows a function that sets one or more of the file status flags for a descriptor.

```
#include     <fcntl.h>
#include     "ourhdr.h"

void
set_fl(int fd, int flags) /* flags are file status flags to turn on */
{
    int      val;

    if ( (val = fcntl(fd, F_GETFL, 0)) < 0)
        err_sys("fcntl F_GETFL error");

    val |= flags;          /* turn on flags */

    if (fcntl(fd, F_SETFL, val) < 0)
        err_sys("fcntl F_SETFL error");
}
```

Program 3.5 Turn on one or more of the file status flags for a descriptor.

If we change the middle statement to

```
    val &= ~flags;         /* turn flags off */
```

we have a function named clr_fl that we'll use in some later examples. This statement logically ANDs the 1's-complement of flags with the current val.

If we call set_fl from Program 3.3 by adding the line

```
    set_fl(STDOUT_FILENO, O_SYNC);
```

at the beginning of the program, we'll turn on the synchronous-write flag This causes each `write` to wait for the data to be written to disk before returning. Normally in Unix, a `write` only queues the data for writing, and the actual I/O operation can take place sometime later. A database system is a likely candidate for using O_SYNC, so that it knows on return from a `write` that the data is actually on the disk, in case of a system crash.

We expect the O_SYNC flag to increase the clock time when the program runs. To test this we can run Program 3.3, copying a 1.5 Mbyte file from one file on disk to another and compare this with a version that does the same thing with the O_SYNC flag set. The results are in Figure 3.6.

Operation	User CPU (seconds)	System CPU (seconds)	Clock time (seconds)
read time from Figure 3.1 for BUFFSIZE = 8192	0.0	0.3	0.3
normal Unix `write` to disk file	0.0	1.0	2.3
`write` to disk file with O_SYNC set	0.0	1.4	13.4

Figure 3.6 Timing results using synchronous writes (O_SYNC).

The three rows in Figure 3.6 were all measured with a BUFFSIZE of 8192. The results in Figure 3.1 were measured reading a disk file and writing to /dev/null, so there was no disk output. The second row in Figure 3.6 corresponds to reading a disk file and writing to another disk file. This is why the first and second rows in Figure 3.6 are different. The system time increases when we write to a disk file because the kernel now copies the data from our process and queues the data to for writing by the disk driver. The clock time increases also when we write to a disk file. When we enable synchronous writes, the system time increases slightly and the clock time increases by a factor of 6.   □

With this example we see the need for `fcntl`. Our program operates on a descriptor (standard output), never knowing name of the file that was opened by the shell on that descriptor. We can't set the O_SYNC flag when the file is opened, since the shell opened the file. `fcntl` allows us to modify the properties of a descriptor, knowing only the descriptor for the open file. We'll see another need for `fcntl` when we describe nonblocking pipes (Section 14.2), since all we have with a pipe is a descriptor.

3.14 `ioctl` Function

The `ioctl` function has always been the catchall for I/O operations. Anything that couldn't be expressed using one of the other functions in this chapter usually ended up being specified with an `ioctl`. Terminal I/O was the biggest user of this function. (When we get to Chapter 11 we'll see that POSIX.1 has replaced the terminal I/O operations with new functions.)

```
#include <unistd.h>        /* SVR4 */
#include <sys/ioctl.h>     /* 4.3+BSD */

int ioctl(int filedes, int request, ...);
```

Returns: −1 on error, something else if OK

The ioctl function is not part of POSIX.1. Both SVR4 and 4.3+BSD, however, use it for many miscellaneous device operations.

The prototype that we show corresponds to SVR4. 4.3+BSD and earlier Berkeley systems declare the second argument as an unsigned long. This detail doesn't matter, since the second argument is always a #defined name from a header.

For the ANSI C prototype an ellipsis is used for the remaining arguments. Normally, however, there is just one more argument, and it's usually a pointer to a variable or a structure.

In this prototype we show only the headers required for the function itself. Normally additional device-specific headers are required. For example, the ioctls for terminal I/O, beyond the basic operations specified by POSIX.1, all require the <termios.h> header.

What are ioctls used for today? We can divide the 4.3+BSD operations into the categories shown in Figure 3.7.

Category	Constant Names	Header	Number of ioctls
disk labels	DIOxxx	<disklabel.h>	10
file I/O	FIOxxx	<ioctl.h>	7
mag tape I/O	MTIOxxx	<mtio.h>	4
socket I/O	SIOxxx	<ioctl.h>	25
terminal I/O	TIOxxx	<ioctl.h>	35

Figure 3.7 4.3+BSD ioctl operations.

The mag tape operations allow us to write end-of-file marks on a tape, rewind a tape, space forward over a specified number of files or records, and the like. None of these operations is easily expressed in terms of the other functions in the chapter (read, write, lseek, etc.) so the easiest way to handle these devices has always been to access their operations using ioctl.

We use the ioctl function in Section 11.12 to fetch and set the size of a terminal's window, in Section 12.4 when we describe the streams system, and in Section 19.7 when we access the advanced features of pseudo terminals.

3.15   /dev/fd

Newer systems provide a directory named /dev/fd whose entries are files named 0, 1, 2, and so on. Opening the file /dev/fd/*n* is equivalent to duplicating descriptor *n* (assuming that descriptor *n* is open).

> The /dev/fd feature was developed by Tom Duff and appeared in the 8th Edition of the Research Unix System. It is supported by SVR4 and 4.3+BSD. It is not part of POSIX.1.

In the function call

```
fd = open("/dev/fd/0", mode);
```

most systems ignore the specified mode, while others require that it be a subset of the mode used when the referenced file (standard input in this case) was originally opened. Since the open above is equivalent to

```
fd = dup(0);
```

the descriptors 0 and fd share the same file table entry (Figure 3.4). For example, if descriptor 0 was opened read-only, we can only read on fd. Even if the system ignores the open mode, and the call

```
fd = open("/dev/fd/0", O_RDWR);
```

succeeds, we still can't write to fd.

We can also call creat with a /dev/fd pathname argument, as well as specifying O_CREAT in a call to open. This allows a program that calls creat to still work if the pathname argument is /dev/fd/1, for example.

Some systems provide the pathnames /dev/stdin, /dev/stdout, and /dev/stderr. These are equivalent to /dev/fd/0, /dev/fd/1, and /dev/fd/2.

The main use of the /dev/fd files is from the shell. It allows programs that use pathname arguments to handle standard input and standard output in the same manner as other pathnames. For example, the cat(1) program specifically looks for an input filename of – and uses this to mean standard input. The command

```
filter file2 | cat file1 - file3 | lpr
```

is an example. First cat reads file1, next its standard input (the output of the filter program on file2), then file3. If /dev/fd is supported, the special handling of – can be removed from cat, and we can enter

```
filter file2 | cat file1 /dev/fd/0 file3 | lpr
```

The special meaning of – as a command-line argument to refer to the standard input or standard output is a kludge that has crept into many programs. There are also problems if we specify – as the first file, since it looks like the start of another command-line option. /dev/fd is a step toward uniformity and cleanliness.

3.16 Summary

This chapter has described the traditional Unix I/O functions. These are often called the unbuffered I/O functions because each read or write invokes a system call into the kernel. Using only read and write we looked at the effect of different I/O sizes on the amount of time required to read a file.

Atomic operations were introduced when multiple processes append to the same file and when multiple processes create the same file. We also looked at the data structures used by the kernel to share information about open files. We'll return to these data structures later in the text.

We also described the ioctl and fcntl functions. We return to both of these functions in Chapter 12—we'll use ioctl with the streams I/O system, and fcntl is used for record locking.

Exercises

3.1 When reading or writing a disk file, are the functions described in this chapter really unbuffered? Explain.

3.2 Write your own function called dup2 that performs the same service as the dup2 function we described in Section 3.12, without calling the fcntl function. Be sure to handle errors correctly.

3.3 Assume a process executes the following three function calls:

```
fd1 = open(pathname, oflags);
fd2 = dup(fd1);
fd3 = open(pathname, oflags);
```

Draw the resulting picture, similar to Figure 3.4. Which descriptors are affected by an fcntl on fd1 with a command of F_SETFD? Which descriptors are affected by an fcntl on fd1 with a command of F_SETFL?

3.4 The following sequence of code has been observed in various programs:

```
dup2(fd, 0);
dup2(fd, 1);
dup2(fd, 2);
if (fd > 2)
    close(fd);
```

To see why the if test is needed, assume fd is 1 and draw a picture of what happens to the three descriptor entries and the corresponding file table entry with each call to dup2. Then assume fd is 3 and draw the same picture.

3.5   The Bourne shell and KornShell notation

digit1 > & *digit2*

says to redirect descriptor *digit1* to the same file as descriptor *digit2*. What is the difference between the two commands

```
a.out > outfile 2>&1
```

```
a.out 2>&1 > outfile
```

(Hint: the shells process their command lines from left to right.)

3.6   If you open a file for read–write with the append flag, can you still read from anywhere in the file using lseek? Can you use lseek to replace existing data in the file? Write a program to verify this.

4

Files and Directories

4.1 Introduction

In the previous chapter we covered the basic functions that perform I/O. The discussion centered around I/O for regular files—opening a file, and reading or writing a file. We'll now look at additional features of the filesystem and the properties of a file. We'll start with the stat functions and go through each member of the stat structure, looking at all the attributes of a file. In this process we'll also describe each of the functions that modify these attributes (change the owner, change the permissions, etc.). We'll also look in more detail at the structure of a Unix filesystem and symbolic links. We finish this chapter with the functions that operate on directories and develop a function that descends through a directory hierarchy.

4.2 `stat`, `fstat`, and `lstat` Functions

The discussion in this chapter is centered around the three stat functions and the information they return.

```
#include <sys/types.h>
#include <sys/stat.h>

int stat(const char *pathname, struct stat *buf);

int fstat(int filedes, struct stat *buf);

int lstat(const char *pathname, struct stat *buf);
```

All three return: 0 if OK, −1 on error

Given a *pathname*, the stat function returns a structure of information about the named file. The fstat function obtains information about the file that is already open on the descriptor *filedes*. The lstat function is similar to stat, but when the named file is a symbolic link, lstat returns information about the symbolic link, not the file referenced by the symbolic link. (We'll need lstat in Section 4.21 when we walk down a directory hierarchy. We describe symbolic links in more detail in Section 4.16.)

> The lstat function is not in the POSIX 1003.1–1990 standard, but will probably be added to 1003.1a. It is supported by SVR4 and 4.3+BSD.

The second argument is a pointer to a structure that we must supply. The function fills in the structure pointed to by *buf*. The actual definition of the structure can differ among implementations, but it could look like

```
struct stat {
  mode_t  st_mode;    /* file type & mode (permissions) */
  ino_t   st_ino;     /* i-node number (serial number) */
  dev_t   st_dev;     /* device number (filesystem) */
  dev_t   st_rdev;    /* device number for special files */
  nlink_t st_nlink;   /* number of links */
  uid_t   st_uid;     /* user ID of owner */
  gid_t   st_gid;     /* group ID of owner */
  off_t   st_size;    /* size in bytes, for regular files */
  time_t  st_atime;   /* time of last access */
  time_t  st_mtime;   /* time of last modification */
  time_t  st_ctime;   /* time of last file status change */
  long    st_blksize; /* best I/O block size */
  long    st_blocks;  /* number of 512-byte blocks allocated */
};
```

> The fields st_rdev, st_blksize, and st_blocks are not defined by POSIX.1. These fields are in SVR4 and 4.3+BSD.

Note that each member, other than the last two, is specified by a primitive system data type (see Section 2.7). We'll go through each member of this structure, to examine the attributes of a file.

The biggest user of the stat functions is probably the ls -l command, to learn all the information about a file.

4.3 File Types

We've talked about two different types of files so far—regular files and directories. Most files on a Unix system are either regular files or directories, but there are additional types of files:

1. Regular file. The most common type of file, which contains data of some form. There is no distinction to the Unix kernel whether this data is text or binary.

Any interpretation of the contents of a regular file is left to the application processing the file.

2. Directory file. A file that contains the names of other files and pointers to information on these files. Any process that has read permission for a directory file can read the contents of the directory, but only the kernel can write to a directory file.

3. Character special file. A type of file used for certain types of devices on a system.

4. Block special file. A type of file typically used for disk devices. All devices on a system are either character special files or block special files.

5. FIFO. A type of file used for interprocess communication between processes. It's sometimes called a named pipe. We describe FIFOs in Section 14.5.

6. Socket. A type of file used for network communication between processes. A socket can also be used for nonnetwork communication between processes on a single host. We use sockets for interprocess communication in Chapter 15.

> A file type of socket is returned only by 4.3+BSD. Although SVR4 supports sockets for interprocess communication, this is currently done through a library of socket functions, not through a file type of socket within the kernel. Future versions of SVR4 may support the socket type.

7. Symbolic link. A type of file that points to another file. We talk more about symbolic links in Section 4.16.

The type of a file is encoded in the st_mode member of the stat structure. We can determine the file type with the macros shown in Figure 4.1. The argument to each of these macros is the st_mode member from the stat structure.

Macro	Type of file
S_ISREG()	regular file
S_ISDIR()	directory file
S_ISCHR()	character special file
S_ISBLK()	block special file
S_ISFIFO()	pipe or FIFO
S_ISLNK()	symbolic link (not in POSIX.1 or SVR4)
S_ISSOCK()	socket (not in POSIX.1 or SVR4)

Figure 4.1 File type macros in <sys/stat.h>.

Example

Program 4.1 takes its command-line arguments and prints the type of file for each command-line argument.

```
#include        <sys/types.h>
#include        <sys/stat.h>
#include        "ourhdr.h"

int
main(int argc, char *argv[])
{
    int         i;
    struct stat buf;
    char        *ptr;

    for (i = 1; i < argc; i++) {
        printf("%s: ", argv[i]);
        if (lstat(argv[i], &buf) < 0) {
            err_ret("lstat error");
            continue;
        }
        if      (S_ISREG(buf.st_mode))  ptr = "regular";
        else if (S_ISDIR(buf.st_mode))  ptr = "directory";
        else if (S_ISCHR(buf.st_mode))  ptr = "character special";
        else if (S_ISBLK(buf.st_mode))  ptr = "block special";
        else if (S_ISFIFO(buf.st_mode)) ptr = "fifo";
#ifdef  S_ISLNK
        else if (S_ISLNK(buf.st_mode))  ptr = "symbolic link";
#endif
#ifdef  S_ISSOCK
        else if (S_ISSOCK(buf.st_mode)) ptr = "socket";
#endif
        else                            ptr = "** unknown mode **";
        printf("%s\n", ptr);
    }
    exit(0);
}
```

Program 4.1 Print type of file for each command-line argument.

Sample output from Program 4.1 is

```
$ a.out /vmunix /etc /dev/ttya /dev/sd0a /var/spool/cron/FIFO \
> /bin /dev/printer
/vmunix: regular
/etc: directory
/dev/ttya: character special
/dev/sd0a: block special
/var/spool/cron/FIFO: fifo
/bin: symbolic link
/dev/printer: socket
```

(Here we have explicitly entered a backslash at the end of the first command line, telling
the shell that we want to continue entering the command on another line. The shell

then prompts us with its secondary prompt, >, on the next line.) We have specifically used the lstat function instead of the stat function, to detect symbolic links. If we used the stat function, we would never see symbolic links. □

Earlier versions of Unix didn't provide the S_ISxxx macros. Instead we had to logically AND the st_mode value with the mask S_IFMT and then compare the result with the constants whose names are S_IFxxx. SVR4 and 4.3+BSD define this mask and the related constants in the file <sys/stat.h>. If we examine this file we'll find the S_ISDIR macro defined as

```
#define  S_ISDIR(mode)  (((mode) & S_IFMT) == S_IFDIR)
```

We've said that regular files are predominant, but it is interesting to see what percentage of the files on a given system are of each file type. Figure 4.2 shows the counts and percentages for a medium-sized system. This data was obtained from the program that we show in Section 4.21.

File type	Count	Percentage
regular file	30,369	91.7 %
directory	1,901	5.7
symbolic link	416	1.3
character special	373	1.1
block special	61	0.2
socket	5	0.0
FIFO	1	0.0

Figure 4.2 Counts and percentages of different file types.

4.4 Set-User-ID and Set-Group-ID

Every process has six or more IDs associated with it. These are shown in Figure 4.3.

real user ID real group ID	who we really are
effective user ID effective group ID supplementary group IDs	used for file access permission checks
saved set-user-ID saved set-group-ID	saved by exec functions

Figure 4.3 User IDs and group IDs associated with each process.

- The real user ID and real group ID identify who we really are. These two fields are taken from our entry in the password file when we log in. Normally these values don't change during a login session, although there are ways for a super-user process to change them, which we describe in Section 8.10.

- The effective user ID, effective group ID, and supplementary group IDs determine our file access permissions, as we describe in the next section. (We defined supplementary group IDs in Section 1.8.)

- The saved set-user-ID and saved set-group-ID contain copies of the effective user ID and the effective group ID when a program is executed. We describe the function of these two saved values when we describe the setuid function in Section 8.10.

> The saved IDs are optional with POSIX.1. An application can test for the constant _POSIX_SAVED_IDS at compile time, or call sysconf with the _SC_SAVED_IDS argument at run time, to see if the implementation supports this feature. SVR4 supports this feature.
>
> FIPS 151-1 requires this optional POSIX.1 feature.

Normally the effective user ID equals the real user ID, and the effective group ID equals the real group ID.

Every file has an owner and a group owner. The owner is specified by the st_uid member of the stat structure, and the group owner by the st_gid member.

When we execute a program file the effective user ID of the process is usually the real user ID, and the effective group ID is usually the real group ID. But the capability exists to set a special flag in the file's mode word (st_mode) that says "when this file is executed, set the effective user ID of the process to be the owner of the file (st_uid)." Similarly, another bit can be set in the file's mode word that causes the effective group ID to be the group owner of the file (st_gid). These two bits in the file's mode word are called the *set-user-ID* bit and the *set-group-ID* bit.

For example, if the owner of the file is the superuser and if the file's set-user-ID bit is set, then while that program file is running as a process, it has superuser privileges. This happens regardless of the real user ID of the process that executes the file. As an example, the Unix program that allows anyone to change his or her password, passwd(1), is a set-user-ID program. This is required so that the program can write the new password to the password file, typically either /etc/passwd or /etc/shadow, files that should be writable only by the superuser. Since a process that is running set-user-ID to some other user usually assumes extra permissions, it must be written carefully. We'll discuss these types of programs in more detail in Chapter 8.

Returning to the stat function, the set-user-ID bit and the set-group-ID bit are contained in the file's st_mode value. These two bits can be tested against the constants S_ISUID and S_ISGID.

4.5   File Access Permissions

The st_mode value also encodes the access permission bits for the file. When we say file we mean any of the file types that we described earlier. All the file types (directories, character special files, etc.) have permissions. Many people think only of regular files as having access permissions.

There are nine permission bits for each file, divided into three categories. These are shown in Figure 4.4.

st_mode mask	Meaning
S_IRUSR	user-read
S_IWUSR	user-write
S_IXUSR	user-execute
S_IRGRP	group-read
S_IWGRP	group-write
S_IXGRP	group-execute
S_IROTH	other-read
S_IWOTH	other-write
S_IXOTH	other-execute

Figure 4.4 The nine file access permission bits, from <sys/stat.h>.

The term user in the first three rows in Figure 4.4 refers to the owner of the file. The chmod(1) command, which is typically used to modify these nine permission bits, allows us to specify u for user (owner), g for group, and o for other. Some books refer to these three as owner, group, and world; this is confusing since the chmod command uses o to mean other, not owner. We'll use the terms user, group, and other, to be consistent with the chmod command.

The three categories in Figure 4.4—read, write, and execute—are used in various ways by different functions. We'll summarize them here, and return to them when we describe the actual functions.

• The first rule is that *whenever* we want to open any type of file by name we must have execute permission in each directory mentioned in the name, including the current directory if it is implied. This is why the execute permission bit for a directory is often called the search bit.

For example, to open the file /usr/dict/words we need execute permission in the directory /, execute permission in the directory /usr, and execute permission in the directory /usr/dict. We then need appropriate permission for the file itself, depending on how we're trying to open it (read-only, read–write, etc.).

If the current directory is /usr/dict then we need execute permission in the current directory to open the file words. This is an example of the current directory being implied, not specifically mentioned. It is identical to our opening the file ./words.

Note that read permission for a directory and execute permission for a directory mean different things. Read permission lets us read the directory, obtaining a list of all the filenames in the directory. Execute permission lets us pass through the directory when it is a component of a pathname that we are trying to access (i.e., search the directory looking for a specific filename).

Another example of an implicit directory reference is if the PATH environment variable (described in Section 8.9) specifies a directory that does not have execute permission enabled. In this case the shell will never find executable files in that directory.

- The read permission for a file determines if we can open an existing file for reading: the O_RDONLY and O_RDWR flags for the open function.

- The write permission for a file determines if we can open an existing file for writing: the O_WRONLY and O_RDWR flags for the open function.

- We must have write permission for a file to specify the O_TRUNC flag in the open function.

- We cannot create a new file in a directory unless we have write permission and execute permission in the directory.

- To delete an existing file, we need write permission and execute permission in the directory containing the file. We do not need read permission or write permission for the file itself.

- Execute permission for a file must be on if we want to execute the file using any of the six exec functions (Section 8.9). The file also has to be a regular file.

The file access tests that the kernel performs each time a process opens, creates, or deletes a file depend on the owners of the file (st_uid and st_gid), the effective IDs of the process (effective user ID and effective group ID), and the supplementary group IDs of the process (if supported). The two owner IDs are properties of the file, while the two effective IDs and the supplementary group IDs are properties of the process. The tests performed by the kernel are

1. If the effective user ID of the process is 0 (the superuser), access is allowed. This gives the superuser free reign throughout the entire filesystem.

2. If the effective user ID of the process equals the owner ID of the file (i.e., the process owns the file):

   a. if the appropriate user access permission bit is set, access is allowed,

   b. else permission is denied.

   By *appropriate access permission bit* we mean if the process is opening the file for reading, the user-read bit must be on. If the process is opening the file for writing, the user-write bit must be on. If the process is executing the file, the user-execute bit must be on.

3. If the effective group ID of the process or one of the supplementary group IDs of the process equals the group ID of the file:

   a. if the appropriate group access permission bit is set, access is allowed,

   b. else permission is denied.

4. If the appropriate other access permission bit is set, access is allowed, else permission is denied.

These four steps are tried in sequence. Note that if the process owns the file (step 2) then access is granted or denied based only on the user access permissions—the group permissions are never looked at. Similarly, if the process does not own the file, but the process belongs to an appropriate group, then access is granted or denied based only on the group access permissions—the other permissions are not looked at.

4.6 Ownership of New Files and Directories

When we described the creation of a new file in Chapter 3, using either open or creat, we never said what values were assigned to the user ID and group ID of the new file. We'll see how to create a new directory in Section 4.20 when we describe the mkdir function. The rules for the ownership of a new directory are identical to the rules in this section for the ownership of a new file.

The user ID of a new file is set to the effective user ID of the process. POSIX.1 allows an implementation to choose one of the following options to determine the group ID of a new file.

1. The group ID of a new file can be the effective group ID of the process.

2. The group ID of a new file can be the group ID of the directory in which the file is being created.

> With SVR4 the group ID of a new file depends on whether the set-group-ID bit is set for the directory in which the file is being created. If this bit is set for the directory, the group ID of the new file is set to the group ID of the directory; otherwise the group ID of the new file is set to the effective group ID of the process.
>
> 4.3+BSD always uses the group ID of the directory as the group ID of the new file.
>
> Other systems allow the choice between these two POSIX.1 options to be done on a filesystem basis, using a special flag to the mount(1) command.
>
> FIPS 151–1 requires that the group ID of a new file be the group ID of the directory in which the file is created.

Using the second POSIX.1 option (inheriting the group ID of the directory) assures us that all files and directories created in that directory will have the group ID belonging to the directory. This group ownership of files and directories will then propagate down the hierarchy from that point. This is used, for example, in the /var/spool directory.

> As we mentioned, this option for group ownership is the default for 4.3+BSD but an option for SVR4. Under SVR4 we have to enable the set-group-ID bit. Furthermore, the SVR4 mkdir function has to propagate a directory's set-group-ID bit automatically (as it does, described in Section 4.20) for this to work.

4.7   access Function

As we described earlier, when accessing a file with the open function, the kernel performs its access tests based on the effective user ID and the effective group ID. There are times when a process wants to test accessibility based on the real user ID and the real group ID. One instance where this is useful is when a process is running as someone else, using either the set-user-ID or the set-group-ID feature. Even though a process might be set-user-ID to root, it could still want to verify that the real user can access a given file. The access function bases its tests on the real user ID and the real group ID. (Go through the four steps at the end of Section 4.5 and replace effective with real.)

```
#include <unistd.h>

int access(const char *pathname, int mode);
```
                                                              Returns: 0 if OK, −1 on error

The *mode* is the bitwise OR of any of the constants shown in Figure 4.5.

mode	Description
R_OK	test for read permission
W_OK	test for write permission
X_OK	test for execute permission
F_OK	test for existence of file

Figure 4.5 The *mode* constants for access function, from <unistd.h>.

Example

Program 4.2 shows the use of the access function. Here is a sample session with this program.

```
$ ls -l a.out
-rwxrwxr-x  1 stevens      105216 Jan 18 08:48 a.out
$ a.out a.out
read access OK
open for reading OK
$ ls -l /etc/uucp/Systems
-rw-r-----  1 uucp           1441 Jul 18 15:05 /etc/uucp/Systems
$ a.out /etc/uucp/Systems
access error for /etc/uucp/Systems: Permission denied
open error for /etc/uucp/Systems: Permission denied
$ su                                        become superuser
Password:                                   enter superuser password
# chown uucp a.out                          change file's user ID to uucp
# chmod u+s a.out                           and turn on set-user-ID bit
```

```
#include     <sys/types.h>
#include     <fcntl.h>
#include     "ourhdr.h"

int
main(int argc, char *argv[])
{
    if (argc != 2)
        err_quit("usage: a.out <pathname>");

    if (access(argv[1], R_OK) < 0)
        err_ret("access error for %s", argv[1]);
    else
        printf("read access OK\n");

    if (open(argv[1], O_RDONLY) < 0)
        err_ret("open error for %s", argv[1]);
    else
        printf("open for reading OK\n");

    exit(0);
}
```

Program 4.2 Example of access function.

```
# ls -l a.out                          check owner and SUID bit
-rwsrwxr-x  1 uucp          105216 Jan 18 08:48 a.out
# exit                                 go back to normal user
$ a.out /etc/uucp/Systems
access error for /etc/uucp/Systems: Permission denied
open for reading OK
```

In this example, the set-user ID program can determine that the real user cannot normally read the file, even though the open function will succeed.   □

> In the preceding example and in Chapter 8, we'll sometimes switch to become the superuser,
> to demonstrate how something works. If you're on a multiuser system and do not have super-
> user permission, you won't be able to duplicate these examples completely.

4.8   umask Function

Now that we've described the nine permission bits associated with every file, we can
describe the file mode creation mask that is associated with every process.

The umask function sets the file mode creation mask for the process and returns the
previous value. (This is one of the few functions that doesn't have an error return.)

```
#include <sys/types.h>
#include <sys/stat.h>

mode_t umask(mode_t cmask);
```
                                      Returns: previous file mode creation mask

The *cmask* argument is formed as the bitwise OR of any of the nine constants from Figure 4.4: S_IRUSR, S_IWUSR, and so on.

The file mode creation mask is used whenever the process creates a new file or a new directory. (Recall Sections 3.3 and 3.4 where we described the open and creat functions. Both accepted a *mode* argument that specified the new file's access permission bits.) We describe how to create a new directory in Section 4.20. Any bits that are *on* in the file mode creation mask are turned *off* in the file's *mode*.

Example

Program 4.3 creates two files, one with a umask of 0 and one with a umask that disables all the group and other permission bits. If we run this program

```
$ umask                          first print the current file mode creation mask
02
$ a.out
$ ls -l foo bar
-rw-------  1 stevens            0 Nov 16 16:23 bar
-rw-rw-rw-  1 stevens            0 Nov 16 16:23 foo
$ umask                          see if the file mode creation mask changed
02
```

we can see how the permission bits have been set.   □

Most Unix users never deal with their umask value. It is usually set once, on log in, by the shell's start-up file, and never changed. Nevertheless, when writing programs that create new files, if we want to assure that specific access permission bits are enabled, we must modify the umask value while the process is running. For example, if we want to assure that anyone can read a file, we should set the umask to 0. Otherwise, the umask value that is in effect when our process is running can cause permission bits to be turned off.

In the preceding example we use the shell's umask command to print the file mode creation mask before we run the program and after. This shows us that changing the file mode creation mask of a process doesn't affect the mask of its parent (often a shell). All three of the shells have a built-in umask command that we can use to set or print the current file mode creation mask.

```
#include     <sys/types.h>
#include     <sys/stat.h>
#include     <fcntl.h>
#include     "ourhdr.h"

int
main(void)
{
    umask(0);
    if (creat("foo", S_IRUSR | S_IWUSR | S_IRGRP | S_IWGRP |
                                       S_IROTH | S_IWOTH) < 0)
        err_sys("creat error for foo");

    umask(S_IRGRP | S_IWGRP | S_IROTH | S_IWOTH);
    if (creat("bar", S_IRUSR | S_IWUSR | S_IRGRP | S_IWGRP |
                                       S_IROTH | S_IWOTH) < 0)
        err_sys("creat error for bar");
    exit(0);
}
```

Program 4.3 Example of umask function.

4.9   chmod **and** fchmod **Functions**

These two functions allow us to change the file access permissions for an existing file.

```
#include <sys/types.h>
#include <sys/stat.h>

int chmod(const char *pathname, mode_t mode);

int fchmod(int filedes, mode_t mode);
```
Both return: 0 if OK, –1 on error

The chmod function operates on the specified file while the fchmod function operates on a file that has already been opened.

> The fchmod function is not part of POSIX.1. It is an extension provided by SVR4 and 4.3+BSD.

To change the permission bits of a file, the effective user ID of the process must equal the owner of the file, or the process must have superuser permissions.

The *mode* is specified as the bitwise OR of the constants shown in Figure 4.6.

mode	Description
S_ISUID	set-user-ID on execution
S_ISGID	set-group-ID on execution
S_ISVTX	saved-text (sticky bit)
S_IRWXU	read, write, and execute by user (owner)
S_IRUSR	read by user (owner)
S_IWUSR	write by user (owner)
S_IXUSR	execute by user (owner)
S_IRWXG	read, write, and execute by group
S_IRGRP	read by group
S_IWGRP	write by group
S_IXGRP	execute by group
S_IRWXO	read, write, and execute by other (world)
S_IROTH	read by other (world)
S_IWOTH	write by other (world)
S_IXOTH	execute by other (world)

Figure 4.6 The *mode* constants for chmod functions, from <sys/stat.h>.

Note that nine of the entries in Figure 4.6 are the nine file access permission bits from Figure 4.4. We've added the two set-ID constants (S_IS[UG]ID), the saved-text constant (S_ISVTX), and the three combined constants (S_IRWX[UGO]). (Here we are using the standard Unix character class operator []. We mean any one of the characters contained within the square brackets. The final example, S_IRWX[UGO], refers to the three constants S_IRWXU, S_IRWXG, and S_IRWXO. This character class operator is a form of a regular expression that is provided by most Unix shells and many standard Unix applications.)

> The saved-text bit (S_ISVTX) is not part of POSIX.1. We describe its purpose in the next section.

Example

Recall the final state of the files foo and bar when we ran Program 4.3 to demonstrate the umask function:

```
$ ls -l foo bar
-rw-------  1 stevens          0 Nov 16 16:23 bar
-rw-rw-rw-  1 stevens          0 Nov 16 16:23 foo
```

Program 4.4 modifies the mode of these two files. After running Program 4.4 we see the final state of the two files is

```
$ ls -l foo bar
-rw-r--r--  1 stevens          0 Nov 16 16:23 bar
-rw-rwlrw-  1 stevens          0 Nov 16 16:23 foo
```

In this example we have set the permissions of foo relative to their current state. To do this we first call stat to obtain the current permissions and then modify them. We

```
#include      <sys/types.h>
#include      <sys/stat.h>
#include      "ourhdr.h"

int
main(void)
{
    struct stat      statbuf;

    /* turn on set-group-ID and turn off group-execute */

    if (stat("foo", &statbuf) < 0)
        err_sys("stat error for foo");
    if (chmod("foo", (statbuf.st_mode & ~S_IXGRP) | S_ISGID) < 0)
        err_sys("chmod error for foo");

    /* set absolute mode to "rw-r--r--" */

    if (chmod("bar", S_IRUSR | S_IWUSR | S_IRGRP | S_IROTH) < 0)
        err_sys("chmod error for bar");

    exit(0);
}
```

Program 4.4 Example of chmod function.

have explicitly turned on the set-group-ID bit and turned off the group-execute bit. Doing this for a regular file enables mandatory record locking, which we'll discuss in Section 12.3. Note that the ls command lists the group-execute permission as l to signify that mandatory record locking is enabled for this file. For the file bar, we set the permissions to an absolute value, regardless of the current permission bits.

Finally note that the time and date listed by the ls command did not change after we ran Program 4.4. We'll see in Section 4.18 that the chmod function updates only the time that the i-node was last changed. By default the ls -l lists the time the contents of the file were last modified.   □

The chmod functions automatically clear two of the permission bits under the following conditions.

- If we try to set the sticky bit (S_ISVTX) of a regular file and we do not have superuser privileges, the sticky bit in the *mode* is automatically turned off. (We describe the sticky bit in the next section.) This means that only the superuser can set the sticky bit of a regular file. The reason is to prevent malicious users from setting the sticky bit and trying to fill up the swap area, if the system supports the saved-text feature.

- It is possible that the group ID of a newly created file is a group that the calling process does not belong to. Recall from Section 4.6 that it's possible for the group ID of the new file to be the group ID of the parent directory. Specifically, if the group ID of the new file does not equal either the effective group ID of the process or one of the process's supplementary group IDs and if the process does not have superuser privileges, then the set-group-ID bit is automatically turned off. This prevents a user from creating a set-group-ID file owned by a group that the user doesn't belong to.

> 4.3+BSD and other Berkeley-derived systems add another security feature to try to prevent misuse of some of the protection bits. If a process that does not have superuser privileges writes to a file, the set-user-ID and set-group-ID bits are automatically turned off. If a malicious user finds a set-group-ID or set-user-ID file they can write to, even though they can modify the file, they lose the special privileges of the file.

4.10 Sticky Bit

The S_ISVTX bit has an interesting history. On earlier versions of Unix this bit was known as the *sticky bit*. If it was set for an executable program file, then the first time the program was executed a copy of the program's text was saved in the swap area when the process terminated. (The text portion of a program is the machine instructions.) This caused the program to load into memory faster the next time it was executed, because the swap area was handled as a contiguous file, compared to the possibly random location of data blocks in a normal Unix filesystem. The sticky bit was often set for common application programs such as the text editor and the passes of the C compiler. Naturally, there was a limit to the number of sticky files that could be contained in the swap area before running out of swap space, but it was a useful technique. The name sticky came about because the text portion of the file stuck around in the swap area until the system was rebooted. Later versions of Unix referred to this as the *saved-text* bit, hence the constant S_ISVTX. With today's newer Unix systems, most of which have a virtual memory system and a faster filesystem, the need for this technique has disappeared.

Both SVR4 and 4.3+BSD allow the sticky bit to be set for a directory. If the bit is set for a directory, a file in the directory can be removed or renamed only if the user has write permission for the directory, and either

- owns the file,
- owns the directory, or
- is the superuser.

The directories /tmp and /var/spool/uucppublic are candidates for the sticky bit—they are directories in which any user can typically create files. The permissions for these two directories are often read, write, and execute for everyone (user, group, and other). But users should not be able to delete or rename files owned by others.

> The sticky bit is not defined by POSIX.1. It is an extension supported by both SVR4 and 4.3+BSD.

4.11 chown, fchown, and lchown Functions

The chown functions allow us to change the user ID of a file and the group ID of a file.

```
#include <sys/types.h>
#include <unistd.h>

int chown(const char *pathname, uid_t owner, gid_t group);

int fchown(int filedes, uid_t owner, gid_t group);

int lchown(const char *pathname, uid_t owner, gid_t group);
```

All three return: 0 if OK, −1 on error

These three functions operate similarly unless the referenced file is a symbolic link. In that case lchown changes the owners of the symbolic link itself, not the file pointed to by the symbolic link.

> The fchown function is not in the POSIX 1003.1–1990 standard, but will probably be added to 1003.1a. It is supported by SVR4 and 4.3+BSD.

> The lchown function is unique to SVR4. Under the non-SVR4 systems (POSIX.1 and 4.3+BSD), if the *pathname* for chown is a symbolic link then the ownership of the symbolic link is changed, not the ownership of the file referenced by the symbolic link. To change the ownership of the file referenced by the symbolic link we have to specify the *pathname* of the actual file itself, not the *pathname* of a symbolic link that points to the file.

> SVR4, 4.3+BSD, and XPG3 allow us to specify either of the arguments *owner* or *group* as −1 to leave the corresponding ID unchanged. This is not part of POSIX.1.

Historically, Berkeley-based systems have enforced the restriction that only the superuser can change the ownership of a file. This is to prevent users from giving away their files to others, thereby defeating any disk space quota restrictions. System V, however, has allowed any user to change the ownership of any files they own.

> POSIX.1 allows either form of operation, depending on the value of _POSIX_CHOWN_RESTRICTED. FIPS 151-1 requires _POSIX_CHOWN_RESTRICTED.

> With SVR4 this functionality is a configuration option, while 4.3+BSD always enforces the chown restriction.

Recall from Figure 2.5 that this constant can optionally be defined in the header <unistd.h> and can always be queried using either the pathconf or fpathconf functions. Also recall that this option can depend on the referenced file—it can be enabled or disabled on a per-filesystem basis. We'll use the phrase, if _POSIX_CHOWN_RESTRICTED is in effect, to mean if it applies to the particular file that we're talking about, regardless whether this actual constant is defined in the header.

If _POSIX_CHOWN_RESTRICTED is in effect for the specified file, then

1. only a superuser process can change the user ID of the file;

2. a nonsuperuser process can change the group ID of the file if

   a. the process owns the file (the effective user ID equals the user ID of the file), and

   b. *owner* equals the user ID of the file and *group* equals either the effective group ID of the process or one of the process's supplementary group IDs.

This means that when _POSIX_CHOWN_RESTRICTED is in effect you can't change the user ID of other users' files. You can change the group ID of files that you own, but only to groups that you belong to.

If these functions are called by a process other than a superuser process, on successful return both the set-user-ID and the set-group-ID bits are cleared.

4.12 File Size

The st_size member of the stat structure contains the size of the file in bytes. This field is meaningful only for regular files, directories, and symbolic links.

> SVR4 also defines the file size for a pipe as the number of bytes that are available for reading from the pipe. We'll discuss pipes in Section 14.2.

For a regular file, a file size of 0 is allowed—we'll get an end-of-file indication on the first read of the file.

For a directory, the file size is usually a multiple of a number such as 16 or 512. We talk about reading directories in Section 4.21.

For a symbolic link, the file size is the actual number of bytes in the filename. For example, in the case

```
lrwxrwxrwx  1 root              7 Sep 25 07:14 lib -> usr/lib
```

the file size of 7 is the length of the pathname usr/lib. (Note that symbolic links do not contain the normal C null byte at the end of the name, since the length is always specified by st_size.)

SVR4 and 4.3+BSD also provide the fields st_blksize and st_blocks. The first is the preferred block size for I/O for the file and the latter is the actual number of 512-byte blocks that are allocated. Recall from Section 3.9 that we encountered the minimum amount of time required to read a file when we used st_blksize for the read operations. The standard I/O library, which we describe in Chapter 5, also tries to read or write st_blksize bytes at a time, for efficiency.

> Be aware that different versions of Unix use units other than 512-byte blocks for st_blocks. Using this value is nonportable.

Holes in a File

In Section 3.6 we mentioned that a regular file can contain "holes." We showed an example of this in Program 3.2. Holes are created by seeking past the current end of file and writing some data. As an example, consider the following:

```
$ ls -l core
-rw-r--r--  1 stevens      8483248 Nov 18 12:18 core
$ du -s core
272     core
```

The size of the file core is just over 8 megabytes, yet the du command reports that the amount of disk space used by the file is 272 512-byte blocks (139,264 bytes). (The du command on many Berkeley-derived systems reports the number of 1024-byte blocks; SVR4 reports the number of 512-byte blocks.) Obviously this file has many holes.

As we mentioned in Section 3.6, the read function returns data bytes of 0 for any byte positions that have not been written. If we execute

```
$ wc -c core
 8483248 core
```

we can see that the normal I/O operations read up through the size of the file. (The wc(1) command with the -c option counts the number of characters (bytes) in the file.)

If we make a copy of this file, using a utility such as cat(1), all these holes are written out as actual data bytes of 0.

```
$ cat core > core.copy
$ ls -l core*
-rw-r--r--  1 stevens      8483248 Nov 18 12:18 core
-rw-rw-r--  1 stevens      8483248 Nov 18 12:27 core.copy
$ du -s core*
272     core
16592   core.copy
```

Here the actual number of bytes used by the new file is 8,495,104 ($512 \times 16,592$). The difference between this size and the size reported by ls is caused by the number of blocks used by the filesystem to hold pointers to the actual data blocks.

Interested readers should refer to Section 4.2 of Bach [1986] and Section 7.2 of Leffler et al. [1989] for additional details on the physical layout of files.

4.13 File Truncation

There are times when we would like to truncate a file by chopping off data at the end of the file. Emptying a file, which we can do with the O_TRUNC flag to open, is a special case of truncation.

```
#include <sys/types.h>
#include <unistd.h>

int truncate(const char *pathname, off_t length);

int ftruncate(int filedes, off_t length);
```

Both return: 0 if OK, −1 on error

These two functions truncate an existing file to *length* bytes. If the previous size of the file was greater than *length*, the data beyond *length* is no longer accessible. If the previous size was less than *length*, the effect is system dependent. If the implementation does extend a file, data between the old end-of-file and the new end-of-file will read as 0 (i.e., a hole is probably created in the file).

> These two functions are provided by SVR4 and 4.3+BSD. They are not part of POSIX.1 or XPG3.
>
> SVR4 truncates or extends a file. 4.3+BSD only truncates a file with these functions—they can't be used to extend a file.
>
> There has never been a standard way of truncating a file with Unix. Truly portable applications must make a copy of the file, copying only the desired bytes of data.
>
> SVR4 also includes an extension to `fcntl` (F_FREESP) that allows us to free any part of a file, not just a chunk at the end of the file.

We use `ftruncate` in Program 12.5 when we need to empty a file after obtaining a lock on the file.

4.14 Filesystems

To appreciate the concept of links to a file, we need a conceptual understanding of the structure of the Unix filesystem. Understanding the difference between an i-node and a directory entry that points to an i-node is also useful.

There are various implementations of the Unix filesystem in use today. SVR4, for example, supports two different types of disk filesystems: the traditional Unix System V filesystem (called S5), and the Unified File System (called UFS). We saw one difference between these two filesystem types in Figure 2.6. UFS is based on the Berkeley fast filesystem. SVR4 also supports additional nondisk filesystems, two distributed filesystems, and a bootstrap filesystem, none of which affects the following discussion. In this section we describe the traditional Unix System V filesystem. This type of filesystem dates back to Version 7.

We can think of a disk drive being divided into one or more partitions. Each partition can contain a filesystem, as shown in Figure 4.7.

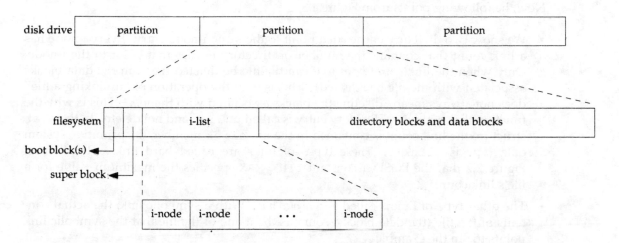

Figure 4.7 Disk drive, partitions, and a filesystem.

The i-nodes are fixed-length entries that contain most of the information about the file.

> In Version 7 an i-node occupied 64 bytes; with 4.3+BSD an i-node occupies 128 bytes. Under SVR4 the size of an i-node on disk depends on the filesystem type: an S5 i-node occupies 64 bytes while a UFS i-node occupies 128 bytes.

If we examine the filesystem in more detail, ignoring the boot blocks and super block, we could have what is shown in Figure 4.8.

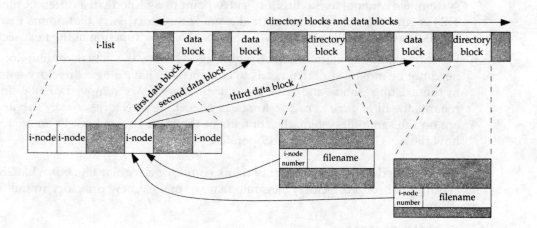

Figure 4.8 Filesystem in more detail.

Note the following points from Figure 4.8:

- We show two directory entries that point to the same i-node entry. Every i-node has a link count that contains the number of directory entries that point to the i-node. Only when the link count goes to 0 can the file be deleted (i.e., can the data blocks associated with the file be released). This is why the operation of "unlinking a file" does not always mean "deleting the blocks associated with the file." This is why the function that removes a directory entry is called `unlink` and not delete. In the `stat` structure the link count is contained in the `st_nlink` member. Its primitive system data type is `nlink_t`. These types of links are called hard links. Recall from Figure 2.7 that the POSIX.1 constant `LINK_MAX` specifies the maximum value for a file's link count.

- The other type of link is called a *symbolic link*. With a symbolic link, the actual contents of the file (the data blocks) contains the name of the file that the symbolic link points to. In the example

```
lrwxrwxrwx  1 root      7 Sep 25 07:14 lib -> usr/lib
```

the filename in the directory entry is the three-character string `lib` and the 7 bytes of data in the file are `usr/lib`. The file type in the i-node would be `S_IFLNK` so that the system knows that this is a symbolic link.

- The i-node contains all the information about the file: the file type, the file's access permission bits, the size of the file, pointers to the data blocks for the file, and so on. Most of the information in the `stat` structure is obtained from the i-node. Only two items are stored in the directory entry: the filename and the i-node number. The data type for the i-node number is `ino_t`.

- Since the i-node number in the directory entry points to an i-node in the same filesystem, we cannot have a directory entry point to an i-node in a different filesystem. This is why the `ln(1)` command (make a new directory entry that points to an existing file) can't cross filesystems. We describe the `link` function in the next section.

- When renaming a file without changing filesystems, the actual contents of the file need not be moved—all that needs to be done is to have a new directory entry point to the existing i-node and have the old directory entry removed. For example, to rename the file `/usr/lib/foo` to `/usr/foo`, if the directories `/usr/lib` and `/usr` are on the same filesystem, the contents of the file `foo` need not be moved. This is how the `mv(1)` command usually operates.

We've talked about the concept of a link count for a regular file, but what about the link count field for a directory? Assume that we make a new directory in the working directory, as in

```
$ mkdir testdir
```

Figure 4.9 shows the result. Note in this figure we explicitly show the entries for dot and dot-dot.

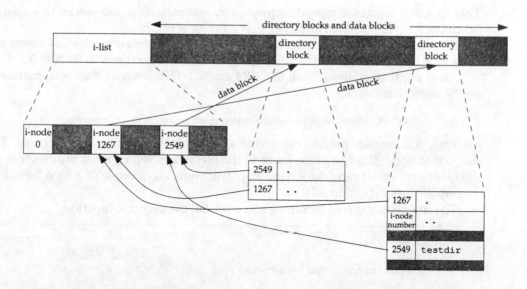

Figure 4.9 Sample filesystem after creating the directory `testdir`.

The i-node whose number is 2549 has a type field of "directory" and a link count equal to 2. Any leaf directory (a directory that does not contain any other directories) always has a link count of 2. The value of 2 is from the directory entry that names the directory (`testdir`) and from the entry for dot in that directory. The i-node whose number is 1267 has a type field of "directory" and a link count that is greater than or equal to 3. The reason we know the link count is greater than or equal to 3 is because minimally it is pointed to from the directory entry that names it (which we don't show in Figure 4.9), from dot, and from dot-dot in the `testdir` directory. Notice that every directory in the working directory causes the working directory's link count to be increased by 1.

As we said, this is the classic format of the Unix filesystem, which is described in detail in Chapter 4 of Bach [1986]. Refer to Chapter 7 of Leffler et al. [1989] for additional information on the changes made with the Berkeley fast filesystem.

4.15 link, unlink, remove, and rename Functions

As we saw in the previous section, any file can have multiple directory entries pointing to its i-node. The way we create a link to an existing file is with the `link` function.

```
#include <unistd.h>

int link(const char *existingpath, const char *newpath);
```
                                                        Returns: 0 if OK, −1 on error

This function creates a new directory entry, *newpath*, that references the existing file *existingpath*. If the *newpath* already exists an error is returned.

The creation of the new directory entry and the increment of the link count must be an atomic operation. (Recall the discussion of atomic operations in Section 3.11)

Most implementations, such as SVR4 and 4.3+BSD, require that both pathnames be on the same filesystem.

> POSIX.1 allows an implementation to support linking across filesystems.

Only a superuser process can create a new link that points to a directory. The reason is that doing this can cause loops in the filesystem, which most utilities that process the filesystem aren't capable of handling. (We show an example of a loop introduced by a symbolic link in Section 4.16.)

To remove an existing directory entry we call the `unlink` function.

```
#include <unistd.h>

int unlink(const char *pathname);
```
                                                            Returns: 0 if OK, –1 on error

This function removes the directory entry and decrements the link count of the file referenced by *pathname*. If there are other links to the file, the data in the file is still accessible through the other links. The file is not changed if an error occurs.

We've mentioned before that to unlink a file we must have write permission and execute permission in the directory containing the directory entry, since it is the directory entry that we may be removing. Also, we mentioned in Section 4.10 that if the sticky bit is set in this directory we must have write permission for the directory and either

- own the file,
- own the directory, or
- have superuser privileges.

Only when the link count reaches 0 can the contents of the file be deleted. One other condition prevents the contents of a file from being deleted—as long as some process has the file open, its contents will not be deleted. When a file is closed the kernel first checks the count of the number of processes that have the file open. If this count has reached 0 then the kernel checks the link count, and if it is 0, the file's contents are deleted.

Example

Program 4.5 opens a file and then `unlink`s it. It then goes to sleep for 15 seconds before terminating.

```
#include        <sys/types.h>
#include        <sys/stat.h>
#include        <fcntl.h>
#include        "ourhdr.h"

int
main(void)
{
    if (open("tempfile", O_RDWR) < 0)
        err_sys("open error");

    if (unlink("tempfile") < 0)
        err_sys("unlink error");

    printf("file unlinked\n");
    sleep(15);
    printf("done\n");

    exit(0);
}
```

Program 4.5 Open a file and then unlink it.

Running this program gives us

```
$ ls -l tempfile                       look at how big the file is
-rw-r--r-- 1 stevens    9240990 Jul 31 13:42 tempfile
$ df /home                             check how much free space is available
Filesystem    kbytes    used    avail capacity  Mounted on
/dev/sd0h     282908   181979   72638   71%     /home
$ a.out &                              run Program 4.5 in the background
1364                                   the shell prints its process ID
$ file unlinked                        the file is unlinked
ls -l tempfile                         see if the filename is still there
tempfile not found                     the directory entry is gone
$ df /home                             see if the space is available yet
Filesystem    kbytes    used    avail capacity  Mounted on
/dev/sd0h     282908   181979   72638   71%     /home
$ done                                 the program is done, all open files are closed
df /home                               now the disk space should be available
Filesystem    kbytes    used    avail capacity  Mounted on
/dev/sd0h     282908   172939   81678   68%     /home
                                       now the 9.2 Mbytes of disk space are available
```

□

This property of unlink is often used by a program to assure that a temporary file
it creates won't be left around in case the program crashes. The process creates a file
using either open or creat and then immediately calls unlink. The file is not deleted,
however, because it is still open. Only when the process either closes the file or terminates (which causes the kernel to close all its open files) is the file deleted.

If *pathname* is a symbolic link, `unlink` references the symbolic link, not the file referenced by the link.

The superuser can call `unlink` with *pathname* specifying a directory, but the function `rmdir` should be used instead to unlink a directory. We describe the `rmdir` function in Section 4.20.

We can also unlink a file or directory with the `remove` function. For a file, `remove` is identical to `unlink`. For a directory, `remove` is identical to `rmdir`.

```
#include <stdio.h>

int remove(const char *pathname);
```
Returns: 0 if OK, −1 on error

> ANSI C specifies the `remove` function to delete a file. The name was changed from the historical Unix name of `unlink` since most non-Unix systems that implement the C standard don't support the concept of links to a file.

A file or directory is renamed with the `rename` function.

```
#include <stdio.h>

int rename(const char *oldname, const char *newname);
```
Returns: 0 if OK, −1 on error

> This function is defined by ANSI C for files. (The C standard doesn't deal with directories.) POSIX.1 expanded the definition to include directories.

There are two conditions to describe, depending whether *oldname* refers to a file or a directory. We must also describe what happens if *newname* already exists.

1. If *oldname* specifies a file that is not a directory then we are renaming a file. In this case if *newname* exists, it cannot refer to a directory. If *newname* exists (and is not a directory), it is removed and *oldname* is renamed to *newname*. We must have write permission for the directory containing *oldname* and for the directory containing *newname*, since we are changing both directories.

2. If *oldname* specifies a directory then we are renaming a directory. If *newname* exists, it must refer to a directory and that directory must be empty. (When we say that a directory is empty, we mean that the only entries in the directory are dot and dot-dot.) If *newname* exists (and is an empty directory), it is removed and *oldname* is renamed to *newname*. Additionally, when we're renaming a directory, *newname* cannot contain a path prefix that names *oldname*. For example, we can't rename /usr/foo to /usr/foo/testdir since the old name (/usr/foo) is a path prefix of the new name and cannot be removed.

3. As a special case, if the oldname and *newname* refer to the same file, the function returns successfully without changing anything.

If *newname* already exists, we need permissions as if we were deleting it. Also, since we're removing the directory entry for *oldname* and possibly creating a directory entry for *newname*, we need write permission and execute permission in the directory containing *oldname* and in the directory containing *newname*.

4.16 Symbolic Links

A symbolic link is an indirect pointer to a file, unlike the hard links from the previous section, which pointed directly to the i-node of the file. Symbolic links were introduced to get around the limitations of hard links: (a) hard links normally require that the link and the file reside in the same filesystem, and (b) only the superuser can create a hard link to a directory. There are no filesystem limitations on a symbolic link and what it points to, and anyone can create a symbolic link to a directory. Symbolic links are typically used to move a file or an entire directory hierarchy to some other location on a system.

> Symbolic links were introduced with 4.2BSD and subsequently supported by SVR4. With SVR4 symbolic links are supported for both the traditional System V filesystem (S5) and the Unified File System (UFS).

> The original POSIX 1003.1–1990 standard does not include symbolic links. These will probably be added in 1003.1a.

When using functions that refer to a file by name we always need to know whether the function follows a symbolic link or not. If the function follows a symbolic link, a pathname argument to the function refers to the file pointed to by the symbolic link. Otherwise a pathname argument refers to the link itself, not the file pointed to by the link. Figure 4.10 summarizes whether the functions described in this chapter follow a symbolic link or not. The function `rmdir` is not in this figure since it is not defined for symbolic links (it returns an error). Also, the functions that take a file descriptor argument (`fstat`, `fchmod`, etc.) are not listed, since the handling of a symbolic link is done by the function that returns the file descriptor (usually `open`). Whether `chown` follows a symbolic link or not depends on the implementation—refer to Section 4.11 for details on the differences.

Example

It is possible to introduce loops into the filesystem using symbolic links. Most functions that look up a pathname return an `errno` of `ELOOP` when this occurs. Consider the following commands:

Function	Does not follow symbolic link	Follows symbolic link
`access`		•
`chdir`		•
`chmod`		•
`chown`	•	•
`creat`		•
`exec`		•
`lchown`	•	
`link`		•
`lstat`	•	
`mkdir`		•
`mkfifo`		•
`mknod`		•
`open`		•
`opendir`		•
`pathconf`		•
`readlink`	•	
`remove`	•	
`rename`	•	
`stat`		•
`truncate`		•
`unlink`	•	

Figure 4.10 Treatment of symbolic links by various functions.

```
$ mkdir foo                              make a new directory
$ touch foo/a                            create a 0-length file
$ ln -s ../foo foo/testdir               create a symbolic link
$ ls -l foo
total 1
-rw-rw-r--  1 stevens          0 Dec   6 06:06 a
lrwxrwxrwx  1 stevens          6 Dec   6 06:06 testdir -> ../foo
```

This creates a directory foo that contains the file a and a symbolic link that points to foo. We show this arrangement in Figure 4.11, drawing a directory as a circle and a file as a square. If we write a simple program that uses the standard function ftw(3) to descend through a file hierarchy, printing each pathname encountered, the output is

```
foo
foo/a
foo/testdir
foo/testdir/a
foo/testdir/testdir
foo/testdir/testdir/a
foo/testdir/testdir/testdir
foo/testdir/testdir/testdir/a
    (many more lines)
ftw returned -1: Too many levels of symbolic links
```

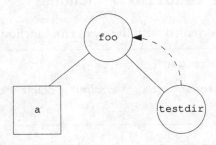

Figure 4.11 Symbolic link `testdir` that creates a loop.

We provide our own version of the `ftw` function in Section 4.21 that uses `lstat` instead of `stat`, to prevent it from following symbolic links.

A loop of this form is easy to remove—we are able to `unlink` the file `foo/testdir` since `unlink` does not follow a symbolic link. But if we create a hard link that forms a loop of this type, its removal is much harder.† This is why the `link` function will not form a hard link to a directory unless the process has superuser privileges.

When we open a file, if the pathname passed to `open` specifies a symbolic link, `open` follows the link to the specified file. If the file pointed to by the symbolic link doesn't exist, `open` returns an error saying that it can't open the file. This can confuse users who aren't familiar with symbolic links. For example,

```
$ ln -s /no/such/file myfile            create a symbolic link
$ ls myfile
myfile                                   ls says it's there
$ cat myfile                             so we try to look at it
cat: myfile: No such file or directory
$ ls -l myfile                           try -l option
lrwxrwxrwx  1 stevens   13 Dec  6 07:27 myfile -> /no/such/file
```

The file `myfile` does exist, yet `cat` says there is no such file, because `myfile` is a symbolic link and the file pointed to by the symbolic link doesn't exist. The `-l` option to `ls` gives us two hints: the first character is an `l`, which means a symbolic link, and the sequence `->` also indicates a symbolic link. The `ls` command has another option (`-F`) that appends an at-sign to filenames that are symbolic links, which can help spot symbolic links in a directory listing without the `-l` option.   □

---

† Indeed, the author did this on his own system as an experiment while writing this section. The filesystem got corrupted and the normal `fsck`(1) utility couldn't fix things. The deprecated tools `clri`(8) and `dcheck`(8) were needed to repair the filesystem.

4.17 `symlink` and `readlink` Functions

A symbolic link is created with the `symlink` function.

```
#include <unistd..h>

int symlink(const char *actualpath, const char *sympath);
```
                                               Returns: 0 if OK, −1 on error

A new directory entry, *sympath*, is created that points to *actualpath*. It is not required that *actualpath* exist when the symbolic link is created. (We saw this in the example at the end of the previous section.) Also, *actualpath* and *sympath* need not reside in the same filesystem.

Since the `open` function follows a symbolic link, we need a way to open the link itself and read the name in the link. The `readlink` function does this.

```
#include <unistd.h>

int readlink(const char *pathname, char *buf, int bufsize);
```
                              Returns: number of bytes read if OK, −1 on error

This function combines the actions of `open`, `read`, and `close`.

If the function is successful it returns the number of bytes placed into *buf*. The contents of the symbolic link that are returned in *buf* are not null terminated.

4.18 File Times

Three time fields are maintained for each file. Their purpose is summarized in Figure 4.12.

Field	Description	Example	`ls(1)` option
`st_atime`	last-access time of file data	`read`	`-u`
`st_mtime`	last-modification time of file data	`write`	default
`st_ctime`	last-change time of i-node status	`chmod`, `chown`	`-c`

Figure 4.12 The three time values associated with each file.

Note the difference between the modification time (`st_mtime`) and the changed-status time (`st_ctime`). The modification time is when the contents of the file were last modified. The changed-status time is when the i-node of the file was last modified. We've described many operations in this chapter that affect the i-node without changing the actual contents of the file: changing the file access permissions, changing the user ID, changing the number of links, and so on. Since all the information in the i-node is stored separate from the actual contents of the file, we need the changed-status time, in addition to the modification time.

Note that the system does not maintain the last-access time for an i-node. This is why the functions access and stat, for example, don't change any of the three times.

The access time is often used by system administrators to delete files that have not been accessed for a certain amount of time. The classic example is the removal of files named a.out or core that haven't been accessed in the past week. The find(1) command is often used for this type of operation.

The modification time and the changed-status time can be used to archive only those files that have had their contents modified or their i-node modified.

The ls command displays or sorts only on one of the three time values. By default (when invoked with either the -l or -t option), it uses the modification time of a file. The -u option causes it to use the access time, and the -c option causes it to use the changed-status time.

Figure 4.13 summarizes the effects of the various functions that we've described on these three times. Recall from Section 4.14 that a directory is just a file containing directory entries (filenames and associated i-node numbers). Adding, deleting, or modifying these directory entries can affect the three times associated with that directory. This is why Figure 4.13 contains one column for the three times associated with the file (or directory), and another column for the three times associated with the parent directory of the referenced file (or directory). For example, creating a new file affects the directory that contains the new file, and it affects the i-node for the new file. Reading or writing a file, however, affects only the i-node of the file and has no effect on the directory. (The mkdir and rmdir functions are covered in Section 4.20. The utime function is covered in the next section. The six exec functions are described in Section 8.9. We describe the mkfifo and pipe functions in Chapter 14.)

4.19 utime Function

The access time and the modification time of a file can be changed with the utime function.

```
#include <sys/types.h>
#include <utime.h>

int utime(const char *pathname, const struct utimbuf *times);
```

Returns: 0 if OK, −1 on error

The structure used by this function is

```
struct utimbuf {
  time_t  actime;   /* access time */
  time_t  modtime;  /* modification time */
}
```

The two time values in the structure are calendar times, which count seconds since the Epoch, as described in Section 1.10.

Function	Referenced file (or directory)			Parent directory of referenced file (or directory)			Note
	a	m	c	a	m	c	
chmod, fchmod			•				
chown, fchown			•				
creat	•	•	•		•	•	O_CREAT new file
creat		•	•				O_TRUNC existing file
exec	•						
lchown			•				
link			•		•	•	
mkdir	•	•	•		•	•	
mkfifo	•	•	•		•	•	
open	•	•	•		•	•	O_CREAT new file
open		•	•				O_TRUNC existing file
pipe	•	•	•				
read	•						
remove			•		•	•	remove file = unlink
remove					•	•	remove directory = rmdir
rename			•		•	•	for both arguments
rmdir					•	•	
truncate, ftruncate		•	•				
unlink			•		•	•	
utime	•	•	•				
write		•	•				

Figure 4.13 Effect of various functions on the access, modification, and changed-status times.

The operation of this function, and the privileges required to execute it, depend on whether the *times* argument is NULL.

1. If *times* is a null pointer, the access time and modification time are both set to the current time. To do this, either (a) the effective user ID of the process must equal the owner ID of the file, or (b) the process must have write permission for the file.

2. If *times* is a nonnull pointer, the access time and the modification time are set to the values in the structure pointed to by *times*. For this case the effective user ID of the process must equal the owner ID of the file, or the process must be a superuser process. Merely having write permission for the file is not adequate.

Note that we are not able to specify a value for the changed-status time, st_ctime (the time the i-node was last changed), since this field is automatically updated when the utime function is called.

On some versions of Unix the touch(1) command uses this function. Also, the standard archive programs, tar(1) and cpio(1), optionally call utime to set the times for a file to their values when they were archived.

Example

Program 4.6 truncates files to zero-length with the O_TRUNC option with the open function, but does not change their access time or modification time. To do this it first obtains the times with the stat function, truncates the file, and then resets the times with the utime function.

```c
#include     <sys/types.h>
#include     <sys/stat.h>
#include     <fcntl.h>
#include     <utime.h>
#include     "ourhdr.h"

int
main(int argc, char *argv[])
{
    int             i;
    struct stat     statbuf;
    struct utimbuf  timebuf;

    for (i = 1; i < argc; i++) {
        if (stat(argv[i], &statbuf) < 0) {   /* fetch current times */
            err_ret("%s: stat error", argv[i]);
            continue;
        }
        if (open(argv[i], O_RDWR | O_TRUNC) < 0) {   /* truncate */
            err_ret("%s: open error", argv[i]);
            continue;
        }
        timebuf.actime  = statbuf.st_atime;
        timebuf.modtime = statbuf.st_mtime;
        if (utime(argv[i], &timebuf) < 0) {      /* reset times */
            err_ret("%s: utime error", argv[i]);
            continue;
        }
    }
    exit(0);
}
```

Program 4.6 Example of utime function.

We can demonstrate Program 4.6 with the following script:

```
$ ls -l changemod times              look at sizes and last-modification times
-rwxrwxr-x  1 stevens   24576 Dec   4 16:13 changemod
-rwxrwxr-x  1 stevens   24576 Dec   6 09:24 times
$ ls -lu changemod times             look at last-access times
-rwxrwxr-x  1 stevens   24576 Feb   1 12:44 changemod
-rwxrwxr-x  1 stevens   24576 Feb   1 12:44 times
$ date                               print today's date
Sun Feb  3 18:22:33 MST 1991
```

```
$ a.out changemod times              run Program 4.6
$ ls -l changemod times              and check the results
-rwxrwxr-x  1 stevens      0 Dec  4 16:13 changemod
-rwxrwxr-x  1 stevens      0 Dec  6 09:24 times
$ ls -lu changemod times             check the last-access times also
-rwxrwxr-x  1 stevens      0 Feb  1 12:44 changemod
-rwxrwxr-x  1 stevens      0 Feb  1 12:44 times
$ ls -lc changemod times             and the changed-status times
-rwxrwxr-x  1 stevens      0 Feb  3 18:23 changemod
-rwxrwxr-x  1 stevens      0 Feb  3 18:23 times
```

As we expect, the last-modification times and the last-access times are not changed. The changed-status times, however, are changed to the time that the program was run. (The reason the last-access times are identical for the two files is because that was the time the directory was archived using tar.)   □

4.20 mkdir and rmdir Functions

Directories are created with the mkdir function and deleted with the rmdir function.

```
#include <sys/types.h>
#include <sys/stat.h>

int mkdir(const char *pathname, mode_t mode);
```
                                                                              Returns: 0 if OK, −1 on error

This function creates a new, empty directory. The entries for dot and dot-dot are automatically created. The specified file access permissions, *mode*, are modified by the file mode creation mask of the process.

A common mistake is to specify the same *mode* as for a file (read and write permissions only). But for a directory we normally want at least one of the execute bits enabled, to allow access to filenames within the directory. (See Exercise 4.18.)

The user ID and group ID of the new directory are established according to the rules we described in Section 4.6.

SVR4 also has the new directory inherit the set-group-ID bit from the parent directory. This is so that files created in the new directory will inherit the group ID of that directory.

4.3+BSD does not require this inheriting of the set-group-ID bit, since newly created files and directories always inherit the group ID of the parent directory, regardless of the set-group-ID bit.

Earlier versions of Unix did not have the mkdir function. It was introduced with 4.2BSD and SVR3. In the earlier versions a process had to call the mknod function to create a new directory. But use of the mknod function was restricted to superuser processes. To circumvent this, the normal command that created a directory, mkdir(1), had to be owned by root with the set-user-ID bit on. To create a directory from a process, the mkdir(1) command had to be invoked with the system(3) function.

An empty directory is deleted with the `rmdir` function.

```
#include <unistd.h>

int rmdir(const char *pathname);
```

Returns: 0 if OK, –1 on error

If the link count of the directory becomes 0 with this call, and no other process has the directory open, then the space occupied by the directory is freed. If one or more processes have the directory open when the link count reaches 0, the last link is removed and the dot and dot-dot entries are removed before this function returns. Additionally, no new files can be created in the directory. The directory is not freed, however, until the last process closes it. (Even though some other process has the directory open, they can't be doing much in the directory since the directory had to be empty for the `rmdir` function to succeed.)

4.21 Reading Directories

Directories can be read by anyone who has access permission to read the directory. But only the kernel can write to a directory (to preserve filesystem sanity). Recall from Section 4.5 that the write permission bits and execute permission bits for a directory determine if we can create new files in the directory and remove files from the directory—they don't specify if we can write to the directory itself.

The actual format of a directory depends on the Unix implementation. Earlier systems, such as Version 7, had a simple structure: each directory entry was 16 bytes, with 14 bytes for the filename and two bytes for the i-node number. When longer filenames were added to 4.2BSD each entry became variable length, which means any program that reads a directory is now system dependent. To simplify this, a set of directory routines were developed and are now part of POSIX.1.

```
#include <sys/types.h>
#include <dirent.h>

DIR *opendir(const char *pathname);
```

Returns: pointer if OK, NULL on error

```
struct dirent *readdir(DIR *dp);
```

Returns: pointer if OK, NULL at end of directory or error

```
void rewinddir(DIR *dp);

int closedir(DIR *dp);
```

Returns: 0 if OK, –1 on error

Recall our use of these functions in Program 1.1, our bare bones implementation of the `ls` command.

The `dirent` structure defined in the file `<dirent.h>` is implementation dependent. SVR4 and 4.3+BSD define the structure to contain at least the following two members:

```
struct dirent {
    ino_t   d_ino;                          /* i-node number */
    char    d_name[NAME_MAX + 1];  /* null-terminated filename */
}
```

The d_ino entry is not defined by POSIX.1, since it's an implementation feature. POSIX.1 defines only the d_name entry in this structure.

Note that `NAME_MAX` is not a defined constant with SVR4—its value depends on the filesystem in which the directory resides, and its value is usually obtained from the `fpathconf` function. A common value for `NAME_MAX` on a BSD-type filesystem is 255. (Recall Figure 2.7.) Since the filename is null terminated, however, it doesn't matter how the array d_name is defined in the header.

The `DIR` structure is an internal structure used by these four functions to maintain information about the directory being read. It serves a purpose similar to the `FILE` structure that is maintained by the standard I/O library (which we describe in Chapter 5).

The pointer to a `DIR` structure that is returned by `opendir` is then used with the other three functions. `opendir` initializes things so that the first `readdir` reads the first entry in the directory. The ordering of entries within the directory is implementation dependent. It is usually not alphabetical.

Example

We'll use these directory routines to write a program that traverses a file hierarchy. The goal is to produce the count of the different types of files that we show in Figure 4.2. Program 4.7 takes a single argument, the starting pathname, and recursively descends the hierarchy from that point. System V provides a function, `ftw(3)`, that performs the actual traversal of the hierarchy, calling a user-defined function for each file. The problem with this function is that it calls the `stat` function for each file, which causes the program to follow symbolic links. For example, if we start at the root and have a symbolic link named `/lib` that points to `/usr/lib`, all the files in the directory `/usr/lib` are counted twice. To correct this, SVR4 provides an additional function, `nftw(3)`, with an option that stops it from following symbolic links. While we could use `nftw`, we'll write our own simple file walker to show the use of the directory routines.

```
#include     <sys/types.h>
#include     <sys/stat.h>
#include     <dirent.h>
#include     <limits.h>
#include     "ourhdr.h"
```

```
typedef int Myfunc(const char *, const struct stat *, int);
                /* function type that's called for each filename */

static Myfunc    myfunc;
static int       myftw(char *, Myfunc *);
static int       dopath(Myfunc *);

static long nreg, ndir, nblk, nchr, nfifo, nslink, nsock, ntot;

int
main(int argc, char *argv[])
{
    int     ret;

    if (argc != 2)
        err_quit("usage:  ftw  <starting-pathname>");

    ret = myftw(argv[1], myfunc);        /* does it all */

    if ( (ntot = nreg + ndir + nblk + nchr + nfifo + nslink + nsock) == 0)
        ntot = 1;        /* avoid divide by 0; print 0 for all counts */
    printf("regular files  = %7ld, %5.2f %%\n", nreg,   nreg*100.0/ntot);
    printf("directories    = %7ld, %5.2f %%\n", ndir,   ndir*100.0/ntot);
    printf("block special  = %7ld, %5.2f %%\n", nblk,   nblk*100.0/ntot);
    printf("char special   = %7ld, %5.2f %%\n", nchr,   nchr*100.0/ntot);
    printf("FIFOs          = %7ld, %5.2f %%\n", nfifo, nfifo*100.0/ntot);
    printf("symbolic links = %7ld, %5.2f %%\n", nslink,nslink*100.0/ntot);
    printf("sockets        = %7ld, %5.2f %%\n", nsock, nsock*100.0/ntot);

    exit(ret);
}

/*
 * Descend through the hierarchy, starting at "pathname".
 * The caller's func() is called for every file.
 */
#define FTW_F   1       /* file other than directory */
#define FTW_D   2       /* directory */
#define FTW_DNR 3       /* directory that can't be read */
#define FTW_NS  4       /* file that we can't stat */

static char *fullpath;        /* contains full pathname for every file */

static int                    /* we return whatever func() returns */
myftw(char *pathname, Myfunc *func)
{
    fullpath = path_alloc(NULL);     /* malloc's for PATH_MAX+1 bytes */
                                     /* (Program 2.2) */
    strcpy(fullpath, pathname);      /* initialize fullpath */

    return(dopath(func));
}
```

```
    /*
     * Descend through the hierarchy, starting at "fullpath".
     * If "fullpath" is anything other than a directory, we lstat() it,
     * call func(), and return.  For a directory, we call ourself
     * recursively for each name in the directory.
     */
    static int                          /* we return whatever func() returns */
    dopath(Myfunc* func)
    {
        struct stat     statbuf;
        struct dirent   *dirp;
        DIR             *dp;
        int             ret;
        char            *ptr;

        if (lstat(fullpath, &statbuf) < 0)
            return(func(fullpath, &statbuf, FTW_NS));    /* stat error */

        if (S_ISDIR(statbuf.st_mode) == 0)
            return(func(fullpath, &statbuf, FTW_F));      /* not a directory */

        /*
         * It's a directory.  First call func() for the directory,
         * then process each filename in the directory.
         */

        if ( (ret = func(fullpath, &statbuf, FTW_D)) != 0)
            return(ret);

        ptr = fullpath + strlen(fullpath);  /* point to end of fullpath */
        *ptr++ = '/';
        *ptr = 0;

        if ( (dp = opendir(fullpath)) == NULL)
            return(func(fullpath, &statbuf, FTW_DNR));
                                            /* can't read directory */

        while ( (dirp = readdir(dp)) != NULL) {
            if (strcmp(dirp->d_name, ".") == 0  ||
                strcmp(dirp->d_name, "..") == 0)
                    continue;       /* ignore dot and dot-dot */

            strcpy(ptr, dirp->d_name);  /* append name after slash */

            if ( (ret = dopath(func)) != 0)      /* recursive */
                break;  /* time to leave */
        }
        ptr[-1] = 0;    /* erase everything from slash onwards */

        if (closedir(dp) < 0)
            err_ret("can't close directory %s", fullpath);

        return(ret);
    }
```

```
static int
myfunc(const char *pathname, const struct stat *statptr, int type)
{
    switch (type) {
    case FTW_F:
        switch (statptr->st_mode & S_IFMT) {
        case S_IFREG:   nreg++;     break;
        case S_IFBLK:   nblk++;     break;
        case S_IFCHR:   nchr++;     break;
        case S_IFIFO:   nfifo++;    break;
        case S_IFLNK:   nslink++;   break;
        case S_IFSOCK:  nsock++;    break;
        case S_IFDIR:
            err_dump("for S_IFDIR for %s", pathname);
                    /* directories should have type = FTW_D */
        }
        break;

    case FTW_D:
        ndir++;
        break;

    case FTW_DNR:
        err_ret("can't read directory %s", pathname);
        break;

    case FTW_NS:
        err_ret("stat error for %s", pathname);
        break;

    default:
        err_dump("unknown type %d for pathname %s", type, pathname);
    }

    return(0);
}
```

Program 4.7 Recursively descend a directory hierarchy, counting file types.

We have provided more generality in this program than needed. This was done to illustrate the actual ftw function. For example, the function myfunc always returns 0, even though the function that calls it is prepared to handle a nonzero return.   □

For additional information on descending through a filesystem and the use of this technique in many standard Unix commands (find, ls, tar, etc.), refer to Fowler, Korn, and Vo [1989]. 4.3+BSD provides a new set of directory traversal functions—see the fts(3) manual page.

4.22 `chdir`, `fchdir`, and `getcwd` Functions

Every process has a current working directory. This directory is where the search for all relative pathnames starts (all pathnames that do not begin with a slash). When a user logs in to a Unix system, the current working directory normally starts at the directory specified by the sixth field in the `/etc/passwd` file—the user's home directory. The current working directory is an attribute of a process; the home directory is an attribute of a login name. We can change the current working directory of the calling process by calling the `chdir` or `fchdir` functions.

```
#include <unistd.h>

int chdir(const char *pathname);

int fchdir(int filedes);
```

Both return: 0 if OK, −1 on error

We can specify the new current working directory as either a *pathname* or through an open file descriptor.

> The `fchdir` function is not part of POSIX.1. It is an extension supported by SVR4 and 4.3+BSD.

Example

Since the current working directory is an attribute of a process it cannot affect processes that invoke the process that executes the `chdir`. (We describe the relationship between processes in more detail in Chapter 8.) This means that Program 4.8 doesn't do what we expect. If we compile Program 4.8 and call the executable `mycd` we get the following:

```
$ pwd
/usr/lib
$ mycd
chdir to /tmp succeeded
$ pwd
/usr/lib
```

The current working directory for the shell that executed the `mycd` program didn't change. For this reason, the `chdir` function has to be called directly from the shell, so the `cd` command is built into the shells.   □

Since the kernel must maintain knowledge of the current working directory, we should be able to fetch its current value. Unfortunately, all the kernel maintains for each process is the i-node number and device identification for the current working directory. The kernel does not maintain the full pathname of the directory.

```
#include    "ourhdr.h"

int
main(void)
{
    if (chdir("/tmp") < 0)
        err_sys("chdir failed");

    printf("chdir to /tmp succeeded\n");
    exit(0);
}
```

Program 4.8 Example of `chdir` function.

What we need is a function that starts at the current working directory (dot) and works its way up the directory hierarchy (using dot-dot to move up one level). At each directory it reads the directory entries until it finds the name that corresponds to the i-node of the directory that it just came from. Repeating this procedure until the root is encountered yields the entire absolute pathname of the current working directory. Fortunately a function is already provided for us that does this task.

```
#include <unistd.h>

char *getcwd(char *buf, size_t size);
```
                                                        Returns: *buf* if OK, NULL on error

We must pass this function the address of a buffer, *buf*, and its *size*. The buffer must be large enough to accommodate the absolute pathname plus a terminating null byte, or an error is returned. (Recall the discussion of allocating space for a maximum-sized pathname in Section 2.5.7.)

> Some implementations of `getcwd` allow the first argument *buf* to be NULL. In this case the function calls `malloc` to allocate *size* number of bytes dynamically. This is not part of POSIX.1 or XPG3 and should be avoided.

Example

Program 4.9 changes to a specific directory and then calls `getcwd` to print the working directory. If we run the program we get

```
$ a.out
cwd = /var/spool/uucppublic
$ ls -l /usr/spool
lrwxrwxrwx  1 root  12 Jan 31 07:57 /usr/spool -> ../var/spool
```

```
#include    "ourhdr.h"

int
main(void)
{
    char    *ptr;
    int     size;

    if (chdir("/usr/spool/uucppublic") < 0)
        err_sys("chdir failed");

    ptr = path_alloc(&size);      /* our own function */
    if (getcwd(ptr, size) == NULL)
        err_sys("getcwd failed");

    printf("cwd = %s\n", ptr);
    exit(0);
}
```

Program 4.9 Example of getcwd function.

Notice that chdir follows the symbolic link (as we expect it to, from Figure 4.10) but when getcwd goes up the directory tree, it has no idea when it hits the /var/spool directory that it is pointed to by the symbolic link /usr/spool. This is a characteristic of symbolic links.   □

4.23 Special Device Files

The two fields st_dev and st_rdev are often confused. We'll need to use these fields in Section 11.9 when we write the ttyname function. The rules are simple.

- Every filesystem is known by its major and minor device number. This device number is encoded in the primitive system data type dev_t. Recall from Figure 4.7 that a disk drive often contains several filesystems.

- We can usually access the major and minor device numbers through two macros defined by most implementations: major and minor. This means we don't care how the two numbers are stored in a dev_t object.

  Early systems stored the device number in a 16-bit integer with 8 bits for the major number and 8 bits for the minor number. SVR4 uses 32 bits: 14 for the major and 18 for the minor. 4.3+BSD uses 16 bits: 8 for the major and 8 for the minor.

  POSIX.1 states that the dev_t type exists, but doesn't define what it contains or how to get at its contents. The macros major and minor are defined by most implementations. Which header they are defined in depends on the system.

- The st_dev value for every filename on a system is the device number of the filesystem containing that filename and its corresponding i-node.

- Only character special files and block special files have an st_rdev value. This value contains the device number for the actual device.

Example

Program 4.10 prints the device number for each command-line argument. Additionally, if the argument refers to a character special file or a block special file, the st_rdev value for the special file is also printed.

```
#include     <sys/types.h>      /* BSD: defines major() and minor() */
#include     <sys/stat.h>
#include     "ourhdr.h"

int
main(int argc, char *argv[])
{
    int          i;
    struct stat buf;

    for (i = 1; i < argc; i++) {
        printf("%s: ", argv[i]);
        if (lstat(argv[i], &buf) < 0) {
            err_ret("lstat error");
            continue;
        }

        printf("dev = %d/%d", major(buf.st_dev),  minor(buf.st_dev));

        if (S_ISCHR(buf.st_mode) || S_ISBLK(buf.st_mode)) {
            printf(" (%s) rdev = %d/%d",
                    (S_ISCHR(buf.st_mode)) ? "character" : "block",
                    major(buf.st_rdev), minor(buf.st_rdev));
        }
        printf("\n");
    }
    exit(0);
}
```

Program 4.10 Print st_dev and st_rdev values.

Under SVR4 the header <sys/sysmacros.h> must be included to define the macros major and minor. Running this program gives us the following output:

```
$ a.out / /home/stevens /dev/tty[ab]
/: dev = 7/0
/home/stevens: dev = 7/7
/dev/ttya: dev = 7/0 (character) rdev = 12/0
/dev/ttyb: dev = 7/0 (character) rdev = 12/1
```

```
$ mount                              which directories are mounted on which devices?
/dev/sd0a on /
/dev/sd0h on /home
$ ls -l /dev/sd0[ah] /dev/tty[ab]
brw-r-----  1 root       7,  0 Jan 31 08:23 /dev/sd0a
brw-r-----  1 root       7,  7 Jan 31 08:23 /dev/sd0h
crw-rw-rw-  1 root      12,  0 Jan 31 08:22 /dev/ttya
crw-rw-rw-  1 root      12,  1 Jul  9 10:11 /dev/ttyb
```

The first two arguments to the program are directories (root and /home/stevens),
and the next two are the device names /dev/tty[ab]. We expect the devices to be
character special files. The output from the program shows that the root directory has a
different device number than the /home/stevens directory. This indicates that they
are on different filesystems. Running the mount(1) command verifies this. We then use
ls to look at the two disk devices reported by mount and the two terminal devices.
The two disk devices are block special files, and the two terminal devices are character
special files. (Normally the only types of devices that are block special files are those
that can contain random-access filesystems: disk drives, floppy disk drives, and
CD-ROMs, for example. Older versions of Unix supported magnetic tapes for filesystems, but this was never widely used.) Note that the filenames and i-nodes for the
two terminal devices (st_dev) are on device 7/0 (the root filesystem, which contains
the /dev filesystem) but their actual device numbers are 12/0 and 12/1.   □

4.24 sync and fsync Functions

Traditional Unix implementations have a buffer cache in the kernel through which most
disk I/O passes. When we write data to a file the data is normally copied by the kernel into one of its buffers and queued for I/O at some later time. This is called *delayed
write*. (Chapter 3 of Bach [1986] discusses this buffer cache in detail.)

The kernel eventually writes all the delayed-write blocks to disk, normally when it
needs to reuse the buffer for some other disk block. To ensure consistency of the actual
filesystem on disk with the contents of the buffer cache, the sync and fsync functions
are provided.

```
#include <unistd.h>

void sync(void);

int fsync(int filedes);
                                                      Returns: 0 if OK, −1 on error
```

sync just queues all the modified block buffers for writing and returns; it does not wait
for the actual I/O to take place.

The function sync is normally called every 30 seconds from a system daemon
(often called update). This guarantees regular flushing of the kernel's block buffers.
The command sync(1) also calls the sync function.

The function `fsync` refers only to a single file (specified by the file descriptor *filedes*), and waits for the I/O to complete before returning. The intended use of `fsync` is for an application such as a database that needs to be sure that the modified blocks have been written to the disk. Compare `fsync`, which updates a file's contents when we say so, with the `O_SYNC` flag (described in Section 3.13), which updates a file's contents every time we `write` to the file.

> `sync` and `fsync` are supported by both SVR4 and 4.3+BSD. Neither is part of POSIX.1, but `fsync` is required by XPG3.

4.25 Summary of File Access Permission Bits

We've covered all the file access permission bits, some of which serve multiple purposes. Figure 4.14 summarizes all these permission bits and their interpretation when applied to a regular file versus their interpretation when applied to a directory.

Constant	Description	Effect on regular file	Effect on directory
S_ISUID	set-user-ID	set effective user ID on execution	(not used)
S_ISGID	set-group-ID	if group-execute set then set effective group ID on execution; otherwise enable mandatory record locking	set group ID of new files created in directory to group ID of directory
S_ISVTX	sticky bit	save program text in swap area (if supported)	restrict removal and renaming of files in directory
S_IRUSR	user-read	user permission to read file	user permission to read directory entries
S_IWUSR	user-write	user permission to write file	user permission to remove and create files in directory
S_IXUSR	user-execute	user permission to execute file	user permission to search for given pathname in directory
S_IRGRP	group-read	group permission to read file	group permission to read directory entries
S_IWGRP	group-write	group permission to write file	group permission to remove and create files in directory
S_IXGRP	group-execute	group permission to execute file	group permission to search for given pathname in directory
S_IROTH	other-read	other permission to read file	other permission to read directory entries
S_IWOTH	other-write	other permission to write file	other permission to remove and create files in directory
S_IXOTH	other-execute	other permission to execute file	other permission to search for given pathname in directory

Figure 4.14 Summary of file access permission bits.

The final nine constants can also be grouped into threes, since

```
S_IRWXU = S_IRUSR | S_IWUSR | S_IXUSR
S_IRWXG = S_IRGRP | S_IWGRP | S_IXGRP
S_IRWXO = S_IROTH | S_IWOTH | S_IXOTH
```

4.26 Summary

This chapter has been centered around the stat function. We've gone through each member in the stat structure in detail. This in turn has led us to examine all the attributes of Unix files. A thorough understanding of all the properties of a file and all the functions that operate on files is essential to all Unix programming.

Exercises

4.1 Modify Program 4.1 to use stat instead of lstat. What changes if one of the command-line arguments is a symbolic link?

4.2 We indicated in Figure 4.1 that SVR4 doesn't currently provide the S_ISLNK macro. But SVR4 does support symbolic links and defines S_IFLNK in <sys/stat.h>. (Perhaps someone forgot to define S_ISLNK?) Devise a way around this omission that can be placed in ourhdr.h, so any programs that need the S_ISLNK macro can use it.

4.3 What happens if the file mode creation mask is set to 777 (octal)? Verify the results using your shell's umask command.

4.4 Verify that turning off user-read permission for a file that you own denies your access to the file.

4.5 Run Program 4.3 *after* creating the files foo and bar. What happens?

4.6 In Section 4.12 we said that a file size of 0 is valid for a regular file. We also said that the st_size field is defined for directories and symbolic links. Should we ever see a file size of 0 for a directory or a symbolic link?

4.7 Write a utility like cp(1) that copies a file containing holes, without writing the bytes of 0 to the output file.

4.8 Note in output from the ls command in Section 4.12 that the files core and core.copy have different access permissions. If the umask value didn't change between the creation of the two files, explain how the difference could have occurred.

4.9 When running Program 4.5 we check the available disk space with the df(1) command. Why didn't we use the du(1) command?

4.10 In Figure 4.13 we show the unlink function as modifying the changed-status time of the file itself. How can this happen?

4.11 In Section 4.21 how does the system's limit on the number of open files affect the myftw function?

4.12 In Section 4.21 our version of ftw never changes its directory. Modify this routine so that each time it encounters a directory it does a chdir to that directory, allowing it to use the filename and not the pathname for each call to lstat. When all the entries in a directory have been processed, execute chdir(".."). Compare the time used by this version and the version in the text.

4.13 Each process also has a root directory that is used for resolution of absolute pathnames. This root directory can be changed with the chroot function. Look up the description for this function in your manuals. When might this function be useful?

4.14 How can you set only one of the two time values with the utime function?

4.15 Some versions of the finger(1) command output "New mail received ..." and "unread since ..." where ... are the corresponding times and dates. How can the program determine these two times and dates?

4.16 Examine the archive formats by the cpio(1) and tar(1) commands. (These descriptions are usually found in Section 5 of the *Unix Programmer's Manual*.) How many of the three possible time values are saved for each file? When a file is restored, what value do you think the access time is set to, and why?

4.17 The command file(1) tries to determine the logical type of a file (C program, Fortran program, shell script, etc.) by reading the first part of the file, examining the contents, and applying some heuristics. Also, some Unix systems provide a command that allows us to execute another command and obtain a trace of all the system calls executed by the command. (Under SVR4 the command is truss(1). Under 4.3+BSD the commands are ktrace(1) and kdump(1). The following example uses the SunOS trace(1) command.) If we run a system call trace of the file command

```
trace file a.out
```

we find it calls the following functions

```
lstat ("a.out", 0xf7fff650) = 0
open ("a.out", 0, 0) = 3
read (3, "".., 512) = 512
fstat (3, 0xf7fff160) = 0
write (1, "a.out: demand paged execu".., 44) = 44
a.out: demand paged executable not stripped
utime ("a.out", 0xf7fff1b0) = 0
```

Why is the file command calling utime?

4.18 Does Unix have a fundamental limitation on the depth of a directory tree? To find out, write a program that creates a directory and then changes to that directory, in a loop. Make certain that the length of the absolute pathname of the leaf of this directory is greater than your system's PATH_MAX limit. Can you call getcwd to fetch the directory's pathname? How do the standard Unix tools deal with this long pathname? Can you archive the directory using either tar or cpio?

4.19 In Section 3.15 we described the /dev/fd feature. For any user to be able to access these files, their permissions must be rw-rw-rw-. Some programs that create an output file delete the file first, in case it already exists (ignoring the return code).

```
unlink(path);
if ( (fd = creat(path, FILE_MODE)) < 0)
    err_sys(...);
```

What happens if path is /dev/fd/1?

5

Standard I/O Library

5.1 Introduction

In this chapter we describe the standard I/O library. This library is specified by the ANSI C standard because it has been implemented on many operating systems other than Unix. This library handles details such as buffer allocation and performing I/O in optimal-sized chunks, obviating our need to worry about using the correct block size (as in Section 3.9). This makes the library easy to use, but at the same time introduces another set of problems if we're not cognizant of what's going on.

> The standard I/O library was written by Dennis Ritchie around 1975. It was a major revision of the Portable I/O library written by Mike Lesk. Surprisingly, little has changed in the standard I/O library after more than 15 years.

5.2 Streams and FILE Objects

In Chapter 3 all the I/O routines centered around file descriptors. When a file is opened a file descriptor is returned, and that descriptor is then used for all subsequent I/O operations. With the standard I/O library the discussion centers around *streams*. (Do not confuse the standard I/O term *stream* with the STREAMS I/O system that is part of System V.) When we open or create a file with the standard I/O library we say that we have associated a stream with the file.

When we open a stream, the standard I/O function fopen returns a pointer to a FILE object. This object is normally a structure that contains all the information required by the standard I/O library to manage the stream: the file descriptor used for actual I/O, a pointer to a buffer for the stream, the size of the buffer, a count of the number of characters currently in the buffer, an error flag, and the like.

Application software should never need to examine a FILE object. To reference the stream we pass its FILE pointer as an argument to each standard I/O function. Throughout this text we'll refer to a pointer to a FILE object, the type FILE * as a *file pointer*.

Throughout this chapter we describe the standard I/O library in the context of a Unix-based system. As we mentioned, this library has already been ported to a wide variety of operating systems other than Unix. But to provide some insight about how this library can be implemented, we need to talk about its typical Unix implementation.

5.3 Standard Input, Standard Output, and Standard Error

Three streams are predefined and automatically available to a process: standard input, standard output, and standard error. These refer to the same files as the file descriptors STDIN_FILENO, STDOUT_FILENO, and STDERR_FILENO, which we mentioned in Section 3.2.

These three standard I/O streams are referenced through the predefined file pointers stdin, stdout, and stderr. These three file pointers are defined in the <stdio.h> header.

5.4 Buffering

The goal of the buffering provided by the standard I/O library is to use the minimum number of read and write calls. (Recall Figure 3.1 where we showed the amount of CPU time required to perform I/O using different buffer sizes.) Also, it tries to do its buffering automatically for each I/O stream, obviating the need for the application to worry about it. Unfortunately, the single aspect of the standard I/O library that generates the most confusion is its buffering.

There are three types of buffering provided.

1. Fully buffered. For this case actual I/O takes place when the standard I/O buffer is filled. Files that reside on disk are normally fully buffered by the standard I/O library. The buffer that's used is normally obtained by one of the standard I/O functions calling malloc (Section 7.8) the first time I/O is performed on a stream.

    The term *flush* describes the writing of a standard I/O buffer. A buffer can be flushed automatically by the standard I/O routines (such as when a buffer fills), or we can call the function fflush to flush a stream. Unfortunately, in the Unix environment *flush* means two different things. In terms of the standard I/O library it means writing out the contents of a buffer (which may be partially filled). In terms of the terminal driver (such as the tcflush function in Chapter 11) it means to discard the data that's already stored in a buffer.

2. Line buffered. In this case the standard I/O library performs I/O when a new-line character is encountered on input or output. This allows us to output a single character at a time (with the standard I/O `fputc` function), knowing that actual I/O will take place only when we finish writing each line. Line buffering is typically used on a stream when it refers to a terminal (e.g., standard input and standard output).

There are two caveats with respect to line buffering. First, since the size of the buffer that the standard I/O library is using to collect each line is fixed, actual I/O might take place if we fill this buffer before writing a newline. Second, whenever input is requested through the standard I/O library from either (a) an unbuffered stream or (b) from a line-buffered stream (that requires data to be requested from the kernel), it is intended that this causes *all* line-buffered output streams to be flushed. The reason for the qualifier on (b) is that the requested data may already be in the buffer, which doesn't require data to be read from the kernel. Obviously, any input from an unbuffered stream, item (a), requires data to be obtained from the kernel.

3. Unbuffered. The standard I/O library does not buffer the characters. If we write 15 characters with the standard I/O `fputs` function, for example, we expect these 15 characters to be output as soon as possible (probably with the `write` function from Section 3.8).

The standard error stream, for example, is normally unbuffered. This is so that any error messages are displayed as quickly as possible, regardless whether they contain a newline or not.

ANSI C requires the following buffering characteristics:

1. Standard input and standard output are fully buffered, if and only if they do not refer to an interactive device.

2. Standard error is never fully buffered.

This, however, doesn't tell us whether standard input and standard output can be unbuffered or line buffered if they refer to an interactive device and whether standard error should be unbuffered or line buffered. Both SVR4 and 4.3+BSD default to the following types of buffering:

- Standard error is always unbuffered.

- All other streams are line buffered if they refer to a terminal device; otherwise they are fully buffered.

If we don't like these defaults for any given stream, we can change the buffering by calling either of the following two functions.

```
#include <stdio.h>

void setbuf(FILE *fp, char *buf);

int setvbuf(FILE *fp, char *buf, int mode, size_t size);
```
                                                        Returns: 0 if OK, nonzero on error

These functions must be called *after* the stream has been opened (obviously, since each requires a valid file pointer as their first argument) but *before* any other operation is performed on the stream.

With setbuf we can turn buffering on or off. To enable buffering, *buf* must point to a buffer of length BUFSIZ (a constant defined in <stdio.h>). Normally the stream is then fully buffered, but some systems may set line buffering if the stream is associated with a terminal device. To disable buffering, we set *buf* to NULL.

With setvbuf we specify exactly which type of buffering we want. This is done with the *mode* argument:

_IOFBF	fully buffered
_IOLBF	line buffered
_IONBF	unbuffered

If we specify an unbuffered stream, the *buf* and *size* arguments are ignored. If we specify fully buffered or line buffered, *buf* and *size* can optionally specify a buffer and its size. If the stream is buffered and *buf* is NULL, then the standard I/O library will automatically allocate its own buffer of the appropriate size for the stream. By appropriate size we mean the value specified by the st_blksize member of the stat structure from Section 4.2. If the system can't determine this value for the stream (if the stream refers to a device or a pipe, for example), then a buffer of length BUFSIZ is allocated.

> Using the st_blksize value for the buffer size came from the Berkeley systems. Earlier versions of System V used the standard I/O constant BUFSIZ (typically 1024). Even 4.3+BSD still sets BUFSIZ to 1024, even though it uses st_blksize to determine the optimal standard I/O buffer size.

Figure 5.1 summarizes the actions of these two functions and their various options.

Function	*mode*	*buf*	Buffer & length	Type of buffering
setbuf		nonnull	user *buf* of length BUFSIZ	fully buffered or line buffered
		NULL	(no buffer)	unbuffered
setvbuf	_IOFBF	nonnull	user *buf* of length *size*	fully buffered
		NULL	system buffer of appropriate length	
	_IOLBF	nonnull	user *buf* of length *size*	line buffered
		NULL	system buffer of appropriate length	
	_IONBF	(ignored)	(no buffer)	unbuffered

Figure 5.1 Summary of the setbuf and setvbuf functions.

Be aware that if we allocate a standard I/O buffer as an automatic variable within a function, we have to close the stream before returning from the function. (We'll discuss this more in Section 7.8.) Also, SVR4 uses part of the buffer for its own bookkeeping, so the actual number of bytes of data that can be stored in the buffer is less than *size*. In general, we should let the system choose the buffer size and automatically allocate the buffer. When we do this the standard I/O library automatically releases the buffer when we close the stream.

At any time we can force a stream to be flushed.

```
#include <stdio.h>

int fflush(FILE *fp);
```
Returns: 0 if OK, EOF on error

This function causes any unwritten data for the stream to be passed to the kernel. As a special case, if *fp* is NULL this function causes all output streams to be flushed.

> The ability to pass a null pointer to force all output streams to be flushed is new with ANSI C. Non-ANSI C libraries (e.g., earlier releases of System V and 4.3BSD) do not support this feature.

5.5 Opening a Stream

The following three functions open a standard I/O stream.

```
#include <stdio.h>

FILE *fopen(const char *pathname, const char *type);

FILE *freopen(const char *pathname, const char *type, FILE *fp);

FILE *fdopen(int filedes, const char *type);
```
All three return: file pointer if OK, NULL on error

The differences in these three functions are as follows:

1. fopen opens a specified file.
2. freopen opens a specified file on a specified stream, closing the stream first, if it is already open. This function is typically used to open a specified file as one of the predefined streams: standard input, standard output, or standard error.
3. fdopen takes an existing file descriptor (which we could obtain from the open, dup, dup2, fcntl, or pipe functions) and associates a standard I/O stream with the descriptor. This function is often used with descriptors that are

returned by the functions that create pipes and network communication channels. Since these special types of files cannot be opened with the standard I/O `fopen` function, we have to call the device-specific function to obtain a file descriptor, and then associate this descriptor with a standard I/O stream using `fdopen`.

> `fopen` and `freopen` are part of ANSI C. `fdopen` is part of POSIX.1, since ANSI C doesn't deal with file descriptors.

ANSI C specifies 15 different values for the *type* argument, shown in Figure 5.2.

type	Description
r or rb	open for reading
w or wb	truncate to 0 length or create for writing
a or ab	append; open for writing at end of file, or create for writing
r+ or r+b or rb+	open for reading and writing
w+ or w+b or wb+	truncate to 0 length or create for reading and writing
a+ or a+b or ab+	open or create for reading and writing at end of file

Figure 5.2   The *type* argument for opening a standard I/O stream.

Using the character b as part of the *type* allows the standard I/O system to differentiate between a text file and a binary file. Since the Unix kernel doesn't differentiate between these types of files, specifying the character b as part of the *type* has no effect.

With `fdopen` the meanings of the *type* argument differ slightly. Since the descriptor has already been opened, opening for write does not truncate the file. (If the descriptor was created by the `open` function, for example, and the file already existed, the `O_TRUNC` flag would determine if the file were truncated or not. The `fdopen` function cannot just truncate any file it opens for writing.) Also, the standard I/O append mode cannot create the file (since the file has to exist if a descriptor refers to it).

When a file is opened with a type of append, each write will take place at the then current end of file. If multiple processes open the same file with the standard I/O append mode, the data from each process will be correctly written to the file.

> Versions of `fopen` from Berkeley before 4.3+BSD, and the simple version shown on page 177 of Kernighan and Ritchie [1988] do not handle the append mode correctly. These versions do an `lseek` to the end of file when the stream is opened. To correctly support the append mode when multiple processes are involved, the file must be opened with the `O_APPEND` flag, which we discussed in Section 3.3. Doing an `lseek` before each write won't work either, as we discussed in Section 3.11.

When a file is opened for reading and writing (the plus sign in the *type*) the following restrictions apply:

- Output cannot be directly followed by input without an intervening `fflush`, `fseek`, `fsetpos`, or `rewind`.

- Input cannot be directly followed by output without an intervening `fseek`, `fsetpos`, or `rewind`, or an input operation that encounters an end of file.

We can summarize the six different ways to open a stream from Figure 5.2 in Figure 5.3.

Restriction	r	w	a	r+	w+	a+
file must already exist	•			•		
previous contents of file discarded		•			•	
stream can be read	•			•	•	•
stream can be written		•	•	•	•	•
stream can be written only at end			•			•

Figure 5.3 Six different ways to open a standard I/O stream.

Note that if a new file is created by specifying a *type* of either w or a, we are not able to specify the file's access permission bits (as we were able to do with the open function and the creat function in Chapter 3). POSIX.1 requires that the file be created with the following permissions

    S_IRUSR | S_IWUSR | S_IRGRP | S_IWGRP | S_IROTH | S_IWOTH

By default, the stream that is opened is fully buffered, unless it refers to a terminal device, in which case it is line buffered. Once the stream is opened, but before we do any other operation on the stream, we can change the buffering if we want to, with the setbuf or setvbuf functions from the previous section.

An open stream is closed by calling fclose.

```
#include <stdio.h>

int fclose(FILE *fp);
```
Returns: 0 if OK, EOF on error

Any buffered output data is flushed before the file is closed. Any input data that may be buffered is discarded. If the standard I/O library had automatically allocated a buffer for the stream, that buffer is released.

When a process terminates normally, either by calling the exit function directly, or by returning from the main function, all standard I/O streams with unwritten buffered data are flushed, and all open standard I/O streams are closed.

5.6 Reading and Writing a Stream

Once we open a stream we can choose among three different types of unformatted I/O. (We describe the formatted I/O functions, such as printf and scanf, in Section 5.11.)

1. Character-at-a-time I/O. We can read or write one character at a time, with the standard I/O functions handling all the buffering (if the stream is buffered).

2. Line-at-a-time I/O. If we want to read or write a line at a time, we use `fgets` and `fputs`. Each line is terminated with a newline character, and we have to specify the maximum line length that we can handle when we call `fgets`. We describe these two functions in Section 5.7.

3. Direct I/O. This type of I/O is supported by the `fread` and `fwrite` functions. For each I/O operation we read or write some number of objects, where each object is of a specified size. These two functions are often used for binary files where we read or write a structure with each operation. We describe these two functions in Section 5.9.

> The term *direct I/O* is from the ANSI C standard. It's known by many names: binary I/O, object-at-a-time I/O, record-oriented I/O, or structure-oriented I/O.

Input Functions

Three functions allow us to read one character at a time.

```
#include <stdio.h>

int getc(FILE *fp);

int fgetc(FILE *fp);

int getchar(void);
```
All three return: next character if OK, EOF on end of file or error

The function `getchar` is defined to be equivalent to `getc(stdin)`. The difference between the first two functions is that `getc` can be implemented as a macro while `fgetc` cannot be implemented as a macro. This means three things:

1. The argument to `getc` should not be an expression with side effects.

2. Since `fgetc` is guaranteed to be a function, we can take its address. This allows us to pass the address of `fgetc` as an argument to another function.

3. Calls to `fgetc` probably take longer than calls to `getc`, since it usually takes more time to call a function. Indeed, examining most implementations of the `<stdio.h>` header shows that `getc` is a macro that has been coded for efficiency.

These three functions return the next character as an `unsigned char` converted to an `int`. The reason for specifying unsigned is so that the high-order bit, if set, doesn't cause the return value to be negative. The reason for requiring an integer return value is so that all possible character values can be returned, along with an indication that either an error occurred or the end of file has been encountered. The constant EOF in `<stdio.h>` is required to be a negative value. Its value is often −1. This representation also means that we cannot store the return value from these three functions in a character variable, and compare this value later against the constant EOF.

Notice that these functions return the same value whether an error occurs or the end of file is reached. To distinguish between the two we must call either ferror or feof.

```
#include <stdio.h>

int ferror(FILE *fp);

int feof(FILE *fp);

                    Both return: nonzero (true) if condition is true, 0 (false) otherwise

void clearerr(FILE *fp);
```

In most implementations, two flags are maintained for each stream in the FILE object:

- an error flag,
- an end-of-file flag.

Both flags are cleared by calling clearerr.

After reading from a stream we can push back characters by calling ungetc.

```
#include <stdio.h>

int ungetc(int c, FILE *fp);

                                                    Returns: c if OK, EOF on error
```

The characters that are pushed back are returned by subsequent reads on the stream in reverse order of their pushing. Be aware, however, that although ANSI C allows an implementation to support any amount of pushback, an implementation is required to provide only a single character of pushback. We should not count on more than a single character.

The character that we push back does not have to be the same character that was read. We are not able to push back EOF. But when we've reached the end of file, we can push back a character. The next read will return that character, and the read after that will return EOF. This works because a successful call to ungetc clears the end-of-file indication for the stream.

Pushback is often used when we're reading an input stream and breaking into words or tokens of some form. Sometimes we need to peek at the next character to determine how to handle the current character. It's then easy to push back the character that we peeked at, for the next call to getc to return. If the standard I/O library didn't provide this pushback capability, we would have to store the character in a variable of our own, along with a flag telling us to use this character instead of calling getc the next time we need a character.

Output Functions

We'll find an output function that corresponds to each of the input functions that we've already described.

```
#include <stdio.h>

int putc(int c, FILE *fp);

int fputc(int c, FILE *fp);

int putchar(int c);
```
All three return: c if OK, EOF on error

Like the input functions, `putchar(c)` is equivalent to `putc(c, stdout)`, and `putc` can be implemented as a macro while `fputc` cannot be implemented as a macro.

5.7   Line-at-a-Time I/O

Line-at-a-time input is provided by the following two functions.

```
#include <stdio.h>

char *fgets(char *buf, int n, FILE *fp);

char *gets(char *buf);
```
Both return: buf if OK, NULL on end of file or error

Both specify the address of the buffer to read the line into. `gets` reads from standard input while `fgets` reads from the specified stream.

With `fgets` we have to specify the size of the buffer, n. This function reads up through and including the next newline, but no more than $n-1$ characters, into the buffer. The buffer is terminated with a null byte. If the line, including the terminating newline, is longer than $n-1$, then only a partial line is returned, but the buffer is always null terminated. Another call to `fgets` will read what follows on the line.

`gets` is a deprecated function. The problem is that it doesn't allow the caller to specify the buffer size. This allows the buffer to overflow, if the line is longer than the buffer, writing over whatever happens to follow the buffer in memory. For a description of how this flaw was used as part of the Internet worm of 1988, see the June 1989 issue (vol. 32, no. 6) of *Communications of the ACM*. An additional difference with `gets` is that it doesn't store the newline in the buffer, as does `fgets`.

> This difference in newline handling between the two functions goes way back in the evolution of Unix. Even the Version 7 manual (1979) states "`gets` deletes a newline, `fgets` keeps it, all in the name of backward compatibility."

Even though ANSI C requires an implementation to provide gets, it should never be used.

Line-at-a-time output is provided by fputs and puts.

```
#include <stdio.h>

int fputs(const char *str, FILE *fp);

int puts(const char *str);
```

> Both return: nonnegative value if OK, EOF on error

The function fputs writes the null terminated string to the specified stream. The null byte at the end is not written. Note that this need not be line-at-a-time output, since the string need not contain a newline as the last nonnull character. Usually this is the case (the last nonnull character is a newline), but it's not required.

puts writes the null terminated string to the standard output (without writing the null byte). But puts then writes a newline character to the standard output.

puts is not unsafe like its counterpart gets. Nevertheless, we'll avoid using it to prevent having to remember whether it appends a newline or not. If we always use fgets and fputs we know that we always have to deal with the newline character at the end of each line.

5.8 Standard I/O Efficiency

Using the functions from the previous section we can get an idea of the efficiency of the standard I/O system. Program 5.1 is like Program 3.3: it just copies standard input to standard output, using getc and putc. These two routines can be implemented as macros.

```
#include    "ourhdr.h"

int
main(void)
{
    int     c;

    while ( (c = getc(stdin)) != EOF)
        if (putc(c, stdout) == EOF)
            err_sys("output error");

    if (ferror(stdin))
        err_sys("input error");

    exit(0);
}
```

Program 5.1 Copy standard input to standard output using getc and putc.

We can make another version of this program that uses `fgetc` and `fputc`, which should be functions and not macros. (We don't show this trivial change to the source code.)

Finally we have a version that reads and writes lines, Program 5.2.

```c
#include     "ourhdr.h"

int
main(void)
{
    char    buf[MAXLINE];

    while (fgets(buf, MAXLINE, stdin) != NULL)
        if (fputs(buf, stdout) == EOF)
            err_sys("output error");

    if (ferror(stdin))
        err_sys("input error");

    exit(0);
}
```

Program 5.2 Copy standard input to standard output using `fgets` and `fputs`.

Note that we do not close the standard I/O streams explicitly in Program 5.1 or Program 5.2. Instead, we know that the `exit` function will flush any unwritten data and then close all open streams. (We'll discuss this in Section 8.5.) It is interesting to compare the timing of these three programs with the timing data from Figure 3.1. We show this data when operating on the same file (1.5 Mbytes with 30,000 lines) in Figure 5.4.

Function	User CPU (seconds)	System CPU (seconds)	Clock time (seconds)	Bytes of program text
best time from Figure 3.1	0.0	0.3	0.3	
fgets, fputs	2.2	0.3	2.6	184
getc, putc	4.3	0.3	4.8	384
fgetc, fputc	4.6	0.3	5.0	152
single byte time from Figure 3.1	23.8	397.9	423.4	

Figure 5.4 Timing results using standard I/O routines.

For each of the three standard I/O versions, the user CPU time is larger than the best `read` version from Figure 3.1, because the character-at-a-time standard I/O versions have a loop that is executed 1.5 million times, and the loop in the line-at-a-time version is executed 30,000 times. In the `read` version, its loop is executed only 180 times (for a buffer size of 8192). This difference in user CPU times accounts for the difference in clock times, since the system CPU times are all the same.

The system CPU time is the same as before, because the same number of kernel requests are being made. Note that an advantage of using the standard I/O routines is that we don't have to worry about buffering or choosing the optimal I/O size. We do have to determine the maximum line size for the version that uses `fgets`, but that's easier than trying to choose the optimal I/O size.

The final column in Figure 5.4 is the number of bytes of text space (the machine instructions generated by the C compiler) for each of the `main` functions. We can see that the version using `getc` expands the `getc` and `putc` macros inline, which takes more instructions than calling the `fgetc` and `fputc` functions. Looking at the difference in user CPU times between the `getc` version and the `fgetc` version, we see that expanding the macros inline versus calling two functions doesn't make a big difference on the system used for these tests.

The version using line-at-a-time I/O is almost twice as fast as the character-at-a-time version (both the user CPU time and the clock time). If the `fgets` and `fputs` functions are implemented using `getc` and `putc` (see Section 7.7 of Kernighan and Ritchie [1988], for example) then we would expect the timing to be similar to the `getc` version. Actually, we might expect the line-at-a-time version to take longer, since we would be adding 3 million macro invocations to the existing 60,000 function calls. What is happening with this example is that the line-at-a-time functions are implemented using `memccpy`(3). Often the `memccpy` function is implemented in assembler, instead of C, for efficiency.

The last point of interest with these timing numbers is that the `fgetc` version is so much faster than the `BUFFSIZE=1` version from Figure 3.1. Both involve the same number of function calls (about 3 million), yet the `fgetc` version is over 5 times faster in user CPU time, and almost 100 times faster in clock time. The difference is that the version using `read` executes 3 million function calls, which in turn execute 3 million system calls. With the `fgetc` version we still execute 3 million function calls but this ends up being only 360 system calls. System calls are usually much more expensive than ordinary function calls.

As a disclaimer you should be aware that these timing results are valid only on the single system they were run on. The results depend on many implementation features that aren't the same on every Unix system. Nevertheless, having a set of numbers such as these, and explaining why the various versions differ, helps us understand the system better. The basic fact that we've learned from this section and Section 3.9 is that the standard I/O library is not much slower than calling the `read` and `write` functions directly. The approximate cost that we've seen is about 3.0 seconds of CPU time to copy a megabyte of data using `getc` and `putc`. For most nontrivial applications, the largest amount of the user CPU time is taken by the application and not by the standard I/O routines.

5.9 Binary I/O

The functions from Section 5.6 operated with one character at a time or one line at a time. If we're doing binary I/O we often would like to read or write an entire structure at a time. To do this using `getc` or `putc` we have to loop through the entire structure, one byte at a time, reading or writing each byte. We can't use the line-at-a-time functions, since `fputs` stops writing when it hits a null byte, and there might be null bytes within the structure. Similarly, `fgets` won't work right on input if any of the data bytes are nulls or newlines. Therefore, the following two functions are provided for binary I/O.

```
#include <stdio.h>

size_t fread(void *ptr, size_t size, size_t nobj, FILE *fp);

size_t fwrite(const void *ptr, size_t size, size_t nobj, FILE *fp);
```
                                                Both return: number of objects read or written

There are two common uses for these functions.

1. Read or write a binary array. For example, to write elements 2 through 5 of a floating point array, we could write

```
float    data[10];

if (fwrite(&data[2], sizeof(float), 4, fp) != 4)
    err_sys("fwrite error");
```

Here we specify *size* as the size of each element of the array, and *nobj* as the number of elements.

2. Read or write a structure. For example, we could write

```
struct {
    short   count;
    long    total;
    char    name[NAMESIZE];
} item;

if (fwrite(&item, sizeof(item), 1, fp) != 1)
    err_sys("fwrite error");
```

Here we specify *size* as the size of structure, and *nobj* as one (the number of objects to write).

The obvious generalization of these two cases is to read or write an array of structures. To do this *size* would be the `sizeof` the structure, and *nobj* would be the number of elements in the array.

Both `fread` and `fwrite` return the number of objects read or written. For the read case, this number can be less than *nobj* if an error occurs or if the end of file is encountered. In this case `ferror` or `feof` must be called. For the write case, if the return value is less than the requested *nobj*, an error has occurred.

A fundamental problem with binary I/O is that it can be used to read only data that has been written on the same system. While this was OK many years ago (when all the Unix systems were PDP-11s), today it is the norm to have heterogeneous systems connected together with networks. It is common to want to write data on one system and process it on another. These two functions won't work because

1. The offset of a member within a structure can differ between compilers and systems (due to different alignment requirements). Indeed, some compilers have an option allowing structures to be packed tightly (to save space with a possible run-time performance penalty) or aligned accurately to optimize run-time access of each member. This means even on a single system the binary layout of a structure can differ, depending on compiler options.

2. The binary formats used to store multibyte integers and floating-point values differs between different machine architectures

The real solution for exchanging binary data between different systems is to use a higher level protocol. Refer to Section 18.2 of Stevens [1990] for a description of some techniques used by various network protocols to exchange binary data.

We'll return to the `fread` function in Section 8.13 when we'll use it to read a binary structure, the Unix process accounting records.

5.10 Positioning a Stream

There are two ways to position a standard I/O stream.

1. `ftell` and `fseek`. These two functions have been around since Version 7, but they assume that a file's position can be stored in a long integer.

2. `fgetpos` and `fsetpos`. These two functions are new with ANSI C. They introduce a new abstract data type, `fpos_t`, that records a file's position. Under non-Unix systems this data type can be made as big as necessary to record a file's position.

Portable applications that need to move to non-Unix systems should use `fgetpos` and `fsetpos`.

```
#include <stdio.h>

long ftell(FILE *fp);
```

                            Returns: current file position indicator if OK, –1L on error

```
int fseek(FILE *fp, long offset, int whence);
```

                                        Returns: 0 if OK, nonzero on error

```
void rewind(FILE *fp);
```

For a binary file, a file's position indicator is measured in bytes from the beginning of the file. The value returned by `ftell` for a binary file is this byte position. To position a binary file using `fseek` we must specify a byte *offset* and how that offset is interpreted. The values for *whence* are the same as for the `lseek` function from Section 3.6;

SEEK_SET means from the beginning of the file, SEEK_CUR means from the current file position, and SEEK_END means from the end of file. ANSI C doesn't require an implementation to support the SEEK_END specification for a binary file, since some systems require a binary file to be padded at the end with zeroes to make the file size a multiple of some magic number. Under Unix, however, SEEK_END is supported for binary files.

For text files, the file's current position may not be measurable as a simple byte offset. Again, this is mainly under non-Unix systems that might store text files in a different format. To position a text file, *whence* has to be SEEK_SET and only two values for *offset* are allowed: 0 (meaning rewind the file to its beginning) or a value that was returned by ftell for that file. A stream can also be set to the beginning of the file with the rewind function.

As we mentioned, the following two functions are new with the C Standard.

```
#include <stdio.h>

int fgetpos(FILE *fp, fpos_t *pos);

int fsetpos(FILE *fp, const fpos_t *pos);
```
                                                    Both return: 0 if OK, nonzero on error

fgetpos stores the current value of the file's position indicator in the object pointed to by *pos*. This value can be used in a later call to fsetpos to reposition the stream to that location.

5.11 Formatted I/O

Formatted Output

Formatted output is handled by the three printf functions.

```
#include <stdio.h>

int printf(const char *format, ...);

int fprintf(FILE *fp, const char *format, ...);
```
                          Both return: number of characters output if OK, negative value if output error

```
int sprintf(char *buf, const char *format, ...);
```
                                                    Returns: number of characters stored in array

printf writes to the standard output, fprintf writes to the specified stream, and sprintf places the formatted characters in the array *buf*. sprintf automatically appends a null byte at the end of the array, but this null byte is not included in the return value.

4.3BSD defines sprintf as returning a char *, its first argument (the buffer pointer), instead of an integer. ANSI C requires that sprintf return an integer.

Note that it's possible for sprintf to overflow the buffer pointed to by *buf*. It's the caller's responsibility to assure the buffer is large enough.

We will not go through all the gory details of the different format conversions possible with these three functions. Refer to your local Unix manual or Appendix B of Kernighan and Ritchie [1988].

The following three variants of the printf family are similar to the previous three, but the variable argument list (. . .) is replaced with *arg*.

```
#include <stdarg.h>
#include <stdio.h>

int vprintf(const char *format, va_list arg);

int vfprintf(FILE *fp, const char *format, va_list arg);
```

Both return: number of characters output if OK, negative value if output error

```
int vsprintf(char *buf, const char *format, va_list arg);
```

Returns: number of characters stored in array

We use the vsprintf function in the error routines in Appendix B.

Refer to Section 7.3 of Kernighan and Ritchie [1988] for additional details on handling variable length argument lists with ANSI Standard C. Be aware that the variable length argument list routines provided with ANSI C (the <stdarg.h> header and its associated routines) differ from the <varargs.h> routines that were provided with SVR3 (and earlier) and 4.3BSD.

Formatted Input

Formatted input is handled by the three scanf functions.

```
#include <stdio.h>

int scanf(const char *format, ...);

int fscanf(FILE *fp, const char *format, ...);

int sscanf(const char *buf, const char *format, ...);
```

All three return: number of input items assigned,
EOF if input error or end of file before any conversion

As with the printf family, refer to your Unix manual for all the details on the various format options.

5.12   Implementation Details

As we've mentioned, under Unix the standard I/O library ends up calling the I/O routines that we described in Chapter 3. Each standard I/O stream has an associated file descriptor, and we can obtain the descriptor for a stream by calling `fileno`.

```
#include <stdio.h>

int fileno(FILE *fp);
```
Returns: the file descriptor associated with the stream

We need this function if we want to call the `dup` or `fcntl` functions, for example.

To look at the implementation of the standard I/O library on your system, the place to start is with the header `<stdio.h>`. This will show how the `FILE` object is defined, the definitions of the per-stream flags, and any standard I/O routines that are defined as macros (such as `getc`). Section 8.5 of Kernighan and Ritchie [1988] has a sample implementation that shows the flavor of many Unix implementations. Chapter 12 of Plauger [1992] provides the complete source code for an implementation of the standard I/O library. The implementation of the standard I/O library in 4.3+BSD (written by Chris Torek) is also publicly available.

Example

Program 5.3 prints the buffering for the three standard streams and for a stream that is associated with a regular file. Note that we perform I/O on each stream before printing its buffering status, since the first I/O operation usually causes the buffers to be allocated for a stream. The structure members `_flag` and `_bufsiz` and the constants `_IONBF` and `_IOLBF` are defined by the system used by the author. Be aware that other Unix systems may have different implementations of the standard I/O library.

If we run Program 5.3 twice, once with the three standard streams connected to the terminal and once with the three standard streams redirected to files, the result is

```
$ a.out                                 stdin, stdout, and stderr connected to terminal
enter any character
                                        we type a newline
one line to standard error
stream = stdin, line buffered, buffer size = 128
stream = stdout, line buffered, buffer size = 128
stream = stderr, unbuffered, buffer size = 8
stream = /etc/motd, fully buffered, buffer size = 8192
$ a.out < /etc/termcap > std.out 2> std.err
                                        run it again with all three streams redirected
$ cat std.err
one line to standard error
$ cat std.out
enter any character
stream = stdin, fully buffered, buffer size = 8192
```

```
#include     "ourhdr.h"

void     pr_stdio(const char *, FILE *);

int
main(void)
{
    FILE     *fp;

    fputs("enter any character\n", stdout);
    if (getchar() == EOF)
        err_sys("getchar error");
    fputs("one line to standard error\n", stderr);

    pr_stdio("stdin",  stdin);
    pr_stdio("stdout", stdout);
    pr_stdio("stderr", stderr);

    if ( (fp = fopen("/etc/motd", "r")) == NULL)
        err_sys("fopen error");
    if (getc(fp) == EOF)
        err_sys("getc error");
    pr_stdio("/etc/motd", fp);
    exit(0);
}

void
pr_stdio(const char *name, FILE *fp)
{
    printf("stream = %s, ", name);
                /* following is nonportable */
    if      (fp->_flag & _IONBF)    printf("unbuffered");
    else if (fp->_flag & _IOLBF)    printf("line buffered");
    else /* if neither of above */  printf("fully buffered");
    printf(", buffer size = %d\n", fp->_bufsiz);
}
```

Program 5.3 Print buffering for various standard I/O streams.

```
stream = stdout, fully buffered, buffer size = 8192
stream = stderr, unbuffered, buffer size = 8
stream = /etc/motd, fully buffered, buffer size = 8192
```

We can see that the default for this system is to have standard input and standard output line buffered when they're connected to a terminal. The line buffer is 128 bytes. Note that this doesn't restrict us to 128-byte input and output lines, that's just the size of the buffer. Writing a 512-byte line to standard output will require four `write` system calls. When we redirect these two streams to regular files they become fully buffered, with buffer sizes equal to the preferred I/O size (the `st_blksize` value from the `stat` structure) for the filesystem. We also see that the standard error is always unbuffered (as it should be) and that a regular file defaults to fully buffered.   □,

5.13 Temporary Files

The standard I/O library provides two functions to assist in creating temporary files.

```
#include <stdio.h>

char *tmpnam(char *ptr);
```

Returns: pointer to unique pathname

```
FILE *tmpfile(void);
```

Returns: file pointer if OK, NULL on error

tmpnam generates a string that is a valid pathname and that is not the same name as an existing file. It generates a different pathname each time it is called, up to TMP_MAX times. TMP_MAX is defined in <stdio.h>.

> Although TMP_MAX is defined by ANSI C, the C standard requires only that its value be at least 25. XPG3, however, requires that its value be at least 10,000. While this minimum value allows an implementation to use four digits (0000–9999), most Unix implementations use lowercase or uppercase characters.

If *ptr* is NULL, the generated pathname is stored in a static area, and a pointer to this static area is returned as the value of the function. Subsequent calls to tmpnam can overwrite this static area. (This means if we call this function more than once and we want to save the pathname, we have to save a copy of the pathname, not a copy of the pointer.) If *ptr* is not NULL, it is assumed that it points to an array of at least L_tmpnam characters. (The constant L_tmpnam is defined in <stdio.h>.) The generated pathname is stored in this array, and *ptr* is also returned as the value of the function.

tmpfile creates a temporary binary file (type wb+) that is automatically removed when it is closed or on program termination. The fact that this file is a binary file makes no difference under Unix.

Example

Program 5.4 demonstrates these two functions. If we execute Program 5.4 we get

```
$ a.out
/usr/tmp/aaaa00470
/usr/tmp/baaa00470
one line of output
```

The five-digit suffix added to each of the temporary names is the process ID. This is how the generated pathnames are known to be unique to each process that may call tmpnam.   □

The standard Unix technique often used by the tmpfile function is to create a unique pathname by calling tmpnam, then create the file, and immediately unlink it.

```
#include    "ourhdr.h"

int
main(void)
{
    char    name[L_tmpnam], line[MAXLINE];
    FILE    *fp;

    printf("%s\n", tmpnam(NULL));        /* first temp name */

    tmpnam(name);                        /* second temp name */
    printf("%s\n", name);

    if ( (fp = tmpfile()) == NULL)       /* create temp file */
        err_sys("tmpfile error");
    fputs("one line of output\n", fp);   /* write to temp file */
    rewind(fp);                          /* then read it back */
    if (fgets(line, sizeof(line), fp) == NULL)
        err_sys("fgets error");
    fputs(line, stdout);                 /* print the line we wrote */

    exit(0);
}
```

Program 5.4 Demonstrate tmpnam and tmpfile functions.

Recall from Section 4.15 that unlinking a file does not delete its contents until the file is closed. This way, when the file is closed, either explicitly or on program termination, the contents of the file are deleted.

tempnam is a variation of tmpnam that allows the caller to specify both the directory and a prefix for the generated pathname.

```
#include <stdio.h>

char *tempnam(const char *directory, const char *prefix);
```

Returns: pointer to unique pathname

There are four different choices for the directory, and the first one that is true is used:

1. If the environment variable TMPDIR is defined, it is used as the directory. (We describe environment variables in Section 7.9.)

2. If *directory* is not NULL, it is used as the directory.

3. The string P_tmpdir in <stdio.h> is used as the directory.

4. A local directory, usually /tmp is used as the directory.

If the *prefix* argument is not NULL, it should be a string of up to five characters to be used as the first characters of the filename.

This function calls the `malloc` function to allocate dynamic storage for the constructed pathname. We can `free` this storage when we're done with the pathname. (We describe the `malloc` and `free` functions in Section 7.8.)

> Although `tempnam` is not part of POSIX.1 or ANSI C, it is part of XPG3.

> The implementation that we've described corresponds to SVR4 and 4.3+BSD. The XPG3 version is identical, except the XPG3 version does not support the TMPDIR environment variable.

Example

Program 5.5 shows use of `tempnam`.

```
#include    "ourhdr.h"

int
main(int argc, char *argv[])
{
    if (argc != 3)
        err_quit("usage: a.out <directory> <prefix>");

    printf("%s\n", tempnam( argv[1][0] != ' ' ? argv[1] : NULL,
                            argv[2][0] != ' ' ? argv[2] : NULL) );
    exit(0);
}
```

Program 5.5 Demonstrate `tempnam` function.

Note that if either command-line argument (the directory or the prefix) begins with a blank, we pass a null pointer to the function. We can now show the various ways to use it:

```
$ a.out /home/stevens TEMP      specify both directory and prefix
/home/stevens/TEMPAAAa00571
$ a.out " " PFX                  use default directory: P_tmpdir
/usr/tmp/PFXAAAa00572
$ TMPDIR=/tmp a.out /usr/tmp " "    use environment variable; no prefix
/tmp/AAAa00573                   environment variable overrides directory
$ TMPDIR=/no/such/dir a.out /tmp QQQQ
/tmp/QQQQAAAa00574               invalid environment directory is ignored
$ TMPDIR=/no/such/file a.out /etc/uucp MMMMM
/usr/tmp/MMMMMAAAa00575          invalid environment; invalid directory; both ignored
```

As the four steps that we listed earlier for specifying the directory name are tried in order, this function also checks if the corresponding directory name makes sense. If the directory doesn't exist (the /no/such/dir example) or if we don't have write permission in the directory (the /etc/uucp example), that case is skipped and the next choice for the directory name is tried. From this example we can see how the process ID is used as part of the pathname, and we can also see that for this implementation the P_tmpdir directory is /usr/tmp. The technique that we used to set the environment variable, specifying TMPDIR= before the program name, is used by both the Bourne shell and the KornShell. □

5.14 Alternatives to Standard I/O

The standard I/O library is not perfect. Korn and Vo [1991] list numerous defects—some in the basic design, but most in the various, different implementations.

One inefficiency inherent in the standard I/O library is the amount of data copying that takes place. When we use the line-at-a-time functions, fgets and fputs, the data is usually copied twice: once between the kernel and the standard I/O buffer (when the corresponding read or write is issued) and again between the standard I/O buffer and our line buffer. The Fast I/O library [fio(3) in AT&T 1990a] gets around this by having the function that reads a line return a pointer to the line instead of copying the line into another buffer. Hume [1988] reports a threefold increase in the speed of a version of the grep(1) utility, just by making this change.

Korn and Vo [1991] describe another replacement for the standard I/O library: *sfio*. This package is similar in speed to the *fio* library and normally faster than the standard I/O library. *sfio* also provides some new features that aren't in the others: I/O streams are generalized to represent both files and regions of memory, processing modules can be written and stacked on an I/O stream to change the operation of a stream, and better exception handling.

Krieger, Stumm, and Unrau [1992] describe another alternative that uses mapped files—the mmap function that we describe in Section 12.9. This new package is called ASI, the Alloc Stream Interface. The programming interface resembles the Unix memory allocation functions (malloc, realloc, and free, described in Section 7.8). As with the *sfio* package, ASI attempts to minimize the amount of data copying by using pointers.

5.15 Summary

The standard I/O library is used by most Unix applications. We have looked at all the functions provided by this library, and some implementation details and efficiency considerations. Be aware of the buffering that takes place with this library, as this is the area that generates the most problems and confusion.

Exercises

5.1   Implement setbuf using setvbuf.

5.2   Type in the program that copies a file using line-at-a-time I/O (fgets and fputs) from Section 5.8, but use a MAXLINE of 4. What happens if you copy lines that exceed this length? Explain what is happening.

5.3   What does a return value of 0 from printf mean?

5.4   The following code works correctly on some machines, but not on others. What could be the problem?

```
#include      <stdio.h>

int
main(void)
{
    char    c;

    while ( (c = getchar()) != EOF )
        putchar(c);
}
```

5.5   Why does tempnam restrict the *prefix* to five characters?

5.6   How would you use the fsync function (Section 4.24) with a standard I/O stream?

5.7   In Programs 1.5 and 1.8 the prompt that is printed does not contain a newline and we don't call fflush. What causes the prompt to be output?

6

System Data Files and
Information

6.1 Introduction

There are numerous data files required for normal operation: the password file
/etc/passwd and the group file /etc/group are two files that are frequently used by
various programs. For example, the password file is used every time a user logs in to a
Unix system and every time someone executes an `ls -l` command.

Historically, these data files have been ASCII text files and were read with the standard I/O library. But for larger systems a sequential scan through the password file
becomes time consuming. We want to be able to store these data files in a format other
than ASCII text, but still provide an interface for an application program that works
with any file format. The portable interfaces to these data files are the subject of this
chapter. We also cover the system identification functions and the time and date functions.

6.2 Password File

The Unix password file, called the user database by POSIX.1, contains the fields shown
in Figure 6.1. These fields are contained in a `passwd` structure that is defined in
`<pwd.h>`.

> Note that POSIX.1 specifies only five of the seven fields in the `passwd` structure. The other
> two elements are supported by both SVR4 and 4.3+BSD.

Description	struct passwd member	POSIX.1
user name	char *pw_name	•
encrypted password	char *pw_passwd	
numerical user ID	uid_t pw_uid	•
numerical group ID	gid_t pw_gid	•
comment field	char *pw_gecos	
initial working directory	char *pw_dir	•
initial shell (user program)	char *pw_shell	•

Figure 6.1 Fields in /etc/passwd file.

Historically the password file has been stored in /etc/passwd and has been an ASCII file. Each line contains the seven fields described in Figure 6.1, separated by colons. For example, three lines from the file could be

```
root:jheVopR58x9Fx:0:1:The superuser:/:/bin/sh
nobody:*:65534:65534::/:
stevens:3hKVD8R58r9Fx:224:20:Richard Stevens:/home/stevens:/bin/ksh
```

Note the following points about these entries.

- There is usually an entry with the user name root. This entry has a user ID of 0 (the superuser).

- The encrypted password field contains a copy of the user's password that has been put through a one-way encryption algorithm. Since this algorithm is one-way, we can't guess the original password from the encrypted version. The algorithm that is currently used (see Morris and Thompson [1979]) always generates 13 printable characters from the 64-character set [a-zA-Z0-9./]. Since the entry for the user name nobody contains a single character, an encrypted password will never match this value. This user name can be used by network servers that allow us to log in to a system, but with a user ID and group ID (65534) that provide no privileges. The only files that we can access with this user ID and group ID are those that are readable or writable by the world. (This assumes that there are no files specifically owned by user ID 65534 or group ID 65534, which should be the case.) We'll discuss a recent change to the password file (shadow passwords) later in this section.

- Some fields in a password file entry can be empty. If the encrypted password field is empty, it usually means the user does not have a password. (This is not recommended.) The entry for nobody has two blank fields: the comment field and the initial shell field. An empty comment field has no effect. The default value for an empty shell field is usually /bin/sh.

- Some Unix systems that support the finger(1) command support additional information in the comment field. Each of these fields are separated by a comma: the user's name, office location, office phone number, and home phone number. Additionally, an ampersand in the comment field is replaced with the login name (capitalized) by some utilities. For example, we could have

```
stevens:3hKVD8R58r9Fx:224:20:Richard &, B232, 555-1111, 555-2222:/home/stevens:/bin/ksh
```

Even if your system doesn't support the finger command, these fields can still go into the comment field, since that field is just a comment and not interpreted by system utilities.

POSIX.1 defines only two functions to fetch entries from the password file. These two functions allow us to look up an entry given a user's login name or numerical user ID.

```
#include <sys/types.h>
#include <pwd.h>

struct passwd *getpwuid(uid_t uid);

struct passwd *getpwnam(const char *name);
```
Both return: pointer if OK, NULL on error

getpwuid is used by the ls(1) program, to map the numerical user ID contained in an i-node into a user's login name. getpwnam is used by the login(1) program, when we enter our login name.

Both functions return a pointer to a passwd structure that the functions fill in. This structure is usually a static variable within the function, so its contents are overwritten each time we call either of these functions.

These two POSIX.1 functions are fine if we want to look up either a login name or a user ID, but there are programs that need to go through the entire password file. The following three functions can be used for this.

```
#include <sys/types.h>
#include <pwd.h>

struct passwd *getpwent(void);
```
Returns: pointer if OK, NULL on error or end of file
```
void setpwent(void);

void endpwent(void);
```

While not part of POSIX.1, these three functions are supported by SVR4 and 4.3+BSD.

We call getpwent to return the next entry in the password file. As with the two POSIX.1 functions, getpwent returns a pointer to a structure that it has filled in. This structure is normally overwritten each time we call this function. If this is the first call to this function, it opens whatever files it uses. There is no order implied when we use this function—the entries can be in any order. (This is because some systems use a hashed version of the file·/etc/passwd.)

The function setpwent rewinds whatever files it uses, and endpwent closes these files. When using getpwent we must always be sure to close these files by calling endpwent when we're through. getpwent is smart enough to know when it has to open its files (the first time we call it) but it never knows when we're through.

Example

Program 6.1 shows an implementation of the function getpwnam.

```
#include <sys/types.h>
#include <pwd.h>
#include <stddef.h>
#include <string.h>

struct passwd *
getpwnam(const char *name)
{
    struct passwd  *ptr;

    setpwent();
    while ( (ptr = getpwent()) != NULL) {
        if (strcmp(name, ptr->pw_name) == 0)
            break;          /* found a match */
    }
    endpwent();
    return(ptr);    /* ptr is NULL if no match found */
}
```

Program 6.1 The getpwnam function.

The call to setpwent at the beginning is self defense—we assure that the files are rewound, in case the caller has already opened them by calling getpwent. The call to endpwent when we're done is because neither getpwnam nor getpwuid should leave any of the files open.   □

6.3   Shadow Passwords

We mentioned in the previous section that the encryption algorithm normally used for Unix passwords is a one-way algorithm. Given an encrypted password, we can't apply an algorithm that inverts it and returns the plaintext password. (The plaintext password is what we enter at the Password: prompt.) But we could guess a password, run it through the one-way algorithm, and compare the result with the encrypted password.

If user passwords were randomly chosen, this brute force approach wouldn't be too useful. Users, however, tend to choose nonrandom passwords (spouse's name, street names, pet names, etc.). A frequently repeated experiment is for someone to obtain a copy of the password file and try guessing the passwords. (Chapter 2 of Garfinkel and Spafford [1991] contains additional details and history on Unix passwords and the password encryption scheme.)

To make it harder to obtain the raw materials (the encrypted passwords), some systems store the encrypted password in another file, often called the *shadow password file*. Minimally this file has to contain the user name and the encrypted password. Other information relating to the password is also stored here. For example, systems with shadow passwords often require the user to choose a new password at certain intervals. This is called password aging, and the time between having to choose new passwords is often stored in the shadow password file also.

> In SVR4 the shadow password file is /etc/shadow. In 4.3+BSD the encrypted passwords are stored in /etc/master.passwd.

The shadow password file should not be readable by the world. Only a few programs need to access encrypted passwords, login(1) and passwd(1), for example, and these programs are often set-user-ID root. With shadow passwords the regular password file, /etc/passwd, can be left readable by the world.

6.4   Group File

The Unix group file, called the group database by POSIX.1, contains the fields shown in Figure 6.2. These fields are contained in a group structure that is defined in <grp.h>.

Description	struct group member	POSIX.1
group name	char *gr_name	•
encrypted password	char *gr_passwd	
numerical group ID	int gr_gid	•
array of pointers to individual user names	char **gr_mem	•

Figure 6.2 Fields in /etc/group file.

POSIX.1 defines only three of the four fields. The other field, gr_passwd, is supported by both SVR4 and 4.3+BSD.

The field gr_mem is an array of pointers to the user names that belong to this group. This array is terminated by a null pointer.

We can look up either a group name or a numerical group ID with the following two functions, which are defined by POSIX.1.

```
#include <sys/types.h>
#include <grp.h>

struct group *getgrid(gid_t gid);

struct group *getgrnam(const char *name);
```

                                                    Both return: pointer if OK, NULL on error

As with the password file functions, both of these functions normally return pointers to a static variable, which is overwritten on each call.

If we want to search the entire group file we need some additional functions. The following three functions are like their counterparts for the password file.

```
#include <sys/types.h>
#include <grp.h>

struct group *getgrent(void);
```

                                            Returns: pointer if OK, NULL on error or end of file

```
void setgrent(void);

void endgrent(void);
```

These three functions are provided by SVR4 and 4.3+BSD. They are not part of POSIX.1.

setgrent opens the group file (if it's not already open) and rewinds it. getgrent reads the next entry from the group file, opening the file first, if it's not already open. endgrent closes the group file.

6.5 Supplementary Group IDs

The use of groups in Unix has changed over time. With Version 7 each user belonged to a single group at any point in time. When we logged in we were assigned the real group ID corresponding to the numerical group ID in our password file entry. We could change this at any point by executing newgrp(1). If the newgrp command succeeded (refer to the manual page for the permission rules), our real group ID was changed to the new group's ID, and this was used for all subsequent file access permission checks. We could always go back to our original group by executing newgrp without any arguments.

This form of group membership persisted until it was changed in 4.2BSD (circa 1983). With 4.2BSD the concept of supplementary group IDs was introduced. Not only did we belong to the group corresponding to the group ID in our password file entry, we could also belong to up to 16 additional groups. The file access permission checks were modified so that not only was the effective group ID compared to the file's group ID, but all the supplementary group IDs were also compared to the file's group ID.

> Supplementary group IDs are an optional feature of POSIX.1. The constant NGROUPS_MAX (Figure 2.7) specifies the number of supplementary group IDs. A common value is 16. This constant is 0 if supplementary group IDs aren't supported.
>
> Both SVR4 and 4.3+BSD support supplementary group IDs.
>
> FIPS 151-1 requires the support of supplementary group IDs and requires that NGROUPS_MAX be at least 8.

The advantage in using supplementary group IDs is that we no longer have to change groups explicitly. It is not uncommon to belong to multiple groups (i.e., participate in multiple projects) at the same time.

Three functions are provided to fetch and set the supplementary group IDs.

```
#include <sys/types.h>
#include <unistd.h>

int getgroups(int gidsetsize, gid_t grouplist[]);
```
> Returns: number of supplementary group IDs if OK, −1 on error

```
int setgroups(int ngroups, const gid_t grouplist[]);

int initgroups(const char *username, gid_t basegid);
```
> Both return: 0 if OK, −1 on error

> Of these three functions, only getgroups is specified by POSIX.1. Since setgroups and initgroups are privileged operations, they are not part of POSIX.1. SVR4 and 4.3+BSD, however, support all three functions.

getgroups fills in the array *grouplist* with the supplementary group IDs. Up to *gidsetsize* elements are stored in the array. The number of supplementary group IDs stored in the array is returned by the function. If the system constant NGROUPS_MAX is 0, the function returns 0, not an error.

As a special case, if *gidsetsize* is 0, the function returns only the number of supplementary group IDs. The array *grouplist* is not modified. (This allows the caller to determine the size of the *grouplist* array to allocate.)

setgroups can be called by the superuser to set the supplementary group ID list for the calling process. *grouplist* contains the array of group IDs, and *ngroups* specifies the number of elements in the array.

The only use of setgroups is usually from the initgroups function, which reads the entire group file (with the functions getgrent, setgrent, and endgrent, which we described earlier) and determines the group membership for *username*. It then calls setgroups to initialize the supplementary group ID list for the user. One must be superuser to call initgroups since it calls setgroups. In addition to finding all the groups that *username* is a member of in the group file, initgroups also includes, *basegid* in the supplementary group ID list. *basegid* is the group ID from the password file for *username*.

initgroups is called by only a few programs—the login(1) program, for example, calls it when we log in.

6.6   Other Data Files

We've discussed only two of the system's data files so far—the password file and the group file. Numerous other files are used by Unix systems in normal day-to-day operation. For example, the BSD networking software has one data file for the services provided by the various network servers (/etc/services), one for the protocols (/etc/protocols), and one for the networks (/etc/networks). Fortunately the interfaces to these various files are like the ones we've already described for the password and group files.

The general principle is that every data file has at least three functions:

1. A get function that reads the next record, opening the file if necessary. These functions normally return a pointer to a structure. A null pointer is returned when the end of the data file is reached. Most of the get functions return a pointer to a static structure, so we always have to copy it if we want to save it.

2. A set function that opens the file (if not already open) and rewinds the file. This function is used when we know we want to start again at the beginning of the file.

3. An end entry that closes the data file. As we mentioned earlier, we always have to call this when we're done, to close all the files.

Additionally, if the data file supports some form of keyed lookup, routines are provided to search for a record with a specific key. For example, two keyed lookup routines are provided for the password file: getpwnam looks for a record with a specific user name, and getpwuid looks for a record with a specific user ID.

Figure 6.3 shows some of these routines, which are common to both SVR4 and 4.3+BSD. In this figure we show the functions for the password file and group file, which we discussed earlier in this chapter, and some of the networking functions. There are get, set, and end functions for all the data files in this figure.

> Under SVR4 the last four data files in Figure 6.3 are symbolic links to files of the same name in the directory /etc/inet.

> Both SVR4 and 4.3+BSD have additional functions that are like these, but the additional functions tend to deal with system administration files and are specific to each implementation.

Description	Data file	Header	Structure	Additional keyed lookup functions
passwords	/etc/passwd	<pwd.h>	passwd	getpwnam, getpwuid
groups	/etc/group	<grp.h>	group	getgrnam, getgrgid
hosts	/etc/hosts	<netdb.h>	hostent	gethostbyname, gethostbyaddr
networks	/etc/networks	<netdb.h>	netent	getnetbyname, getnetbyaddr
protocols	/etc/protocols	<netdb.h>	protoent	getprotobyname, getprotobynumber
services	/etc/services	<netdb.h>	servent	getservbyname, getservbyport

Figure 6.3 Similar routines for accessing system data files.

6.7 Login Accounting

Two data files that have been provided with most Unix systems are the utmp file, which keeps track of all the users currently logged in, and the wtmp file, which keeps track of all logins and logouts.

With Version 7, one type of record was written to both files, a binary record consisting of the following structure:

```
struct utmp {
  char  ut_line[8]; /* tty line: "ttyh0", "ttyd0", "ttyp0", ... */
  char  ut_name[8]; /* login name */
  long  ut_time;    /* seconds since Epoch */
};
```

On login, one of these structures was filled in and written to the utmp file by the login program, and the same structure was appended to the wtmp file. On logout, the entry in the utmp file was erased (filled with 0 bytes) by the init process, and a new entry was appended to the wtmp file. This logout entry in the wtmp file had the ut_name field zeroed out. Special entries were appended to the wtmp file to indicate when the system was rebooted and right before and after the system's time and date was changed. The who(1) program read the utmp file and printed its contents in a readable form. Later versions of Unix provided the last(1) command, which read through the wtmp file and printed selected entries.

Most versions of Unix still provide the utmp and wtmp files, but as expected, the amount of the information in these files has grown. The 20-byte structure that was written by Version 7 grew to 36 bytes with SVR2, and the extended utmp structure with SVR4 takes over 350 bytes!

The detailed format of these records in SVR4 is given in the utmp(4) and utmpx(4) manual pages. With SVR4 both files are in the /var/adm directory. SVR4 provides numerous functions described in getut(3) and getutx(3) to read and write these two files.

The 4.3+BSD utmp(5) manual page gives the format of its version of these login records. The pathnames of these two files are /var/run/utmp and /var/log/wtmp.

6.8   System Identification

POSIX.1 defines the `uname` function to return information on the current host and operating system.

```
#include <sys/utsname.h>

int uname(struct utsname *name);
```

Returns: nonnegative value if OK, –1 on error

We pass the address of a `utsname` structure, and the function fills it in. POSIX.1 defines only the minimum fields in the structure (which are all character arrays), and it's up to each implementation to set the size of each array. Some implementations provide additional fields in the structure. Historically, System V has allocated 8 bytes for each element, with room for a null byte at the end.

```
struct utsname {
   char   sysname[9];      /* name of the operating system */
   char   nodename[9];     /* name of this node */
   char   release[9];      /* current release of operating system */
   char   version[9];      /* current version of this release */
   char   machine[9];      /* name of hardware type */
};
```

The information in the `utsname` structure can usually be printed with the uname(1) command.

> POSIX.1 warns that the nodename element may not be adequate to reference the host on a communications network. This function is from System V, and in older days the nodename element was adequate for referencing the host on a UUCP network.
>
> Realize also that the information in this structure does not give any information on the POSIX.1 level. This should be obtained using _POSIX_VERSION as described in Section 2.5.2.
>
> Finally, this function gives us a way only to fetch the information in the structure—there is nothing specified by POSIX.1 about initializing this information. Most versions of System V have this information compiled into the kernel when the kernel is built.

Berkeley-derived systems provide the `gethostname` function to return just the name of the host. This name is usually the name of the host on a TCP/IP network.

```
#include <unistd.h>

int gethostname(char *name, int namelen);
```

Returns: 0 if OK, –1 on error

The string returned through *name* is null terminated, unless insufficient room is provided. The constant MAXHOSTNAMELEN in `<sys/param.h>` specifies the maximum length of this name (normally 64 bytes). If the host is connected to a TCP/IP network, the host name is normally the fully qualified domain name of the host.

There is also a hostname(1) command that can fetch or set the host name. (The host name is set by the superuser using a similar function, sethostname.) The host name is normally set at bootstrap time from one of the start-up files invoked by /etc/rc.

> Although this function is Berkeley-specific, SVR4 provides the gethostname and sethostname functions, and the hostname command as part of the BSD compatibility package. SVR4 also extends MAXHOSTNAMELEN to 256 bytes.

6.9   Time and Date Routines

The basic time service provided by the Unix kernel is to count the number of seconds that have passed since the Epoch: 00:00:00 January 1, 1970, UTC. In Section 1.10 we said that these seconds are represented in a time_t data type, and we call them *calendar times*. These calendar times represent both the time and date. Unix has always differed from other operating systems in (a) keeping time in UTC instead of the local time, (b) automatically handling conversions such as daylight saving time, and (c) keeping the time and date as a single quantity.

The time function returns the current time and date.

```
#include <time.h>

time_t time(time_t *calptr);
```
                                                    Returns: value of time if OK, −1 on error

The time value is always returned as the value of the function. If the argument is non-null, the time value is also stored at the location pointed to by *calptr*.

> In many Berkeley-derived systems time(3) is just a function that invokes the gettimeofday(2) system call.

> We haven't said how the kernel's notion of the current time is initialized. Under SVR4 the stime(2) function is called, while Berkeley-derived systems use settimeofday(2).

> The BSD gettimeofday and settimeofday functions provide greater resolution (up to a microsecond) than the time and stime functions. This is important for some applications.

Once we have this large integer value that counts the number of seconds since the Epoch, we normally call one of the other time functions to convert it to a human-readable time and date. Figure 6.4 shows the relationships between the various time functions. (The four functions in this figure that are shown with dashed lines, localtime, mktime, ctime, and strftime, are all affected by the TZ environment variable, which we describe later in this section.)

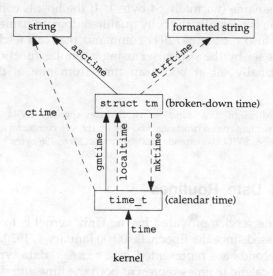

Figure 6.4 Relationship of the various time functions.

The two functions `localtime` and `gmtime` convert a calendar time into what's called a broken-down time, a `tm` structure.

```
struct tm {  /* a broken-down time */
  int  tm_sec;   /* seconds after the minute: [0, 61] */
  int  tm_min;   /* minutes after the hour: [0, 59] */
  int  tm_hour;  /* hours after midnight: [0, 23] */
  int  tm_mday;  /* day of the month: [1, 31] */
  int  tm_mon;   /* month of the year: [0, 11] */
  int  tm_year;  /* years since 1900 */
  int  tm_wday;  /* days since Sunday: [0, 6] */
  int  tm_yday;  /* days since January 1: [0, 365] */
  int  tm_isdst; /* daylight saving time flag: <0, 0, >0 */
};
```

The reason that the seconds can be greater than 59 is to allow for leap seconds. Notice that all the fields except the day of the month are 0-based. The daylight saving time flag is positive if daylight saving time is in effect, 0 if it's not in effect, and negative if the information isn't available.

```
#include <time.h>

struct tm *gmtime(const time_t *calptr);

struct tm *localtime(const time_t *calptr);
```
                                          Both return: pointer to broken-down time

The difference between localtime and gmtime is that the first converts the calendar time to the local time (taking into account the local time zone and daylight saving time flag), while the latter converts the calendar time into a broken-down time expressed as UTC.

The function mktime takes a broken-down time (expressed as a local time) and converts it into a time_t value.

```
#include <time.h>

time_t mktime(struct tm *tmptr);
```
                                                    Returns: calendar time if OK, –1 on error

The asctime and ctime functions produce the familiar 26-byte string that is similar to the default output of the date(1) command:

```
Tue Jan 14 17:49:03 1992\n\0
```

```
#include <time.h>

char *asctime(const struct tm *tmptr);

char *ctime(const time_t *calptr);
```
                                                    Both return: pointer to null terminated string

The argument to asctime is a pointer to a broken-down string, while the argument to ctime is a pointer to a calendar time.

The final time function is the most complicated. strftime is a printf-like function for time values.

```
#include <time.h>

size_t strftime(char *buf, size_t maxsize, const char *format,
                const struct tm *tmptr);
```
                                        Returns: number of characters stored in array if room, else 0

The final argument is the time value to format, specified by a pointer to a broken-down time value. The formatted result is stored in the array *buf* whose size is *maxsize* characters. If the size of the result, including the terminating null, fits in the buffer, the function returns the number of characters stored in *buf* (excluding the terminating null). Otherwise the function returns 0.

The *format* argument controls the formatting of the time value. Like the printf functions, conversion specifiers are given as a percent followed by a special character. All other characters in the *format* string are copied to the output. Two percents in a row generate a single percent in the output. Unlike the printf functions, each conversion specified generates a fixed size output string—there are no field widths in the *format* string. Figure 6.5 describes the 21 different ANSI C conversion specifiers.

Format	Description	Example
%a	abbreviated weekday name	Tue
%A	full weekday name	Tuesday
%b	abbreviated month name	Jan
%B	full month name	January
%c	date and time	Tue Jan 14 19:40:30 1992
%d	day of the month: [01, 31]	14
%H	hour of the 24-hour day: [00, 23]	19
%I	hour of the 24-hour day: [01, 12]	07
%j	day of the year: [001, 366]	014
%m	month: [01, 12]	01
%M	minute: [00, 59]	40
%p	AM/PM	PM
%S	second: [00, 61]	30
%U	Sunday week number: [00, 53]	02
%w	weekday: [0=Sunday, 6]	2
%W	Monday week number: [00, 53]	02
%x	date	01/14/92
%X	time	19:40:30
%y	year without century: [00, 99]	92
%Y	year with century	1992
%Z	time zone name	MST

Figure 6.5 Conversion specifiers for `strftime`.

The third column of this figure is from the output of `strftime` under SVR4 corresponding to the time and date

```
Tue Jan 14 19:40:30 MST 1992
```

The only two specifiers that are not self-evident are %U and %W. The first is the week number of the year where the week containing the first Sunday is week 1. %W is the week number of the year where the week containing the first Monday is week 1.

Both SVR4 and 4.3+BSD support additional, nonstandard extensions to the *format* string for `strftime`.

We mentioned that the four functions in Figure 6.4 with dashed lines were affected by the TZ environment variable: `localtime`, `mktime`, `ctime`, and `strftime`. If defined, the value of this environment variable is used by these functions instead of the default time zone. If the variable is defined to be a null string (e.g., TZ=) then UTC is normally used. The value of this environment variable is often something like TZ=EST5EDT, but POSIX.1 allows a much more detailed specification. Refer to Section 8.1.1 of the POSIX.1 standard [IEEE 1990], the SVR4 environ(5) manual page [AT&T 1990e], or the 4.3+BSD ctime(3) manual page for all the details on the TZ variable.

All the time and date functions described in this section are defined by the ANSI C standard. POSIX.1, however, added the TZ environment variable.

Five of the seven functions in Figure 6.4 date back to Version 7 (or earlier): time, localtime, gmtime, asctime, and ctime. Many of the recent additions to the Unix time keeping have dealt with non-U.S. time zones and the changing rules for daylight saving time.

6.10 Summary

The password file and group file are used on all Unix systems. We've looked at the various functions that read these files. We've also talked about shadow passwords, which can help system security. Supplementary group IDs are becoming common and provide a way to participate in multiple groups at the same time. We also looked at how similar functions are provided by most systems to access other system-related data files. We finished the chapter with a look at the time and date functions provided by ANSI C and POSIX.1.

Exercises

6.1   If the system uses a shadow file and we need to obtain the encrypted password, how do we do it?

6.2   If you have superuser access and your system uses shadow passwords, implement the previous exercise.

6.3   Write a program that calls uname and prints all the fields in the utsname structure. Compare the output to the output from the uname(1) command.

6.4   Write a program to obtain the current time and print it using strftime so that it looks like the default output from date(1). Set the TZ environment variable to different values and see what happens.

7

The Environment of a Unix Process

7.1 Introduction

Before looking at the process control primitives in the next chapter, we need to examine the environment of a single process. We'll see how the main function is called when the program is executed, how command-line arguments are passed to the new program, what the typical memory layout looks like, how to allocate additional memory, how the process can use environment variables, and different ways for the process to terminate. Additionally we'll look at the longjmp and setjmp functions and their interaction with the stack. We finish the chapter by examining the resource limits of a process.

7.2 main Function

A C program starts execution with a function called main. The prototype for the main function is

```
int main(int argc, char *argv[]);
```

argc is the number of command-line arguments and *argv* is an array of pointers to the arguments. We describe these in Section 7.4.

When a C program is started by the kernel (by one of the exec functions, which we describe in Section 8.9), a special start-up routine is called before the main function is called. The executable program file specifies this start-up routine as the starting address for the program—this is set up by the link editor when it is invoked by the C compiler, usually cc. This start-up routine takes values from the kernel (the command-line arguments and the environment) and sets things up so that the main function is called as shown earlier.

7.3   Process Termination

There are five ways for a process to terminate.

1. Normal termination:
   (a) return from `main`
   (b) calling `exit`
   (c) calling `_exit`
2. Abnormal termination:
   (a) calling `abort` (Chapter 10)
   (b) terminated by a signal (Chapter 10)

The start-up routine that we mentioned in the previous section is also written so that if the `main` function returns, the `exit` function is called. If the start-up routine were coded in C (it is often coded in assembler) the call to `main` could look like

```
exit( main(argc, argv) );
```

exit and _exit Functions

Two functions terminate a program normally: `_exit`, which returns to the kernel immediately, and `exit`, which performs certain cleanup processing and then returns to the kernel.

```
#include <stdlib.h>

void exit(int status);

#include <unistd.h>

void _exit(int status);
```

We'll discuss the effect of these two functions on other processes, such as the children and the parent of the terminating process, in Section 8.5.

> The reason for the different headers is that `exit` is specified by ANSI C, while `_exit` is specified by POSIX.1.

Historically the `exit` function has always performed a clean shutdown of the standard I/O library: the `fclose` function is called for all open streams. Recall from Section 5.5 that this causes all buffered output data to be flushed (written to the file).

Both the `exit` and `_exit` functions expect a single integer argument, which we call the *exit status*. Most Unix shells provide a way to examine the exit status of a process. If (a) either of these functions is called without an exit status, (b) `main` does a return without a return value, or (c) `main` "falls off the end" (an implicit return), the exit status of the process is undefined. This means that the classic example

```
#include     <stdio.h>
main()
{
    printf("hello, world\n");
}
```

is incomplete, since the `main` function falls off the end, returning to the C start-up routine, but without returning a value (the exit status). Adding either

```
return(0);
```

or

```
exit(0);
```

provides an exit status of 0 to the process that executed this program (often a shell). Also, the declaration of `main` should really be

```
int main(void)
```

In the next chapter we'll see how any process can cause a program to be executed, wait for the process to complete, then fetch its exit status.

> The declaration of `main` as returning an integer and the use of `exit` (instead of `return`) produces needless warnings from some compilers and the Unix `lint(1)` program. The problem is that these compilers don't know that an `exit` from `main` is the same as a `return`. The warning message is something like "control reaches end of nonvoid function." One way around these warnings (which become annoying after a while) is to use `return` instead of `exit` from `main`. But doing this prevents us from using the Unix `grep` utility to locate all calls to `exit` from a program. Another solution is to declare `main` as returning `void`, instead of `int`, and continue calling `exit`. This gets rid of the compiler warnings but doesn't look right (especially in a programming text). In this text we show `main` as returning an integer, since that is the definition specified by both ANSI C and POSIX.1. We'll just put up with the extraneous compiler warnings.

`atexit` Function

With ANSI C a process can register up to 32 functions that are automatically called by `exit`. These are called *exit handlers* and are registered by calling the `atexit` function.

```
#include <stdlib.h>

int atexit(void (*func)(void));
```
                                                    Returns: 0 if OK, nonzero on error

This declaration says that we pass the address of a function as the argument to `atexit`. When this function is called it is not passed any arguments and it is not expected to return a value. The `exit` function calls these functions in reverse order of their registration. Each function is called as many times as it was registered.

These exit handlers are new with ANSI C. They are provided by both SVR4 and 4.3+BSD. Earlier releases of System V and 4.3BSD did not provide these exit handlers.

With ANSI C and POSIX.1, exit first calls the exit handlers and then fcloses all open streams. Figure 7.1 summarizes how a C program is started and the various ways it can terminate.

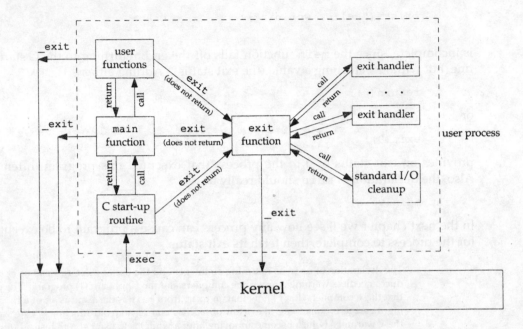

Figure 7.1 How a C program is started and how it terminates.

Note that the only way a program is executed by the kernel is when one of the exec functions is called. The only way a process voluntarily terminates is when _exit is called, either explicitly or implicitly (by calling exit). A process can also be involuntarily terminated by a signal (not shown in Figure 7.1).

Example

Program 7.1 demonstrates the use of the atexit function. Executing Program 7.1 yields

```
$ a.out
main is done
first exit handler
first exit handler
second exit handler
```

Note that we don't call exit, instead we return from main.

```
#include     "ourhdr.h"

static void my_exit1(void), my_exit2(void);

int
main(void)
{
    if (atexit(my_exit2) != 0)
        err_sys("can't register my_exit2");

    if (atexit(my_exit1) != 0)
        err_sys("can't register my_exit1");
    if (atexit(my_exit1) != 0)
        err_sys("can't register my_exit1");

    printf("main is done\n");
    return(0);
}

static void
my_exit1(void)
{
    printf("first exit handler\n");
}

static void
my_exit2(void)
{
    printf("second exit handler\n");
}
```

Program 7.1 Example of exit handlers.

7.4   Command-Line Arguments

When a program is executed, the process that does the exec can pass command-line arguments to the new program. This is part of the normal operation of the Unix shells. We have already seen this in many of the examples from earlier chapters.

Example

Program 7.2 echoes all its command-line arguments to standard output. (The normal Unix echo(1) program doesn't echo the zeroth argument.) If we compile this program and name the executable echoarg, we have

```
$ ./echoarg arg1 TEST foo
argv[0]: ./echoarg
argv[1]: arg1
argv[2]: TEST
argv[3]: foo
```

```
#include      "ourhdr.h"

int
main(int argc, char *argv[])
{
    int     i;

    for (i = 0; i < argc; i++)           /* echo all command-line args */
        printf("argv[%d]: %s\n", i, argv[i]);
    exit(0);
}
```

Program 7.2 Echo all command-line arguments to standard output.

We are guaranteed by both ANSI C and POSIX.1 that `argv[argc]` is a null pointer. This lets us alternatively code the argument processing loop as

```
for (i = 0; argv[i] != NULL; i++)
```

                                                                                        □

7.5 Environment List

Each program is also passed an environment list. Like the argument list, the environment list is an array of character pointers, with each pointer containing the address of a null-terminated C string. The address of the array of pointers is contained in the global variable `environ`.

```
extern char **environ;
```

For example, if the environment consisted of five strings it could look like

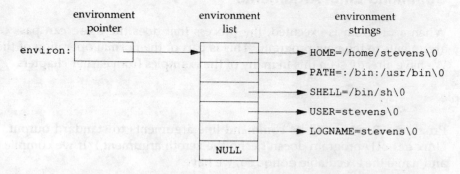

Figure 7.2 Environment consisting of five C character strings.

Here we explicitly show the null bytes at the end of each string. We'll call `environ` the environment pointer, the array of pointers the environment list, and the strings they point to the environment strings.

By convention the environment consists of

name=value

strings, as shown in Figure 7.2. Most predefined names are entirely uppercase, but this is only a convention.

Historically, most Unix systems have provided a third argument to the `main` function that is the address of the environment list:

```
int main(int argc, char *argv[], char *envp[]);
```

Since ANSI C specifies that the `main` function be written with two arguments, and since this third argument provides no benefit over the global variable `environ`, POSIX.1 specifies that `environ` should be used instead of the (possible) third argument. Access to specific environment variables is normally through the `getenv` and `putenv` functions (described in Section 7.9), instead of through the `environ` variable. But to go through the entire environment, the `environ` pointer must be used.

7.6   Memory Layout of a C Program

Historically a C program has been composed of the following pieces:

- Text segment. This is the machine instructions that are executed by the CPU. Usually the text segment is sharable so that only a single copy needs to be in memory for frequently executed programs (text editors, the C compiler, the shells, etc.). Also, the text segment is often read-only, to prevent a program from accidentally modifying its instructions.

- Initialized data segment. This is usually just called the data segment and it contains variables that are specifically initialized in the program. For example, the C declaration

  ```
  int   maxcount = 99;
  ```

  appearing outside any function causes this variable to be stored in the initialized data segment with its initial value.

- Uninitialized data segment. This segment is often called the "bss" segment, named after an ancient assembler operator that stood for "block started by symbol." Data in this segment is initialized by the kernel to arithmetic 0 or null pointers before the program starts executing. The C declaration

  ```
  long   sum[1000];
  ```

  appearing outside any function causes this variable to be stored in the uninitialized data segment.

- Stack. This is where automatic variables are stored, along with information that is saved each time a function is called. Each time a function is called, the address of where to return to, and certain information about the caller's environment (such as some of the machine registers) is saved on the stack. The newly called function then allocates room on the stack for its automatic and temporary variables. By utilizing a stack in this fashion, C functions can be recursive.

- Heap. Dynamic memory allocation usually takes place on the heap. Historically the heap has been located between the top of the uninitialized data and the bottom of the stack.

Figure 7.3 shows the typical arrangement of these segments. This is a logical picture of how a program looks—there is no requirement that a given implementation arrange its memory in this fashion. Nevertheless, this gives us a typical arrangement to describe.

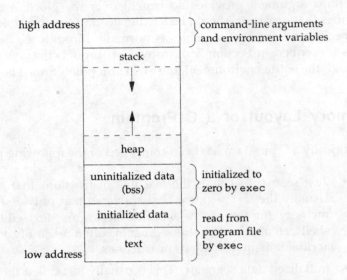

Figure 7.3 Typical memory arrangement.

With 4.3+BSD on a VAX, the text segment starts at location 0 and the top of the stack starts just below 0x7fffffff. On the VAX the unused virtual address space between the top of the heap and the bottom of the stack is large.

Note from Figure 7.3 that the contents of the uninitialized data segment are not stored in the program file on disk. This is because the kernel sets it to 0 before the program starts running. The only portions of the program that need to be saved in the program file are the text segment and the initialized data.

The size(1) command reports the sizes in bytes of the text, data, and bss segments. For example

```
$ size /bin/cc /bin/sh
text    data   bss    dec      hex
81920   16384  664    98968    18298    /bin/cc
90112   16384  0      106496   1a000    ./bin/sh
```

The fourth and fifth columns are the total of the sizes in decimal and hexadecimal.

7.7   Shared Libraries

Many Unix systems today support shared libraries. Arnold [1986] describes an early implementation under System V and Gingell et al. [1987] describe a different implementation under SunOS. Shared libraries remove the common library routines from the executable file, instead maintaining a single copy of the library routine somewhere in memory that all processes reference. This reduces the size of each executable file but may add some run-time overhead, either when the program is first execed, or the first time each shared library function is called. Another advantage of shared libraries is that library functions can be replaced with new versions without having to re-link edit every program that uses the library. (This assumes that the number and type of arguments haven't changed.)

Different systems provide different ways for a program to say that it wants to use or not use the shared libraries. Options for the cc(1) and ld(1) commands are typical. As an example of the size differences, the following executable file (the classic hello.c program) was first created without shared libraries.

```
$ ls -l a.out
-rwxrwxr-x  1 stevens        104859 Aug  2 14:25 a.out
$ size a.out
text    data    bss     dec     hex
49152   49152   0       98304   18000
```

If we compile this program to use shared libraries, the text and data sizes of the executable file are greatly decreased.

```
$ ls -l a.out
-rwxrwxr-x  1 stevens         24576 Aug  2 14:26 a.out
$ size a.out
text    data    bss     dec     hex
8192    8192    0       16384   4000
```

7.8   Memory Allocation

There are three functions specified by ANSI C for memory allocation.

1. malloc. Allocates a specified number of bytes of memory. The initial value of the memory is indeterminate.

2. calloc. Allocates space for a specified number of objects of a specified size. The space is initialized to all 0 bits.

3. realloc. Changes the size of a previously allocated area (increases or decreases). When the size increases, it may involve moving the previously allocated area somewhere else, to provide the additional room at the end. Also, when the size increases, the initial value of the space between the old contents and the end of the new area is indeterminate.

```
#include <stdlib.h>

void *malloc(size_t size);

void *calloc(size_t nobj, size_t size);

void *realloc(void *ptr, size_t newsize);

                          All three return: nonnull pointer if OK, NULL on error

void free(void *ptr);
```

The pointer returned by the three allocation functions is guaranteed to be suitably aligned so that it can be used for any data object. For example, if the most restrictive alignment requirement on a particular system requires that doubles must start at memory locations that are multiples of 8, then all pointers returned by these three functions would be so aligned.

Recall our discussion of the generic void * pointer and function prototypes in Section 1.6. Since the three alloc functions return generic pointers, if we #include <stdlib.h> (to obtain the function prototypes), we do not explicitly have to cast the pointer returned by these functions when we assign it to a pointer of a different type.

The function free causes the space pointed to by *ptr* to be deallocated. This freed space is usually put into a pool of available memory and can be allocated in a later call to one of the three alloc functions.

realloc lets us increase or decrease the size of a previously allocated area. (The most common usage is to increase an area.) For example, if we allocate room for 512 elements in an array that we fill in at run time, and find we need room for more than 512 elements, we can call realloc. If there is room beyond the end of the existing region for the requested space, then realloc doesn't have to move anything, it just allocates the additional area at the end and returns the same pointer that we passed it. But if there isn't room at the end of the existing region, realloc allocates another area that is large enough, copies the existing 512-element array to the new area, frees the old area, and returns the pointer to the new area. Since the area may move, we shouldn't have any pointers into this area. Exercise 4.18 shows the use of realloc with getcwd to handle any length pathname. Program 15.27 shows an example that uses realloc to avoid arrays with fixed, compile-time sizes.

Notice that the final argument to realloc is the *newsize* of the region, not the difference between the old and new sizes. As a special case, if *ptr* is a null pointer, realloc behaves like malloc and allocates a region of the specified *newsize*.

This feature is new with ANSI C. Older versions of realloc can fail miserably if passed a null pointer.

Older versions of these routines allowed us to realloc a block that we had freed since the last call to malloc, realloc, or calloc. This trick dates back to Version 7 and exploited the search strategy of malloc to perform storage compaction. 4.3+BSD still supports this feature, but SVR4 doesn't. This feature is deprecated and should not be used.

The allocation routines are usually implemented with the sbrk(2) system call. This system call expands (or contracts) the heap of the process. (Refer to Figure 7.3.) A sample implementation of malloc and free is given in Section 8.7 of Kernighan and Ritchie [1988].

Although sbrk can expand or contract the memory of a process, most versions of malloc and free never decrease their memory size. The space that we free is available for a later allocation, but the freed space is not returned to the kernel—it is kept in the malloc pool.

It is important to realize that most implementations allocate a little more space than is requested and use the additional space for record keeping—the size of the allocated block, a pointer to the next allocated block, and the like. This means that writing past the end of an allocated area could overwrite this record keeping information in a later block. These types of errors are often catastrophic, but hard to find, because the error may not show up until much later. Also, it is possible to overwrite this record keeping in the current block by moving the pointer to the block backward.

Other possible errors that can be fatal are freeing a block that was already freed and calling free with a pointer that was not obtained from one of the three alloc functions. If a process calls malloc and thinks it's calling free, but its memory usage continually increases, this is called leakage. It is usually caused by not calling free to return unused space.

Since memory allocation errors are hard to track down, some systems provide versions of these functions that do additional error checking every time one of the three alloc functions or free is called. These versions of the functions are often specified by including a special library for the link editor. There are also publicly available sources (such as the one provided with 4.3+BSD) that you can compile with special flags to enable additional run-time checking.

Since the operation of the memory allocator is often crucial to the run-time performance of certain applications, some systems provide additional capabilities. For example, SVR4 provides a function named mallopt that allows a process to set certain variables that control the operation of the storage allocator. A function called mallinfo is also available to provide statistics on the memory allocator. Check the malloc(3) manual page for your system to see if any of these features are available.

alloca Function

One additional function is also worth mentioning. The function alloca has the same calling sequence as malloc, however instead of allocating memory from the heap, the memory is allocated from the stack frame of the current function. The advantage to this is that we don't have to free the space—it goes away automatically when the function returns. alloca increases the size of the stack frame. The disadvantage is that some systems can't support alloca, if it's impossible to increase the size of the stack frame after the function has been called. Nevertheless, many software packages use it, and implementations exist for a wide variety of systems.

7.9   Environment Variables

As we mentioned earlier, the environment strings are usually of the form

name=value

The Unix kernel never looks at these strings—their interpretation is up to the various applications. The shells, for example, use numerous environment variables. Some are set automatically at login (HOME, USER, etc.) and others are for us to set. We normally set environment variables in a shell start-up file to control the shell's actions. If we set the environment variable MAILPATH, for example, it tells the Bourne shell and Korn-Shell where to look for mail.

ANSI C defines a function that we can use to fetch values from the environment, but this standard says that the contents of the environment are implementation defined.

```
#include <stdlib.h>

char *getenv(const char *name);
```

                                Returns: pointer to *value* associated with *name*, NULL if not found

---

Note that this function returns a pointer to the *value* of a *name=value* string. We should always use getenv to fetch a specific value from the environment, instead of accessing environ directly.

Some environment variables are defined by POSIX.1 and XPG3. Figure 7.4 lists the ones defined by these standards and which are supported by SVR4 and 4.3+BSD. There are many additional implementation-dependent environment variables used in SVR4 and 4.3+BSD. Note that ANSI C doesn't define any environment variables.

> FIPS 151–1 requires that a login shell must define the environment variables HOME and LOGNAME.

Variable	Standards		Implementations		Description
	POSIX.1	XPG3	SVR4	4.3+BSD	
HOME	•	•	•	•	home directory
LANG	•	•	•		name of locale
LC_ALL	•	•	•		name of locale
LC_COLLATE	•	•	•		name of locale for collation
LC_CTYPE	•	•	•		name of locale for character classification
LC_MONETARY	•	•	•		name of locale for monetary editing
LC_NUMERIC	•	•	•		name of locale for numeric editing
LC_TIME	•	•	•		name of locale for date/time formatting
LOGNAME	•	•	•	•	login name
NLSPATH		•	•		sequence of templates for message catalogs
PATH	•	•	•	•	list of path prefixes to search for executable file
TERM	•	•	•	•	terminal type
TZ	•	•	•	•	time zone information

Figure 7.4 Environment variables.

In addition to fetching the value of an environment variable, sometimes we want to set an environment variable. We may want to change the value of an existing variable, or add a new variable to the environment. (In the next chapter we'll see that we can affect the environment of only the current process and any child processes that we invoke. We cannot affect the environment of the parent process, which is often a shell. Nevertheless, it is still useful to be able to modify the environment list.) Unfortunately, not all systems support this capability. Figure 7.5 shows the various functions that are supported by the different standards and implementations.

Function	Standards			Implementations	
	ANSI C	POSIX.1	XPG3	SVR4	4.3+BSD
getenv	•	•	•	•	•
putenv		(maybe)	•	•	•
setenv					•
unsetenv					•
clearenv		(maybe)			

Figure 7.5 Support for various environment list functions.

The Rationale in the POSIX.1 standard states that putenv and clearenv are being considered for an amendment to POSIX.1.

The prototypes for the middle three functions listed in Figure 7.5 are

```
#include <stdlib.h>

int putenv(const char *str);

int setenv(const char *name, const char *value, int rewrite);

                                    Both return: 0 if OK, nonzero on error

void unsetenv(const char *name);
```

The operation of these three functions is

- putenv takes a string of the form *name=value* and places it in the environment list. If the *name* already exists, its old definition is first removed.

- setenv sets *name* to *value*. If *name* already exists in the environment then (a) if *rewrite* is nonzero, the existing definition for *name* is first removed; (b) if *rewrite* is 0, an existing definition for *name* is not removed (and *name* is not set to the new *value*, and no error occurs).

- unsetenv removes any definition of *name*. It is not an error if such a definition does not exist.

It is interesting to examine how these functions must operate when modifying the environment list. Recall Figure 7.3 where the environment list (the array of pointers to the actual *name=value* strings) and the environment strings are typically stored at the top of a process's memory space (above the stack). Deleting a string is simple—we just find the pointer in the environment list and move all subsequent pointers down one—but adding a string, or modifying an existing string, is harder. The space at the top of the stack cannot be expanded because it is often at the top of the address space of the process. Since it's at the top it can't expand upward and it can't be expanded downward because all the stack frames below it can't be moved.

1. If we're modifying an existing *name*:

   (a) If the size of the new *value* is less than or equal to the size of the existing *value*, we can just copy the new string over the old string.

   (b) If the new *value* is larger than the old one, however, we must `malloc` to obtain room for the new string, copy the new string to this area, then replace the old pointer in the environment list for *name* with the pointer to this `malloc`ed area.

2. If we're adding a new *name* it's more complicated. First we have to call `malloc` to allocate room for the *name=value* string and copy the string to this area.

   (a) Then, if it's the first time we've added a new *name*, we have to call `malloc` to obtain room for a new list of pointers. We copy the old environment list to this new area and store a pointer to the *name=value* string at the end of this list of pointers. We also store a null pointer at the end of this list, of course. Finally we set `environ` to point to this new list of pointers. Note from Figure 7.3 that if the original environment list was contained above the top of the stack (as is common), then we have moved this list of pointers to the heap. But most of the pointers in this list still point to *name=value* strings above the top of the stack.

   (b) If this isn't the first time we've added new strings to the environment list, then we know we've already `malloc`ed room for the list on the heap, so we just call `realloc` to allocate room for one more pointer. The pointer to the new *name=value* string is stored at the end of the list (on top of the previous null pointer), followed by a null pointer.

7.10 `setjmp` and `longjmp` Functions

In C we can't `goto` a label that's in another function. Instead we must use the `setjmp` and `longjmp` functions to perform this type of branching. As we'll see, these two functions are useful for handling error conditions that occur in a deeply nested function call.

Consider the skeleton in Program 7.3. It consists of a main loop that reads lines from standard input and calls the function `do_line` to process each line. This function then calls `get_token` to fetch the next token from the input line. The first token of a line is assumed to be a command of some form and a `switch` statement selects each command. For the single command shown, the function `cmd_add` is called.

```
#include     "ourhdr.h"

#define TOK_ADD     5

void     do_line(char *);
void     cmd_add(void);
int      get_token(void);

int
main(void)
{
    char     line[MAXLINE];

    while (fgets(line, MAXLINE, stdin) != NULL)
        do_line(line);
    exit(0);
}

char     *tok_ptr;          /* global pointer for get_token() */

void
do_line(char *ptr)          /* process one line of input */
{
    int      cmd;

    tok_ptr = ptr;
    while ( (cmd = get_token()) > 0) {
        switch (cmd) {  /* one case for each command */
        case TOK_ADD:
                cmd_add();
                break;
        }
    }
}

void
cmd_add(void)
{
    int      token;

    token = get_token();
    /* rest of processing for this command */
}

int
get_token(void)
{
    /* fetch next token from line pointed to by tok_ptr */
}
```

Program 7.3 Typical program skeleton for command processing.

Program 7.3 is typical for programs that read commands, determine the command type, and then call functions to process each command. Figure 7.6 shows what the stack could look like after cmd_add has been called.

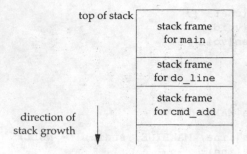

Figure 7.6 Stack frames after cmd_add has been called.

Storage for the automatic variables is within the stack frame for each function. The array line is in the stack frame for main, the integer cmd is in the stack frame for do_line, and the integer token is in the stack frame for cmd_add.

As we've said, this type of arrangement of the stack is typical, but not required. Stacks do not have to grow toward lower memory addresses. On systems that don't have built-in hardware support for stacks, a C implementation might use a linked list for its stack frames.

The coding problem that's often encountered with programs like Program 7.3 is how to handle nonfatal errors. For example, if the cmd_add function encounters an error, say an invalid number, it might want to print an error, ignore the rest of the input line, and return to the main function to read the next input line. But when we're deeply nested numerous levels down from the main function, this is hard to do in C. (In this example, in the cmd_add function, we're only two levels down from main, but it's not uncommon to be 5 or more levels down from where we want to return to.) It becomes messy if we have to code each function with a special return value that tells it to return one level.

The solution to this problem is to use a nonlocal goto—the setjmp and longjmp functions. The adjective nonlocal is because we're not doing a normal C goto statement within a function; instead we're branching back through the call frames to a function that is in the call path of the current function.

```
#include <setjmp.h>

int setjmp(jmp_buf env);

                Returns: 0 if called directly, nonzero if returning from a call to longjmp

void longjmp(jmp_buf env, int val);
```

We call set jmp from the location that we want to return to, which in this example is in the main function. set jmp returns 0 in this case, because we called it directly. In the call to set jmp the argument *env* is of the special type jmp_buf. This data type is some form of array that is capable of holding all the information required to restore the status of the stack to the state when we call long jmp. Normally the *env* variable is a global variable, since we'll need to reference it from another function.

When we encounter an error, say in the cmd_add function, we call long jmp with two arguments. The first is the same *env* that we used in a call to set jmp, and the second, *val*, is a nonzero value that becomes the return value from set jmp. The reason for the second argument is to allow us to have more than one long jmp for each set jmp. For example, we could long jmp from cmd_add with a *val* of 1 and also call long jmp from get_token with a *val* of 2. In the main function, the return value from set jmp is either 1 or 2, and we can test this value (if we want) and determine if the long jmp was from cmd_add or get_token.

Let's return to the example. Program 7.4 shows both the main and cmd_add functions. (The other two functions, do_line and get_token haven't changed.)

```
#include    <setjmp.h>
#include    "ourhdr.h"

#define TOK_ADD    5

jmp_buf jmpbuffer;

int
main(void)
{
    char    line[MAXLINE];

    if (setjmp(jmpbuffer) != 0)
        printf("error");
    while (fgets(line, MAXLINE, stdin) != NULL)
        do_line(line);
    exit(0);
}

    . . .

void
cmd_add(void)
{
    int     token;

    token = get_token();
    if (token < 0)          /* an error has occurred */
        longjmp(jmpbuffer, 1);
    /* rest of processing for this command */
}
```

Program 7.4 Example of set jmp and long jmp.

When main is executed, we call setjmp and it records whatever information it needs to in the variable jmpbuffer and returns 0. We then call do_line, which calls cmd_add, and assume an error of some form is detected. Before the call to longjmp in cmd_add, the stack looks like that in Figure 7.6. But longjmp causes the stack to be "unwound" back to the main function, throwing away the stack frames for cmd_add and do_line. Calling longjmp causes the setjmp in main to return, but this time it returns with a value of 1 (the second argument for longjmp).

Automatic, Register, and Volatile Variables

The next question is "what are the states of the automatic variables and register variables in the main function?" When main is returned to by the longjmp, do these variables have values corresponding to when the setjmp was previously called (i.e., are their values rolled back), or are their values left alone so that their values are whatever they were when do_line was called (which caused cmd_add to be called, which caused longjmp to be called)? Unfortunately, the answer is "it depends." Most implementations do not try to roll back these automatic variables and register variables, but all that the standards say is that their values are indeterminate. If you have an automatic variable that you don't want rolled back, define it with the volatile attribute. Variables that are declared global or static are left alone when longjmp is executed.

Example

Program 7.5 demonstrates the different behavior that can be seen with automatic, register, and volatile variables, after calling longjmp. If we compile and test Program 7.5, with and without compiler optimizations, the results are different:

```
$ cc testjmp.c                        compile without any optimization
$ a.out
in f1(): count = 97, val = 98, sum = 99
after longjmp: count = 97, val = 98, sum = 99
$ cc -O testjmp.c                     compile with full optimization
$ a.out
in f1(): count = 97, val = 98, sum = 99
after longjmp: count = 2, val = 3, sum = 99
```

Note that the volatile variable (sum) isn't affected by the optimizations—its value after the longjmp is the last value that it assumed. The setjmp(3) manual page on one system states that variables stored in memory will have values as of the time of the longjmp, while variables in the CPU and floating point registers are restored to their values when setjmp was called. This is indeed what we see when we run Program 7.5. Without optimization all three variables are stored in memory (i.e., the register hint is ignored for val). When we enable optimization, both count and val go into registers (even though the former wasn't declared register) and the volatile variable stays in memory. The thing to realize with this example is that you must use the volatile attribute if you're writing portable code that uses nonlocal jumps. Anything else can change from one system to the next.   □

```
#include    <setjmp.h>
#include    "ourhdr.h"

static void f1(int, int, int);
static void f2(void);

static jmp_buf  jmpbuffer;

int
main(void)
{
    int             count;
    register int    val;
    volatile int    sum;

    count = 2; val = 3; sum = 4;
    if (setjmp(jmpbuffer) != 0) {
        printf("after longjmp: count = %d, val = %d, sum = %d\n",
                count, val, sum);
        exit(0);
    }
    count = 97; val = 98; sum = 99;
                /* changed after setjmp, before longjmp */
    f1(count, val, sum);        /* never returns */
}

static void
f1(int i, int j, int k)
{
    printf("in f1(): count = %d, val = %d, sum = %d\n", i, j, k);
    f2();
}

static void
f2(void)
{
    longjmp(jmpbuffer, 1);
}
```

Program 7.5 Effect of longjmp on automatic, register, and volatile variables.

We'll return to these two functions, setjmp and longjmp in Chapter 10 when we discuss signal handlers and their signal versions sigsetjmp and siglongjmp.

Potential Problem with Automatic Variables

Having looked at the way stack frames are usually handled, it is worth looking at a potential error in dealing with automatic variables. The basic rule is that an automatic variable can never be referenced after the function that declared the automatic variable returns. There are numerous warnings about this throughout the Unix manuals.

Program 7.6 is a function called `open_data` that opens a standard I/O stream and sets the buffering for the stream.

```
#include        <stdio.h>

#define DATAFILE    "datafile"

FILE *
open_data(void)
{
    FILE    *fp;
    char    databuf[BUFSIZ];  /* setvbuf makes this the stdio buffer */

    if ( (fp = fopen(DATAFILE, "r")) == NULL)
        return(NULL);

    if (setvbuf(fp, databuf, _IOLBF, BUFSIZ) != 0)
        return(NULL);

    return(fp);       /* error */
}
```

Program 7.6 Incorrect usage of an automatic variable.

The problem is that when `open_data` returns, the space it used on the stack will be used by the stack frame for the next function that is called. But the standard I/O library will still be using that portion of memory for its buffer for the stream. Chaos is sure to result. To correct this problem the array `databuf` needs to be allocated from global memory, either statically (`static` or `extern`) or dynamically (one of the `alloc` functions).

7.11 `getrlimit` and `setrlimit` Functions

Every process has a set of resource limits, some of which can be queried and changed by the `getrlimit` and `setrlimit` functions.

```
#include <sys/time.h>
#include <sys/resource.h>

int getrlimit(int resource, struct rlimit *rlptr);

int setrlimit(int resource, const struct rlimit *rlptr);
```
Both return: 0 if OK, nonzero on error

Each call to these two functions specifies a single *resource* and a pointer to the following structure.

```
struct rlimit {
    rlim_t  rlim_cur;  /* soft limit: current limit */
    rlim_t  rlim_max;  /* hard limit: maximum value for rlim_cur */
};
```

These two functions are not part of POSIX.1, but SVR4 and 4.3+BSD provide them.

SVR4 uses the primitive system data type `rlim_t` in the preceding structure. Other systems define these two members as integers or long integers.

The resource limits for a process are normally established by process 0 when the system is initialized and then inherited by each successive process. In SVR4 the defaults can be examined in the file `/etc/conf/cf.d/mtune`. In 4.3+BSD the defaults are scattered among various headers.

Three rules govern the changing of the resource limits:

1. A soft limit can be changed by any process to a value less than or equal to its hard limit.

2. Any process can lower its hard limit to a value greater than or equal to its soft limit. This lowering of the hard limit is irreversible for normal users.

3. Only a superuser process can raise a hard limit.

An infinite limit is specified by the constant `RLIM_INFINITY`.

The *resource* argument takes on one of the following values. Note that not all resources are supported by both SVR4 and 4.3+BSD.

RLIMIT_CORE   (SVR4 and 4.3+BSD) The maximum size in bytes of a core file. A limit of 0 prevents the creation of a core file.

RLIMIT_CPU   (SVR4 and 4.3+BSD) The maximum amount of CPU time in seconds. When the soft limit is exceeded, the `SIGXCPU` signal is sent to the process.

RLIMIT_DATA   (SVR4 and 4.3+BSD) The maximum size in bytes of the data segment. This is the sum of the initialized data, uninitialized data, and heap from Figure 7.3.

RLIMIT_FSIZE   (SVR4 and 4.3+BSD) The maximum size in bytes of a file that may be created. When the soft limit is exceeded, the `SIGXFSZ` signal is sent to the process.

RLIMIT_MEMLOCK   (4.3+BSD only) Locked-in-memory address space (not implemented yet).

RLIMIT_NOFILE   (SVR4 only) The maximum number of open files per process. Changing this limit affects the value returned by the `sysconf` function for its `_SC_OPEN_MAX` argument (Section 2.5.4). See Program 2.3 also.

`RLIMIT_NPROC`	(4.3+BSD only) The maximum number of child processes per real user ID. Changing this limit affects the value returned for `_SC_CHILD_MAX` by the `sysconf` function (Section 2.5.4).
`RLIMIT_OFILE`	(4.3+BSD) Same as the SVR4 `RLIMIT_NOFILE`.
`RLIMIT_RSS`	(4.3+BSD only) Maximum resident set size (RSS) in bytes. If physical memory is tight, the kernel takes memory from processes that exceed their RSS.
`RLIMIT_STACK`	(SVR4 and 4.3+BSD) The maximum size in bytes of the stack. See Figure 7.3.
`RLIMIT_VMEM`	(SVR4 only) The maximum size in bytes of the mapped address space. This affects the `mmap` function (Section 12.9).

The resource limits affect the calling process and are inherited by any of its children. This means that the setting of resource limits really needs to be built into the shells to affect all our future processes. Indeed, the Bourne shell and KornShell have the built-in `ulimit` command, and the C shell has the built-in `limit` command. (The `umask` and `chdir` functions also have to be handled as shell built-ins.)

> Older Bourne shells, such as the one distributed by Berkeley, don't support the `ulimit` command.

> Newer versions of the KornShell have undocumented `-H` and `-S` options for the `ulimit` command, to examine or modify the hard or soft limits, respectively.

Example

Program 7.7 prints out the current soft limit and the hard limit for all the resource limits supported on the system. To run this program under both SVR4 and 4.3+BSD we have conditionally compiled the resource names that differ.

```
#include     <sys/types.h>
#include     <sys/time.h>
#include     <sys/resource.h>
#include     "ourhdr.h"

#define doit(name)  pr_limits(#name, name)

static void pr_limits(char *, int);

int
main(void)
{
    doit(RLIMIT_CORE);
    doit(RLIMIT_CPU);
    doit(RLIMIT_DATA);
    doit(RLIMIT_FSIZE);
```

```
#ifdef  RLIMIT_MEMLOCK
    doit(RLIMIT_MEMLOCK);
#endif
#ifdef  RLIMIT_NOFILE    /* SVR4 name */
    doit(RLIMIT_NOFILE);
#endif
#ifdef  RLIMIT_OFILE     /* 4.3+BSD name */
    doit(RLIMIT_OFILE);
#endif
#ifdef  RLIMIT_NPROC
    doit(RLIMIT_NPROC);
#endif
#ifdef  RLIMIT_RSS
    doit(RLIMIT_RSS);
#endif
    doit(RLIMIT_STACK);
#ifdef  RLIMIT_VMEM
    doit(RLIMIT_VMEM);
#endif
    exit(0);
}

static void
pr_limits(char *name, int resource)
{
    struct rlimit   limit;

    if (getrlimit(resource, &limit) < 0)
        err_sys("getrlimit error for %s", name);
    printf("%-14s  ", name);
    if (limit.rlim_cur == RLIM_INFINITY)
        printf("(infinite)  ");
    else
        printf("%10ld  ", limit.rlim_cur);
    if (limit.rlim_max == RLIM_INFINITY)
        printf("(infinite)\n");
    else
        printf("%10ld\n", limit.rlim_max);
}
```

Program 7.7 Print the current resource limits.

Note that we've used the new ANSI C string-creation operator (#) in the doit macro, to generate the string value for each resource name. When we say

```
doit(RLIMIT_CORE);
```

this is expanded by the C preprocessor into

```
pr_limits("RLIMIT_CORE", RLIMIT_CORE);
```

Running this program under SVR4 gives us the following:

```
$ a.out
RLIMIT_CORE            1048576         1048576
RLIMIT_CPU           (infinite)      (infinite)
RLIMIT_DATA          16777216        16777216
RLIMIT_FSIZE          2097152         2097152
RLIMIT_NOFILE              64            1024
RLIMIT_STACK         16777216        16777216
RLIMIT_VMEM          16777216        16777216
```

4.3+BSD gives us the following results:

```
$ a.out
RLIMIT_CORE          (infinite)      (infinite)
RLIMIT_CPU           (infinite)      (infinite)
RLIMIT_DATA           8388608        16777216
RLIMIT_FSIZE         (infinite)      (infinite)
RLIMIT_MEMLOCK       (infinite)      (infinite)
RLIMIT_OFILE              64         (infinite)
RLIMIT_NPROC              40         (infinite)
RLIMIT_RSS           27070464        27070464
RLIMIT_STACK           524288        16777216
```

Exercise 10.11 continues the discussion of resource limits, after we've covered signals.

7.12 Summary

Understanding the environment of a C program in a Unix environment is a requisite to understanding the process control features of Unix. In this chapter we've looked at how a process is started, how it can terminate, and how it's passed an argument list and an environment. Although both are uninterpreted by the kernel, it is the kernel that passes both from the caller of exec to the new process.

We've also examined the typical memory layout of a C program and how a process can dynamically allocate and free memory. It is worthwhile to look in detail at the functions available for manipulating the environment, since they involve memory allocation. The functions setjmp and longjmp were presented, providing a way to perform nonlocal branching within a process. We finished the chapter describing the resource limits that are provided by SVR4 and 4.3+BSD.

Exercises

7.1 On an 80386 system under both SVR4 and 4.3+BSD, if we execute the program that prints "hello, world", without calling exit or return, the termination status of the program (which we can examine with the shell) is 13. Why?

7.2 When is the output from the printfs in Program 7.1 actually output?

7.3 Is there any way for a function that is called by main to examine the command-line arguments, without (a) passing argc and argv as arguments from main to the function, or (b) having main copy argc and argv into global variables?

7.4 Some Unix implementations purposely arrange that, when a program is executed, location 0 in the data segment is not accessible. Why?

7.5 Use the typdef facility of C to define a new data type Exitfunc for an exit handler. Redo the prototype for atexit using this data type.

7.6 If we allocate an array of longs using calloc is the array initialized to 0? If we allocate an array of pointers using calloc is the array initialized to null pointers?

7.7 In the output from the size command at the end of Section 7.6, why aren't any sizes given for the heap and the stack?

7.8 In Section 7.7 the two file sizes (104859 and 24576) don't equal the sums of their respective text and data sizes. Why?

7.9 In Section 7.7 why is there such a difference in the size of the executable file when using shared libraries for such a trivial program?

7.10 At the end of Section 7.10 we showed how a function can't return a pointer to an automatic variable. Is the following code correct?

```
int
f1(int val)
{
    int     *ptr;

    if (val == 0) {
        int     val;

        val = 5;
        ptr = &val;
    }
    return(*ptr + 1);
}
```

8

Process Control

8.1 Introduction

We now turn to the process control provided by Unix. This includes the creation of new processes, executing programs, and process termination. We also look at the various IDs that are the property of the process—real, effective, and saved; user and group IDs—and how they're affected by the process control primitives. Interpreter files and the system function are also covered. We conclude the chapter by looking at the process accounting that is provided by most Unix systems. This lets us look at the process control functions from a different perspective.

8.2 Process Identifiers

Every process has a unique process ID, a nonnegative integer. Since the process ID is the only well-known identifier of a process that is always unique, it is often used as a piece of other identifiers, to guarantee uniqueness. The tmpnam function in Section 5.13 created unique pathnames by incorporating the process ID in the name.

There are some special processes. Process ID 0 is usually the scheduler process and is often known as the *swapper*. No program on disk corresponds to this process—it is part of the kernel and is known as a system process. Process ID 1 is usually the init process and is invoked by the kernel at the end of the bootstrap procedure. The program file for this process was /etc/init in older versions of Unix and is /sbin/init in newer versions. This process is responsible for bringing up a Unix system after the kernel has been bootstrapped. init usually reads the system-dependent initialization files (the /etc/rc* files) and brings the system to a certain state (such as multiuser). The init process never dies. It is a normal user process (not a system process within the kernel like the swapper), although it does run with superuser privileges. Later in this chapter we'll see how init becomes the parent process of any orphaned child process.

On some virtual memory implementations of Unix, process ID 2 is the *pagedaemon*. This process is responsible for supporting the paging of the virtual memory system. Like the swapper, the pagedaemon is a kernel process.

In addition to the process ID, there are other identifiers for every process. The following functions return these identifiers.

```
#include <sys/types.h>
#include <unistd.h>

pid_t getpid(void);                          Returns: process ID of calling process

pid_t getppid(void);                         Returns: parent process ID of calling process

uid_t getuid(void);                          Returns: real user ID of calling process

uid_t geteuid(void);                         Returns: effective user ID of calling process

gid_t getgid(void);                          Returns: real group ID of calling process

gid_t getegid(void);                         Returns: effective group ID of calling process
```

Note that none of these functions has an error return. We'll return to the parent process ID in the next section when we discuss the fork function. The real and effective user and group IDs were discussed in Section 4.4.

8.3 `fork` Function

The *only* way a new process is created by the Unix kernel is when an existing process calls the fork function. (This doesn't apply to the special processes that we mentioned in the previous section—the swapper, init, and the pagedaemon. These processes are created specially by the kernel as part of the bootstrapping.)

```
#include <sys/types.h>
#include <unistd.h>

pid_t fork(void);

                        Returns: 0 in child, process ID of child in parent, −1 on error
```

The new process created by fork is called the *child process*. This function is called once but returns twice. The only difference in the returns is that the return value in the child is 0 while the return value in the parent is the process ID of the new child. The reason the child's process ID is returned to the parent is because a process can have more than one child, so there is no function that allows a process to obtain the process IDs of its children. The reason fork returns 0 to the child is because a process can have only a single parent, so the child can always call getppid to obtain the process ID of its parent. (Process ID 0 is always in use by the swapper, so it's not possible for 0 to be the process ID of a child.)

Both the child and parent continue executing with the instruction that follows the call to fork. The child is a copy of the parent. For example, the child gets a copy of the parent's data space, heap, and stack. Note that this is a copy for the child—the parent and child do not share these portions of memory. Often the parent and child share the text segment (Section 7.6), if it is read-only.

Many current implementations don't perform a complete copy of the parent's data, stack, and heap, since a fork is often followed by an exec. Instead, a technique called *copy-on-write* (COW) is used. These regions are shared by the parent and child and have their protection changed by the kernel to read-only. If either process tries to modify these regions, the kernel then makes a copy of that piece of memory only, typically a "page" in a virtual memory system. Section 9.2 of Bach [1986] and Section 5.7 of Leffler et al. [1989] provide more detail on this feature.

Example

Program 8.1 demonstrates the fork function. If we execute this program we get

```
$ a.out
a write to stdout
before fork
pid = 430, glob = 7, var = 89      child's variables were changed
pid = 429, glob = 6, var = 88      parent's copy were not changed
$ a.out > temp.out
$ cat temp.out
a write to stdout
before fork
pid = 432, glob = 7, var = 89
before fork
pid = 431, glob = 6, var = 88
```

In general, we never know if the child starts executing before the parent or vice versa. This depends on the scheduling algorithm used by the kernel. If it's required that the child and parent synchronize with each other, some form of interprocess communication is required. In Program 8.1 we just have the parent put itself to sleep for 2 seconds, to let the child execute. There is no guarantee that this is adequate, and we talk about this and other types of synchronization in Section 8.8 when we talk about race conditions. In Section 10.16 we show how to synchronize a parent and child after a fork using signals.

Note the interaction of fork with the I/O functions in Program 8.1. Recall from Chapter 3 that the write function is not buffered. Since write is called before the fork, its data is written once to standard output. The standard I/O library, however, is buffered. Recall from Section 5.12 that standard output is line buffered if it's connected to a terminal device, otherwise it's fully buffered. When we run the program interactively we get only a single copy of the printf line, because the standard output buffer

```
#include        <sys/types.h>
#include        "ourhdr.h"

int     glob = 6;           /* external variable in initialized data */
char    buf[] = "a write to stdout\n";

int
main(void)
{
    int     var;            /* automatic variable on the stack */
    pid_t   pid;

    var = 88;
    if (write(STDOUT_FILENO, buf, sizeof(buf)-1) != sizeof(buf)-1)
        err_sys("write error");
    printf("before fork\n");    /* we don't flush stdout */

    if ( (pid = fork()) < 0)
        err_sys("fork error");
    else if (pid == 0) {        /* child */
        glob++;                 /* modify variables */
        var++;
    } else
        sleep(2);               /* parent */

    printf("pid = %d, glob = %d, var = %d\n", getpid(), glob, var);
    exit(0);
}
```

Program 8.1 Example of fork function.

is flushed by the newline. But when we redirect standard output to a file we get two copies of the printf line. What has happened in this second case is that the printf before the fork is called once, but the line remains in the buffer when fork is called. This buffer is then copied into the child, when the parent's data space is copied to the child. Both the parent and child now have a standard I/O buffer with this line in it. The second printf, right before the exit, just appends its data to the existing buffer. When each process terminates, its copy of the buffer is finally flushed.   □

File Sharing

Another point to note from Program 8.1 is, when we redirect the standard output of the parent, the child's standard output is also redirected. Indeed, one characteristic of fork is that all descriptors that are open in the parent are duplicated in the child. We say "duplicated" because it's as if the dup function had been called for each descriptor. The parent and child share a file table entry for every open descriptor (recall Figure 3.4).

Consider a process that has three different files opened for standard input, standard output, and standard error. On return from fork we have the arrangement shown in Figure 8.1.

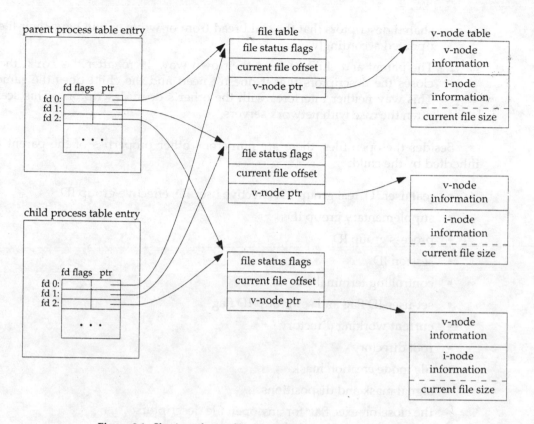

Figure 8.1 Sharing of open files between parent and child after fork.

It is important that the parent and child share the same file offset. Consider a process that forks a child, then waits for the child to complete. Assume that both processes write to standard output as part of their normal processing. If the parent has its standard output redirected (by a shell, perhaps) it is essential that the parent's file offset be updated by the child, if the child writes to standard output. In this case the child can write to standard output while the parent is waiting for it, and on completion of the child the parent can continue writing to standard output, knowing that its output will be appended to whatever the child wrote. If the parent and child did not share the same file offset, this type of interaction would be harder to accomplish and would require explicit actions by the parent.

If both parent and child write to the same descriptor, without any form of synchronization (such as having the parent wait for the child), their output will be intermixed (assuming it's a descriptor that was open before the fork). While this is possible (we saw it in Program 8.1), it's not the normal mode of operation.

There are two normal cases for handling the descriptors after a fork.

1. The parent waits for the child to complete. In this case, the parent does not need to do anything with its descriptors. When the child terminates, any of the

shared descriptors that the child read from or wrote to will have their file offsets updated accordingly.

2. The parent and child each go their own way. Here, after the `fork`, the parent closes the descriptors that it doesn't need and the child does the same thing. This way neither interferes with the other's open descriptors. This scenario is often the case with network servers.

Besides the open files, there are numerous other properties of the parent that are inherited by the child:

*   real user ID, real group ID, effective user ID, effective group ID
*   supplementary group IDs
*   process group ID
*   session ID
*   controlling terminal
*   set-user-ID flag and set-group-ID flag
*   current working directory
*   root directory
*   file mode creation mask
*   signal mask and dispositions
*   the close-on-exec flag for any open file descriptors
*   environment
*   attached shared memory segments
*   resource limits

The differences between the parent and child are

*   the return value from `fork`
*   the process IDs are different
*   the two processes have different parent process IDs—the parent process ID of the child is the parent; the parent process ID of the parent doesn't change
*   the child's values for `tms_utime`, `tms_stime`, `tms_cutime`, and `tms_ustime` are set to 0
*   file locks set by the parent are not inherited by the child
*   pending alarms are cleared for the child
*   the set of pending signals for the child is set to the empty set

Many of these features haven't been discussed yet—we'll cover them in later chapters.

The two main reasons for `fork` to fail are (a) if there are already too many processes in the system (which usually means something else is wrong), or (b) if the total number of processes for this real user ID exceeds the system's limit. Recall from Figure 2.7 that `CHILD_MAX` specifies the maximum number of simultaneous processes per real user ID. There are two uses for `fork`.

1. When a process wants to duplicate itself so that the parent and child can each execute different sections of code at the same time. This is common for network servers—the parent waits for a service request from a client. When the request arrives, the parent calls `fork` and lets the child handle the request. The parent goes back to waiting for the next service request to arrive.

2. When a process wants to execute a different program. This is common for shells. In this case the child does an `exec` (which we describe in Section 8.9) right after it returns from the `fork`.

Some operating systems combine the operations from step 2 (a `fork` followed by an `exec`) into a single operation called a spawn. Unix separates the two as there are numerous uses for `fork` without doing an `exec`. Also, separating the two allows the child to change the per-process attributes between the `fork` and `exec`, such as I/O redirection, user ID, signal disposition, and so on. We'll see numerous examples of this in Chapter 14.

8.4   `vfork` Function

The function `vfork` has the same calling sequence and same return values as `fork`. But the semantics of the two functions differ.

> `vfork` originated with the early virtual-memory releases of 4BSD. In Section 5.7 of Leffler et al. [1989] they state, "Although it is extremely efficient, `vfork` has peculiar semantics and is generally considered to be an architectural blemish."
>
> Nevertheless, both SVR4 and 4.3+BSD support `vfork`.
>
> Some systems have a header `<vfork.h>` that should be included when calling `vfork`.

`vfork` is intended to create a new process when the purpose of the new process is to `exec` a new program (step 2 at the end of previous section). The bare bones shell in Program 1.5 is also an example of this type of program. `vfork` creates the new process, just like `fork`, without fully copying the address space of the parent into the child, since the child won't reference that address space—the child just calls `exec` (or `exit`) right after the `vfork`. Instead, while the child is running, until it calls either `exec` or `exit`, the child runs in the address space of the parent. This optimization provides an efficiency gain on some paged virtual-memory implementations of Unix. (As we mentioned in the previous section, some implementations use copy-on-write to improve the efficiency of a `fork` followed by an `exec`.)

Another difference between the two functions is that vfork guarantees that the child runs first, until the child calls exec or exit. When the child calls either of these functions, the parent resumes. (This can lead to deadlock if the child depends on further actions of the parent before calling either of these two functions.)

Example

Let's look at Program 8.1, replacing the call to fork with vfork. We've removed the write to standard output. Also, we don't need to have the parent call sleep, since we're guaranteed that it is put to sleep by the kernel until the child calls either exec or exit.

```
#include     <sys/types.h>
#include     "ourhdr.h"

int      glob = 6;        /* external variable in initialized data */

int
main(void)
{
    int      var;         /* automatic variable on the stack */
    pid_t    pid;

    var = 88;
    printf("before vfork\n");    /* we don't flush stdio */

    if ( (pid = vfork()) < 0)
        err_sys("vfork error");
    else if (pid == 0) {         /* child */
        glob++;                  /* modify parent's variables */
        var++;
        _exit(0);                /* child terminates */
    }

    /* parent */
    printf("pid = %d, glob = %d, var = %d\n", getpid(), glob, var);
    exit(0);
}
```

Program 8.2 Example of vfork function.

Running this program gives us

```
$ a.out
before vfork
pid = 607, glob = 7, var = 89
```

Here the incrementing of the variables done by the child changes the values in the parent. Since the child runs in the address space of the parent, this doesn't surprise us. This behavior, however, differs from fork.

Notice in Program 8.2 that we call _exit instead of exit. As we described in Section 8.5, _exit does not perform any flushing of standard I/O buffers. If we call exit instead, the output is different.

```
$ a.out
before vfork
```

Here the output from the parent's printf has disappeared! What's happening here is that the child calls exit, which flushes and closes all the standard I/O streams. This includes standard output. Even though this is done by the child, it's done in the parent's address space, so all the standard I/O FILE objects that are modified are modified in the parent. When the parent calls printf later, standard output has been closed, and printf returns −1. □

Section 5.7 of Leffler et al. [1989] contains additional information on the implementation issues of fork and vfork. Exercises 8.1 and 8.2 continue the discussion of vfork.

8.5 exit Functions

There are three ways for a process to terminate normally, as we described in Section 7.3, and two forms of abnormal termination.

1. Normal termination:

   (a) Executing a return from the main function. As we saw in Section 7.3, this is equivalent to calling exit.

   (b) Calling the exit function. This function is defined by ANSI C and includes the calling of all exit handlers that have been registered by calling atexit and closing all standard I/O streams. Since ANSI C does not deal with file descriptors, multiple processes (parents and children), and job control, the definition of this function is incomplete for a Unix system.

   (c) Calling the _exit function. This function is called by exit and handles the Unix-specific details. _exit is specified by POSIX.1.

   > In most Unix implementations exit(3) is a function in the standard C library while _exit(2) is a system call.

2. Abnormal termination:

   (a) Calling abort. This is a special case of the next item, since it generates the SIGABRT signal.

   (b) When the process receives certain signals. (We describe signals in more detail in Chapter 10). The signal can be generated by the process itself (e.g., calling the abort function), by some other process, or by the kernel. Examples of signals generated by the kernel could be because the process references a memory location not within its address space or dividing by 0.

Regardless how a process terminates, the same code in the kernel is eventually executed. This kernel code closes all the open descriptors for the process, releases the memory that it was using, and the like.

For any of the preceding cases we want the terminating process to be able to notify its parent how it terminated. For the exit and _exit functions this is done by passing an exit status as the argument to these two functions. In the case of an abnormal termination, however, the kernel (not the process) generates a termination status to indicate the reason for the abnormal termination. In any case, the parent of the process can obtain the termination status from either the wait or waitpid function (described in the next section).

Note that we're differentiating between the "exit status" (which is the argument to either exit or _exit, or the return value from main) and the "termination status." The exit status is converted into a termination status by the kernel when _exit is finally called (recall Figure 7.1). Figure 8.2 describes the different ways the parent can examine the termination status of a child. If the child terminated normally, then the parent can obtain the exit status of the child.

When we described the fork function it was obvious that the child has a parent process after the call to fork. Now we're talking about returning a termination status to the parent, but what happens if the parent terminates before the child? The answer is that the init process becomes the parent process of any process whose parent terminates. We say that the process has been inherited by init. What normally happens is that whenever a process terminates the kernel goes through all active processes to see if the terminating process is the parent of any process that still exists. If so, the parent process ID of the still existing process is changed to be 1 (the process ID of init). This way we're guaranteed that every process has a parent.

Another condition we have to worry about is when the child terminates before the parent. If the child completely disappeared, the parent wouldn't be able to fetch its termination status, when (and if) the parent were finally ready to check if the child had terminated. The answer is that the kernel has to keep a certain amount of information for every terminating process, so that the information is available when the parent of the terminating process calls wait or waitpid. Minimally, this information consists of the process ID, the termination status of the process, and the amount of CPU time taken by the process. The kernel can discard all the memory used by the process and close its open files. In Unix terminology the process that has terminated, but whose parent has not yet waited for it, is called a *zombie*. The ps(1) command prints the state of a zombie process as Z. If we write a long running program that forks many child processes, unless we wait for these processes to fetch their termination status, they become zombies.

System V provides a nonstandard way to avoid zombies, as we describe in Section 10.7.

The final condition to consider is this: what happens when a process that has been inherited by init terminates? Does it become a zombie? The answer is "no," because init is written so that whenever one of its children terminates, init calls one of the wait functions to fetch the termination status. By doing this init prevents the system from being clogged by zombies. When we say "one of init's children" we mean either a process that init generates directly (such as getty, which we describe in Section 9.2) or a process whose parent has terminated and has been inherited by init.

8.6 `wait` and `waitpid` Functions

When a process terminates, either normally or abnormally, the parent is notified by the kernel sending the parent the SIGCHLD signal. Since the termination of a child is an asynchronous event (it can happen at any time while the parent is running) this signal is the asynchronous notification from the kernel to the parent. The parent can choose to ignore this signal, or it can provide a function that is called when the signal occurs (a signal handler). The default action for this signal is to be ignored. We describe these options in Chapter 10. For now we need to be aware that a process that calls wait or waitpid can

- block (if all of its children are still running), or
- return immediately with the termination status of a child (if a child has terminated and is waiting for its termination status to be fetched), or
- return immediately with an error (if it doesn't have any child processes).

If the process is calling wait because it received the SIGCHLD signal, we expect wait to return immediately. But if we call it at any random point in time, it can block.

```
#include <sys/types.h>
#include <sys/wait.h>

pid_t wait(int *statloc);

pid_t waitpid(pid_t pid, int *statloc, int options);
```
Both return: process ID if OK, 0 (see later), or −1 on error

The differences between these two functions are

- wait can block the caller until a child process terminates, while waitpid has an option that prevents it from blocking.
- waitpid doesn't wait for the first child to terminate—it has a number of options that control which process it waits for.

If a child has already terminated and is a zombie, wait returns immediately with that child's status. Otherwise it blocks the caller until a child terminates. If the caller blocks and has multiple children, wait returns when one terminates. We can always tell which child terminated because the process ID is returned by the function.

For both functions the argument *statloc* is a pointer to an integer. If this argument is not a null pointer, the termination status of the terminated process is stored in the location pointed to by the argument. If we don't care about the termination status, we just pass a null pointer as this argument.

Traditionally the integer status that is returned by these two functions has been defined by the implementation with certain bits indicating the exit status (for a normal return), other bits indicating the signal number (for an abnormal return), one bit to indicate if a core file was generated, and so on. POSIX.1 specifies that the termination status is to be looked at using various macros that are defined in <sys/wait.h>. There are three mutually exclusive macros that tell us how the process terminated, and they all begin with WIF. Based on which of these three macros is true, other macros are used to obtain the exit status, signal number, and the like. These are shown in Figure 8.2. We'll discuss how a process can be stopped in Section 9.8 when we discuss job control.

Macro	Description
WIFEXITED (*status*)	True if status was returned for a child that terminated normally. In this case we can execute WEXITSTATUS (*status*) to fetch the low-order 8 bits of the argument that the child passed to exit or _exit.

WIFSIGNALED (*status*)	True if status was returned for a child that terminated abnormally (by receipt of a signal that it didn't catch). In this case we can execute
	
	        WTERMSIG (*status*)
	
	to fetch the signal number that caused the termination.
	
	Additionally, SVR4 and 4.3+BSD (but not POSIX.1) define the macro
	
	        WCOREDUMP (*status*)
	
	that returns true if a core file of the terminated process was generated.

WIFSTOPPED (*status*)	True if status was returned for a child that is currently stopped. In this case we can execute WSTOPSIG (*status*) to fetch the signal number that caused the child to stop.

Figure 8.2 Macros to examine the termination status returned by wait and waitpid.

Example

The function pr_exit in Program 8.3 uses the macros from Figure 8.2 to print a description of the termination status. We'll call this function from numerous programs in the text. Note that this function handles the WCOREDUMP macro, if it is defined.

Program 8.4 calls the pr_exit function, demonstrating the different values for the termination status. If we run Program 8.4 we get

```
$ a.out
normal termination, exit status = 7
abnormal termination, signal number = 6 (core file generated)
abnormal termination, signal number = 8 (core file generated)
```

```
#include     <sys/types.h>
#include     <sys/wait.h>
#include     "ourhdr.h"

void
pr_exit(int status)
{
    if (WIFEXITED(status))
        printf("normal termination, exit status = %d\n",
                WEXITSTATUS(status));
    else if (WIFSIGNALED(status))
        printf("abnormal termination, signal number = %d%s\n",
                WTERMSIG(status),
#ifdef  WCOREDUMP
                WCOREDUMP(status) ? " (core file generated)" : "");
#else
                "");
#endif
    else if (WIFSTOPPED(status))
        printf("child stopped, signal number = %d\n",
                WSTOPSIG(status));
}
```

Program 8.3 Print a description of the exit status.

Unfortunately, there is no portable way to map the signal numbers from WTERMSIG into descriptive names. (See Section 10.21 for one method.) We have to look at the <signal.h> header to verify that SIGABRT has a value of 6, and SIGFPE has a value of 8.   □

As we mentioned, if we have more than one child, wait returns on termination of any of the children. What if we want to wait for a specific process to terminate (assuming we know which process ID we want to wait for)? In older versions of Unix we would have to call wait and compare the returned process ID with the one we're interested in. If the terminated process isn't the one we want, we have to save the process ID and termination status and call wait again. We continue doing this until the desired process terminates. The next time we want to wait for a specific process we would go through the list of already-terminated processes to see if we had already waited for it, and if not, call wait again. What we need is a function that waits for a specific process. This functionality (and more) is provided by the POSIX.1 waitpid function.

> The waitpid function is new with POSIX.1. It is provided by both SVR4 and 4.3+BSD. Earlier releases of System V and 4.3BSD, however, didn't support it.

```
#include        <sys/types.h>
#include        <sys/wait.h>
#include        "ourhdr.h"

int
main(void)
{
    pid_t   pid;
    int     status;

    if ( (pid = fork()) < 0)
        err_sys("fork error");
    else if (pid == 0)          /* child */
        exit(7);

    if (wait(&status) != pid)           /* wait for child */
        err_sys("wait error");
    pr_exit(status);                    /* and print its status */

    if ( (pid = fork()) < 0)
        err_sys("fork error");
    else if (pid == 0)          /* child */
        abort();                /* generates SIGABRT */

    if (wait(&status) != pid)           /* wait for child */
        err_sys("wait error");
    pr_exit(status);                    /* and print its status */

    if ( (pid = fork()) < 0)
        err_sys("fork error");
    else if (pid == 0)          /* child */
        status /= 0;            /* divide by 0 generates SIGFPE */

    if (wait(&status) != pid)           /* wait for child */
        err_sys("wait error");
    pr_exit(status);                    /* and print its status */

    exit(0);
}
```

Program 8.4 Demonstrate different `exit` statuses.

Constant	Description
WNOHANG	`waitpid` will not block if a child specified by *pid* is not immediately available. In this case the return value is 0.
WUNTRACED	If the implementation supports job control, the status of any child specified by *pid* that has stopped, and whose status has not been reported since it has stopped, is returned. The `WIFSTOPPED` macro determines if the return value corresponds to a stopped child process.

Figure 8.3 The *options* constants for `waitpid`.

The interpretation of the *pid* argument for `waitpid` depends on its value:

pid == −1   waits for any child process. In this respect, `waitpid` is equivalent to `wait`.

pid > 0   waits for the child whose process ID equals *pid*.

pid == 0   waits for any child whose process group ID equals that of the calling process.

pid < −1   waits for any child whose process group ID equals the absolute value of *pid*.

(We describe process groups in Section 9.4.) `waitpid` returns the process ID of the child that terminated, and its termination status is returned through *statloc*. With `wait` the only error is if the calling process has no children. (Another error return is possible, in case the function call is interrupted by a signal. We'll discuss this in Chapter 10.) With `waitpid`, however, it's also possible to get an error if the specified process or process group does not exist or is not a child of the calling process.

The *options* argument lets us further control the operation of `waitpid`. This argument is either 0 or is constructed from the bitwise OR of the constants in Figure 8.3.

> SVR4 supports two additional, but nonstandard, *option* constants. WNOWAIT has the system keep the process whose termination status is returned by `waitpid` in a wait state, so that it may be waited for again. With WCONTINUED, the status of any child specified by *pid* that has been continued, and whose status has not been reported, is returned.

The `waitpid` function provides three features that aren't provided by the `wait` function.

1. `waitpid` lets us wait for one particular process (whereas `wait` returns the status of any terminated child). We'll return to this feature when we discuss the `popen` function.

2. `waitpid` provides a nonblocking version of `wait`. There are times when we want to fetch a child's status, but we don't want to block.

3. `waitpid` supports job control (with the WUNTRACED option).

Example

Recall our discussion in Section 8.5 about zombie processes. If we want to write a process so that it `fork`s a child but we don't want to wait for the child to complete and we don't want the child to become a zombie until we terminate, the trick is to call `fork` twice. Program 8.5 does this.

We call `sleep` in the second child to assure that the first child terminates before printing the parent process ID. After a fork either the parent or child can continue executing—we never know which will resume execution first. If we didn't put the second child to sleep, and if it resumed execution after the `fork` before its parent, the parent process ID that it printed would be that of its parent, not process ID 1.

```
#include        <sys/types.h>
#include        <sys/wait.h>
#include        "ourhdr.h"

int
main(void)
{
    pid_t    pid;

    if ( (pid = fork()) < 0)
        err_sys("fork error");
    else if (pid == 0) {            /* first child */
        if ( (pid = fork()) < 0)
            err_sys("fork error");
        else if (pid > 0)
            exit(0);    /* parent from second fork == first child */

        /* We're the second child; our parent becomes init as soon
           as our real parent calls exit() in the statement above.
           Here's where we'd continue executing, knowing that when
           we're done, init will reap our status. */

        sleep(2);
        printf("second child, parent pid = %d\n", getppid());
        exit(0);
    }

    if (waitpid(pid, NULL, 0) != pid)   /* wait for first child */
        err_sys("waitpid error");

    /* We're the parent (the original process); we continue executing,
       knowing that we're not the parent of the second child. */

    exit(0);
}
```

Program 8.5 Avoid zombie processes by forking twice.

Executing Program 8.5 gives us

```
$ a.out
$ second child, parent pid = 1
```

Note that the shell prints its prompt when the original process terminates, which is before the second child prints its parent process ID.   □

8.7 `wait3` and `wait4` Functions

4.3+BSD provides two additional functions, `wait3` and `wait4`. The only feature provided by these two functions that isn't provided by the POSIX.1 functions `wait` and waitpid is an additional argument that allows the kernel to return a summary of the resources used by the terminated process and all its child processes.

```
#include <sys/types.h>
#include <sys/wait.h>
#include <sys/time.h>
#include <sys/resource.h>

pid_t wait3(int *statloc, int options, struct rusage *rusage);

pid_t wait4(pid_t pid, int *statloc, int options, struct rusage *rusage);
```

                              Both return: process ID if OK, 0, or −1 on error

SVR4 also provides the wait3 function in the BSD compatibility library.

The resource information includes information such as the amount of use CPU time, the amount of system CPU time, number of page faults, number of signals received, and the like. Refer to the getrusage(2) manual page for additional details. This resource information is available only for terminated child processes, not for stopped child processes. (This resource information differs from the resource limits we described in Section 7.11.) Figure 8.4 details the different arguments supported by the various wait functions.

Function	*pid*	*options*	*rusage*	POSIX.1	SVR4	4.3+BSD
wait				•	•	•
waitpid	•	•		•	•	•
wait3		•	•		•	•
wait4	•	•	•			•

Figure 8.4 Arguments supported by various wait functions on different systems.

8.8 Race Conditions

For our purposes a race condition occurs when multiple processes are trying to do something with shared data and the final outcome depends on the order in which the processes run. The fork function is a lively breeding ground for race conditions, if any of the logic after the fork either explicitly or implicitly depends on whether the parent or child runs first after the fork. In general we cannot predict which process runs first. Even if we knew which process would run first, what happens after that process starts running depends on the system load and the kernel's scheduling algorithm.

We saw a potential race condition in Program 8.5 when the second child printed its parent process ID. If the second child runs before the first child, then its parent process will be the first child. But if the first child runs first and has enough time to exit, then the parent process of the second child is init. Even calling sleep, as we did, guarantees nothing. If the system was heavily loaded, the second child could resume after, sleep returns, before the first child has a chance to run. Problems of this form can be hard to debug because they tend to work "most of the time."

If a process wants to wait for a child to terminate, it must call one of the wait functions. If a process wants to wait for its parent to terminate, as in Program 8.5, a loop of the following form could be used

```
while (getppid() != 1)
    sleep(1);
```

The problem with this type of loop (called *polling*) is that it wastes CPU time, since the caller is woken up every second to test the condition.

To avoid race conditions and to avoid polling, some form of signaling is required between multiple processes. Signals can be used, and we describe one way to do this in Section 10.16. Various forms of interprocess communication (IPC) can also be used. We'll discuss some of these in Chapters 14 and 15.

For a parent and child relationship, we often have the following scenario. After the fork both the parent and child have something to do. For example, the parent could update a record in a log file with the child's process ID, and the child might have to create a file for the parent. In this example we require that each process tell the other when it has finished its initial set of operations, and that each wait for the other to complete, before heading off on its own. The scenario is

```
#include  "ourhdr.h"

TELL_WAIT();      /* set things up for TELL_xxx & WAIT_xxx */

if ( (pid = fork()) < 0)
    err_sys("fork error");
else if (pid == 0) {              /* child */

    /* child does whatever is necessary ... */

    TELL_PARENT(getppid());      /* tell parent we're done */

    WAIT_PARENT();               /* and wait for parent */

    /* and the child continues on its way ... */
    exit(0);
}

/* parent does whatever is necessary ... */

TELL_CHILD(pid);                 /* tell child we're done */

WAIT_CHILD();                    /* and wait for child */

/* and the parent continues on its way ... */
exit(0);
```

We assume that the header ourhdr.h defines whatever variables are required. The five routines TELL_WAIT, TELL_PARENT, TELL_CHILD, WAIT_PARENT, and WAIT_CHILD can be either macros or actual functions.

We'll show various ways to implement these TELL and WAIT routines in later chapters: Section 10.16 shows an implementation using signals, Program 14.3 shows an implementation using stream pipes. Let's look at an example that uses these five routines.

Example

Program 8.6 outputs two strings: one from the child and one from the parent. It contains a race condition because the output depends on the order in which the processes are run by the kernel and for how long each process runs.

```
#include     <sys/types.h>
#include     "ourhdr.h"

static void charatatime(char *);

int
main(void)
{
    pid_t    pid;

    if ( (pid = fork()) < 0)
        err_sys("fork error");
    else if (pid == 0) {
        charatatime("output from child\n");
    } else {
        charatatime("output from parent\n");
    }
    exit(0);
}

static void
charatatime(char *str)
{
    char    *ptr;
    int     c;

    setbuf(stdout, NULL);                /* set unbuffered */
    for (ptr = str; c = *ptr++; )
        putc(c, stdout);
}
```

Program 8.6 Program with a race condition.

We set the standard output unbuffered, so that every character output generates a write. The goal in this example is to allow the kernel to switch between the two processes as often as possible to demonstrate the race condition. (If we didn't do this we might never see the type of output that follows. Not seeing the erroneous output doesn't mean that the race condition doesn't exist, it just means that we can't see it on this particular system.) The following actual output shows how the results can vary.

```
$ a.out
output from child
output from parent
$ a.out
oouuttppuutt  ffrroomm  cphairledn
t
$ a.out
oouuttppuutt  ffrroomm  pcahrielndt

$ a.out
ooutput from parent
utput from child
```

We need to change Program 8.6 to use the TELL and WAIT functions. Program 8.7 does this. The lines preceded by a plus sign are new lines.

```
     #include    <sys/types.h>
     #include    "ourhdr.h"

     static void charatatime(char *);

     int
     main(void)
     {
         pid_t    pid;

+        TELL_WAIT();
+
         if ( (pid = fork()) < 0)
             err_sys("fork error");
         else if (pid == 0) {
+            WAIT_PARENT();        /* parent goes first */
             charatatime("output from child\n");
         } else {
             charatatime("output from parent\n");
+            TELL_CHILD(pid);
         }
         exit(0);
     }

     static void
     charatatime(char *str)
     {
         char    *ptr;
         int     c;

         setbuf(stdout, NULL);             /* set unbuffered */
         for (ptr = str; c = *ptr++; )
             putc(c, stdout);
     }
```

Program 8.7 Modification of Program 8.6 to avoid race condition.

When we run this program the output is as we expect—there is no intermixing of output from the two processes.

In Program 8.7 the parent goes first. If we change the lines following the fork to be

```
else if (pid == 0) {
    charatatime("output from child\n");
    TELL_PARENT(getppid());
} else {
    WAIT_CHILD();            /* child goes first */
    charatatime("output from parent\n");
}
```

the child goes first. Exercise 8.3 continues this example.   □

8.9   exec Functions

We mentioned in Section 8.3 that one use of the fork function was to create a new process (the child) that then causes another program to be executed by calling one of the exec functions. When a process calls one of the exec functions, that process is completely replaced by the new program, and the new program starts executing at its main function. The process ID does not change across an exec because a new process is not created. exec merely replaces the current process (its text, data, heap, and stack segments) with a brand new program from disk.

There are six different exec functions, but we'll often just refer to "the exec function," which means we could use any of the six different functions. These six functions round out the Unix process control primitives. With fork we can create new processes, and with the exec functions we can initiate new programs. The exit function and the two wait functions handle termination and waiting for termination. These are the only process control primitives we need. We'll use these primitives in later sections to build additional functions such as popen and system.

```
#include <unistd.h>

int execl(const char *pathname, const char *arg0, ... /* (char *) 0 */ );

int execv(const char *pathname, char *const argv[]);

int execle(const char *pathname, const char *arg0, ...
        /* (char *) 0, char *const envp[] */ );

int execve(const char *pathname, char *const argv[], char *const envp[]);

int execlp(const char *filename, const char *arg0, ... /* (char *) 0 */ );

int execvp(const char *filename, char *const argv[]);
```
                                    All six return: -1 on error, no return on success

The first difference in these functions is that the first four take a pathname argument while the last two take a filename argument. When a *filename* argument is specified

- if *filename* contains a slash, it is taken as a pathname,
- otherwise, the executable file is searched for in the directories specified by the PATH environment variable.

The PATH variable contains a list of directories (called path prefixes) that are separated by colons. For example, the *name=value* environment string

```
PATH=/bin:/usr/bin:/usr/local/bin/:.
```

specifies four directories to search. (A zero-length prefix also means the current directory. It can be specified as a colon at the beginning of the *value*, two colons in a row, or a colon at the end of the *value*.)

> There are security reasons for *never* including the current directory in the search path. See Garfinkel and Spafford [1991].

If either of the two functions, execlp or execvp, finds an executable file using one of the path prefixes, but the file isn't a machine executable that was generated by the link editor, it assumes the file is a shell script and tries to invoke /bin/sh with the *filename* as input to the shell.

The next difference concerns the passing of the argument list (l stands for list and v stands for vector). The functions execl, execlp, and execle require each of the command-line arguments to the new program to be specified as separate arguments. We mark the end of the arguments with a null pointer. For the other three functions (execv, execvp, and execve) we have to build an array of pointers to the arguments, and the address of this array is the argument to these three functions.

Before using ANSI C prototypes, the normal way to show the command-line arguments for the three functions execl, execle, and execlp was

```
char *arg0, char *arg1, ..., char *argn, (char *) 0
```

This specifically shows that the final command-line argument is followed by a null pointer. If this null pointer is specified by the constant 0, we must explicitly cast it to a pointer, because if we don't it's interpreted as an integer argument. If the size of an integer is different from the size of a char *, the actual arguments to the exec function will be wrong.

The final difference is the passing of the environment list to the new program. The two functions whose name ends in an e (execle and execve) allow us to pass a pointer to an array of pointers to the environment strings. The other four functions, however, use the environ variable in the calling process to copy the existing environment for the new program. (Recall our discussion of the environment strings in Section 7.9 and Figure 7.5. We mentioned that if the system supported functions such as setenv and putenv we could change the current environment and the environment of any subsequent child processes, but we couldn't affect the environment of the parent process.) Normally a process allows its environment to be propagated to its children, but there are cases when a process wants to specify a certain environment for a child. One example of the latter is the `login` program when a new login shell is initiated. Normally `login` creates a specific environment with only a few variables defined and lets us, through the shell start-up file, add variables to the environment when we log in.

Before using ANSI C prototypes, the arguments to `execle` were shown as

```
char *pathname, char *arg0, ..., char *argn, (char *) 0, char *envp[]
```

This specifically shows that the final argument is the address of the array of character pointers to the environment strings. The ANSI C prototype doesn't show this, since all the command-line arguments, the null pointer, and the *envp* pointer are shown with the ellipsis notation (. . .).

The arguments for these six `exec` functions are hard to remember. The letters in the function names help somewhat. The letter p means the function takes a *filename* argument and uses the PATH environment variable to find the executable file. The letter l means the function takes a list of arguments and is mutually exclusive with the letter v, which means it takes an *argv[]* vector. Finally the letter e means the function takes an *envp[]* array, instead of using the current environment. Figure 8.5 shows the differences between these six functions.

Function	*pathname*	*filename*	Arg list	*argv[]*	environ	*envp[]*
execl	•		•		•	
execlp		•	•		•	
execle	•		•			•
execv	•			•	•	
execvp		•		•	•	
execve	•			•		•
(letter in name)		p	l	v		e

Figure 8.5 Differences between the six `exec` functions.

Every system has a limit on the total size of the argument list and the environment list. From Figure 2.7 this limit is given by ARG_MAX. This value must be at least 4096 bytes on a POSIX.1 system. We sometimes encounter this limit when using the shell's filename expansion feature to generate a list of filenames. For example, the command

```
grep _POSIX_SOURCE /usr/include/*/*.h
```

can generate a shell error of the form

```
arg list too long
```

on some systems.

Historically, System V has had a limit of 5120 bytes. 4.3BSD and 4.3+BSD are distributed with a limit of 20,480 bytes. The system used by the author (see the output from Program 2.1) allows up to a megabyte!

We've mentioned that the process ID does not change after an exec, but there are additional properties that the new program inherits from the calling process:

- process ID and parent process ID
- real user ID and real group ID
- supplementary group IDs
- process group ID
- session ID
- controlling terminal
- time left until alarm clock
- current working directory
- root directory
- file mode creation mask
- file locks
- process signal mask
- pending signals
- resource limits
- tms_utime, tms_stime, tms_cutime, and tms_ustime values

The handling of open files depends on the value of the close-on-exec flag for each descriptor. Recall from Figure 3.2 and our mention of the FD_CLOEXEC flag in Section 3.13, that every open descriptor in a process has a close-on-exec flag. If this flag is set, the descriptor is closed across an exec. Otherwise the descriptor is left open across the exec. Note that the default is to leave the descriptor open across the exec, unless we specifically set the close-on-exec flag using fcntl.

POSIX.1 specifically requires that open directory streams (recall the opendir function from Section 4.21) be closed across an exec. This is normally done by the opendir function calling fcntl to set the close-on-exec flag for the descriptor corresponding to the open directory stream.

Note that the real user ID and the real group ID remain the same across the exec, but the effective IDs can change, depending on the status of the set-user-ID and the set-group-ID bits for the program file that is executed. If the set-user-ID bit is set for the new program, the effective user ID becomes the owner ID of the program file. Otherwise the effective user ID is not changed (it's not set to the real user ID). The group ID is handled in the same way.

In many Unix implementations only one of these six functions, execve, is a system call within the kernel. The other five are just library functions that eventually invoke this system call. We can picture the relationship between these six functions as shown in Figure 8.6. In this arrangement the library functions execlp and execvp process the PATH environment variable, looking for the first path prefix that contains an executable file named *filename*.

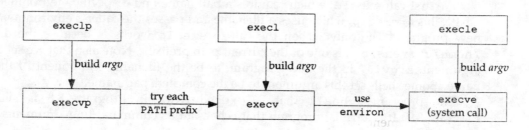

Figure 8.6 Relationship of the six exec functions.

Example

Program 8.8 demonstrates the exec functions.

```c
#include        <sys/types.h>
#include        <sys/wait.h>
#include        "ourhdr.h"

char    *env_init[] = { "USER=unknown", "PATH=/tmp", NULL };

int
main(void)
{
    pid_t   pid;

    if ( (pid = fork()) < 0)
        err_sys("fork error");
    else if (pid == 0) {    /* specify pathname, specify environment */
        if (execle("/home/stevens/bin/echoall",
                    "echoall", "myarg1", "MY ARG2", (char *) 0,
                    env_init) < 0)
            err_sys("execle error");
    }
    if (waitpid(pid, NULL, 0) < 0)
        err_sys("wait error");

    if ( (pid = fork()) < 0)
        err_sys("fork error");
    else if (pid == 0) {    /* specify filename, inherit environment */
        if (execlp("echoall",
                    "echoall", "only 1 arg", (char *) 0) < 0)
            err_sys("execlp error");
    }
    exit(0);
}
```

Program 8.8 Example of exec functions.

We first call execle, which requires a pathname and a specific environment. The next call is to execlp, which uses a filename and passes the caller's environment to the new program. The only reason the call to execlp works is because the directory /home/stevens/bin is one of the current path prefixes. Note also that we set the first argument, argv[0] in the new program, to be the filename component of the pathname. Some shells set this argument to be the complete pathname.

The program echoall that is execed twice in Program 8.8 is shown in Program 8.9. It is a trivial program that echoes all its command-line arguments and its entire environment list.

```
#include     "ourhdr.h"

int
main(int argc, char *argv[])
{
    int         i;
    char        **ptr;
    extern char **environ;

    for (i = 0; i < argc; i++)        /* echo all command-line args */
        printf("argv[%d]: %s\n", i, argv[i]);

    for (ptr = environ; *ptr != 0; ptr++)   /* and all env strings */
        printf("%s\n", *ptr);

    exit(0);
}
```

Program 8.9 Echo all command-line arguments and all environment strings.

When we execute Program 8.8 we get

```
$ a.out
argv[0]: echoall
argv[1]: myarg1
argv[2]: MY ARG2
USER=unknown
PATH=/tmp
argv[0]: echoall
$ argv[1]: only 1 arg
USER=stevens
HOME=/home/stevens
LOGNAME=stevens
```
                              31 more lines that aren't shown
```
EDITOR=/usr/ucb/vi
```

Notice that the shell prompt appeared between the printing of argv[0] and argv[1] from the second exec. This is because the parent did not wait for this child process to finish.   □

8.10 Changing User IDs and Group IDs

We can set the real user ID and effective user ID with the setuid function. Similarly we can set the real group ID and the effective group ID with the setgid function.

```
#include <sys/types.h>
#include <unistd.h>

int setuid(uid_t uid);

int setgid(gid_t gid);
```
Both return: 0 if OK, −1 on error

There are rules for who can change the IDs. Let's consider only the user ID for now. (Everything we describe for the user ID also applies to the group ID.)

1. If the process has superuser privileges, the setuid function sets the real user ID, effective user ID, and saved set-user-ID to *uid*.

2. If the process does not have superuser privileges, but *uid* equals either the real user ID or the saved set-user-ID, setuid sets only the effective user ID to *uid*. The real user ID and the saved set-user-ID are not changed.

3. If neither of these two conditions is true, errno is set to EPERM and an error is returned.

Here we are assuming that _POSIX_SAVED_IDS is true. If this feature isn't provided, then delete all references above to the saved set-user-ID.

> FIPS 151−1 requires this feature.
>
> SVR4 supports the _POSIX_SAVED_IDS feature.

We can make a couple of statements about the three user IDs that the kernel maintains.

1. Only a superuser process can change the real user ID. Normally the real user ID is set by the login(1) program when we log in and never changes. Since login is a superuser process, when it calls setuid it sets all three user IDs.

2. The effective user ID is set by the exec functions, only if the set-user-ID bit is set for the program file. If the set-user-ID bit is not set, the exec functions leave the effective user ID as its current value. We can call setuid at any time to set the effective user ID to either the real user ID or the saved set-user-ID. Naturally, we can't set the effective user ID to any random value.

3. The saved set-user-ID is copied from the effective user ID by exec. This copy is saved after exec stores the effective user ID from the file's user ID (if the file's set-user-ID bit is set).

Figure 8.7 summarizes the different ways these three user IDs can be changed.

ID	exec		setuid(*uid*)	
	set-user-ID bit off	set-user-ID bit on	superuser	unprivileged user
real user ID	unchanged	unchanged	set to *uid*	unchanged
effective user ID	unchanged	set from user ID of program file	set to *uid*	set to *uid*
saved set-user ID	copied from effective user ID	copied from effective user ID	set to *uid*	unchanged

Figure 8.7 Different ways to change the three user IDs.

Note that we can obtain only the current value of the real user ID and the effective user ID with the functions getuid and geteuid from Section 8.2. We can't obtain the current value of the saved set-user-ID.

Example

To see the utility of the saved set-user-ID feature, let's examine the operation of a program that uses it. We'll look at the Berkeley tip(1) program. (The System V cu(1) program is similar.) Both programs connect to a remote system, either through a direct connection or by dialing a modem. When tip uses a modem, it has to obtain exclusive use of the modem through the use of a lock file. This lock file is also shared with the UUCP program, since both programs can want to use the same modem at the same time. The following steps take place.

1. The tip program file is owned by the user name uucp and has its set-user-ID bit set. When we exec it, we have

   real user ID = our user ID
   effective user ID = uucp
   saved set-user-ID = uucp

2. tip accesses the required lock files. These lock files are owned by the user name uucp, but since the effective user ID is uucp, file access is allowed.

3. tip executes setuid(getuid()). Since we are not a superuser process, this changes only the effective user ID. We have

   real user ID = our user ID (unchanged)
   effective user ID = our user ID
   saved set-user-ID = uucp (unchanged)

Now the tip process is running with our user ID as its effective user ID. This means we can access only the files that we have normal access to. We have no additional permissions.

4. When we are done, `tip` executes `setuid(uucpuid)`, where *uucpuid* is the numerical user ID for the user name uucp. (This was probably saved by `tip` when it started by calling `geteuid`. We are not implying that it searches the password file for this numerical user ID.) This call is allowed because the argument to `setuid` equals the saved set-user-ID. (This is why we need the saved set-user-ID.) Now we have

$$
\begin{aligned}
\text{real user ID} &= \text{our user ID (unchanged)} \\
\text{effective user ID} &= \texttt{uucp} \\
\text{saved set-user-ID} &= \texttt{uucp (unchanged)}
\end{aligned}
$$

5. `tip` can now operate on its lock files, to release them, since its effective user ID is uucp.

By using the saved set-user-ID in this fashion, we can use the extra privileges allowed us by the set-user-ID of the program file at the beginning of the process and at the end of the process. Most of the time the process is running, however, it runs with our normal permissions. If we weren't able to switch back to the saved set-user-ID at the end, we might be tempted to retain the extra permissions the whole time we were running (which is asking for trouble).

Let's look at what happens if `tip` spawns a shell for us while it is running. (The shell is spawned using `fork` and `exec`.) Since the real user ID and effective user ID are both our normal user ID (step 3 above), the shell has no extra permissions. The shell can't access the saved set-user-ID that is set to uucp while `tip` is running, because the saved set-user-ID for the shell is copied from the effective user ID by `exec`. So in the child process that does the `exec`, all three user IDs are our normal user ID.

Our description of how the `setuid` function is used by `tip` is not correct if the program is set-user-ID to root. This is because a call to `setuid` with superuser privileges sets all three user IDs. For the example to work as described, we need `setuid` to set only the effective user ID.   □

setreuid and setregid Functions

4.3+BSD supports the swapping of the real user ID and the effective user ID with the `setreuid` function.

```
#include <sys/types.h>
#include <unistd.h>

int setreuid(uid_t ruid, uid_t euid);

int setregid(gid_t rgid, gid_t egid);
```
                                                                    Both return: 0 if OK, −1 on error

The rule is simple: an unprivileged user can always swap between the real user ID and the effective user ID. This allows a set-user-ID program to swap to the user's normal permissions and swap back again later for set-user-ID operations. When the saved set-user-ID feature was introduced with POSIX.1, the rule was enhanced to also allow an unprivileged user to set its effective user ID to its saved set-user-ID.

SVR4 also provides these two functions in the BSD compatibility library.

4.3BSD didn't have the saved set-user-ID feature described earlier. It used setreuid and setregid instead. This allowed an unprivileged user to swap back and forth between the two values, and the tip program under 4.3BSD was written to use this feature. Be aware, however, that when this version of tip spawned a shell it had to set the real user ID to the normal user ID before the exec. If it didn't do this, the real user ID could be uucp (from the swap done by setreuid) and the shell process could call setreuid to swap the two and assume the permissions of uucp. tip sets both the real user ID and the effective user ID to the normal user ID in the child as a defensive programming measure.

seteuid and setegid Functions

A proposed change to POSIX.1 includes the two functions seteuid and setegid. Only the effective user ID or effective group ID is changed.

```
#include <sys/types.h>
#include <unistd.h>

int seteuid(uid_t uid);

int setegid(gid_t gid);
```
                                                                 Both return: 0 if OK, –1 on error

An unprivileged user can set its effective user ID to either its real user ID or its saved set-user-ID. For a privileged user only the effective user ID is set to *uid*. (This differs from the setuid function, which changes all three user IDs.) This proposed POSIX.1 change also requires that the saved set-user-ID always be supported.

Both SVR4 and 4.3+BSD support these two functions.

Figure 8.8 summarizes all the functions that we've described in this section that modify the three different user IDs.

Group IDs

Everything that we've said so far in this section also applies in a similar fashion to group IDs. The supplementary group IDs are not affected by the setgid function.

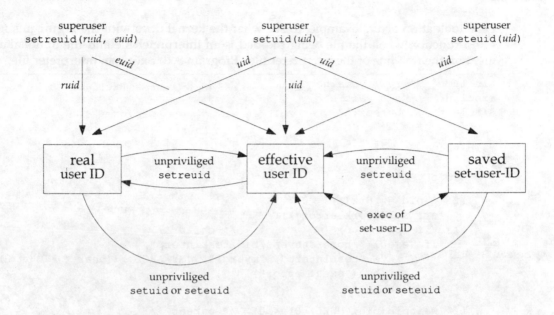

Figure 8.8 Summary of all the functions that set the different user IDs.

8.11 Interpreter Files

Both SVR4 and 4.3+BSD support interpreter files. These files are text files that begin with a line of the form

    #! pathname [optional-argument]

The space between the exclamation point and the *pathname* is optional. The most common of these begin with the line

    #!/bin/sh

The *pathname* is normally an absolute pathname, since no special operations are performed on it (i.e., PATH is not used). The recognition of these files is done within the kernel as part of processing the exec system call. The actual file that gets execed by the kernel is not the interpreter file, but the file specified by the *pathname* on the first line of the interpreter file. Be sure to differentiate between the interpreter file (a text file that begins with #!) and the interpreter (specified by the *pathname* on the first line of the interpreter file).

Be aware that many systems have a limit of 32 characters for the first line of an interpreter file. This includes the #!, the *pathname*, the optional argument, and any spaces.

Example

Let's look at an actual example, to see what the kernel does with the arguments to the exec function when the file being execed is an interpreter file and the optional argument on the first line of the interpreter file. Program 8.10 execs an interpreter file.

```
#include     <sys/types.h>
#include     <sys/wait.h>
#include     "ourhdr.h"

int
main(void)
{
    pid_t    pid;

    if ( (pid = fork()) < 0)
        err_sys("fork error");
    else if (pid == 0) {                /* child */
        if (execl("/home/stevens/bin/testinterp",
                "testinterp", "myarg1", "MY ARG2", (char *) 0) < 0)
            err_sys("execl error");
    }

    if (waitpid(pid, NULL, 0) < 0)   /* parent */
        err_sys("waitpid error");
    exit(0);
}
```

Program 8.10 A program that execs an interpreter file.

The following shows the contents of the one line interpreter file that is execed, and the result from running Program 8.10:

```
$ cat /home/stevens/bin/testinterp
#!/home/stevens/bin/echoarg foo
$ a.out
argv[0]: /home/stevens/bin/echoarg
argv[1]: foo
argv[2]: /home/stevens/bin/testinterp
argv[3]: myarg1
argv[4]: MY ARG2
```

The program echoarg (the interpreter) just echoes each of its command-line arguments. (This is Program 7.2.) Note that when the kernel execs the interpreter (/home/stevens/bin/echoarg), argv[0] is the *pathname* of the interpreter, argv[1] is the optional argument from the interpreter file, and the remaining arguments are the *pathname* (/home/stevens/bin/testinterp) and the second and third arguments from the call to execl in Program 8.10 (myarg1 and MY ARG2). argv[1] and argv[2] from the call to execl have been shifted right two positions. Note that the kernel takes the *pathname* from the execl call, instead of the first argument (testinterp), on the assumption that the *pathname* might contain more information than the first argument.   □

Example

A common use for the optional argument following the interpreter *pathname* is to specify the $-f$ option for programs that support this option. For example, an awk(1) program can be executed as

```
awk -f myfile
```

which tells awk to read the awk program from the file myfile.

> There are two versions of the awk language on many systems. awk is often called "old awk" and corresponds to the original version distributed with Version 7. nawk (new awk) contains numerous enhancements and corresponds to the language described in Aho, Kernighan, and Weinberger [1988]. This newer version provides access to the command-line arguments, which we need for the example that follows. SVR4 provides both, with awk and oawk being the same, and a note that awk will be nawk in a future release. The POSIX.2 draft specifies the new language as just awk, and that's what we'll use in this text.

Using the $-f$ option with an interpreter file lets us write

```
#!/bin/awk -f
```
(awk program follows in the interpreter file)

For example, Program 8.11 shows /usr/local/bin/awkexample (an interpreter file).

```
#!/bin/awk -f

BEGIN {
    for (i = 0; i < ARGC; i++)
        printf "ARGV[%d] = %s\n", i, ARGV[i]
    exit
}
```

Program 8.11 An awk program as an interpreter file.

If one of the path prefixes is /usr/local/bin, we can execute Program 8.11 (assuming we've turned on the execute bit for the file) as

```
$ awkexample file1 FILENAME2 f3
ARGV[0] = /bin/awk
ARGV[1] = file1
ARGV[2] = FILENAME2
ARGV[3] = f3
```

When /bin/awk is executed, its command-line arguments are

```
/bin/awk -f /usr/local/bin/awkexample file1 FILENAME2 f3
```

The pathname of the interpreter file (/usr/local/bin/awkexample) is passed to the interpreter. The filename portion of this pathname (what we typed to the shell) isn't adequate, because the interpreter (/bin/awk in this example) can't be expected to use the PATH variable to locate files. When awk reads the interpreter file it ignores the first line, since the pound sign is awk's comment character.

We can verify these command-line arguments with the following commands.

```
$ su                                     become superuser
Password:                                enter superuser password
# mv /bin/awk /bin/awk.save              save the original program
# cp /home/stevens/bin/echoarg /bin/awk      and replace it temporarily
# suspend                                suspend the superuser shell using job control
[1] + Stopped            su
$ awkexample file1 FILENAME2 f3
argv[0]: /bin/awk
argv[1]: -f
argv[2]: /usr/local/bin/awkexample
argv[3]: file1
argv[4]: FILENAME2
argv[5]: f3
$ fg                                     resume superuser shell using job control
su
# mv /bin/awk.save /bin/awk              restore the original program
# exit                                   and exit the superuser shell
```

In this example the $-f$ option for the interpreter is required. As we said, this tells awk where to look for the awk program. If we remove the $-f$ option from the interpreter file, the results are

```
$ awkexample file1 FILENAME2 f3
/bin/awk: syntax error at source line 1
 context is
        >>> /usr/local <<< /bin/awkexample
/bin/awk: bailing out at source line 1
```

This is because the command-line arguments in this case are

```
/bin/awk /usr/local/bin/awkexample file1 FILENAME2 f3
```

and awk is trying to interpret the string /usr/local/bin/awkexample as an awk program. If we couldn't pass at least a single optional argument to the interpreter ($-f$ in this case), these interpreter files would be usable only with the shells.   □

Are interpreter files required? Not really. They provide an efficiency gain for the user at some expense in the kernel (since it's the kernel that recognizes these files). Interpreter files are useful for the following reasons.

1. They hide the fact that certain programs are scripts in some other language. For example, to execute Program 8.11 we just say

    ```
    awkexample optional-arguments
    ```

    instead of needing to know that the program is really an awk script that we would otherwise have to execute as

    ```
    awk -f awkexample optional-arguments
    ```

2. Interpreter scripts provide an efficiency gain. Consider the previous example again. We could still hide the fact that the program is an awk script, by wrapping it in a shell script:

```
awk 'BEGIN {
    for (i = 0; i < ARGC; i++)
        printf "ARGV[%d] = %s\n", i, ARGV[i]
    exit
}' $*
```

The problem with this solution is that more work is required. First the shell reads the command and tries to execlp the filename. Since the shell script is an executable file, but isn't a machine executable, an error is returned and execlp assumes the file is a shell script (which it is). Then /bin/sh is execed with the pathname of the shell script as its argument. The shell correctly runs our script, but to run the awk program, it does a fork, exec, and wait. There is more overhead in replacing an interpreter script with a shell script.

3. Interpreter scripts let us write shell scripts using shells other than /bin/sh. When execlp finds an executable file that isn't a machine executable it has to choose a shell to invoke, and it always uses /bin/sh. Using an interpreter script, however, we can just write

```
#!/bin/csh
```
(C shell script follows in the interpreter file)

Again, we could wrap this all in a /bin/sh script (that invokes the C shell), as we described earlier, but more overhead is required.

None of this would work as we've shown if the three shells and awk didn't use the pound sign as their comment character.

8.12 system Function

It is convenient to execute a command string from within a program. For example, assume we want to put a time and date stamp into a certain file. We could use the functions we describe in Section 6.9 to do this—call time to get the current calendar time, next call localtime to convert it to a broken-down time, then call strftime to format the result, and write the results to the file. It is much easier, however, to say

```
system("date > file");
```

ANSI C defines the system function, but its operation is strongly system dependent.

> The system function is not defined by POSIX.1 because it is not an interface to the operating system, but really an interface to a shell. Therefore it is being standardized by POSIX.2. The following description corresponds to Draft 11.2 of the POSIX.2 standard.

```
#include <stdlib.h>

int system(const char *cmdstring);
```

Returns: (see below)

If *cmdstring* is a null pointer, system returns nonzero only if a command processor is available. This feature determines if the system function is supported on a given operating system. Under Unix system is always available.

Since system is implemented by calling fork, exec, and waitpid, there are three different types of return values:

1. If either the fork fails or waitpid returns an error other than EINTR, system returns −1 with errno set to indicate the error.

2. If the exec fails (implying that the shell can't be executed) the return value is as if the shell had executed exit(127).

3. Otherwise all three functions succeed (fork, exec, and waitpid) and the return value from system is the termination status of the shell, in the format specified for waitpid.

> Many current implementations of system return an error if waitpid is interrupted by a caught signal (EINTR). The requirement that system not return an error in this case was added to a recent draft of POSIX.2. (We discuss interrupted system calls in Section 10.5.)

Program 8.12 is an implementation of the system function. The one feature that it doesn't handle is signals. We'll update this function with signal handling in Section 10.18.

The shell's −c option tells it to take the next command-line argument (*cmdstring* in this case) as its command input (instead of reading from standard input or from a given file). The shell parses this null terminated C string and breaks it up into separate command-line arguments for the actual command. The actual command string that is passed to the shell can contain any valid shell commands. For example, input and output redirection using < and > can be used.

If we didn't use the shell to execute the command, but tried to execute the command ourself, it would be harder. First, we would want to call execlp instead of execl, to use the PATH variable, like the shell. We would also have to break up the null terminated C string into separate command-line arguments for the call to execlp. Finally, we wouldn't be able to use any of the shell metacharacters.

Note that we call _exit instead of exit. This is to prevent any standard I/O buffers (which would have been copied from the parent to the child across the fork) from being flushed in the child.

```
#include        <sys/types.h>
#include        <sys/wait.h>
#include        <errno.h>
#include        <unistd.h>

int
system(const char *cmdstring)    /* version without signal handling */
{
    pid_t   pid;
    int     status;

    if (cmdstring == NULL)
        return(1);         /* always a command processor with Unix */

    if ( (pid = fork()) < 0) {
        status = -1;       /* probably out of processes */

    } else if (pid == 0) {                      /* child */
        execl("/bin/sh", "sh", "-c", cmdstring, (char *) 0);
        _exit(127);        /* execl error */

    } else {                                    /* parent */
        while (waitpid(pid, &status, 0) < 0)
            if (errno != EINTR) {
                status = -1; /* error other than EINTR from waitpid() */
                break;
            }
    }

    return(status);
}
```

Program 8.12 The system function (without signal handling).

We can test this version of system with Program 8.13. (The pr_exit function was defined in Program 8.3.) Running Program 8.13 gives us

```
$ a.out
Thu Aug 29 14:24:19 MST 1991
normal termination, exit status = 0        for date
sh: nosuchcommand: not found
normal termination, exit status = 1        for nosuchcommand
stevens  console Aug 25 11:49
stevens  ttyp0   Aug 29 05:56
stevens  ttyp1   Aug 29 05:56
stevens  ttyp2   Aug 29 05:56
normal termination, exit status = 44       for exit
```

```
#include        <sys/types.h>
#include        <sys/wait.h>
#include        "ourhdr.h"

int
main(void)
{
    int         status;

    if ( (status = system("date")) < 0)
        err_sys("system() error");
    pr_exit(status);

    if ( (status = system("nosuchcommand")) < 0)
        err_sys("system() error");
    pr_exit(status);

    if ( (status = system("who; exit 44")) < 0)
        err_sys("system() error");
    pr_exit(status);

    exit(0);
}
```

Program 8.13 Calling the system function.

The advantage in using system, instead of using fork and exec directly, is that system does all the required error handling and (in our next version of this function in Section 10.18) all the required signal handling.

Earlier versions of Unix, including SVR3.2 and 4.3BSD, didn't have the waitpid function available. Instead, the parent waited for the child, using a statement such as

```
while ((lastpid = wait(&status)) != pid && lastpid != -1)
```

A problem occurs if the process that calls system has spawned its own children before calling system. Since the while statement above keeps looping until the child that was generated by system terminates, if any children of the process terminate before the process identified by pid, then the process ID and termination status of these other children is just discarded by the while statement. Indeed, this inability to wait for a specific child is one of the reasons given in the POSIX.1 Rationale for including the waitpid function. We'll see in Section 14.3 that the same problem occurs with the popen and pclose functions, if the system doesn't provide a waitpid function.

Set-User-ID Programs

What happens if we call system from a set-user-ID program? This is a security hole and should never be done. Program 8.14 is a simple program that just calls system for its command-line argument.

```
#include     "ourhdr.h"

int
main(int argc, char *argv[])
{
    int     status;

    if (argc < 2)
        err_quit("command-line argument required");

    if ( (status = system(argv[1])) < 0)
        err_sys("system() error");
    pr_exit(status);

    exit(0);
}
```

Program 8.14 Execute the command-line argument using system.

We'll compile this program into the executable file tsys.

Program 8.15 is another simple program that prints its real and effective user IDs.

```
#include     "ourhdr.h"

int
main(void)
{
    printf("real uid = %d, effective uid = %d\n", getuid(), geteuid());
    exit(0);
}
```

Program 8.15 Print real and effective user IDs.

We'll compile this program into the executable file printuids. Running both programs gives us the following.

```
$ tsys printuids                            normal execution, no special privileges
real uid = 224, effective uid = 224
normal termination, exit status = 0
$ su                                        become superuser
Password:                                   enter superuser password
# chown root tsys                           change owner
# chmod u+s tsys                            make set-user-ID
# ls -l tsys                                verify file's permissions and owner
-rwsrwxr-x  1 root     105737 Aug 18 11:21 tsys
# exit                                      leave superuser shell
$ tsys printuids
real uid = 224, effective uid = 0           oops, this is a security hole
normal termination, exit status = 0
```

The superuser permissions that we gave the tsys program are retained across the fork and exec that are done by system.

If a process is running with special permissions (either set-user-ID or set-group-ID) and it wants to spawn another process, it should use fork and exec directly, being certain to change back to normal permissions after the fork, before calling exec. The system function should *never* be used from a set-user-ID or a set-group-ID program.

> One reason for this admonition is that system invokes the shell to parse the command string and the shell uses its IFS variable as the input field separator. Older versions of the shell didn't reset this variable to a normal set of characters when invoked. This allowed a malicious user to set IFS before system was called, causing system to execute a different program.

8.13 Process Accounting

Most Unix systems provide an option to do process accounting. When enabled the kernel writes an accounting record each time a process terminates. These accounting records are typically 32 bytes of binary data with the name of the command, the amount of CPU time used, the user ID and group ID, the starting time, and so on. We'll take a closer look at these accounting records in this section, since it gives us a chance to look at processes again, and a chance to use the fread function from Section 5.9.

> Process accounting is not specified by any of the standards. What we describe in this section corresponds to the implementation under SVR4 and 4.3+BSD. SVR4 provides numerous programs to process this raw accounting data—see runacct and acctcom, for example. 4.3+BSD provides the sa(8) command to process and summarize the raw accounting data.

A function we haven't described (acct) enables and disables process accounting. The only use of this function is from the SVR4 and 4.3+BSD accton(8) command. A superuser executes accton with a pathname argument to enable accounting. The pathname is usually /var/adm/pacct, although on older systems it is /usr/adm/acct. Accounting is turned off by executing accton without any arguments.

The structure of the accounting records is defined in the header <sys/acct.h> and looks like

```
typedef  u_short comp_t;   /* 3-bit base 8 exponent; 13-bit fraction */

struct  acct
{
  char    ac_flag;   /* flag (see Figure 8.9) */
  char    ac_stat;   /* termination status (signal & core flag only) */
                     /* (not provided by BSD systems) */
  uid_t   ac_uid;    /* real user ID */
  gid_t   ac_gid;    /* real group ID */
  dev_t   ac_tty;    /* controlling terminal */
  time_t  ac_btime;  /* starting calendar time */
  comp_t  ac_utime;  /* user CPU time (clock ticks) */
  comp_t  ac_stime;  /* system CPU time (clock ticks) */
  comp_t  ac_etime;  /* elapsed time (clock ticks) */
  comp_t  ac_mem;    /* average memory usage */
  comp_t  ac_io;     /* bytes transferred (by read and write) */
```

```
    comp_t  ac_rw;     /* blocks read or written */
    char    ac_comm[8];/* command name: [8] for SVR4, [10] for 4.3+BSD */
};
```

Historically, Berkeley systems, including 4.3+BSD, don't provide the ac_stat variable.

The ac_flag member records certain events during the execution of the process. These are described in Figure 8.9.

ac_flag	Description
AFORK	process is the result of fork, but never called exec
ASU	process used superuser privileges
ACOMPAT	process used compatibility mode (VAXes only)
ACORE	process dumped core (not in SVR4)
AXSIG	process was killed by a signal (not in SVR4)

Figure 8.9 Values for ac_flag from accounting record.

The data required for the accounting record (CPU times, number of characters transferred, etc.) are all kept by the kernel in the process table and initialized whenever a new process is created (e.g., in the child after a fork). Each accounting record is written when the process terminates. This means that the order of the records in the accounting file corresponds to the termination order of the processes, not the order in which they were started. To know the starting order we would have to go through the accounting file and sort by the starting calendar time. But this isn't perfect, since calendar times are in units of seconds (Section 1.10) and it's possible for many processes to be started in any given second. Alternatively, the elapsed time is given in clock ticks, which are usually between 50 and 100 ticks per second. But we don't know the ending time of a process, all we know is its starting time and ending order. This means that even though the elapsed time is more accurate than the starting time, we still can't reconstruct the exact starting order of various processes, given the data in the accounting file.

The accounting records correspond to processes, not programs. A new record is initialized by the kernel for the child after a fork, not when a new program is execed. Although exec doesn't create a new accounting record, the command name changes and the AFORK flag is cleared. This means that, if we have a chain of three programs (A execs B, then B execs C, and C exits), only a single accounting record is written. The command name in the record corresponds to program C but the CPU times, for example, are the sum for programs A, B, and C.

Example

To have some accounting data to examine, we'll run Program 8.16, which calls fork four times. Each child does something different and then terminates. A picture of what this program is doing is shown in Figure 8.10.

Program 8.17 prints out selected fields from the accounting records.

```
#include      <signal.h>
#include      "ourhdr.h"

int
main(void)
{
    pid_t   pid;

    if ( (pid = fork()) < 0)
        err_sys("fork error");
    else if (pid != 0) {                /* parent */
        sleep(2);
        exit(2);                        /* terminate with exit status 2 */
    }

                                        /* first child */
    if ( (pid = fork()) < 0)
        err_sys("fork error");
    else if (pid != 0) {
        sleep(4);
        abort();                        /* terminate with core dump */
    }

                                        /* second child */
    if ( (pid = fork()) < 0)
        err_sys("fork error");
    else if (pid != 0) {
        execl("/usr/bin/dd", "dd", "if=/boot", "of=/dev/null", NULL);
        exit(7);                        /* shouldn't get here */
    }

                                        /* third child */
    if ( (pid = fork()) < 0)
        err_sys("fork error");
    else if (pid != 0) {
        sleep(8);
        exit(0);                        /* normal exit */
    }

                                        /* fourth child */
    sleep(6);
    kill(getpid(), SIGKILL);            /* terminate with signal, no core dump */
    exit(6);                            /* shouldn't get here */
}
```

Program 8.16 Program to generate accounting data.

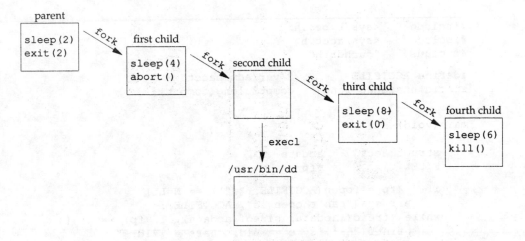

Figure 8.10 Process structure for accounting example.

We then do the following steps:

1. Become superuser and enable accounting, with the `accton` command. Note that, when this command terminates, accounting should be on, therefore the first record in the accounting file should be from this command.

2 Run Program 8.16. This should append five records to the accounting file (one for the parent and one for each of the four children).

   A new process is not created by the `execl` in the second child. There is only a single accounting record for the second child.

3. Become superuser and turn accounting off. Since accounting is off when this `accton` command terminates, it should not appear in the accounting file.

4. Run Program 8.17 to print the selected fields from the accounting file.

The output from step 4 follows. We have appended to each line the description of the process in italics, for the discussion later.

```
accton      e =       7, chars =      64, stat =   0:  S
dd          e =      37, chars =  221888, stat =   0:          second child
a.out       e =     128, chars =       0, stat =   0:          parent
a.out       e =     274, chars =       0, stat = 134: F   D X  first child
a.out       e =     360, chars =       0, stat =   9: F     X  fourth child
a.out       e =     484, chars =       0, stat =   0: F        third child
```

```
#include        <sys/types.h>
#include        <sys/acct.h>
#include        "ourhdr.h"

#define ACCTFILE        "/var/adm/pacct"
static unsigned long     compt2ulong(comp_t);

int
main(void)
{
    struct acct     acdata;
    FILE            *fp;

    if ( (fp = fopen(ACCTFILE, "r")) == NULL)
        err_sys("can't open %s", ACCTFILE);
    while (fread(&acdata, sizeof(acdata), 1, fp) == 1) {
        printf("%-*.*s  e = %6ld, chars = %7ld, "
                "stat = %3u: %c %c %c %c\n", sizeof(acdata.ac_comm),
                sizeof(acdata.ac_comm), acdata.ac_comm,
                compt2ulong(acdata.ac_etime), compt2ulong(acdata.ac_io),
                (unsigned char) acdata.ac_stat,
#ifdef  ACORE           /* SVR4 doesn't define ACORE */
                acdata.ac_flag & ACORE ? 'D' : ' ',
#else
                ' ',
#endif
#ifdef  AXSIG           /* SVR4 doesn't define AXSIG */
                acdata.ac_flag & AXSIG ? 'X' : ' ',
#else
                ' ',
#endif
                acdata.ac_flag & AFORK ? 'F' : ' ',
                acdata.ac_flag & ASU   ? 'S' : ' ');
    }
    if (ferror(fp))
        err_sys("read error");
    exit(0);
}

static unsigned long
compt2ulong(comp_t comptime)        /* convert comp_t to unsigned long */
{
    unsigned long   val;
    int             exp;

    val = comptime & 017777;    /* 13-bit fraction */
    exp = (comptime >> 13) & 7; /* 3-bit exponent (0-7) */
    while (exp-- > 0)
        val *= 8;
    return(val);
}
```

Program 8.17 Print selected fields from system's accounting file.

The elapsed time values are measured in units of CLK_TCK. From Figure 2.6 the value on this system is 60. For example, the sleep(2) in the parent corresponds to the elapsed time of 128 clock ticks. For the first child the sleep(4) becomes 274 clock ticks. Notice that the amount of time a process sleeps is not exact. (We'll return to the sleep function in Chapter 10.) Also, the calls to fork and exit take some amount of time.

Note that the ac_stat member is not the true termination status of the process. It corresponds to a portion of the termination status that we discussed in Section 8.6. The only information in this byte is a core-flag bit (usually the high-order bit) and the signal number (usually the seven low-order bits), if the process terminated abnormally. If the process terminated normally, we are not able to obtain the exit status from the accounting file. For the first child this value is 128+6. The 128 is the core flag bit and 6 happens to be the value on this system for SIGABRT (which is generated by the call to abort). The value 9 for the fourth child corresponds to the value of SIGKILL. We can't tell from the accounting data that the parent's argument to exit was 2, and the third child's argument to exit was 0.

The size of the file /boot that the dd process copies in the second child is 110,888 bytes. The number of characters of I/O is just over twice this value. It is twice the value since 110,888 bytes are read in, then 110,888 bytes are written out. Even though the output goes to the null device, they are still accounted for.

The ac_flag values are as we expect. The F flag is set for all the child processes except the second child that does the execl. The F flag is not set for the parent because the interactive shell that executed the parent did a fork and then an exec of the a.out file. The core dump flag (D) is on for the first child process that calls abort. Since abort generates a SIGABRT signal to generate the core dump, the X flag is also on for this process, since it was terminated by a signal. The X flag is also on for the fourth child, but the SIGKILL signal does not generate a core dump—it only terminates the process.

As a final note, the first child has a 0 count for the number of characters of I/O, yet this process generated a core file. It appears that the I/O required to write the core file is not charged to the process. □

8.14 User Identification

Any process can find out its real and effective user ID and group ID. Sometimes, however, we want to find out the login name of the user who's running the program. We could call getpwuid(getuid()), but what if a single user has multiple login names, each with the same user ID? (A person might have multiple entries in the password file with the same user ID to have a different login shell for each entry.) The system normally keeps track of the name we log in under (Section 6.7), and the getlogin function provides a way to fetch that login name.

```
#include <unistd.h>

char *getlogin(void);
```

                                     Returns: pointer to string giving login name if OK, NULL on error

This function can fail if the process is not attached to a terminal that a user logged into. We normally call these processes *daemons*. We discuss them in Chapter 13.

Given the login name, we can then use it to look up the user in the password file (to determine the login shell, for example) using getpwnam.

To find the login name, Unix systems have historically called the ttyname function (Section 11.9) and then tried to find a matching entry in the utmp file (Section 6.7). 4.3+BSD stores the login name in the process table entry and provides system calls to fetch and store this name.

System V provided the cuserid function to return the login name. This function called getlogin and, if that failed, did a getpwuid(getuid()). The IEEE Std. 1003.1–1988 specified cuserid, but it called for the effective user ID to be used, instead of the real user ID. The final 1990 version of POSIX.1 dropped the cuserid function.

FIPS 151–1 requires a login shell to define the environment variable LOGNAME with the user's login name. In 4.3+BSD this variable is set by login and inherited by the login shell. Realize, however, that a user can modify an environment variable, so we shouldn't use LOGNAME to validate the user in any way. Instead, getlogin should be used.

8.15 Process Times

In Section 1.10 we described three times that we can measure: wall clock time, user CPU time, and system CPU time. Any process can call the times function to obtain these values for itself and any terminated children.

```
#include <sys/times.h>

clock_t times(struct tms *buf);
```

                                     Returns: elapsed wall clock time in clock ticks if OK, –1 on error

This function fills in the tms structure pointed to by *buf*.

```
struct tms {
  clock_t  tms_utime;  /* user CPU time */
  clock_t  tms_stime;  /* system CPU time */
  clock_t  tms_cutime; /* user CPU time, terminated children */
  clock_t  tms_cstime; /* system CPU time, terminated children */
};
```

Note that the structure does not contain any measurement for the wall clock time. Instead, the function returns the wall clock time as the value of the function, each time it's called. This value is measured from some arbitrary point in the past, so we can't use its absolute value, instead we use its relative value. For example, we call times and save the return value. At some later time we call times again, and subtract the earlier return value from the new return value. The difference is the wall clock time. (It is possible, though unlikely, for a long running process to overflow the wall clock time—see Exercise 1.6.)

The two structure fields for child processes contain values only for children that we have waited for.

All the clock_t values returned by this function are converted to seconds using the number of clock ticks per second—the _SC_CLK_TCK value returned by sysconf (Section 2.5.4).

> Berkeley-derived systems, including 4.3BSD, inherited a version of times from Version 7 that did not return the wall clock time. Instead, this older version returned 0 if OK or −1 on error. 4.3+BSD supports the POSIX.1 version.

> 4.3+BSD and SVR4 (in the BSD compatibility library) provide the getrusage(2) function. This function returns the CPU times, and 14 other values indicating resource usage.

Example

Program 8.18 executes each command-line argument as a shell command string, timing the command and printing the values from the tms structure. If we run this program we get:

```
$ a.out "sleep 5" "date"

command: sleep 5
  real:      5.25
  user:      0.00
  sys:       0.00
  child user:      0.02
  child sys:       0.13
normal termination, exit status = 0

command: date
Sun Aug 18 09:25:38 MST 1991
  real:      0.27
  user:      0.00
  sys:       0.00
  child user:      0.05
  child sys:       0.10
normal termination, exit status = 0
```

In these two examples all the CPU time appears in the child process, which is where the shell and the command execute.

```
#include     <sys/times.h>
#include     "ourhdr.h"

static void pr_times(clock_t, struct tms *, struct tms *);
static void do_cmd(char *);

int
main(int argc, char *argv[])
{
    int     i;

    for (i = 1; i < argc; i++)
        do_cmd(argv[i]);     /* once for each command-line arg */
    exit(0);
}
static void
do_cmd(char *cmd)          /* execute and time the "cmd" */
{
    struct tms  tmsstart, tmsend;
    clock_t     start, end;
    int         status;

    fprintf(stderr, "\ncommand: %s\n", cmd);

    if ( (start = times(&tmsstart)) == -1)  /* starting values */
        err_sys("times error");

    if ( (status = system(cmd)) < 0)            /* execute command */
        err_sys("system() error");

    if ( (end = times(&tmsend)) == -1)          /* ending values */
        err_sys("times error");

    pr_times(end-start, &tmsstart, &tmsend);
    pr_exit(status);
}
static void
pr_times(clock_t real, struct tms *tmsstart, struct tms *tmsend)
{
    static long     clktck = 0;

    if (clktck == 0)     /* fetch clock ticks per second first time */
        if ( (clktck = sysconf(_SC_CLK_TCK)) < 0)
            err_sys("sysconf error");
    fprintf(stderr, "  real:  %7.2f\n", real / (double) clktck);
    fprintf(stderr, "  user:  %7.2f\n",
            (tmsend->tms_utime - tmsstart->tms_utime) / (double) clktck);
    fprintf(stderr, "  sys:   %7.2f\n",
            (tmsend->tms_stime - tmsstart->tms_stime) / (double) clktck);
    fprintf(stderr, "  child user: %7.2f\n",
            (tmsend->tms_cutime - tmsstart->tms_cutime) / (double) clktck);
    fprintf(stderr, "  child sys:  %7.2f\n",
            (tmsend->tms_cstime - tmsstart->tms_cstime) / (double) clktck);
}
```

Program 8.18 Time and execute all command-line arguments.

Let's rerun the example from Section 1.10.

```
$ a.out "cd /usr/include; grep _POSIX_SOURCE */*.h > /dev/null"

command: cd /usr/include; grep _POSIX_SOURCE */*.h > /dev/null
   real:     18.67
   user:      0.00
   sys:       0.02
   child user:      0.43
   child sys:       4.13
normal termination, exit status = 0
```

As we expect, all three values (the real time and the child CPU times) are similar to the values in Section 1.10.   □

8.16 Summary

A thorough understanding of Unix process control is essential for advanced programming. There are only a few functions to master: fork, the exec family, _exit, wait, and waitpid. These primitives are used in many applications. The fork function also gave us an opportunity to look at race conditions.

Our examination of the system function and process accounting gave us another look at all these process control functions. We also looked at another variation of the exec functions: interpreter files and how they operate. An understanding of the different user IDs and group IDs that are provided (real, effective, and saved) is critical to writing safe set-user-ID programs.

Given an understanding of a single process and its children, in the next chapter we examine the relationship of a process to other processes—sessions and job control. We then complete our discussion of processes in Chapter 10 when we describe signals.

Exercises

8.1   In Program 8.2 we said that replacing the call to _exit with a call to exit causes the standard output to be closed. Modify the program to verify that printf does return −1.

8.2   Recall the typical arrangement of memory in Figure 7.3. Since the stack frames corresponding to each function call are usually stored in the stack, and since after a vfork the child runs in the address space of the parent, what happens if the call to vfork is from a function other than main, and the child does a return from this function after the vfork? Write a test program to verify this and draw a picture of what's happening.

8.3   When we execute Program 8.7 one time, as in

```
$ a.out
```

the output is correct. But if we execute the program multiple times, one right after the other, as in

```
$ a.out ; a.out ; a.out
output from parent
ooutput from parent
ouotuptut from child
put from parent
output from child
utput from child
```

the output is not correct. What's happening? How can we correct this? Can this problem happen if we let the child write its output first?

8.4   In Program 8.10 we call execl, specifying the *pathname* of the interpreter file. If we called execlp instead, specifying a *filename* of testinterp, and if the directory /home/stevens/bin was a path prefix, what would be printed as argv[2] when the program is run?

8.5   How can a process obtain its saved set-user-ID?

8.6   Write a program that creates a zombie and then call system to execute the ps(1) command to verify that the process is a zombie.

8.7   We mentioned in Section 8.9 that POSIX.1 requires that open directory streams be closed across an exec. Verify this as follows: call opendir for the root directory, peek at your system's implementation of the DIR structure, and print the close-on-exec flag. Then open the same directory for reading and print the close-on-exec flag.

9

Process Relationships

9.1 Introduction

We learned in the previous chapter that there are relationships between different processes. First, every process has a parent process. The parent is notified when the child terminates, and the parent can obtain the child's exit status. We also mentioned process groups when we described the waitpid function (Section 8.6) and how we can wait for any process in a process group to terminate.

In this chapter we'll look at process groups in more detail, and the new concept of sessions that was introduced by POSIX.1. We also look at the relationship between the login shell that is invoked for us when we log in and all the processes that we start from our login shell.

It is impossible to describe these relationships without talking about signals, and to talk about signals we need many of the concepts in this chapter. If you are unfamiliar with Unix signals you may want to skim through Chapter 10 at this point.

9.2 Terminal Logins

Let's start by looking at the programs that are executed when we log in to a Unix system. In early Unix systems, such as Version 7, users logged in using dumb terminals that were connected to the host with RS-232 connections. The terminals were either local (directly connected) or remote (connected through a modem). In either case, these logins came through a terminal device driver in the kernel. For example, on PDP-11s the common devices were DH-11s and DZ-11s. There were a fixed number of these terminal devices on a host, so there was a known upper limit on the number of simultaneous logins. The procedure that we now describe is used to log in to a Unix system using an RS-232 terminal.

4.3+BSD Terminal Logins

This procedure has not changed much over the past 15 years. The system administrator creates a file, usually /etc/ttys, that has one line per terminal device. Each line specifies the name of the device and other parameters that are passed to the getty program. One parameter is the baud rate of the terminal, for example. When the system is bootstrapped the kernel creates process ID 1, the init process, and it is init that brings the system up multiuser. init reads the file /etc/ttys and, for every terminal device that allows a login, init does a fork followed by an exec of the program getty. This gives us the processes shown in Figure 9.1.

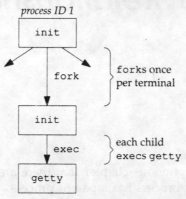

Figure 9.1 Processes invoked by init to allow terminal logins.

All the processes shown in Figure 9.1 have a real user ID of 0 and an effective user ID of 0 (i.e., they all have superuser privileges). init also execs the getty program with an empty environment.

It is getty that calls open for the terminal device. The terminal is opened for reading and writing. If the device is a modem, the open may delay inside the device driver until the modem is dialed and the call is answered. Once the device is open, file descriptors 0, 1, and 2 are set to the device. Then getty outputs something like login: and waits for us to enter our user name. If the terminal supports multiple speeds, getty can detect special characters that tell it to change the terminal's speed (baud rate). Consult your Unix manuals for additional details on the getty program and the data files (gettytab) that can drive its actions.

getty is done when we enter our user name. It then invokes the login program, similar to

```
execle("/usr/bin/login", "login", "-p", username, (char *) 0, envp);
```

(There can be options in the gettytab file to have it invoke other programs, but the default is the login program.) init invokes getty with an empty environment. getty creates an environment for login (the envp argument) with the name of the terminal (something like TERM=foo, where the type of terminal foo is taken from the gettytab file) and any environment strings that are specified in the gettytab. The

-p flag to `login` tells it to preserve the environment that it is passed and to add to that environment, not replace it. Figure 9.2 shows the state of these processes right after `login` has been invoked.

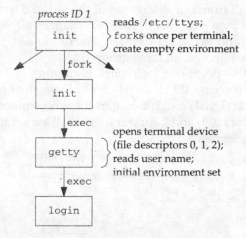

Figure 9.2 State of processes after `login` has been invoked.

All the processes shown in Figure 9.2 have superuser privileges, since the original `init` process has superuser privileges. The process ID of the bottom three processes in Figure 9.2 is the same, since the process ID does not change across an `exec`. Also, all the processes other than the original `init` process have a parent process ID of one.

Now `login` does many things. Since it has our user name it can call `getpwnam` to fetch our password file entry. It then calls `getpass`(3) to display the prompt `Password:` and read our password (with echoing disabled, of course). It calls `crypt`(3) to encrypt the password that we entered and compares the encrypted result with the `pw_passwd` field from our password file entry. If the login attempt fails because of an invalid password (after a few tries), `login` calls `exit` with an argument of 1. This termination will be noticed by the parent (`init`) and it will do another `fork` followed by an `exec` of `getty`, starting the procedure over again for this terminal.

If we log in correctly, `login` changes to our home directory (`chdir`). The ownership of our terminal device is changed (`chown`) so we are the owner and group owner. The access permissions are also changed for the terminal device, so that user-read, user-write, and group-write are enabled. Our group IDs are set, by calling `setgid` and then `initgroups`. The environment is then initialized with all the information that `login` has: our home directory (`HOME`), shell (`SHELL`), user name (`USER` and `LOGNAME`), and a default path (`PATH`). Finally it changes to our user ID (`setuid`) and invokes our login shell, as in

```
execl("/bin/sh", "-sh", (char *) 0);
```

The minus sign as the first character of `argv[0]` is a flag to all the shells that they are being invoked as a login shell. The shells can look at this character and modify their start-up accordingly.

`login` really does more than we've described here. It optionally prints the message-of-the-day file, checks for new mail, and does other functions. We're interested only in the features that we've described.

Recall from our discussion of the `setuid` function in Section 8.10 that since `setuid` is called by a superuser process it changes all three user IDs: the real user ID, effective user ID, and saved set-user-ID. The call to `setgid` that was done earlier by `login` has the same effect on all three group IDs.

At this point our login shell is running. Its parent process ID is the original `init` process (process ID 1), so when our login shell terminates, `init` is notified (it is sent a `SIGCHLD` signal) and it can start the whole procedure over again for this terminal. File descriptors 0, 1, and 2 for our login shell are set to the terminal device. Figure 9.3 shows this arrangement.

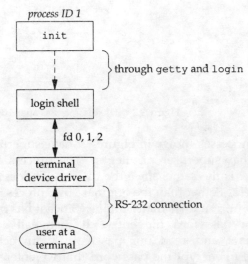

Figure 9.3 Arrangement of processes after everything is set for a terminal login.

Our login shell now reads its start-up files (`.profile` for the Bourne shell and KornShell, `.cshrc` and `.login` for the C shell). These start-up files usually change some of the environment variables and add many additional variables to the environment. For example, most users set their own `PATH` and often prompt for the actual terminal type (`TERM`). When the start-up files are done, we finally get the shell's prompt and can enter commands.

SVR4 Terminal Logins

SVR4 supports two forms of terminal logins: (a) `getty` style, as described previously for 4.3+BSD, and (b) `ttymon` logins, a new feature with SVR4. Normally `getty` is used for the console and `ttymon` is used for other terminal logins.

`ttymon` is part of a larger facility termed SAF, the Service Access Facility. For our purposes we end up with the same picture as in Figure 9.3, with a different set of steps between init and the login shell. init is the parent of sac (the service access controller), which does a fork and exec of the ttymon program when the system enters multiuser state. ttymon monitors all the terminal ports listed in its configuration file and does a fork when we've entered our login name. This child of ttymon does an exec of login, and login prompts us for our password. Once this is done it execs our login shell, and we're at the position shown in Figure 9.3. One difference is that the parent of our login shell is now ttymon, whereas the parent of the login shell from a getty login is init.

9.3   Network Logins

4.3+BSD Network Logins

With the terminal logins that we described in the previous section, init knows which terminal devices are enabled for logins and spawns a getty process for each device. In the case of network logins, however, all the logins come through the kernel's network interface drivers (e.g., the Ethernet driver), and we don't know ahead of time how many of these will occur. Instead of having a process waiting for each possible login, we now have to wait for a network connection request to arrive. In 4.3+BSD there is a single process that waits for most network connections, the inetd process, sometimes called the *Internet superserver*. In this section we'll look at the sequence of processes involved in network logins for a 4.3+BSD system. We are not interested in the detailed network programming aspects of these processes—refer to Stevens [1990] for all the details.

As part of the system start-up, init invokes a shell that executes the shell script /etc/rc. One of the daemons that is started by this shell script is inetd. Once the shell script terminates, the parent process of inetd becomes init. inetd waits for TCP/IP connection requests to arrive at the host, and when a connection request arrives for it to handle, it does a fork and exec of the appropriate program.

Let's assume that a TCP connection request arrives for the TELNET server. TELNET is a remote login application that uses the TCP protocol. A user on another host (that is connected to the server's host through a network of some form) or on the same host initiates the login by starting the TELNET client:

    telnet *hostname*

The client opens a TCP connection to *hostname* and the program that's started on *hostname* is called the TELNET server. The client and server then exchange data across the TCP connection using the TELNET application protocol. What has happened is that the user who started the client program is now logged into the server's host. (This assumes, of course, that the user has a valid account on the server's host.) Figure 9.4 shows the sequence of processes that are involved in executing the TELNET server, called telnetd.

The telnetd process then opens a pseudo-terminal device and splits into two processes using fork. (In Chapter 19 we talk about pseudo terminals in detail.) The

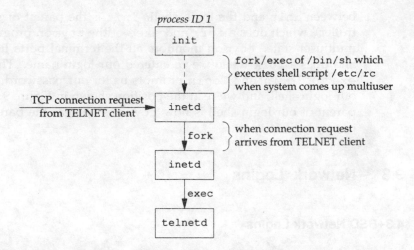

process ID 1

```
init
```

fork/exec of /bin/sh which
executes shell script /etc/rc
when system comes up multiuser

TCP connection request
from TELNET client

```
inetd
```

```
fork
```

when connection request
arrives from TELNET client

```
inetd
```

```
exec
```

```
telnetd
```

Figure 9.4 Sequence of processes involved in executing TELNET server.

parent handles the communication across the network connection, and the child does an
`exec` of the `login` program. The parent and child are connected through the pseudo
terminal. Before doing the `exec`, the child sets up file descriptors 0, 1, and 2 to the
pseudo terminal. If we log in correctly, `login` performs the same steps we described in
Section 9.2—it changes to our home directory, sets our group IDs and user ID, and our
initial environment. Then `login` replaces itself with our login shell by calling `exec`.
Figure 9.5 shows the arrangement of the processes at this point.

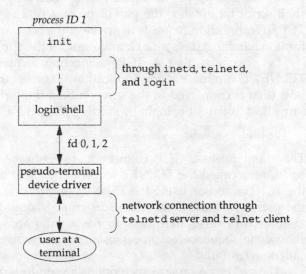

process ID 1

```
init
```

through inetd, telnetd,
and login

```
login shell
```

```
fd 0, 1, 2
```

```
pseudo-terminal
device driver
```

network connection through
telnetd server and telnet client

user at a
terminal

Figure 9.5 Arrangement of processes after everything is set for a network login.

Obviously a lot is going on between the pseudo-terminal device driver and the actual user at the terminal. We show all the processes involved in this type of arrangement in Chapter 19 when we talk about pseudo terminals in more detail.

The important thing to understand is whether we log in through a terminal (Figure 9.3) or a network (Figure 9.5) we have a login shell with its standard input, standard output, and standard error connected to either a terminal device or a pseudo-terminal device. We'll see in the coming sections that this login shell is the start of a POSIX.1 session, and the terminal or pseudo terminal is the controlling terminal for the session.

SVR4 Network Logins

The scenario for network logins under SVR4 is almost identical to the steps under 4.3+BSD. The same inetd server is used, but instead of its parent being init, under SVR4 inetd is invoked as a service by the service access controller, sac. We end up with the same overall picture as in Figure 9.5.

9.4 Process Groups

In addition to having a process ID, each process also belongs to a process group. We'll encounter process groups again when we discuss signals in Chapter 10.

A process group is a collection of one or more processes. Each process group has a unique process group ID. Process·group IDs are similar to process IDs—they are positive integers and they can be stored in a pid_t data type. The function getpgrp returns the process group ID of the calling process.

```
#include <sys/types.h>
#include <unistd.h>

pid_t getpgrp(void);
```

Returns: process group ID of calling process

> In many Berkeley-derived systems, including 4.3+BSD, this function takes a *pid* argument and returns the process group for that process. The prototype shown is the POSIX.1 version.

Each process group can have a process group leader. The leader is identified by having its process group ID equal its process ID.

It is possible for a process group leader to create a process group, create processes in the group, and then terminate. The process group still exists, as long as there is at least one process in the group, regardless whether the group leader terminates or not. This is called the process group lifetime—the period of time that begins when the group is created and ends when the last remaining process in the group leaves the group. The last remaining process in the process group can either terminate or enter some other process group.

A process joins an existing process group, or creates a new process group by calling setpgid. (In the next section we'll see that setsid also creates a new process group.)

```
#include <sys/types.h>
#include <unistd.h>

int setpgid(pid_t pid, pid_t pgid);
```
                                                            Returns: 0 if OK, –1 on error

This sets the process group ID to *pgid* of the process *pid*. If the two arguments are equal, the process specified by *pid* becomes a process group leader.

A process can set the process group ID of only itself or one of its children. Furthermore, it can't change the process group ID of one of its children after that child has called one of the exec functions.

If *pid* is 0, the process ID of the caller is used. Also, if *pgid* is 0, the process ID specified by *pid* is used as the process group ID.

If the system does not support job control (we talk about job control in Section 9.8), _POSIX_JOB_CONTROL won't be defined, and this function returns an error with errno set to ENOSYS.

In most job-control shells this function is called after a fork to have the parent set the process group ID of the child, and to have the child set its own process group ID. One of these calls is redundant, but by doing both we are guaranteed that the child is placed into its own process group before either process assumes that this has happened. If we didn't do this we have a race condition, since it depends on which process executes first.

When we discuss signals we'll see how we can send a signal to either a single process (identified by its process ID) or to a process group (identified by its process group ID). Similarly, the waitpid function from Section 8.6 lets us wait for either a single process or one process from a specified process group.

9.5   Sessions

A session is a collection of one or more process groups. For example, we could have the arrangement shown in Figure 9.6. Here we have three process groups in a single session. The processes in a process group are usually grouped together into the process group by a shell pipeline. For example, the arrangement shown in Figure 9.6 could have been generated by shell commands of the form

```
proc1 | proc2 &
proc3 | proc4 | proc5
```

A process establishes a new session by calling the setsid function.

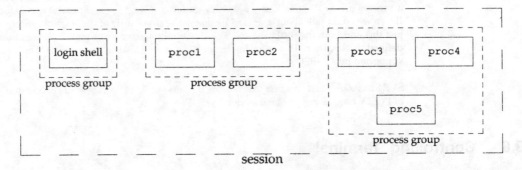

Figure 9.6 Arrangement of processes into process groups and sessions.

```
#include <sys/types.h>
#include <unistd.h>

pid_t setsid(void);
```
Returns: process group ID if OK, −1 on error

If the calling process is not a process group leader, this function creates a new session. Three things happen:

1. The process becomes the *session leader* of this new session. (A session leader is the process that creates a session.) The process is the only process in this new session.

2. The process becomes the process group leader of a new process group. The new process group ID is the process ID of the calling process.

3. The process has no controlling terminal. (We discuss controlling terminals in the next section.) If the process had a controlling terminal before calling setsid, that association is broken.

This function returns an error if the caller is already a process group leader. To ensure this is not the case, the usual practice is to call fork and have the parent terminate and the child continue. We are guaranteed that the child is not a process group leader because the process group ID of the parent is inherited by the child, but the child gets a new process ID. Hence it is impossible for the child's process ID to equal its inherited process group ID.

POSIX.1 talks only about a "session leader." There is no "session ID" similar to a process ID or a process group ID. Obviously a session leader is a single process that has a unique process ID, so we could talk about a session ID that is the process ID of the session leader. SVR4 does just this and both the SVID and the SVR4 manual page for setsid(2) talk about a session ID defined in this way. This is an implementation detail that is not part of POSIX.1 and is not supported by 4.3+BSD.

SVR4 has a getsid function that returns the session ID of a process. This function is not part of POSIX.1 and is not available under 4.3+BSD.

9.6 Controlling Terminal

There are a few other characteristics of sessions and process groups.

- A session can have a single *controlling terminal*. This is usually the terminal device (in the case of a terminal login) or pseudo-terminal device (in the case of a network login) on which we log in.

- The session leader that establishes the connection to the controlling terminal is called the *controlling process*.

- The process groups within a session can be divided into a single *foreground process group* and one or more *background process groups*.

- If a session has a controlling terminal, then it has a single foreground process group, and all other process groups in the session are background process groups.

- Whenever we type our terminal's interrupt key (often DELETE or Control-C) or quit key (often Control-backslash) this causes either the interrupt signal or the quit signal to be sent to all processes in the foreground process group.

- If a modem disconnect is detected by the terminal interface, the hang-up signal is sent to the controlling process (the session leader).

These characteristics are shown in Figure 9.7.

Usually we don't have to worry about our controlling terminal—it is established automatically for us when we log in.

How a system allocates a controlling terminal is left to the implementation by POSIX.1. We show the actual steps in Section 19.4.

SVR4 allocates the controlling terminal for a session when the session leader opens the first terminal device that is not already associated with a session. This assumes that the call to open by the session leader does not specify the O_NOCTTY flag (Section 3.3).

4.3+BSD allocates the controlling terminal for a session when the session leader calls ioctl with a *request* of TIOCSCTTY (the third argument is a null pointer). The session cannot already have a controlling terminal for this call to succeed. (Normally this call to ioctl follows a call to setsid, which guarantees that the process is a session leader without a controlling terminal.) The POSIX.1 O_NOCTTY flag to open is not used by 4.3+BSD.

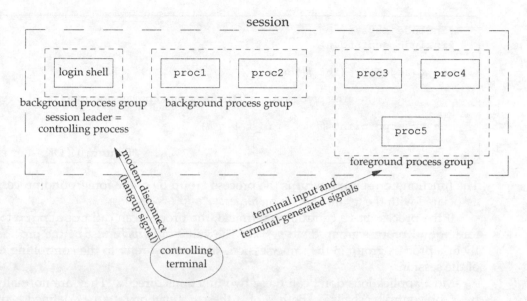

Figure 9.7 Process groups and sessions showing controlling terminal.

There are times when a program wants to talk to the controlling terminal, regardless whether the standard input or standard output is redirected. The way a program guarantees that it is talking to the controlling terminal is to `open` the file `/dev/tty`. This special file is a synonym within the kernel for the controlling terminal. Naturally, if the program doesn't have a controlling terminal, the `open` of this device will fail.

The classic example is the `getpass`(3) function that reads a password (with terminal echoing turned off, of course). This function is called by the `crypt`(1) program and can be used in a pipeline. For example

```
crypt < salaries | lpr
```

decrypts the file `salaries` and pipes the output to the print spooler. Because `crypt` reads its input file on its standard input, standard input can't be used to enter the password. Also, a design feature of `crypt` is that we should have to enter the encryption password each time we run the program, to prevent us from saving the password in a file.

There are known ways to break the encoding used by the `crypt` program. See Garfinkel and Spafford [1991] for more details on encrypting files.

9.7 `tcgetpgrp` and `tcsetpgrp` Functions

We need a way to tell the kernel which process group is the foreground process group, so that the terminal device driver knows where to send the terminal input and the terminal-generated signals (Figure 9.7).

```
#include <sys/types.h>
#include <unistd.h>

pid_t tcgetpgrp(int filedes);
```

                    Returns: process group ID of foreground process group if OK, –1 on error

```
int tcsetpgrp(int filedes, pid_t pgrpid);
```

                                                              Returns: 0 if OK, –1 on error

The function `tcgetpgrp` returns the process group ID of the foreground process group associated with the terminal open on *filedes*.

If the process has a controlling terminal, the process can call `tcsetpgrp` to set the foreground process group ID to *pgrpid*. The value of *pgrpid* must be the process group ID of a process group in the same session. *filedes* must refer to the controlling terminal of the session.

Most applications don't call these two functions directly. They are normally called by job-control shells. Both of these functions are defined only if `_POSIX_JOB_CONTROL` is defined. Otherwise they both return an error.

9.8   Job Control

Job control is a feature added by Berkeley around 1980. It allows us to start multiple jobs (groups of processes) from a single terminal and control which jobs can access the terminal and which jobs are to run in the background. Job control requires three forms of support.

1.   A shell that supports job control.
2.   The terminal driver in the kernel must support job control.
3.   Support for certain job-control signals must be provided.

> A different form of job control, termed shell layers, was provided by SVR3. The Berkeley form of job control, however, was selected by POSIX.1 and is what we describe here. Recall from Figure 2.7 that the constant `_POSIX_JOB_CONTROL` defines whether the system supports job control.
>
> FIPS 151–1 requires POSIX.1 job control.
>
> Both SVR4 and 4.3+BSD support POSIX.1 job control.

From our perspective, using job control from a shell, we can start a job in either the foreground or the background. A job is just a collection of processes, often a pipeline of processes. For example,

```
vi main.c
```

starts a job consisting of one process in the foreground. The commands

```
pr *.c | lpr &
make all &
```

start two jobs in the background. All the processes invoked by these background jobs
are in the background.

As we said, we need to be using a shell that supports job control, to use the features
provided by job control. With older systems it was simple to say which shells supported job control and which didn't. The C shell supported job control, the Bourne shell
didn't, and it was an option with the KornShell, depending whether the host supported
job control or not. But the C shell has been ported to systems that don't support job
control (e.g., earlier versions of System V) and the SVR4 Bourne shell, when invoked by
the name jsh instead of sh, supports job control. The KornShell continues to support
job control if the host does. We'll just talk generically about a shell that supports job
control, versus one that doesn't, when the difference between the various shells doesn't
matter.

When we start a background job, the shell assigns it a job identifier and prints one
or more of the process IDs. The following script shows how the KornShell handles this.

```
$ make all > Make.out &
[1]     1475
$ pr *.c | lpr &
[2]     1490
$                             just press RETURN
[2] +  Done           pr *.c | lpr &
[1] +  Done           make all > Make.out &
```

The make is job number 1 and the starting process ID is 1475. The next pipeline is job
number 2 and the process ID of the first process is 1490. When the jobs are done and
when we press RETURN, the shell tells us that the jobs are complete. The reason we
have to press RETURN is to have the shell print its prompt. The shell doesn't print the
changed status of background jobs at any random time—only right before it prints its
prompt, to let us enter a new command line. If it didn't do this, it could output while
we were entering an input line.

The interaction with the terminal driver arises because there is a special terminal
character that we can enter that affects the foreground job—the suspend key (typically
Control-Z). Entering this character causes the terminal driver to send the SIGTSTP signal to all processes in the foreground process group. The jobs in any background process groups aren't affected. The terminal driver really looks for three special characters,
which generate signals to the foreground process group:

- the interrupt character (typically DELETE or Control-C) generates SIGINT

- the quit character (typically Control-backslash) generates SIGQUIT

- the suspend character (typically Control-Z) generates SIGTSTP

In Chapter 11 we'll see how we can change these three characters to be any characters
we choose, and how we can disable the terminal driver's processing of these special
characters.

Another condition can arise with job control that must be handled by the terminal driver. Since we can have a foreground job and one or more background jobs, which of these receives the characters that we enter at the terminal? Only the foreground job receives terminal input. It is not an error for a background job to try to read from the terminal, but the terminal driver detects this and sends a special signal to the background job: SIGTTIN. This normally stops the background job, and by using the shell we are notified of this, and we can bring the job into the foreground so that it can read from the terminal. The following demonstrates this.

```
$ cat > temp.foo &              start in background, but it'll read from standard input
[1]    1681
$                               we press RETURN
[1] + Stopped (tty input)       cat > temp.foo &
$ fg %1                         bring job number 1 into the foreground
cat > temp.foo                  the shell tells us which job is now in the foreground
hello, world                    enter one line
^D                              type our end-of-file character
$ cat temp.foo                  check that the one line was put into the file
hello, world
```

The shell starts the cat process in the background, but when cat tries to read its standard input (the controlling terminal), the terminal driver, knowing that it is a background job, sends the SIGTTIN signal to the background job. The shell detects this change in status of its child (recall our discussion of the wait and waitpid function in Section 8.6) and tells us that the job has been stopped. We then move the stopped job into the foreground with the shell's fg command. (Refer to the manual page for the shell that you are using, for all the details on its job control commands, such as fg and bg, and the various ways to identify the different jobs.) Doing this causes the shell to place the job into the foreground process group (tcsetpgrp) and send the continue signal (SIGCONT) to the process group. Since the job is now in the foreground process group it can read from the controlling terminal.

What happens if a background job outputs to the controlling terminal? This is an option that we can allow or disallow. Normally we use the stty(1) command to change this option. (We'll see in Chapter 11 how we can change this option from a program.) The following shows how this works.

```
$ cat temp.foo &                execute in background
[1]    1719
$ hello, world                  the output from the background job appears after the prompt
                                we press RETURN
[1] + Done          cat temp.foo &
$ stty tostop                   disable ability of background jobs to output to controlling terminal
$ cat temp.foo &                try it again in the background
[1]    1721
$                               we press RETURN and find the job is stopped
[1] + Stopped(tty output)       cat temp.foo &
$ fg %1                         resume stopped job in the foreground
cat temp.foo                    the shell tells us which job is now in the foreground
hello, world                    and here is its output
```

Figure 9.8 summarizes some of the features of job control that we've been describing.

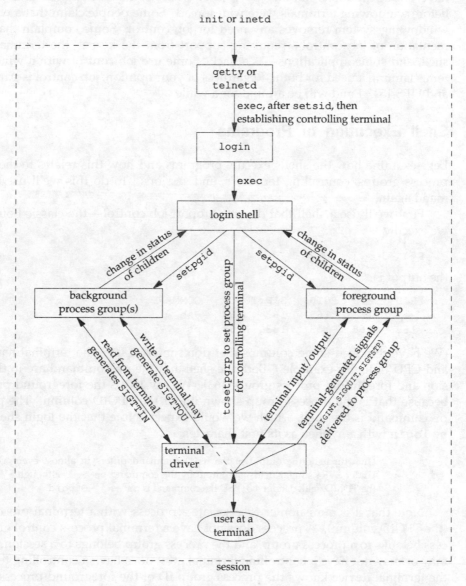

Figure 9.8 Summary of job control features with foreground and background jobs, and terminal driver.

The solid lines through the terminal driver box mean that the terminal I/O and the terminal-generated signals are always connected from the foreground process group to the actual terminal. The dashed line corresponding to the SIGTTOU signal means that whether the output from a process in the background process group appears on the terminal is an option.

Is job control necessary or desirable? This is a controversial topic that some users have strong opinions about. Job control was originally designed and implemented before windowing terminals were widespread. Some people claim that a well-designed windowing system removes any need for job control. Some complain that the implementation of job control—requiring support from the kernel, the terminal driver, the shell, and some applications—is a hack. Some use job control with a windowing system, claiming a need for both. Regardless of your opinion, job control is part of POSIX.1 and FIPS 151-1 and will be around for a while.

9.9 Shell Execution of Programs

Let's examine how the shells execute programs and how this relates to the concepts of process groups, controlling terminals, and sessions. To do this we'll use the ps command again.

First we'll use a shell that doesn't support job control—the classic Bourne shell. If we execute

```
ps -xj
```

the output is

```
PPID   PID  PGID   SID TPGID   COMMAND
   1   163   163   163   163   -sh
 163   168   163   163   163   ps
```

(We have removed some columns that don't interest us—the terminal name, user ID, and CPU time, for example.) Both the shell and the ps command are in the same session and foreground process group (163). We say 163 is the foreground process group because that is the process group shown under the TPGID column. The parent of the ps command is the shell, which we would expect. Note that the login shell is invoked by login with a hyphen as its first character.

> Unfortunately, the output of the ps(1) command differs in almost every version of Unix. Under SVR4 similar fields are output by the command ps -jl, although SVR4 never prints the TPGID field. Under 4.3+BSD the command is ps -xj -Otpgid.

Note that it is a misnomer to associate a process with a terminal process group ID (the TPGID column). A process does not have a terminal process control group. A process belongs to a process group, and the process group belongs to a session. The session may or may not have a controlling terminal. If it does have a controlling terminal, then the terminal device knows the process group ID of the foreground process. This value can be set in the terminal driver with the tcsetpgrp function, as we show in Figure 9.8. The foreground process group ID is an attribute of the terminal, not the process. This value from the terminal device driver is what ps prints as the TPGID. If ps finds that the session doesn't have a controlling terminal, it prints -1.

If we execute the command in the background,

```
ps -xj &
```

the only value that changes is the process ID of the command.

```
PPID  PID  PGID   SID TPGID  COMMAND
   1  163   163   163   163  -sh
 163  169   163   163   163  ps
```

The background job is not put into its own process group, and the controlling terminal isn't taken away from the background job, because this shell doesn't know about job control.

Let's now look at how the Bourne shell handles a pipeline. When we execute

```
ps -xj | cat1
```

the output is

```
PPID  PID  PGID   SID TPGID  COMMAND
   1  163   163   163   163  -sh
 163  200   163   163   163  cat1
 200  201   163   163   163  ps
```

(The program cat1 is just a copy of the standard cat program, with a different name. We have another copy of cat with the name cat2, which we'll use later in this section. When we have two copies of cat in a pipeline, the different names let us differentiate between the two programs.) Note that the last process in the pipeline is the child of the shell, and the first process in the pipeline is a child of the last process. It appears that the shell forks a copy of itself and this copy then forks to make each of the previous processes in the pipeline.

If we execute the pipeline in the background

```
ps -xj | cat1 &
```

only the process IDs change. Since the shell doesn't handle job control, the process group ID of the background processes remains 163, as does the terminal process group ID.

What happens in this case if a background process tries to read from its controlling terminal? For example if we execute

```
cat > temp.foo &
```

With job control this is handled by placing the background job into a background process group, which causes the signal SIGTTIN to be generated if the background job tries to read from the controlling terminal. The way this is handled without job control is that the shell automatically redirects the standard input of a background process to /dev/null, if the process doesn't redirect standard input itself. A read from /dev/null generates an end of file. This means that our background cat process immediately reads an end of file and terminates normally.

The previous paragraph adequately handles the case of a background process accessing the controlling terminal through its standard input, but what happens if a background process specifically opens /dev/tty and reads from the controlling terminal? The answer is "it depends," but it's probably not what we want. For example,

```
crypt < salaries | lpr &
```

is such a pipeline. We run it in the background, but the crypt program opens
/dev/tty, changes the terminal characteristics (to disable echoing), reads from the device, and resets the terminal characteristics. When we execute this background pipeline,
the prompt Password: from crypt is printed on the terminal, but what we enter (the
encryption password) is read by the shell and the shell tries to execute a command of
that name. The next line we enter to the shell is taken as the password, and the file is
not encrypted correctly, sending junk to the printer. Here we have two processes trying
to read from the same device at the same time, and the result depends on the system.
Job control, as we described earlier, handles this multiplexing of a single terminal
between multiple processes in a better fashion.

Returning to our Bourne shell example, executing three processes in the pipeline

```
ps -xj | cat1 | cat2
```

lets us examine the process control employed by this shell.

```
PPID    PID   PGID   SID  TPGID   COMMAND
   1    163    163   163    163   -sh
 163    202    163   163    163   cat2
 202    203    163   163    163   ps
 202    204    163   163    163   cat1
```

Again, the last process in the pipeline is the child of the shell, and all previous processes
in the pipeline are children of the last process. Figure 9.9 shows what is happening.

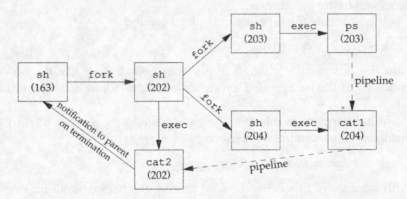

Figure 9.9 Processes in the pipeline "ps -xj | cat1 | cat2" when invoked by Bourne shell.

Since the last process in the pipeline is the child of the login shell, when that process
(cat2) terminates, the shell is notified.

Now let's examine the same examples using a job-control shell. This shows the way
these shells handle background jobs. We'll use the KornShell in this example—the C
shell results are almost identical.

```
ps -xj
```

gives us

```
PPID  PID  PGID   SID TPGID   COMMAND
   1  700  700    700   708   -ksh
 700  708  708    700   708   ps
```

(Starting with this example we show the foreground process group in a **bolder font**.) We immediately have a difference from our Bourne shell example. The KornShell places the foreground job (ps) into its own process group (708). The ps command is the process group leader and the only process in this process group. Furthermore this process group is the foreground process group since it has the controlling terminal. Our login shell is a background process group while the ps command executes. Note, however, that both process groups, 700 and 708, are members of the same session. Indeed, we'll see that the session never changes through our examples in this section.

Executing this process in the background

```
ps -xj &
```

gives us

```
PPID  PID  PGID   SID TPGID   COMMAND
   1  700  700    700   700   -ksh
 700  709  709    700   700   ps
```

Again, the ps command is placed into its own process group but this time the process group (709) is no longer the foreground process group. It is a background process group. The TPGID of 700 indicates that the foreground process group is our login shell.

Executing two processes in a pipeline, as in

```
ps -xj | cat1
```

gives us

```
PPID  PID  PGID   SID TPGID   COMMAND
   1  700  700    700   710   -ksh
 700  710  710    700   710   ps
 700  711  710    700   710   cat1
```

Both processes, ps and cat1, are placed into a new process group (710), and this is the foreground process group. We can also see another difference between this example and the similar Bourne shell example. The Bourne.shell created the last process in the pipeline first, and this final process was the parent of the first process. Here the Korn-Shell is the parent of both processes. But if we execute this pipeline in the background

```
ps -xj | cat1 &
```

the results show that now the KornShell generates the processes in the same fashion as the Bourne shell.

```
PPID  PID  PGID   SID TPGID   COMMAND
   1  700  700    700   700   -ksh
 700  712  712    700   700   cat1
 712  713  712    700   700   ps
```

Both processes, 712 and 713, are placed into a background process group, 712.

9.10 Orphaned Process Groups

We've talked about the fact that a process whose parent terminates is called an orphan and is inherited by the init process. We now look at entire process groups that can be orphaned and how POSIX.1 handles this.

Example

Consider a process that forks a child and then terminates. While this is nothing abnormal (it happens all the time), what happens if the child is stopped (using job control) when the parent terminates? How will the child ever be continued, and does the child know that it has been orphaned? Program 9.1 shows a specific example. There are some new features in this program that we describe below. Figure 9.10 shows the status after Program 9.1 has been started and the parent has forked the child.

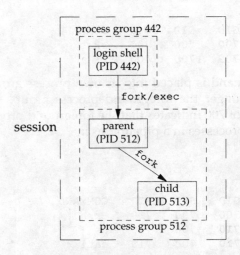

Figure 9.10 Example of a process group about to be orphaned.

Here we are assuming a job-control shell. Recall from the previous section that the shell places the foreground process into its own process group (512 in this example) and the shell stays in its own process group (442). The child inherits the process group of its parent (512). After the fork,

- The parent sleeps for 5 seconds. This is our (imperfect) way of letting the child execute before the parent terminates.

- The child establishes a signal handler for the hang-up signal (SIGHUP). This is so we can see if SIGHUP is sent to the child. (We discuss signal handlers in Chapter 10.)

- The child sends itself the stop signal (SIGTSTP) with the kill function. This stops the child, similar to our stopping a foreground job with our terminal's suspend character (Control-Z).

```
#include        <sys/types.h>
#include        <errno.h>
#include        <fcntl.h>
#include        <signal.h>
#include        "ourhdr.h"

static void sig_hup(int);
static void pr_ids(char *);

int
main(void)
{
    char    c;
    pid_t   pid;

    pr_ids("parent");
    if ( (pid = fork()) < 0)
        err_sys("fork error");

    else if (pid > 0) { /* parent */
        sleep(5);           /* sleep to let child stop itself */
        exit(0);            /* then parent exits */

    } else {                /* child */
        pr_ids("child");
        signal(SIGHUP, sig_hup);    /* establish signal handler */
        kill(getpid(), SIGTSTP);    /* stop ourself */
        pr_ids("child");    /* this prints only if we're continued */
        if (read(0, &c, 1) != 1)
            printf("read error from control terminal, errno = %d\n", errno);
        exit(0);
    }
}

static void
sig_hup(int signo)
{
    printf("SIGHUP received, pid = %d\n", getpid());
    return;
}

static void
pr_ids(char *name)
{
    printf("%s: pid = %d, ppid = %d, pgrp = %d\n",
            name, getpid(), getppid(), getpgrp());
    fflush(stdout);
}
```

Program 9.1 Creating an orphaned process group.

- When the parent terminates, the child is orphaned, so the child's parent process ID becomes 1, the `init` process ID.

- At this point the child is now a member of an *orphaned process group*. The POSIX.1 definition of an orphaned process group is one in which the parent of every member is either itself a member of the group or is not a member of the group's session. Another way of wording this is that the process group is not orphaned as long as there is a process in the group that has a parent in a different process group but in the same session. If the process group is not orphaned, there is a chance that one of those parents in a different process group but in the same session will restart a stopped process in the process group that is not orphaned.

  Here the parent of every process in the group (e.g., process 1 is the parent of process 513) belongs to another session.

- Since the process group is orphaned when the parent terminates, POSIX.1 requires that every process in the newly orphaned process group that is stopped (as our child is) be sent the hang-up signal (`SIGHUP`) followed by the continue signal (`SIGCONT`).

- This causes the child to be continued, after processing the hang-up signal. The default action for the hang-up signal is to terminate the process, which is why we have to provide a signal handler to catch the signal. We therefore expect the `printf` in the `sig_hup` function to appear before the `printf` in the `pr_ids` function.

Here is the output from Program 9.1.

```
$ a.out
parent: pid = 512, ppid = 442, pgrp = 512
child: pid = 513, ppid = 512, pgrp = 512
$ SIGHUP received, pid = 513
child: pid = 513, ppid = 1, pgrp = 512
read error from control terminal, errno = 5
```

Note that our shell prompt appears with the output from the child, since two processes, our login shell and the child, are writing to the terminal. As we expect, the parent process ID of the child has become 1.

Note that after calling `pr_ids` in the child, the program tries to read from standard input. As we saw earlier in this chapter, when a background process group tries to read from its controlling terminal, `SIGTTIN` is generated for the background process group. But here we have an orphaned process group—if the kernel were to stop it with this signal, the processes in the process group would probably never be continued. POSIX.1 specifies that the `read` is to return an error with `errno` set to `EIO` (whose value is 5 on this system).

Finally, notice that our child becomes a background process group when the parent terminates, since the parent was executed as a foreground job by the shell.   □

We'll see another example of orphaned process groups in Section 19.5 with the `pty` program.

9.11   4.3+BSD Implementation

Having talked about the various attributes of a process, process group, session, and controlling terminal, it's worth looking at how all of this can be implemented. We'll look briefly at the implementation used by 4.3+BSD. Some details of the SVR4 implementation of these features can be found in Williams [1989]. Figure 9.11 shows the various data structures used by 4.3+BSD.

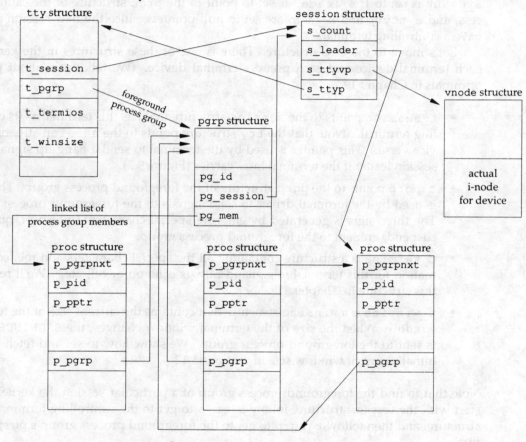

Figure 9.11   4.3+BSD implementation of sessions and process groups.

Let's look at all the fields that we've labeled. We'll start with the `session` structure. One of these structures is allocated for each session (e.g., each time `setsid` is called).

- `s_count` is the number of process groups in the session. When this counter is decremented to 0, the structure can be freed.

- `s_leader` is a pointer to the `proc` structure of the session leader. As we mentioned earlier, 4.3+BSD doesn't keep a session ID field, as SVR4 does.

- `s_ttyvp` is a pointer to the `vnode` structure of the controlling terminal.

- `s_ttyp` is a pointer to the `tty` structure of the controlling terminal.

When `setsid` is called, a new `session` structure is allocated within the kernel. `s_count` is set to 1, `s_leader` is set to point to the `proc` structure of the calling process, and `s_ttyvp` and `s_ttyp` are set to null pointers, since the new session doesn't have a controlling terminal.

Let's move to the `tty` structure. There is one of these structures in the kernel for each terminal device and each pseudo-terminal device. (We talk more about pseudo terminals in Chapter 19.)

- `t_session` points to the `session` structure that has this terminal as its controlling terminal. (Note that the `tty` structure points to the `session` structure and vice versa.) This pointer is used by the terminal to send a hang-up signal to the session leader if the terminal loses carrier (Figure 9.7).

- `t_pgrp` points to the `pgrp` structure of the foreground process group. This field is used by the terminal driver to send signals to the foreground process group. The three signals generated by entering special characters (interrupt, quit, and suspend) are sent to the foreground process group.

- `t_termios` is a structure containing all the special characters and related information for this terminal (e.g., baud rate, is echo on or off, etc.). We'll return to this structure in Chapter 11.

- `t_winsize` is a `winsize` structure that contains the current size of the terminal window. When the size of the terminal window changes, the `SIGWINCH` signal is sent to the foreground process group. We show how to set and fetch the terminal's current window size in Section 11.12.

Note that to find the foreground process group of a particular session the kernel has to start with the session structure, follow `s_ttyp` to get to the controlling terminal's `tty` structure, and then follow `t_pgrp` to get to the foreground process group's `pgrp` structure.

The `pgrp` structure contains the information for a particular process group.

- `pg_id` is the process group ID.

- `pg_session` points to the `session` structure that this process group belongs to.

- `pg_mem` is a pointer to the `proc` structure of the first process that is a member of this process group. The `p_pgrpnxt` in that `proc` structure points to the next process in the group, and so on, until a null pointer is encountered in the `proc` structure of the last process in the group.

The proc structure contains all the information for a single process.

- p_pid contains the process ID.
- p_pptr is a pointer to the proc structure of the parent process.
- p_pgrp points to the pgrp structure of the process group that this process belongs to.
- p_pgrpnxt is a pointer to the next process in the process group, as we mentioned earlier.

Finally we have the vnode structure. This structure is allocated when the controlling terminal device is opened. All references to /dev/tty in a process go through this vnode structure. We show the actual i-node as being part of the v-node. In Section 3.10 we said that this is the implementation used by 4.3+BSD, while SVR4 stores the v-node in the i-node.

9.12 Summary

This chapter has described the relationships between groups of processes—sessions, which are made up of process groups. Job control is a feature supported by many Unix systems today, and we've described how it's implemented by a shell that supports job control. The controlling terminal for a process, /dev/tty, is also involved in these process relationships.

We've made numerous references to the signals that are used in all these process relationships. The next chapter continues the discussion of signals, looking at all the Unix signals in detail.

Exercises

9.1 Refer back to our discussion of the utmp and wtmp files in Section 6.7. Why are the logout records written by the 4.3+BSD init process? Is this handled the same way for a network login?

9.2 Write a small program that calls fork and has the child create a new session. Verify that the child becomes a process group leader, and that the child no longer has a controlling terminal.

10

Signals

10.1 Introduction

Signals are software interrupts. Most nontrivial application programs need to deal with signals. Signals provide a way of handling asynchronous events: a user at a terminal typing the interrupt key to stop a program or the next program in a pipeline terminating prematurely.

Signals have been provided since the early versions of Unix, but the signal model provided with systems such as Version 7 was not reliable. Signals could get lost and it was hard for a process to turn off selected signals when executing critical regions of code. Both 4.3BSD and SVR3 made changes to the signal model, adding what are called *reliable signals*. But the changes made by Berkeley and AT&T were incompatible. Fortunately POSIX.1 standardizes the reliable signal routines, and that is what we describe in this chapter.

In this chapter we start with an overview of signals and a description of what each signal is normally used for. Then we look at the problems with earlier implementations. It is often important to understand what is wrong with an implementation, before seeing how to do things correctly. This chapter contains numerous examples that are not 100% correct and a discussion of the defects.

10.2 Signal Concepts

First, every signal has a name. These names all begin with the three characters SIG. For example, SIGABRT is the abort signal that is generated when a process calls the abort function. SIGALRM is the alarm signal that is generated when the timer set by the alarm function goes off. Version 7 had 15 different signals; SVR4 and 4.3+BSD both have 31 different signals.

These names are all defined by positive integer constants (the signal number) in the header <signal.h>. No signal has a signal number of 0. We'll see in Section 10.9 that the kill function uses the signal number of 0 for a special case. POSIX.1 calls this value the null signal.

Numerous conditions can generate a signal.

- The terminal-generated signals occur when users press certain terminal keys. Pressing the DELETE key on the terminal normally causes the interrupt signal to be generated (SIGINT). This is how to stop a runaway program. (We'll see in Chapter 11 how this signal can be mapped to any character on the terminal.)

- Hardware exceptions generate signals: divide by 0, invalid memory reference, and the like. These conditions are usually detected by the hardware, and the kernel is notified. The kernel then generates the appropriate signal for the process that was running at the time the condition occurred. For example, SIGSEGV is generated for a process that executes an invalid memory reference.

- The kill(2) function allows a process to send any signal to another process or process group. Naturally there are limitations: we have to be the owner of the process that we're sending the signal to, or we have to be the superuser.

- The kill(1) command allows us to send signals to other processes. This program is just an interface to the kill function. This command is often used to terminate a runaway background process.

- Software conditions can generate signals when something happens that the process should be made aware of. These aren't hardware-generated conditions (as is the divide-by-0 condition) but software conditions. Examples are SIGURG (generated when out-of-band data arrives over a network connection), SIGPIPE (generated when a process writes to a pipe after the reader of the pipe has terminated), and SIGALRM (generated when an alarm clock set by the process expires).

Signals are classic examples of asynchronous events. They occur at what appear to be random times to the process. The process can't just test a variable (such as errno) to see if a signal has occurred, instead the process has to tell the kernel "if and when this signal occurs, do the following."

There are three different things that we can tell the kernel to do when a signal occurs. We call this the *disposition* of the signal or the *action* associated with a signal.

1. Ignore the signal. This works for most signals, but there are two signals that can never be ignored: SIGKILL and SIGSTOP. The reason these two signals can't be ignored is to provide the superuser with a surefire way of either killing or stopping any process. Also, if we ignore some of the signals that are generated by a hardware exception (such as illegal memory reference or divide-by-0) the behavior of the process is undefined.

2. Catch the signal. To do this we tell the kernel to call a function of ours when-
    ever the signal occurs. In our function we can do whatever we want to handle
    the condition. If we're writing a command interpreter, for example, when the
    user generates the interrupt signal at the keyboard, we probably want to return
    to the main loop of the program, terminating whatever command we were exe-
    cuting for the user. If the SIGCHLD signal is caught, it means a child process has
    terminated, so the signal-catching function can call waitpid to fetch the pro-
    cess ID of the child and its termination status. As another example, if the pro-
    cess has created temporary files we may want to write a signal-catching
    function for SIGTERM signal (the termination signal that is the default signal
    sent by the kill command) to clean up the temporary files.

3. Let the default action apply. Every signal has a default action, shown in
    Figure 10.1. Notice that the default action for most signals is to terminate the
    process.

Figure 10.1 lists the names of all the signals and an indication of which systems support
the signal and the default action for the signal. The POSIX.1 column contains • if the
signal is required, or "job" if the signal is a job-control signal (which is required only if
job control is supported).

When the default action is labeled "terminate w/core" it means that a memory
image of the process is left in the file named core of the current working directory of
the process. (The fact that the file is named core shows how long this feature has been
part of Unix.) This file can be used with most Unix debuggers to examine the state of
the process at the time it terminated. The file will not be generated if (a) the process was
set-user-ID and the current user is not the owner of the program file, or (b) the process
was set-group-ID and the current user is not the group owner of the file, (c) the user
does not have permission to write in the current working directory, or (d) the file is too
big (recall the RLIMIT_CORE limit in Section 7.11). The permissions of the core file
(assuming the file doesn't already exist) are usually user-read, user-write, group-read,
and other-read.

> The generation of the core file is an implementation feature of most versions of Unix. It is not
> part of POSIX.1.
>
> Unix Version 6 didn't check for conditions (a) and (b) and the source code contained the com-
> ment "If you are looking for protection glitches, there are probably a wealth of them here when
> this occurs to a set-user-ID command."
>
> 4.3+BSD now generates a file with the name core.*prog*, where *prog* is the first 16 characters of
> the program name that was executed. This is a nice feature as it gives some identity to the core
> file.

The signals in Figure 10.1 with a description "hardware fault" correspond to implementation-defined hardware faults. Many of these names are taken from the original
PDP-11 implementation of Unix. Check your system's manuals to determine exactly
what type of error these signals correspond to.

Name	Description	ANSI C	POSIX.1	SVR4	4.3+BSD	Default action
SIGABRT	abnormal termination (abort)	•	•	•	•	terminate w/core
SIGALRM	time out (alarm)		•	•	•	terminate
SIGBUS	hardware fault			•	•	terminate w/core
SIGCHLD	change in status of child		job	•	•	ignore
SIGCONT	continue stopped process		job	•	•	continue/ignore
SIGEMT	hardware fault			•	•	terminate w/core
SIGFPE	arithmetic exception	•	•	•	•	terminate w/core
SIGHUP	hangup		•	•	•	terminate
SIGILL	illegal hardware instruction	•	•	•	•	terminate w/core
SIGINFO	status request from keyboard				•	ignore
SIGINT	terminal interrupt character	•	•	•	•	terminate
SIGIO	asynchronous I/O			•	•	terminate/ignore
SIGIOT	hardware fault			•	•	terminate w/core
SIGKILL	termination		•	•	•	terminate
SIGPIPE	write to pipe with no readers		•	•	•	terminate
SIGPOLL	pollable event (poll)			•		terminate
SIGPROF	profiling time alarm (setitimer)			•	•	terminate
SIGPWR	power fail/restart			•		ignore
SIGQUIT	terminal quit character		•	•	•	terminate w/core
SIGSEGV	invalid memory reference	•	•	•	•	terminate w/core
SIGSTOP	stop		job	•	•	stop process
SIGSYS	invalid system call			•	•	terminate w/core
SIGTERM	termination	•	•	•	•	terminate
SIGTRAP	hardware fault			•	•	terminate w/core
SIGTSTP	terminal stop character		job	•	•	stop process
SIGTTIN	background read from control tty		job	•	•	stop process
SIGTTOU	background write to control tty		job	•	•	stop process
SIGURG	urgent condition			•	•	ignore
SIGUSR1	user-defined signal		•	•	•	terminate
SIGUSR2	user-defined signal		•	•	•	terminate
SIGVTALRM	virtual time alarm (setitimer)			•	•	terminate
SIGWINCH	terminal window size change			•	•	ignore
SIGXCPU	CPU limit exceeded (setrlimit)			•	•	terminate w/core
SIGXFSZ	file size limit exceeded (setrlimit)			•	•	terminate w/core

Figure 10.1 Unix signals.

We'll now describe each of these signals in more detail.

SIGABRT   This signal is generated by calling the abort function (Section 10.17). The process terminates abnormally.

SIGALRM   This signal is generated when a timer that we've set with the alarm function expires. See Section 10.10 for more details.

This signal is also generated when an interval timer set by the setitimer(2) function expires.

SIGBUS   This indicates an implementation-defined hardware fault.

SIGCHLD   Whenever a process terminates or stops, the SIGCHLD signal is sent to the parent. By default this signal is ignored, so the parent must catch this signal if it wants to be notified whenever a child's status changes. The normal action in the signal-catching function is to call one of the wait functions to fetch the child's process ID and termination status.

Earlier releases of System V had a similar signal named SIGCLD (without the H). This signal had nonstandard semantics, and as far back as SVR2 the manual page warned that its use in new programs was strongly discouraged. Applications should use the standard SIGCHLD signal. We discuss these two signals in Section 10.7.

SIGCONT   This job-control signal is sent to a stopped process when it is continued. If the process was stopped the default action is to continue the process, otherwise the default action is to ignore the signal. The vi editor, for example, catches this signal and redraws the terminal screen. Refer to Section 10.20 for additional details.

SIGEMT   This indicates an implementation-defined hardware fault.

> The name EMT comes from the PDP-11 "emulator trap" instruction.

SIGFPE   This signals an arithmetic exception, such as divide-by-0, floating point overflow, and so on.

SIGHUP   This signal is sent to the controlling process (session leader) associated with a controlling terminal if a disconnect is detected by the terminal interface. Referring to Figure 9.11 the signal is sent to the process pointed to by the s_leader field in the session structure. This signal is generated for this condition only if the terminal's CLOCAL flag is not set. (The CLOCAL flag for a terminal is set if the attached terminal is local. It tells the terminal driver to ignore all modem status lines. We describe how to set this flag in Chapter 11.) Note that the session leader that receives this signal may be in the background; see Figure 9.7 for an example. This differs from the normal terminal-generated signals (interrupt, quit, and suspend) that are always delivered to the foreground process group.

This signal is also generated if the session leader terminates. In this case the signal is sent to each process in the foreground process group.

This signal is commonly used to notify daemon processes (Chapter 13) to reread their configuration files. The reason SIGHUP is chosen for this is because a daemon should not have a controlling terminal and would normally never receive this signal.

SIGILL   This signal indicates that the process has executed an illegal hardware instruction.

> 4.3BSD generated this signal from the abort function. SIGABRT is now used for this.

SIGINFO   This 4.3+BSD signal is generated by the terminal driver when we type the status key (often Control-T). It is sent to all processes in the foreground process group (refer to Figure 9.8). This signal normally causes status information on processes in the foreground process group to be displayed on the terminal.

SIGINT   This signal is generated by the terminal driver when we type the interrupt key (often DELETE or Control-C). It is sent to all processes in the foreground process group (refer to Figure 9.8). This signal is often used to terminate a runaway program, especially when it's generating a lot of output on the screen that we don't want.

SIGIO   This signal indicates an asynchronous I/O event. We discuss it in Section 12.6.2.

> In Figure 10.1 we labeled the default action for SIGIO as either terminate or ignore. Unfortunately the default depends on the system. Under SVR4 SIGIO is identical to SIGPOLL, so its default action is to terminate the process. Under 4.3+BSD (the signal originated with 4.2BSD), the default is to be ignored.

SIGIOT   This indicates an implementation-defined hardware fault.

> The name IOT comes from the PDP-11 mnemonic for the "input/output TRAP" instruction.
>
> Earlier versions of System V generated this signal from the abort function. SIGABRT is now used for this.

SIGKILL   This signal is one of the two that can't be caught or ignored. It provides the system administrator a sure way to kill any process.

SIGPIPE   If we write to a pipeline but the reader has terminated, SIGPIPE is generated. We describe pipes in Section 14.2. This signal is also generated when a process writes to a socket when the other end has terminated.

SIGPOLL   This SVR4 signal can be generated when a specific event occurs on a pollable device. We describe this signal with the poll function in Section 12.5.2. It loosely corresponds to the 4.3+BSD SIGIO and SIGURG signals.

SIGPROF   This signal is generated when a profiling interval timer set by the setitimer(2) function expires.

SIGPWR   This SVR4 signal is system dependent. Its main use is on a system that has an uninterruptible power supply (UPS). If power fails, the UPS takes over and the software can usually be notified. Nothing needs to be done at this point, as the system continues running on battery power. But if the battery gets low (if the power is off for an extended period), the software is usually notified again, and at this point it behooves the system to shut everything down within about 15–30 seconds. This is when SIGPWR should be sent. Most systems have the process that is notified of the low battery condition send the SIGPWR signal to the init process, and init handles the shutdown. Many System V implementations of init provide two entries in the inittab file for this purpose: powerfail and powerwait.

This signal is becoming more important with the availability of low cost UPS systems that can easily notify the computer of a low battery condition with an RS-232 serial connection.

SIGQUIT   This signal is generated by the terminal driver when we type the terminal quit key (often Control-backslash). It is sent to all processes in the foreground process group (refer to Figure 9.8). This signal not only terminates the foreground process group (as does SIGINT), but it generates a core file.

SIGSEGV   This signal indicates that the process has made an invalid memory reference.

The name SEGV stands for "segmentation violation."

SIGSTOP   This job-control signal stops a process. It is like the interactive stop signal (SIGTSTP), but SIGSTOP cannot be caught or ignored.

SIGSYS   This signals an invalid system call. Somehow the process executed a machine instruction that the kernel thought was a system call, but the parameter with the instruction that indicates the type of system call was invalid.

SIGTERM   This is the termination signal sent by the kill(1) command by default.

SIGTRAP   This indicates an implementation-defined hardware fault.

The signal name comes from the PDP-11 TRAP instruction.

SIGTSTP   This interactive stop signal is generated by the terminal driver when we type the terminal suspend key (often Control-Z).† It is sent to all processes in the foreground process group (refer to Figure 9.8).

SIGTTIN   This signal is generated by the terminal driver when a process in a background process group tries to read from its controlling terminal. (Refer to the discussion of this topic in Section 9.8.) As special cases, if either (a) the reading process is ignoring or blocking this signal or (b) the process group of the reading process is orphaned, then the signal is not generated and instead the read operation returns an error with errno set to EIO.

SIGTTOU   This signal is generated by the terminal driver when a process in a background process group tries to write to its controlling terminal. (Refer to

---

† Unfortunately the term *stop* has different meanings. When discussing job control and signals we talk about stopping and continuing jobs. The terminal driver, however, has historically used the term stop to refer to stopping and starting the terminal output using the Control-S and Control-Q characters. Therefore the terminal driver calls the character that generates the interactive stop signal the suspend character, not the stop character.

the discussion of this topic in Section 9.8.) Unlike the SIGTTIN signal just described, a process has a choice of allowing background writes to the controlling terminal. We describe how to change this option in Chapter 11.

If background writes are not allowed, then like the SIGTTIN signal there are two special cases: if either (a) the writing process is ignoring or blocking this signal or (b) the process group of the writing process is orphaned, then the signal is not generated and instead the write operation returns an error with errno set to EIO.

Regardless whether background writes are allowed or not, certain terminal operations (other than writing) can also generate the SIGTTOU signal: tcsetattr, tcsendbreak, tcdrain, tcflush, tcflow, and tcsetpgrp. We describe these terminal operations in Chapter 11.

SIGURG   This signal notifies the process that an urgent condition has occurred. This is optionally generated when out-of-band data is received on a network connection.

SIGUSR1   This is a user-defined signal, for use in application programs.

SIGUSR2   This is a user-defined signal, for use in application programs.

SIGVTALRM   This signal is generated when a virtual interval timer set by the setitimer(2) function expires.

SIGWINCH   The SVR4 and 4.3+BSD kernels maintain the size of the window associated with each terminal and pseudo terminal. A process can get and set the window size with the ioctl function, which we describe in Section 11.12. If a process changes the window size from its previous value, with the ioctl set-window-size command, the kernel generates the SIGWINCH signal for the foreground process group.

SIGXCPU   SVR4 and 4.3+BSD support the concept of resource limits; refer to Section 7.11. If the process exceeds its soft CPU time limit, the SIGXCPU signal is generated.

SIGXFSZ   This signal is generated by SVR4 and 4.3+BSD if the process exceeds its soft file size limit; refer to Section 7.11.

10.3 signal Function

The simplest interface to the signal features of Unix is the signal function.

```
#include <signal.h>

void (*signal(int signo, void (*func)(int)))(int);
```
                    Returns: previous disposition of signal (see following) if OK, SIG_ERR on error

The `signal` function is defined by ANSI C. Since ANSI C doesn't involve multiple processes, process groups, terminal I/O, and the like, its definition of signals is vague enough to be almost useless for Unix systems. Indeed, the ANSI C description of signals takes 2 pages while the POSIX.1 description takes over 15 pages.

SVR4 also provides the `signal` function, but using it causes SVR4 to provide the old SVR2 unreliable signal semantics. (We describe these older semantics in Section 10.4.) This function is provided for backward compatibility for applications that require the older semantics. New applications should not use these unreliable signals.

4.3+BSD also provides the `signal` function, but it is defined in terms of the `sigaction` function (which we describe in Section 10.14), so using it under 4.3+BSD provides the newer reliable signal semantics.

When we describe the `sigaction` function we provide an implementation of `signal` that uses it. All the examples in this text use the `signal` function that we show in Program 10.12.

The *signo* argument is just the name of the signal from Figure 10.1. The value of *func* is either (a) the constant `SIG_IGN`, (b) the constant `SIG_DFL`, or (c) the address of a function to be called when the signal occurs. If we specify `SIG_IGN` we are telling the system to ignore the signal. (Remember that there are two signals, `SIGKILL` and `SIGSTOP`, that we cannot ignore.) By specifying `SIG_DFL` we are setting the action associated with the signal to its default action (see the final column in Figure 10.1). When we specify the address of a function to be called when the signal occurs, we call this "catching" the signal. We call the function either the *signal handler* or the *signal-catching function*.

The prototype for the `signal` function states that the function requires two arguments and returns a pointer to a function that returns nothing (`void`). The first argument, *signo*, is an integer. The second argument is a pointer to a function that takes a single integer argument and returns nothing. The function whose address is returned as the value of `signal` takes a single integer argument (the final (`int`)). In plain English, this declaration says that the signal handler is passed a single integer argument (the signal number) and it returns nothing. When we call `signal` to establish the signal handler, the second argument is a pointer to the function. The return value from `signal` is the pointer to the previous signal handler.

Many systems call the signal handler with additional, implementation-dependent arguments. We mention the optional SVR4 and 4.3+BSD arguments in Section 10.21.

The perplexing prototype shown at the beginning of this section for the `signal` function can be made much simpler through the use of the following `typedef` [Plauger 1992].

```
typedef void    Sigfunc(int);
```

Then the prototype becomes

```
Sigfunc *signal(int, Sigfunc *);
```

We've included this `typedef` in `ourhdr.h` (Appendix B) and use it with the functions in this chapter.

If we examine the system's header `<signal.h>` we probably find declarations of
the form

```
#define SIG_ERR    (void (*)())-1
#define SIG_DFL    (void (*)())0
#define SIG_IGN    (void (*)())1
```

These constants can be used in place of the "pointer to a function that takes an integer
argument and returns nothing," the second argument to `signal`, and the return value
from `signal`. The three values used for these constants need not be −1, 0, and 1. They
must be three values that can never be the address of any declarable function. Most
Unix systems use the values shown.

Example

Program 10.1 shows a simple signal handler that catches either of the two user defined
signals and prints the signal number. We describe the `pause` function in
Section 10.10—it just puts the calling process to sleep.

```
#include    <signal.h>
#include    "ourhdr.h"

static void sig_usr(int);    /* one handler for both signals */

int
main(void)
{
    if (signal(SIGUSR1, sig_usr) == SIG_ERR)
        err_sys("can't catch SIGUSR1");
    if (signal(SIGUSR2, sig_usr) == SIG_ERR)
        err_sys("can't catch SIGUSR2");

    for ( ; ; )
        pause();
}

static void
sig_usr(int signo)         /* argument is signal number */
{
    if (signo == SIGUSR1)
        printf("received SIGUSR1\n");
    else if (signo == SIGUSR2)
        printf("received SIGUSR2\n");
    else
        err_dump("received signal %d\n", signo);
    return;
}
```

Program 10.1 Simple program to catch `SIGUSR1` and `SIGUSR2`.

We invoke the program in the background and use the kill(1) command to send it signals. Note that the term *kill* in Unix is a misnomer. The kill(1) command and the kill(2) function just send a signal to a process or process group. Whether or not that signal terminates the process depends on which signal is sent and whether the process has arranged to catch the signal.

```
$ a.out &                                   start process in background
[1]       4720                               job-control shell prints job number and process ID
$ kill -USR1 4720                            send it SIGUSR1
received SIGUSR1
$ kill -USR2 4720                            send it SIGUSR2
received SIGUSR2
$ kill 4720                                  now send it SIGTERM
[1] + Terminated        a.out &
```

When we send the SIGTERM signal the process is terminated, since it doesn't catch the signal and the default action for the signal is termination.   □

Program Start-up

When a program is execed the status of all signals is either default or ignore. Normally all signals are set to their default action, unless the process that calls exec is ignoring the signal. Specifically, the exec functions change the disposition of any signals that are being caught to their default action and leave the status of all other signals alone. (Naturally a signal that is being caught by a process that calls exec cannot be caught in the new program, since the address of the signal-catching function in the caller probably has no meaning in the new program file that is execed.)

One specific example that we encounter daily (but may not be cognizant of) is how an interactive shell treats the interrupt and quit signals for a background process. With a non-job-control shell, when we execute a process in the background, as in

```
cc main.c &
```

the shell automatically sets the disposition of the interrupt and quit signals in the background process to be ignored. This is so that if we type the interrupt character it doesn't affect the background process. If this weren't done; and we typed the interrupt character, not only would it terminate the foreground process, but it would also terminate all the background processes.

Many interactive programs that catch these two signals have code that looks like

```
int   sig_int(), sig_quit();

if (signal(SIGINT, SIG_IGN) != SIG_IGN)
    signal(SIGINT, sig_int);
if (signal(SIGQUIT, SIG_IGN) != SIG_IGN)
    signal(SIGQUIT, sig_quit);
```

Doing this, the process catches the signal only if the signal is not currently being ignored.

These two calls to `signal` also show a limitation of the `signal` function: we are not able to determine the current disposition of a signal without changing the disposition. We'll see later in this chapter how the `sigaction` function allows us to determine a signal's disposition without changing it.

Process Creation

When a process calls `fork` the child inherits the parent's signal dispositions. Here, since the child starts off with a copy of the parent's memory image, the address of a signal-catching function has meaning in the child.

10.4 Unreliable Signals

In earlier versions of Unix (such as Version 7), signals were unreliable. By this we mean that signals could get lost—a signal could occur and the process would never know about it. Also, a process had little control over a signal—it could catch the signal or ignore it. Sometimes we would like to tell the kernel to block a signal—don't ignore it, just remember if it occurs, and tell us later when we're ready.

> Changes were made with 4.2BSD to provide what are called *reliable signals*. A different set of changes was then made in SVR3 to provide reliable signals under System V. POSIX.1 chose the BSD model to standardize.

One problem with these early versions is that the action for a signal was reset to its default each time the signal occurred. (In the previous example, when we ran Program 10.1, we avoided this detail by catching each signal only once.) The classic example from many programming books that described these earlier systems concerns how to handle the interrupt signal. The code that was described usually looked like

```
int     sig_int();          /* my signal handling function */

...
signal(SIGINT, sig_int); /* establish handler */
...

sig_int()
{
signal(SIGINT, sig_int);
                /* reestablish handler for next occurrence */

...                         /* process the signal ... */
}
```

(The reason the signal handler is declared as returning an integer is that these early systems didn't support the ANSI C `void` data type.)

The problem with this code fragment is that there is a window of time after the signal has occurred, but before the call to `signal` in the signal handler, when the interrupt signal could occur another time. This second signal would cause the default action to occur, which for this signal terminates the process. This is one of those conditions that works correctly most of the time, causing us to think that it is correct, when it isn't.

Another problem with these earlier systems is that the process was unable to turn a signal off when it didn't want the signal to occur. All the process could do was ignore the signal. There are times when we would like to tell the system "prevent the following signals from occurring, but remember if they do occur." The classic example that demonstrates this flaw is shown by a piece of code that catches a signal and sets a flag for the process that indicates that the signal occurred.

```
int    sig_int_flag;            /* set nonzero when signal occurs */

main()
{
    int    sig_int();           /* my signal handling function */
    ...
    signal(SIGINT, sig_int); /* establish handler */
    ...
    while (sig_int_flag == 0)
        pause();                /* go to sleep, waiting for signal */
    ...
}

sig_int()
{
    signal(SIGINT, sig_int); /* reestablish handler for next time */
    sig_int_flag = 1;           /* set flag for main loop to examine */
}
```

Here the process is calling the pause function to put it to sleep, until a signal is caught. When the signal is caught, the signal handler just sets the flag sig_int_flag nonzero. The process is automatically woken up by the kernel after the signal handler returns, notices the flag is nonzero, and does whatever it needs to do. But there is a window of time when things can go wrong. If the signal occurs after the test of sig_int_flag, but before the call to pause, the process could go to sleep forever (assuming the signal is never generated again). This occurrence of the signal is lost. This is another example of some code that isn't right, yet it works most of the time. Debugging this type of problem can be hard.

10.5 Interrupted System Calls

A characteristic of earlier Unix systems is that if a process caught a signal while the process was blocked in a "slow" system call, the system call was interrupted. The system call returned an error and errno was set to EINTR. This was done under the assumption that since a signal occurred and the process caught it, there is a good chance that something has happened that should wake up the blocked system call.

Here we have to differentiate between a system call and a function. It is a system call within the kernel that is interrupted when some signal is caught.

To support this feature all the system calls are divided into two categories: the "slow" system calls, and all the others. The slow system calls are those that can block forever. Included in this category are

- reads from files that can block the caller forever if data isn't present (pipes, terminal devices, and network devices),

- writes to these same files that can block the caller forever if the data can't be accepted immediately,

- opens of files that block until some condition occurs (such as an open of a terminal device that waits until an attached modem answers the phone),

- pause (which by definition puts the calling process to sleep until a signal is caught) and wait,

- certain ioctl operations,

- some of the interprocess communication functions (Chapter 14).

The notable exception to these slow system calls is anything related to disk I/O. Although the read or a write of a disk file can block the caller temporarily (while the disk driver queues the request and then the request is executed), unless a hardware error occurs, the I/O operation always returns and unblocks the caller quickly.

One condition that is handled by interrupted system calls, for example, is when a process initiates a read from a terminal device and the user at the terminal walks away from the terminal for an extended period. In this example the process could be blocked for hours or days and would remain so unless the system was taken down.

The problem with interrupted system calls is that we now have to handle the error return explicitly. The typical code sequence (assuming a read operation and assuming we want to restart the read even if it's interrupted) would be

```
again:
    if ( (n = read(fd, buff, BUFFSIZE)) < 0) {
        if (errno == EINTR)
            goto again;      /* just an interrupted system call */
        /* handle other errors */
    }
```

To prevent the applications from having to handle interrupted system calls 4.2BSD introduced the automatic restarting of certain interrupted system calls. The system calls that were automatically restarted are ioctl, read, readv, write, writev, wait, and waitpid. As we've mentioned, the first five of these functions are interrupted by a signal only if they are operating on a slow device. wait and waitpid are always interrupted when a signal is caught. Since this caused a problem for some applications that didn't want the operation restarted if it was interrupted, 4.3BSD allowed the process to disable this feature on a per-signal basis.

POSIX.1 allows an implementation to restart system calls, but it is not required.

System V has never restarted system calls by default. But when `sigaction` is used with SVR4 (Section 10.14), the `SA_RESTART` option can be specified to restart system calls that are interrupted by that signal.

With 4.3+BSD the automatic restarting of system calls depends on which function is called to set the signal's disposition. The older, 4.3BSD-compatible `sigvec` function, causes system calls interrupted by that signal to be restarted automatically. But using the newer, POSIX.1-compatible `sigaction` causes them not to be restarted. As with SVR4, however, the `SA_RESTART` option can be used with `sigaction` to have the kernel restart system calls interrupted by that signal.

One of the reasons 4.2BSD introduced the automatic restart feature is because sometimes we don't know that the input or output device is a slow device. If the program we write can be used interactively, then it might be reading or writing a slow device, since terminals fall into this category. If we catch signals in this program, and if the system doesn't provide the restart capability, then we have to test every read or write for the interrupted error return and reissue the read or write.

Figure 10.2 summarizes the different signal functions and their semantics provided by the different implementations.

Functions	System	Signal handler remains installed	Ability to block signals	Automatic restart of interrupted system calls?
`signal`	V7, SVR2, SVR3, SVR4			never
`sigset, sighold, sigrelse sigignore, sigpause`	SVR3, SVR4	•	•	never
`signal, sigvec, sigblock`	4.2BSD	•	•	always
`sigsetmask, sigpause`	4.3BSD, 4.3+BSD	•	•	default
`sigaction, sigprocmask sigpending, sigsuspend`	POSIX.1	•	•	unspecified
	SVR4	•	•	optional
	4.3+BSD	•	•	optional

Figure 10.2 Features provided by different signal implementations.

Be aware that Unix systems from other vendors can have values different from those shown in this figure. For example, `sigaction` under SunOS 4.1.2 restarts an interrupted system call by default, different from both SVR4 and 4.3+BSD.

In Program 10.12 we provide our own version of the `signal` function that automatically tries to restart interrupted system calls (other than for the `SIGALRM` signal). In Program 10.13 we provide another function, `signal_intr`, that tries to never do the restart.

In all our code examples, we purposely show the `return` from a signal handler (if it returns) to remind ourselves that the return may interrupt a system call.

We talk more about interrupted system calls in Section 12.5 with regard to the `select` and `poll` functions.

10.6 Reentrant Functions

When a signal that is being caught is handled by a process, the normal sequence of instructions being executed by the process are temporarily interrupted by the signal handler. The process then continues executing, but the instructions in the signal handler are now executed. If the signal handler returns (instead of calling exit or longjmp, for example) then the normal sequence of instructions that the process was executing when the signal was caught continues executing. (This is similar to what happens when a hardware interrupt occurs.) But in the signal handler we can't tell where the process was executing when the signal was caught. What if the process was in the middle of allocating additional memory on its heap using malloc, and we call malloc from the signal handler? Or, what if the process was in the middle of a call to a function such as getpwnam (Section 6.2) that stores its result in a static location, and we call the same function from the signal handler? In the malloc example, havoc can result for the process, since malloc usually maintains a linked list of all its allocated areas, and it may have been in the middle of changing this list. In the case of getpwnam the information returned to the normal caller can get overwritten with the information returned to the signal handler.

POSIX.1 specifies the functions that are guaranteed to be reentrant. Figure 10.3 lists these reentrant functions. The four functions marked with an asterisk in this figure are not specified as being reentrant by POSIX.1, but are listed in the SVR4 SVID [AT&T 1989] as being reentrant.

_exit	fork	pipe	stat
abort*	fstat	read	sysconf
access	getegid	rename	tcdrain
alarm	geteuid	rmdir	tcflow
cfgetispeed	getgid	setgid	tcflush
cfgetospeed	getgroups	setpgid	tcgetattr
cfsetispeed	getpgrp	setsid	tcgetpgrp
cfsetospeed	getpid	setuid	tcsendbreak
chdir	getppid	sigaction	tcsetattr
chmod	getuid	sigaddset	tcsetpgrp
chown	kill	sigdelset	time
close	link	sigemptyset	times
creat	longjmp*	sigfillset	umask
dup	lseek	sigismember	uname
dup2	mkdir	signal*	unlink
execle	mkfifo	sigpending	utime
execve	open	sigprocmask	wait
exit*	pathconf	sigsuspend	waitpid
fcntl	pause	sleep	write

Figure 10.3 Reentrant functions that may be called from a signal handler.

Most functions that are not in Figure 10.3 are missing because (a) they are known to use static data structures, (b) they call malloc or free, or (c) they are part of the standard I/O library. Most implementations of the standard I/O library use global data structures in a nonreentrant way.

Be aware that even if we call a function listed in Figure 10.3 from a signal handler, there is only one errno variable per process, and we might modify its value. Consider a signal handler that is invoked right after main has set errno. If the signal handler calls read, for example, this call can change the value of errno, wiping out the value that was just stored in main. Therefore, as a general rule, when calling the functions listed in Figure 10.3 from a signal handler, we should save and restore errno. (Be aware that a commonly caught signal is SIGCHLD and its signal handler usually calls one of the wait functions. All the wait functions can change errno.)

POSIX.1 does not include longjmp and siglongjmp in Figure 10.3. (We describe the latter function in Section 10.15.) This is because the signal may have occurred while the main routine was updating a data structure in a nonreentrant way. Not returning from the signal handler, but calling siglongjmp instead, could leave this data structure half updated. If the application is going to do things such as update global data structures as we describe here, while catching signals that cause sigsetjmp to be executed, then we need to block the signal while we're updating the data structure.

Example

Program 10.2 calls the nonreentrant function getpwnam from a signal handler that is called every second. We describe the alarm function in Section 10.10. We use it here to generate a SIGALRM every second.

When this program was run the results were random. Usually the program would be terminated by a SIGSEGV signal when the signal handler returned the first time. An examination of the core file showed that the main function had called getpwnam, but some internal pointers had been corrupted when the signal handler called the same function. Occasionally the program would run for several seconds before crashing with a SIGSEGV error. When the main function did run correctly after the signal had been caught, sometimes the return value was corrupted and sometimes it was fine. Once the call to getpwnam from the signal handler returned an error of EBADF (invalid file descriptor).

As shown by this example, if we call a nonreentrant function from a signal handler, the results are unpredictable.   □

10.7 SIGCLD Semantics

Two signals that continually generate confusion are SIGCLD and SIGCHLD. First, SIGCLD (without the H) is the System V name, and this signal has different semantics from the BSD signal, named SIGCHLD. The POSIX.1 signal is also named SIGCHLD.

The semantics of the BSD SIGCHLD signal are normal, in that its semantics are similar to all other signals. When the signal occurs, the status of a child has changed and we need to call one of the wait functions to determine what has happened.

System V, however, has traditionally handled the SIGCLD signal differently from other signals. SVR4 continues this questionable tradition (i.e., compatibility constraint), if we set its disposition using either signal or sigset (the older, SVR3-compatible

```
#include     <pwd.h>
#include     <signal.h>
#include     "ourhdr.h"

static void my_alarm(int);

int
main(void)
{
    struct passwd    *ptr;

    signal(SIGALRM, my_alarm);
    alarm(1);

    for ( ; ; ) {
        if ( (ptr = getpwnam("stevens")) == NULL)
            err_sys("getpwnam error");
        if (strcmp(ptr->pw_name, "stevens") != 0)
            printf("return value corrupted!, pw_name = %s\n",
                    ptr->pw_name);
    }
}

static void
my_alarm(int signo)
{
    struct passwd    *rootptr;

    printf("in signal handler\n");
    if ( (rootptr = getpwnam("root")) == NULL)
            err_sys("getpwnam(root) error");
    alarm(1);
    return;
}
```

Program 10.2 Call a nonreentrant function from a signal handler.

functions to set the disposition of a signal). This older handling of SIGCLD consists of the following:

1. If the process specifically sets its disposition to SIG_IGN, children of the calling process will not generate zombie processes. Note that this is different from its default action (SIG_DFL), which from Figure 10.1 is to be ignored. Instead, on termination the status of these child processes is just discarded. If the calling process subsequently calls one of the wait functions, it will block until all of its children have terminated, and then wait returns −1 with errno set to ECHILD. (The default disposition of this signal is to be ignored, but this default will not cause the above semantics to occur. Instead, we specifically have to set its disposition to SIG_IGN.)

POSIX.1 does not specify what happens when SIGCHLD is ignored, so this behavior is allowed.

4.3+BSD always generates zombies if SIGCHLD is ignored. If we want to avoid zombies, we have to wait for our children.

With SVR4, if either signal or sigset is called to set the disposition of SIGCHLD to be ignored, zombies are never generated. Also, with the SVR4 version of sigaction, we can set the SA_NOCLDWAIT flag (Figure 10.5) to avoid zombies.

2. If we set the disposition of SIGCLD to be caught, the kernel immediately checks if there are any child processes ready to be waited for and, if so, calls the SIGCLD handler.

Item 2 changes the way we have to write a signal handler for this signal.

Example

Recall in Section 10.4 we said the first thing to do on entry to a signal handler is to call signal again, to reestablish the handler. (This was to minimize the window of time when the signal is reset back to its default, and could get lost.) We show this in Program 10.3. This program doesn't work. If we compile and run it under SVR2 the output is a continual string of SIGCLD received lines. Eventually the process runs out of stack space and terminates abnormally.

The problem with this program is that the call to signal at the beginning of the signal handler invokes item 2 from the preceding discussion—the kernel checks if there is a child that needs to be waited for (which there is, since we're processing a SIGCLD signal), so it generates another call to the signal handler. The signal handler calls signal, and the whole process starts over again.

To fix this program we have to move the call to signal after the call to wait. By doing this we call signal after fetching the child's termination status—the signal is generated again by the kernel only if some other child has since terminated.

POSIX.1 states that when we establish a signal handler for SIGCHLD, and there exists a terminated child who we have not yet waited for, it is unspecified whether the signal is generated. This allows the behavior described previously. But since POSIX.1 does not reset a signal's disposition to its default when the signal occurs (assuming we're using the POSIX.1 sigaction function to set its disposition), there is no need for us to ever establish a signal handler for SIGCHLD within that handler.   ☐

Be cognizant of the semantics that your implementation associates with the SIGCHLD signal. Be especially aware of some systems that #define SIGCHLD to be SIGCLD or vice versa. Changing the name may allow you to compile a program that was written for another system, but if that program depends on the other semantics, it may not work.

```c
#include     <sys/types.h>
#include     <signal.h>
#include     <stdio.h>

static void sig_cld();

int
main()
{
    pid_t   pid;

    if (signal(SIGCLD, sig_cld) == -1)
        perror("signal error");

    if ( (pid = fork()) < 0)
        perror("fork error");
    else if (pid == 0) {            /* child */
        sleep(2);
        _exit(0);
    }
    pause();     /* parent */
    exit(0);
}

static void
sig_cld()
{
    pid_t   pid;
    int     status;

    printf("SIGCLD received\n");
    if (signal(SIGCLD, sig_cld) == -1)  /* reestablish handler */
        perror("signal error");

    if ( (pid = wait(&status)) < 0)       /* fetch child status */
        perror("wait error");
    printf("pid = %d\n", pid);
    return;      /* interrupts pause() */
}
```

Program 10.3 System V SIGCLD handler that doesn't work.

10.8 Reliable Signal Terminology and Semantics

There are terms used throughout our discussion of signals that we need to define. First, a signal is *generated* for a process (or sent to a process) when the event that causes the signal occurs. The event could be a hardware exception (e.g., divide by 0), a software condition (e.g., an alarm timer expiring), a terminal-generated signal, or a call to the kill function. When the signal is generated the kernel usually sets a flag of some form in the process table.

We say that a signal is *delivered* to a process when the action for a signal is taken. During the time between the generation of a signal and its delivery, the signal is said to be *pending*.

A process has the option of *blocking* the delivery of a signal. If a signal that is blocked is generated for a process, and if the action for that signal is either the default action or to catch the signal, then the signal remains pending for the process until the process either (a) unblocks the signal or (b) changes the action to ignore the signal. The system determines what to do with a blocked signal when the signal is delivered, not when it's generated. This allows the process to change the action for the signal before it's delivered. The `sigpending` function (Section 10.13) can be called by a process to determine which signals are blocked and pending.

What happens if a blocked signal is generated more than once before the process unblocks the signal? POSIX.1 allows the system to deliver the signal either once or more than once. If the system delivers the signal more than once, we say that the signals are queued. Most Unix systems, however, do *not* queue signals. Instead the Unix kernel just delivers the signal once.

> The manual pages for earlier versions of System V claimed that the SIGCLD signal was queued, but it really wasn't. Instead the signal was regenerated by the kernel as we described in Section 10.7.

> The sigaction(2) manual page in AT&T [1990e] claims that the SA_SIGINFO flag (Figure 10.5) causes signals to be reliably queued. This is wrong. Apparently this feature exists within the kernel, but it is not enabled in SVR4.

What happens if more than one signal is ready to be delivered to a process? POSIX.1 does not specify the order in which the signals are delivered to the process. The Rationale for POSIX.1 does suggest, however, that signals related to the current state of the process, such as SIGSEGV, be delivered before other signals.

Each process has a *signal mask* that defines the set of signals currently blocked from delivery to that process. We can think of this mask as having one bit for each possible signal. If the bit is on for a given signal, that signal is currently blocked. A process can examine and change its current signal mask by calling `sigprocmask`, which we describe in Section 10.12.

Since it is possible for the number of signals to exceed the number of bits in an integer, POSIX.1 defines a new data type, `sigset_t` that holds a *signal set*. The signal mask, for example, is stored in one of these signal sets. We describe five functions that operate on signal sets in Section 10.11.

10.9 `kill` and `raise` Functions

The `kill` function sends a signal to a process or a group of processes. The `raise` function allows a process to send a signal to itself.

> raise is defined by ANSI C, not POSIX.1. Since ANSI C does not deal with multiple processes it could not define a function such as `kill` that requires a process ID argument.

```
#include <sys/types.h>
#include <signal.h>

int kill(pid_t pid, int signo);

int raise(int signo);
```
                                                                    Both return: 0 if OK, −1 on error

There are four different conditions for the *pid* argument to kill.

pid > 0   The signal is sent to the process whose process ID is *pid*.

pid == 0   The signal is sent to all processes whose process group ID equals the process group ID of the sender and for which the sender has permission to send the signal.

           The term "all processes" excludes an implementation-defined set of system processes. For most Unix systems this set of system processes includes the swapper (pid 0), init (pid 1), and the pagedaemon (pid 2).

pid < 0   The signal is sent to all processes whose process group ID equals the absolute value of *pid* and for which the sender has permission to send the signal.

           Again, the set of "all processes" excludes certain system processes, as described earlier.

pid == −1   POSIX.1 leaves this condition as unspecified.

> SVR4 and 4.3+BSD use this for what they call *broadcast signals*. These broadcast signals are never sent to the set of system processes described previously. 4.3+BSD also never sends a broadcast signal to the process sending the signal. If the caller is the superuser, the signal is sent to all processes. If the caller is not the superuser, the signal is sent to all processes whose real user ID or saved set-user-ID equals the real user ID or effective user ID of the caller. These broadcast signals should be used only for administrative purposes (such as a superuser process that is about to shut down the system).

As we've mentioned, a process needs permission to send a signal to some other process. The superuser can send a signal to any process. For others, the basic rule is that the real or effective user ID of the sender has to equal the real or effective user ID of the receiver. If the implementation supports _POSIX_SAVED_IDS (as does SVR4) then the saved set-user-ID of the receiver is checked instead of its effective user ID.

There is also one special case for the permission testing: if the signal being sent is SIGCONT then a process can send it to any other process that is a member of the same session.

POSIX.1 defines signal number 0 as the null signal. If the *signo* argument is 0, then the normal error checking is performed by kill, but no signal is sent. This is often used to determine if a specific process still exists. If we send the process the null signal and it doesn't exist, kill returns −1 and errno is set to ESRCH. Be aware, however, that Unix systems recycle process IDs after some amount of time, so the existence of a process with a given process ID does not mean it's the process that you think it is.

If the call to kill causes the signal to be generated for the calling process and, if the signal is not blocked, either *signo* or some other pending, unblocked signal is delivered to the process before kill returns.

10.10 alarm and pause Functions

The alarm function allows us to set a timer that will expire at a specified time in the future. When the timer expires, the SIGALRM signal is generated. If we ignore or don't catch this signal, its default action is to terminate the process.

```
#include <unistd.h>

unsigned int alarm(unsigned int seconds);
```
                                    Returns: 0 or number of seconds until previously set alarm

The *seconds* value is the number of clock seconds in the future when the signal should be generated. Be aware that when that time occurs, the signal is generated by the kernel, but there could be additional time before the process gets control to handle the signal because of processor scheduling delays.

> Earlier versions of Unix warned that the signal could also be sent up to 1 second early. POSIX.1 does not allow this.

There is only one of these alarm clocks per process. If, when we call alarm, there is a previously registered alarm clock for the process that has not yet expired, the number of seconds left for that alarm clock is returned as the value of this function. That previously registered alarm clock is replaced by the new value.

If there is a previously registered alarm clock for the process that has not yet expired and if the *seconds* value is 0, the previous alarm clock is cancelled. The number of seconds left for that previous alarm clock is still returned as the value of the function.

Although the default action for SIGALRM is to terminate the process, most processes that use an alarm clock catch this signal. If the process then wants to terminate, it can perform whatever cleanup is required before terminating.

The pause function suspends the calling process until a signal is caught.

```
#include <unistd.h>

int pause(void);
```
                                                      Returns: −1 with errno set to EINTR

The only time pause returns is if a signal handler is executed and that handler returns. In that case, pause returns −1 with errno set to EINTR.

Example

Using `alarm` and `pause` we can put ourself to sleep for a specified amount of time. The `sleep1` function in Program 10.4 does this.

```
#include     <signal.h>
#include     <unistd.h>

static void
sig_alrm(int signo)
{
    return;  /* nothing to do, just return to wake up the pause */
}

unsigned int
sleep1(unsigned int nsecs)
{
    if (signal(SIGALRM, sig_alrm) == SIG_ERR)
        return(nsecs);
    alarm(nsecs);           /* start the timer */
    pause();                /* next caught signal wakes us up */
    return( alarm(0) );     /* turn off timer, return unslept time */
}
```

Program 10.4 Simple, incomplete implementation of `sleep`.

This function looks like the `sleep` function, which we describe in Section 10.19, but this simple implementation has problems.

1. If the caller already has an alarm set, that alarm is erased by the first call to `alarm`.

    We can correct this by looking at the return value from the first call to `alarm`. If the number of seconds until some previously set alarm is less than the argument, then we should wait only until the previously set alarm expires. If the previously set alarm will go off after ours, then before returning we should reset this alarm to occur at its designated time in the future.

2. We have modified the disposition for `SIGALRM`. If we're writing a function for others to call, we should save the disposition when we're called and restore it when we're done.

    We can correct this by saving the return value from `signal` and resetting the disposition before we return.

3. There is a race condition between the first call to `alarm` and the call to `pause`. It's possible on a busy system for the alarm to go off and the signal handler be called before we call `pause`. If that happens, the caller is suspended forever in the call to `pause` (assuming some other signal isn't caught).

Earlier implementations of `sleep` looked like our program, with problems 1 and 2 corrected as described. There are two ways to correct problem 3. The first uses `setjmp`, which we show later. The other uses `sigprocmask` and `sigsuspend`, and we describe it in Section 10.19.   □

Example

The SVR2 implementation of `sleep` used `setjmp` and `longjmp` (Section 7.10) to avoid the race condition described in problem 3 earlier. A simple version of this function, called `sleep2` is shown in Program 10.5. (To reduce the size of this example, we don't handle problems 1 and 2 described earlier.)

```c
#include    <setjmp.h>
#include    <signal.h>
#include    <unistd.h>

static jmp_buf  env_alrm;

static void
sig_alrm(int signo)
{
    longjmp(env_alrm, 1);
}

unsigned int
sleep2(unsigned int nsecs)
{
    if (signal(SIGALRM, sig_alrm) == SIG_ERR)
        return(nsecs);
    if (setjmp(env_alrm) == 0) {
        alarm(nsecs);           /* start the timer */
        pause();                /* next caught signal wakes us up */
    }
    return( alarm(0) );         /* turn off timer, return unslept time */
}
```

Program 10.5 Another (imperfect) implementation of `sleep`.

In this function the race condition from Program 10.4 has been avoided. Even if the pause is never executed, when the SIGALRM occurs, the `sleep2` function returns.

There is, however, another subtle problem with the `sleep2` function that involves its interaction with other signals. If the SIGALRM interrupts some other signal handler, when we call `longjmp` it aborts the other signal handler. Program 10.6 shows this scenario. The loop in the SIGINT handler was written so that it executes for longer than 5 seconds on the system used by the author. We just want it to execute longer than the argument to `sleep2`. The integer `j` is declared `volatile` to prevent an optimizing compiler from discarding the loop. Executing Program 10.6 gives us

```
$ a.out
^?                              we type our interrupt character
sig_int starting
sleep2 returned: 0
```

```
#include    <signal.h>
#include    "ourhdr.h"

unsigned int    ·sleep2(unsigned int);
static void     sig_int(int);

int
main(void)
{
    unsigned int    unslept;

    if (signal(SIGINT, sig_int) == SIG_ERR)
        err_sys("signal(SIGINT) error");

    unslept = sleep2(5);
    printf("sleep2 returned: %u\n", unslept);

    exit(0);
}

static void
sig_int(int signo)
{
    int             i;
    volatile int    j;

    printf("\nsig_int starting\n");
    for (i = 0; i < 2000000; i++)
        j += i * i;
    printf("sig_int finished\n");
    return;
}
```

Program 10.6 Calling `sleep2` from a program that catches other signals.

We can see that the `longjmp` from the `sleep2` function aborted the other signal handler, `sig_int`, even though it wasn't finished. This is what you'll encounter if you mix the SVR2 `sleep` function with other signal handling. See Exercise 10.3.   □

The purpose of these two examples, the `sleep1` and `sleep2` functions, is to show the pitfalls in dealing naively with signals. The following sections will show ways around all these problems, so we can handle signals reliably, without interfering with other pieces of code.

Example

A common use for `alarm`, in addition to implementing the `sleep` function, is to put an upper time limit on operations that can block. For example, if we have a read operation on a device that can block (a "slow" device, as described in Section 10.5) we might want the read to timeout after some amount of time. Program 10.7 does this, reading one line from standard input and writing it to standard output.

```
#include        <signal.h>
#include        "ourhdr.h"

static void sig_alrm(int);

int
main(void)
{
    int     n;
    char    line[MAXLINE];

    if (signal(SIGALRM, sig_alrm) == SIG_ERR)
        err_sys("signal(SIGALRM) error");
    alarm(10);
    if ( (n = read(STDIN_FILENO, line, MAXLINE)) < 0)
        err_sys("read error");
    alarm(0);

    write(STDOUT_FILENO, line, n);

    exit(0);
}

static void
sig_alrm(int signo)
{
    return; /* nothing to do, just return to interrupt the read */
}
```

Program 10.7 Calling read with a time out.

This sequence of code is seen in many Unix applications, but there are two problems with this program.

1. Program 10.7 has the same flaw that we described in Program 10.4: there is a race condition between the first call to alarm and the call to read. If the kernel blocks the process between these two function calls for longer than the alarm period, the read could block forever. Most operations of this type use a long alarm period, such as a minute or more, making this unlikely, but nevertheless it is a race condition.

2. If system calls are automatically restarted, the read is not interrupted when the SIGALRM signal handler returns. In this case the time out does nothing.

Here we specifically want a slow system call to be interrupted. POSIX.1, however, does not give us a portable way to do this.   □

Example

Let's redo the preceding example using longjmp. This way we don't need to worry whether a slow system call is interrupted or not.

```c
#include     <setjmp.h>
#include     <signal.h>
#include     "ourhdr.h"

static void      sig_alrm(int);
static jmp_buf   env_alrm;

int
main(void)
{
    int     n;
    char    line[MAXLINE];

    if (signal(SIGALRM, sig_alrm) == SIG_ERR)
        err_sys("signal(SIGALRM) error");

    if (setjmp(env_alrm) != 0)
        err_quit("read timeout");

    alarm(10);
    if ( (n = read(STDIN_FILENO, line, MAXLINE)) < 0)
        err_sys("read error");
    alarm(0);

    write(STDOUT_FILENO, line, n);

    exit(0);
}

static void
sig_alrm(int signo)
{
    longjmp(env_alrm, 1);
}
```

Program 10.8 Calling read with a time out, using longjmp.

This version works as expected, regardless of whether the system restarts interrupted system calls or not. Realize, however, that we still have the problem of interactions with other signal handlers, as in Program 10.5.   □

If we want to set a time limit on an I/O operation we need to use longjmp, as shown previously, realizing its possible interaction with other signal handlers. Another option is to use the select or poll functions, described in Sections 12.5.1 and 12.5.2.

10.11 Signal Sets

We need a data type to represent multiple signals—a *signal set*. We'll use this with functions such as sigprocmask (in the next section) to tell the kernel not to allow any of the signals in the set to occur. As we mentioned earlier, the number of different signals can exceed the number of bits in an integer, so in general we can't use one bit per signal in an integer. POSIX.1 defines the data type sigset_t to contain a signal set and the following five functions to manipulate signal sets.

```
#include <signal.h>

int sigemptyset(sigset_t *set);

int sigfillset(sigset_t *set);

int sigaddset(sigset_t *set, int signo);

int sigdelset(sigset_t *set, int signo);

                                                       All four return: 0 if OK, –1 on error

int sigismember(const sigset_t *set, int signo);

                                                       Returns: 1 if true, 0 if false
```

The function sigemptyset initializes the signal set pointed to by *set* so that all signals are excluded. The function sigfillset initializes the signal set so that all signals are included. All applications have to call either sigemptyset or sigfillset once for each signal set, before using the signal set. This is because we cannot assume that the C initialization for external and static variables (0) corresponds to the implementation of signal sets on a given system.

Once we have initialized a signal set, we can add and delete specific signals in the set. The function sigaddset adds a single signal to an existing set, and sigdelset removes a single signal from a set. We'll see in all the functions that take a signal set as an argument that we always pass the address of the signal set as the argument.

Implementation

If the implementation has fewer signals than bits in an integer, a signal set can be implemented using one bit per signal. Most implementations of 4.3+BSD, for example, have 31 signals and 32-bit integers. sigemptyset zeroes the integer and sigfillset turns on all the bits in the integer. These two functions can be implemented as macros in the <signal.h> header:

```
#define sigemptyset(ptr)   ( *(ptr) = 0 )
#define sigfillset(ptr)    ( *(ptr) = ~(sigset_t)0, 0 )
```

Note that `sigfillset` must return 0, in addition to setting all the bits on in the signal set, so we use C's comma operator, which returns the value after the comma as the value of the expression.

Using this implementation `sigaddset` turns on a single bit and `sigdelset` turns off a single bit. `sigismember` tests a certain bit. Since there is never a signal numbered 0, we subtract 1 from the signal number to obtain the bit to manipulate. Program 10.9 implements these functions.

```
#include      <signal.h>
#include      <errno.h>

#define SIGBAD(signo)    ((signo) <= 0 || (signo) >= NSIG)
    /* <signal.h> usually defines NSIG to include signal number 0 */

int
sigaddset(sigset_t *set, int signo)
{
    if (SIGBAD(signo)) { errno = EINVAL; return(-1); }

    *set |= 1 << (signo - 1);           /* turn bit on */
    return(0);
}

int
sigdelset(sigset_t *set, int signo)
{
    if (SIGBAD(signo)) { errno = EINVAL; return(-1); }

    *set &= ~(1 << (signo - 1));    /* turn bit off */
    return(0);
}

int
sigismember(const sigset_t *set, int signo)
{
    if (SIGBAD(signo)) { errno = EINVAL; return(-1); }

    return( (*set & (1 << (signo - 1))) != 0 );
}
```

Program 10.9 An implementation of `sigaddset`, `sigdelset`, and `sigismember`.

We might be tempted to implement these three functions as one-line macros in the `<signal.h>` header, but POSIX.1 requires us to check the signal number argument for validity and set `errno` if it is invalid. This is harder to do in a macro than a function.

10.12 `sigprocmask` Function

Recall from Section 10.8 that the signal mask of a process is the set of signals currently blocked from delivery to that process. A process can examine or change (or both) its signal mask by calling the following function.

```
#include <signal.h>

int sigprocmask(int how, const sigset_t *set, sigset_t *oset);
```
                                                                    Returns: 0 if OK, −1 on error

First, if *oset* is a nonnull pointer, the current signal mask for the process is returned through *oset*.

Second, if *set* is a nonnull pointer, then the *how* argument indicates how the current signal mask is modified. Figure 10.4 describes the different values for *how*. SIG_BLOCK is an inclusive-OR operation while SIG_SETMASK is an assignment.

how	Description
SIG_BLOCK	The new signal mask for the process is the union of its current signal mask and the signal set pointed to by *set*. That is, *set* contains the additional signals that we want to block.
SIG_UNBLOCK	The new signal mask for the process is the intersection of its current signal mask and the complement of the signal set pointed to by *set*. That is, *set* contains the signals that we want to unblock.
SIG_SETMASK	The new signal mask for the process is the value pointed to by *set*.

Figure 10.4 Ways to change current signal mask using sigprocmask.

If *set* is a null pointer, the signal mask of the process is not changed, and the value of *how* is not significant.

If there are any pending, unblocked signals after the call to sigprocmask, at least one of these signals is delivered to the process before sigprocmask returns.

Example

Program 10.10 shows a function that prints the names of the signals in the signal mask of the calling process. We call this function from Program 10.14 and Program 10.15. To save space we don't test the signal mask for every signal that we listed in Figure 10.1. (See Exercise 10.9.)   □

10.13 sigpending Function

sigpending returns the set of signals that are blocked from delivery and currently pending for the calling process. The set of signals is returned through the *set* argument.

```
#include <signal.h>

int sigpending(sigset_t *set);
```
                                                                    Returns: 0 if OK, −1 on error

```
#include      <errno.h>
#include      <signal.h>
#include      "ourhdr.h"

void
pr_mask(const char *str)
{
    sigset_t      sigset;
    int           errno_save;

    errno_save = errno;        /* we can be called by signal handlers */
    if (sigprocmask(0, NULL, &sigset) < 0)
        err_sys("sigprocmask error");

    printf("%s", str);
    if (sigismember(&sigset, SIGINT))   printf("SIGINT ");
    if (sigismember(&sigset, SIGQUIT))  printf("SIGQUIT ");
    if (sigismember(&sigset, SIGUSR1))  printf("SIGUSR1 ");
    if (sigismember(&sigset, SIGALRM))  printf("SIGALRM ");
        /* remaining signals can go here */
    printf("\n");
    errno = errno_save;
}
```

Program 10.10   Print the signal mask for the process.

Example

Program 10.11 shows many of the signal features that we've been describing. The process blocks SIGQUIT, saving its current signal mask (to reset later), and then goes to sleep for 5 seconds. Any occurrence of the quit signal during this period is blocked and won't be delivered until the signal is unblocked. At the end of the 5 second sleep we check if the signal is pending and unblock the signal.

Note that we saved the old mask when we blocked the signal. To unblock the signal we did a SIG_SETMASK of the old mask. Alternately, we could SIG_UNBLOCK only the signal that we had blocked. Be aware, however, if we write a function that can be called by others and if we need to block a signal in our function, we can't use SIG_UNBLOCK to unblock the signal. In this case we have to use SIG_SETMASK and reset the signal mask to its prior value, because it's possible that the caller had specifically blocked this signal before calling our function. We'll see an example of this in the system function in Section 10.18.

If we generate the quit signal during this sleep period, the signal is now pending and unblocked, so it is delivered before sigprocmask returns. We'll see this occur because the printf in the signal handler is output before the printf that follows the call to sigprocmask.

```
#include    <signal.h>
#include    "ourhdr.h"

static void sig_quit(int);

int
main(void)
{
    sigset_t    newmask, oldmask, pendmask;

    if (signal(SIGQUIT, sig_quit) == SIG_ERR)
        err_sys("can't catch SIGQUIT");

    sigemptyset(&newmask);
    sigaddset(&newmask, SIGQUIT);
                    /* block SIGQUIT and save current signal mask */
    if (sigprocmask(SIG_BLOCK, &newmask, &oldmask) < 0)
        err_sys("SIG_BLOCK error");

    sleep(5);       /* SIGQUIT here will remain pending */

    if (sigpending(&pendmask) < 0)
        err_sys("sigpending error");
    if (sigismember(&pendmask, SIGQUIT))
        printf("\nSIGQUIT pending\n");

                    /* reset signal mask which unblocks SIGQUIT */
    if (sigprocmask(SIG_SETMASK, &oldmask, NULL) < 0)
        err_sys("SIG_SETMASK error");
    printf("SIGQUIT unblocked\n");

    sleep(5);       /* SIGQUIT here will terminate with core file */

    exit(0);
}

static void
sig_quit(int signo)
{
    printf("caught SIGQUIT\n");

    if (signal(SIGQUIT, SIG_DFL) == SIG_ERR)
        err_sys("can't reset SIGQUIT");
    return;
}
```

Program 10.11 Example of signal sets and sigprocmask.

The process then goes to sleep for another 5 seconds. If we generate the quit signal during this sleep period, it should terminate the process, since we reset the handling of the signal to its default when we caught it. In the following output, the terminal prints ^\ when we input Control-backslash, the terminal quit character.

```
$ a.out
^\                              generate signal once (before 5 seconds are up)
SIGQUIT pending                 after return from sleep
caught SIGQUIT                  in signal handler
SIGQUIT unblocked               after return from sigprocmask
^\Quit(coredump)                generate signal again
$ a.out
^\^\^\^\^\^\^\^\^\^\             generate signal 10 times (before 5 seconds are up)
SIGQUIT pending
caught SIGQUIT                  signal is generated only once
SIGQUIT unblocked
^\Quit(coredump)                generate signal again
```

(The message Quit(coredump) is printed by the shell when it sees that its child terminated abnormally.) Notice that when we run the program the second time we generate the quit signal 10 times while the process is asleep, yet the signal is delivered only once to the process when it's unblocked. This demonstrates that signals are not queued on this system.   □

10.14 sigaction Function

The sigaction function allows us to examine or modify (or both) the action associated with a particular signal. This function supersedes the signal function from earlier releases of Unix. Indeed, at the end of this section we show an implementation of signal using sigaction.

```
#include <signal.h>

int sigaction(int signo, const struct sigaction *act,
                          struct sigaction *oact);
```
                                                                Returns: 0 if OK, −1 on error

The argument *signo* is the signal number whose action we are examining or modifying. If the *act* pointer is nonnull, we are modifying the action. If the *oact* pointer is nonnull, the system returns the previous action for the signal. This function uses the following structure

```
struct sigaction {
   void     (*sa_handler)(); /* addr of signal handler,
                                or SIG_IGN, or SIG_DFL */
   sigset_t sa_mask;         /* additional signals to block */
   int      sa_flags;        /* signal options, Figure 10.5 */
};
```

When changing the action for a signal, if the sa_handler points to a signal-catching function (as opposed to the constants SIG_IGN or SIG_DFL) then the sa_mask field specifies a set of signals that are added to the signal mask of the process before the signal-catching function is called. If and when the signal-catching function returns, the signal mask of the process is reset to its previous value. This way we are able to block certain signals whenever a signal handler is invoked. This new signal mask that is installed by the system when the signal handler is invoked automatically includes the signal being delivered. Hence, we are guaranteed that whenever we are processing a given signal, another occurrence of that same signal is blocked until we're finished processing the first occurrence. Recall from Section 10.8 that additional occurrences of the same signal are usually not queued. If the signal occurs five times while it is blocked, when we unblock the signal the signal-handling function for that signal will usually be invoked only one time.

Once we install an action for a given signal, that action remains installed until we explicitly change it by calling sigaction. Unlike earlier systems with their unreliable signals, POSIX.1 requires that a signal handler remain installed until explicitly changed.

The sa_flags field of the *act* structure specifies various options for the handling of this signal. Figure 10.5 details the meaning of these options when set.

Option	POSIX.1	SVR4	4.3+BSD	Description
SA_NOCLDSTOP	•	•	•	If *signo* is SIGCHLD, do not generate this signal when a child process stops (job control). This signal is still generated, of course, when a child terminates (but see the SVR4-specific SA_NOCLDWAIT option below).
SA_RESTART		•	•	System calls interrupted by this signal are automatically restarted. (Refer to Section 10.5.)
SA_ONSTACK		•	•	If an alternate stack has been declared with sigaltstack(2), this signal is delivered to the process on the alternate stack.
SA_NOCLDWAIT		•		If *signo* is SIGCHLD, this option causes the system not to create zombie processes when children of the calling process terminate. If the calling process subsequently calls wait, it blocks until all its child processes have terminated and then returns −1 with errno set to ECHILD. (Recall Section 10.7.)
SA_NODEFER		•		When this signal is caught, the signal is not automatically blocked by the system while the signal-catching function executes. Note that this type of operation corresponds to the earlier unreliable signals.
SA_RESETHAND		•		The disposition for this signal is reset to SIG_DFL on entry to the signal-catching function. Note that this type of operation corresponds to the earlier unreliable signals.
SA_SIGINFO		•		This option provides additional information to a signal handler. Refer to Section 10.21 for additional details.

Figure 10.5 Option flags (sa_flags) for the handling of each signal.

Example—signal Function

Let's now implement the signal function using sigaction. This is what 4.3+BSD does (and what a note in the POSIX.1 Rationale states was the intent of POSIX). SVR4, on the other hand, provides a signal function that provides the older, unreliable signal semantics. Unless you specifically require these older, unreliable semantics (for backward compatibility), under SVR4 you should use the following implementation of signal or call sigaction directly. (As you might guess, an implementation of signal under SVR4 with the old semantics could call sigaction specifying SA_RESETHAND and SA_NODEFER.) All the examples in this text that call signal call the function shown in Program 10.12.

```
/* Reliable version of signal(), using POSIX sigaction().  */

#include     <signal.h>
#include     "ourhdr.h"

Sigfunc *
signal(int signo, Sigfunc *func)
{
    struct sigaction     act, oact;

    act.sa_handler = func;
    sigemptyset(&act.sa_mask);
    act.sa_flags = 0;
    if (signo == SIGALRM) {
#ifdef  SA_INTERRUPT
        act.sa_flags |= SA_INTERRUPT;     /* SunOS */
#endif
    } else {
#ifdef  SA_RESTART
        act.sa_flags |= SA_RESTART;       /* SVR4, 4.3+BSD */
#endif
    }
    if (sigaction(signo, &act, &oact) < 0)
        return(SIG_ERR);
    return(oact.sa_handler);
}
```

Program 10.12 An implementation of signal using sigaction.

Note that we must use sigemptyset to initialize the sa_mask member of the structure. We're not guaranteed that

```
    act.sa_mask = 0;
```

does the same thing.

We intentionally try to set the SA_RESTART flag, for all signals other than SIGALRM, so that any system call interrupted by these other signals is automatically restarted. The reason we don't want SIGALRM restarted is to allow us to set a time out for I/O operations. (Recall the discussion of Program 10.7.)

Some systems (such as SunOS) define the SA_INTERRUPT flag. These systems restart interrupted system calls by default, so specifying this flag causes system calls to be interrupted. □

Example—`signal_intr` Function

Program 10.13 is a version of the signal function that tries to prevent any interrupted system calls from being restarted.

```
#include    <signal.h>
#include    "ourhdr.h"

Sigfunc *
signal_intr(int signo, Sigfunc *func)
{
    struct sigaction    act, oact;

    act.sa_handler = func;
    sigemptyset(&act.sa_mask);
    act.sa_flags = 0;
#ifdef  SA_INTERRUPT    /* SunOS */
    act.sa_flags |= SA_INTERRUPT;
#endif
    if (sigaction(signo, &act, &oact) < 0)
        return(SIG_ERR);
    return(oact.sa_handler);
}
```

Program 10.13 The signal_intr function.

We specify the SA_INTERRUPT flag, if defined by the system, to prevent interrupted system calls from being restarted. □

10.15 `sigsetjmp` and `siglongjmp` Functions

In Section 7.10 we described the setjmp and longjmp functions that can be used for nonlocal branching. The longjmp function is often called from a signal handler to return to the main loop of a program, instead of returning from the handler. Indeed, the ANSI C standard states that a signal handler can either return or call abort, exit, or longjmp. We saw this in Programs 10.5 and 10.8.

There is a problem in calling longjmp. When a signal is caught, the signal-catching function is entered with the current signal automatically being added to the signal mask of the process. This prevents subsequent occurrences of that signal from interrupting the signal handler. If we longjmp out of the signal handler, what happens to the signal mask for the process?

> Under 4.3+BSD setjmp and longjmp save and restore the signal mask. SVR4, however, does not do this. 4.3+BSD provides the functions _setjmp and _longjmp that do not save and restore the signal mask.

To allow either form of behavior, POSIX.1 does not specify the effect of setjmp and longjmp on signal masks. Instead, two new functions, sigsetjmp and siglongjmp, are defined by POSIX.1. These two functions should always be used when branching from a signal handler.

```
#include <setjmp.h>

int sigsetjmp(sigjmp_buf env, int savemask);
```

        Returns: 0 if called directly, nonzero if returning from a call to siglongjmp

```
void siglongjmp(sigjmp_buf env, int val);
```

The only difference between these functions and the setjmp and longjmp functions is that sigsetjmp has an additional argument. If *savemask* is nonzero then sigsetjmp also saves the current signal mask of the process in *env*. When siglongjmp is called, if the *env* argument was saved by a call to sigsetjmp with a nonzero *savemask*, then siglongjmp restores the saved signal mask.

Example

Program 10.14 demonstrates how the signal mask that is installed by the system when a signal handler is invoked automatically includes the signal being caught. It also illustrates the use of the sigsetjmp and siglongjmp functions.

```c
#include     <signal.h>
#include     <setjmp.h>
#include     <time.h>
#include     "ourhdr.h"

static void              sig_usr1(int), sig_alrm(int);
static sigjmp_buf        jmpbuf;
static volatile sig_atomic_t    canjump;

int
main(void)
{
    if (signal(SIGUSR1, sig_usr1) == SIG_ERR)
        err_sys("signal(SIGUSR1) error");
    if (signal(SIGALRM, sig_alrm) == SIG_ERR)
        err_sys("signal(SIGALRM) error");
    pr_mask("starting main: ");      /* Program 10.10 */

    if (sigsetjmp(jmpbuf, 1)) {
        pr_mask("ending main: ");
        exit(0);
    }
    canjump = 1;    /* now sigsetjmp() is OK */

    for ( ; ; )
        pause();
```

```
static void
sig_usr1(int signo)
{
    time_t  starttime;

    if (canjump == 0)
        return;        /* unexpected signal, ignore */

    pr_mask("starting sig_usr1: ");

    alarm(3);                    /* SIGALRM in 3 seconds */

    starttime = time(NULL);
    for ( ; ; )                  /* busy wait for 5 seconds */
        if (time(NULL) > starttime + 5)
            break;

    pr_mask("finishing sig_usr1: ");

    canjump = 0;
    siglongjmp(jmpbuf, 1);   /* jump back to main, don't return */
}
static void
sig_alrm(int signo)
{
    pr_mask("in sig_alrm: ");
    return;
}
```

Program 10.14 Example of signal masks, sigsetjmp, and siglongjmp.

This program demonstrates another technique that should be used whenever siglongjmp is being called from a signal handler. We set the variable canjump nonzero only after we've called sigsetjmp. This variable is also examined in the signal handler, and siglongjmp is called only if the flag canjump is nonzero. This provides protection against the signal handler being called at some earlier or later time, when the jump buffer isn't initialized by sigsetjmp. (In this trivial program we terminate quickly after the siglongjmp, but in larger programs the signal handler may remain installed long after the siglongjmp.) Providing this type of protection usually isn't required with longjmp in normal C code (as opposed to a signal handler). Since a signal can occur at *any* time, however, we need the added protection in a signal handler.

Here we use the data type sig_atomic_t, which is defined by the ANSI C standard to be the type of variable that can be written without being interrupted. By this we mean that a variable of this type should not extend across page boundaries on a system with virtual memory and can be accessed with a single machine instruction, for example. We always include the ANSI type qualifier volatile for these data types too, since the variable is being accessed by two different threads of control—the main function and the asynchronously executing signal handler.

Figure 10.6 shows a time line for this program. We can divide Figure 10.6 into three parts: the left part (corresponding to main), the center part (sig_usr1), and the right part (sig_alrm). While the process is executing in the left part its signal mask is 0 (no

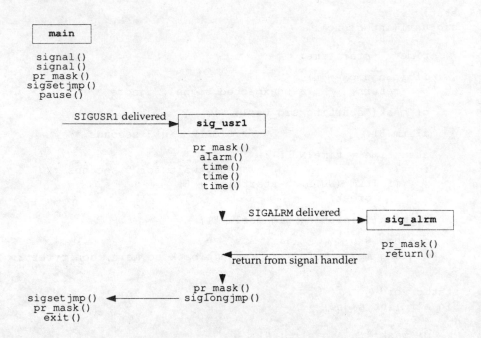

Figure 10.6 Time line for example program handling two signals.

signals are blocked). While executing in the center part its signal mask is SIGUSR1. While executing in the right part its signal mask is SIGUSR1 | SIGALRM.

Let's examine the actual output when Program 10.14 is executed.

```
$ a.out &                                start process in background
starting main:
[1]    531                               the job-control shell prints its process ID
$ kill -USR1 531                         send the process SIGUSR1
starting sig_usr1: SIGUSR1
$ in sig_alrm: SIGUSR1 SIGALRM
finishing sig_usr1: SIGUSR1
ending main:
                                         just press RETURN
[1] +  Done            a.out &
```

The output is as we expect: when a signal handler is invoked, the signal being caught is added to the current signal mask of the process. The original mask is restored when the signal handler returns. Also, siglongjmp restores the signal mask that was saved by sigsetjmp.

If we change Program 10.14 so that the calls to sigsetjmp and siglongjmp are replaced with calls to _setjmp and _longjmp instead, under 4.3+BSD the final line of output becomes

```
ending main: SIGUSR1
```

This means that the main function is executing with the SIGUSR1 signal blocked, after the call to _setjmp. This probably isn't what we want. □

10.16 sigsuspend Function

We have seen how we can change the signal mask for a process to block and unblock selected signals. We can use this to protect critical regions of code that we don't want interrupted by a signal. What if we want to unblock a signal and then pause, waiting for the previously blocked signal to occur? Assuming the signal is SIGINT, the incorrect way to do this is

```
sigset_t      newmask, oldmask;

sigemptyset(&newmask);
sigaddset(&newmask, SIGINT);
                    /* block SIGINT and save current signal mask */
if (sigprocmask(SIG_BLOCK, &newmask, &oldmask) < 0)
    err_sys("SIG_BLOCK error");

/* critical region of code */

                    /* reset signal mask, which unblocks SIGINT */
if (sigprocmask(SIG_SETMASK, &oldmask, NULL) < 0)
    err_sys("SIG_SETMASK error");

pause();          /* wait for signal to occur */

/* continue processing */
```

There is a problem if the signal occurs between the unblocking and the pause. Any occurrence of the signal in this window of time is lost. This is another problem with the earlier unreliable signals.

To correct this problem we need a way to both reset the signal mask and put the process to sleep in a single atomic operation. This feature is provided by the sigsuspend function.

```
#include <signal.h>

int sigsuspend(const sigset_t *sigmask);
```
                                              Returns: −1 with errno set to EINTR

The signal mask of the process is set to the value pointed to by *sigmask*. The process is also suspended until a signal is caught or until a signal occurs that terminates the process. If a signal is caught and if the signal handler returns, then sigsuspend returns and the signal mask of the process is set to its value before the call to sigsuspend.

Note that there is no successful return from this function. If it returns to the caller, it always returns −1 with errno set to EINTR (indicating an interrupted system call).

Example

Program 10.15 shows the correct way to protect a critical region of code from a specific
signal.

```
#include      <signal.h>
#include      "ourhdr.h"

static void sig_int(int);

int
main(void)
{
    sigset_t    newmask, oldmask, zeromask;

    if (signal(SIGINT, sig_int) == SIG_ERR)
        err_sys("signal(SIGINT) error");

    sigemptyset(&zeromask);

    sigemptyset(&newmask);
    sigaddset(&newmask, SIGINT);
                    /* block SIGINT and save current signal mask */
    if (sigprocmask(SIG_BLOCK, &newmask, &oldmask) < 0)
        err_sys("SIG_BLOCK error");

                    /* critical region of code */
    pr_mask("in critical region: ");

                    /* allow all signals and pause */
    if (sigsuspend(&zeromask) != -1)
        err_sys("sigsuspend error");
    pr_mask("after return from sigsuspend: ");

                    /* reset signal mask which unblocks SIGINT */
    if (sigprocmask(SIG_SETMASK, &oldmask, NULL) < 0)
        err_sys("SIG_SETMASK error");

                    /* and continue processing ... */
    exit(0);
}

static void
sig_int(int signo)
{
    pr_mask("\nin sig_int: ");
    return;
}
```

Program 10.15 Protecting a critical region from a signal.

Note that when `sigsuspend` returns it sets the signal mask to its value before the call. In this example the `SIGINT` signal will be blocked. We therefore reset the signal mask to the value that we saved earlier (`oldmask`).

Running Program 10.15 produces the following output.

```
$ a.out
in critical region: SIGINT
^?                                  type our interrupt character
in sig_int: SIGINT
after return from sigsuspend: SIGINT
```

We can see that when `sigsuspend` returns, it restores the signal mask to its value before the call.   □

Example

Another use of `sigsuspend` is to wait for a signal handler to set a global variable. In Program 10.16 we catch both the interrupt signal and the quit signal, but want only to wake up the main routine when the quit signal is caught. Sample output from this program is

```
$ a.out
^?                                  type our interrupt character
interrupt
^?                                  type our interrupt character again
interrupt
^?                                  and again
interrupt
^\ $                                now terminate with quit character
```

□

For portability between non-POSIX systems that support ANSI C, and POSIX.1 systems, the only thing we should do within a signal handler is assign a value to a variable of type `sig_atomic_t`, and nothing else. POSIX.1 goes farther and specifies a list of functions that are safe to call from within a signal handler (Figure 10.3), but if we do this our code may not run correctly on non-POSIX systems.

Example

As another example of signals we show how signals can be used to synchronize a parent and child. Program 10.17 implements the five routines `TELL_WAIT`, `TELL_PARENT`, `TELL_CHILD`, `WAIT_PARENT`, and `WAIT_CHILD` from Section 8.8. We use the two user-defined signals: `SIGUSR1` is sent by the parent to the child, and `SIGUSR2` is sent by the child to the parent. In Program 14.3 we show another implementation of these five functions using pipes.   □

```c
#include     <signal.h>
#include     "ourhdr.h"

volatile sig_atomic_t   quitflag;    /* set nonzero by signal handler */

int
main(void)
{
    void        sig_int(int);
    sigset_t    newmask, oldmask, zeromask;

    if (signal(SIGINT, sig_int) == SIG_ERR)
        err_sys("signal(SIGINT) error");
    if (signal(SIGQUIT, sig_int) == SIG_ERR)
        err_sys("signal(SIGQUIT) error");

    sigemptyset(&zeromask);

    sigemptyset(&newmask);
    sigaddset(&newmask, SIGQUIT);
                    /* block SIGQUIT and save current signal mask */
    if (sigprocmask(SIG_BLOCK, &newmask, &oldmask) < 0)
        err_sys("SIG_BLOCK error");

    while (quitflag == 0)
        sigsuspend(&zeromask);

    /* SIGQUIT has been caught and is now blocked; do whatever */
    quitflag = 0;
                    /* reset signal mask which unblocks SIGQUIT */
    if (sigprocmask(SIG_SETMASK, &oldmask, NULL) < 0)
        err_sys("SIG_SETMASK error");

    exit(0);
}

void
sig_int(int signo)  /* one signal handler for SIGINT and SIGQUIT */
{
    if (signo == SIGINT)
        printf("\ninterrupt\n");
    else if (signo == SIGQUIT)
        quitflag = 1;   /* set flag for main loop */
    return;
}
```

Program 10.16 Using sigsuspend to wait for a global variable to be set.

```
#include     <signal.h>
#include     "ourhdr.h"

static volatile sig_atomic_t     sigflag;
                                 /* set nonzero by signal handler */
static sigset_t          newmask, oldmask, zeromask;

static void
sig_usr(int signo)   /* one signal handler for SIGUSR1 and SIGUSR2 */
{
    sigflag = 1;
    return;
}

void
TELL_WAIT(void)
{
    if (signal(SIGUSR1, sig_usr) == SIG_ERR)
        err_sys("signal(SIGUSR1) error");
    if (signal(SIGUSR2, sig_usr) == SIG_ERR)
        err_sys("signal(SIGUSR2) error");

    sigemptyset(&zeromask);

    sigemptyset(&newmask);
    sigaddset(&newmask, SIGUSR1);
    sigaddset(&newmask, SIGUSR2);
        /* block SIGUSR1 and SIGUSR2, and save current signal mask */
    if (sigprocmask(SIG_BLOCK, &newmask, &oldmask) < 0)
        err_sys("SIG_BLOCK error");
}

void
TELL_PARENT(pid_t pid)
{
    kill(pid, SIGUSR2);      /* tell parent we're done */
}

void
WAIT_PARENT(void)
{
    while (sigflag == 0)
        sigsuspend(&zeromask);   /* and wait for parent */

    sigflag = 0;
            /* reset signal mask to original value */
    if (sigprocmask(SIG_SETMASK, &oldmask, NULL) < 0)
        err_sys("SIG_SETMASK error");
}
```

```
void
TELL_CHILD(pid_t pid)
{
    kill(pid, SIGUSR1);          /* tell child we're done */
}

void
WAIT_CHILD(void)
{
    while (sigflag == 0)
        sigsuspend(&zeromask);   /* and wait for child */

    sigflag = 0;
            /* reset signal mask to original value */
    if (sigprocmask(SIG_SETMASK, &oldmask, NULL) < 0)
        err_sys("SIG_SETMASK error");
}
```

Program 10.17 Routines to allow a parent and child to synchronize.

The sigsuspend function is fine if we want to go to sleep while waiting for a signal to occur (as we've shown in the previous two examples), but what if we want to call other system functions while we're waiting? Unfortunately there is no bulletproof solution to this problem.

In Program 17.13 we encounter this scenario. We catch both SIGINT and SIGALRM, setting a global variable in each of the signal handlers if the signal occurs. Both signal handlers are installed using the signal_intr function, so that they interrupt any slow system call that is blocked. The signals are most likely to occur when we're blocked in a call to the select function (Section 12.5.1), waiting for input from a slow device. (This is especially true for SIGALRM, since we set the alarm clock to prevent us from blocking forever waiting for input.) The best we can do is the following.

```
if (intr_flag)          /* flag set by our SIGINT handler */
    handle_intr();
if (alrm_flag)          /* flag set by our SIGALRM handler */
    handle_alrm();
            /* signals occurring in here are lost */
while (select( ... ) < 0) {
    if (errno == EINTR) {
        if (alrm_flag)
            handle_alrm();
        else if (intr_flag)
            handle_intr();
    } else
        /* some other error */
}
```

We test each of the global flags before calling select and again if select returns an interrupted system call error. The problem occurs if either signal is caught between the first two if statements and the subsequent call to select. Signals occurring in here are lost, as indicated by the code comment. The signal handlers are called, and they set the appropriate global variable, but the select never returns (unless some data is ready to be read).

What we would like to be able to do is the following sequence of steps, in order.

1. Block SIGINT and SIGALRM.

2. Test the two global variables to see if either signal has occurred and, if so, handle the condition.

3. Call select (or any other system function, such as read) and unblock the two signals, as an atomic operation.

The sigsuspend function helps us only if step 3 is a pause operation.

10.17 abort Function

We mentioned earlier that the abort function causes abnormal program termination.

```
#include <stdlib.h>

void abort(void);
```
                                                                        This function never returns

This function sends the SIGABRT signal to the process. A process should not ignore this signal.

ANSI C requires that if the signal is caught and the signal handler returns, abort still doesn't return to its caller. If this signal is caught, the only way the signal handler can't return is if it calls exit, _exit, longjmp, or siglongjmp. (Section 10.15 discusses the differences between longjmp and siglongjmp.) POSIX.1 also specifies that abort overrides the blocking or ignoring of the signal by the process.

The intent of letting the process catch the SIGABRT is to allow it to perform any cleanup that it wants to do, before the process terminates. If the process doesn't terminate itself from this signal handler, POSIX.1 states that, when the signal handler returns, abort terminates the process.

The ANSI C specification of this function leaves it up to the implementation whether output streams are flushed and whether temporary files (Section 5.13) are deleted. POSIX.1 goes further and requires that if the call to abort terminates the process, then it shall have the effect of calling fclose on all open standard I/O streams. But if the call to abort doesn't terminate the process, then it should have no effect on open streams. As we see later, this requirement is hard to implement.

Earlier versions of System V generated the SIGIOT signal from the abort function. Furthermore it was possible for a process to ignore this signal or to catch it and return from the signal handler, in which case abort returned to its caller.

4.3BSD generated the SIGILL signal. Before doing this the 4.3BSD function unblocked the signal and reset its disposition to SIG_DFL (terminate with core file). This prevented a process from either ignoring the signal or catching it.

SVR4 closes all standard I/O streams before generating the signal. On the other hand, 4.3+BSD does not. For defensive programming, if we want standard I/O streams to be flushed, we specifically do it before calling abort. We do this in the err_dump function (Appendix B).

Since most Unix implementations of tmpfile call unlink immediately after creating the file, the ANSI C warning about temporary files does not usually concern us.

Example

Program 10.18 implements the abort function, as specified by POSIX.1. The required handling of open standard I/O streams is hard to accomplish. We first see if the default action will occur, and if so we flush all the standard I/O streams. This is not equivalent to an fclose on all the open streams (since it just flushes and doesn't close them), but when the process terminates the system closes all open files. If the process catches the signal and returns, we flush all the streams. (If the process catches the signal and doesn't return, we're not supposed to touch the standard I/O streams.) The only condition we don't handle is if the process catches the signal and calls _exit. In this case any unflushed standard I/O buffers in memory are discarded. We assume that a caller who catches the signal and specifically calls _exit, doesn't want the buffers flushed.

Recall from Section 10.9 that if calling kill causes the signal to be generated for the caller, and if the signal is not blocked (which we guarantee in Program 10.18), then the signal is delivered to the process before kill returns. This way we know that, if the call to kill returns, the process caught the signal and the signal handler returned.   □

10.18 system Function

In Section 8.12 we showed an implementation of the system function. That version, however, did not do any signal handling. POSIX.2 requires that system ignore SIGINT and SIGQUIT and block SIGCHLD. Before showing a version that correctly handles these signals, let's see why we need to worry about signal handling.

```
#include <sys/signal.h>
#include <stdio.h>
#include <stdlib.h>
#include <unistd.h>

void
abort(void)                /* POSIX-style abort() function */
{
    sigset_t            mask;
    struct sigaction    action;

        /* caller can't ignore SIGABRT, if so reset to default */
    sigaction(SIGABRT, NULL, &action);
    if (action.sa_handler == SIG_IGN) {
        action.sa_handler = SIG_DFL;
        sigaction(SIGABRT, &action, NULL);
    }

    if (action.sa_handler == SIG_DFL)
        fflush(NULL);               /* flush all open stdio streams */

        /* caller can't block SIGABRT; make sure it's unblocked */
    sigfillset(&mask);
    sigdelset(&mask, SIGABRT);   /* mask has only SIGABRT turned off */
    sigprocmask(SIG_SETMASK, &mask, NULL);

    kill(getpid(), SIGABRT);     /* send the signal */

        /* if we're here, process caught SIGABRT and returned */
    fflush(NULL);                   /* flush all open stdio streams */

    action.sa_handler = SIG_DFL;
    sigaction(SIGABRT, &action, NULL);  /* reset disposition to default */
    sigprocmask(SIG_SETMASK, &mask, NULL);  /* just in case ... */

    kill(getpid(), SIGABRT);                /* and one more time */

    exit(1);    /* this should never be executed ... */
}
```

Program 10.18 POSIX.1 implementation of abort.

Example

Program 10.19 uses the version of system from Section 8.12 to invoke the ed(1) editor. (This editor has been part of Unix systems for a long time. We use it here because it is an interactive program that catches the interrupt and quit signals. If we invoke ed from a shell, and type the interrupt character, it catches the interrupt signal and prints a question mark. It also sets the disposition of the quit signal so that it is ignored.)

```c
#include     <sys/types.h>
#include     <signal.h>
#include     "ourhdr.h"

static void sig_int(int), sig_chld(int);

int
main(void)
{
    int      status;

    if (signal(SIGINT, sig_int) == SIG_ERR)
        err_sys("signal(SIGINT) error");
    if (signal(SIGCHLD, sig_chld) == SIG_ERR)
        err_sys("signal(SIGCHLD) error");

    if ( (status = system("/bin/ed")) < 0)
        err_sys("system() error");
    exit(0);
}

static void
sig_int(int signo)
{
    printf("caught SIGINT\n");
    return;
}

static void
sig_chld(int signo)
{
    printf("caught SIGCHLD\n");
    return;
}
```

Program 10.19 Using system to invoke the ed editor.

Program 10.19 catches both SIGINT and SIGCHLD. If we invoke it we get

```
$ a.out
a                              append text to the editor's buffer
Here is one line of text
and another
                               period on a line by itself stops append mode
```

```
1,$p                             print first through last lines of buffer to see what's there
Here is one line of text
and another
w temp.foo                       write the buffer to a file
37                               editor says it wrote 37 bytes
q                                and leave the editor
caught SIGCHLD
```

What is happening when the editor terminates is that SIGCHLD is generated for the parent (the a.out process). We catch it and return from the signal handler. But if the parent is catching the SIGCHLD signal, it should be doing so because it has created its own children, so that it knows when its children have terminated. The delivery of this signal in the parent should be blocked while the system function is executing. Indeed, this is what POSIX.2 specifies. Otherwise, when the child created by system terminates, it would fool the caller of system into thinking that one of its own children terminated.

If we execute the program again, this time sending an interrupt signal to the editor, we get

```
$ a.out
a                                append text to the editor's buffer
_hello, world
                                 period on a line by itself stops append mode
1,$p                             print first through last lines to see what's there
hello, world
w temp.foo                       write the buffer to a file
13                               editor says it wrote 13 bytes
^?                               type our interrupt character
?                                editor catches signal, prints question mark
caught SIGINT                    and so does the parent process
q                                leave editor
caught SIGCHLD
```

Recall from Section 9.6 that typing the interrupt character causes the interrupt signal to be sent to all the processes in the foreground process group. Figure 10.7 shows the arrangement of the processes when the editor is running.

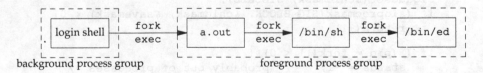

Figure 10.7 Foreground and background process groups for Program 10.19.

In this example SIGINT is sent to all three foreground processes. (The shell ignores it.) As we can see from the output, both the a.out process and the editor catch the signal. But when we're running another program with the system function, we shouldn't have both the parent and the child catching the two terminal-generated signals: interrupt and quit. These two signals should really be sent to the program that is running: the child. Since the command that is executed by system can be an interactive command (as is

the ed program in this example) and since the caller of system gives up control while
the program executes, waiting for it to finish, the caller of system should not be receiving these two terminal-generated signals. This is why POSIX.2 specifies that the caller
of system should ignore these two signals.   □

Example

Program 10.20 shows an implementation of the system function with the required signal handling.

```c
#include        <sys/types.h>
#include        <sys/wait.h>
#include        <errno.h>
#include        <signal.h>
#include        <unistd.h>

int
system(const char *cmdstring)    /* with appropriate signal handling */
{
    pid_t              pid;
    int                status;
    struct sigaction   ignore, saveintr, savequit;
    sigset_t           chldmask, savemask;

    if (cmdstring == NULL)
        return(1);         /* always a command processor with Unix */

    ignore.sa_handler = SIG_IGN;     /* ignore SIGINT and SIGQUIT */
    sigemptyset(&ignore.sa_mask);
    ignore.sa_flags = 0;
    if (sigaction(SIGINT, &ignore, &saveintr) < 0)
        return(-1);
    if (sigaction(SIGQUIT, &ignore, &savequit) < 0)
        return(-1);

    sigemptyset(&chldmask);             /* now block SIGCHLD */
    sigaddset(&chldmask, SIGCHLD);
    if (sigprocmask(SIG_BLOCK, &chldmask, &savemask) < 0)
        return(-1);

    if ( (pid = fork()) < 0) {
        status = -1;    /* probably out of processes */

    } else if (pid == 0) {              /* child */
            /* restore previous signal actions & reset signal mask */
        sigaction(SIGINT, &saveintr, NULL);
        sigaction(SIGQUIT, &savequit, NULL);
        sigprocmask(SIG_SETMASK, &savemask, NULL);

        execl("/bin/sh", "sh", "-c", cmdstring, (char *) 0);
        _exit(127);       /* exec error */
```

```
        } else {                               /* parent */
            while (waitpid(pid, &status, 0) < 0)
                if (errno != EINTR) {
                    status = -1; /* error other than EINTR from waitpid() */
                    break;
                }
        }

        /* restore previous signal actions & reset signal mask */
    if (sigaction(SIGINT, &saveintr, NULL) < 0)
        return(-1);
    if (sigaction(SIGQUIT, &savequit, NULL) < 0)
        return(-1);
    if (sigprocmask(SIG_SETMASK, &savemask, NULL) < 0)
        return(-1);

    return(status);
}
```

Program 10.20 Correct POSIX.2 implementation of system function.

Many older texts show the ignoring of the interrupt and quit signals as follows:

```
    if ( (pid = fork()) < 0)
        err_sys("fork error");
    else if (pid == 0) {      /* child */
        execl(...);
        _exit(127);
    }
    /* parent */
    old_intr = signal(SIGINT, SIG_IGN);
    old_quit = signal(SIGQUIT, SIG_IGN);
    waitpid(pid, &status, 0)
    signal(SIGINT, old_intr);
    signal(SIGQUIT, old_quit);
```

The problem with this sequence of code is that we have no guarantee after the fork whether the parent or child runs first. If the child runs first and the parent doesn't run for some time after, it's possible for an interrupt signal to be generated before the parent is able to change its disposition to be ignored. For this reason, in Program 10.20 we change the disposition of the signals before the fork.

Notice that we have to reset the dispositions of these two signals in the child before the call to execl. This allows execl to change their dispositions to the default, based on the caller's dispositions, as we described in Section 8.9. □

Return Value from system

Beware of the return value from system. It is the termination status of the shell, which isn't always the termination status of the command string. We saw some examples in

Program 8.13, and the results were as we expected: if we execute a simple command such as date, the termination status is 0. Executing the shell command exit 44 gave us a termination status of 44. What happens with signals?

Let's run Program 8.14 and send some signals to the command that's executing.

```
$ tsys "sleep 30"
^?normal termination, exit status = 130    we type our interrupt key
$ tsys "sleep 30"
^\sh: 946 Quit                             we type our quit key
normal termination, exit status = 131
```

When we terminate the sleep with the interrupt signal, the pr_exit function (Program 8.3) thinks it terminated normally. The same thing happens when we kill the sleep with the quit key. What is happening here is that the Bourne shell has a poorly documented feature that its termination status is 128 plus the signal number, when the command it was executing is terminated by a signal. We can see this with the shell interactively.

```
$ sh                                       make sure we're running the Bourne shell
$ sh -c "sleep 30"
^?                                         type our interrupt key
$ echo $?                                  print termination status of last command
130
$ sh -c "sleep 30"
^\sh: 962 Quit - core dumped               type our quit key
$ echo $?                                  print termination status of last command
131
$ exit                                     leave Bourne shell
```

On the system being used, SIGINT has a value of 2 and SIGQUIT has a value of 3, giving us the shell's termination statuses of 130 and 131.

Let's try a similar example, but this time we'll send a signal directly to the shell and see what gets returned by system.

```
$ tsys "sleep 30" &                        start it in background this time
[1]      980
$ ps                                       look at the process IDs
  PID TT STAT  TIME COMMAND
  980 p3 S     0:00 tsys sleep 30
  981 p3 S     0:00 sh -c sleep 30
  982 p3 S     0:00 sleep 30
  985 p3 R     0:00 ps
$ kill -KILL 981                           kill the shell itself
abnormal termination, signal number = 9
[1] + Done        tsys "sleep 30" &
```

Here we can see that the return value from system reports an abnormal termination only when the shell itself abnormally terminates.

When writing programs that use the system function, be sure to interpret the return value correctly. If we call fork, exec, and wait ourself, the termination status is different than if we call system.

10.19 `sleep` Function

We've used the `sleep` function in numerous examples throughout the text, and we showed two flawed implementations of it in Programs 10.4 and 10.5.

```
#include <unistd.h>

unsigned int sleep(unsigned int seconds);
```
                                                            Returns: 0 or number of unslept seconds

This function causes the calling process to be suspended until either

1. the amount of wall clock time specified by *seconds* has elapsed, or
2. a signal is caught by the process and the signal handler returns.

As with an `alarm` signal, the actual return may be at a time later than requested, because of other system activity.

In case 1 the return value is 0. When `sleep` returns early, because of some signal being caught (case 2), the return value is the number of unslept seconds (the requested time minus the actual time slept).

`sleep` can be implemented with the `alarm` function (Section 10.10), but this isn't required. If `alarm` is used, however, there can be interactions between the two functions. The POSIX.1 standard leaves all these interactions unspecified. For example, if we do an `alarm(10)` and 3 wall clock seconds later do a `sleep(5)`, what happens? The `sleep` will return in 5 seconds (assuming some other signal isn't caught in that time), but will another `SIGALRM` be generated 2 seconds later? These details depend on the implementation.

> SVR4 implements `sleep` using `alarm`. The `sleep(3)` manual page says that a previously scheduled alarm is properly handled. For example, in the preceding scenario, before `sleep` returns it will reschedule the alarm to happen 2 seconds later. `sleep` returns 0 in this case. (Obviously, `sleep` must save the address of the signal handler for `SIGALRM` and reset it before returning.) Also, if we do an `alarm(6)` and 3 wall clock seconds later do a `sleep(5)`, the `sleep` returns in 3 seconds (when the alarm goes off), not in 5 seconds. Here the return value from `sleep` is 2 (the number of unslept seconds).

> 4.3+BSD, on the other hand, uses another technique: the interval timer provided by `setitimer(2)`. This timer is independent of the `alarm` function, but there can still be interaction between a previously set interval timer and `sleep`. Also, even though the alarm timer (`alarm`) and interval timer (`setitimer`) are separate, they (unfortunately) use the same `SIGALRM` signal. Since `sleep` temporarily changes the address of the signal handler for this signal to its own function, there can still be unwanted interactions between `alarm` and `sleep`.

> The moral in all this is to be intimately aware of how your system implements `sleep` if you have any intentions of mixing calls to `sleep` with any other timing functions.

> Previous Berkeley-derived implementations of `sleep` did not provide any useful return information. This has been fixed in 4.3+BSD.

Example

Program 10.21 shows an implementation of the POSIX.1 `sleep` function. This function is a modification of Program 10.4 that handles signals reliably, avoiding the race condition in the earlier implementation. We still do not handle any interactions with previously set alarms. (As we mentioned, these interactions are explicitly undefined by POSIX.1.)

```c
#include     <signal.h>
#include     <stddef.h>
#include     "ourhdr.h"

static void
sig_alrm(void)
{
    return; /* nothing to do, just returning wakes up sigsuspend() */
}

unsigned int
sleep(unsigned int nsecs)
{
    struct sigaction    newact, oldact;
    sigset_t            newmask, oldmask, suspmask;
    unsigned int        unslept;

    newact.sa_handler = sig_alrm;
    sigemptyset(&newact.sa_mask);
    newact.sa_flags = 0;
    sigaction(SIGALRM, &newact, &oldact);
                    /* set our handler, save previous information */

    sigemptyset(&newmask);
    sigaddset(&newmask, SIGALRM);
                    /* block SIGALRM and save current signal mask */
    sigprocmask(SIG_BLOCK, &newmask, &oldmask);

    alarm(nsecs);

    suspmask = oldmask;
    sigdelset(&suspmask, SIGALRM);   /* make sure SIGALRM isn't blocked */

    sigsuspend(&suspmask);           /* wait for any signal to be caught */

    /* some signal has been caught, SIGALRM is now blocked */

    unslept = alarm(0);
    sigaction(SIGALRM, &oldact, NULL);  /* reset previous action */

                    /* reset signal mask, which unblocks SIGALRM */
    sigprocmask(SIG_SETMASK, &oldmask, NULL);

    return(unslept);
}
```

Program 10.21 Reliable implementation of `sleep`.

It takes more code to write this reliable implementation than Program 10.4. We don't use any form of nonlocal branching (as we did in Program 10.5 to avoid the race condition between the alarm and pause), so there is no effect on other signal handlers that may be executing when the SIGALRM is handled.   □

10.20 Job-Control Signals

From Figure 10.1 there are six signals that POSIX.1 considers the job-control signals.

SIGCHLD	Child process has stopped or terminated.
SIGCONT	Continue process, if stopped.
SIGSTOP	Stop signal (can't be caught or ignored).
SIGTSTP	Interactive stop signal.
SIGTTIN	Read from controlling terminal by member of a background process group.
SIGTTOU	Write to controlling terminal by member of a background process group.

> Although POSIX.1 requires the system to support SIGCHLD only if the system supports job control, almost every version of Unix supports the signal. We have already described how this signal is generated when a child process terminates.

Most application programs don't handle these signals—interactive shells usually do all the work required to handle these signals. When we type the suspend character (usually Control-Z), SIGTSTP is sent to all processes in the foreground process group. When we tell the shell to resume a job in the foreground or background, the shell sends all the processes in the job the SIGCONT signal. Similarly, if SIGTTIN or SIGTTOU is delivered to a process, the process is stopped by default, and the job-control shell recognizes this and notifies us.

An exception is a process that is managing the terminal—the vi(1) editor, for example. It needs to know when the user wants to suspend it, so that it can restore the terminal's state to the way it was when vi was started. Also, when it resumes in the foreground it needs to set the terminal state back to way it wants it, and it needs to redraw the terminal screen. We see how a program such as vi handles this in the example that follows.

There are some interactions between the job-control signals. When any of the four stop signals are generated for a process (SIGTSTP, SIGSTOP, SIGTTIN, or SIGTTOU), any pending SIGCONT signal for that process is discarded. Similarly, when the SIGCONT signal is generated for a process, any pending stop signals for that same process are discarded.

Notice that the default action for SIGCONT is to continue the process, if it is stopped, otherwise the signal is ignored. Normally we don't have to do anything with this signal. When SIGCONT is generated for a process that is stopped, the process is continued, even if the signal is blocked or ignored.

Example

Program 10.22 demonstrates the normal sequence of code used when a program handles job control. This program just copies its standard input to its standard output, but comments are given in the signal handler for typical actions performed by a program that manages a screen. When Program 10.22 starts, it arranges to catch the SIGTSTP signal only if the signal's disposition is SIG_DFL. The reason is that when the program is started by a shell that doesn't support job control (/bin/sh, for example), the signal's disposition should be set to SIG_IGN. Actually, the shell doesn't explicitly ignore this signal, init sets the disposition of the three job-control signals SIGTSTP, SIGTTIN, and SIGTTOU to SIG_IGN. This disposition is then inherited by all login shells. Only a job-control shell should reset the disposition of these three signals to SIG_DFL.

When we type the suspend character, the process receives the SIGTSTP signal, and the signal handler is invoked. At this point we would do any terminal-related processing: move the cursor to the lower left corner, restore the terminal mode, and so on. We then send ourself the same signal, SIGTSTP, after resetting its disposition to its default (stop the process) and unblocking the signal. We have to unblock it since we're currently handling that same signal, and the system blocks it automatically while it's being caught. At this point the system stops the process. It is continued only when someone (usually the job-control shell, in response to an interactive fg command) sends it a SIGCONT signal. We don't catch SIGCONT. Its default disposition is to continue the stopped process, and when this happens the program continues as though it returned from the kill function. When the program is continued we reset the disposition for the SIGTSTP signal and do whatever terminal processing we want (we could redraw the screen, for example).   □

We'll see another way to handle the special job-control suspend character in Chapter 18, when we don't use the signal, but recognize the special character ourself.

10.21 Additional Features

In this section we describe some additional implementation-dependent features of signals.

Signal Names

Some systems provide the array

```
extern char *sys_siglist[];
```

The array index is the signal number, giving a pointer to the character string name of the signal.

```
#include    <signal.h>
#include    "ourhdr.h"

#define BUFFSIZE    1024

static void sig_tstp(int);

int
main(void)
{
    int     n;
    char    buf[BUFFSIZE];

    /* only catch SIGTSTP if we're running with a job-control shell */
    if (signal(SIGTSTP, SIG_IGN) == SIG_DFL)
        signal(SIGTSTP, sig_tstp);

    while ( (n = read(STDIN_FILENO, buf, BUFFSIZE)) > 0)
        if (write(STDOUT_FILENO, buf, n) != n)
            err_sys("write error");
    if (n < 0)
        err_sys("read error");

    exit(0);
}

static void
sig_tstp(int signo)  /* signal handler for SIGTSTP */
{
    sigset_t    mask;

    /* ... move cursor to lower left corner, reset tty mode ... */

    /* unblock SIGTSTP, since it's blocked while we're handling it */
    sigemptyset(&mask);
    sigaddset(&mask, SIGTSTP);
    sigprocmask(SIG_UNBLOCK, &mask, NULL);

    signal(SIGTSTP, SIG_DFL);    /* reset disposition to default */

    kill(getpid(), SIGTSTP);     /* and send the signal to ourself */

        /* we won't return from the kill until we're continued */

    signal(SIGTSTP, sig_tstp);   /* reestablish signal handler */

    /* ... reset tty mode, redraw screen ... */
    return;
}
```

Program 10.22 How to handle SIGTSTP.

These systems normally provide the function psignal also.

```
#include <signal.h>

void psignal(int signo, const char *msg);
```

The string *msg* (which is normally the name of the program) is output to the standard error, followed by a colon and a space, followed by a description of the signal, followed by a newline. This function is similar to perror (Section 1.7).

> Both SVR4 and 4.3+BSD provide sys_siglist and the psignal function.

Additional Arguments to SVR4 Signal Handler

When we call sigaction to set the disposition for a signal, we can specify an sa_flags value of SA_SIGINFO (Figure 10.5). This causes two additional arguments to be passed to the signal handler. The integer signal number is always passed as the first argument. The second argument is either a null pointer or a pointer to a siginfo structure. (The third argument provides information about different threads of control within a single process, which we don't discuss.)

```
struct siginfo {
    int    si_signo;   /* signal number */
    int    si_errno;   /* if nonzero, errno value from <errno.h> */
    int    si_code;    /* additional info (depends on signal) */
    pid_t  si_pid;     /* sending process ID */
    uid_t  si_uid;     /* sending process real user ID */
    /* other fields also */
};
```

For hardware generated signals, such as SIGFPE, the si_code value gives additional information: FPE_INTDIV means integer divide by 0, FPE_FLTDIV means floating point divide by 0, and so on. If si_code is less than or equal to 0, it means the signal was generated by a user process that called kill(2). In this case the two elements si_pid and si_uid give additional information on the process that sent us the signal. Other information is available that depends on the signal being caught; see the SVR4 siginfo(5) manual page.

Additional Arguments to 4.3+BSD Signal Handler

4.3+BSD always calls a signal handler with three arguments.

```
handler(int signo, int code, struct sigcontext *scp);
```

The argument *signo* is the signal number, and *code* gives additional information for certain signals. For example, a *code* of FPE_INTDIV_TRAP for SIGFPE means integer divide by 0. The third argument, *scp*, is hardware dependent.

10.22 Summary

Signals are used in most nontrivial applications. An understanding of the hows and whys of signal handling is essential to advanced Unix programming. This chapter has been a long and thorough look at Unix signals. We started by looking at the warts in previous implementations of signals and how they manifest themselves. We then proceeded to the POSIX.1 reliable signal concept and all the related functions. Once we covered all these details, we were able to provide implementations of the POSIX.1 `abort`, `system`, and `sleep` functions. We finished with a look at the job-control signals.

Exercises

10.1 In Program 10.1 remove the `for (;;)` statement? What happens and why?

10.2 Implement the `raise` function.

10.3 Draw pictures of the stack frames when we run Program 10.6.

10.4 In Program 10.8 we showed a technique that's often used to set a time out on an I/O operation using `setjmp` and `longjmp`. The following code has also been seen:

```
signal(SIGALRM, sig_alrm);
alarm(60);
if (setjmp(env_alrm) != 0) {
    /* handle time out */
    ...
}
...
```

What else is wrong with this sequence of code?

10.5 Using only a single timer (either `alarm` or the higher precision `setitimer`) provide a set of functions that allows a process to set any number of timers.

10.6 Write the following program to test the parent–child synchronization functions in Program 10.17. The process creates a file and writes the integer 0 to the file. The process then calls `fork` and the parent and child alternate incrementing the counter in the file. Each time the counter is incremented, print which process is doing the increment (parent or child).

10.7 In Program 10.18 if the caller catches `SIGABRT` and returns from the signal handler, why do we go to the trouble of resetting the disposition to its default and call `kill` the second time, instead of just calling `_exit`?

10.8 Why do you think the designers of the SVR4 `siginfo` feature (Section 10.21) chose to pass the real user ID, instead of the effective user ID, in the `si_uid` field?

10.9 Rewrite Program 10.10 to handle all the signals from Figure 10.1. The function should consist of a single loop that iterates once for every signal in the current signal mask (not once for every possible signal).

10.10 Write a program that calls `sleep(60)` in an infinite loop. Every five times through the loop (every 5 minutes) fetch the current time-of-day and print the `tm_sec` field. Run the program overnight and explain the results. How would a program such as the BSD `cron` daemon, which runs every minute on the minute, handle this?

10.11 Modify Program 3.3 as follows: (a) change `BUFFSIZE` to 100; (b) catch the `SIGXFSZ` signal using the `signal_intr` function, printing a message when it's caught, and returning from the signal handler; and (c) print the return value from `write` if the requested number of bytes weren't written. Modify the soft `RLIMIT_FSIZE` resource limit (Section 7.11) to 1024 bytes and run your new program, copying a file that is larger than 1024 bytes. (Try to set the soft resource limit from your shell. If you can't do this from your shell, call `setrlimit` directly from the program.) Run this program on the different systems that you have access to. What happens and why?

10.12 Write a program that calls `fwrite` with a large buffer (a few megabytes). Before calling `fwrite`, call `alarm` to schedule a signal in 1 second. In your signal handler print that the signal was caught and return. Does the call to `fwrite` complete? What's happening?

11

Terminal I/O

11.1 Introduction

The handling of terminal I/O is a messy area, regardless of the operating system. Unix is no exception. The manual page for terminal I/O is usually one of the longest in most editions of the Unix manuals. The `termio` manual page in the SVID exceeds 16 pages.

With Unix, a schism formed in the late 1970s when System III developed a different set of terminal routines from Version 7. The System III style of terminal I/O continued through System V, and the Version 7 style became the standard for the Berkeley-derived systems. As with signals, this difference between the two worlds has been conquered by POSIX.1. In this chapter we look at all the POSIX.1 terminal functions, and some of the SVR4 and 4.3+BSD additions.

Part of the complexity of the terminal I/O system is because people use terminal I/O for so many different things: terminals, hardwired lines between computers, modems, printers, and so on. In later chapters we develop two programs to demonstrate terminal I/O: one communicates with a PostScript printer (Chapter 17) and the other allows us to talk to a modem and log in to a remote computer (Chapter 18).

11.2 Overview

There are two different modes for terminal I/O:

1. Canonical mode input processing. In this mode terminal input is processed as lines. The terminal driver returns at most one line per read request.

2. Noncanonical mode input processing. The input characters are not assembled into lines.

If we don't do anything special, canonical mode is the default. For example, if the shell redirects standard input to the terminal and we copy standard input to standard output using read and write, the terminal is in the canonical mode and each read returns at most one line. Programs that manipulate the entire screen, such as the vi editor, use noncanonical mode, since the commands may be single characters and are not terminated by newlines. Also, this editor doesn't want processing by the system of the special characters since the special characters may overlap with the editor commands. For example, the Control-D character is often the end-of-file character for the terminal, but it's also a vi command to scroll down one-half screen.

> The Version 7 and BSD-style terminal drivers support three different modes for terminal input: (a) cooked mode (the input is collected into lines and the special characters are processed), (b) raw mode (the input is not assembled into lines and there is no processing of special characters), and (c) cbreak mode (the input is not assembled into lines, but some of the special characters are processed). Program 11.10 shows a POSIX.1 function that places a terminal in cbreak or raw mode.

POSIX.1 defines 11 special input characters, 9 of which we can change. We've been using some of these throughout the text: the end-of-file character (usually Control-D) and the suspend character (usually Control-Z), for example. Section 11.3 describes each of these characters.

We can think of a terminal device as being controlled by a terminal driver, probably within the kernel. Each terminal device has an input queue and an output queue, shown in Figure 11.1.

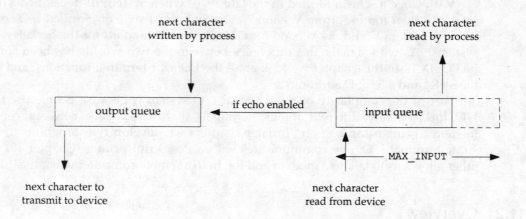

Figure 11.1 Logical picture of input and output queues for a terminal device.

There are several points to consider from this picture.

- There is an implied link between the input queue and the output queue, if echoing is enabled.

- The size of the input queue, MAX_INPUT (refer to Figure 2.5), may be finite. What the system does when the input queue for a particular device fills is implementation dependent. Most Unix systems echo the bell character when this happens.

- There is another input limit that we don't show here, MAX_CANON. This is the maximum number of bytes in a canonical input line.

- Although the output queue is normally of a finite size, there are no constants defining its size that are accessible to the program. This is because when the output queue starts to fill up, the kernel just puts the writing process to sleep until room is available.

- We'll see how the tcflush flush function allows us to flush either the input queue or the output queue. Similarly, when we describe the tcsetattr function, we'll see how we can tell the system to change the attributes of a terminal device only after the output queue is empty. (We want to do this, for example, if we're changing the output attributes.) We can also tell the system that when it changes the terminal attributes, to discard everything in the input queue also. (We want to do this if we're changing the input attributes or changing between canonical and noncanonical modes, so that previously entered characters aren't interpreted in the wrong mode.)

Most Unix systems implement all the canonical processing in a module called the *terminal line discipline*. We can think of this as a box that sits between the kernel's generic read and write functions and the actual device driver. We show this in Figure 11.2.

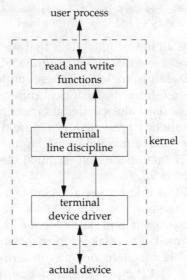

Figure 11.2 Terminal line discipline.

We'll return to this picture in Section 12.4 when we discuss the stream I/O system, and in Chapter 19 when we discuss pseudo terminals.

All the characteristics of a terminal device that we can examine and change are contained in a `termios` structure. This is defined in the header `<termios.h>`, which we use throughout this chapter.

```
struct termios {
  tcflag_t  c_iflag;        /* input flags */
  tcflag_t  c_oflag;        /* output flags */
  tcflag_t  c_cflag;        /* control flags */
  tcflag_t  c_lflag;        /* local flags */
  cc_t      c_cc[NCCS];     /* control characters */
};
```

Roughly speaking, the input flags control the input of characters by the terminal device driver (strip eighth bit on input, enable input parity checking, etc.), the output flags control the driver output (perform output processing, map newline to CR/LF, etc.), the control flags affect the RS-232 serial lines (ignore modem status lines, one or two stop bits per character, etc.), and the local flags affect the interface between the driver and the user (echo on or off, visually erase characters, enable terminal-generated signals, job control stop signal for background output, etc.).

The type `tcflag_t` is big enough to hold each of the flag values. It is often defined as an `unsigned long`. The `c_cc` array contains all the special characters that we can change. `NCCS` is the number of elements in this array and is typically between 11 and 18 (since most Unix implementations support more than the 11 POSIX-defined special characters). The `cc_t` type is large enough to hold each special character and is typically an `unsigned char`.

> Earlier versions of System V had a header named `<termio.h>` and a structure named `termio`. POSIX.1 added an s to the names, to differentiate them from their predecessors.

Figure 11.3 lists all the terminal flags that we can change to affect the characteristics of a terminal device. Note that even though POSIX.1 defines a common subset that both SVR4 and 4.3+BSD start from, both of these implementations have their own additions. These additions come from the historical differences between the two systems. We'll discuss each of these flag values in detail in Section 11.5.

Given all the options presented in Figure 11.3, how do we examine and change these characteristics of a terminal device? Figure 11.4 summarizes the various functions defined by POSIX.1 that operate on terminal devices. (We described `tcgetpgrp` and `tcsetpgrp` in Section 9.7.)

Note that POSIX.1 doesn't use the classic `ioctl` on terminal devices. Instead, it uses the 12 functions shown in Figure 11.4. The reason is that the `ioctl` function for terminal devices uses a different data type for its final argument, which depends on the action being performed. This makes type checking of the arguments impossible.

Although only 12 functions operate on terminal devices, realize that the first two functions in Figure 11.4, `tcgetattr` and `tcsetattr`, manipulate about 50 different flags (Figure 11.3). The large number of options available for terminal devices and trying to determine which options are required for a particular device (be it a terminal, modem, laser printer, or whatever) complicates the handling of terminal devices.

Field	Flag	Description	POSIX.1	SVR4	4.3+BSD extension
c_iflag	BRKINT	generate SIGINT on BREAK	•		
	ICRNL	map CR to NL on input	•		
	IGNBRK	ignore BREAK condition	•		
	IGNCR	ignore CR	•		
	IGNPAR	ignore characters with parity errors	•		
	IMAXBEL	ring bell on input queue full		•	•
	INLCR	map NL to CR on input	•		
	INPCK	enable input parity checking	•		
	ISTRIP	strip eighth bit off input characters	•		
	IUCLC	map uppercase to lowercase on input		•	
	IXANY	enable any characters to restart output		•	•
	IXOFF	enable start/stop input flow control	•		
	IXON	enable start/stop output flow control	•		
	PARMRK	mark parity errors	•		
c_oflag	BSDLY	backspace delay mask		•	
	CRDLY	CR delay mask		•	
	FFDLY	form feed delay mask		•	
	NLDLY	NL delay mask		•	
	OCRNL	map CR to NL on output		•	
	OFDEL	fill is DEL, else NUL		•	
	OFILL	use fill character for delay		•	
	OLCUC	map lowercase to uppercase on output		•	
	ONLCR	map NL to CR-NL (ala CRMOD)		•	•
	ONLRET	NL performs CR function		•	
	ONOCR	no CR output at column 0		•	
	ONOEOT	discard EOTs (^D) on output			•
	OPOST	perform output processing	•		
	OXTABS	expand tabs to spaces			•
	TABDLY	horizontal tab delay mask		•	
	VTDLY	vertical tab delay mask		•	
c_cflag	CCTS_OFLOW	CTS flow control of output			•
	CIGNORE	ignore control flags			•
	CLOCAL	ignore modem status lines	•		
	CREAD	enable receiver	•		
	CRTS_IFLOW	RTS flow control of input			•
	CSIZE	character size mask	•		
	CSTOPB	send two stop bits, else one	•		
	HUPCL	hangup on last close	•		
	MDMBUF	flow control output via Carrier			•
	PARENB	parity enable	•		
	PARODD	odd parity, else even	•		
c_lflag	ALTWERASE	use alternate WERASE algorithm			•
	ECHO	enable echo	•		
	ECHOCTL	echo control chars as ^(Char)		•	•
	ECHOE	visually erase chars	•		
	ECHOK	echo kill	•		
	ECHOKE	visual erase for kill		•	•
	ECHONL	echo NL	•		
	ECHOPRT	visual erase mode for hardcopy		•	•
	FLUSHO	output being flushed		•	•
	ICANON	canonical input	•		
	IEXTEN	enable extended input char processing	•		
	ISIG	enable terminal-generated signals	•		
	NOFLSH	disable flush after interrupt or quit	•		
	NOKERNINFO	no kernel output from STATUS			•
	PENDIN	retype pending input		•	•
	TOSTOP	send SIGTTOU for background output	•		
	XCASE	canonical upper/lower presentation		•	

Figure 11.3 Terminal flags.

Function	Description
tcgetattr	fetch attributes (termios structure)
tcsetattr	set attributes (termios structure)
cfgetispeed	get input speed
cfgetospeed	get output speed
cfsetispeed	set input speed
cfsetospeed	set output speed
tcdrain	wait for all output to be transmitted
tcflow	suspend transmit or receive
tcflush	flush pending input and/or output
tcsendbreak	send BREAK character
tcgetpgrp	get foreground process group ID
tcsetpgrp	set foreground process group ID

Figure 11.4 Summary of POSIX.1 terminal I/O functions.

The relationships among the 12 functions shown in Figure 11.4 are shown in Figure 11.5.

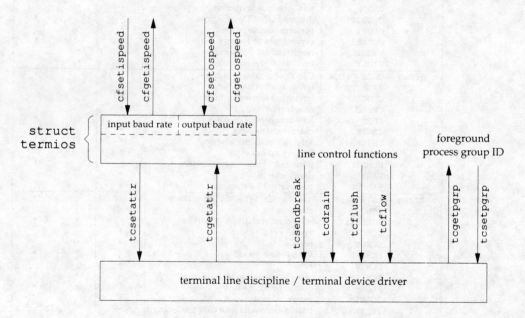

Figure 11.5 Relationship between the terminal-related functions.

POSIX.1 doesn't specify where in the termios structure the baud rate information is stored, that is an implementation feature. Many older systems stored this information in the c_cflag field. 4.3+BSD has two separate fields in the structure—one for the input speed and one for the output speed.

11.3 Special Input Characters

POSIX.1 defines 11 different characters that are handled specially on input. SVR4 adds another 6 special characters and 4.3+BSD adds 7. Figure 11.6 summarizes these special characters.

Character	Description	c_cc subscript	Enabled by field	flag	Typical value	POSIX.1	SVR4	4.3+BSD extension
CR	carriage return	(can't change)	c_lflag	ICANON	\r	•		
DISCARD	discard output	VDISCARD	c_lflag	IEXTEN	^O		•	•
DSUSP	delayed suspend (SIGTSTP)	VDSUSP	c_lflag	ISIG	^Y		•	•
EOF	end-of-file	VEOF	c_lflag	ICANON	^D	•		
EOL	end-of-line	VEOL	c_lflag	ICANON		•		
EOL2	alternate end-of-line	VEOL2	c_lflag	ICANON			•	•
ERASE	backspace one character	VERASE	c_lflag	ICANON	^H	•		
INTR	interrupt signal (SIGINT)	VINTR	c_lflag	ISIG	?,^C	•		
KILL	erase line	VKILL	c_lflag	ICANON	^U	•		
LNEXT	literal next	VLNEXT	c_lflag	IEXTEN	^V		•	•
NL	linefeed	(can't change)	c_lflag	ICANON	\n	•		
QUIT	quit signal (SIGQUIT)	VQUIT	c_lflag	ISIG	^\	•		
REPRINT	reprint all input	VREPRINT	c_lflag	ICANON	^R		•	•
START	resume output	VSTART	c_iflag	IXON/IXOFF	^Q	•		
STATUS	status request	VSTATUS	c_lflag	ICANON	^T			•
STOP	stop output	VSTOP	c_iflag	IXON/IXOFF	^S	•		
SUSP	suspend signal (SIGTSTP)	VSUSP	c_lflag	ISIG	^Z	•		
WERASE	backspace one word	VWERASE	c_lflag	ICANON	^W		•	•

Figure 11.6 Summary of special terminal input characters.

Of the 11 POSIX.1 special characters, we can change nine of them to almost any value that we like. The exceptions are the newline and carriage-return characters, (\n and \r respectively), and perhaps the STOP and START characters (depends on the implementation). To do this we modify the appropriate entry in the c_cc array of the termios structure. The elements in this array are referred to by name, with each name beginning with a V (the third column in Figure 11.6).

POSIX.1 optionally allows us to disable these characters. If _POSIX_VDISABLE is in effect, then the value of _POSIX_VDISABLE can be stored in the appropriate entry in the c_cc array to disable that special character. This feature can be queried with the pathconf and fpathconf functions (Section 2.5.4).

FIPS 151−1 requires support for _POSIX_VDISABLE.

SVR4 and 4.3+BSD also support this feature. SVR4 defines _POSIX_VDISABLE as 0, while 4.3+BSD defines it as octal 377.

Some earlier Unix systems disabled a feature if the corresponding special input character was 0.

Example

Before describing all the special characters in detail, let's look at a small program that changes them. Program 11.1 disables the interrupt character and sets the end-of-file character to Control-B.

```
#include    <termios.h>
#include    "ourhdr.h"

int
main(void)
{
    struct termios  term;
    long            vdisable;

    if (isatty(STDIN_FILENO) == 0)
        err_quit("standard input is not a terminal device");

    if ( (vdisable = fpathconf(STDIN_FILENO, _PC_VDISABLE)) < 0)
        err_quit("fpathconf error or _POSIX_VDISABLE not in effect");

    if (tcgetattr(STDIN_FILENO, &term) < 0)  /* fetch tty state */
        err_sys("tcgetattr error");

    term.c_cc[VINTR] = vdisable;        /* disable INTR character */
    term.c_cc[VEOF]  = 2;               /* EOF is Control-B */

    if (tcsetattr(STDIN_FILENO, TCSAFLUSH, &term) < 0)
        err_sys("tcsetattr error");

    exit(0);
}
```

Program 11.1 Disable interrupt character and change end-of-file character.

There are a few things to note in this program.

1. We modify the terminal characters only if standard input is a terminal device. We call isatty (Section 11.9) to check this.

2. We fetch the _POSIX_VDISABLE value using fpathconf.

3. The function tcgetattr (Section 11.4) fetches a termios structure from the kernel. After we've modified this structure we call tcsetattr to set the attributes. The only attributes that change are the ones we specifically modified.

4. Disabling the interrupt key is different from ignoring the interrupt signal. All Program 11.1 does is disable the special character that causes the terminal driver to generate SIGINT. We can still use the kill function to send the process the signal.   □

We now describe each of the special characters in more detail. We call these the special input characters, but two of the characters, STOP and START (Control-S and Control-Q), are also handled specially when output. Note that most of these special characters, when they are recognized by the terminal driver and processed specially, are then discarded: they are not returned to the process in a read operation. The exceptions to this are the newline characters (NL, EOL, EOL2) and the carriage return (CR).

CR   The POSIX.1 carriage return character. We cannot change this character. This character is recognized on input in canonical mode. When both ICANON (canonical mode) and ICRNL (map CR to NL) are set and IGNCR (ignore CR) is not set, the CR character is translated to NL and has the same effect as an NL character.

            This character is returned to the reading process (perhaps after being translated to an NL).

DISCARD   The SVR4 and 4.3+BSD discard character. This character is recognized on input in extended mode (IEXTEN). It causes subsequent output to be discarded, until another DISCARD character is entered or the discard condition is cleared (see the FLUSHO option). This character is discarded when processed (i.e., it is not passed to the process).

DSUSP   The SVR4 and 4.3+BSD delayed-suspend job-control character. This character is recognized on input in extended mode (IEXTEN) if job control is supported and if the ISIG flag is set. Like the SUSP character, this delayed-suspend character generates the SIGTSTP signal that is sent to all processes in the foreground process group (refer to Figure 9.7). But the delayed-suspend character is sent to the process group only when a process reads from the controlling terminal, not when the character is typed. This character is discarded when processed (i.e., it is not passed to the process).

EOF   The POSIX.1 end-of-file character. This character is recognized on input in canonical mode (ICANON). When we type this character, all bytes waiting to be read are immediately passed to the reading process. If there are no bytes waiting to be read, a count of 0 is returned. Entering an EOF character at the beginning of the line is the normal way to indicate an end-of-file to a program. This character is discarded when processed in canonical mode (i.e., it is not passed to the process).

EOL   The POSIX.1 additional line delimiter character, like NL. This character is recognized on input in canonical mode (ICANON).

            This character is not normally used. This character is returned to the reading process.

EOL2   The SVR4 and 4.3+BSD additional line delimiter character, like NL. This character is recognized on input in canonical mode (ICANON).

            This character is not normally used. This character is returned to the reading process.

ERASE   The POSIX.1 erase character (backspace). This character is recognized on input in canonical mode (ICANON). It erases the previous character in the line, not erasing beyond the beginning of the line. This character is discarded when processed in canonical mode (i.e., it is not passed to the process).

INTR The POSIX.1 interrupt character. This character is recognized on input if the ISIG flag is set. It generates the SIGINT signal that is sent to all processes in the foreground process group (refer to Figure 9.7). This character is discarded when processed (i.e., it is not passed to the process).

KILL The POSIX.1 kill character. (The name "kill" is once again a misnomer. This character should be called the line erase character.) It is recognized on input in canonical mode (ICANON). It erases the entire line. It is discarded when processed (i.e., it is not passed to the process).

LNEXT The SVR4 and 4.3+BSD literal-next character. This character is recognized on input in extended mode (IEXTEN). It causes any special meaning of the next character to be ignored. This works for all the special characters mentioned in this section. Using this we can type any character to a program. The LNEXT character is discarded when processed, but the next character entered is passed to the process.

NL The POSIX.1 newline character, which is also called the line delimiter. We cannot change this character. This character is recognized on input in canonical mode (ICANON).

This character is returned to the reading process.

QUIT The POSIX.1 quit character. This character is recognized on input if the ISIG flag is set. It generates the SIGQUIT signal that is sent to all processes in the foreground process group (refer to Figure 9.7). This character is discarded when processed (i.e., it is not passed to the process).

Recall from Figure 10.1 that the difference between INTR and QUIT is that the QUIT character not only terminates the process by default, but it also generates a core file.

REPRINT The SVR4 and 4.3+BSD reprint character. This character is recognized on input in extended, canonical mode (both IEXTEN and ICANON flags set). It causes all unread input to be output (reechoed). This character is discarded when processed (i.e., it is not passed to the process).

START The POSIX.1 start character. This character is recognized on input if the IXON flag is set, and it is automatically generated as output if the IXOFF flag is set. A received START character with IXON set causes stopped output (from a previously entered STOP character) to restart. In this case the START character is discarded when processed (i.e., it is not passed to the process).

When IXOFF is set, the terminal driver automatically generates a START character to resume input that it had previously stopped, when the new input will not overflow the input buffer.

STATUS The 4.3+BSD status-request character. This character is recognized on input in extended, canonical mode (both IEXTEN and ICANON flags set). It generates the SIGINFO signal that is sent to all processes in the foreground process group (refer to Figure 9.7). Additionally, if the NOKERNINFO flag is not set, status information on the foreground process group is also displayed on the terminal. This character is discarded when processed (i.e., it is not passed to the process).

STOP   The POSIX.1 stop character. This character is recognized on input if the IXON flag is set, and it is automatically generated as output if the IXOFF flag is set. A received STOP character with IXON set stops the output. In this case the STOP character is discarded when processed (i.e., it is not passed to the process). The stopped output is restarted when a START character is entered.

When IXOFF is set, the terminal driver automatically generates a STOP character to prevent the input buffer from overflowing.

SUSP   The POSIX.1 suspend job-control character. This character is recognized on input if job control is supported and if the ISIG flag is set. It generates the SIGTSTP signal that is sent to all processes in the foreground process group (refer to Figure 9.7). This character is discarded when processed (i.e., it is not passed to the process).

WERASE   The SVR4 and 4.3+BSD word erase character. This character is recognized on input in extended, canonical mode (both IEXTEN and ICANON flags set). It causes the previous word to be erased. First it skips backward over any whitespace (spaces or tabs), then backward over the previous token, leaving the cursor positioned where the first character of the previous token was located. Normally the previous token ends when a whitespace character is encountered. We can change this, however, by setting the ALTWERASE flag. This flag causes the previous token to end when the first nonalphanumeric character is encountered. The word erase character is discarded when processed (i.e., it is not passed to the process).

Another "character" that we need to define for terminal devices is the BREAK character. BREAK is not really a character, but a condition that occurs during asynchronous serial data transmission. A BREAK condition is signaled to the device driver in various ways, depending on the serial interface. Most terminals have a key labeled BREAK that generates the BREAK condition, which is why most people think of BREAK as a character. For asynchronous serial data transmission, a BREAK is a sequence of zero-valued bits that continues for longer than the time required to send one byte. The entire sequence of zero-valued bits is considered a single BREAK. In Section 11.8 we'll see how to send a BREAK.

11.4   Getting and Setting Terminal Attributes

We call two functions to get and set a termios structure: tcgetattr and tcsetattr. This is how we examine and modify the various option flags and special characters to make the terminal operate the way we want it to.

```
#include <termios.h>

int tcgetattr(int filedes, struct termios *termptr);

int tcsetattr(int filedes, int opt, const struct termios *termptr);
```
Both return: 0 if OK, −1 on error

Both functions take a pointer to a `termios` structure and either return the current terminal attributes or set the terminal's attributes. Since these two functions operate only on terminal devices, if *filedes* does not refer to a terminal device, an error is returned and `errno` is set to `ENOTTY`.

The argument *opt* for `tcsetattr` lets us specify when we want the new terminal attributes to take effect. *opt* is specified as one of the following constants:

TCSANOW   The change occurs immediately.

TCSADRAIN   The change occurs after all output has been transmitted. This option should be used if we are changing the output parameters.

TCSAFLUSH   The change occurs after all output has been transmitted. Furthermore, when the change takes place, all input data that has not been read is discarded (flushed).

The return status of `tcsetattr` confuses the programming. This function returns OK if it was able to perform *any* of the requested actions, even if it couldn't perform all the requested actions. If the function returns OK it is our responsibility to see if all the requested actions were performed. This means that after we call `tcsetattr` to set the desired attributes, we need to call `tcgetattr` and compare the actual terminal's attributes with the desired attributes to detect any differences.

11.5 Terminal Option Flags

In this section we list all the various terminal option flags, expanding the descriptions of all the options from Figure 11.3. This list is alphabetical, and indicates in which of the four terminal flag fields the option appears. (The field a given option is controlled by is usually not apparent from just the option name.) We also list whether each option is POSIX defined or supported by either SVR4 or 4.3+BSD.

All the flags listed specify one or more bits that we turn on or clear, unless we call the flag a *mask*. A mask defines multiple bits. We have a defined name for the mask, and a name for each value. For example, to set the character size, we first zero the bits using the character-size mask `CSIZE`, and then set one of the values `CS5`, `CS6`, `CS7`, or `CS8`.

The six delay values supported by SVR4 are also masks: `BSDLY`, `CRDLY`, `FFDLY`, `NLDLY`, `TABDLY`, and `VTDLY`. Refer to the `termio(7)` manual page in AT&T [1991] for the length of each delay value. In all cases a delay mask of 0 means no delay. If a delay is specified, the OFILL and OFDEL flags determine if the driver does an actual delay or if fill characters are transmitted instead.

Example

Program 11.2 demonstrates the use of these masks to extract a value and to set a value.

```
#include     <termios.h>
#include     "ourhdr.h"

int
main(void)
{
    struct termios   term;
    int              size;

    if (tcgetattr(STDIN_FILENO, &term) < 0)
        err_sys("tcgetattr error");

    size = term.c_cflag & CSIZE;
    if      (size == CS5)   printf("5 bits/byte\n");
    else if (size == CS6)   printf("6 bits/byte\n");
    else if (size == CS7)   printf("7 bits/byte\n");
    else if (size == CS8)   printf("8 bits/byte\n");
    else                    printf("unknown bits/byte\n");

    term.c_cflag &= ~CSIZE;       /* zero out the bits */
    term.c_cflag |= CS8;          /* set 8 bits/byte */

    if (tcsetattr(STDIN_FILENO, TCSANOW, &term) < 0)
        err_sys("tcsetattr error");

    exit(0);
}
```

Program 11.2 Example of tcgetattr.

□

We now describe each of the flags.

ALTWERASE   (c_lflag, 4.3+BSD) When set, an alternate word erase algorithm is used when the WERASE character is entered. Instead of moving backward until the previous whitespace character, this flag causes the WERASE character to move backward until the first nonalphanumeric character is encountered.

BRKINT   (c_iflag, POSIX.1) If this flag is set and IGNBRK is not set, when a BREAK is received the input and output queues are flushed and a SIGINT signal is generated. This signal is generated for the foreground process group if the terminal device is a controlling terminal.

If neither IGNBRK nor BRKINT is set, then a BREAK is read as a single character \0, unless PARMRK is set, in which case the BREAK is read as the three byte sequence \377, \0, \0.

BSDLY   (c_oflag, SVR4) Backspace delay mask. The values for the mask are BS0 or BS1.

CCTS_OFLOW   (c_cflag, 4.3+BSD) CTS flow control of output. (See Exercise 11.4.)

CIGNORE   (c_cflag, 4.3+BSD) Ignore control flags.

CLOCAL   (c_cflag, POSIX.1) If set, the modem status lines are ignored. This usually means that the device is locally attached. When this flag is not set, an open of a terminal device usually blocks until the modem is answered, for example.

CRDLY   (c_oflag, SVR4) Carriage return delay mask. The values for the mask are CR0, CR1, CR2, or CR3.

CREAD   (c_cflag, POSIX.1) If set, the receiver is enabled and characters can be received.

CRTS_IFLOW   (c_cflag, 4.3+BSD) RTS flow control of input. (See Exercise 11.4.)

CSIZE   (c_cflag, POSIX.1) This field is a mask that specifies the number of bits per byte for both transmission and reception. This size does not include the parity bit, if any. The values for the field defined by this mask are CS5, CS6, CS /, and CS8, for 5, 6, 7, and 8 bits per byte, respectively.

CSTOPB   (c_cflag, POSIX.1) If set, two stop bits are used, otherwise one stop bit is used.

ECHO   (c_lflag, POSIX.1) If set, input characters are echoed back to the terminal device. Input characters can be echoed in either canonical or non-canonical mode.

ECHOCTL   (c_lflag, SVR4 and 4.3+BSD) If set and if ECHO is set, ASCII control characters (those character in the range 0 through octal 37, inclusive) other than the ASCII TAB, the ASCII NL, and the START and STOP characters, are echoed as ^X, where X is the character formed by adding octal 100 to the control character. This means the ASCII Control-A character (octal 1) is echoed as ^A. Also, the ASCII DELETE character (octal 177) is echoed as ^?. If this flag is not set, the ASCII control characters are echoed as themselves. As with the ECHO flag, this flag affects the echoing of control characters in both canonical and noncanonical modes.

Be aware that some systems echo the EOF character differently, since its typical value is Control-D. (Control-D is the ASCII EOT character, which can cause some terminals to hangup.) Check your manual.

ECHOE   (c_lflag, POSIX.1) If set and if ICANON is set, the ERASE character erases the last character in the current line from the display. This is usually done in the terminal driver by writing the three-character sequence: backspace, space, backspace.

If the WERASE character is supported, ECHOE causes the previous word to be erased using one or more of the same three-character sequence.

If the ECHOPRT flag is supported, the actions described here for ECHOE assume that the ECHOPRT flag is not set.

ECHOK   (c_lflag, POSIX.1) If set and if ICANON is set, the KILL character erases the current line from the display or outputs the NL character (to emphasize that the entire line was erased).

If the ECHOKE flag is supported, this description of ECHOK assumes that ECHOKE is not set.

ECHOKE   (c_lflag, SVR4 and 4.3+BSD) If set and if ICANON is set, the KILL character is echoed by erasing each character on the line. The way in which each character is erased is selected by the ECHOE and ECHOPRT flags.

ECHONL   (c_lflag, POSIX.1) If set and if ICANON is set, the NL character is echoed, even if ECHO is not set.

ECHOPRT   (c_lflag, SVR4 and 4.3+BSD) If set and if both ICANON and ECHO are set, then the ERASE character (and WERASE character, if supported) cause all the characters being erased to be printed as they are erased. This is often useful on a hardcopy terminal to see exactly which characters are being deleted.

FFDLY   (c_oflag, SVR4) Form feed delay mask. The values for the mask are FF0 or FF1.

FLUSHO   (c_lflag, SVR4 and 4.3+BSD) If set, output is being flushed. This flag is set when we type the DISCARD character, and it is cleared when we type another DISCARD character. We can also set or clear this condition by setting or clearing this terminal flag.

HUPCL   (c_cflag, POSIX.1) If set, when the last process closes the device, the modem control lines are lowered (i.e., the modem connection is broken).

ICANON   (c_lflag, POSIX.1) If set, canonical mode is in effect (Section 11.10). This enables the following characters: EOF, EOL, EOL2, ERASE, KILL, REPRINT, STATUS, and WERASE. The input characters are assembled into lines.

If canonical mode is not enabled, read requests are satisfied directly from the input queue. A read does not return until at least MIN bytes have been received or the time-out value TIME has expired between bytes. Refer to Section 11.11 for additional details.

ICRNL   (c_iflag, POSIX.1) If set and if IGNCR is not set, a received CR character is translated into an NL character.

IEXTEN   (c_lflag, POSIX.1) If set, the extended, implementation-defined special characters are recognized and processed.

IGNBRK   (c_iflag, POSIX.1) When set, a BREAK condition on input is ignored. See BRKINT for a way to have a BREAK condition either generate a SIGINT signal, or be read as data.

IGNCR   (c_iflag, POSIX.1) If set, a received CR character is ignored. If this flag is not set, it is possible to translate the received CR into an NL character if the ICRNL flag is set.

IGNPAR   (c_iflag, POSIX.1) When set, an input byte with a framing error (other than a BREAK) or an input byte with a parity error is ignored.

IMAXBEL   (c_iflag, SVR4 and 4.3+BSD) Ring bell when input queue is full.

INLCR   (c_iflag, POSIX.1) If set, a received NL character is translated into a CR character.

INPCK   (c_iflag, POSIX.1) When set, input parity checking is enabled. If INPCK is not set, input parity checking is disabled.

                Parity "generation and detection" and "input parity checking" are two different things. The generation and detection of parity bits is controlled by the PARENB flag. Setting this flag usually causes the device driver for the serial interface to generate parity for outgoing characters and to verify the parity of incoming characters. The flag PARODD determines if the parity should be odd or even. If an input character arrives with the wrong parity, then the state of the INPCK flag is checked. If this flag is set, then the IGNPAR flag is checked (to see if the input byte with the parity error should be ignored); and if the byte should not be ignored, then the PARMRK flag is checked to see what characters should be passed to the reading process.

ISIG   (c_lflag, POSIX.1) If set, the input characters are compared against the special characters that cause the terminal-generated signals to be generated (INTR, QUIT, SUSP, and DSUSP), and if equal, the corresponding signal is generated.

ISTRIP   (c_iflag, POSIX.1) When set, valid input bytes are stripped to seven bits. When this flag is not set, all eight bits are processed.

IUCLC   (c_iflag, SVR4) Map uppercase to lowercase on input.

IXANY   (c_iflag, SVR4 and 4.3+BSD) Enable any characters to restart output.

IXOFF   (c_iflag, POSIX.1) If set, start–stop input control is enabled. When the terminal driver notices that the input queue is getting full, it outputs a STOP character. This character should be recognized by the device that is sending the data and cause the device to stop. Later, when the characters on the input queue have been processed, the terminal driver will output a START character. This should cause the device to resume sending data.

IXON   (c_iflag, POSIX.1) If set, start–stop output control is enabled. When the terminal driver receives a STOP character, output stops. While the output is stopped, the next START character resumes the output. If this flag is not set, the START and STOP characters are read by the process as normal characters.

MDMBUF   (c_cflag, 4.3+BSD) Flow control the output according to the modem carrier flag.

NLDLY   (c_oflag, SVR4) Newline delay mask. The values for the mask are NL0 or NL1.

NOFLSH   (c_lflag, POSIX.1) By default, when the terminal driver generates the SIGINT and SIGQUIT signals, both the input and output queues are flushed. Also, when it generates the SIGSUSP signal, the input queue is flushed. If the NOFLSH flag is set, this normal flushing of the queues does not occur when these signals are generated.

NOKERNINFO (c_lflag, 4.3+BSD) When set, this flag prevents the STATUS character from printing information on the foreground process group. Regardless of this flag, however, the STATUS character still causes the SIGINFO signal to be sent to the foreground process group.

OCRNL   (c_oflag, SVR4) If set, map CR to NL on output.

OFDEL   (c_oflag, SVR4) If set, the output fill character is ASCII DEL, otherwise it's ASCII NUL. See the OFILL flag.

OFILL   (c_oflag, SVR4) If set, fill characters (either ASCII DEL or ASCII NUL, see the OFDEL flag) are transmitted for a delay, instead of using a timed delay. See the six delay masks: BSDLY, CRDLY, FFDLY, NLDLY, TABDLY, and VTDLY.

OLCUC   (c_oflag, SVR4) If set, map lowercase to uppercase on output.

ONLCR   (c_oflag, SVR4 and 4.3+BSD) If set, map NL to CR-NL on output.

ONLRET   (c_oflag, SVR4) If set, the NL character is assumed to perform the carriage-return function on output.

ONOCR   (c_oflag, SVR4) If set, a CR is not output at column 0.

ONOEOT   (c_oflag, 4.3+BSD) If set, EOT characters (^D) are discarded on output. This may be necessary on some terminals that interpret the Control-D as a hangup.

OPOST   (c_oflag, POSIX.1) If set, implementation-defined output processing takes place. Refer to Figure 11.3 for the various implementation-defined flags for the c_oflag word.

OXTABS   (c_oflag, 4.3+BSD) If set, tabs are expanded to spaces on output. This produces the same effect as setting the horizontal tab delay (TABDLY) to XTABS or TAB3.

PARENB   (c_cflag, POSIX.1) If set, parity generation is enabled for outgoing characters, and parity checking is performed on incoming characters.

The parity is odd if PARODD is set, otherwise it is even parity. See also the discussion of the INPCK, IGNPAR, and PARMRK flags.

PARMRK   (c_iflag, POSIX.1) When set and if IGNPAR is not set, a byte with a framing error (other than a BREAK) or a byte with a parity error, is read by the process as the three character sequence \377, \0, X, where X is the byte received in error. If ISTRIP is not set, a valid \377 is passed to the process as \377, \377. If neither IGNPAR nor PARMRK is set, a byte with a framing error (other than a BREAK) or a byte with a parity error is read as a single character \0.

PARODD   (c_cflag, POSIX.1) If set, the parity for outgoing and incoming characters is odd parity. Otherwise, the parity is even parity. Note that the PARENB flag controls the generation and detection of parity.

PENDIN   (c_lflag, SVR4 and 4.3+BSD) If set, any input that has not been read is reprinted by the system when the next character is input. This action is similar to what happens when we type the REPRINT character.

TABDLY   (c_oflag, SVR4) Horizontal tab delay mask. The values for the mask are TAB0, TAB1, TAB2, or TAB3.

The value XTABS is equal to TAB3. This value causes the system to expand tabs into spaces. The system assumes a tab stop every eight spaces, and we can't change this assumption.

TOSTOP   (c_lflag, POSIX.1) If set and if the implementation supports job control, the SIGTTOU signal is sent to the process group of a background process that tries to write to its controlling terminal. By default, this signal stops all the processes in the process group. This signal is not generated by the terminal driver if the background process that is writing to the controlling terminal is either ignoring or blocking the signal.

VTDLY   (c_oflag, SVR4) Vertical tab delay mask. The values for the mask are VT0 or VT1.

XCASE   (c_lflag, SVR4) If set and if ICANON is also set, the terminal is assumed to be uppercase only, and all input is converted to lowercase. To input an uppercase character, precede it with a backslash. Similarly, an uppercase character is output by the system by being preceded by a backslash. (This option flag is obsolete today, since most, if not all, uppercase only terminals have disappeared.)

11.6 stty Command

All the options described in the previous section can be examined and changed from within a program, with the tcgetattr and tcsetattr functions (Section 11.4), or from the command line (or a shell script), with the stty(1) command. This command is just an interface to the first six functions that we listed in Figure 11.4. If we execute this command with its −a option, it displays all the terminal options.

```
$ stty -a
speed 9600 baud; 34 rows; 80 columns;
lflags: icanon isig iexten echo echoe echok echoke -echonl echoctl
        -echoprt -altwerase -noflsh -tostop -mdmbuf -flusho -pendin
        -nokerninfo -extproc
iflags: istrip icrnl -inlcr -igncr ixon -ixoff ixany imaxbel -ignbrk
        brkint -inpck -ignpar -parmrk
oflags: opost onlcr -oxtabs
cflags: cread cs7 parenb -parodd hupcl -clocal -cstopb -crtscts
cchars: discard = ^O; dsusp = ^Y; eof = ^D; eol = <undef>;
        eol2 = <undef>; erase = ^H; intr = ^?; kill = ^U; lnext = ^V;
        quit = ^\; reprint = ^R; start = ^Q; status = ^T; stop = ^S;
        susp = ^Z; werase = ^W;
```

Option names preceded by a hyphen are disabled. The last four lines display the current settings for each of the terminal special characters (Section 11.3). The first line displays the number of rows and columns for the current terminal window—we discuss this in Section 11.12.

Since the stty command is a user command and not an operating system function, it is specified by POSIX.2, not POSIX.1.

> Historically, System V versions of stty operate on the standard input and write any output to standard output. Version 7 and BSD systems operate on the standard output and write any output to standard error. The current draft of POSIX.2 follows the System V convention, as does the 4.3+BSD version.
>
> The Version 7 manual page for stty required a single page, while the SVR4 version requires over six pages. Terminal drivers tend to acquire more and more options over time.

11.7 Baud Rate Functions

The term baud rate is a historical term that should be referred to today as "bits per second." Although most terminal devices use the same baud rate for both input and output, the capability exists to set the two to different values, if the hardware allows this.

```
#include <termios.h>

speed_t cfgetispeed(const struct termios *termptr);

speed_t cfgetospeed(const struct termios *termptr);
```

Both return: baud rate value

```
int cfsetispeed(struct termios *termptr, speed_t speed);

int cfsetospeed(struct termios *termptr, speed_t speed);
```

Both return: 0 if OK, –1 on error

The return value from the two cfget functions and the *speed* argument to the two cfset functions are one of the following constants: B50, B75, B110, B134, B150, B200, B300, B600, B1200, B1800, B2400, B4800, B9600, B19200, or B38400. The constant B0 means "hangup." When B0 is specified as the output baud rate when tcsetattr is called, the modem control lines are no longer asserted.

To use these functions we must realize that the input and output baud rates are stored in the device's termios structure, as shown in Figure 11.5. Before calling either of the cfget functions we first have to obtain the device's termios structure using tcgetattr. Similarly, after calling either of the two cfset functions, all we've done is set the baud rate in a termios structure. For this change to affect the device we have to call tcsetattr.

If there is an error in either of the baud rates that we set, we may not find out about the error until we call tcsetattr.

11.8   Line Control Functions

The following four functions provide line control capability for terminal devices. All four require that *filedes* refer to a terminal device, otherwise an error is returned with errno set to ENOTTY.

```
#include <termios.h>

int tcdrain(int filedes);

int tcflow(int filedes, int action);

int tcflush(int filedes, int queue);

int tcsendbreak(int filedes, int duration);
```

                                                                All four return: 0 if OK, –1 on error

The tcdrain function waits for all output to be transmitted. tcflow gives us control over both input and output flow control. The *action* argument must be one of the following four values:

TCOOFF   Output is suspended.

TCOON   Output that was previously suspended is restarted.

TCIOFF   The system transmits a STOP character. This should cause the terminal
          device to stop sending data.

TCION   The system transmits a START character. This should cause the terminal
          device to resume sending data.

The `tcflush` function lets us flush (throw away) either the input buffer (data that has been received by the terminal driver, which we have not read) or the output buffer (data that we have written, which has not yet been transmitted). The *queue* argument must be one of the following three constants:

TCIFLUSH   The input queue is flushed.

TCOFLUSH   The output queue is flushed.

TCIOFLUSH   Both the input and output queues are flushed.

The `tcsendbreak` function transmits a continuous stream of zero bits for a specified duration. If the *duration* argument is 0, the transmission lasts between 0.25 and 0.5 seconds. POSIX.1 specifies that if *duration* is nonzero, the transmission time is implementation dependent.

> The SVR4 SVID states that if *duration* is nonzero, no zero bits are transmitted. The SVR4 manual page, however, states that if *duration* is nonzero, then `tcsendbreak` behaves like `tcdrain`. Yet another system's manual page states that if *duration* is nonzero, the time that the zero bits are transmitted is *duration*×N, where *N* is between 0.25 and 0.5 seconds. Clearly there is little agreement on how to handle this condition.

11.9 Terminal Identification

Historically, the name of the controlling terminal in most versions of Unix has been `/dev/tty`. POSIX.1 provides a run-time function that we can call to determine the name of the controlling terminal.

```
#include <stdio.h>

char *ctermid(char *ptr);
```

                                                              Returns: (see following)

If *ptr* is nonnull, it is assumed to point to an array of at least `L_ctermid` bytes and the name of the controlling terminal of the process is stored in the array. The constant `L_ctermid` is defined in `<stdio.h>`. If *ptr* is a null pointer, the function allocates room for the array (usually as a static variable). Again, the name of the controlling terminal of the process is stored in the array.

In both cases, the starting address of the array is returned as the value of the function. Since most Unix systems use `/dev/tty` as the name of the controlling terminal, this function is intended to aid portability to other operating systems.

Example—`ctermid` Function

Program 11.3 is an implementation of the POSIX.1 `ctermid` function.

```
#include      <stdio.h>
#include      <string.h>

static char ctermid_name[L_ctermid];

char *
ctermid(char *str)
{
    if (str == NULL)
        str = ctermid_name;
    return(strcpy(str, "/dev/tty"));      /* strcpy() returns str */
}
```

Program 11.3 Implementation of POSIX.1 ctermid function.

Two functions that are more interesting for a Unix system are isatty, which returns true if a file descriptor refers to a terminal device, and ttyname, which returns the pathname of the terminal device that is open on a file descriptor.

```
#include <unistd.h>

int isatty(int filedes);
```

Returns: 1 (true) if terminal device, 0 (false) otherwise

```
char *ttyname(int filedes);
```

Returns: pointer to pathname of terminal, NULL on error

Example—isatty Function

The isatty function is trivial to implement as we show in Program 11.4. We just try one of the terminal-specific functions (that doesn't change anything if it succeeds) and look at the return value.

```
#include      <termios.h>
int
isatty(int fd)
{
    struct termios  term;

    return(tcgetattr(fd, &term) != -1); /* true if no error (is a tty) */
}
```

Program 11.4 Implementation of POSIX.1 isatty function.

```
#include     "ourhdr.h"

int
main(void)
{
    printf("fd 0: %s\n", isatty(0) ? "tty" : "not a tty");
    printf("fd 1: %s\n", isatty(1) ? "tty" : "not a tty");
    printf("fd 2: %s\n", isatty(2) ? "tty" : "not a tty");
    exit(0);
}
```

Program 11.5 Test the isatty function.

We test our isatty function with Program 11.5, giving us

```
$ a.out
fd 0: tty
fd 1: tty
fd 2: tty
$ a.out </etc/passwd 2>/dev/null
-fd 0: not a tty
fd 1: tty
fd 2: not a tty
```

□

Example—ttyname Function

The ttyname function (Program 11.6) is longer, as we have to search all the device entries, looking for a match. The technique is to read the /dev directory, looking for an entry with the same device number and i-node number. Recall from Section 4.23 that each filesystem has a unique device number (the st_dev field in the stat structure, from Section 4.2), and each directory entry in that filesystem has a unique i-node number (the st_ino field in the stat structure). We assume in this function that when we hit a matching device number and matching i-node number, we've located the desired directory entry. We could also verify that the two entries have matching st_rdev fields (the major and minor device numbers for the terminal device) and that the directory entry is also a character special file. But since we've already verified that the file descriptor argument is both a terminal device and a character special file, and since a matching device number and i-node number is unique on a Unix system, there is no need for the additional comparisons.

We can test this implementation with Program 11.7. Running Program 11.7 gives us

```
$ a.out < /dev/console 2> /dev/null
fd 0: /dev/console
fd 1: /dev/ttyp3
fd 2: not a tty
```

□

```
#include     <sys/types.h>
#include     <sys/stat.h>
#include     <dirent.h>
#include     <limits.h>
#include     <string.h>
#include     <termios.h>
#include     <unistd.h>

#define DEV      "/dev/"           /* device directory */
#define DEVLEN   sizeof(DEV)-1     /* sizeof includes null at end */

char *
ttyname(int fd)
{
    struct stat      fdstat, devstat;
    DIR              *dp;
    struct dirent    *dirp;
    static char      pathname[_POSIX_PATH_MAX + 1];
    char             *rval;

    if (isatty(fd) == 0)
        return(NULL);
    if (fstat(fd, &fdstat) < 0)
        return(NULL);
    if (S_ISCHR(fdstat.st_mode) == 0)
        return(NULL);

    strcpy(pathname, DEV);
    if ( (dp = opendir(DEV)) == NULL)
        return(NULL);
    rval = NULL;
    while ( (dirp = readdir(dp)) != NULL) {
        if (dirp->d_ino != fdstat.st_ino)
            continue;          /* fast test to skip most entries */

        strncpy(pathname + DEVLEN, dirp->d_name, _POSIX_PATH_MAX - DEVLEN);
        if (stat(pathname, &devstat) < 0)
            continue;
        if (devstat.st_ino == fdstat.st_ino &&
            devstat.st_dev == fdstat.st_dev) {   /* found a match */
                rval = pathname;
                break;
        }
    }
    closedir(dp);
    return(rval);
}
```

Program 11.6 Implementation of POSIX.1 ttyname function.

```
#include    "ourhdr.h"

int
main(void)
{
    printf("fd 0: %s\n", isatty(0) ? ttyname(0) : "not a tty");
    printf("fd 1: %s\n", isatty(1) ? ttyname(1) : "not a tty");
    printf("fd 2: %s\n", isatty(2) ? ttyname(2) : "not a tty");
    exit(0);
}
```

Program 11.7 Test the ttyname function.

11.10 Canonical Mode

Canonical mode is simple—we issue a read and the terminal driver returns when a line has been entered. Several conditions cause the read to return:

- The read returns when the requested number of bytes has been read. We don't have to read a complete line. If we read a partial line, no information is lost—the next read starts where the previous read stopped.

- The read returns when a line delimiter is encountered. Recall from Section 11.3 that the following characters are interpreted as "end-of-line" in canonical mode: NL, EOL, EOL2, and EOF. Also, from Section 11.5 recall that if ICRNL is set, and if IGNCR is not set, then the CR character also terminates a line since it acts just like the NL character.

    Realize that of these five line delimiters, one (EOF) is discarded by the terminal driver when it's processed. The other four are returned to the caller as the last character of the line.

- The read also returns if a signal is caught and if the function is not automatically restarted (Section 10.5).

Example—getpass Function

We now show the function getpass that reads a password of some type from the user at a terminal. This function is called by the Unix login(1) and crypt(1) programs. To read the password it must turn off echoing, but it can leave the terminal in canonical mode, as whatever we type as the password forms a complete line. Program 11.8 shows a typical Unix implementation.

```c
#include      <signal.h>
#include      <stdio.h>
#include      <termios.h>

#define MAX_PASS_LEN    8         /* max #chars for user to enter */

char *
getpass(const char *prompt)
{
    static char      buf[MAX_PASS_LEN + 1];  /* null byte at end */
    char             *ptr;
    sigset_t         sig, sigsave;
    struct termios   term, termsave;
    FILE             *fp;
    int              c;

    if ( (fp = fopen(ctermid(NULL), "r+")) == NULL)
        return(NULL);
    setbuf(fp, NULL);

    sigemptyset(&sig);  /* block SIGINT & SIGTSTP, save signal mask */
    sigaddset(&sig, SIGINT);
    sigaddset(&sig, SIGTSTP);
    sigprocmask(SIG_BLOCK, &sig, &sigsave);

    tcgetattr(fileno(fp), &termsave);    /* save tty state */
    term = termsave;                     /* structure copy */
    term.c_lflag &=  (ECHO | ECHOE | ECHOK | ECHONL);
    tcsetattr(fileno(fp), TCSAFLUSH, &term);

    fputs(prompt, fp);

    ptr = buf;
    while ( (c = getc(fp)) != EOF && c != '\n') {
        if (ptr < &buf[MAX_PASS_LEN])
            *ptr++ = c;
    }
    *ptr = 0;             /* null terminate */
    putc('\n', fp);       /* we echo a newline */

                          /* restore tty state */
    tcsetattr(fileno(fp), TCSAFLUSH, &termsave);

                          /* restore signal mask */
    sigprocmask(SIG_SETMASK, &sigsave, NULL);
    fclose(fp);           /* done with /dev/tty */

    return(buf);
}
```

Program 11.8 Implementation of getpass function.

There are several points to consider in this example.

- We call the function `ctermid` to open the controlling terminal, instead of hardwiring `/dev/tty` into the program.

- We read and write only to the controlling terminal and return an error if we can't open this device for reading and writing. There are other conventions to use. The 4.3+BSD version of `getpass` reads from standard input and writes to standard error if the controlling terminal can't be opened for reading and writing. The SVR4 version always writes to standard error but only reads from the controlling terminal.

- We block the two signals `SIGINT` and `SIGTSTP`. If we didn't do this, entering the INTR character would abort the program and leave the terminal with echoing disabled. Similarly, entering the SUSP character would stop the program and return to the shell with echoing disabled. We choose to block the signals while we have echoing disabled. If they are generated while we're reading the password, they are held until we return. There are other ways to handle these signals. Some versions just ignore `SIGINT` (saving its previous action) while in `getpass`, resetting the action for this signal to its previous value before returning. This means that any occurrence of the signal while it's ignored is lost. Other versions catch `SIGINT` (saving its previous action) and if the signal is caught, then after resetting the terminal state and signal action, just send themselves the signal with the `kill` function. None of the versions of `getpass` catch, ignore, or block `SIGQUIT`, so entering the QUIT character aborts the program and probably leaves the terminal with echoing disabled.

- Be aware that some shells, notably the KornShell, turn echoing back on whenever they read interactive input. These shells are the ones that provide command-line editing and therefore manipulate the state of the terminal every time we enter an interactive command. So, if we invoke this program under one of these shells and abort it with the QUIT character, it may reenable echoing for us. Other shells that don't provide this form of command-line editing, such as the Bourne shell and C shell, will abort the program and leave the terminal in a noecho mode. If we do this to our terminal, the `stty` command can reenable echoing.

- We use standard I/O to read and write the controlling terminal. We specifically set the stream to be unbuffered, otherwise there might be some interactions between the writing and reading of the stream (we would need some calls to `fflush`). We could have also used unbuffered I/O (Chapter 3), but we would have to simulate the `getc` function using `read`.

- We store only up to eight characters as the password. Any additional characters that are entered are just ignored.

Program 11.9 calls `getpass` and prints what we entered. This is just to let us verify that the ERASE and KILL characters work (as they should in canonical mode).

```
#include    "ourhdr.h"

char    *getpass(const char *);

int
main(void)
{
    char    *ptr;

    if ( (ptr = getpass("Enter password:")) == NULL)
        err_sys("getpass error");
    printf("password: %s\n", ptr);

    /* now use password (probably encrypt it) ... */

    while (*ptr != 0)
        *ptr++ = 0;         /* zero it out when we're done with it */

    exit(0);
}
```

Program 11.9 Call the getpass function.

Whenever a program that calls getpass is done with the cleartext password, it should zero it out in memory, just to be safe. If the program were to generate a core file that others could read (recall from Section 10.2 that the default permissions on a core file allow everyone to read it), or if some other process were somehow able to read our memory, they might be able to read the cleartext password. (By "cleartext" we mean the password that we type at the prompt that is printed by getpass. Most Unix programs then modify this cleartext password into an "encrypted" password. The field pw_passwd in the password file, for example, contains the encrypted password, not the cleartext password.)   □

11.11 Noncanonical Mode

Noncanonical mode is specified by turning off the ICANON flag in the c_lflag field of the termios structure. In noncanonical mode the input data is not assembled into lines. The following special characters (Section 11.3) are not processed: ERASE, KILL, EOF, NL, EOL, EOL2, CR, REPRINT, STATUS, and WERASE.

As we said, canonical mode is easy—the system returns up to one line at a time. But with noncanonical mode, how does the system know when to return data to us? If it returned one byte at a time, there would be excessive overhead. (Recall Figure 3.1 where we saw how much overhead there was in reading one byte at a time. Each time we doubled the amount of data returned we halved the system call overhead.) The system can't always return multiple bytes at a time, since sometimes we don't know how much data to read, until we start reading it.

The solution is to tell the system to return when either a specified amount of data has been read or after a given amount of time has passed. This technique uses two variables in the `c_cc` array in the `termios` structure: MIN and TIME. These two elements of the array are indexed by the names `VMIN` and `VTIME`.

MIN specifies the minimum number of bytes before a `read` returns. TIME specifies the number of tenths-of-a-second to wait for data to arrive. There are four cases.

Case A: MIN > 0, TIME > 0

TIME specifies an interbyte timer that is started only when the first byte is received. If MIN bytes are received before the timer expires, `read` returns MIN bytes. If the timer expires before MIN bytes are received, `read` returns the bytes received. (At least one byte is returned if the timer expires, because the timer is not started until the first byte is received.) In this case the caller blocks until the first byte is received. If data is already available when `read` is called, it is as if the data had been received immediately after the `read`.

Case B: MIN > 0, TIME == 0

The `read` does not return until MIN bytes have been received. This can cause a `read` to block indefinitely.

Case C: MIN == 0, TIME > 0

TIME specifies a read timer that is started when `read` is called. (Compare this to case A, where a nonzero TIME represented an interbyte timer that was not started until the first byte was received.) `read` returns when a single byte is received or when the timer expires. If the timer expires, `read` returns 0.

Case D: MIN == 0, TIME == 0

If some data is available, `read` returns up to the number of bytes requested. If no data is available, `read` returns 0 immediately.

Realize in all these cases that MIN is only a minimum. If the program requests more than MIN bytes of data, it's possible to receive up to the requested amount. This also applies to cases C and D where MIN is 0.

Figure 11.7 summarizes the four different cases for noncanonical input. In this figure *nbytes* is the third argument to `read` (the maximum number of bytes to return).

	MIN > 0	MIN == 0
TIME > 0	A: read returns [MIN, *nbytes*] before timer expires; read returns [1, MIN) if timer expires. (TIME = interbyte timer. Caller can block indefinitely.)	C: read returns [1, *nbytes*] before timer expires; read returns 0 if timer expires. (TIME = read timer.)
TIME == 0	B: read returns [MIN, *nbytes*] when available. (Caller can block indefinitely.)	D: read returns [0, *nbytes*] immediately.

Figure 11.7 Four cases for noncanonical input.

Be aware that POSIX.1 allows the subscripts VMIN and VTIME to have the same values as VEOF and VEOL, respectively. Indeed, SVR4 does this. This provides backward compatibility for older versions of System V. The problem is that in going from noncanonical to canonical mode, we must now restore VEOF and VEOL also. If we don't do this, and VMIN equals VEOF, and we set VMIN to its typical value of 1, the end-of-file character becomes Control-A. The easiest way around this problem is to save the entire termios structure when going into non-canonical mode and restore it when going back to canonical mode.

Example

Program 11.10 defines the functions tty_cbreak and tty_raw that set the terminal in a *cbreak mode* and a *raw mode*. (The terms cbreak and raw come from the Version 7 terminal driver.) We can reset the terminal to its prior state by calling the function tty_reset. Two additional functions are also provided: tty_atexit can be established as an exit handler to assure that the terminal mode is reset by exit, and tty_termios returns a pointer to the original canonical mode termios structure. We use all these functions in the modem dialer in Chapter 18.

```c
#include      <termios.h>
#include      <unistd.h>

static struct termios   save_termios;
static int              ttysavefd = -1;
static enum { RESET, RAW, CBREAK }  ttystate = RESET;

int
tty_cbreak(int fd)   /* put terminal into a cbreak mode */
{
    struct termios  buf;

    if (tcgetattr(fd, &save_termios) < 0)
        return(-1);

    buf = save_termios; /* structure copy */

    buf.c_lflag &= ~(ECHO | ICANON);
                     /* echo off, canonical mode off */

    buf.c_cc[VMIN] = 1; /* Case B: 1 byte at a time, no timer */
    buf.c_cc[VTIME] = 0;

    if (tcsetattr(fd, TCSAFLUSH, &buf) < 0)
        return(-1);
    ttystate = CBREAK;
    ttysavefd = fd;
    return(0);
}

int
tty_raw(int fd)        /* put terminal into a raw mode */
{
    struct termios  buf;

    if (tcgetattr(fd, &save_termios) < 0)
        return(-1);
```

```
            buf = save_termios; /* structure copy */

            buf.c_lflag &= ~(ECHO | ICANON | IEXTEN | ISIG);
                            /* echo off, canonical mode off, extended input
                               processing off, signal chars off */

            buf.c_iflag &= ~(BRKINT | ICRNL | INPCK | ISTRIP | IXON);
                            /* no SIGINT on BREAK, CR-to-NL off, input parity
                               check off, don't strip 8th bit on input,
                               output flow control off */

            buf.c_cflag &= ~(CSIZE | PARENB);
                            /* clear size bits, parity checking off */
            buf.c_cflag |= CS8;
                            /* set 8 bits/char */

            buf.c_oflag &= ~(OPOST);
                            /* output processing off */

            buf.c_cc[VMIN] = 1; /* Case B: 1 byte at a time, no timer */
            buf.c_cc[VTIME] = 0;

            if (tcsetattr(fd, TCSAFLUSH, &buf) < 0)
                return(-1);
            ttystate = RAW;
            ttysavefd = fd;
            return(0);
}
int
tty_reset(int fd)           /* restore terminal's mode */
{
        if (ttystate != CBREAK && ttystate != RAW)
            return(0);

        if (tcsetattr(fd, TCSAFLUSH, &save_termios) < 0)
            return(-1);
        ttystate = RESET;
        return(0);
}

void
tty_atexit(void)            /* can be set up by atexit(tty_atexit) */
{
        if (ttysavefd >= 0)
            tty_reset(ttysavefd);
}

struct termios *
tty_termios(void)           /* let caller see original tty state */
{
        return(&save_termios);
}
```

Program 11.10 Set terminal mode to raw or cbreak.

Our definition of cbreak mode is the following:

- Noncanonical mode. As we mentioned at the beginning of this section, this mode turns off some input character processing. It does not turn off signal handling, so the user can always type one of the terminal-generated signals. Be aware, that the caller should catch these signals, or there's a chance that the signal will terminate the program, and the terminal will be left in cbreak mode.

  As a general rule, whenever we write a program that changes the terminal mode, we should catch most signals. This allows us to reset the terminal mode before terminating.

- Echo off.

- One byte at a time input. To do this we set MIN to 1 and TIME to 0. This is Case B from Figure 11.7. A read won't return until at least one byte is available.

We define raw mode as follows:

- Noncanonical mode. Additionally we turn off processing of the signal-generating characters (ISIG) and the extended input character processing (IEXTEN). We also disable a BREAK character from generating a signal by turning off BRKINT.

- Echo off.

- We disable the CR-to-NL mapping on input (ICRNL), input parity detection (INPCK), the stripping of the eighth bit on input (ISTRIP), and output flow control (IXON).

- Eight bit characters (CS8), and parity checking is disabled (PARENB).

- All output processing is disabled (OPOST).

- One byte at a time input (MIN = 1, TIME = 0).

Program 11.11 tests the raw and cbreak modes. Running Program 11.11 we can see what happens with these two terminal modes.

```
$ a.out
Enter raw mode characters, terminate with DELETE
                                                         4
                                                  33
                                                     133
                                                        62
                                                          63
                                                           60
                                                             172
                        type DELETE
Enter cbreak mode characters, terminate with SIGINT
1                                type Control-A
10                               type backspace
signal caught                    type interrupt key
```

```
#include    <signal.h>
#include    "ourhdr.h"

static void sig_catch(int);

int
main(void)
{
    int     i;
    char    c;

    if (signal(SIGINT, sig_catch) == SIG_ERR)    /* catch signals */
        err_sys("signal(SIGINT) error");
    if (signal(SIGQUIT, sig_catch) == SIG_ERR)
        err_sys("signal(SIGQUIT) error");
    if (signal(SIGTERM, sig_catch) == SIG_ERR)
        err_sys("signal(SIGTERM) error");

    if (tty_raw(STDIN_FILENO) < 0)
        err_sys("tty_raw error");
    printf("Enter raw mode characters, terminate with DELETE\n");
    while ( (i = read(STDIN_FILENO, &c, 1)) == 1) {
        if ((c &= 255) == 0177)    /* 0177 = ASCII DELETE */
            break;
        printf("%o\n", c);
    }
    if (tty_reset(STDIN_FILENO) < 0)
        err_sys("tty_reset error");
    if (i <= 0)
        err_sys("read error");

    if (tty_cbreak(STDIN_FILENO) < 0)
        err_sys("tty_raw error");
    printf("\nEnter cbreak mode characters, terminate with SIGINT\n");
    while ( (i = read(STDIN_FILENO, &c, 1)) == 1) {
        c &= 255;
        printf("%o\n", c);
    }
    tty_reset(STDIN_FILENO);
    if (i <= 0)
        err_sys("read error");
    exit(0);
}

static void
sig_catch(int signo)
{
    printf("signal caught\n");
    tty_reset(STDIN_FILENO);
    exit(0);
}
```

Program 11.11 Test the raw and cbreak modes.

In raw mode the characters entered were Control-D (04) and the special function key F7. On the terminal being used, this function key generated six characters: *ESC* (033), *[* (0133), *2* (062), *3* (063), *0* (060), and *z* (0172). Notice with the output processing turned off in raw mode (˜OPOST) we do not get a carriage-return output after each character. Also notice that special character processing is disabled in cbreak mode (so Control-D, the end-of-file character, and backspace aren't handled specially), while the terminal-generated signals are still processed.   □

11.12 Terminal Window Size

SVR4 and Berkeley systems provide a way to keep track of the current terminal window size and to have the kernel notify the foreground process group when the size changes. The kernel maintains a winsize structure for every terminal and pseudo terminal.

```
struct winsize {
  unsigned short  ws_row;     /* rows, in characters */
  unsigned short  ws_col;     /* columns, in characters */
  unsigned short  ws_xpixel;  /* horizontal size, pixels (not used) */
  unsigned short  ws_ypixel;  /* vertical size, pixels (not used) */
};
```

The rules for this structure are as follows:

1. We can fetch the current value of this structure using an ioctl (Section 3.14) of TIOCGWINSZ.

2. We can store a new value of this structure in the kernel using an ioctl of TIOCSWINSZ. If this new value differs from the current value stored in the kernel, a SIGWINCH signal is sent to the foreground process group. (Note from Figure 10.1 that the default action for this signal is to be ignored.)

3. Other than storing the current value of the structure and generating a signal when the value changes, the kernel does nothing else with the values in this structure. Interpreting the values in the structure is entirely up to the application.

The reason for providing this feature is to notify applications (such as the vi editor) when the window size changes. When the application receives the signal it can fetch the new size and redraw the screen.

Example

Program 11.12 prints the current window size and goes to sleep. Each time the window size changes, SIGWINCH is caught and the new size is printed. We have to terminate this program with a signal.

```
#include      <signal.h>
#include      <termios.h>
#ifndef TIOCGWINSZ
#include      <sys/ioctl.h>    /* 4.3+BSD requires this too */
#endif
#include      "ourhdr.h"

static void pr_winsize(int), sig_winch(int);

int
main(void)
{
    if (isatty(STDIN_FILENO) == 0)
        exit(1);

    if (signal(SIGWINCH, sig_winch) == SIG_ERR)
        err_sys("signal error");

    pr_winsize(STDIN_FILENO);    /* print initial size */
    for ( ; ; )                  /* and sleep forever */
        pause();
}

static void
pr_winsize(int fd)
{
    struct winsize  size;

    if (ioctl(fd, TIOCGWINSZ, (char *) &size) < 0)
        err_sys("TIOCGWINSZ error");
    printf("%d rows, %d columns\n", size.ws_row, size.ws_col);
}

static void
sig_winch(int signo)
{
    printf("SIGWINCH received\n");
    pr_winsize(STDIN_FILENO);
    return;
}
```

Program 11.12 Print window size.

Running Program 11.12 on a windowed terminal gives us

```
$ a.out
35 rows, 80 columns              initial size
SIGWINCH received               change window size: signal is caught
40 rows, 123 columns
SIGWINCH received               and again
42 rows, 33 columns
^? $                            type the interrupt key to terminate
```

11.13 `termcap`, `terminfo`, and `curses`

`termcap` stands for "terminal capability," and it refers to the text file `/etc/termcap` and a set of routines to read this file. The `termcap` scheme was developed at Berkeley to support the `vi` editor. The `termcap` file contains descriptions of various terminals: what features the terminal supports (how many lines and rows, does the terminal support backspace, etc.) and how to make the terminal perform certain operations (clear the screen, move the cursor to a given location, etc.). By taking this information out of the compiled program and placing it into a text file that can easily be edited, it allows the `vi` editor to run on many different terminals.

The routines that support the `termcap` file were then extracted from the `vi` editor and placed into a separate `curses` library. Lots of features were added to make this library usable for any program that wanted to manipulate the screen.

The `termcap` scheme was not perfect. As more and more terminals were added to the data file, it took longer to scan the file looking for a specific terminal. The data file also used two-character names to identify the different terminal attributes. These deficiencies led to development of the `terminfo` scheme and its associated `curses` library. The terminal descriptions in `terminfo` are basically compiled versions of a textual description and can be located faster at run time. `terminfo` appeared with SVR2 and has been in all System V releases since then.

> SVR4 uses `terminfo`, while 4.3+BSD uses `termcap`.

A description of `terminfo` and the `curses` library is provided by Goodheart [1991]. Strang, Mui, and O'Reilly [1991] provide a description of `termcap` and `terminfo`.

Neither `termcap` nor `terminfo`, by itself, addresses the problems we've been looking at in this chapter—changing the terminal's mode, changing one of the terminal special characters, handling the window size, and so on. What they do provide is a way to perform typical operations (clear the screen, move the cursor) on a wide variety of terminals. On the other hand, `curses` does help with some of the details that we've addressed in this chapter. Functions are provided by `curses` to set raw mode, set cbreak mode, turn echo on and off, and the like. But `curses` is designed for character-based dumb terminals, while the trend today is toward pixel-based graphics terminals.

11.14 Summary

Terminals have many features and options, most of which we're able to change to suit our needs. In this chapter we've described numerous functions that change a terminal's operation—special input characters and the option flags. We've looked at all the terminal special characters and the many options that can be set or reset for a terminal device.

There are two modes of terminal input—canonical (line at a time) and noncanonical. We showed examples of both modes and provided functions that map between the POSIX.1 terminal options and the older BSD cbreak and raw modes. We also described how to fetch and change the window size of a terminal. Chapters 17 and 18 show additional examples of terminal I/O.

Exercises

11.1 Write a program that calls `tty_raw` and terminates (without resetting the terminal mode). If your system provides the `reset`(1) command (both SVR4 and 4.3+BSD provide it) use it to restore the terminal mode.

11.2 The `PARODD` flag in the `c_cflag` field allows us to specify even or odd parity. The BSD `tip` program, however, also allows the parity bit to be 0 or 1. How does it do this?

11.3 If your system's `stty`(1) command outputs the MIN and TIME values, do the following exercise. Log in to the system twice and start the `vi` editor from one login. Use the `stty` command from your other login to determine what values `vi` sets MIN and TIME to (since it sets the terminal to noncanonical mode).

11.4 As the terminal interface moves to faster line speeds (19,200 and 38,400 are becoming common nowadays) the need for hardware flow control becomes important. This involves the RS-232 RTS (request to send) and CTS (clear to send) signals, instead of the XON and XOFF characters. Hardware flow control is not specified by POSIX.1. Under SVR4 and 4.3+BSD how can a process enable or disable hardware flow control?

12

Advanced I/O

12.1 Introduction

This chapter covers numerous topics and functions that we lump under the term "advanced I/O." This includes nonblocking I/O, record locking, System V streams, I/O multiplexing (the select and poll functions), the readv and writev functions, and memory mapped I/O (mmap). We need to cover these topics before describing interprocess communication in Chapters 14 and 15, and many of the examples in later chapters.

12.2 Nonblocking I/O

In Section 10.5 we said that the system calls are divided into two categories: the "slow" ones, and all the others. The slow system calls are those that can block forever:

- reads from files that can block the caller forever, if data isn't present (pipes, terminal devices, and network devices),

- writes to these same files that can block forever, if the data can't be accepted immediately,

- opens of files block until some condition occurs (such as an open of a terminal device that waits until an attached modem answers the phone, or an open of a FIFO for writing-only when no other process has the FIFO open for reading),

- reads and writes of files that have mandatory record locking enabled,

- certain ioctl operations,

- some of the interprocess communication functions (Chapter 14).

We also said that system calls related to disk I/O are not considered slow, even though the read or write of a disk file can block the caller temporarily.

Nonblocking I/O lets us issue an I/O operation, such as an open, read, or write, and not have it block forever. If the operation cannot be completed, return is made immediately with an error noting that the operation would have blocked.

There are two ways to specify nonblocking I/O for a given descriptor.

1. If we call open to get the descriptor, we can specify the O_NONBLOCK flag (Section 3.3).

2. For a descriptor that is already open, we call fcntl to turn on the O_NONBLOCK file status flag (Section 3.13). Program 3.5 shows a function that we can call to turn on any of the file status flags for a descriptor.

> Earlier versions of System V used the flag O_NDELAY to specify the nonblocking mode. These versions of System V returned a value of 0 from the read function if there wasn't any data to be read. Since this use of a return value of 0 overlapped with the normal Unix convention of 0 meaning the end of file, POSIX.1 chose to provide a nonblocking flag with a different name and different semantics. Indeed, with these older versions of System V we don't know when we get a return of 0 from read whether the call would have blocked, or if the end of file was encountered. We'll see that POSIX.1 requires that read return −1 with errno set to EAGAIN if there is no data to read from a nonblocking descriptor. SVR4 supports both the older O_NDELAY and the POSIX.1 O_NONBLOCK, but in this text we'll only use the POSIX.1 feature. The older O_NDELAY is for backward compatibility and should not be used in new applications.

> 4.3BSD provided the FNDELAY flag for fcntl, and its semantics were slightly different. Instead of just affecting the file status flags for the descriptor, the flags for either the terminal device or the socket were also changed to be nonblocking, affecting all users of the terminal or socket, not just the users sharing the same file table entry (4.3BSD nonblocking I/O only worked on terminals and sockets). Also, 4.3BSD returned EWOULDBLOCK if an operation on a nonblocking descriptor could not complete without blocking. 4.3+BSD provides the POSIX.1 O_NONBLOCK flag, but the semantics are similar to those for FNDELAY under 4.3BSD. A common use for nonblocking I/O is for dealing with a terminal device or a network connection, and these devices are normally used by one process at a time. This means that the change in the BSD semantics normally doesn't affect us. The different error return, EWOULDBLOCK, instead of the POSIX.1 EAGAIN, continues to be a portability difference that we must deal with. 4.3+BSD also supports FIFOs, and nonblocking I/O works with FIFOs too.

Example

Let's look at an example of nonblocking I/O. Program 12.1 reads up to 100,000 bytes from the standard input and attempts to write it to the standard output. The standard output is first set nonblocking. The output is in a loop, with the results of each write being printed on the standard error. The function clr_fl is similar to the function set_fl that we showed in Program 3.5. This new function just clears one or more of the flag bits.

```
#include        <sys/types.h>
#include        <errno.h>
#include        <fcntl.h>
#include        "ourhdr.h"

char    buf[100000];

int
main(void)
{
    int     ntowrite, nwrite;
    char    *ptr;

    ntowrite = read(STDIN_FILENO, buf, sizeof(buf));
    fprintf(stderr, "read %d bytes\n", ntowrite);

    set_fl(STDOUT_FILENO, O_NONBLOCK);  /* set nonblocking */

    for (ptr = buf; ntowrite > 0; ) {
        errno = 0;
        nwrite = write(STDOUT_FILENO, ptr, ntowrite);
        fprintf(stderr, "nwrite = %d, errno = %d\n", nwrite, errno);
        if (nwrite > 0) {
            ptr += nwrite;
            ntowrite -= nwrite;
        }
    }

    clr_fl(STDOUT_FILENO, O_NONBLOCK);  /* clear nonblocking */
    exit(0);
}
```

Program 12.1 Large nonblocking write.

If the standard output is a regular file, we expect the write to be executed once.

```
$ ls -l /etc/termcap                                  print file size
-rw-rw-r--  1 root       133439 Oct 11  1990 /etc/termcap
$ a.out < /etc/termcap > temp.file                    try a regular file first
read 100000 bytes
nwrite = 100000, errno = 0                             a single write
$ ls -l temp.file                                     verify size of output file
-rw-rw-r--  1 stevens   100000 Nov 21 16:27 temp.file
```

But if the standard output is a terminal, we expect the write to return a partial count sometimes and an error at other times. This is what we see.

```
$ a.out < /etc/termcap 2>stderr.out                    output to terminal
                                                       lots of output to terminal ...
$ cat stderr.out
read 100000 bytes
nwrite = 8192, errno = 0
nwrite = 8192, errno = 0
nwrite = -1, errno = 11                                211 of these errors
. . .
nwrite = 4096, errno = 0
nwrite = -1, errno = 11                                658 of these errors
. . .
nwrite = 4096, errno = 0
nwrite = -1, errno = 11                                604 of these errors
. . .
nwrite = 4096, errno = 0
nwrite = -1, errno = 11                                1047 of these errors
. . .
nwrite = -1, errno = 11                                1046 of these errors
. . .
nwrite = 4096, errno = 0
                                                       and so on ...
```

On this system the `errno` of 11 is `EAGAIN`. The terminal driver on this system always accepted 4096 or 8192 bytes at a time. On another system the first three `writes` returned 2005, 1822, and 1811, followed by 96 errors, followed by a `write` of 1846, and so on. How much data is accepted on each `write` is system dependent.

The behavior of this program under SVR4 is completely different from the preceding—when the output was to the terminal only a single `write` was needed to output the entire input file. Apparently the nonblocking mode makes no difference! A bigger input file was created and the program's buffer was increased. This behavior of the program (one `write` for the entire file) continued until the size of the input file was about 700,000 bytes. At that point every `write` returned the error `EAGAIN`. (The input file was never output to the terminal—the program just generated a continual stream of error messages.)

What's going on here is that the terminal driver in SVR4 is connected to the program through the stream I/O system. (We describe streams in detail in Section 12.4.) The streams system has its own buffers and is capable of accepting more data at a time from the program. The SVR4 behavior also depends on the type of terminal—hardwired terminal, console device, or a pseudo terminal.   □

In this example the program issues thousands of `write` calls, when only around 20 are required to output the data. The rest just return an error. This type of loop, called *polling*, is a waste of CPU time on a multiuser system. In Section 12.5 we'll see that I/O multiplexing with a nonblocking descriptor is a more efficient way to do this.

We'll encounter nonblocking I/O in Chapter 17 when we output to a terminal device (a PostScript printer) and want to make certain we don't block on a `write`.

12.3 Record Locking

What happens when two people edit the same file at the same time? In most Unix systems the final state of the file corresponds to the last process that wrote the file. There are applications, however, such as a database system, when a process needs to be certain that it alone is writing to a file. To provide this capability for processes that need it, newer Unix systems provide record locking. (We develop a database library in Chapter 16 that uses record locking.)

Record locking is the term normally used to describe the ability of a process to prevent other processes from modifying a region of a file, while the first process is reading or modifying that portion of the file. Under Unix the adjective "record" is a misnomer, since the Unix kernel does not have a notion of records in a file. A better term is "range locking," since it is a range of a file (possibly the entire file) that is locked.

History

Figure 12.1 shows the different forms of record locking provided by various Unix systems.

System	Advisory	Mandatory	fcntl	lockf	flock
POSIX.1	•		•		
XPG3	•		•		
SVR2	•		•	•	
SVR3, SVR4	•	•	•	•	
4.3BSD	•				•
4.3BSD Reno	•		•		•

Figure 12.1 Forms of record locking supported by various Unix systems.

We describe the difference between advisory locking and mandatory locking later in this section. As shown in this figure, POSIX.1 selected the System V style of record locking, which is based on the fcntl function. This style is also supported by the latest version of 4.3BSD Reno.

Earlier Berkeley releases supported only the BSD flock function. This function locks only entire files, not regions of a file. But the POSIX.1 fcntl function can lock any region of a file, from the entire file down to a single byte within the file.

In this text we describe only the POSIX.1 fcntl locking. The System V lockf function is just an interface to the fcntl function.

> Record locking was originally added to Version 7 in 1980 by John Bass. The system call entry into the kernel was a function named locking. This function provided mandatory record locking and propagated through many vendor's versions of System III. Xenix systems picked up this function, and SVR4 still supports it in its Xenix compatibility library.
>
> SVR2 was the first release of System V to support the fcntl style of record locking, in 1984.

fcntl Record Locking

Let's repeat the prototype for the fcntl function from Section 3.13.

```
#include <sys/types.h>
#include <unistd.h>
#include <fcntl.h>

int fcntl(int filedes, int cmd, ... /* struct flock *flockptr */ );
```

Returns: depends on *cmd* if OK (see below), −1 on error

For record locking *cmd* is F_GETLK, F_SETLK, or F_SETLKW. The third argument (which we'll call *flockptr*) is a pointer to an flock structure.

```
struct flock {
  short   l_type;   /* F_RDLCK, F_WRLCK, or F_UNLCK */
  off_t   l_start;  /* offset in bytes, relative to l_whence */
  short   l_whence; /* SEEK_SET, SEEK_CUR, or SEEK_END */
  off_t   l_len;    /* length, in bytes; 0 means lock to EOF */
  pid_t   l_pid;    /* returned with F_GETLK */
};
```

This structure describes

- the type of lock desired: F_RDLCK (a shared read lock), F_WRLCK (an exclusive write lock), or F_UNLCK (unlocking a region),
- the starting byte offset of the region being locked or unlocked (l_start and l_whence), and
- the size of the region (l_len).

There are numerous rules about the specification of the region to be locked or unlocked.

- The two elements that specify the starting offset of the region are similar to the last two arguments of the lseek function (Section 3.6). Indeed, the l_whence member is specified as SEEK_SET, SEEK_CUR, or SEEK_END.
- Locks can start and extend beyond the current end of file, but cannot start or extend before the beginning of the file.
- If the l_len is 0, it means that the lock extends to the largest possible offset of the file. This allows us to lock a region starting anywhere in the file, up through and including any data that is appended to the file. (We don't have to try to guess how many bytes might be appended to the file.)
- To lock the entire file, we set l_start and l_whence to point to the beginning of the file, and specify a length (l_len) of 0. (There are several ways to specify the beginning of the file, but most applications specify l_start as 0 and l_whence as SEEK_SET.)

We mentioned two types of locks: a shared read lock (1_type of F_RDLCK) and an exclusive write lock (F_WRLCK). The basic rule is that any number of processes can have a shared read lock on a given byte, but only one process can have an exclusive write lock on a given byte. Furthermore, if there are one or more read locks on a byte, there can't be any write locks on that byte, and if there is an exclusive write lock on a byte, there can't be any read locks on that byte. We show this compatibility rule in Figure 12.2.

		request for	
		read lock	write lock
region currently has	no locks	OK	OK
	one or more read locks	OK	denied
	one write lock	denied	denied

Figure 12.2 Compatibility between different lock types.

To obtain a read lock the descriptor must be open for reading, and to obtain a write lock the descriptor must be open for writing.

We can now describe the three different commands for the fcntl function.

F_GETLK   Determine if the lock described by *flockptr* is blocked by some other lock. If a lock exists that would prevent ours from being created, the information on that existing lock overwrites the information pointed to by *flockptr*. If no lock exists that would prevent ours from being created, the structure pointed to by *flockptr* is left unchanged except for the 1_type member, which is set to F_UNLCK.

F_SETLK   Set the lock described by *flockptr*. If we are trying to obtain a read lock (1_type of F_RDLCK) or a write lock (1_type of F_WRLCK) and the compatibility rule prevents the system from giving us the lock (Figure 12.2), fcntl returns immediately with errno set to either EACCES or EAGAIN.

> SVR2 returned EACCES, but the manual page warned that in the future EAGAIN would be returned. SVR4 continues this tradition (returning EACCES with the same warning about the future). 4.3+BSD returns EAGAIN. POSIX.1 allows either error to be returned.

This command is also used to clear the lock described by *flockptr* (1_type of F_UNLCK).

F_SETLKW   This command is a blocking version of F_SETLK. (The W in the command name means "wait.") If the requested read lock or write lock cannot be granted because another process currently has some part of the requested region locked, the calling process is put to sleep. This sleep is interrupted if a signal is caught.

Be aware that testing for a lock with F_GETLK and then trying to obtain that lock with F_SETLK or F_SETLKW is not an atomic operation. We have no guarantee that between the two fcntl calls some other process won't come in and obtain the same lock. If we don't want to block while waiting for a lock to become available to us, we must handle the possible error returns from F_SETLK.

When setting or releasing a lock on a file, the system combines or splits adjacent areas as required. For example, if we set a read lock on bytes 0 through 99 and then set a write lock on bytes 0 through 49, we then have two locked regions: bytes 0 through 49 (write locked) and bytes 50 through 99 (read locked). Similarly, if we lock bytes 100 through 199 and then unlock byte 150, the kernel still maintains the locks on bytes 100 through 149, and bytes 151 through 199.

Example—Requesting and Releasing A Lock

To save ourselves from having to allocate an flock structure and fill in all the elements each time, the function lock_reg in Program 12.2 handles all these details.

```
#include      <sys/types.h>
#include      <fcntl.h>
#include      "ourhdr.h"

int
lock_reg(int fd, int cmd, int type, off_t offset, int whence, off_t len)
{
    struct flock    lock;

    lock.l_type = type;      /* F_RDLCK, F_WRLCK, F_UNLCK */
    lock.l_start = offset;   /* byte offset, relative to l_whence */
    lock.l_whence = whence;  /* SEEK_SET, SEEK_CUR, SEEK_END */
    lock.l_len = len;        /* #bytes (0 means to EOF) */

    return( fcntl(fd, cmd, &lock) );
}
```

Program 12.2 Function to lock or unlock a region of a file.

Since most locking calls are to lock or unlock a region (the command F_GETLK is rarely used) we normally use one of the following five macros, which are defined in ourhdr.h (Appendix B).

```
#define read_lock(fd, offset, whence, len) \
            lock_reg(fd, F_SETLK, F_RDLCK, offset, whence, len)
#define readw_lock(fd, offset, whence, len) \
            lock_reg(fd, F_SETLKW, F_RDLCK, offset, whence, len)
#define write_lock(fd, offset, whence, len) \
            lock_reg(fd, F_SETLK, F_WRLCK, offset, whence, len)
#define writew_lock(fd, offset, whence, len) \
            lock_reg(fd, F_SETLKW, F_WRLCK, offset, whence, len)
#define un_lock(fd, offset, whence, len) \
            lock_reg(fd, F_SETLK, F_UNLCK, offset, whence, len)
```

We have purposely defined the first three arguments to these macros in the same order as the lseek function.   □

Example—Testing for A Lock

Program 12.3 defines the function lock_test that we'll use to test for a lock.

```
#include     <sys/types.h>
#include     <fcntl.h>
#include     "ourhdr.h"

pid_t
lock_test(int fd, int type, off_t offset, int whence, off_t len)
{
    struct flock    lock;

    lock.l_type = type;      /* F_RDLCK or F_WRLCK */
    lock.l_start = offset;   /* byte offset, relative to l_whence */
    lock.l_whence = whence;  /* SEEK_SET, SEEK_CUR, SEEK_END */
    lock.l_len = len;        /* #bytes (0 means to EOF) */

    if (fcntl(fd, F_GETLK, &lock) < 0)
        err_sys("fcntl error");

    if (lock.l_type == F_UNLCK)
        return(0);           /* false, region is not locked by another proc */
    return(lock.l_pid);  /* true, return pid of lock owner */
}
```

Program 12.3 Function to test for a locking condition.

If a lock exists that would block the request specified by the arguments, this function returns the process ID of the process holding the lock. Otherwise the function returns 0 (false). We normally call this function from the following two macros (defined in ourhdr.h).

```
#define is_readlock(fd, offset, whence, len) \
            lock_test(fd, F_RDLCK, offset, whence, len)
#define is_writelock(fd, offset, whence, len) \
            lock_test(fd, F_WRLCK, offset, whence, len)
```
                                                                                                    □

Example—Deadlock

Deadlock occurs when two processes are each waiting for a resource that the other has locked. The potential for deadlock exists if a process that controls a locked region is put to sleep when it tries to lock another region that is controlled by a different process.

Program 12.4 shows an example of deadlock. The child locks byte 0 and the parent locks byte 1. Then each tries to lock the other's already locked byte. We use the parent–child synchronization routines from Section 8.8 (TELL_xxx and WAIT_xxx) so that each process can wait for the other to obtain its lock. Running Program 12.4 gives us

```
#include        <sys/types.h>
#include        <sys/stat.h>
#include        <fcntl.h>
#include        "ourhdr.h"

static void lockabyte(const char *, int, off_t);

int
main(void)
{
    int     fd;
    pid_t   pid;

        /* Create a file and write two bytes to it */
    if ( (fd = creat("templock", FILE_MODE)) < 0)
        err_sys("creat error");
    if (write(fd, "ab", 2) != 2)
        err_sys("write error");

    TELL_WAIT();
    if ( (pid = fork()) < 0)
        err_sys("fork error");

    else if (pid == 0) {                /* child */
        lockabyte("child", fd, 0);
        TELL_PARENT(getppid());
        WAIT_PARENT();
        lockabyte("child", fd, 1);

    } else {                            /* parent */
        lockabyte("parent", fd, 1);
        TELL_CHILD(pid);
        WAIT_CHILD();
        lockabyte("parent", fd, 0);
    }
    exit(0);
}

static void
lockabyte(const char *name, int fd, off_t offset)
{
    if (writew_lock(fd, offset, SEEK_SET, 1) < 0)
        err_sys("%s: writew_lock error", name);

    printf("%s: got the lock, byte %d\n", name, offset);
}
```

Program 12.4 Example of deadlock detection.

```
$ a.out
child: got the lock, byte 0
parent: got the lock, byte 1
child: writew_lock error: Deadlock situation detected/avoided
parent: got the lock, byte 0
```

When a deadlock is detected, the kernel has to choose one process to receive the error return. In this example the child was chosen, but this is an implementation detail. When this program was run on another system, half the time the child received the error and half the time the parent received the error.   □

Implied Inheritance and Release of Locks

There are three rules that govern the automatic inheritance and release of record locks.

1. Locks are associated with a process and a file. This has two implications. The first is obvious: when a process terminates all its locks are released. The second is far from obvious: whenever a descriptor is closed, any locks on the file referenced by that descriptor for that process are released. This means that if we do the following four steps

    ```
    fd1 = open(pathname, ...);
    read_lock(fd1, ...);
    fd2 = dup(fd1);
    close(fd2);
    ```

    after the close(fd2) the lock that was obtained on fd1 is released. The same thing would happen if we replaced the dup with open, as in

    ```
    fd1 = open(pathname, ...);
    read_lock(fd1, ...);
    fd2 = open(pathname, ...)
    close(fd2);
    ```

    to open the same file on another descriptor.

2. Locks are never inherited by the child across a fork. This means that if a process obtains a lock and then calls fork, the child is considered "another process" with regard to the lock that was obtained by the parent. The child has to call fcntl to obtain its own locks on any descriptors that were inherited across the fork. This makes sense, because locks are meant to prevent multiple processes from writing to the same file at the same time. If the child inherited locks across a fork, both the parent and child could write to the same file at the same time.

3. Locks may be inherited by a new program across an exec.

    We have to say *may* here because POSIX.1 doesn't require this. Under SVR4 and 4.3+BSD, however, locks are inherited across an exec.

4.3+BSD Implementation

Let's take a brief look at the data structures used in the 4.3+BSD implementation. This should help clarify rule 1, that locks are associated with a process and a file.

Consider a process that executes the following statements (ignoring error returns):

```
fd1 = open(pathname, ...);
write_lock(fd1, 0, SEEK_SET, 1);      /* parent write locks byte 0 */
if (fork() > 0) {      /* parent */
    fd2 = dup(fd1);
    fd3 = open(pathname, ...);
    pause();
} else {
    read_lock(fd1, 1, SEEK_SET, 1); /* child read locks byte 1 */
    pause();
}
```

Figure 12.3 shows the resulting data structures after both the parent and child have paused.

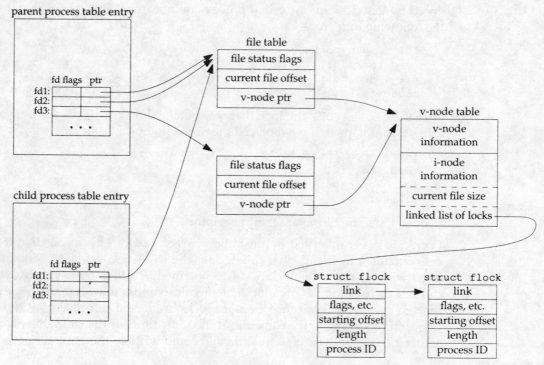

Figure 12.3 The 4.3+BSD data structures for record locking.

We've shown the data structures that result from the open, fork, and dup earlier (Figures 3.4 and 8.1). What is new are the flock structures that are linked together from the i-node structure. Notice that each flock structure describes one locked region (defined by an offset and length) for a given process. We show two of these structures, one for the parent's call to write_lock and one for the child's call to read_lock. Each structure contains the corresponding process ID.

In the parent, closing any one of fd1, fd2, or fd3 causes the parent's lock to be released. When any one of these three descriptors is closed, the kernel goes through the linked list of locks for the corresponding i-node, and releases the locks held by the calling process. The kernel can't tell (and doesn't care) which descriptor of the three the parent's lock was obtained on.

Example

Advisory locks can be used by a daemon to assure that only one copy of the daemon is running. When started, many daemons write their process ID to a file. This process ID can be used when it is time to shut down the system. The way to prevent multiple copies of the daemon from running is to have the daemon obtain a lock on its process ID file when it starts. If it holds the lock for as long as it runs, no more copies of itself will be started. Program 12.5 implements this technique.

We specifically truncate the file in case the file previously contained a process ID that was longer than the current process ID. If the previous contents of the file were 12345\n and the new process ID was 654, we want the file to contain just the four bytes 654\n, and not 654\n5\n. Note that we call ftruncate after we get the lock—we cannot specify O_TRUNC in the call to open, because that could empty the file even though it was locked by another copy of the daemon. (We could use O_TRUNC if we were using mandatory locking, instead of advisory locking. We discuss mandatory locking later in this section.)

In this example we also set the close-on-exec flag for the descriptor. This is because daemons often fork and exec other processes, and there is no need for this file to remain open in another process.   □

Example

Use caution when locking or unlocking relative to the end of file. Most implementations convert an l_whence value of SEEK_CUR or SEEK_END into an absolute file offset, using l_start and the file's current position or current length. Often, however, we need to specify a lock relative to the file's current position or current length, because we can't call lseek to obtain the current file offset, since we don't have a lock on the file. (There's a chance another process could change the file's length between the call to lseek and the lock call.)

Program 12.6 writes a large file, one byte at a time. Each time around the loop it locks from the current end of file through any future end of file (the final argument, the length of 0), and writes one byte. It then unlocks from the current end of file through any future end of file, and writes another byte. If the system kept track of locks using the notation ("from the current end of file through any future end of file") this should work. But if the system converts this notation into absolute file offsets, we could have a problem. Running this program under SVR4 shows that we do have a problem.

```c
#include    <sys/types.h>
#include    <sys/stat.h>
#include    <errno.h>
#include    <fcntl.h>
#include    "ourhdr.h"

#define PIDFILE     "daemon.pid"

int
main(void)
{
    int     fd, val;
    char    buf[10];

    if ( (fd = open(PIDFILE, O_WRONLY | O_CREAT, FILE_MODE)) < 0)
        err_sys("open error");

            /* try and set a write lock on the entire file */
    if (write_lock(fd, 0, SEEK_SET, 0) < 0) {
        if (errno == EACCES || errno == EAGAIN)
            exit(0);      /* gracefully exit, daemon is already running */
        else
            err_sys("write_lock error");
    }

            /* truncate to zero length, now that we have the lock */
    if (ftruncate(fd, 0) < 0)
        err_sys("ftruncate error");

            /* and write our process ID */
    sprintf(buf, "%d\n", getpid());
    if (write(fd, buf, strlen(buf)) != strlen(buf))
        err_sys("write error");

            /* set close-on-exec flag for descriptor */
    if ( (val = fcntl(fd, F_GETFD, 0)) < 0)
        err_sys("fcntl F_GETFD error");
    val |= FD_CLOEXEC;
    if (fcntl(fd, F_SETFD, val) < 0)
        err_sys("fcntl F_SETFD error");

    /* leave file open until we terminate: lock will be held */

    /* do whatever ... */

    exit(0);
}
```

Program 12.5 Daemon start-up code to prevent multiple copies of itself from running.

```
#include       <sys/types.h>
#include       <sys/stat.h>
#include       <fcntl.h>
#include       "ourhdr.h"

int
main(void)
{
    int     i, fd;

    if ( (fd = open("temp.lock", O_RDWR | O_CREAT | O_TRUNC,
                                        FILE_MODE)) < 0)
        err_sys("open error");

    for (i = 0; i < 1000000; i++) { /* try to write 2 Mbytes */
                /* lock from current EOF to EOF */
        if (writew_lock(fd, 0, SEEK_END, 0) < 0)
            err_sys("writew_lock error");

        if (write(fd, &fd, 1) != 1)
            err_sys("write error");

        if (un_lock(fd, 0, SEEK_END, 0) < 0)
            err_sys("un_lock error");

        if (write(fd, &fd, 1) != 1)
            err_sys("write error");
    }
    exit(0);
}
```

Program 12.6 Program displaying problems with locking relative to end of file.

```
$ a.out
writew_lock error: No record locks available
$ ls -l temp.lock
-rw-r--r--   1 stevens  other      592 Nov  1 04:41 temp.lock
```

(The error ENOLCK is returned by the kernel. It indicates that the kernel's lock table is full.) It is instructive to see what the system is doing. Figure 12.4 shows the state of the file after the first call to writew_lock and the first call to write.

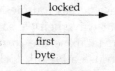

Figure 12.4 State of file after first writew_lock and first write.

We show the locked region extending past the byte that we wrote, since we specified "through any future end of file" in the call to `writew_lock`.

We then call `un_lock`. This unlocks from the current end of file through any future end of file, which moves the right end of the arrow in Figure 12.4 back to the end of the first byte. We then write the second byte to the file. Figure 12.5 shows the state of the file after calling `un_lock` and the `write` that follows.

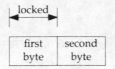

Figure 12.5 State of file after `un_lock` and second `write`.

After going through the `for` loop one more time, we have written four bytes to the file. Figure 12.6 shows the state of the file and its locks.

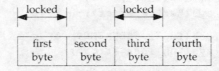

Figure 12.6 State of file and locks after second time through `for` loop.

What happens when we run Program 12.6 is that this form of file locking (every other byte locked) continues until the kernel runs out of lock structures for the process. When this happens, `fcntl` returns an error of ENOLCK.

Since we know how many bytes we are writing to the file each time, we can correct this problem by replacing the second argument to `un_lock` (the `l_start` specifier) with the negative of the number of bytes (−1 in this case). This causes each lock to be removed by `un_lock`.

> This problem actually occurred to the author when developing the `_db_writedat` and `_db_writeidx` functions in Section 16.7. A slightly different way around the problem is shown there.   □

Advisory versus Mandatory Locking

Consider a library of database access routines. If all the functions in the library handle record locking in a consistent way, then we say that any set of processes that are using these functions to access a database are *cooperating processes*. It is feasible for these database access functions to use advisory locking if these functions are the only ones being used to access the database. But advisory locking doesn't prevent some other process that has write permission for the database file from writing whatever it wants to the database file. This rogue process would be an uncooperating process since it's not using the accepted method (the library of database functions) to access the database.

Mandatory locking causes the kernel to check every open, read, and write to verify that the calling process isn't violating a lock on the file being accessed. Mandatory locking is sometimes called enforcement-mode locking.

We saw in Figure 12.1 that SVR4 provides mandatory record locking. It is not part of POSIX.1.

Mandatory locking is enabled for a particular file by turning on the set-group-ID bit and turning off the group-execute bit. (Recall Program 4.4.) Since the set-group-ID bit makes no sense when the group-execute bit is off, the designers of SVR3 chose this way to specify that the locking for a file is to be mandatory locking and not advisory locking. (Many people consider this multiplexing of the set-group-ID bit to be a hack.)

What happens to a process that tries to read or write a file that has mandatory locking enabled and the specified part of the file is currently read or write locked by another process? The answer depends on the type of operation (read or write), the type of lock held by the other process (read lock or write lock), and whether the descriptor for the read or write is nonblocking. Figure 12.7 shows the eight possibilities.

	Blocking descriptor, tries to		Nonblocking descriptor, tries to	
	read	write	read	write
read lock exists on region	OK	blocks	OK	EAGAIN
write lock exists on region	blocks	blocks	EAGAIN	EAGAIN

Figure 12.7 Effect of mandatory locking on reads and writes by other processes.

In addition to the read and write functions in Figure 12.7, the open function can also be affected by mandatory record locks held by another process. Normally, open succeeds, even if the file being opened has outstanding mandatory record locks. The next read or write follows the rules listed in Figure 12.7. But if the file being opened has outstanding mandatory record locks (either read locks or write locks); and if the flags in the call to open specify either O_TRUNC, or O_CREAT, then open returns an error of EAGAIN immediately, regardless whether O_NONBLOCK is specified. (Generating the open error for O_TRUNC makes sense, because the file cannot be truncated if it is read locked or write locked by another process. Generating the error for O_CREAT, however, makes little sense, since this flag says to create the file only if it doesn't already exist, but it has to exist to be record locked by another process.)

This handling of locking conflicts with open can lead to surprising results. While developing the exercises in this section a test program was run that opened a file (whose mode specified mandatory locking), established a read lock on an entire file, then went to sleep for a while. (Recall from Figure 12.7 that a read lock should prevent writing to the file by other processes.) During this sleep period the following behavior was seen in other "normal" Unix programs.

- The same file could be edited with the ed editor, and the results written back to disk! The mandatory record locking had no effect at all. Using the system call trace feature provide by some versions of Unix it was seen that ed wrote the new contents to a temporary file, removed the original file, then renamed the temporary file to be the original file. The mandatory record locking has no effect on the unlink function, which allowed this to happen.

> Under SVR4 the system call trace of a process is obtained by the truss(1) command. 4.3+BSD uses the ktrace(1) and kdump(1) commands.

- The vi editor was never able to edit the file. It could read the file's contents, but whenever we tried to write new data to the file, EAGAIN was returned. If we tried to append new data to the file, the write blocked. This behavior from vi is what we expect.
- Using the KornShell's > and >> operators to overwrite or append to the file resulted in the error "cannot create."
- Using the same two operators with the Bourne shell resulted in an error for >, but the >> operator just blocked until the mandatory lock was removed, and then proceeded. (The difference in the handling of the append operator is because the KornShell opens the file with O_CREAT and O_APPEND, and we mentioned above that specifying O_CREAT generates an error. The Bourne shell, however, doesn't specify O_CREAT if the file already exists, so the open succeeds but the next write blocks.)

The bottom line with this exercise is to be wary of mandatory record locking. As seen with the ed example, it can be circumvented.

Mandatory record locking can also be used by a malicious user to hold a read lock on a file that is publicly readable. This can prevent anyone from writing to the file. (Of course, the file has to have mandatory record locking enabled for this to occur, which may require the user be able to change the permission bits of the file.) Consider a database file that is world readable and has mandatory record locking enabled. If a malicious user were to hold a read lock on the entire file, the file could not be written to by other processes.

Example

Program 12.7 determines whether mandatory locking is supported by a system.

```
#include    <sys/types.h>
#include    <sys/stat.h>
#include    <sys/wait.h>
#include    <errno.h>
#include    <fcntl.h>
#include    "ourhdr.h"

int
main(void)
{
    int         fd;
    pid_t       pid;
    char        buff[5];
    struct stat statbuf;
```

```
        if ( (fd = open("templock", O_RDWR | O_CREAT | O_TRUNC,
                                               FILE_MODE)) < 0)
            err_sys("open error");
        if (write(fd, "abcdef", 6) != 6)
            err_sys("write error");

            /* turn on set-group-ID and turn off group-execute */
        if (fstat(fd, &statbuf) < 0)
            err_sys("fstat error");
        if (fchmod(fd, (statbuf.st_mode & ~S_IXGRP) | S_ISGID) < 0)
            err_sys("fchmod error");

    TELL_WAIT();
    if ( (pid = fork()) < 0) {
        err_sys("fork error");

    } else if (pid > 0) {    /* parent */
                /* write lock entire file */
        if (write_lock(fd, 0, SEEK_SET, 0) < 0)
            err_sys("write_lock error");
        TELL_CHILD(pid);

        if (waitpid(pid, NULL, 0) < 0)
            err_sys("waitpid error");

    } else {                    /* child */
        WAIT_PARENT();          /* wait for parent to set lock */

        set_fl(fd, O_NONBLOCK);

            /* first let's see what error we get if region is locked */
        if (read_lock(fd, 0, SEEK_SET, 0) != -1)      /* no wait */
            err_sys("child: read_lock succeeded");
        printf("read_lock of already-locked region returns %d\n", errno);

            /* now try to read the mandatory locked file */
        if (lseek(fd, 0, SEEK_SET) == -1)
            err_sys("lseek error");
        if (read(fd, buff, 2) < 0)
            err_ret("read failed (mandatory locking works)");
        else
            printf("read OK (no mandatory locking), buff = %2.2s\n", buff);
    }
    exit(0);
}
```

Program 12.7 Determine whether mandatory locking is supported.

This program creates a file and enables mandatory locking for the file. It then splits into
a parent and child, with the parent obtaining a write lock on the entire file. The child
first sets its descriptor nonblocking and then attempts to obtain a read lock on the file,
expecting to get an error. This lets us see if the system returns EACCES or EAGAIN.
Next the child rewinds the file and tries to read from the file. If mandatory locking is

provided, the read should return EACCES or EAGAIN (since the descriptor is non-blocking). Otherwise the read returns the data that it read. Running this program under SVR4 (which supports mandatory locking) gives us

```
$ a.out
read_lock of already-locked region returns 13
read failed (mandatory locking works): No more processes
```

If we look at either the system's headers or the intro(2) manual page, we see that an errno of 13 corresponds to EACCES. We can also see from this example that the errno returned by the read (EAGAIN) has the nondescriptive message "No more processes" associated with it. Normally this error comes from fork when we are out of processes.

Under 4.3+BSD we get

```
$ a.out
read_lock of already-locked region returns 35
read OK (no mandatory locking), buff = ab
```

Here an errno of 35 corresponds to EAGAIN. Mandatory locking is not supported.   □

Example

Let's return to the first question of this section: what happens when two people edit the same file at the same time? The normal Unix text editors do not employ record locking, so the answer is still that the final result of the file corresponds to the last process that wrote the file. (The 4.3+BSD vi editor does have a compile-time option to enable run-time advisory record locking, but this option is not enabled by default.) Even if we were to put advisory locking into one editor, say vi, it still doesn't prevent users from using another editor that doesn't employ advisory record locking.

If the system provides mandatory record locking, we could modify our favorite editor to use it (if we have the sources). Not having the source code to the editor, we might try the following. We write our own program that is a front-end to vi. This program immediately calls fork and the parent just waits for the child to complete. The child opens the file specified on the command line, enables mandatory locking, obtains a write lock on the entire file, and then execs vi. While vi is running, the file is write locked, so other users can't modify it. When vi terminates, the parent's wait returns, and our front-end terminates. Assumed in this example is that locks are inherited across an exec, which we said earlier is the case for SVR4 (the only system we've described that provides mandatory locking).

A small front-end program of this type can be written, but it doesn't work. The problem is that most editors (vi and ed, at least) read their input file and then close it. A lock is released on a file whenever a descriptor that references that file is closed. This means that when the editor closes the file after reading its contents, the lock is gone. There is no way to prevent this in the front-end program.   □

We use record locking in Chapter 16 in our database library to provide concurrent access to multiple processes. In this chapter we also provide some timing measurements to see what effect record locking has on a process.

12.4   Streams

Streams are provided by System V as a general way to interface communication drivers
into the kernel. We need to discuss streams to understand (a) the terminal interface in
System V, (b) the use of the `poll` function for I/O multiplexing (Section 12.5.2), (c) the
implementation of stream pipes and named stream pipes (Sections 15.2 and 15.5).

> Streams were developed by Dennis Ritchie [Ritchie 1984] as a way of cleaning up the tradi-
> tional character I/O system (clists) and to accommodate networking protocols. It was later
> added to SVR3. Complete support for streams (i.e., a streams-based terminal I/O system) was
> provided with SVR4. The SVR4 implementation is described in [AT&T 1990d]. SVR4 calls the
> feature STREAMS. We'll just use the all lowercase name.

> Be careful not to confuse this usage of the word streams with our previous usage of it in the
> standard I/O library (Section 5.2).

A stream provides a full-duplex path between a user process and a device driver.
There is no need for a stream to talk to an actual hardware device—streams can also be
used with pseudo device drivers. Figure 12.8 shows the basic picture for what is called
a simple stream.

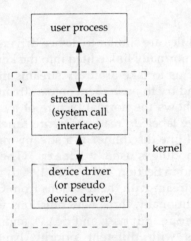

Figure 12.8   A Simple stream.

Beneath the stream head we can push processing modules onto the stream. This is
done using an `ioctl`. Figure 12.9 shows a stream with a single processing module. We
also show the connection between these boxes with two arrows, to stress the full-duplex
nature of streams.

Any number of processing modules can be pushed onto a stream. We use the term
push, because each new module goes beneath the stream head, pushing any previously
pushed modules down. (This is similar to a last-in, first-out stack.) In Figure 12.9 we
have labeled the downstream and upstream sides of the stream. Data that we write to a
stream head is sent downstream. Data read by the device driver is sent upstream.

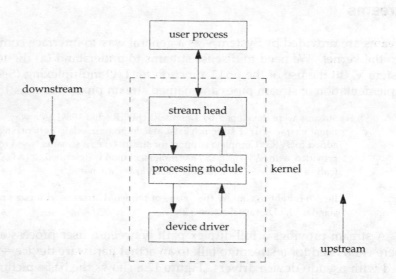

Figure 12.9 A stream with a processing module.

Streams modules are similar to device drivers in that they execute as part of the kernel, and they are normally link edited into the kernel when the kernel is built. Most systems don't allow us to take arbitrary streams modules that have not been link edited into the kernel and try to push them onto a stream.

Figure 11.2 shows the normal picture of a streams-based terminal system. In this figure what we've labeled "read and write functions" is the stream head, and the box labeled "terminal line discipline" is a streams processing module. The actual name of this processing module is usually `ldterm`. (The manual pages for the various streams modules are found in Section 7 of [AT&T 1990d] and Section 7 of [AT&T 1991].)

We access a stream with the functions from Chapter 3: `open`, `close`, `read`, `write`, and `ioctl`. Additionally, three new functions were added to the SVR3 kernel to support streams (`getmsg`, `putmsg`, and `poll`), and another two were added with SVR4 to handle messages with different priority bands within a stream (`getpmsg` and `putpmsg`). We describe these five new functions later in this section. The *pathname* that we open for a stream normally lives beneath the /dev directory. Just looking at the device name using `ls -l`, we can't tell if the device is a streams device or not. All streams devices are character special files.

Although some streams documentation implies that we can write processing modules and push them willy-nilly onto a stream, the writing of these modules requires the same skills and care as writing a device driver. It is generally specialized applications or functions that push and pop streams modules.

Before streams, terminals were handled with the existing clist mechanism. (Section 10.3.1 of Bach [1986] and Section 9.6 of Leffler et al. [1989] describe clists in SVR2 and 4.3BSD, respectively.) Adding other character-based devices to the kernel usually involved writing a device driver and putting everything into the driver. Access to the new device was typically through the raw device, meaning every user read or write ended up directly in the device driver. The streams mechanism cleans up this way of interaction, allowing the data to flow between the stream head and the driver in streams messages and allowing any number of intermediate processing modules to operate on the data.

Streams Messages

All input and output under streams is based on messages. The stream head and user process exchange messages using read, write, ioctl, getmsg, getpmsg, putmsg, and putpmsg. Messages are also passed up and down a stream between the stream head, the processing modules, and the device driver.

Between the user process and the stream head a message consists of (a) a message type, (b) optional control information, and (c) optional data. We show in Figure 12.10 how the different message types are generated by the various arguments to write, putmsg, and putpmsg. The control information and data are specified by strbuf structures.

```
struct strbuf
    int   maxlen;   /* size of buffer */
    int   len;      /* number of bytes currently in buffer */
    char *buf;      /* pointer to buffer */
};
```

When we send a message with putmsg or putpmsg, len specifies the number of bytes of data in the buffer. When we receive a message with getmsg or getpmsg, maxlen specifies the size of the buffer (so the kernel won't overflow the buffer) and len is set by the kernel to the amount of data stored in the buffer. We'll see that a zero-length message is OK, and a len of −1 can specify that there is no control or data.

Why do we need to pass both control information and data? Providing both allows us to implement service interfaces between a user process and a stream. Olander, McGrath, and Israel [1986] describe the original implementation of service interfaces in System V. Chapter 5 of AT&T [1990d] describes service interfaces in detail, along with a simple example. Probably the best-known service interface is the System V Transport Layer Interface (TLI), described in Chapter 7 of Stevens [1990], which provides an interface to the networking system.

Another example of control information is sending a connectionless network message (a datagram). To send the message we need to specify the contents of the message (the data) and the destination address for the message (the control information). If we couldn't send control and data together, some ad hoc scheme would be required. For example, we could specify the address using an ioctl, followed by a write of the data. Another technique would be to require that the address occupy the first N bytes of the data that is written using write. Separating the control information from the data, and providing functions that handle both (putmsg and getmsg) is a cleaner way to handle this.

There are about 25 different types of messages, but only a few of these are used between the user process and the stream head. The rest are passed up and down a stream within the kernel. (These are of interest to people writing streams-processing modules, but can safely be ignored by people writing user-level code.) We'll encounter only three of these message types with the functions we use (read, write, getmsg, getpmsg, putmsg, and putpmsg):

- M_DATA (user data for I/O),
- M_PROTO (protocol control information), and
- M_PCPROTO (high-priority protocol control information).

Every message on a stream has a queueing priority:

- high-priority messages (highest priority)
- priority band messages
- ordinary messages (lowest priority)

Ordinary messages are priority band messages with a band of 0. Priority band messages have a band of 1–255, with a higher band specifying a higher priority.

Each streams module has two input queues. One receives messages from the module above (messages moving downstream from the stream head toward the driver), and one receives messages from the module below (messages moving upstream from the driver toward the stream head). The messages on an input queue are arranged by priority. We show in Figure 12.10 how the different arguments to write, putmsg, and putpmsg cause these different priority messages to be generated.

There are other types of messages that we don't consider. For example, if the stream head receives an M_SIG message from below, it generates a signal. This is how a terminal line discipline module sends the terminal-generated signals to the foreground process group associated with a controlling terminal.

putmsg and putpmsg Functions

A streams message (control information or data, or both) is written to a stream using either putmsg or putpmsg. The difference in these two functions is that the latter allows us to specify a priority band for the message.

```
#include <stropts.h>

int putmsg(int filedes, const struct strbuf *ctlptr,
                   const struct strbuf *dataptr, int flag);

int putpmsg(int filedes, const struct strbuf *ctlptr,
                   const struct strbuf *dataptr, int band, int flag);
                                              Both return: 0 if OK, −1 on error
```

We can also write to a stream, and that is equivalent to a putmsg without any control information and with a flag of 0.

These two functions can generate the three different priorities of messages: ordinary, priority band, and high-priority. Figure 12.10 details the different combinations of the arguments to these two functions that generate the different types of messages.

Function	Control?	Data?	*band*	*flag*	Message type generated
write	N/A	yes	N/A	N/A	M_DATA (ordinary)
putmsg	no	no	N/A	0	no message sent, returns 0
putmsg	no	yes	N/A	0	M_DATA (ordinary)
putmsg	yes	yes or no	N/A	0	M_PROTO (ordinary)
putmsg	yes	yes or no	N/A	RS_HIPRI	M_PCPROTO (high-priority)
putmsg	no	yes or no	N/A	RS_HIPRI	error, EINVAL
putpmsg	yes or no	yes or no	0–255	0	error, EINVAL
putpmsg	no	no	0–255	MSG_BAND	no message sent, returns 0
putpmsg	no	yes	0	MSG_BAND	M_DATA (ordinary)
putpmsg	no	yes	1–255	MSG_BAND	M_DATA (priority band)
putpmsg	yes	yes or no	0	MSG_BAND	M_PROTO (ordinary)
putpmsg	yes	yes or no	1–255	MSG_BAND	M_PROTO (priority band)
putpmsg	yes	yes or no	0	MSG_HIPRI	M_PCPROTO (high-priority)
putpmsg	no	yes or no	0	MSG_HIPRI	error, EINVAL
putpmsg	yes or no	yes or no	nonzero	MSG_HIPRI	error, EINVAL

Figure 12.10 Type of streams message generated for write, putmsg, and putpmsg.

The notation "N/A" means not applicable. In this figure a "no" for the control portion of the message corresponds to either a null *ctlptr* argument, or *ctlptr–>len* being −1. A "yes" for the control portion corresponds to *ctlptr* being nonnull and *ctlptr–>len* being greater than or equal to 0. The data portion of the message is handled equivalently (using *dataptr* instead of *ctlptr*).

Streams ioctl Operations

We mentioned in Section 3.14 that the ioctl function is the catchall for anything that can't be done with the other I/O functions. The streams system continues this tradition.

Under SVR4 there are 29 different operations that can be performed on a stream using ioctl. These operations are documented in the streamio(7) manual page (part of [AT&T 1990d]) and the header <stropts.h> must be included in C code that uses any of these operations. The second argument for ioctl, *request*, specifies which of the 29 operations to perform. All the *request*s begin with I_. The third argument depends on the *request*. Sometimes the third argument is an integer value and sometimes it's a pointer to an integer or a structure.

Example—isastream Function

We sometimes need to determine if a descriptor refers to a stream or not. This is similar to calling the isatty function to determine if a descriptor refers to a terminal device (Section 11.9). SVR4 provides the isastream function.

```
    int isastream(int filedes);
```

Returns: 1 (true) if streams device, 0 (false) otherwise

(For some reason, the designers of SVR4 forgot to put the prototype for this function in
a header, so we can't show an #include for this function.)

Like isatty, this is usually a trivial function that just tries an ioctl that is valid
only on a streams device. Program 12.8 is one possible implementation of this function.
We use the I_CANPUT ioctl, which checks if the band specified by the third argument
(0 in the example) is writable. If the ioctl succeeds, the stream is not changed.

```
#include     <stropts.h>
#include     <unistd.h>

int
isastream(int fd)
{
    return(ioctl(fd, I_CANPUT, 0) != -1);
}
```

Program 12.8 Check if descriptor is a streams device.

We can use Program 12.9 to test this function.

```
#include     <sys/types.h>
#include     <sys/fcntl.h>
#include     "ourhdr.h"

int
main(int argc, char *argv[])
{
    int      i, fd;

    for (i = 1; i < argc; i++) {
        printf("%s: ", argv[i]);
        if ( (fd = open(argv[i], O_RDONLY)) < 0) {
            err_ret("%s: can't open", argv[i]);
            continue;
        }

        if (isastream(fd) == 0)
            err_ret("%s: not a stream", argv[i]);
        else
            err_msg("%s: streams device", argv[i]);
    }
    exit(0);
}
```

Program 12.9 Test the isastream function.

Running this program shows the various errors returned by the `ioctl` function.

```
$ a.out /dev/tty /dev/vidadm /dev/null /etc/motd
/dev/tty: /dev/tty: streams device
/dev/vidadm: /dev/vidadm: not a stream: Invalid argument
/dev/null: /dev/null: not a stream: No such device
/etc/motd: /etc/motd: not a stream: Not a typewriter
```

`/dev/tty` is a streams device, as we expect under SVR4. `/dev/vidadm` is not a streams device, but it is a character special file that supports other `ioctl` requests. These devices return `EINVAL` when the `ioctl` request is unknown. `/dev/null` is a character special file that does not support any `ioctl` operations, so the error `ENODEV` is returned. Finally, `/etc/motd` is a regular file, not a character special file, so the classic error `ENOTTY` is returned. We never receive the error we might expect: `ENOSTR` ("Device is not a stream").

> "Not a typewriter" is a historical artifact because the Unix kernel returns `ENOTTY` whenever an `ioctl` is attempted on a descriptor that doesn't refer to a character special device.   □

Example

If the `ioctl` *request* is `I_LIST`, the system returns the names of all the modules on the stream—the ones that have been pushed onto the stream, including the topmost driver. (We say topmost because in the case of a multiplexing driver there may be more than one driver. Chapter 10 of AT&T [1990d] discusses multiplexing drivers in detail.) The third argument must be a pointer to a `str_list` structure.

```
struct str_list {
    int              sl_nmods;   /* number of entries in array */
    struct str_mlist  *sl_modlist; /* ptr to first element of array */
};
```

We have to set `sl_modlist` to point to the first element of an array of `str_mlist` structures, and set `sl_nmods` to the number of entries in the array.

```
struct str_mlist {
    char  l_name[FMNAMESZ+1];   /* null terminated module name */
};
```

The constant `FMNAMESZ` is defined in the header `<sys/conf.h>` and is often 8. The extra byte in `l_name` is for the terminating null byte.

If the third argument to the `ioctl` is 0, the count of the number of modules is returned (as the value of `ioctl`) instead of the module names. We'll use this to determine the number of modules and then allocate the required number of `str_mlist` structures.

Program 12.10 illustrates the `I_LIST` operation. Since the returned list of names doesn't differentiate between the modules and the driver, when we print the module names we know that the final entry in the list is the driver at the bottom of the stream.

If we run Program 12.10 from both a network login and a console login, to see which streams modules are pushed onto the controlling terminal, we get the following:

```
#include        <sys/conf.h>
#include        <sys/types.h>
#include        <fcntl.h>
#include        <stropts.h>
#include        "ourhdr.h"

int
main(int argc, char *argv[])
{
    int             fd, i, nmods;
    struct str_list list;

    if (argc != 2)
        err_quit("usage: a.out <pathname>");

    if ( (fd = open(argv[1], O_RDONLY)) < 0)
        err_sys("can't open %s", argv[1]);
    if (isastream(fd) == 0)
        err_quit("%s is not a stream", argv[1]);

            /* fetch number of modules */
    if ( (nmods = ioctl(fd, I_LIST, (void *) 0)) < 0)
        err_sys("I_LIST error for nmods");
    printf("#modules = %d\n", nmods);

            /* allocate storage for all the module names */
    list.sl_modlist = calloc(nmods, sizeof(struct str_mlist));
    if (list.sl_modlist == NULL)
        err_sys("calloc error");
    list.sl_nmods = nmods;

            /* and fetch the module names */
    if (ioctl(fd, I_LIST, &list) < 0)
        err_sys("I_LIST error for list");

            /* print the module names */
    for (i = 1; i <= nmods; i++)
        printf("  %s: %s\n", (i == nmods) ? "driver" : "module",
                             list.sl_modlist++);

    exit(0);
}
```

Program 12.10 List the names of the modules on a stream.

```
$ who
stevens     console       Sep 25 06:12
stevens     pts001        Oct 12 07:12
$ a.out /dev/pts001
#modules = 4
  module: ttcompat
  module: ldterm
  module: ptem
  driver: pts
```

```
$ a.out /dev/console
#modules = 5
  module: ttcompat
  module: ldterm
  module: ansi
  module: char
  driver: cmux
```

The top two streams modules are the same for both cases (ttcompat and ldterm), but the remaining modules and the topmost driver differ. We'll return to the pseudo-terminal case (the network login) in Chapter 19.   □

write to Streams Devices

In Figure 12.10 we said that a write to a streams device generates an M_DATA message. While this is generally true, there are some additional details to consider. First, with a stream the topmost processing module specifies the minimum and maximum packet sizes that can be sent downstream. (We are unable to query the module for these values.) If we write more than the maximum, the stream head normally breaks the data into packets of the maximum size, with one final packet that can be smaller than the maximum.

The next thing to consider is what happens if we write zero bytes to a stream. Unless the stream refers to a pipe or FIFO, a zero-length message is sent downstream. With a pipe or FIFO, the default is to ignore the zero-length write, for compatibility with previous versions. We can change this default for pipes and FIFOs using an ioctl to set the write mode for the stream.

Write Mode

There are two ioctls that fetch and set the "write mode" for a stream. Setting *request* to I_GWROPT requires that the third argument be a pointer to an integer, and the current write mode for the stream is returned in that integer. If *request* is I_SWROPT then the third argument is an integer whose value becomes the new write mode for the stream. As with the file descriptor flags and the file status flags (Section 3.13) we should always fetch the current write mode value and modify it, rather than setting the write mode to some absolute value (possibly turning off some other bits that were enabled).

Currently only two write mode values are defined.

SNDZERO   A zero-length write to a pipe or FIFO will cause a zero-length message to be sent downstream. By default this zero-length write sends no message.

SNDPIPE   Causes SIGPIPE to be sent to the calling process that calls either write or putmsg after an error has occurred on a stream.

A stream also has a read mode, and we'll look at it after describing the getmsg and getpmsg functions.

getmsg and getpmsg Functions

Streams messages are read from a stream head using read, getmsg, or getpmsg.

```
#include <stropts.h>

int getmsg(int filedes, struct strbuf *ctlptr,
                   struct strbuf *dataptr, int *flagptr);

int getpmsg(int filedes, struct strbuf *ctlptr,
                   struct strbuf *dataptr, int *bandptr, int *flagptr);
```

Both return: nonnegative value if OK, −1 on error

Note that *flagptr* and *bandptr* are pointers to integers. The integer pointed to by these two pointers must be set before the call to specify the type of message desired, and the integer is also set on return to the type of message that was read.

If the integer pointed to by *flagptr* is 0, getmsg returns the next message on the stream head's read queue. If the next message is a high-priority message, on return the integer pointed to by *flagptr* is set to RS_HIPRI. If we want to receive only high-priority messages, we must set the integer pointed to by *flagptr* to RS_HIPRI before calling getmsg.

A different set of constants are used by getpmsg. It can also use *bandptr* to specify a particular priority band.

These two functions have many conditions that dictate what type of message is returned to the caller, based on (a) the values pointed to by *flagptr* and *bandptr*, (b) what types of messages are on the stream's queue, (c) whether we specify a nonnull *dataptr* and *ctlptr*, and (d) the values of *ctlptr–>maxlen* and *dataptr–>maxlen*. We won't need all these details for our use of getmsg. Refer to the getmsg(2) manual page for all the gory details.

Read Mode

We also need to consider what happens if we read from a streams device. There are two potential problems: (1) what happens to the record boundaries associated with the messages on a stream, and (2) what happens if we call read and the next message on the stream has control information? The default handling for condition 1 is called byte-stream mode. In this mode a read takes data from the stream until the requested number of bytes has been read or until there is no more data. The message boundaries associated with the streams messages are ignored in this mode. The default handling for condition 2 causes the read to return an error if there is a control message at the front of the queue. We can change either of these defaults.

Using ioctl, if we set *request* to I_GRDOPT the third argument is a pointer to an integer, and the current read mode for the stream is returned in that integer. A *request* of I_SRDOPT takes the integer value of the third argument and sets the read mode to that value. The read mode is specified by one of the following three constants.

RNORM   Normal, byte-stream mode, as described previously. This is the
               default.

RMSGN   Message nondiscard mode. A read takes data from a stream until it
               reads the requested number of bytes or until a message boundary is
               encountered. If the read uses a partial message, the rest of the data
               in the message is left on the stream for a subsequent read.

RMSGD   Message discard mode. This is like the nondiscard mode, but if a
               partial message is used, the remainder of the message is discarded.

Three additional constants can be specified in the read mode to set the behavior of read
when it encounters messages containing protocol information on a stream.

RPROTNORM   Protocol-normal mode: read returns an error of EBADMSG. This is
               the default.

RPROTDAT   Protocol-data mode: read returns the control portion as data to the
               caller.

RPROTDIS   Protocol-discard mode: read discards the control information but
               returns any data in the message.

Example

Program 12.11 is Program 3.3 recoded to use getmsg instead of read. If we run this
program under SVR4, where both pipes and terminals are implemented using streams,
we get the following output.

```
$ echo hello, world | a.out          requires pipes to be implemented using streams
flag = 0, ctl.len = -1, dat.len = 13
hello, world
flag = 0, ctl.len = 0, dat.len = 0   indicates a streams hangup
$ a.out                              requires terminals to be implemented using streams
this is line 1
flag = 0, ctl.len = -1, dat.len = 15
this is line 1
and line 2
flag = 0, ctl.len = -1, dat.len = 11
and line 2
^D                                   type our terminal EOF character
flag = 0, ctl.len = -1, dat.len = 0  tty end of file is not the same as a hangup
$ a.out < /etc/motd
getmsg error: Not a stream device
```

When the pipe is closed (when echo terminates) it appears to Program 12.11 as a
streams hangup—both the control length and the data length are set to 0. (We discuss
pipes in Section 14.2.) With a terminal, however, typing the end of file character only
causes the data length to be returned as 0. This terminal end of file is not the same as a
streams hangup. As expected, when we redirect standard input to be a nonstreams device, an error is returned by getmsg.   □

```
#include    <stropts.h>
#include    "ourhdr.h"

#define BUFFSIZE    8192

int
main(void)
{
    int             n, flag;
    char            ctlbuf[BUFFSIZE], datbuf[BUFFSIZE];
    struct strbuf   ctl, dat;

    ctl.buf = ctlbuf;
    ctl.maxlen = BUFFSIZE;
    dat.buf = datbuf;
    dat.maxlen = BUFFSIZE;
    for ( ; ; ) {
        flag = 0;           /* return any message */
        if ( (n = getmsg(STDIN_FILENO, &ctl, &dat, &flag)) < 0)
            err_sys("getmsg error");
        fprintf(stderr, "flag = %d, ctl.len = %d, dat.len = %d\n",
                        flag, ctl.len, dat.len);
        if (dat.len == 0)
            exit(0);
        else if (dat.len > 0)
            if (write(STDOUT_FILENO, dat.buf, dat.len) != dat.len)
                err_sys("write error");
    }
}
```

Program 12.11 Copy standard input to standard output using getmsg.

12.5 I/O Multiplexing

When we read from one descriptor and write to another, we can use blocking I/O in a loop such as

```
while ( (n = read(STDIN_FILENO, buf, BUFSIZ)) > 0)
    if (write(STDOUT_FILENO, buf, n) != n)
        err_sys("write error");
```

We see this form of blocking I/O over and over again. What if we have to read from two descriptors? In this case we can't do a blocking read on either descriptor, as data may appear on one descriptor while we're blocked in a read on the other. A different technique is required to handle this case.

Let's skip ahead and look at the modem dialer in Chapter 18. In this program we read from the terminal (standard input) and write to the modem, and we read from the modem and write to the terminal (standard output). Figure 12.11 shows a picture of this.

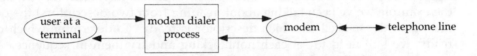

Figure 12.11 Overview of modem dialer program.

The process has two inputs and two outputs. We can't do a blocking `read` on either of the inputs, as we never know which input will have data for us.

One way to handle this particular problem is to divide the process in two pieces (using `fork`) with each half handling one direction of data. We show this in Figure 12.12.

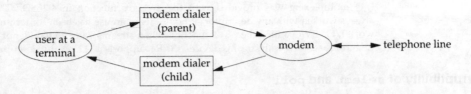

Figure 12.12 Modem dialer using two processes.

If we use two processes we can let each process do a blocking `read`. But this leads to a problem when the operation terminates. If an end of file is received by the child (the modem is hung up by the other end of the phone line) then the child terminates and the parent is notified by the `SIGCHLD` signal. But if the parent terminates (the user enters an end of file at the terminal) then the parent has to tell the child to stop. We can use a signal for this (`SIGUSR1`, for example) but it does complicate the program somewhat.

We could use nonblocking I/O in a single process. To do this we set both descriptors nonblocking, and issue a `read` on the first descriptor. If data is present, we read it and process it. If there is no data to read, the call returns immediately. We then do the same thing with the second descriptor. After this we wait for some amount of time (a few seconds perhaps), then try to read from the first descriptor again. This type of loop is called *polling*. The problem is that it is a waste of CPU time. Most of the time there won't be data to read, so we waste the time performing the `read` system calls. We also have to guess how long to wait each time around the loop. Although polling works on any system that supports nonblocking I/O, it should be avoided on a multitasking system.

Another technique is called *asynchronous I/O*. To do this we tell the kernel to notify us with a signal when a descriptor is ready for I/O. There are two problems with this. First, not all systems support this feature (it is not yet part of POSIX, but may be in the future). SVR4 provides the `SIGPOLL` signal for this technique, but this signal works only if the descriptor refers to a streams device. 4.3+BSD has a similar signal, `SIGIO`, but it has similar limitations—it works only on descriptors that refer to terminal devices or networks. The second problem with this technique is that there is only one of these signals per process (SIGPOLL or SIGIO). If we enable this signal for two descriptors (in the example we've been talking about, reading from two descriptors) the occurrence of the signal doesn't tell us which descriptor is ready. To determine which descriptor is ready, we still need to set each nonblocking and try them in sequence. We describe asynchronous I/O briefly in Section 12.6.

A better technique is to use *I/O multiplexing*. To do this we build a list of the descriptors that we are interested in (usually more than one descriptor) and call a function that doesn't return until one of the descriptors is ready for I/O. On return from the function we are told which descriptors are ready for I/O.

> I/O multiplexing is not yet part of POSIX. The select function is provided by both SVR4 and 4.3+BSD to do I/O multiplexing. The poll function is provided only by SVR4. SVR4 actually implements select using poll.

> I/O multiplexing was provided with the select function in 4.2BSD. This function has always worked with any descriptor, although its main use has been for terminal I/O and network I/O. SVR3 added the poll function when streams were added. Until SVR4, however, poll only worked with streams devices. SVR4 supports poll on any descriptor.

Interruptibility of select and poll

When the automatic restarting of interrupted system calls was introduced with 4.2BSD (Section 10.5), the select function was never restarted. This characteristic continues with 4.3+BSD (and most systems derived from earlier BSD systems) even if the SA_RESTART option is specified. But under SVR4, if SA_RESTART is specified, even select and poll are automatically restarted. To prevent this from catching us when we port software to SVR4, we'll always use the signal_intr function (Program 10.13) if the signal could interrupt a call to select or poll.

12.5.1 select Function

The select function lets us do I/O multiplexing under both SVR4 and 4.3+BSD. The arguments we pass to select tell the kernel

1. Which descriptors we're interested in.
2. What conditions we're interested in for each descriptor. (Do we want to read from a given descriptor? Do we want to write to a given descriptor? Are we interested in an exception condition for a given descriptor?)
3. How long we want to wait. (We can wait forever, wait a fixed amount of time, or not wait at all.)

On the return from select the kernel tells us

1. The total count of the number of descriptors that are ready.
2. Which descriptors are ready for each of the three conditions (read, write, or exception condition).

With this return information we can call the appropriate I/O function (usually `read` or `write`) and know that the function won't block.

```
#include <sys/types.h> /* fd_set data type */
#include <sys/time.h>  /* struct timeval */
#include <unistd.h>    /* function prototype might be here */

int select(int maxfdp1, fd_set *readfds, fd_set *writefds, fd_set *exceptfds,
           struct timeval *tvptr);
```
                                        Returns: count of ready descriptors, 0 on timeout, –1 on error

Let's look at the last argument first. This specifies how long we want to wait.

```
struct timeval {
  long  tv_sec;   /* seconds */
  long  tv_usec;  /* and microseconds */
};
```

There are three conditions.

tvptr == NULL

> Wait forever. This infinite wait can be interrupted if we catch a signal. Return is made when one of the specified descriptors is ready or when a signal is caught. If a signal is caught, `select` returns –1 with `errno` set to EINTR.

tvptr->*tv_sec* == 0 && *tvptr*->*tv_usec* == 0

> Don't wait at all. All the specified descriptors are tested and return is made immediately. This is a way to poll the system to find out the status of multiple descriptors, without blocking in the `select` function.

tvptr->*tv_sec* != 0 || *tvptr*->*tv_usec* != 0

> Wait the specified number of seconds and microseconds. Return is made when one of the specified descriptors is ready or when the time-out value expires. If the timeout expires before any of the descriptors is ready, the return value is 0. (If the system doesn't provide microsecond resolution, the *tvptr*->*tv_usec* value is rounded up to the nearest supported value.) As with the first condition, this wait can also be interrupted by a caught signal.

The middle three arguments, *readfds*, *writefds*, and *exceptfds*, are pointers to *descriptor sets*. These three sets specify which descriptors we're interested in and for which conditions (readable, writable, or an exception condition). A descriptor set is stored in an `fd_set` data type. This data type is chosen by the implementation so that it can hold one bit for each possible descriptor. We can consider it just a big array of bits, as shown in Figure 12.13.

The only thing we can do with the `fd_set` data type is (a) allocate a variable of this type, (b) assign a variable of this type to another variable of the same type, or (c) use one of the following four macros on a variable of this type:

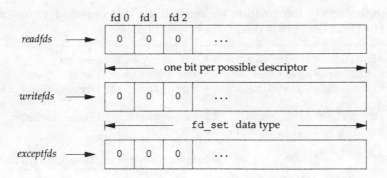

Figure 12.13 Specifying the read, write, and exception descriptors for `select`.

```
FD_ZERO(fd_set *fdset);              /* clear all bits in fdset */
FD_SET(int fd, fd_set *fdset);       /* turn on bit for fd in fdset */
FD_CLR(int fd, fd_set *fdset);       /* turn off bit for fd in fdset */
FD_ISSET(int fd, fd_set *fdset);     /* test bit for fd in fdset */
```

After declaring a descriptor set, as in

```
fd_set    rset;
int       fd;
```

we must zero the set using `FD_ZERO`.

```
FD_ZERO(&rset);
```

We then set bits in the set for each descriptor that we're interested in:

```
FD_SET(fd, &rset);
FD_SET(STDIN_FILENO, &rset);
```

On return from `select` we can test whether a given bit in the set is still on using `FD_ISSET`:

```
if (FD_ISSET(fd, &rset)) {
    ...
}
```

Any (or all) of the middle three arguments to `select` (the pointers to the descriptor sets) can be null pointers, if we're not interested in that condition. If all three pointers are NULL, then we have a higher precision timer than provided by `sleep`. (Recall from Section 10.19 that `sleep` waits for an integral number of seconds. With `select` we can wait for intervals less than 1 second; the actual resolution depending on the system's clock.) Exercise 12.6 shows such a function.

The first argument to `select`, *maxfdp1*, stands for "max fd plus 1." We calculate the highest descriptor that we're interested in, in any of the three descriptor sets, add 1, and that's the first argument. We could just set the first argument to FD_SETSIZE, a constant in `<sys/types.h>` that specifies the maximum number of descriptors (often

256 or 1024), but this value is too large for most applications. Indeed, most applications probably use between 3 and 10 descriptors. (There are applications that need many more descriptors, but these aren't the typical Unix program.) By specifying the highest descriptor that we're interested in, the kernel can avoid going through hundreds of unused bits in the three descriptor sets, looking for bits that are turned on.

As an example, if we write

```
fd_set   readset, writeset;

FD_ZERO(&readset);
FD_ZERO(&writeset);

FD_SET(0, &readset);
FD_SET(3, &readset);
FD_SET(1, &writeset);
FD_SET(2, &writeset);

select(4, &readset, &writeset, NULL, NULL);
```

then Figure 12.14 shows what the two descriptor sets look like.

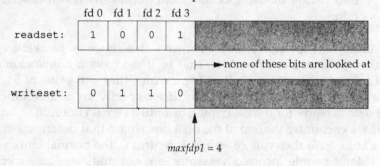

Figure 12.14 Example descriptor sets for `select`.

The reason we have to add 1 to the maximum descriptor number is because descriptors start at 0, and the first argument is really a count of the number of descriptors to check (starting with descriptor 0).

There are three possible return values from `select`.

1. A return value of –1 means an error occurred. This can happen, for example, if a signal is caught before any of the specified descriptors are ready.

2. A return value of 0 means no descriptors are ready. This happens if the time limit expires before any of the descriptors are ready.

3. A positive return value specifies the number of descriptors that are ready. In this case the only bits left on in the three descriptor sets are the bits corresponding to the descriptors that are ready.

> Be careful not to check the descriptor sets on return unless the return value is greater than 0. The return state of the descriptor sets is implementation dependent if either a signal is caught or the timer expires. Indeed, if the timer expires 4.3+BSD doesn't change the descriptor sets while SVR4 clears the descriptor sets.

There is another discrepancy between the SVR4 and BSD implementations of select. BSD systems have always returned the sum of the number of ready descriptors in each set. If the same descriptor is ready in two sets (say the read set and the write set), that descriptor is counted twice. .SVR4 unfortunately changes this and if the same descriptor is ready in multiple sets, that descriptor is counted only once. This again shows the problems we'll encounter until functions such as select are standardized by POSIX.

We now need to be more specific about what "ready" means.

1. A descriptor in the read set (*readfds*) is considered ready if a read from that descriptor won't block.

2. A descriptor in the write set (*writefds*) is considered ready if a write to that descriptor won't block.

3. A descriptor in the exception set (*exceptfds*) is considered ready if there is an exception condition pending on that descriptor. Currently an exception condition corresponds to (a) the arrival of out-of-band data on a network connection, or (b) certain conditions occurring on a pseudo terminal that has been placed into packet mode. (Section 15.10 of Stevens [1990] describes this latter condition.)

It is important to realize that whether a descriptor is blocking or not doesn't affect whether select blocks or not. That is, if we have a nonblocking descriptor that we want to read from and we call select with a time-out value of 5 seconds, select will block for up to 5 seconds. Similarly, if we specify an infinite timeout, select blocks until data is ready for the descriptor, or until a signal is caught.

If we encounter the end of file on a descriptor, that descriptor is considered readable by select. We then call read and it returns 0, the normal Unix way to signify end of file. (Many people incorrectly assume select indicates an exception condition on a descriptor when the end of file is reached.)

12.5.2 poll Function

The SVR4 poll function is similar to select, but the programmer interface is different. As we'll see, poll is tied to the streams system, although in SVR4 we are able to use it with any descriptor.

```
#include <stropts.h>
#include <poll.h>

int poll(struct pollfd fdarray[], unsigned long nfds, int timeout);
```
                                    Returns: count of ready descriptors, 0 on timeout, −1 on error

Instead of building a set of descriptors for each condition (readability, writability, and exception condition), as we did with select, with poll we build an array of pollfd structures, with each array element specifying a descriptor number and the conditions that we're interested in for that descriptor.

```
struct pollfd {
  int     fd;        /* file descriptor to check, or <0 to ignore */
  short   events;    /* events of interest on fd */
  short   revents;   /* events that occurred on fd */
};
```

The number of elements in the *fdarray* array is specified by *nfds*.

> For some unknown reason, SVR3 specified the number of elements in the array as an
> unsigned long, which seems excessive. In the SVR4 manual [AT&T 1990d], the prototype
> for poll shows the data type of the second argument as size_t. (Recall the primitive system
> data types, Figure 2.8.) But the actual prototype in the <poll.h> header still shows the sec-
> ond argument as an unsigned long.

> The SVID for SVR4 [AT&T 1989] shows the first argument to poll as struct pollfd *fdar-
> ray*[], while the SVR4 manual page [AT&T 1990d] shows this argument as struct pollfd
> *fdarray*. In the C language both declarations are equivalent. We use the first declaration to
> reiterate that fdarray points to an array of structures and not a pointer to a single structure.

We have to set the events member of each array element to one or more of the values in Figure 12.15. This is how we tell the kernel what events we're interested in for
that descriptor. On return the revents member is set by the kernel, specifying which
events have occurred for that descriptor. (Notice that poll doesn't change the events
member—this differs from select, which modifies its arguments to indicate what is
ready.)

Name	Input to events ?	Result from revents ?	Description
POLLIN	•	•	Data other than high priority can be read without blocking.
POLLRDNORM	•	•	Normal data (priority band 0) can be read without blocking.
POLLRDBAND	•	•	Data from a nonzero priority band can be read without blocking.
POLLPRI	•	•	High-priority data can be read without blocking.
POLLOUT	•	•	Normal data can be written without blocking.
POLLWRNORM	•	•	Same as POLLOUT.
POLLWRBAND	•	•	Data for a nonzero priority band can be written without blocking.
POLLERR		•	An error has occurred.
POLLHUP		•	A hangup has occurred.
POLLNVAL		•	The descriptor does not reference an open file.

Figure 12.15 The events and revents flags for poll.

The first four rows of Figure 12.15 test for readability, the next three test for writability,
and the final three are for exception conditions.

The last three rows in Figure 12.15 are set by the kernel on return. These three values are returned in revents when the condition occurs, even if they weren't specified
in the events field.

When a descriptor is hung up (POLLHUP) we can no longer write to the descriptor.
There may, however, still be data to be read from the descriptor.

The final argument to `poll` specifies how long we want to wait. As with `select`, there are three different cases.

timeout == INFTIM

> Wait forever. The constant INFTIM is defined in <stropts.h>, and its value is usually −1. Return is made when one of the specified descriptors is ready or when a signal is caught. If a signal is caught, `poll` returns −1 with `errno` set to EINTR.

timeout == 0

> Don't wait. All the specified descriptors are tested and return is made immediately. This is a way to poll the system to find out the status of multiple descriptors, without blocking in the call to `poll`.

timeout > 0

> Wait *timeout* milliseconds. Return is made when one of the specified descriptors is ready or when the *timeout* expires. If the *timeout* expires before any of the descriptors is ready, the return value is 0. (If your system doesn't provide millisecond resolution, *timeout* is rounded up to the nearest supported value.)

It is important to realize the difference between an end of file and a hangup. If we're entering data from the terminal and type the end of file character, POLLIN is turned on so we can `read` the end of file indication (the `read` returns 0). POLLHUP is not turned on in `revents`. If we're reading from a modem and the telephone line is hung up, we'll receive the POLLHUP notification.

As with `select`, whether a descriptor is blocking or not doesn't affect whether `poll` blocks or not.

12.6 Asynchronous I/O

Using `select` and `poll`, as described in the previous section, is a synchronous form of notification. The system doesn't tell us anything until we ask (by calling either `select` or `poll`). As we saw in Chapter 10, signals provide an asynchronous form of notification that something has happened. Both SVR4 and 4.3+BSD provide asynchronous I/O, using a signal (SIGPOLL in SVR4, and SIGIO in 4.3+BSD) to notify the process that something of interest has happened on a descriptor.

> We saw that `select` and `poll` work with any descriptors under SVR4. Under 4BSD `select` has always worked with any descriptor. But with asynchronous I/O, we now encounter restrictions. Under SVR4 asynchronous I/O works only with streams devices. Under 4.3+BSD asynchronous I/O works only with terminals and networks.

One limitation of asynchronous I/O, as supported by both SVR4 and 4.3+BSD, is that there is only one signal per process. If we enable more than one descriptor for asynchronous I/O, when the signal is delivered we cannot tell which descriptor the signal corresponds to.

12.6.1 System V Release 4

Asynchronous I/O in SVR4 is part of the streams system. It works only with streams devices. The SVR4 asynchronous I/O signal is SIGPOLL.

To enable asynchronous I/O for a streams device we have to call ioctl with a second argument (*request*) of I_SETSIG. The third argument is an integer value formed from one or more of the constants in Figure 12.16. These constants are defined in <stropts.h>.

Constant	Description
S_INPUT	A message other than a high-priority message has arrived.
S_RDNORM	An ordinary message has arrived.
S_RDBAND	A message with a nonzero priority band has arrived.
S_BANDURG	If this constant is specified with S_RDBAND, the SIGURG signal is generated instead of SIGPOLL when a nonzero priority band message has arrived.
S_HIPRI	A high-priority message has arrived.
S_OUTPUT	The write queue is no longer full.
S_WRNORM	Same as S_OUTPUT.
S_WRBAND	We can send a nonzero priority band message.
S_MSG	A streams signal message that contains the SIGPOLL signal has arrived.
S_ERROR	An M_ERROR message has arrived.
S_HANGUP	An M_HANGUP message has arrived.

Figure 12.16 Conditions for generating SIGPOLL signal.

In Figure 12.16, whenever we say "has arrived" we mean "has arrived at the stream head's read queue."

In addition to calling ioctl to specify the conditions that should generate the SIGPOLL signal, we also have to establish a signal handler for this signal. Recall from Figure 10.1 that the default action for SIGPOLL is to terminate the process, so we should establish the signal handler before calling ioctl.

12.6.2 4.3+BSD

Asynchronous I/O in 4.3+BSD is a combination of two different signals: SIGIO and SIGURG. The former is the general asynchronous I/O signal and the latter is used only to notify the process that out-of-band data has arrived on a network connection.

To receive the SIGIO signal we need to perform three steps.

1. Establish a signal handler for the signal, by calling either signal or sigaction.

2. Set the process ID or process group ID to receive the signal for the descriptor, by calling fcntl with a command of F_SETOWN (Section 3.13).

3. Enable asynchronous I/O on the descriptor by calling fcntl with a command of F_SETFL to set the O_ASYNC file status flag (Figure 3.5).

Step 3 can be performed only on descriptors that refer to terminals or networks, which is a fundamental limitation of the 4.3+BSD asynchronous I/O facility.

For the SIGURG signal we need only perform steps 1 and 2. This signal is generated only for descriptors that refer to network connections that support out-of-band data.

12.7 `readv` and `writev` Functions

The `readv` and `writev` functions let us read into and write from multiple noncontiguous buffers in a single function call. These are called *scatter read* and *gather write*.

```
#include <sys/types.h>
#include <sys/uio.h>

ssize_t readv(int filedes, const struct iovec iov[], int iovcnt);

ssize_t writev(int filedes, const struct iovec iov[], int iovcnt);
```
                    Both return: number of bytes read or written, –1 on error

The second argument to both functions is a pointer to an array of `iovec` structures:

```
struct iovec {
   void   *iov_base;   /* starting address of buffer */
   size_t  iov_len;    /* size of buffer */
};
```

The number of elements in the *iov* array is specified by *iovcnt*.

These two functions originated in 4.2BSD. They are now in SVR4 also.

The prototypes for these two functions, and the `iovec` structure that they both use, exemplify the continuing differences that appear in functions that have not been standardized by either POSIX.1 or XPG3. If we compare the definitions in the SVR4 Programmer's Manual [AT&T 1990e], the SVID for SVR4 [AT&T 1989], and both the SVR4 and 4.3+BSD `<sys/uio.h>` headers, all are different! Part of the problem is that the SVID and the SVR4 Programmer's Manual correspond to the 1988 POSIX.1 standard, not the 1990 version. The prototype and structure definition that we show above correspond to the POSIX.1 definitions for `read` and `write`: the buffer addresses are `void *`, the buffer lengths are `size_t`, and the return value is `ssize_t`.

Note that we have specified the second argument to `readv` as `const`. This corresponds to the 4.3+BSD function prototype, but the SVR4 manuals omit this qualifier. The qualifier is valid with `readv`, since the members of the `iovec` structure are not modified—only the memory locations pointed to by the `iov_base` members are modified by the function.

4.3BSD and SVR4 limit *iovcnt* to 16. 4.3+BSD defines the constant `UIO_MAXIOV`, which is currently 1024. The SVID claims the constant `IOV_MAX` provides the System V limit, but it's not defined in any of the SVR4 headers.

Figure 12.17 shows a picture relating the arguments to these two functions and the `iovec` structure. `writev` gathers the output data from the buffers in order: *iov[0]*,

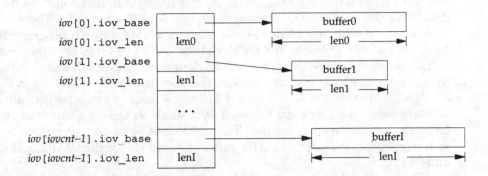

Figure 12.17 The iovec structure for readv and writev.

iov[1], through iov[iovcnt−1]. writev returns the total number of bytes output, which should normally equal the sum of all the buffer lengths.

readv scatters the data into the buffers in order. readv always fills one buffer before proceeding to the next. readv returns the total number of bytes that were read. A count of 0 is returned if there is no more data and the end of file is encountered.

Example

In Section 16.7, in the function _db_writeidx, we need to write two buffers consecutively to a file. The second buffer to output is an argument passed by the caller, and the first buffer is one we create, containing the length of the second buffer and a file offset of other information in the file. There are three ways we can do this.

1. Call write twice, once for each buffer.

2. Allocate a buffer of our own that is large enough to contain both buffers, and copy both into the new buffer. We then call write once for this new buffer.

3. Call writev to output both buffers.

The solution we use in Section 16.7 is to use writev, but it's instructive to compare it to the other two solutions.

Figure 12.18 shows the results from the three different methods just described.

Operation	SPARC			80386		
	User	System	Clock	User	System	Clock
two writes	0.2	7.2	17.2	0.5	13.1	13.7
buffer copy, then one write	0.5	4.4	17.2	0.7	7.3	8.1
one writev	0.3	4.6	17.1	0.3	7.8	8.2

Figure 12.18 Timing results comparing writev and other techniques.

The test program that we measured output a 100-byte header followed by 200 bytes of data. This was done 10,000 times, generating a 3-million-byte file. Three versions of the program were written, and three times were measured for each program: the user CPU time, the system CPU time, and the clock time. All three times are in seconds.

As we expect, the system time almost doubles when we call `write` twice, compared to calling `write` once or `writev` once. This correlates with the results in Figure 3.1.

Next, note that the sum of the CPU times (user plus system) is almost constant whether we do a buffer copy followed by a single `write` or a single `writev`. The difference is whether we pay for the CPU time executing in user space (the buffer copy) or in system space (the `writev`). This sum is 4.9 seconds for the SPARC and about 8.0 seconds for the 80386.

There is one final point to note from Figure 12.18, which is unrelated to our discussion of `readv` and `writev`. The clock time for the SPARC system used for this test is dominated by the disk speed (the clock time is double the CPU time, and the tests were run on an otherwise idle system) while the clock time for the 80386 is dominated by the CPU speed (the clock time almost equals the CPU time).   □

In summary, we should always use `readv` and `writev`, instead of multiple `read`s and `write`s. The timing results show that a buffer copy followed by a single `write` often takes the same amount of CPU time as a single `writev`, but usually it is more complicated to allocate the storage for a temporary buffer and do the copy, compared to calling `writev` once.

12.8 `readn` and `writen` Functions

Some devices, notably terminals, networks, and any SVR4 streams devices, have the following two properties.

1. A `read` operation may return less than asked for, even though we have not encountered the end of file. This is not an error, and we should just continue reading from the device.

2. A `write` operation can also return less than we specified. This may be caused by flow control constraints by downstream modules, for example. Again, it's not an error, and we should continue writing the remainder of the data. (Normally this short return from a `write` only occurs with a nonblocking descriptor or if a signal is caught.)

We'll never see this happen when reading or writing a disk file.

In Chapter 18 we'll be writing to a stream pipe (which is based on SVR4 streams or BSD Unix domain sockets) and need to take these characteristics into consideration. We can use the following two functions to `read` or `write` N bytes of data, letting these functions handle a possible return value that's less than requested. These two functions just call `read` or `write` as many times as required to read or write the entire N bytes of data.

```
#include "ourhdr.h"

ssize_t readn(int filedes, void *buff, size_t nbytes);

ssize_t writen(int filedes, void *buff, size_t nbytes);
```
Both return: number of bytes read or written, −1 on error

We call `writen` anytime we're writing to one of the device types that we mentioned, but we call `readn` only when we know ahead of time that we will be receiving a certain number of bytes. (Often we issue a `read` to one of these devices and take whatever is returned.)

Program 12.12 is an implementation of `writen` that we use in later examples. Program 12.13 is an implementation of `readn`.

12.9 Memory Mapped I/O

Memory mapped I/O lets us map a file on disk into a buffer in memory so that, when we fetch bytes from the buffer, the corresponding bytes of the file are read. Similarly, when we store data in the buffer, the corresponding bytes are automatically written to the file. This lets us perform I/O without using `read` or `write`.

To use this feature we have to tell the kernel to map a given file to a region in memory. This is done by the `mmap` function.

```
#include <sys/types.h>
#include <sys/mman.h>

caddr_t mmap(caddr_t addr, size_t len, int prot, int flag,
             int filedes, off_t off);
```
Returns: starting address of mapped region if OK, −1 on error

> Memory mapped I/O has been in use with virtual memory systems for many years. 4.1BSD (1981) provided a different form of memory mapped I/O with its `vread` and `vwrite` functions. These two functions were then removed in 4.2BSD and were intended to be replaced with the `mmap` function. The `mmap` function, however, was not included with 4.2BSD (for reasons described in Section 2.5 of Leffler et al. [1989]). Gingell, Moran, and Shannon [1987] describe an implementation of `mmap`. The `mmap` function is now supported by both SVR4 and 4.3+BSD.

The data type `caddr_t` is often defined as `char *`. The *addr* argument lets us specify the starting address of where we want the mapped region to start. We normally set this to 0 to allow the system to choose the starting address. The return value of this function is the starting address of the mapped area.

filedes is the file descriptor specifying the file that is to be mapped. We have to open this file before we can map it into the address space. *len* is the number of bytes to map,

```
#include     "ourhdr.h"

ssize_t                      /* Write "n" bytes to a descriptor. */
writen(int fd, const void *vptr, size_t n)
{
    size_t      nleft;
    ssize_t     nwritten;
    const char  *ptr;

    ptr = vptr; /* can't do pointer arithmetic on void* */
    nleft = n;
    while (nleft > 0) {
        if ( (nwritten = write(fd, ptr, nleft)) <= 0)
            return(nwritten);          /* error */

        nleft -= nwritten;
        ptr   += nwritten;
    }
    return(n);
}
```

Program 12.12 The writen function.

```
#include     "ourhdr.h"

ssize_t                      /* Read "n" bytes from a descriptor. */
readn(int fd, void *vptr, size_t n)
{
    size_t  nleft;
    ssize_t nread;
    char    *ptr;

    ptr = vptr;
    nleft = n;
    while (nleft > 0) {
        if ( (nread = read(fd, ptr, nleft)) < 0)
            return(nread);          /* error, return < 0 */
        else if (nread == 0)
            break;                  /* EOF */

        nleft -= nread;
        ptr   += nread;
    }
    return(n - nleft);       /* return >= 0 */
}
```

Program 12.13 The readn function.

and *off* is the starting offset in the file of the bytes to map. (There are some restrictions on the value of *off*, described later.)

Before looking at the remaining arguments, let's see what's going on here. Figure 12.19 shows a memory mapped file. (Recall the memory layout of a typical process, Figure 7.3.)

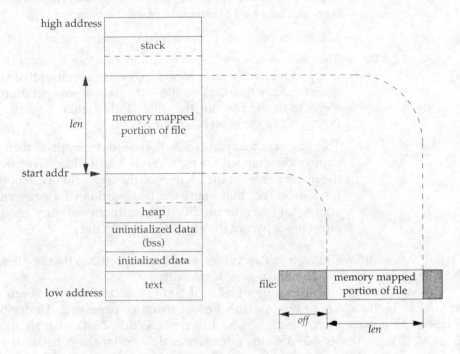

Figure 12.19 Example of a memory mapped file.

In this figure, "start addr" is the return value from mmap. We have shown the mapped memory being somewhere between the heap and the stack: this is an implementation detail and may differ from one implementation to the next.

The *prot* argument specifies the protection of the mapped region.

prot	Description
PROT_READ	region can be read
PROT_WRITE	region can be written
PROT_EXEC	region can be executed
PROT_NONE	region cannot be accessed (not in 4.3+BSD)

Figure 12.20 Protection of memory mapped region.

The protection specified for a region has to match the open mode of the file. For example, we can't specify PROT_WRITE if the file was opened read-only.

The *flag* argument affects various attributes of the mapped region.

MAP_FIXED   The return value must equal *addr*. Use of this flag is discouraged, as it hinders portability.

If this flag is not specified, and *addr* is nonzero, then the kernel uses *addr* as a hint of where to place the mapped region.

Maximum portability is obtained by specifying *addr* as 0.

MAP_SHARED   This flag describes the disposition of store operations into the mapped region by this process. This flag specifies that store operations modify the mapped file—that is, a store operation is equivalent to a `write` to the file. Either this flag or the next (MAP_PRIVATE) must be specified.

MAP_PRIVATE   This flag says that store operations into the mapped region cause a copy of the mapped file to be created. All successive references to the mapped region then reference the copy. (One use of this flag is for a debugger that maps the text portion of a program file but allows the user to modify the instructions. Any modifications affect the copy, not the original program file.)

4.3+BSD has additional MAP_xxx flag values, which are specific to that implementation. Check the 4.3+BSD mmap(2) manual page for details.

The value of *off* and the value of *addr* (if MAP_FIXED is specified) are normally required to be multiples of the system's virtual memory page size. Under SVR4 this value can be obtained from the `sysconf` function (Section 2.5.4) with an argument of _SC_PAGESIZE. Under 4.3+BSD the page size is defined by the constant NBPG in the header `<sys/param.h>`. Since *off* and *addr* are often specified as 0, this requirement is not a problem.

Since the starting offset of the mapped file is tied to the system's virtual memory page size, what happens if the length of the mapped region isn't a multiple of the page size? Assume the file size is 12 bytes and the system's page size is 512 bytes. In this case the system normally provides a mapped region of 512 bytes and the final 500 bytes of this region are set to 0. We can modify the final 500 bytes, but any changes we make to them are not reflected in the file.

Two signals are normally used with mapped regions. SIGSEGV is the signal normally used to indicate that we have tried to access memory that is not available to us. It can also be generated if we try to store into a mapped region that we specified to `mmap` as read-only. The SIGBUS signal can be generated if we access a portion of the mapped region that does not make sense at the time of the access. For example, assume we map a file using the file's size, but before we reference the mapped region the file's size is truncated by some other process. If we then try to access the memory mapped region corresponding to the end portion of the file that was truncated, we'll receive SIGBUS.

A memory mapped region is inherited by a child across a `fork` (since it's part of the parent's address space), but for the same reason is not inherited by the new program across an `exec`.

A memory mapped region is automatically unmapped when the process terminates, or by calling `munmap` directly. Closing the file descriptor *filedes* does not unmap the region.

```
#include <sys/types.h>
#include <sys/mman.h>

int munmap(caddr_t addr, size_t len);
```

Returns: 0 if OK, −1 on error

`munmap` does not affect the object that was mapped—that is, the call to `munmap` does not cause the contents of the mapped region to be written to the disk file. The updating of the disk file for a `MAP_SHARED` region happens automatically by the kernel's virtual memory algorithm as we store into the memory mapped region.

> Some systems provide an `msync` function that is similar to `fsync` (Section 4.24), but works on memory mapped regions.

Example

Program 12.14 copies a file (similar to the `cp`(1) command) using memory mapped I/O. We first open both files and then call `fstat` to obtain the size of the input file. We need this size for the call to `mmap` for the input file, plus we need to set the size of the output file. We call `lseek` and then `write` one byte to set the size of the output file. If we don't set the output file's size, the call to `mmap` for the output file is OK, but the first reference to the associated memory region generates `SIGBUS`. We might be tempted to use `ftruncate` to set the size of the output file, but not all systems extend the size of a file with this function. (See Section 4.13.)

We then call `mmap` for each file, to map the file into memory, and finally call `memcpy` to copy from the input buffer to the output buffer. As the bytes of data are fetched from the input buffer (`src`), the input file is automatically read by the kernel; and as the data is stored in the output buffer (`dst`), the data is automatically written to the output file.

Let's compare this memory mapped file copy to a copy that is done by calling `read` and `write` (with a buffer size of 8192). Figure 12.21 shows the results.

Operation	SPARC			80386		
	User	System	Clock	User	System	Clock
read/write	0.0	2.6	11.0	0.0	5.3	11.2
mmap/memcpy	0.9	1.7	3.7	0.3	2.7	5.7

Figure 12.21 Timing results comparing read/write versus mmap/memcpy.

The times are given in seconds and the size of the file being copied was almost 3 million bytes.

For the SPARC the total CPU time (user + system) is the same for both types of copies: 2.6 seconds. (This is similar to what we found for `writev` in Figure 12.18.) For

```
#include        <sys/types.h>
#include        <sys/stat.h>
#include        <sys/mman.h>        /* mmap() */
#include        <fcntl.h>
#include        "ourhdr.h"

#ifndef MAP_FILE      /* 4.3+BSD defines this & requires it to mmap files */
#define MAP_FILE     0    /* to compile under systems other than 4.3+BSD */
#endif

int
main(int argc, char *argv[])
{
    int            fdin, fdout;
    char           *src, *dst;
    struct stat statbuf;

    if (argc != 3)
        err_quit("usage: a.out <rromfile> <tofile>");

    if ( (fdin = open(argv[1], O_RDONLY)) < 0)
        err_sys("can't open %s for reading", argv[1]);

    if ( (fdout = open(argv[2], O_RDWR | O_CREAT | O_TRUNC,
                                      FILE_MODE)) < 0)
        err_sys("can't creat %s for writing", argv[2]);

    if (fstat(fdin, &statbuf) < 0)  /* need size of input file */
        err_sys("fstat error");

            /* set size of output file */
    if (lseek(fdout, statbuf.st_size - 1, SEEK_SET) == -1)
        err_sys("lseek error");
    if (write(fdout, "", 1) != 1)
        err_sys("write error");

    if ( (src = mmap(0, statbuf.st_size, PROT_READ,
                    MAP_FILE | MAP_SHARED, fdin, 0)) == (caddr_t) -1)
        err_sys("mmap error for input");

    if ( (dst = mmap(0, statbuf.st_size, PROT_READ | PROT_WRITE,
                    MAP_FILE | MAP_SHARED, fdout, 0)) == (caddr_t) -1)
        err_sys("mmap error for output");

    memcpy(dst, src, statbuf.st_size);  /* does the file copy */

    exit(0);
}
```

Program 12.14 Copy a file using memory mapped I/O.

the 386 the total CPU time is almost halved when we use mmap and memcpy.

When we use mmap, the reason that the system time decreases for both the SPARC and the 386 is because the kernel is doing I/O directly to and from the mapped memory buffers. When we call read and write, the kernel has to copy the data between our buffers and its buffers and then do I/O from its buffers.

The final point to note is that the clock time is at least halved when we use mmap and memcpy.   □

Memory mapped I/O is faster, when copying one regular file to another. There are limitations. We can't use it to copy between certain devices (such as a network device or a terminal device), and we have to be careful if the size of the underlying file could change after we map it. Nevertheless, there are some applications that can benefit from memory mapped I/O, as it can often simplify the algorithms since we manipulate memory instead of reading and writing a file. One example that can benefit from memory mapped I/O is the manipulation of a frame buffer device that references a bit-mapped display.

Krieger, Stumm, and Unrau [1992] describe an alternative to the standard I/O library (Chapter 5) that uses memory mapped I/O.

We return to memory mapped I/O in Section 14.9, showing an example of how it can be used under both SVR4 and 4.3+BSD to provide shared memory between related processes.

12.10 Summary

In this chapter we've described numerous advanced I/O functions, most of which are used in the examples in later chapters:

- nonblocking I/O—issuing an I/O operation without letting it block (we'll need this for the PostScript printer driver in Chapter 17);

- record locking (which we'll look at in more detail through an actual example, the database library in Chapter 16);

- System V streams (which we'll need in Chapter 15 to understand SVR4 stream pipes, passing file descriptors, and SVR4 client–server connections);

- I/O multiplexing—the select and poll functions (we'll use these in many of the later examples);

- the readv and writev functions (also used in many of the later examples);

- memory mapped I/O (mmap).

Exercises

12.1 Remove the second call to `write` in the `for` loop in Program 12.6. What happens and why?

12.2 Take a look at your system's `<sys/types.h>` header and examine the implementation of `select` and the four `FD_` macros.

12.3 The `<sys/types.h>` header usually has a built-in limit on the maximum number of descriptors that the `fd_set` data type can handle. Assume we need to increase this to handle up to 2048 descriptors. How can we do this?

12.4 Compare the different functions provided for signal sets (Section 10.11) and the `fd_set` descriptor sets. Also compare the implementation of the two on your system.

12.5 How many different types of information does `getmsg` return?

12.6 Implement the function `sleep_us` that is similar to `sleep`, but waits for a specified number of microseconds. Use either `select` or `poll`. Compare this function to the BSD `usleep` function.

12.7 Can you implement the functions `TELL_WAIT`, `TELL_PARENT`, `TELL_CHILD`, `WAIT_PARENT`, and `WAIT_CHILD` from Program 10.17 using advisory record locking instead of signals? If so, code and test your implementation.

12.8 Determine the capacity of a pipe using either `select` or `poll`. Compare this value with the value of `PIPE_BUF` from Chapter 2.

12.9 Run Program 12.14 to copy a file and determine whether the last-access time for the input file is updated.

12.10 In Program 12.14 `close` the input file after calling `mmap` to verify that closing the descriptor does not invalidate the memory mapped I/O.

13

Daemon Processes

13.1 Introduction

Daemons are processes that live for a long time. They are often started when the system is bootstrapped and terminate only when the system is shutdown. We say they run in the background, because they don't have a controlling terminal. Unix systems have numerous daemons that perform day-to-day activities.

In this chapter we look at the process structure of daemons, and how to write a daemon. Since a daemon does not have a controlling terminal, we need to see how a daemon can report error conditions when something goes wrong.

13.2 Daemon Characteristics

Let's look at some common system daemons and how they relate to the concepts of process groups, controlling terminals, and sessions that we described in Chapter 9. The ps(1) command prints the status of various processes in the system. There are a multitude of options—consult your system's manual for all the details. We'll execute

```
ps -axj
```

under 4.3+BSD or SunOS to see the information we need for this discussion. The -a option shows the status of processes owned by others, and -x shows processes that don't have a controlling terminal. The -j option displays the job-related information: the session ID, process group ID, controlling terminal, and terminal process group ID. Under SVR4 a similar command is ps -efjc. (On some Unix systems that conform to the Department of Defense security guidelines, we are not able to use ps to look at any processes other than our own.) The output from ps looks like

```
PPID    PID   PGID    SID TT  TPGID   UID   COMMAND
   0      0      0      0 ?      -1     0   swapper
   0      1      0      0 ?      -1     0   /sbin/init -
   0      2      0      0 ?      -1     0   pagedaemon
   1     80     80     80 ?      -1     0   syslogd
   1     88     88     88 ?      -1     0   /usr/lib/sendmail -bd -q1h
   1    105     37     37 ?      -1     0   update
   1    108    108    108 ?      -1     0   cron
   1    114    114    114 ?      -1     0   inetd
   1    117    117    117 ?      -1     0   /usr/lib/lpd
```

We have removed a few columns that don't interest us, such as the accumulated CPU time. The columns headings, in order, are the parent process ID, process ID, process group ID, session ID, terminal name, terminal process group ID (the foreground process group associated with the controlling terminal), user ID, and actual command string.

> The system that these ps commands were run on (SunOS) supports the notion of a session ID, which we mentioned with the setsid function in Section 9.5. It is just the process ID of the session leader. A 4.3+BSD system, however, will print the address of the session structure corresponding to the process group that the process belongs to (Section 9.11).

Processes 0, 1, and 2 are the ones described in Section 8.2. These three are special and exist for the entire lifetime of the system. They have no parent process ID, no process group ID, and no session ID. The syslogd daemon is available to any program to log system messages for an operator. The messages may be printed on an actual console device and also written to a file. (We describe the syslog facility in Section 13.4.2.) sendmail is the standard mailer daemon. update is a program that flushes the kernel's buffer cache to disk at regular intervals (usually every 30 seconds). To do this it just calls the sync(2) function every 30 seconds. (We described sync in Section 4.24.) The cron daemon executes commands at specified dates and times. Numerous system administration tasks are handled by having programs executed regularly by cron. We talked about the inetd daemon in Section 9.3. It listens on the system's network interfaces for incoming requests for various network servers. The final daemon, lpd, handles print requests on the system.

Notice that all the daemons run with superuser privilege (a user ID of 0). None of the daemons has a controlling terminal—the terminal name is set to a question mark and the terminal foreground process group is –1. The lack of a controlling terminal is probably the result of the daemon having called setsid. All the daemons other than update are process group leaders and session leaders and are the only processes in their process group and session. update is the only process in its process group (37) and session (37), but the process group leader (which was probably also the session leader) has already exited. Finally, note that the parent of all these daemons is the init process.

13.3 Coding Rules

There are some basic rules to coding a daemon, to prevent unwanted interactions from happening. We state these rules and then show a function, `daemon_init`, that implements them.

1. The first thing to do is call `fork` and have the parent `exit`. This does several things. First, if the daemon was started as a simple shell command, having the parent terminate makes the shell think that the command is done. Second, the child inherits the process group ID of the parent but gets a new process ID, so we're guaranteed that the child is not a process group leader. This is a prerequisite for the call to `setsid` that is done next.

2. Call `setsid` to create a new session. The three steps listed in Section 9.5 occur. The process (1) becomes a session leader of a new session, (2) becomes the process group leader of a new process group, and (3) has no controlling terminal.

   > Under SVR4, some people recommend calling `fork` again at this point and having the parent terminate. The second child continues as the daemon. This guarantees that the daemon is not a session leader, which prevents it from acquiring a controlling terminal under the SVR4 rules (Section 9.6). Alternately, to avoid acquiring a controlling terminal be sure to specify `O_NOCTTY` whenever opening a terminal device.

3. Change the current working directory to the root directory. The current working directory inherited from the parent could be on a mounted filesystem. Since daemons normally exist until the system is rebooted, if the daemon stays on a mounted filesystem, that filesystem cannot be unmounted.

   Alternately, some daemons might change the current working directory to some specific location, where they will do all their work. For example, line printer spooling daemons often change to their spool directory.

4. Set the file mode creation mask to 0. The file mode creation mask that's inherited could be set to deny certain permissions. If the daemon process is going to create files, it may want to set specific permissions. For example, if it specifically creates files with group-read and group-write enabled, a file mode creation mask that turns off either of these permissions would undo its efforts.

5. Unneeded file descriptors should be closed. This prevents the daemon from holding open any descriptors that it may have inherited from its parent (which could be a shell or some other process). Exactly which descriptors to close, however, depends on the daemon, so we don't show this step in our example. It can use our `open_max` function (Program 2.3) to determine the highest descriptor and close all descriptors up to that value.

Example

Program 13.1 is a function that can be called from a program that wants to initialize itself as a daemon.

```
#include     <sys/types.h>
#include     <sys/stat.h>
#include     <fcntl.h>
#include     "ourhdr.h"

int
daemon_init(void)
{
    pid_t    pid;

    if ( (pid = fork()) < 0)
        return(-1);
    else if (pid != 0)
        exit(0);    /* parent goes bye-bye */

    /* child continues */
    setsid();       /* become session leader */

    chdir("/");     /* change working directory */

    umask(0);       /* clear our file mode creation mask */

    return(0);
}
```

Program 13.1 Initialize a daemon process.

If the daemon_init function is called from a main program that then goes to sleep, we can check the status of the daemon with the ps command:

```
$ a.out
$ ps -axj
 PPID   PID  PGID   SID TT TPGID  UID  COMMAND
    1   735   735   735 ?    -1  224  a.out
```

We can see that our daemon has been initialized correctly.   □

13.4 Error Logging

One problem a daemon has is how to handle error messages. It can't just write to standard error, since it shouldn't have a controlling terminal. We don't want all the daemons writing to the console device, since on many workstations the console device runs a windowing system. We also don't want each daemon writing its own error messages into a separate file. It would be a headache for anyone administering the system to keep up with which daemon writes to which log file and to check these files on a regular basis. A central daemon error logging facility is required.

The BSD `syslog` facility was developed at Berkeley and used widely in 4.2BSD. Most systems derived from 4.xBSD support `syslog`. We describe this facility in Section 13.4.2.

There has never been a central daemon logging facility in System V. SVR4 supports the BSD-style `syslog` facility, and the `inetd` daemon under SVR4 uses `syslog`. The basis for `syslog` in SVR4 is the `/dev/log` streams device driver, which we describe in the next section.

13.4.1 SVR4 Streams `log` Driver

SVR4 provides a streams device driver, documented in `log(7)` in [AT&T 1990d], with an interface for streams error logging, streams event tracing, and console logging. Figure 13.1 details the overall structure of this facility.

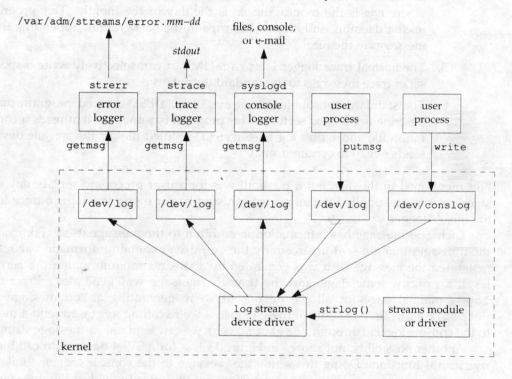

Figure 13.1 The SVR4 `log` facility.

Each `log` message can be destined for one of three loggers: the error logger, the trace logger, or the console logger.

We show three ways to generate `log` messages and three ways to read them.

- Generating `log` messages.
  1. Routines within the kernel can call `strlog` to generate log messages. This is normally used by streams modules and streams device drivers for either error messages or trace messages. (Trace messages are often used in the

debugging of new streams modules or drivers.) We won't consider this type of message generation, since we're not interested in the coding of kernel routines.

2. A user process (such as a daemon) can putmsg to /dev/log. This message can be sent to any of the three loggers.

3. A user process (such as a daemon) can write to /dev/conslog. This message is sent only to the console logger.

• Reading log messages.

4. The normal error logger is strerr(1M). It appends these messages to a file in the directory /var/adm/streams. The file's name is error.*mm-dd*, where *mm* is the month and *dd* is the day of the month. This program is itself a daemon, and it normally runs in the background, appending the log messages to the file.

5. The normal trace logger is strace(1M). It can selectively write a specified set of trace messages to its standard output.

6. The standard console logger is syslogd, a BSD-derived program that we describe in the next section. This program is a daemon that reads a configuration file and writes log messages to specified files or the console device or sends e-mail to certain users.

Not mentioned in this list, but a possibility, is for a user process to replace any of the standard system-supplied daemons: we can supply our own error logger, trace logger, or console logger.

Each log message has information in addition to the message itself. For example, the messages that are sent upstream by the log driver contain information about who generated the message (if it was generated by a streams module within the kernel), a level, a priority, some flags, and the time the message was generated. Refer to the log(7) manual page for all the details. If we're generating a log message using putmsg, we can also set some of these fields. If we're calling write to send a message to the console logger (through /dev/conslog), we can send only a message string.

Another possibility, not shown in Figure 13.1, is for a SVR4 daemon to call the BSD syslog(3) function. Doing this sends the message to the console logger, similar to a putmsg to /dev/log. With syslog, we can set the priority field of the message. We describe this function in the next section.

If the appropriate type of logger isn't running when a log message of that type is generated, the log driver just throws away the message.

Unfortunately, in SVR4 the use of this log facility is haphazard. A few daemons use it, but most system-supplied daemons are hardcoded to write directly to the console.

The syslog(3) function and syslogd(1M) daemon are documented in the BSD Compatibility Library [AT&T 1990c], but they are not in this library—they are in the standard C library, available to all user processes (daemons).

13.4.2 4.3+BSD `syslog` Facility

The BSD `syslog` facility has been widely used since 4.2BSD. Most daemons use this facility. Figure 13.2 details its organization.

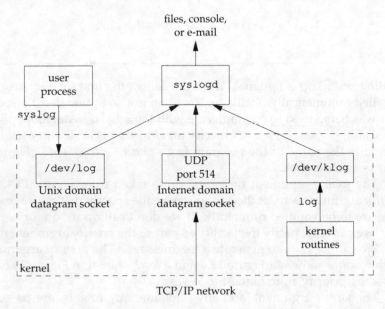

Figure 13.2 The 4.3+BSD `syslog` facility.

There are three ways to generate log messages:

1. Kernel routines can call the `log` function. These messages can be read by any user process that `opens` and `reads` the `/dev/klog` device. We won't describe this function any further, since we're not interested in writing kernel routines.

2. Most user processes (daemons) call the `syslog`(3) function to generate log messages. We describe its calling sequence later. This causes the message to be sent to the Unix domain datagram socket `/dev/log`.

3. A user process on this host, or on some other host that is connected to this host by a TCP/IP network, can send log messages to UDP port 514. Note that the `syslog` function never generates these UDP datagrams—they require explicit network programming by the process generating the log message.

Refer to Stevens [1990] for details on Unix domain sockets and UDP sockets.

Normally the `syslogd` daemon reads all three forms of log messages. This daemon reads a configuration file on start-up, usually `/etc/syslog.conf`, that determines where different classes of messages are to be sent. For example, urgent messages can be sent to the system administrator via e-mail and printed on the console, while warnings may be logged to a file.

Our interface to this facility is through the `syslog` function.

```
#include <syslog.h>

void openlog(char *ident, int option, int facility);

void syslog(int priority, char *format, ...);

void closelog(void);
```

Calling `openlog` is optional. If it's not called, the first time `syslog` is called, `openlog` is called automatically. Calling `closelog` is also optional—it just closes the descriptor that was being used to communicate with the `syslogd` daemon.

Calling `openlog` lets us specify an *ident* that is added to each log message. This is normally the name of the program (e.g., `cron`, `inetd`, etc.). Figure 13.3 describes the four possible *option*s.

The *facility* argument for `openlog` is taken from Figure 13.4. The reason for the *facility* argument is to let the configuration file specify that messages from different facilities are to be handled differently. If we don't call `openlog`, or we call it with a *facility* of 0, we can still specify the facility as part of the *priority* argument to `syslog`.

We call `syslog` to generate a log message. The *priority* argument is a combination of the *facility* shown in Figure 13.4 and a *level*, shown in Figure 13.5. These *level*s are ordered by priority, from highest to lowest.

The *format* argument, and any remaining arguments, are passed to the `vsprintf` function for formatting. Any occurrence of the two characters `%m` in the *format* are first replaced with the error message string (`strerror`) corresponding to the value of `errno`.

The `logger(1)` program is also provided by both SVR4 and 4.3+BSD as a way to send log messages to the `syslog` facility. Optional arguments to this program can specify the *facility*, *level*, and *ident*. It is intended for a shell script running noninteractively that needs to generate log messages.

A form of the `logger` command is being standardized by POSIX.2.

Example

In our PostScript printer daemon in Chapter 17 we will encounter the sequence

```
openlog("lprps", LOG_PID, LOG_LPR);
syslog(LOG_ERR, "open error for %s: %m", filename);
```

The first call sets the *ident* string to the program name, specifies that the process ID should always be printed, and sets the default *facility* to the line printer system. The actual call to `syslog` specifies an error condition and a message string. If we had not called `openlog`, the second call could have been

```
syslog(LOG_ERR | LOG_LPR, "open error for %s: %m", filename);
```

Here we specify the *priority* argument as a combination of a *level* and a *facility*.   □

option	Description
LOG_CONS	If the log message can't be sent to syslogd via the Unix domain datagram, the message is written to the console instead.
LOG_NDELAY	Open the Unix domain datagram socket to the syslogd daemon immediately—don't wait until the first message is logged. Normally the socket is not opened until the first message is logged.
LOG_PERROR	Write the log message to standard error in addition to sending it to syslogd. This option is supported only by the 4.3BSD Reno releases and later.
LOG_PID	Log the process ID with each message. This is intended for daemons that fork a child process to handle different requests (as compared to daemons such as syslogd that never call fork).

Figure 13.3 The *option* argument for openlog.

facility	Description
LOG_AUTH	authorization programs: login, su, getty, ...
LOG_CRON	cron and at
LOG_DAEMON	system daemons: ftpd, routed, ...
LOG_KERN	messages generated by the kernel
LOG_LOCAL0	reserved for local use
LOG_LOCAL1	reserved for local use
LOG_LOCAL2	reserved for local use
LOG_LOCAL3	reserved for local use
LOG_LOCAL4	reserved for local use
LOG_LOCAL5	reserved for local use
LOG_LOCAL6	reserved for local use
LOG_LOCAL7	reserved for local use
LOG_LPR	line printer system: lpd, lpc, ...
LOG_MAIL	the mail system
LOG_NEWS	the Usenet network news system
LOG_SYSLOG	the syslogd daemon itself
LOG_USER	messages from other user processes (default)
LOG_UUCP	the UUCP system

Figure 13.4 The *facility* argument for openlog.

level	Description
LOG_EMERG	emergency (system is unusable) (highest priority)
LOG_ALERT	condition that must be fixed immediately
LOG_CRIT	critical condition (e.g., hard device error)
LOG_ERR	error condition
LOG_WARNING	warning condition
LOG_NOTICE	normal, but significant condition
LOG_INFO	informational message
LOG_DEBUG	debug message (lowest priority)

Figure 13.5 The syslog *level*s (ordered).

13.5 Client–Server Model

A common use for a daemon process is as a server process. Indeed, in Figure 13.2 we can call the `syslogd` process a server that has messages sent to it by user processes (clients) using a Unix domain datagram socket.

   In general a *server* is a process that waits for a *client* to contact it, requesting some type of service. In Figure 13.2 the service being provided by the `syslogd` server is the logging of an error message.

   In Figure 13.2 the communication between the client and server is one-way. The client just sends its service request to the server—the server sends nothing back to the client. In the following chapters on interprocess communication we'll see numerous examples where there is a two-way communication between the client and server. The client sends a request to the server, and the server sends a reply back to the client.

13.6 Summary

Daemon processes are running all the time on most Unix systems. To initialize our own process that is to run as a daemon takes some care and an understanding of the process relationships that we described in Chapter 9. In this chapter we developed a function that can be called by a daemon process to initialize itself correctly.

   We also discussed the ways a daemon can log error messages, since a daemon normally doesn't have a controlling terminal. Under SVR4 the streams `log` driver is available, and under 4.3+BSD the `syslog` facility is provided. Since the BSD `syslog` facility is also provided by SVR4, in later chapters when we need to log error messages from a daemon, we'll call the `syslog` function. We'll encounter this in Chapter 17 with our PostScript printer daemon.

Exercises

13.1 As we might guess from Figure 13.2, when the `syslog` facility is initialized, either by calling `openlog` directly or on the first call to `syslog`, the special device file for the Unix domain datagram socket, `/dev/log`, has to be opened. What happens if the user process (the daemon) calls `chroot` before calling `openlog`?

13.2 List all the daemons active on your system and identify the function of each one.

13.3 Write a program that calls the `daemon_init` function in Program 13.1. After calling this function, call `getlogin` (Section 8.14) to see if the process has a login name now that it has become a daemon. Print the login name to file descriptor 3 and redirect this descriptor to a temporary file when the program is run with the notation `3>/tmp/name1` (Bourne shell or KornShell).

   Now rerun the program closing descriptors 0, 1, and 2 after the call to `daemon_init`, but before the call to `getlogin`. Does this make any difference?

13.4 Write an SVR4 daemon that establishes itself as a console logger. Refer to log(7) in [AT&T 1990d] for the details. Each time a message is received, print the relevant information. Also write a test program that sends console log messages to /dev/log to test the daemon.

13.5 Modify Program 13.1 as we mentioned in rule 2 of Section 13.3 by doing a second fork so that it can never acquire a controlling terminal under SVR4. Test your function to verify that it is no longer a session leader.

14

Interprocess Communication

14.1 Introduction

In Chapter 8 we described the process control primitives and saw how to invoke multiple processes. But the only way for these processes to exchange information is by passing open files across a `fork` or an `exec`, or through the filesystem. We'll now describe other techniques for processes to communicate with each other—IPC or interprocess communication.

Unix IPC has been, and continues to be, a hodgepodge of different approaches, few of which are portable across all Unix implementations. Figure 14.1 summarizes the different forms of IPC that are supported by different implementations.

IPC type	POSIX.1	XPG3	V7	SVR2	SVR3.2	SVR4	4.3BSD	4.3+BSD
pipes (half duplex)	•	•	•	•	•	•		•
FIFOs (named pipes)	•	•		•	•	•		•
stream pipes (full duplex)					•	•	•	•
named stream pipes					•	•	•	•
message queues		•		•	•	•		
semaphores		•		•	•	•		
shared memory		•		•	•	•		
sockets						•	•	•
streams					•	•		

Figure 14.1 Summary of Unix IPC.

As this figure shows, about the only form of IPC that we can count on, regardless of the Unix implementation, is half-duplex pipes. The first seven forms of IPC in this figure are usually restricted to IPC between processes on the same host. The final two rows, sockets and streams, are the only two that are generally supported for IPC between processes on different hosts. (See Stevens [1990] for details on networked IPC.) Although the three forms of IPC in the middle of this figure (message queues, semaphores, and shared memory) are shown as being supported only by System V, in most vendor-supported Unix systems that are derived from Berkeley Unix (such as SunOS and Ultrix), support has been added by the vendors for these three forms of IPC.

> Work is underway in different POSIX groups on IPC, but the final outcome is far from clear. It appears that nothing final will come from POSIX regarding IPC until 1994 or later.

We have divided the discussion of IPC into two chapters. In this chapter we examine classical IPC: pipes, FIFOs, message queues, semaphores, and shared memory. In the next chapter we take a look at some advanced features of IPC, supported by both SVR4 and 4.3+BSD: stream pipes, named stream pipes, and some of the things we can do with these more advanced forms of IPC.

14.2 Pipes

Pipes are the oldest form of Unix IPC and are provided by all Unix systems. They have two limitations:

1. They are half-duplex. Data flows only in one direction.
2. They can be used only between processes that have a common ancestor. Normally a pipe is created by a process, that process calls `fork`, and the pipe is used between the parent and child.

We'll see that stream pipes (Section 15.2) get around the first limitation, and FIFOs (Section 14.5) and named stream pipes (Section 15.5) get around the second limitation. Despite these limitations, half-duplex pipes are still the most commonly used form of IPC.

A pipe is created by calling the `pipe` function.

```
#include <unistd.h>

int pipe(int filedes[2]);
```
                                                              Returns: 0 if OK, −1 on error

Two file descriptors are returned through the *filedes* argument: *filedes[0]* is open for reading and *filedes[1]* is open for writing. The output of *filedes[1]* is the input for *filedes[0]*.

There are two ways to picture a pipe, as shown in Figure 14.2. The left half of the figure shows the two ends of the pipe connected in a single process. The right half of the figure reiterates the fact that the data in the pipe flows through the kernel.

> Under SVR4 a pipe is full duplex. Both descriptors can be written to and read from. The arrows in Figure 14.2 would have heads on both ends. We call these full-duplex pipes "stream

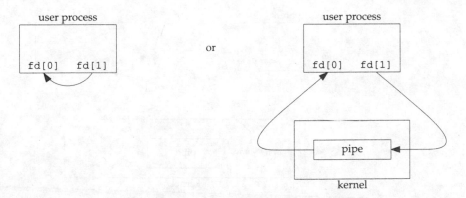

Figure 14.2 Two ways to view a Unix pipe.

pipes" and discuss them in detail in the next chapter. Since POSIX.1 only provides half-duplex pipes, for portability we'll assume the pipe function creates a one-way pipe.

The fstat function (Section 4.2) returns a file type of FIFO for the file descriptor of either end of a pipe. We can test for a pipe with the S_ISFIFO macro.

> POSIX.1 states that the st_size member of the stat structure is undefined for pipes. But when the fstat function is applied to the file descriptor for the read end of the pipe, many systems store in st_size the number of bytes available for reading in the pipe. This is, however, nonportable.

A pipe in a single process is next to useless. Normally the process that calls pipe then calls fork, creating an IPC channel from the parent to the child or vice versa. Figure 14.3 shows this scenario.

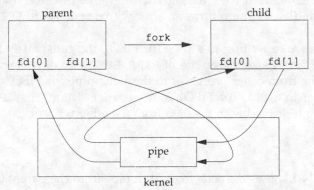

Figure 14.3 Half-duplex pipe after a fork.

What happens after the fork depends on which direction of data flow we want. For a pipe from the parent to the child, the parent closes the read end of the pipe (fd[0]) and the child closes the write end (fd[1]). Figure 14.4 shows the resulting arrangement of descriptors.

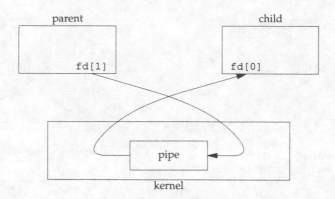

Figure 14.4 Pipe from parent to child.

For a pipe from the child to the parent, the parent closes `fd[1]` and the child closes `fd[0]`.

When one end of a pipe is closed, the following rules apply:

1. If we `read` from a pipe whose write end has been closed, after all the data has been read, `read` returns 0 to indicate an end of file. (Technically we should say that this end of file is not generated until there are no more writers for the pipe. It's possible to duplicate a pipe descriptor so that multiple processes have the pipe open for writing. Normally, however, there is a single reader and a single writer for a pipe. When we get to FIFOs in the next section, we'll see that often there are multiple writers for a single FIFO.)

2. If we `write` to a pipe whose read end has been closed, the signal `SIGPIPE` is generated. If we either ignore the signal or catch it and return from the signal handler, `write` returns an error with `errno` set to `EPIPE`.

When we're writing to a pipe (or FIFO), the constant `PIPE_BUF` specifies the kernel's pipe buffer size. A `write` of `PIPE_BUF` bytes or less will not be interleaved with the `writes` from other processes to the same pipe (or FIFO). But if multiple processes are writing to a pipe (or FIFO), and we `write` more than `PIPE_BUF` bytes, the data might be interleaved with the data from the other writers.

Example

Program 14.1 shows the code to create a pipe from the parent to the child, and send data down the pipe.   □

In the previous example we called `read` and `write` directly on the pipe descriptors. What is more interesting is to duplicate the pipe descriptors onto standard input or standard output. Often the child then `execs` some other program and that program can either read from its standard input (the pipe that we created) or write to its standard output (the pipe).

Before calling `fork` we create a pipe. After the `fork` the parent closes its read end and the child closes its write end. The child then calls `dup2` to have its standard input be the read end of the pipe. When the pager program is executed, its standard input will be the read end of the pipe.

When we duplicate a descriptor onto another (`fd[0]` onto standard input in the child), we have to be careful that the descriptor doesn't already have the desired value. If the descriptor already had the desired value and we called `dup2` and `close`, the single copy of the descriptor would be closed. (Recall the operation of `dup2` from Section 3.12 when its two arguments are equal.) In this program, if standard input had not been opened by the shell, the `fopen` at the beginning of the program should have used descriptor 0, the lowest unused descriptor, so `fd[0]` should never equal standard input. Nevertheless, whenever we call `dup2` and `close` to duplicate a descriptor onto another, as a defensive programming measure we'll always compare the descriptors first.

Note how we try to use the environment variable PAGER to obtain the name of the user's pager program. If this doesn't work, we use a default. This is a common usage of environment variables.   □

Example

Recall the five functions TELL_WAIT, TELL_PARENT, TELL_CHILD, WAIT_PARENT, and WAIT_CHILD from Section 8.8. In Program 10.17 we showed an implementation using signals. Program 14.3 shows an implementation using pipes.

We create two pipes before the `fork`, as shown in Figure 14.5.

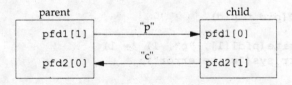

Figure 14.5 Using two pipes for parent–child synchronization.

The parent writes the character "p" across the top pipe when TELL_CHILD is called, and the child writes the character "c" across the bottom pipe when TELL_PARENT is called. The corresponding WAIT_xxx functions do a blocking `read` for the single character.

Note that each pipe has an extra reader, which doesn't matter. That is, in addition to the child reading from `pfd1[0]`, the parent also has this end of the top pipe open for reading. This doesn't affect us since the parent doesn't try to read from this pipe.   □

```
#include     "ourhdr.h"

static int  pfd1[2], pfd2[2];

void
TELL_WAIT(void)
{
    if (pipe(pfd1) < 0 || pipe(pfd2) < 0)
        err_sys("pipe error");
}

void
TELL_PARENT(pid_t pid)
{
    if (write(pfd2[1], "c", 1) != 1)
        err_sys("write error");
}


void
WAIT_PARENT(void)
{
    char    c;

    if (read(pfd1[0], &c, 1) != 1)
        err_sys("read error");
    if (c != 'p')
        err_quit("WAIT_PARENT: incorrect data");
}

void
TELL_CHILD(pid_t pid)
{
    if (write(pfd1[1], "p", 1) != 1)
        err_sys("write error");
}

void
WAIT_CHILD(void)
{
    char    c;

    if (read(pfd2[0], &c, 1) != 1)
        err_sys("read error");
    if (c != 'c')
        err_quit("WAIT_CHILD: incorrect data");
}
```

Program 14.3 Routines to let a parent and child synchronize.

14.3   popen and pclose Functions

Since a common operation is to create a pipe to another process, to either read its output or send it input, the standard I/O library has historically provided the popen and pclose functions. These two functions handle all the dirty work that we've been doing ourselves: the creation of a pipe, the fork of a child, closing the unused ends of the pipe, execing a shell to execute the command, and waiting for the command to terminate.

```
#include <stdio.h>

FILE *popen(const char *cmdstring, const char *type);
```
Returns: file pointer if OK, NULL on error

```
int pclose(FILE *fp);
```
Returns: termination status of cmdstring, or −1 on error

The function popen does a fork and exec to execute the *cmdstring*, and returns a standard I/O file pointer. If *type* is "r", the file pointer is connected to the standard output of *cmdstring* (Figure 14.6).

Figure 14.6   Result of fp = popen(*command*, "r").

If *type* is "w", the file pointer is connected to the standard input of *cmdstring* (Figure 14.7).

Figure 14.7   Result of fp = popen(*command*, "w")

One way to remember the final argument to popen is to remember that like fopen, the returned file pointer is readable if *type* is "r", or writable if *type* is "w".

The pclose function closes the standard I/O stream, waits for the command to terminate, and returns the termination status of the shell. (The termination status is what we described in Section 8.6. This is what the system function (Section 8.12) also returns.) If the shell cannot be executed, the termination status returned by pclose is as if the shell had executed exit (127).

The *cmdstring* is executed by the Bourne shell as in

    sh -c *cmdstring*

This means that the shell expands any of its special characters in *cmdstring*. This allows us to say, for example,

    fp = popen ("ls *.c", "r");

or

    fp = popen ("cmd 2>&1", "r");

> popen and pclose are not specified by POSIX.1, since they interact with a shell, which is covered by POSIX.2. Our description of these functions corresponds to Draft 11.2 of POSIX.2. There are some differences between the proposed POSIX.2 specification and prior implementations.

```
#include    <sys/wait.h>
#include    "ourhdr.h"

#define PAGER    "${PAGER:-more}" /* environment variable, or default */

int
main(int argc, char *argv[])
{
    char    line[MAXLINE];
    FILE    *fpin, *fpout;

    if (argc != 2)
        err_quit("usage: a.out <pathname>");
    if ( (fpin = fopen(argv[1], "r")) == NULL)
        err_sys("can't open %s", argv[1]);

    if ( (fpout = popen(PAGER, "w")) == NULL)
        err_sys("popen error");

        /* copy argv[1] to pager */
    while (fgets(line, MAXLINE, fpin) != NULL) {
        if (fputs(line, fpout) == EOF)
            err_sys("fputs error to pipe");
    }
    if (ferror(fpin))
        err_sys("fgets error");
    if (pclose(fpout) == -1)
        err_sys("pclose error");
    exit(0);
}
```

Program 14.4 Copy file to pager program using popen.

Example

Let's redo Program 14.2 using popen. This is shown in Program 14.4. Using popen reduces the amount of code we have to write.

The shell command ${PAGER:-more} says to use the value of the shell variable PAGER if it is defined and nonnull, otherwise use the string more.   □

Example—popen Function

Program 14.5 shows our version of popen and pclose. Although the core of popen is similar to the code we've used earlier in this chapter, there are many details that we need to take care of. First, each time popen is called we have to remember the process ID of the child that we create and either its file descriptor or FILE pointer. We choose to save the child's process ID in the array childpid, which we index by the file descriptor. This way, when pclose is called with the FILE pointer as its argument, we call the standard I/O function fileno to get the file descriptor, and then have the child process ID for the call to waitpid. Since it's possible for a given process to call popen more than once, we dynamically allocate the childpid array (the first time popen is called), with room for as many children as there are file descriptors.

Calling pipe, fork, and then duplicating the appropriate descriptors for each process is similar to what we've done earlier in this chapter.

POSIX.2 requires that popen close any streams in the child that are still open from previous calls to popen. To do this we go through the childpid array in the child, closing any descriptors that are still open.

What happens if the caller of pclose has established a signal handler for SIGCHLD? waitpid would return an error of EINTR. Since the caller is allowed to catch this signal (or any other signal that might interrupt the call to waitpid) we just call waitpid again if it is interrupted by a caught signal.

> Earlier versions of pclose returned an error of EINTR if a signal interrupted the wait.

> Earlier versions of pclose blocked or ignored the signals SIGINT, SIGQUIT, and SIGHUP during the wait. This is not allowed by POSIX.2.   □

```
#include     <sys/wait.h>
#include     <errno.h>
#include     <fcntl.h>
#include     "ourhdr.h"

static pid_t     *childpid = NULL;
                         /* ptr to array allocated at run-time */
static int       maxfd;  /* from our open_max(), Program 2.3 */

#define SHELL    "/bin/sh"

FILE *
popen(const char *cmdstring, const char *type)
```

```
{
    int     i, pfd[2];
    pid_t   pid;
    FILE    *fp;

                /* only allow "r" or "w" */
    if ((type[0] != 'r' && type[0] != 'w') || type[1] != 0) {
        errno = EINVAL;       /* required by POSIX.2 */
        return(NULL);
    }

    if (childpid == NULL) {        /* first time through */
                /* allocate zeroed out array for child pids */
        maxfd = open_max();
        if ( (childpid = calloc(maxfd, sizeof(pid_t))) == NULL)
            return(NULL);
    }

    if (pipe(pfd) < 0)
        return(NULL);    /* errno set by pipe() */

    if ( (pid = fork()) < 0)
        return(NULL);    /* errno set by fork() */
    else if (pid == 0) {                              /* child */
        if (*type == 'r') {
            close(pfd[0]);
            if (pfd[1] != STDOUT_FILENO) {
                dup2(pfd[1], STDOUT_FILENO);
                close(pfd[1]);
            }
        } else {
            close(pfd[1]);
            if (pfd[0] != STDIN_FILENO) {
                dup2(pfd[0], STDIN_FILENO);
                close(pfd[0]);
            }
        }
            /* close all descriptors in childpid[] */
        for (i = 0; i < maxfd; i++)
            if (childpid[i] > 0)
                close(i);

        execl(SHELL, "sh", "-c", cmdstring, (char *) 0);
        _exit(127);
    }
                                /* parent */
    if (*type == 'r') {
        close(pfd[1]);
        if ( (fp = fdopen(pfd[0], type)) == NULL)
            return(NULL);
    } else {
```

```
            close(pfd[0]);
            if ( (fp = fdopen(pfd[1], type)) == NULL)
                return(NULL);
        }
        childpid[fileno(fp)] = pid; /* remember child pid for this fd */
        return(fp);
    }

    int
    pclose(FILE *fp)
    {
        int     fd, stat;
        pid_t   pid;

        if (childpid == NULL)
            return(-1);        /* popen() has never been called */

        fd = fileno(fp);
        if ( (pid = childpid[fd]) == 0)
            return(-1);        /* fp wasn't opened by popen() */

        childpid[fd] = 0;
        if (fclose(fp) == EOF)
            return(-1);

        while (waitpid(pid, &stat, 0) < 0)
            if (errno != EINTR)
                return(-1); /* error other than EINTR from waitpid() */

        return(stat);    /* return child's termination status */
    }
```

Program 14.5 The popen and pclose functions.

Example

Consider an application that writes a prompt to standard output and reads a line from standard input. With popen we can intersperse a program between the application and its input, to transform the input. Figure 14.8 shows the arrangement of processes.

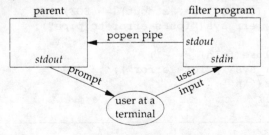

Figure 14.8 Transforming input using popen.

```
#include      <ctype.h>
#include      "ourhdr.h"

int
main(void)
{
    int       c;

    while ( (c = getchar()) != EOF) {
        if (isupper(c))
            c = tolower(c);
        if (putchar(c) == EOF)
            err_sys("output error");
        if (c == '\n')
            fflush(stdout);
    }
    exit(0);
}
```

Program 14.6 Filter to convert uppercase characters to lowercase.

```
#include      <sys/wait.h>
#include      "ourhdr.h"

int
main(void)
{
    char      line[MAXLINE];
    FILE      *fpin;

    if ( (fpin = popen("myuclc", "r")) == NULL)
        err_sys("popen error");

    for ( ; ; ) {
        fputs("prompt> ", stdout);
        fflush(stdout);
        if (fgets(line, MAXLINE, fpin) == NULL)  /* read from pipe */
            break;
        if (fputs(line, stdout) == EOF)
            err_sys("fputs error to pipe");
    }
    if (pclose(fpin) == -1)
        err_sys("pclose error");
    putchar('\n');
    exit(0);
}
```

Program 14.7 Invoke uppercase/lowercase filter to read commands.

The transformation could be pathname expansion, for example, or providing a history mechanism (remembering previously entered commands). (This example comes from the Rationale for popen in the POSIX.2 draft.)

Program 14.6 shows a simple filter to demonstrate this operation. It just copies standard input to standard output, converting any uppercase character to lowercase. The reason we're careful to fflush standard output after writing a newline is discussed in the next section when we talk about coprocesses.

We compile this filter into the executable file myuclc, which we then invoke from Program 14.7 using popen.

We need to call fflush after writing the prompt because the standard output is normally line buffered, and the prompt does not contain a newline.   □

14.4 Coprocesses

A Unix filter is a program that reads from standard input and writes to standard output. Filters are normally connected linearly in shell pipelines. A filter becomes a *coprocess* when the same program generates its input and reads its output.

The KornShell provides coprocesses [Bolsky and Korn 1989]. The Bourne shell and C shell don't provide a way to connect processes together as coprocesses. A coprocess normally runs in the background from a shell and its standard input and standard output are connected to another program using a pipe. Although the shell syntax required to initiate a coprocess and connect its input and output to other processes is quite contorted (see pp. 65–66 of Bolsky and Korn [1989] for all the details), coprocesses are also useful from a C program.

Whereas popen gives us a one-way pipe to the standard input or from the standard output of another process, with a coprocess we have two one-way pipes to the other process—one to its standard input and one from its standard output. We want to write to its standard input, let it operate on the data, then read from its standard output.

Example

Let's look at coprocesses with an example. The process creates two pipes: one is the standard input of the coprocess and the other is the standard output of the coprocess. Figure 14.9 shows this arrangement.

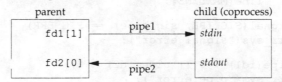

Figure 14.9 Driving a coprocess by writing its standard input and reading its standard output.

Program 14.8 is a simple coprocess that reads two numbers from its standard input, computes their sum, and writes the sum to its standard output.

```
#include     "ourhdr.h"

int
main(void)
{
    int     n, int1, int2;
    char    line[MAXLINE];

    while ( (n = read(STDIN_FILENO, line, MAXLINE)) > 0) {
        line[n] = 0;                /* null terminate */
        if (sscanf(line, "%d%d", &int1, &int2) == 2) {
            sprintf(line, "%d\n", int1 + int2);
            n = strlen(line);
            if (write(STDOUT_FILENO, line, n) != n)
                err_sys("write error");
        } else {
            if (write(STDOUT_FILENO, "invalid args\n", 13) != 13)
                err_sys("write error");
        }
    }
    exit(0);
}
```

Program 14.8 Simple filter to add two numbers.

We compile this program and leave the executable in the file add2.

Program 14.9 invokes the add2 coprocess, after reading two numbers from its standard input. The value from the coprocess is written to its standard output.

```
#include     <signal.h>
#include     "ourhdr.h"

static void sig_pipe(int);        /* our signal handler */

int
main(void)
{
    int     n, fd1[2], fd2[2];
    pid_t   pid;
    char    line[MAXLINE];

    if (signal(SIGPIPE, sig_pipe) == SIG_ERR)
        err_sys("signal error");

    if (pipe(fd1) < 0 || pipe(fd2) < 0)
        err_sys("pipe error");

    if ( (pid = fork()) < 0)
        err_sys("fork error");
```

```
            else if (pid > 0) {                          /* parent */
                close(fd1[0]);
                close(fd2[1]);
                while (fgets(line, MAXLINE, stdin) != NULL) {
                    n = strlen(line);
                    if (write(fd1[1], line, n) != n)
                        err_sys("write error to pipe");
                    if ( (n = read(fd2[0], line, MAXLINE)) < 0)
                        err_sys("read error from pipe");
                    if (n == 0) {
                        err_msg("child closed pipe");
                        break;
                    }
                    line[n] = 0;      /* null terminate */
                    if (fputs(line, stdout) == EOF)
                        err_sys("fputs error");
                }
                if (ferror(stdin))
                    err_sys("fgets error on stdin");
                exit(0);

        } else {                                          /* child */
                close(fd1[1]);
                close(fd2[0]);
                if (fd1[0] != STDIN_FILENO) {
                    if (dup2(fd1[0], STDIN_FILENO) != STDIN_FILENO)
                        err_sys("dup2 error to stdin");
                    close(fd1[0]);
                }
                if (fd2[1] != STDOUT_FILENO) {
                    if (dup2(fd2[1], STDOUT_FILENO) != STDOUT_FILENO)
                        err_sys("dup2 error to stdout");
                    close(fd2[1]);
                }
                if (execl("./add2", "add2", (char *) 0) < 0)
                    err_sys("execl error");
            }
}

static void
sig_pipe(int signo)
{
    printf("SIGPIPE caught\n");
    exit(1);
}
```

Program 14.9 Program to drive the add2 filter.

Here we create two pipes, with the parent and child closing the ends they don't need.
We have to use two pipes: one for the standard input of the coprocess, and one for its

standard output. The child then calls dup2 to move the pipe descriptors onto its standard input and standard output, before calling execl.

If we compile and run Program 14.9, it works as expected. Furthermore, if we kill the add2 coprocess while Program 14.9 is waiting for our input, and then enter two numbers, when the program writes to the pipe that has no reader, the signal handler is invoked. (See Exercise 14.4.)

In Program 15.1 we provide another version of this example using a single full-duplex pipe instead of two half-duplex pipes.   □

Example

In the coprocess add2 (Program 14.8) we purposely used Unix I/O: read and write. What happens if we rewrite this coprocess to use standard I/O? Program 14.10 shows the new version.

```
#include     "ourhdr.h"

int
main(void)
{
    int     int1, int2;
    char    line[MAXLINE];

    while (fgets(line, MAXLINE, stdin) != NULL) {
        if (sscanf(line, "%d%d", &int1, &int2) == 2)
            if (printf("%d\n", int1 + int2) == EOF)
                err_sys("printf error");
        } else {
            if (printf("invalid args\n") == EOF)
                err_sys("printf error");
        }
    }
    exit(0);
}
```

Program 14.10 Filter to add two numbers, using standard I/O.

If we invoke this new coprocess from Program 14.9 it no longer works. The problem is the default standard I/O buffering. When Program 14.10 is invoked, the first fgets on the standard input causes the standard I/O library to allocate a buffer and choose the type of buffering. Since the standard input is a pipe, isatty is false, and the standard I/O library defaults to fully buffered. The same thing happens with the standard output. While add2 is blocked reading from its standard input, Program 14.9 is blocked reading from the pipe. We have a deadlock.

Here we have control over the coprocess that's being execed. We can change Program 14.10 by adding the following four lines before the while loop is entered.

```
if (setvbuf(stdin, NULL, _IOLBF, 0) != 0)
    err_sys("setvbuf error");
```

```
        if (setvbuf(stdout, NULL, _IOLBF, 0) != 0)
            err_sys("setvbuf error");
```

This causes the fgets to return when a line is available, and it causes printf to do an fflush when a newline is output. Making these explicit calls to setvbuf fixes Program 14.10.

If we aren't able to modify the program that we're piping the output into, other techniques are required. For example, if we use awk(1) as a coprocess from our program (instead of the add2 program), the following won't work:

```
#! /bin/awk -f
{ print $1 + $2 }
```

The reason this won't work is again the standard I/O buffering. But in this case we cannot change the way awk works (unless we have the source code for it). We are unable to modify the executable of awk in any way to change the way the standard I/O buffering is handled.

The solution for this general problem is to make the coprocess being invoked (awk in this case) think that its standard input and standard output are connected to a terminal. That causes the standard I/O routines in the coprocess to line buffer these two I/O streams, similar to what we did with the explicit calls to setvbuf previously. We use pseudo terminals to do this in Chapter 19.   □

14.5 FIFOs

FIFOs are sometimes called named pipes. Pipes can be used only between related processes when a common ancestor has created the pipe. With FIFOs, however, unrelated processes can exchange data.

We saw in Chapter 4 that a FIFO is a type of file. One· of the codings of the st_mode member of the stat structure (Section 4.2) indicates that a file is a FIFO. We can test for this with the S_ISFIFO macro.

Creating a FIFO is similar to creating a file. Indeed, the *pathname* for a FIFO exists in the filesystem.

```
#include <sys/types.h>
#include <sys/stat.h>

int mkfifo(const char *pathname, mode_t mode);
```
Returns: 0 if OK, −1 on error

The specification of the *mode* argument for the mkfifo function is the same as for the open function (Section 3.3). The rules for the user and group ownership of the new FIFO are the same as we described in Section 4.6.

Once we have created a FIFO using mkfifo, we open it using open. Indeed, the normal file I/O functions (close, read, write, unlink, etc.) all work with FIFOs.

The mkfifo function is an invention of POSIX.1. SVR3, for example, used the mknod(2) system call to create a FIFO. In SVR4 mkfifo just calls mknod to create the FIFO.

POSIX.2 has proposed a mkfifo(1) command. Both SVR4 and 4.3+BSD currently support this command. This allows a FIFO to be created using a shell command, and then accessed with the normal shell I/O redirection.

When we open a FIFO, the nonblocking flag (O_NONBLOCK) affects what happens.

1. In the normal case (O_NONBLOCK not specified), an open for read-only blocks until some other process opens the FIFO for writing. Similarly, an open for write-only blocks until some other process opens the FIFO for reading.

2. If O_NONBLOCK is specified, an open for read-only returns immediately. But an open for write-only returns an error with an errno of ENXIO if no process has the FIFO open for reading.

Like a pipe, if we write to a FIFO that no process has open for reading, the signal SIGPIPE is generated. When the last writer for a FIFO closes the FIFO, an end of file is generated for the reader of the FIFO.

It is common to have multiple writers for a given FIFO. This means we have to worry about atomic writes if we don't want the writes from multiple processes to be interleaved. As with pipes, the constant PIPE_BUF specifies the maximum amount of data that can be written atomically to a FIFO.

There are two uses for FIFOs.

1. FIFOs are used by shell commands to pass data from one shell pipeline to another, without creating intermediate temporary files.

2. FIFOs are used in a client–server application to pass data between the clients and server.

We discuss each of these with an example.

Example—Using FIFOs to Duplicate Output Streams

FIFOs can be used to duplicate an output stream in a series of shell commands. This prevents writing the data to an intermediate disk file (similar to using pipes to avoid intermediate disk files). But while pipes can be used only for linear connections between processes, since a FIFO has a name, it can be used for nonlinear connections.

Consider a procedure that needs to process a filtered input stream twice. Figure 14.10 shows this arrangement.

With a FIFO and the Unix program tee(1) we can accomplish this procedure without using a temporary file. (The tee program copies its standard input to both its standard output and to the file named on its command line.)

```
mkfifo fifo1
prog3 < fifo1 &
prog1 < infile | tee fifo1 | prog2
```

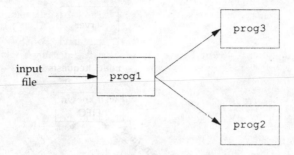

Figure 14.10 Procedure that processes a filtered input stream twice.

We create the FIFO and then start prog3 in the background, reading from the FIFO. We then start prog1 and use tee to send its input to both the FIFO and prog2. Figure 14.11 shows the process arrangement pictorially.

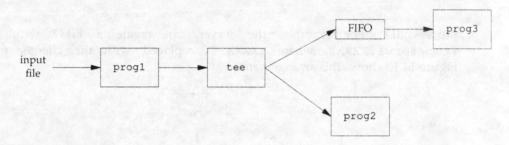

Figure 14.11 Using a FIFO and tee to send a stream to two different processes.

□

Example—Client–Server Communication Using a FIFO

Another use for FIFOs is to send data between a client and server. If we have a server that is contacted by numerous clients, each client can write its request to a well-known FIFO that the server creates. (By "well-known" we mean that the pathname of the FIFO is known to all the clients that need to contact it.) Figure 14.12 shows this arrangement. Since there are multiple writers for the FIFO, the requests sent by the clients to the server need to be less than PIPE_BUF bytes in size. This prevents any interleaving of the client writes.

The problem in using FIFOs for this type of client–server communication is how to send replies back from the server to each client. A single FIFO can't be used, as the clients would never know when to read their response, versus responses for other clients. One solution is for each client to send its process ID with the request. The server then creates a unique FIFO for each client, using a pathname based on the client's

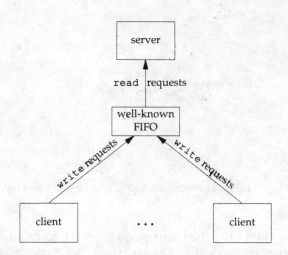

Figure 14.12 Clients sending requests to a server using a FIFO.

process ID. For example, the server can create a FIFO with the name
/tmp/serv1.XXXXX, where XXXXX is replaced with the client's process ID.
Figure 14.13 shows this arrangement.

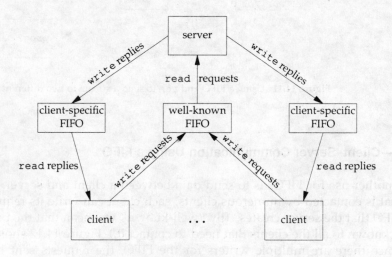

Figure 14.13 Client–server communication using FIFOs.

This arrangement works, although it is impossible for the server to tell if a client
crashes. This causes the client-specific FIFOs to be left in the filesystem. The server also
must catch SIGPIPE, since it's possible for a client to send a request and terminate
before reading the response, leaving the client-specific FIFO with one writer (the server)
and no reader.

With the arrangement shown in Figure 14.13, if the server opens its well-known FIFO read-only (since it only `reads` from it) each time the number of clients goes from 1 to 0 the server will `read` an end of file on the FIFO. To prevent the server having to handle this case, a common trick is just to have the server open its well-known FIFO for read–write. (See Exercise 14.10.)   □

14.6 System V IPC

There are many similarities between the three types of IPC that we call System V IPC—message queues, semaphores, and shared memory. In this section we cover these similar features, before looking at the specific functions for each of the three IPC types in the following sections.

> These three types of IPC originated in the 1970s in an internal version of Unix called "Columbus Unix." These IPC features were later added to System V.

14.6.1 Identifiers and Keys

Each *IPC structure* (message queue, semaphore, or shared memory segment) in the kernel is referred to by a nonnegative integer *identifier*. To send or fetch a message to or from a message queue, for example, all we need know is the identifier for the queue. Unlike file descriptors, IPC identifiers are not small integers. Indeed, when a given IPC structure is created and then removed, the identifier associated with that structure continually increases until it reaches the maximum positive value for an integer, and then wraps around to 0. (This value that is remembered even after an IPC structure is deleted, and incremented each time the structure is used, is called the "slot usage sequence number." It is in the `ipc_perm` structure, which we show in the next section.)

Whenever an IPC structure is being created (by calling `msgget`, `semget`, or `shmget`), a *key* must be specified. The data type of this key is the primitive system data type `key_t`, which is often defined as a long integer in the header `<sys/types.h>`. This key is converted into an identifier by the kernel.

There are various ways for a client and server to rendezvous at the same IPC structure.

1. The server can create a new IPC structure by specifying a key of `IPC_PRIVATE` and store the returned identifier somewhere (such as a file) for the client to obtain. The key `IPC_PRIVATE` guarantees that the server creates a brand new IPC structure. The disadvantage to this technique is that filesystem operations are required for the server to write the integer identifier to a file, and then for the clients to retrieve this identifier later.

    The `IPC_PRIVATE` key is also used in a parent–child relationship. The parent creates a new IPC structure specifying `IPC_PRIVATE` and the resulting identifier is then available to the child after the `fork`. The child can pass the identifier to a new program as an argument to one of the `exec` functions.

2. The client and server can agree on a key by defining the key in a common header, for example. The server then creates a new IPC structure specifying this key. The problem with this approach is that it's possible for the key to already be associated with an IPC structure, in which case the get function (msgget, semget, or shmget) returns an error. The server must handle t¹   error, deleting the existing IPC structure, and try to create it again.

3. The client and server can agree on a pathname and project ID (the project ID is just a character value between 0 and 255) and call the function ftok to convert these two values into a key. (The function ftok is described in the stdipc(3) manual page.) This key is then used in step 2. The only service provided by ftok is a way of generating a key from a pathname and project ID. Since the client and server typically share at least one header, an easier technique is to avoid using ftok and just store the well-known key in this header, avoiding yet another function.

The three get functions (msgget, semget, and shmget) all have two similar arguments: a *key* and an integer *flag*. A new IPC structure is created (normally by a server) if either

1. *key* is IPC_PRIVATE, or

2. *key* is not currently associated with an IPC structure of the particular type and the IPC_CREAT bit of *flag* is specified.

To reference an existing queue (normally done by a client), *key* must equal the key that was specified when the queue was created and IPC_CREAT must not be specified.

Note that it's never possible to specify IPC_PRIVATE to reference an existing queue, since this special *key* value always creates a new queue. To reference an existing queue that was created with a *key* of IPC_PRIVATE we must know the associated identifier, and then use that identifier in the other IPC calls (such as msgsnd and msgrcv), bypassing the get function.

If we want to create a new IPC structure, making sure that we don't reference an existing one with the same identifier, we must specify a *flag* with both the IPC_CREAT and IPC_EXCL bits set. Doing this causes an error return of EEXIST if the IPC structure already exists. (This is similar to an open that specifies the O_CREAT and O_EXCL flags.)

14.6.2 Permission Structure

System V IPC associates an ipc_perm structure with each IPC structure. This structure defines the permissions and owner.

```
struct ipc_perm {
  uid_t  uid;   /* owner's effective user id */
  gid_t  gid;   /* owner's effective group id */
  uid_t  cuid;  /* creator's effective user id */
  gid_t  cgid;  /* creator's effective group id */
```

```
    mode_t mode;  /* access modes */
    ulong  seq;   /* slot usage sequence number */
    key_t  key;   /* key */
};
```

All the fields other than seq are initialized when the IPC structure is created. At a later time we can modify the uid, gid, and mode fields, by calling msgctl, semctl, or shmctl. To change these values the calling process must either be the creator of the IPC structure, or it must be the superuser. Changing these fields is similar to calling chown or chmod for a file.

The values in the mode field are similar to the values we saw in Figure 4.4, but there is nothing corresponding to execute permission for any of the IPC structures. Also, whereas message queues and shared memory use the terms read and write, semaphores use the terms read and alter. Figure 14.14 specifies the six permissions for each form of IPC.

Permission	Message queue	Semaphore	Shared memory
user-read	MSG_R	SEM_R	SHM_R
user-write (alter)	MSG_W	SEM_A	SHM_W
group-read	MSG_R >> 3	SEM_R >> 3	SHM_R >> 3
group-write (alter)	MSG_W >> 3	SEM_A >> 3	SHM_W >> 3
other-read	MSG_R >> 6	SEM_R >> 6	SHM_R >> 6
other-write (alter)	MSG_W >> 6	SEM_A >> 6	SHM_W >> 6

Figure 14.14 System V IPC permissions.

14.6.3 Configuration Limits

All three forms of System V IPC have built-in limits that we may encounter. Most of these can be changed by reconfiguring the kernel. We describe the limits when we describe each of the three forms of IPC.

> Under SVR4 these values, and their minimum and maximum values, are in the file /etc/conf/cf.d/mtune.

14.6.4 Advantages and Disadvantages

A fundamental problem with System V IPC is that the IPC structures are systemwide and do not have a reference count. For example, if we create a message queue, place some messages on the queue, and then terminate, the message queue and its contents are not deleted. They remain in the system until specifically read or deleted: by some process calling msgrcv or msgctl, by someone executing the ipcrm(1) command, or by the system being rebooted. Compare this with a pipe, which is completely removed when the last process to reference it terminates. With a FIFO, although the name stays in the filesystem until explicitly removed, any data left in a FIFO is removed when the last process to reference the FIFO terminates.

Another problem with System V IPC is that these IPC structures are not known by names in the filesystem. We can't access them and modify their properties with the functions we described in Chapters 3 and 4. Almost a dozen brand new system calls were added to the kernel to support them (msgget, semop, shmat, etc.). We can't see them with an ls command, we can't remove them with the rm command, and we can't change their permissions with the chmod command. Instead, brand new commands, ipcs(1) and ipcrm(1), were added.

Since these forms of IPC don't use file descriptors, we can't use the multiplexed I/O functions with them: select and poll. This makes it harder to use more than one of these IPC structures at a time, or to use any of these IPC structures with file or device I/O. For example, we can't have a server wait for a message to be placed on one of two message queues without some form of busy–wait loop.

An overview of an actual transaction processing system built using System V IPC is given in Andrade, Carges, and Kovach [1989]. They claim that the name space used by System V IPC (the identifiers) is an advantage, and not a problem as we said earlier, because using identifiers allows a process to send a message to a message queue with just a single function call (msgsnd), while other forms of IPC normally require an open, write, and close. This argument is false. Somehow the clients still have to obtain the identifier for the server's queue, to avoid using a key and calling msgget. The identifier assigned to a particular queue depends on how many other message queues exist when the queue is created and how many times the table in the kernel assigned to the new queue has been used since the kernel was bootstrapped. This is a dynamic value that can't be guessed or stored in a header. As we mentioned in Section 14.6.1, minimally the server has to write the identifier assigned to a queue to a file for the clients to read.

Other advantages listed by these authors for message queues are that they're (a) reliable, (b) flow controlled, (c) record oriented, and (d) can be processed in other than first-in, first-out order. As we saw in Section 12.4, streams also possess all these properties, although an open is required before sending data to a stream, and a close is required when we're finished. Figure 14.15 compares some of the features of these different forms of IPC.

IPC type	connectionless?	reliable?	flow control?	records?	message types or priorities?
message queues	no	yes	yes	yes	yes
streams	no	yes	yes	yes	yes
Unix stream socket	no	yes	yes	no	no
Unix datagram socket	yes	yes	no	yes	no
FIFOs	no	yes	yes	no	no

Figure 14.15 Comparison of features of different forms of IPC.

(We describe Unix stream and datagram sockets briefly in Chapter 15.) By connectionless we mean the ability to send a message without having to call some form of an open function first. As described previously, we don't consider message queues connection-less, since some technique is required to obtain the identifier for a queue. Since all these forms of IPC are restricted to a single host, all are reliable. When the messages are sent across a network, the possibility of messages being lost becomes a concern. Flow control means that the sender is put to sleep if there is a shortage of system resources (buffers) or if the receiver can't accept any more messages. When the flow control condition subsides, the sender should automatically be awakened.

One feature that we don't show in Figure 14.15 is whether the IPC facility can automatically create a unique connection to a server for each client. We'll see in Chapter 15 that streams and Unix stream sockets provide this capability.

The next three sections describe each of the three forms of System V IPC in detail.

14.7 Message Queues

Message queues are a linked list of messages stored within the kernel and identified by a message queue identifier. We'll call the message queue just a "queue" and its identifier just a "queue ID." A new queue is created, or an existing queue is opened by msgget. New messages are added to the end of a queue by msgsnd. Every message has a positive long integer type field, a nonnegative length, and the actual data bytes (corresponding to the length), all of which are specified to msgsnd when the message is added to a queue. Messages are fetched from a queue by msgrcv. We don't have to fetch the messages in a first-in, first-out order. Instead, we can fetch messages based on their type field.

Each queue has the following msqid_ds structure associated with it. This structure defines the current status of the queue.

```
struct msqid_ds {
  struct ipc_perm  msg_perm; /* see Section 14.6.2 */
  struct msg *msg_first;  /* ptr to first message on queue */
  struct msg *msg_last;   /* ptr to last message on queue */
  ulong        msg_cbytes; /* current # bytes on queue */
  ulong        msg_qnum;   /* # of messages on queue */
  ulong        msg_qbytes; /* max # of bytes on queue */
  pid_t        msg_lspid;  /* pid of last msgsnd() */
  pid_t        msg_lrpid;  /* pid of last msgrcv() */
  time_t       msg_stime;  /* last-msgsnd() time */
  time_t       msg_rtime;  /* last-msgrcv() time */
  time_t       msg_ctime;  /* last-change time */
};
```

The two pointers, msg_first and msg_last are worthless to a user process, as these point to where the corresponding messages are stored within the kernel. The remaining members of the structure are self-defining.

Figure 14.16 lists the system limits (Section 14.6.3) that affect message queues.

Name	Description	Typical Value
MSGMAX	The size in bytes of the largest message we can send.	2048
MSGMNB	The maximum size in bytes of a particular queue (i.e., the sum of all the messages on the queue).	4096
MSGMNI	The maximum number of messages queues, systemwide.	50
MSGTQL	The maximum number of messages, systemwide.	40

Figure 14.16 System limits that affect message queues.

The first function normally called is `msgget` to either open an existing queue or create a new queue.

```
#include <sys/types.h>
#include <sys/ipc.h>
#include <sys/msg.h>

int msgget(key_t key, int flag);
```

Returns: message queue ID if OK, –1 on error

In Section 14.6.1 we described the rules for converting the *key* into an identifier and discussed whether a new queue is created or an existing queue is referenced. When a new queue is created the following members of the `msqid_ds` structure are initialized.

- The `ipc_perm` structure is initialized as described in Section 14.6.2. The `mode` member of this structure is set to the corresponding permission bits of *flag*. These permissions are specified with the constants from Figure 14.14.

- `msg_qnum`, `msg_lspid`, `msg_lrpid`, `msg_stime`, and `msg_rtime` are all set to 0.

- `msg_ctime` is set to the current time.

- `msg_qbytes` is set to the system limit.

On success, `msgget` returns the nonnegative queue ID. This value is then used with the other three message queue functions.

The `msgctl` function performs various operations on a queue. It, and the related functions for semaphores and shared memory (`semctl` and `shmctl`) are the `ioctl`-like functions for System V IPC (i.e., the garbage-can functions).

```
#include <sys/types.h>
#include <sys/ipc.h>
#include <sys/msg.h>

int msgctl(int msqid, int cmd, struct msqid_ds *buf);
```

Returns: 0 if OK, –1 on error

The *cmd* argument specifies the command to be performed, on the queue specified by *msqid*.

IPC_STAT   Fetch the `msqid_ds` structure for this queue, storing it in the structure pointed to by *buf*.

IPC_SET   Set the following four fields from the structure pointed to by *buf* in the structure associated with this queue: `msg_perm.uid`, `msg_perm.gid`, `msg_perm.mode`, and `msg_qbytes`. This command can be executed only by a process whose effective user ID equals `msg_perm.cuid` or `msg_perm.uid`, or by a process with superuser privileges. Only the superuser can increase the value of `msg_qbytes`.

IPC_RMID   Remove the message queue from the system and any data still on the queue. This removal is immediate. Any other process still using the message queue will get an error of `EIDRM` on its next attempted operation on the queue. This command can be executed only by a process whose effective user ID equals `msg_perm.cuid` or `msg_perm.uid`, or by a process with superuser privileges.

We'll see that these three commands (`IPC_STAT`, `IPC_SET`, and `IPC_RMID`) are also provided for semaphores and shared memory.

Data is placed onto a message queue by calling `msgsnd`.

```
#include <sys/types.h>
#include <sys/ipc.h>
#include <sys/msg.h>

int msgsnd(int msqid, const void *ptr, size_t nbytes, int flag);
```
Returns: 0 if OK, –1 on error

As we mentioned earlier, each message is composed of a positive long integer type field, a nonnegative length (*nbytes*), and the actual data bytes (corresponding to the length). Messages are always placed at the end of the queue.

ptr points to a long integer that contains the positive integer message type, and it is immediately followed by the message data. (There is no message data if *nbytes* is 0.) If the largest message we send is 512 bytes, we can define the following structure

```
struct mymesg {
    long  mtype;       /* positive message type */
    char  mtext[512];  /* message data, of length nbytes */
};
```

The *ptr* argument is then a pointer to a mymesg structure. The message type can be used by the receiver to fetch messages in an order other than first-in, first-out.

A *flag* value of `IPC_NOWAIT` can be specified. This is similar to the nonblocking I/O flag for file I/O (Section 12.2). If the message queue is full (either the total number of messages on the queue equals the system limit, or the total number of bytes on the queue equals the system limit), specifying IPC_NOWAIT causes msgsnd to return immediately with an error of EAGAIN. If IPC_NOWAIT is not specified, we are blocked until (a) there is room for the message, (b) the queue is removed from the system, or (c) a signal is caught and the signal handler returns. In the second case an error of EIDRM is returned ("identifier removed"), and in the last case the error returned is EINTR.

Notice how ungracefully the removal of a message queue is handled. Since a reference count is not maintained with each message queue (as there is for open files), the removal of a queue just generates errors on the next queue operation by processes still using the queue. Semaphores handle this removal in the same fashion. Removing a file doesn't delete the file's contents until the last process using the file closes it.

Messages are retrieved from a queue by msgrcv.

```
#include <sys/types.h>
#include <sys/ipc.h>
#include <sys/msg.h>

int msgrcv(int msqid, void *ptr, size_t nbytes, long type, int flag);
```

                                    Returns: size of data portion of message if OK, −1 on error

As with msgsnd, the *ptr* argument points to a long integer (where the message type of the returned message is stored) followed by a data buffer for the actual message data. *nbytes* specifies the size of the data buffer. If the returned message is larger than *nbytes*, the message is truncated if the MSG_NOERROR bit in *flag* is set. (In this case, no notification is given us that the message was truncated.) If the message is too big and this *flag* value is not specified, an error of E2BIG is returned instead (and the message stays on the queue).

The *type* argument lets us specify which message we want.

type == 0   The first message on the queue is returned.

type > 0   The first message on the queue whose message type equals *type* is returned.

type < 0   The first message on the queue whose message type is the lowest value less than or equal to the absolute value of *type* is returned.

A nonzero *type* is used to read the messages in an order other than first-in, first-out. For example, the *type* could be a priority value if the application assigns priorities to the messages. Another use of this field is to contain the process ID of the client if a single message queue is being used by multiple clients and a single server.

We can specify a *flag* value of IPC_NOWAIT to make the operation nonblocking. This causes msgrcv to return an error of ENOMSG if a message of the specified type is not available. If IPC_NOWAIT is not specified, we are blocked until (a) a message of the specified type is available, (b) the queue is removed from the system (an error of EIDRM is returned), or (c) a signal is caught and the signal handler returns (an error of EINTR is returned).

Example—Timing Comparison of Message Queues versus Stream Pipes

If we need a bidirectional flow of data between a client and server, we can use either message queues or stream pipes. (We cover stream pipes in Section 15.2. They are similar to pipes but full duplex.)

Figure 14.17 shows a timing comparison of these two techniques, on two different systems. The test consisted of a program that created the IPC channel, called `fork`, and then sent 20 megabytes of data from the parent to the child. The data was sent using 10,000 calls to `msgsnd`, with a message length of 2,000 bytes, for the message queue, and 10,000 calls to `write`, with a length of 2,000 bytes, for the stream pipe. The times are all in seconds.

Operation	SPARC, SunOS 4.1.1			80386, SVR4		
	User	System	Clock	User	System	Clock
message queue	0.8	10.7	11.6	0.7	19.6	20.1
stream pipe	0.3	10.6	11.0	0.5	21.4	21.9

Figure 14.17 Timing comparison of message queues and stream pipes.

On the SPARC, stream pipes are implemented using Unix domain sockets. Under SVR4 the `pipe` function provides stream pipes (using streams, as we described in Section 12.4).

What these numbers show us is that message queues, originally implemented to provide higher-than-normal speed IPC, are no longer any faster than other forms of IPC. (When message queues were implemented, the only other form of IPC available was half-duplex pipes.) When we consider the problems in using message queues (Section 14.6.4), we come to the conclusion that we shouldn't use them for new applications.   □

14.8 Semaphores

A semaphore isn't really a form of IPC similar to the others that we've described (pipes, FIFOs, and message queues). A semaphore is a counter used to provide access to a shared data object for multiple processes. To obtain a shared resource a process needs to do the following:

1. Test the semaphore that controls the resource.

2. If the value of the semaphore is positive the process can use the resource. The process decrements the semaphore value by 1, indicating that it has used one unit of the resource.

3. If the value of the semaphore is 0, the process goes to sleep until the semaphore value is greater than 0. When the process wakes up it returns to step 1.

When a process is done with a shared resource that is controlled by a semaphore, the semaphore value is incremented by 1. If any other processes are asleep, waiting for the semaphore, they are awakened.

To implement semaphores correctly, the test of a semaphore's value and the decrementing of this value must be an atomic operation. For this reason, semaphores are normally implemented inside the kernel.

A common form of semaphore is called a *binary semaphore*. It controls a single resource and its value is initialized to 1. In general, however, a semaphore can be initialized to any positive value, with the value indicating how many of units of the shared resource are available for sharing.

System V semaphores are, unfortunately, more complicated than this. Three features contribute to this unnecessary complication.

1. A semaphore is not just a single nonnegative value. Instead we have to define a semaphore as a set of one or more semaphore values. When we create a semaphore we specify the number of values in the set.

2. The creation of a semaphore (semget) is independent of its initialization (semctl). This is a fatal flaw, since we cannot atomically create a new semaphore set and initialize all the values in the set.

3. Since all forms of System V IPC remain in existence even when no process is using them, we have to worry about a program that terminates without releasing the semaphores it has been allocated. The "undo" feature that we describe later is supposed to handle this.

The kernel maintains a semid_ds structure for each semaphore.

```
struct semid_ds {
  struct ipc_perm  sem_perm;  /* see Section 14.6.2 */
  struct sem  *sem_base;  /* ptr to first semaphore in set */
  ushort        sem_nsems; /* # of semaphores in set */
  time_t        sem_otime; /* last-semop() time */
  time_t        sem_ctime; /* last-change time */
};
```

The sem_base pointer is worthless to a user process, since it points to memory in the kernel. What it points to is an array of sem structures, containing sem_nsems elements, one element in the array for each semaphore value in the set.

```
struct sem {
  ushort  semval;   /* semaphore value, always >= 0 */
  pid_t   sempid;   /* pid for last operation */
  ushort  semncnt;  /* # processes awaiting semval > currval */
  ushort  semzcnt;  /* # processes awaiting semval = 0 */
};
```

Figure 14.18 lists the system limits (Section 14.6.3) that affect semaphore sets.

Name	Description	Typical Value
SEMVMX	The maximum value of any semaphore.	32,767
SEMAEM	The maximum value of any semaphore's adjust-on-exit value.	16,384
SEMMNI	The maximum number of semaphore sets, systemwide.	10
SEMMNS	The maximum number of semaphores, systemwide.	60
SEMMSL	The maximum number of semaphores per semaphore set.	25
SEMMNU	The maximum number of undo structures, systemwide.	30
SEMUME	The maximum number of undo entries per undo structures.	10
SEMOPM	The maximum number of operations per semop call.	10

Figure 14.18 System limits that affect semaphores.

The first function to call is semget to obtain a semaphore ID.

```
#include <sys/types.h>
#include <sys/ipc.h>
#include <sys/sem.h>

int semget(key_t key, int nsems, int flag);
```

Returns: semaphore ID if OK, –1 on error

In Section 14.6.1 we described the rules for converting the *key* into an identifier and discussed whether a new set is created or an existing set is referenced. When a new set is created the following members of the semid_ds structure are initialized.

- The ipc_perm structure is initialized as described in Section 14.6.2. The mode member of this structure is set to the corresponding permission bits of *flag*. These permissions are specified with the constants from Figure 14.14.
- sem_otime is set to 0.
- sem_ctime is set to the current time.
- sem_nsems is set to *nsems*.

nsems is the number of semaphores in the set. If a new set is being created (typically in the server) we must specify *nsems*. If we are referencing an existing set (a client) we can specify *nsems* as 0.

The semctl function is the catchall for various semaphore operations.

```
#include <sys/types.h>
#include <sys/ipc.h>
#include <sys/sem.h>

int semctl(int semid, int semnum, int cmd, union semun arg);
```

Returns: (see following)

Notice that the final argument is the actual union, not a pointer to the union.

```
union semun {
  int              val;    /* for SETVAL */
  struct semid_ds  *buf;   /* for IPC_STAT and IPC_SET */
  ushort           *array; /* for GETALL and SETALL */
};
```

The *cmd* argument specifies one of the following 10 commands to be performed, on the set specified by *semid*. The five commands that refer to one particular semaphore value use *semnum* to specify one member of the set. The value of *semnum* is between 0 and *nsems–1*, inclusive.

IPC_STAT   Fetch the `semid_ds` structure for this set, storing it in the structure pointed to by *arg.buf*.

IPC_SET   Set the following three fields from the structure pointed to by *arg.buf* in the structure associated with this set: `sem_perm.uid`, `sem_perm.gid`, and `sem_perm.mode`. This command can be executed only by a process whose effective user ID equals `sem_perm.cuid` or `sem_perm.uid`, or by a process with superuser privileges.

IPC_RMID   Remove the semaphore set from the system. This removal is immediate. Any other process still using the semaphore will get an error of `EIDRM` on its next attempted operation on the semaphore. This command can be executed only by a process whose effective user ID equals `sem_perm.cuid` or `sem_perm.uid`, or by a process with superuser privileges.

GETVAL   Return the value of `semval` for the member *semnum*.

SETVAL   Set the value of `semval` for the member *semnum*. The value is specified by *arg.val*.

GETPID   Return the value of `sempid` for the member *semnum*.

GETNCNT   Return the value of `semncnt` for the member *semnum*.

GETZCNT   Return the value of `semzcnt` for the member *semnum*.

GETALL   Fetch all the semaphore values in the set. These values are stored in the array pointed to by *arg.array*.

SETALL   Set all the semaphore values in the set to the values pointed to by *arg.array*.

For all the GET commands other than GETALL, the function returns the corresponding value. For the remaining commands, the return value is 0.

The function `semop` atomically performs an array of operations on a semaphore set.

```
#include <sys/types.h>
#include <sys/ipc.h>
#include <sys/sem.h>

int semop(int semid, struct sembuf semoparray[], size_t nops);
```

Returns: 0 if OK, −1 on error

semoparray is a pointer to an array of semaphore operations.

```
struct sembuf {
  ushort  sem_num;  /* member # in set (0, 1, ..., nsems-1) */
  short   sem_op;   /* operation (negative, 0, or positive) */
  short   sem_flg;  /* IPC_NOWAIT, SEM_UNDO */
};
```

nops specifies the number of operations (elements) in the array.

The operation on each member of the set is specified by the corresponding sem_op value. This value can be negative, 0, or positive. (In the following discussion we refer to the "undo" flag for a semaphore. This flag corresponds to the SEM_UNDO bit in the corresponding sem_flg member.)

1. The easiest case is when sem_op is positive. This corresponds to the returning of resources by the process. The value of sem_op is added to the semaphore's value. If the undo flag is specified, sem_op is also subtracted from the semaphore's adjustment value for this process.

2. If sem_op is negative this means we want to obtain resources that the semaphore controls.

   If the semaphore's value is greater than or equal to the absolute value of sem_op (the resources are available), the absolute value of sem_op is subtracted from the semaphore's value. This guarantees that the resulting value for the semaphore is greater than or equal to 0. If the undo flag is specified, the absolute value of sem_op is also added to the semaphore's adjustment value for this process.

   If the semaphore's value is less than the absolute value of sem_op (the resources are not available):

   a. if IPC_NOWAIT is specified, return is made with an error of EAGAIN;

   b. if IPC_NOWAIT is not specified, the semncnt value for this semaphore is incremented (since we're about to go to sleep) and the calling process is suspended until one of the following occurs.

      i. The semaphore's value becomes greater than or equal to the absolute value of sem_op (i.e., some other process has released some resources).

The value of semncnt for this semaphore is decremented (since we're done waiting) and the absolute value of sem_op is subtracted from the semaphore's value. If the undo flag is specified, the absolute value of sem_op is also added to the semaphore's adjustment value for this process.

ii.   The semaphore is removed from the system. In this case the function returns an error of ERMID.

iii. A signal is caught by the process and the signal handler returns. In this case the value of semncnt for this semaphore is decremented (since we're no longer waiting) and the function returns an error of EINTR.

3. If sem_op is 0 this means we want to wait until the semaphore's value becomes 0.

If the semaphore's value is currently 0, the function returns immediately.

If the semaphore's value is nonzero:

a. if IPC_NOWAIT is specified, return is made with an error of EAGAIN;

b. if IPC_NOWAIT is not specified, the semzcnt value for this semaphore is incremented (since we're about to go to sleep) and the calling process is suspended until one of the following occurs.

i.   The semaphore's value becomes 0. The value of semzcnt for this semaphore is decremented (since we're done waiting).

ii. The semaphore is removed from the system. In this case the function returns an error of ERMID.

iii. A signal is caught by the process and the signal handler returns. In this case the value of semzcnt for this semaphore is decremented (since we're no longer waiting) and the function returns an error of EINTR.

The atomicity of semop is because it either does all the operations in the array or it does none of them.

Semaphore Adjustment on exit

As we mentioned earlier, it is a problem if a process terminates while it has resources allocated through a semaphore. Whenever we specify the SEM_UNDO flag for a semaphore operation, and we allocate resources (a sem_op value less than 0), the kernel remembers how many resources we allocated from that particular semaphore (the absolute value of sem_op). When the process terminates, either voluntary or involuntary, the kernel checks to see if the process has any outstanding semaphore adjustments and, if so, applies the adjustment to the corresponding semaphore.

If we set the value of a semaphore using semctl, with either the SETVAL or SETALL commands, the adjustment value for that semaphore in all processes is set to 0.

Example—Timing Comparison of Semaphores versus Record Locking

If we are sharing a single resource among multiple processes, we can use either a semaphore or record locking. It's interesting to compare the timing differences between the two techniques.

With a semaphore we create a semaphore set consisting of a single member and initialize the semaphore's value to 1. To allocate the resource we call semop with a sem_op of −1, and to release the resource we perform a sem_op of +1. We also specify SEM_UNDO with each operation, to handle the case of a process that terminates without releasing its resource.

With record locking we create an empty file and use the first byte of the file (which need not exist) as the lock byte. To allocate the resource we obtain a write lock on the byte, and to release it we unlock the byte. The properties of record locking guarantee that any process that terminates while holding a lock, has the lock automatically released by the kernel.

Figure 14.19 shows the time required to perform these two locking techniques on two different systems. In each case the resource was allocated and then released 10,000 times. This was done simultaneously by three different processes. The times in Figure 14.19 are the totals in seconds for all three processes.

Operation	SPARC, SunOS 4.1.1			80386, SVR4		
	User	System	Clock	User	System	Clock
semaphores with undo	0.9	13.9	15.0	0.5	13.1	13.7
advisory record locking	1.1	15.2	16.5	2.1	20.6	22.9

Figure 14.19 Timing comparison of semaphore locking and record locking.

On the SPARC, there is about a 10% penalty in the system time for record locking compared of semaphore locking. On the 80386 this penalty increases to about 50%.

Even though record locking is slightly slower than semaphore locking, if we're locking a single resource (such as a shared memory segment) and don't need all the fancy features of System V semaphores, record locking is preferred. The reasons are (a) it is much simpler to use, and (b) the system takes care of any lingering locks when a process terminates. □

14.9 Shared Memory

Shared memory allows two or more processes to share a given region of memory. This is the fastest form of IPC because the data does not need to be copied between the client and server. The only trick in using shared memory is synchronizing access to a given region among multiple processes. If the server is placing data into a shared memory region, the client shouldn't try to access the data until the server is done. Often semaphores are used to synchronize shared memory access. (But as we saw at the end of the previous section, record locking can also be used.)

The kernel maintains the following structure for each shared memory segment.

```
struct shmid_ds {
    struct ipc_perm  shm_perm; /* see Section 14.6.2 */
    struct anon_map *shm_amp;  /* pointer in kernel */
    int       shm_segsz;   /* size of segment in bytes */
    ushort    shm_lkcnt;   /* number of times segment is being locked */
    pid_t     shm_lpid;    /* pid of last shmop() */
    pid_t     shm_cpid;    /* pid of creator */
    ulong     shm_nattch;  /* number of current attaches */
    ulong     shm_cnattch; /* used only for shminfo */
    time_t    shm_atime;   /* last-attach time */
    time_t    shm_dtime;   /* last-detach time */
    time_t    shm_ctime;   /* last-change time */
};
```

Figure 14.20 lists the system limits (Section 14.6.3) that affect shared memory.

Name	Description	Typical Value
SHMMAX	The maximum size in bytes of a shared memory segment.	131,072
SHMMIN	The minimum size in bytes of a shared memory segment.	1
SHMMNI	The maximum number of shared memory segments, systemwide.	100
SHMSEG	The maximum number of shared memory segments, per process.	6

Figure 14.20 System limits that affect shared memory.

The first function called is usually shmget, to obtain a shared memory identifier.

```
#include <sys/types.h>
#include <sys/ipc.h>
#include <sys/shm.h>

int shmget(key_t key, int size, int flag);
```
                                        Returns: shared memory ID if OK, −1 on error

In Section 14.6.1 we described the rules for converting the *key* into an identifier and whether a new segment is created or an existing segment is referenced. When a new segment is created the following members of the shmid_ds structure are initialized.

- The ipc_perm structure is initialized as described in Section 14.6.2. The mode member of this structure is set to the corresponding permission bits of *flag*. These permissions are specified with the constants from Figure 14.14.
- shm_lpid, shm_nattach, shm_atime, and shm_dtime are all set to 0.
- shm_ctime is set to the current time.

size is the minimum size of the shared memory segment. If a new segment is being created (typically in the server) we must specify its *size*. If we are referencing an existing segment (a client) we can specify *size* as 0.

The `shmctl` function is the catchall for various shared memory operations.

```
#include <sys/types.h>
#include <sys/ipc.h>
#include <sys/shm.h>

int shmctl(int shmid, int cmd, struct shmid_ds *buf);
```

Returns: 0 if OK, −1 on error

The *cmd* argument specifies one of the following five commands to be performed, on the segment specified by *shmid*.

IPC_STAT   Fetch the shmid_ds structure for this segment, storing it in the structure pointed to by *buf*.

IPC_SET   Set the following three fields from the structure pointed to by *buf* in the structure associated with this segment: shm_perm.uid, shm_perm.gid, and shm_perm.mode. This command can be executed only by a process whose effective user ID equals shm_perm.cuid or shm_perm.uid, or by a process with superuser privileges.

IPC_RMID   Remove the shared memory segment set from the system. Since an attachment count is maintained for shared memory segments (the shm_nattch field in the shmid_ds structure) the segment is not actually removed until the last process using the segment terminates or detaches it. Regardless whether the segment is still in use or not, the segment's identifier is immediately removed so that shmat can no longer attach the segment. This command can be executed only by a process whose effective user ID equals shm_perm.cuid or shm_perm.uid, or by a process with superuser privileges.

SHM_LOCK   Lock the shared memory segment in memory. This command can be executed only by the superuser.

SHM_UNLOCK Unlock the shared memory segment. This command can be executed only by the superuser.

Once a shared memory segment has been created, a process attaches it to its address space by calling shmat.

```
#include <sys/types.h>
#include <sys/ipc.h>
#include <sys/shm.h>

void *shmat(int shmid, void *addr, int flag);
```

Returns: pointer to shared memory segment if OK, −1 on error

The address in the calling process at which the segment is attached depends on the *addr* argument and whether the SHM_RND bit is specified in *flag*.

1. If *addr* is 0, the segment is attached at the first available address selected by the kernel. This is the recommended technique.

2. If *addr* is nonzero and SHM_RND is not specified, the segment is attached at the address given by *addr*.

3. If *addr* is nonzero and SHM_RND is specified, the segment is attached at the address given by *(addr − (addr modulus SHMLBA))*. The SHM_RND command stands for "round." SHMLBA stands for "low boundary address multiple" and is always a power of 2. What the arithmetic does is round the address down to the next multiple of SHMLBA.

Unless we plan to run the application on only a single type of hardware (which is highly unlikely today), we should not specify the address where the segment is to be attached. Instead we should specify an *addr* of 0 and let the system choose the address.

If the SHM_RDONLY bit is specified in *flag*, the segment is attached read-only. Otherwise the segment is attached read–write.

The value returned by shmat is the actual address that the segment is attached at, or −1 if an error occurred.

When we're done with a shared memory segment we call shmdt to detach it. Note that this does not remove the identifier and its associated data structure from the system. The identifier remains in existence until some process (often a server) specifically removes it by calling shmctl with a command of IPC_RMID.

```
#include <sys/types.h>
#include <sys/ipc.h>
#include <sys/shm.h>

int shmdt(void *addr);
```
                                                    Returns: 0 if OK, −1 on error

The *addr* argument is the value that was returned by a previous call to shmat.

Example

Where a kernel places shared memory segments that are attached with an address of 0 is highly system dependent. Program 14.11 prints some information on where one particular system places different types of data. Running this program on one particular system gives us the following output:

```
$ a.out
array[] from 18f48 to 22b88
stack around f7fffb2c
malloced from 24c28 to 3d2c8
shared memory attached from f77d0000 to f77e86a0
```

```
#include        <sys/types.h>
#include        <sys/ipc.h>
#include        <sys/shm.h>
#include        "ourhdr.h"

#define ARRAY_SIZE      40000
#define MALLOC_SIZE    100000
#define SHM_SIZE       100000
#define SHM_MODE        (SHM_R | SHM_W) /* user read/write */

char    array[ARRAY_SIZE];   /* uninitialized data = bss */

int
main(void)
{
    int     shmid;
    char    *ptr, *shmptr;

    printf("array[] from %x to %x\n", &array[0], &array[ARRAY_SIZE]);
    printf("stack around %x\n", &shmid);

    if ( (ptr = malloc(MALLOC_SIZE)) == NULL)
        err_sys("malloc error");
    printf("malloced from %x to %x\n", ptr, ptr+MALLOC_SIZE);

    if ( (shmid = shmget(IPC_PRIVATE, SHM_SIZE, SHM_MODE)) < 0)
        err_sys("shmget error");
    if ( (shmptr = shmat(shmid, 0, 0)) == (void *) -1)
        err_sys("shmat error");
    printf("shared memory attached from %x to %x\n",
                shmptr, shmptr+SHM_SIZE);
    if (shmctl(shmid, IPC_RMID, 0) < 0)
        err_sys("shmctl error");

    exit(0);
}
```

Program 14.11 Print where different types of data are stored.

Figure 14.21 shows a picture of this, similar to what we said was a typical memory layout in Figure 7.3. Notice that the shared memory segment is placed well below the stack. In fact, there is about eight megabytes of unused address space between the shared memory segment and the stack.   □

Example—Memory Mapping of /dev/zero

Shared memory can be used between unrelated processes. But if the processes are related, SVR4 provides a different technique.

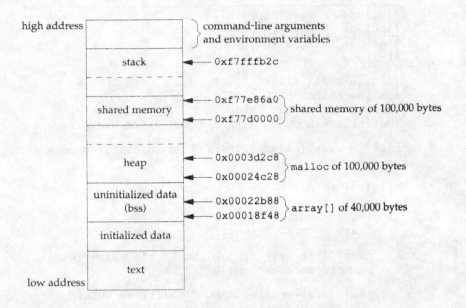

Figure 14.21 Memory layout on one particular system.

The device /dev/zero is an infinite source of 0 bytes when read. This device also accepts any data that is written to it, ignoring the data. Our interest in this device for IPC arises from its special properties when it is memory mapped.

- An unnamed memory region is created whose size is the second argument to mmap, rounded up to the nearest page size on the system.
- The memory region is initialized to 0.
- Multiple processes can share this region if a common ancestor specifies the MAP_SHARED flag to mmap.

Program 14.12 is an example that uses this special device. It opens the /dev/zero device and calls mmap specifying a size of a long integer. Notice that once the region is mapped, we can close the device. The process then creates a child. Since MAP_SHARED was specified in the call to mmap, writes to the memory mapped region by one process are seen by the other process. (If we had specified MAP_PRIVATE instead, this example wouldn't work.)

The parent and child then alternate running, incrementing a long integer in the shared memory mapped region, using the synchronization functions from Section 8.8. The memory mapped region is initialized to 0 by mmap. The parent increments it to 1, then the child increments it to 2, then the parent increments it to 3, and so on. Notice that we have to use parentheses when we increment the value of the long integer in the update function, since we are incrementing the value and not the pointer.

```
#include     <sys/types.h>
#include     <sys/mman.h>
#include     <fcntl.h>
#include     "ourhdr.h"

#define NLOOPS      1000
#define SIZE        sizeof(long)     /* size of shared memory area */

static int  update(long *);

int
main()
{
    int      fd, i, counter;
    pid_t    pid;
    caddr_t  area;

    if ( (fd = open("/dev/zero", O_RDWR)) < 0)
        err_sys("open error");
    if ( (area = mmap(0, SIZE, PROT_READ | PROT_WRITE,
                              MAP_SHARED, fd, 0)) == (caddr_t) -1)
        err_sys("mmap error");
    close(fd);          /* can close /dev/zero now that it's mapped */

    TELL_WAIT();
    if ( (pid = fork()) < 0) {
        err_sys("fork error");
    } else if (pid > 0) {               /* parent */
        for (i = 0; i < NLOOPS; i += 2) {
            if ( (counter = update((long *) area)) != i)
                err_quit("parent: expected %d, got %d", i, counter);
            TELL_CHILD(pid);
            WAIT_CHILD();
        }

    } else {                            /* child */
        for (i = 1; i < NLOOPS + 1; i += 2) {
            WAIT_PARENT();
            if ( (counter = update((long *) area)) != i)
                err_quit("child: expected %d, got %d", i, counter);
            TELL_PARENT(getppid());
        }
    }
    exit(0);
}
static int
update(long *ptr)
{
    return( (*ptr)++ ); /* return value before increment */
}
```

Program 14.12 IPC between parent and child using memory mapped I/O of /dev/zero.

The advantage of using /dev/zero in the manner that we've shown is that an actual file need not exist before we call mmap to create the mapped region. Mapping /dev/zero automatically creates a mapped region of the specified size. The disadvantage in this technique is that it works only between related processes. If shared memory is required between unrelated processes, the shmXXX functions must be used.   □

Example—Anonymous Memory Mapping

4.3+BSD provides a facility similar to the /dev/zero feature, called anonymous memory mapping. To use this feature we specify the MAP_ANON flag to mmap and specify the file descriptor as −1. The resulting region is anonymous (since it's not associated with a pathname through a file descriptor) and creates a memory region that can be shared with descendant processes.

To modify Program 14.12 to use this feature under 4.3+BSD we make two changes: (a) remove the open of /dev/zero, and (b) change the call to mmap to the following

```
if ( (area = mmap(0, SIZE, PROT_READ | PROT_WRITE,
                MAP_ANON | MAP_SHARED, -1, 0)) == (caddr_t) -1)
```

In this call we specify the MAP_ANON flag, and set the file descriptor to −1. The rest of Program 14.12 is unchanged.   □

14.10 Client–Server Properties

Let's detail some of the properties of clients and servers that are affected by the different types of IPC used between them.

The simplest type of relationship is to have the client fork and exec the desired server. Two one-way pipes can be created before the fork to allow data to be transferred in both directions. Figure 14.9 is an example of this. The server that is execed can be a set-user-ID program, giving it special privileges. Also, it can determine the real identity of the client by looking at its real user ID. (Recall from Section 8.9 that the real user ID and real group ID don't change across an exec.)

With this arrangement we can build an "open server." (We show an implementation of this client–server in Section 15.4.) It opens files for the client, instead of client calling the open function. This way additional permission checking can be added, above and beyond the normal Unix user/group/other permissions. We assume that the server is a set-user-ID program, giving it additional permissions (root permission, perhaps). The server uses the real user ID of the client to determine whether to give it access to the requested file or not. This way we can build a server that allows certain users permissions that they don't normally have.

In this example, since the server is a child of the parent, all it can do is pass back the contents of the file to the parent. While this works fine for regular files, it can't be used for special device files, for example. What we would like to be able to do is have the server open the requested file and pass back the file descriptor. While a parent can pass a child an open descriptor, a child cannot pass a descriptor back to the parent (unless special programming techniques are used, which we cover in the next chapter).

The next type of server we showed in Figure 14.13. The server is a daemon process that is contacted using some form of IPC by all clients. We can't use pipes for this type of client–server. A form of named IPC is required, such as FIFOs or message queues. With FIFOs we saw that an individual per-client FIFO is also required, if the server is to send data back to the client. If the client–server application sends data only from the client to the server, a single well-known FIFO suffices. (The System V line printer spooler uses this form of client–server. The client is the lp(1) command and the server is the lpsched process. A single FIFO is used since the flow of data is only from the client to the server. Nothing is sent back to the client.)

Multiple possibilities exist with message queues.

1. A single queue can be used between the server and all the clients, using the type field of each message to indicate who the message is for. For example, the clients can send their requests with a type field of 1. Included in the request must be the client's process ID. The server then sends the response with the type field set to the client's process ID. The server receives only the messages with a type field of 1 (the fourth argument for msgrcv), and the clients receive only the messages with a type field equal to their process IDs.

2. Alternately, an individual message queue can be used for each client. Before sending the first request to a server, each client creates its own message queue with a key of IPC_PRIVATE. The server also has its own queue, with a key or identifier known to all clients. The client sends its first request to the server's well-known queue, and this request must contain the message queue ID of the client's queue. The server sends its first response to the client's queue, and all future requests and responses are exchanged on this queue.

   One problem with this technique is that each client-specific queue usually has only a single message on it—a request for the server or a response for a client. This seems wasteful of a limited systemwide resource (a message queue) and a FIFO can be used instead. Another problem is that the server has to read messages from multiple queues. Neither select or poll work with message queues.

Either of these two techniques using message queues can be implemented using shared memory segments and a synchronization method (a semaphore or record locking). The problem with shared memory is that only a single "message" can be in a shared memory segment at a time—similar to a message queue with a limit of one message per queue. For this reason shared memory IPC normally uses one shared memory segment per client.

The problem with this type of client–server relationship (the client and the server being unrelated processes) is for the server to identify the client accurately. Unless the server is performing a nonprivileged operation, it is essential that the server know who the client is. This is required, for example, if the server is a set-user-ID program. Although all these forms of IPC go through the kernel, there is no facility provided by them to have the kernel identify the sender.

With message queues, if a single queue is used between the client and server (so that only a single message is on the queue at a time, for example), the `msg_lspid` of the queue contains the process ID of the other process. But when writing the server, we want the effective user ID of the client, not its process ID. There is no portable way to obtain the effective user ID, given the process ID. (Naturally the kernel maintains both values in the process table entry, but other than rummaging around through the kernel's memory, we can't obtain one, given the other.)

We'll use the following technique in Section 15.5.2 to allow the server to identify the client. The same technique can be used with either FIFOs, message queues, semaphores, or shared memory. For the following description, assume FIFOs are being used, as in Figure 14.13. The client must create its own FIFO and set the file access permissions of the FIFO so that only user-read and user-write are on. We assume the server has superuser privileges (or else it probably wouldn't care about the client's true identity), so the server can still read and write to this FIFO. When the server receives the client's first request on the server's well-known FIFO (which must contain the identity of the client-specific FIFO) the server calls either `stat` or `fstat` on the client-specific FIFO. The assumption made by the server is that the effective user ID of the client is the owner of the FIFO (the `st_uid` field of the `stat` structure). The server verifies that only the user-read and user-write permissions are enabled. As another check the server should also look at the three times associated with the FIFO (the `st_atime`, `st_mtime`, and `st_ctime` fields of the `stat` structure) to verify that they are recent (no older than 15 or 30 seconds, for example). If a malicious client can create a FIFO with someone else as the owner and set the file's permission bits to user-read and user-write only, then there are other fundamental security problems in the system.

To use this technique with System V IPC, recall that the `ipc_perm` structure associated with each message queue, semaphore, and shared memory segment identifies the creator of the IPC structure (the `cuid` and `cgid` fields). As with the FIFO example, the server should require the client to create the IPC structure and have the client set the access permissions to user-read and user-write only. The times associated with the IPC structure should also be verified by the server to be recent (since these IPC structures hang around until explicitly deleted).

We'll see in Section 15.5.1 that a far better way of doing this authentication is for the kernel to provide the effective user ID and effective group ID of the client. This is done by SVR4 when file descriptors are passed between processes.

14.11 Summary

We've detailed numerous forms of interprocess communication: pipes, named pipes (FIFOs), and the three forms of IPC commonly called System V IPC—message queues, semaphores, and shared memory. Semaphores are really a synchronization primitive, not true IPC, and are often used to synchronize access to a shared resource, such as a shared memory segment. With pipes we looked at the implementation of the `popen` function, at coprocesses, and the pitfalls that can be encountered with the standard I/O library's buffering.

After comparing the timing of message queues versus stream pipes, and semaphores versus record locking, we can make the following recommendations: learn pipes and FIFOs, since there are numerous applications where these two basic techniques can still be used effectively. Avoid using message queues and semaphores in any new applications. Stream pipes and record locking should be considered instead, as they integrate with the rest of the Unix kernel far better. Shared memory still has its use, although the mmap function (Section 12.9) may assume some of its capabilities in future releases.

In the next chapter we look at some advanced forms of IPC that are provided with newer systems, such as SVR4 and 4.3+BSD.

Exercises

14.1 In Program 14.2, at the end of the parent code, remove the close right before the waitpid. Explain what happens.

14.2 In Program 14.2, at the end of the parent code, remove the waitpid. Explain what happens.

14.3 What happens if the argument to popen is a nonexistent command? Write a small program to test this.

14.4 In Program 14.9 remove the signal handler, execute the program and then terminate the child. After entering a line of input, how can you tell that the parent was terminated by SIGPIPE?

14.5 In Program 14.9 use the standard I/O library for reading and writing the pipes instead of read and write.

14.6 The Rationale for POSIX.1 gives as one of the reasons for adding the waitpid function the fact that most pre-POSIX.1 systems can't handle the following:

```
if ( (fp = popen("/bin/true", "r")) == NULL)
    ...
if ( (rc = system("sleep 100")) == -1)
    ...
if (pclose(fp) == -1)
    ...
```

What happens in this code if waitpid isn't available, and wait is used instead?

14.7 Explain how select and poll handle an input descriptor that is a pipe, when the pipe is closed by the writer. Write two small test programs, one using select and one using poll to determine the answer.

Redo this exercise looking at an output descriptor that is a pipe, when the read end is closed.

14.8 What happens if the *cmdstring* executed by popen with a *type* of "r" writes to its standard error?

14.9 Since popen invokes a shell to execute its *cmdstring* argument, what happens when cmdstring terminates? (Hint: draw all the processes involved.)

14.10 POSIX.1 specifically states that opening a FIFO for read–write is undefined. While most Unix systems allow this, show another method for opening a FIFO for both reading and writing, without blocking.

14.11 Unless a file contains sensitive or confidential data, allowing other users to read the file causes no harm. (It is usually considered antisocial, however, to go snooping around in other's files.) But what happens if a malicious process reads a message from a message queue that is being used by a server and several clients? What information does the malicious process need to know to read the message queue?

14.12 Write a program that does the following. Execute a loop five times: create a message queue, print the queue identifier, delete the message queue. Then execute the next loop five times: create a message queue with a key of IPC_PRIVATE, and place a message on the queue. After the program terminates look at the message queues using ipcs(1). Explain what is happening with the queue identifiers.

14.13 Describe how to build a linked list of data objects in a shared memory segment. What would you store as the list pointers?

14.14 Draw a time line of Program 14.12 showing the value of the variable i in both the parent and child, the value of the long integer in the shared memory region, and the value returned by the update function. Assume the child runs first after the fork.

14.15 Redo Program 14.12 using the shmXXX functions from Section 14.9 instead of the shared memory mapped region.

14.16 Redo Program 14.12 using the System V semaphore functions from Section 14.8 to alternate between the parent and child.

14.17 Redo Program 14.12 using advisory record locking to alternate between the parent and child.

14.18 Explain how the file descriptor argument for mmap can be used with 4.3+BSD anonymous memory mapping to allow unrelated processes to share memory.

Advanced

Interprocess Communication

15.1 Introduction

In the previous chapter we looked at the classical methods of IPC provided by various Unix systems: pipes, FIFOs, message queues, semaphores, and shared memory. In this chapter we look at some advanced forms of IPC and what we can do with them: stream pipes and named stream pipes. With these two forms of IPC we can pass open file descriptors between processes, and clients can rendezvous with a daemon server with the system providing a unique IPC channel per client. These advanced forms of IPC were provided with 4.2BSD and SVR3.2, but have not been widely documented or used. Many of the ideas in this chapter come from the paper by Presotto and Ritchie [1990].

15.2 Stream Pipes

A stream pipe is just a bidirectional (full-duplex) pipe. To obtain bidirectional data flow between a parent and child, only a single stream pipe is required. Figure 15.1 shows the two ways to view a stream pipe. The only difference between this picture and Figure 14.2 is that the arrows have heads on both ends, since the stream pipe is full duplex.

Example

Let's redo the coprocess example, Program 14.9, with a single stream pipe. Program 15.1 is the new main function. The add2 coprocess is the same (Program 14.8). We call a new function, s_pipe, to create a single stream pipe. (We show versions of this function for SVR4 and 4.3+BSD in the following sections.)

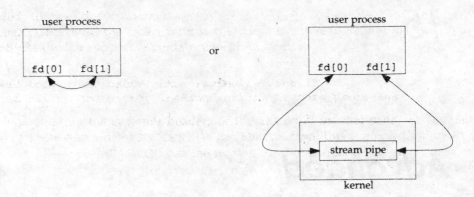

Figure 15.1 Two ways to view a stream pipe.

```
#include     <signal.h>
#include     "ourhdr.h"

static void sig_pipe(int);          /* our signal handler */

int
main(void)
{
    int     n, fd[2];
    pid_t   pid;
    char    line[MAXLINE];

    if (signal(SIGPIPE, sig_pipe) == SIG_ERR)
        err_sys("signal error");

    if (s_pipe(fd) < 0)             /* only need a single stream pipe */
        err_sys("pipe error");

    if ( (pid = fork()) < 0)
        err_sys("fork error");
    else if (pid > 0) {                              /* parent */
        close(fd[1]);
        while (fgets(line, MAXLINE, stdin) != NULL) {
            n = strlen(line);
            if (write(fd[0], line, n) != n)
                err_sys("write error to pipe");
            if ( (n = read(fd[0], line, MAXLINE)) < 0)
                err_sys("read error from pipe");
            if (n == 0) {
                err_msg("child closed pipe");
                break;
            }
            line[n] = 0;     /* null terminate */
```

```
                    if (fputs(line, stdout) == EOF)
                        err_sys("fputs error");
            }
            if (ferror(stdin))
                err_sys("fgets error on stdin");
            exit(0);

    } else {                                        /* child */
        close(fd[0]);
        if (fd[1] != STDIN_FILENO) {
            if (dup2(fd[1], STDIN_FILENO) != STDIN_FILENO)
                err_sys("dup2 error to stdin");
        }
        if (fd[1] != STDOUT_FILENO) {
            if (dup2(fd[1], STDOUT_FILENO) != STDOUT_FILENO)
                err_sys("dup2 error to stdout");
        }
        if (execl("./add2", "add2", NULL) < 0)
            err_sys("execl error");
    }
}

static void
sig_pipe(int signo)
{
    printf("SIGPIPE caught\n");
    exit(1);
}
```

Program 15.1 Program to drive the add2 filter, using a stream pipe.

The parent uses only fd[0] and the child uses only fd[1]. Since each end of the stream pipe is full duplex, the parent reads and writes fd[0] and the child duplicates fd[1] to both standard input and standard output. Figure 15.2 shows the resulting descriptors.

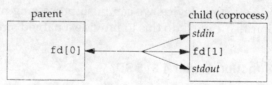

Figure 15.2 Arrangement of descriptors for coprocess.

We define the function s_pipe to be similar to the standard pipe function. It takes the same argument as pipe, but the returned descriptors are open for reading and writing.

Example—s_pipe Function Under SVR4

Program 15.2 shows the SVR4 version of the s_pipe function. It just calls the standard pipe function, which creates a full-duplex pipe.

```
#include    "ourhdr.h"

int
s_pipe(int fd[2])  /* two file descriptors returned in fd[0] & fd[1] */
{
    return( pipe(fd) );
}
```

Program 15.2 SVR4 version of the s_pipe function.

Stream pipes can also be created under earlier versions of System V, but it takes more work. See Section 7.9 of Stevens [1990] for the details involved under SVR3.2.

Figure 15.3 shows what a pipe looks like under SVR4. It is just two stream heads that are connected to each other.

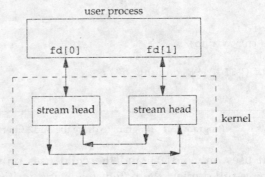

Figure 15.3 Arrangement of a pipe under SVR4.

Since a pipe is a streams device, we can push processing modules onto either end of the pipe. In Section 15.5.1 we'll do this to provide a named stream that can be mounted. □

Example—s_pipe Function Under 4.3+BSD

Program 15.3 shows the BSD version of the s_pipe function. This function works under 4.2BSD and any later versions. It creates a pair of connected Unix domain stream sockets.

Normal pipes have been implemented in this fashion since 4.2BSD. But when pipe is called, the write end of the first descriptor and the read end of the second descriptor are both closed. To get a full-duplex pipe we must call socketpair directly. □

```
#include      <sys/types.h>
#include      <sys/socket.h>
#include      "ourhdr.h"

int
s_pipe(int fd[2]) /* two file descriptors returned in fd[0] & fd[1] */
{
      return( socketpair(AF_UNIX, SOCK_STREAM, 0, fd) );
}
```

Program 15.3 BSD version of the s_pipe function.

15.3 Passing File Descriptors

The ability to pass an open file descriptor between processes is powerful. It can lead to different ways of designing client–server applications. It allows one process (typically a server) to do everything that is required to open a file (involving details such as translation of a network name to a network address, dialing a modem, negotiating locks for the file, etc.) and just pass back to the calling process a descriptor that can be used with all the I/O functions. All the details involved in opening the file or device are transparent to the client.

> 4.2BSD supported the passing of open descriptors, but there were some bugs in the implementation. 4.3BSD fixed these bugs. SVR3.2 and above also support the passing of open descriptors.

We must be more specific about what we mean by "passing an open file descriptor" from one process to another. Recall Figure 3.3 where we showed two processes that have opened the same file. Although they share the same v-node table, each process has its own file table entry.

When we pass an open file descriptor from one process to another, we want the passing process and the receiving process to also share the same file table entry. Figure 15.4 shows the desired arrangement. Technically we are really passing a pointer to an open file table entry from one process to another. This pointer is assigned the first available descriptor in the receiving process. (Saying that we are passing an open descriptor mistakenly gives the impression that the descriptor number in the receiving process is the same as in the sending process, which usually isn't true.) Having two processes share an open file table is exactly what happens after a fork (recall Figure 8.1).

What normally happens when a descriptor is passed from one process to another is that the sending process, after passing the descriptor, then closes the descriptor. Closing the descriptor by the sender doesn't really close the file or device, since the descriptor is still considered open by the receiving process (even if the receiver hasn't specifically received the descriptor yet).

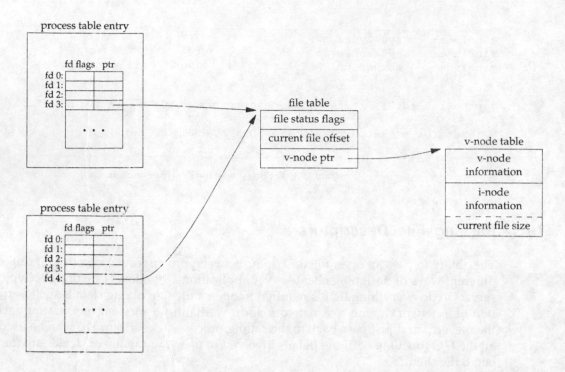

Figure 15.4 Passing an open file from the top process to the bottom process.

We define the following three functions that we use in this chapter (and in Chapter 18) to send and receive file descriptors. Later in this section we'll show the actual code for these three functions, for both SVR4 and 4.3+BSD.

```
#include "ourhdr.h"

int send_fd(int spipefd, int filedes);

int send_err(int spipefd, int status, const char *errmsg);

                                                Both return: 0 if OK, −1 on error

int recv_fd(int spipefd, ssize_t (*userfunc)(int, const void *, size_t));

                                                Returns: file descriptor if OK, <0 on error
```

When a process (normally a server) wants to pass a descriptor to another process it calls either send_fd or send_err. The process waiting to receive the descriptor (the client) calls recv_fd.

send_fd sends the descriptor *filedes* across the stream pipe *spipefd*. send_err sends the *errmsg* across the stream pipe *spipefd*, followed by the *status* byte. The value of *status* must be in the range −1 through −255.

recv_fd is called by the client to receive a descriptor. If all is OK (the sender called send_fd), the nonnegative descriptor is returned as the value of the function. Otherwise the value returned is the *status* that was sent by send_err (a negative value in the range −1 through −255). Additionally, if an error message was sent by the server, the client's *userfunc* is called to process the message. The first argument to *userfunc* is the constant STDERR_FILENO, followed by a pointer to the error message and its length. Often the client specifies the normal Unix write function as the *userfunc*.

We implement our own protocol that is used by these three functions. To send a descriptor, send_fd sends two bytes of 0, followed by the actual descriptor. To send an error, send_err sends the *errmsg*, followed by a byte of 0, followed by the absolute value of the *status* byte (1 through 255). recv_fd just reads everything on the stream pipe until it encounters a null byte. Any characters read up to this point are passed to the caller's *userfunc*. The next byte read by recv_fd is the status byte. If the status byte is 0, a descriptor was passed, otherwise there is no descriptor to receive.

The function send_err just calls the send_fd function, after writing the error message to the stream pipe. This is shown in Program 15.4.

```
#include     "ourhdr.h"

/* Used when we had planned to send an fd using send_fd(),
 * but encountered an error instead.  We send the error back
 * using the send_fd()/recv_fd() protocol. */

int
send_err(int clifd, int errcode, const char *msg)
{
    int     n;

    if ( (n = strlen(msg)) > 0)
        if (writen(clifd, msg, n) != n)  /* send the error message */
            return(-1);

    if (errcode >= 0)
        errcode = -1;    /* must be negative */

    if (send_fd(clifd, errcode) < 0)
        return(-1);

    return(0);
}
```

Program 15.4 The send_err function.

The following three sections look at the actual implementation of the two functions send_fd and recv_fd under SVR4, 4.3BSD, and 4.3+BSD.

15.3.1 System V Release 4

Under SVR4 file descriptors are exchanged on a stream pipe using two ioctl commands: I_SENDFD and I_RECVFD. To send a descriptor we just set the third argument for ioctl to the actual descriptor. This is shown in Program 15.5.

```
#include     <sys/types.h>
#include     <stropts.h>
#include     "ourhdr.h"

/* Pass a file descriptor to another process.
 * If fd<0, then -fd is sent back instead as the error status. */

int
send_fd(int clifd, int fd)
{
    char    buf[2];         /* send_fd()/recv_fd() 2-byte protocol */

    buf[0] = 0;             /* null byte flag to recv_fd() */
    if (fd < 0) {
        buf[1] = -fd;       /* nonzero status means error */
        if (buf[1] == 0)
            buf[1] = 1; /* -256, etc. would screw up protocol */
    } else {
        buf[1] = 0;         /* zero status means OK */
    }

    if (write(clifd, buf, 2) != 2)
        return(-1);

    if (fd >= 0)
        if (ioctl(clifd, I_SENDFD, fd) < 0)
            return(-1);
    return(0);
}
```

Program 15.5 The send_fd function for SVR4.

When we receive a descriptor the third argument for ioctl is a pointer to a
strrecvfd structure.

```
struct strrecvfd {
  int    fd;        /* new descriptor */
  uid_t  uid;       /* effective user ID of sender */
  gid_t  gid;       /* effective group ID of sender */
  char   fill[8];
};
```

recv_fd just reads the stream pipe until the first byte of the two-byte protocol (the null
byte) is received. When we issue the ioctl of I_RECVFD the next message at the
stream's read head must be a descriptor from a I_SENDFD, or we get an error. This is
shown in Program 15.6.

```
#include     <sys/types.h>
#include     <stropts.h>
#include     "ourhdr.h"

/* Receive a file descriptor from another process (a server).
 * In addition, any data received from the server is passed
```

```
 * to (*userfunc)(STDERR_FILENO, buf, nbytes).  We have a
 * 2-byte protocol for receiving the fd from send_fd(). */

int
recv_fd(int servfd, ssize_t (*userfunc)(int, const void *, size_t))
{
    int                 newfd, nread, flag, status;
    char                *ptr, buf[MAXLINE];
    struct strbuf       dat;
    struct strrecvfd    recvfd;

    status = -1;
    for ( ; ; ) {
        dat.buf = buf;
        dat.maxlen = MAXLINE;
        flag = 0;
        if (getmsg(servfd, NULL, &dat, &flag) < 0)
            err_sys("getmsg error");
        nread = dat.len;
        if (nread == 0) {
            err_ret("connection closed by server");
            return(-1);
        }
            /* See if this is the final data with null & status.
               Null must be next to last byte of buffer, status
               byte is last byte.  Zero status means there must
               be a file descriptor to receive. */
        for (ptr = buf; ptr < &buf[nread]; ) {
            if (*ptr++ == 0) {
                if (ptr != &buf[nread-1])
                    err_dump("message format error");
                status = *ptr & 255;
                if (status == 0) {
                    if (ioctl(servfd, I_RECVFD, &recvfd) < 0)
                        return(-1);
                    newfd = recvfd.fd;   /* new descriptor */
                } else
                    newfd = -status;
                nread -= 2;
            }
        }
        if (nread > 0)
            if ((*userfunc)(STDERR_FILENO, buf, nread) != nread)
                return(-1);

        if (status >= 0)     /* final data has arrived */
            return(newfd);   /* descriptor, or -status */
    }
}
```

Program 15.6 The recv_fd function for SVR4.

15.3.2 4.3BSD

Unfortunately, we have to provide different implementations for 4.3BSD (and vendor's systems built on 4.3BSD, such as SunOS and Ultrix), and later versions starting with 4.3BSD Reno.

To exchange file descriptors we call the sendmsg(2) and recvmsg(2) functions. Both functions take a pointer to a msghdr structure that contains all the information on what to send or receive. This structure is defined in the <sys/socket.h> header and under 4.3BSD it looks like

```
struct msghdr {
   caddr_t        msg_name;       /* optional address */
   int            msg_namelen; /* size of address */
   struct iovec *msg_iov;       /* scatter/gather array */
   int            msg_iovlen;  /* # elements in msg_iov array */
   caddr_t        msg_accrights;   /* access rights sent/received */
   int            msg_accrightslen; /* size of access rights buffer */
};
```

The first two elements are normally used for sending datagrams on a network connection, where the destination address can be specified with each datagram. The next two elements allow us to specify an array of buffers (scatter read or gather write) as we described for the readv and writev functions (Section 12.7). The final two elements deal with the passing or receiving of access rights. The only access rights currently defined are file descriptors. Access rights can be passed only across a Unix domain socket (i.e., what we use as stream pipes under 4.3BSD). To send or receive a file descriptor we set msg_accrights to point to the integer descriptor and msg_accrightslen to be the length of the descriptor (i.e., the size of an integer). A descriptor is passed or received only if this length is nonzero.

Program 15.7 is the send_fd function for 4.3BSD.

```
#include        <sys/types.h>
#include        <sys/socket.h>        /* struct msghdr */
#include        <sys/uio.h>           /* struct iovec */
#include        <errno.h>
#include        <stddef.h>
#include        "ourhdr.h"

/* Pass a file descriptor to another process.
 * If fd<0, then -fd is sent back instead as the error status. */

int
send_fd(int clifd, int fd)
{
    struct iovec     iov[1];
    struct msghdr    msg;
    char             buf[2]; /* send_fd()/recv_fd() 2-byte protocol */

    iov[0].iov_base = buf;
    iov[0].iov_len  = 2;
```

```
        msg.msg_iov     = iov;
        msg.msg_iovlen  = 1;
        msg.msg_name    = NULL;
        msg.msg_namelen = 0;

        if (fd < 0) {
            msg.msg_accrights    = NULL;
            msg.msg_accrightslen = 0;
            buf[1] = fd;    /* nonzero status means error */
            if (buf[1] == 0)
                buf[1] = 1; /* -256, etc. would screw up protocol */
        } else {
            msg.msg_accrights    = (caddr_t) &fd;   /* addr of descriptor */
            msg.msg_accrightslen = sizeof(int);     /* pass 1 descriptor */
            buf[1] = 0;     /* zero status means OK */
        }
        buf[0] = 0;             /* null byte flag to recv_fd() */

        if (sendmsg(clifd, &msg, 0) != 2)
            return(-1);

        return(0);
}
```

Program 15.7 The send_fd function for 4.3BSD.

In the sendmsg call we send both the two bytes of protocol data (the null and the status byte) and the descriptor.

To receive a file descriptor we read from the stream pipe until we read the null byte that precedes the final status byte. Everything up to this null byte is an error message from the sender. This is shown in Program 15.8.

```
#include        <sys/types.h>
#include        <sys/socket.h>      /* struct msghdr */
#include        <sys/uio.h>         /* struct iovec */
#include        <stddef.h>
#include        "ourhdr.h"

/* Receive a file descriptor from another process (a server).
 * In addition, any data received from the server is passed
 * to (*userfunc)(STDERR_FILENO, buf, nbytes).  We have a
 * 2-byte protocol for receiving the fd from send_fd(). */

int
recv_fd(int servfd, ssize_t (*userfunc)(int, const void *, size_t))
{
    int             newfd, nread, status;
    char            *ptr, buf[MAXLINE];
    struct iovec    iov[1];
    struct msghdr   msg;
```

```
        status = -1;
        for ( ; ; ) {
            iov[0].iov_base = buf;
            iov[0].iov_len  = sizeof(buf);
            msg.msg_iov       = iov;
            msg.msg_iovlen    = 1;
            msg.msg_name      = NULL;
            msg.msg_namelen = 0;
            msg.msg_accrights = (caddr_t) &newfd;/* addr of descriptor */
            msg.msg_accrightslen = sizeof(int);  /* receive 1 descriptor */

            if ( (nread = recvmsg(servfd, &msg, 0)) < 0)
                err_sys("recvmsg error");
            else if (nread == 0) {
                err_ret("connection closed by server");
                return(-1);
            }

                /* See if this is the final data with null & status.
                   Null must be next to last byte of buffer, status
                   byte is last byte.  Zero status means there must
                   be a file descriptor to receive. */
            for (ptr = buf; ptr < &buf[nread]; ) {
                if (*ptr++ == 0) {
                    if (ptr != &buf[nread-1])
                        err_dump("message format error");
                    status = *ptr & 255;
                    if (status == 0) {
                        if (msg.msg_accrightslen != sizeof(int))
                            err_dump("status = 0 but no fd");
                        /* newfd = the new descriptor */
                    } else
                        newfd = -status;
                    nread -= 2;
                }
            }
            if (nread > 0)
                if ((*userfunc)(STDERR_FILENO, buf, nread) != nread)
                    return(-1);

            if (status >= 0)    /* final data has arrived */
                return(newfd);  /* descriptor, or -status */
        }
    }
```

Notice that we are always prepared to receive a descriptor (we set msg_accrights
and msg_accrightslen before each call to recvmsg), but only if
msg_accrightslen is nonzero on return did we receive a descriptor.

15.3.3 4.3+BSD

Starting with 4.3BSD Reno the definition of the msghdr structure changed. The final two elements, which were called "access rights" in previous releases, became "ancillary data." Also, a new member, msg_flags, was added to end of the structure.

```
struct msghdr {
    caddr_t        msg_name;      /* optional address */
    int            msg_namelen;   /* size of address */
    struct iovec  *msg_iov;       /* scatter/gather array */
    int            msg_iovlen;    /* # elements in msg_iov array */
    caddr_t        msg_control;   /* ancillary data */
    u_int          msg_controllen; /* size of ancillary data */
    int            msg_flags;     /* flags on received message */
};
```

The msg_control field now points to a cmsghdr (control message header) structure.

```
struct cmsghdr {
    u_int  cmsg_len;    /* data byte count, including header */
    int    cmsg_level;  /* originating protocol */
    int    cmsg_type;   /* protocol-specific type */
    /* followed by the actual control message data */
};
```

To send a file descriptor we set cmsg_len to the size of the cmsghdr structure, plus the size of an integer (the descriptor). cmsg_level is set to SOL_SOCKET, and cmsg_type is set to SCM_RIGHTS, to indicate that we are passing access rights. ("SCM" stands for "socket-level control message.") The actual descriptor is stored right after the cmsg_type field, using the macro CMSG_DATA to obtain the pointer to this integer. Program 15.9 shows the send_fd function for 4.3BSD Reno.

```
#include     <sys/types.h>
#include     <sys/socket.h>     /* struct msghdr */
#include     <sys/uio.h>        /* struct iovec */
#include     <errno.h>
#include     <stddef.h>
#include     "ourhdr.h"

static struct cmsghdr   *cmptr = NULL;  /* buffer is malloc'ed first time */
#define CONTROLLEN  (sizeof(struct cmsghdr) + sizeof(int))
        /* size of control buffer to send/recv one file descriptor */

/* Pass a file descriptor to another process.
 * If fd<0, then -fd is sent back instead as the error status. */

int
send_fd(int clifd, int fd)
{
    struct iovec    iov[1];
    struct msghdr   msg;
    char            buf[2]; /* send_fd()/recv_fd() 2-byte protocol */
```

```
            iov[0].iov_base = buf;
            iov[0].iov_len  = 2;
            msg.msg_iov     = iov;
            msg.msg_iovlen  = 1;
            msg.msg_name    = NULL;
            msg.msg_namelen = 0;
            if (fd < 0) {
                msg.msg_control    = NULL;
                msg.msg_controllen = 0;
                buf[1] = -fd;   /* nonzero status means error */
                if (buf[1] == 0)
                    buf[1] = 1; /* -256, etc. would screw up protocol */
            } else {
                if (cmptr == NULL && (cmptr = malloc(CONTROLLEN)) == NULL)
                    return(-1);
                cmptr->cmsg_level  = SOL_SOCKET;
                cmptr->cmsg_type   = SCM_RIGHTS;
                cmptr->cmsg_len    = CONTROLLEN;
                msg.msg_control    = (caddr_t) cmptr;
                msg.msg_controllen = CONTROLLEN;
                *(int *)CMSG_DATA(cmptr) = fd;      /* the fd to pass */
                buf[1] = 0;      /* zero status means OK */
            }
            buf[0] = 0;                /* null byte flag to recv_fd() */

            if (sendmsg(clifd, &msg, 0) != 2)
                return(-1);
            return(0);
        }
```

Program 15.9 The send_fd function for 4.3BSD Reno.

To receive a descriptor (Program 15.10) we allocate enough room for a cmsghdr structure and a descriptor, set msg_control to point to the allocated area, and call recvmsg.

```
#include      <sys/types.h>
#include      <sys/socket.h>      /* struct msghdr */
#include      <sys/uio.h>         /* struct iovec */
#include      <stddef.h>
#include      "ourhdr.h"

static struct cmsghdr   *cmptr = NULL;         /* malloc'ed first time */
#define CONTROLLEN  (sizeof(struct cmsghdr) + sizeof(int))
        /* size of control buffer to send/recv one file descriptor */
/* Receive a file descriptor from another process (a server).
 * In addition, any data received from the server is passed
 * to (*userfunc)(STDERR_FILENO, buf, nbytes).  We have a
 * 2-byte protocol for receiving the fd from send_fd(). */
int
recv_fd(int servfd, ssize_t (*userfunc)(int, const void *, size_t))
```

```
{
    int             newfd, nread, status;
    char            *ptr, buf[MAXLINE];
    struct iovec    iov[1];
    struct msghdr   msg;

    status = -1;
    for ( ; ; ) {
        iov[0].iov_base = buf;
        iov[0].iov_len  = sizeof(buf);
        msg.msg_iov     = iov;
        msg.msg_iovlen  = 1;
        msg.msg_name    = NULL;
        msg.msg_namelen = 0;
        if (cmptr == NULL && (cmptr = malloc(CONTROLLEN)) == NULL)
            return(-1);
        msg.msg_control    = (caddr_t) cmptr;
        msg.msg_controllen = CONTROLLEN;

        if ( (nread = recvmsg(servfd, &msg, 0)) < 0)
            err_sys("recvmsg error");
        else if (nread == 0) {
            err_ret("connection closed by server");
            return(-1);
        }
            /* See if this is the final data with null & status.
               Null must be next to last byte of buffer, status
               byte is last byte.  Zero status means there must
               be a file descriptor to receive. */
        for (ptr = buf; ptr < &buf[nread]; ) {
            if (*ptr++ == 0) {
                if (ptr != &buf[nread-1])
                    err_dump("message format error");
                status = *ptr & 255;
                if (status == 0) {
                    if (msg.msg_controllen != CONTROLLEN)
                        err_dump("status = 0 but no fd");
                    newfd = *(int *)CMSG_DATA(cmptr); /* new descriptor */
                } else
                    newfd = -status;
                nread -= 2;
            }
        }
        if (nread > 0)
            if ((*userfunc)(STDERR_FILENO, buf, nread) != nread)
                return(-1);
        if (status >= 0)    /* final data has arrived */
            return(newfd);  /* descriptor, or -status */
    }
}
```

Program 15.10 The recv_fd function for 4.3BSD Reno.

15.4 An Open Server, Version 1

Using file descriptor passing, we now develop an open server: an executable program that is execed by a process to open one or more files. But instead of the server sending the file back to the calling process, it sends back an open file descriptor instead. This lets the server work with any type of file (such as a modem line or a network connection) and not just regular files. It also means that a minimum of information is exchanged using IPC—the filename and open mode from the client to the server, and the returned descriptor from the server to the client. The contents of the file are not exchanged using IPC.

There are several advantages in designing the server to be a separate executable program (either one that is execed by the client, as we develop in this section, or a daemon server, which we develop in Section 15.6).

1. The server can easily be contacted by any client, similar to the client calling a library function. We are not hardcoding a particular service into the application, but designing a general facility that others can reuse.

2. If we need to change the server, only a single program is affected. Conversely, updating a library function can require that all programs that call the function be updated (i.e., relinked with the link editor). Shared libraries can simplify this updating (Section 7.7).

3. The server can be a set-user-ID program, providing it additional permissions that the client does not have. Notice that a library function (or shared library function) can't provide this capability.

The client process creates a stream pipe, and then calls fork and exec to invoke the server. The client sends requests across the stream pipe, and the server sends back responses across the pipe. We define the following application protocol between the client and server.

1. The client sends a request of the form

   open *<pathname>* *<openmode>*\0

   across the stream pipe to the server. The *<openmode>* is the numeric value, in decimal, of the second argument to the open function. This request string is terminated by a null byte.

2. The server sends back an open descriptor or an error by calling either send_fd or send_err.

This is an example of a process sending an open descriptor to its parent. In Section 15.6 we'll modify this example to use a single daemon server, where the server sends a descriptor to a completely unrelated process.

We first have the header, open.h (Program 15.11), which includes the standard system headers and defines the function prototypes.

```
#include      <sys/types.h>
#include      <errno.h>
#include      "ourhdr.h"

#define CL_OPEN "open"             /* client's request for server */

              /* our function prototypes */
int      csopen(char *, int);
```

Program 15.11 The open.h header.

The main function (Program 15.12) is a loop that reads a pathname from standard input and copies the file to standard output. It calls the function csopen to contact the open server, and return an open descriptor.

```
#include      "open.h"
#include      <fcntl.h>

#define BUFFSIZE      8192

int
main(int argc, char *argv[])
{
    int      n, fd;
    char     buf[BUFFSIZE], line[MAXLINE];

                  /* read filename to cat from stdin */
    while (fgets(line, MAXLINE, stdin) != NULL) {
        line[strlen(line) - 1] = 0; /* replace newline with null */

                  /* open the file */
        if ( (fd = csopen(line, O_RDONLY)) < 0)
            continue;   /* csopen() prints error from server */

                  /* and cat to stdout */
        while ( (n = read(fd, buf, BUFFSIZE)) > 0)
            if (write(STDOUT_FILENO, buf, n) != n)
                err_sys("write error");
        if (n < 0)
            err_sys("read error");
        close(fd);
    }

    exit(0);
}
```

Program 15.12 The main function.

The function csopen (Program 15.13) does the fork and exec of the server, after creating the stream pipe.

```
#include    "open.h"
#include    <sys/uio.h>        /* struct iovec */

/* Open the file by sending the "name" and "oflag" to the
 * connection server and reading a file descriptor back. */
int
csopen(char *name, int oflag)
{
    pid_t           pid;
    int             len;
    char            buf[10];
    struct iovec    iov[3];
    static int      fd[2] = { -1, -1 };

    if (fd[0] < 0) {      /* fork/exec our open server first time */
        if (s_pipe(fd) < 0)
            err_sys("s_pipe error");
        if ( (pid = fork()) < 0)
            err_sys("fork error");
        else if (pid == 0) {          /* child */
            close(fd[0]);
            if (fd[1] != STDIN_FILENO) {
                if (dup2(fd[1], STDIN_FILENO) != STDIN_FILENO)
                    err_sys("dup2 error to stdin");
            }
            if (fd[1] != STDOUT_FILENO) {
                if (dup2(fd[1], STDOUT_FILENO) != STDOUT_FILENO)
                    err_sys("dup2 error to stdout");
            }
            if (execl("./opend", "opend", NULL) < 0)
                err_sys("execl error");
        }
        close(fd[1]);                     /* parent */
    }

    sprintf(buf, " %d", oflag);        /* oflag to ascii */
    iov[0].iov_base = CL_OPEN " ";
    iov[0].iov_len  = strlen(CL_OPEN) + 1;
    iov[1].iov_base = name;
    iov[1].iov_len  = strlen(name);
    iov[2].iov_base = buf;
    iov[2].iov_len  = strlen(buf) + 1;  /* +1 for null at end of buf */
    len = iov[0].iov_len + iov[1].iov_len + iov[2].iov_len;
    if (writev(fd[0], &iov[0], 3) != len)
        err_sys("writev error");

        /* read descriptor, returned errors handled by write() */
    return( recv_fd(fd[0], write) );
}
```

Program 15.13 The csopen function.

The child closes one end of the pipe, and the parent closes the other. The child also duplicates its end of the pipe onto its standard input and standard output, for the server that it execs. (Another option would have been to pass the ASCII representation of the descriptor `fd[1]` as an argument to the server.)

The parent sends the request to the server containing the pathname and open mode. Finally the parent calls `recv_fd` to return either the descriptor or an error. If an error is returned by the server, `write` is called to output the message to standard error.

Now let's look at the open server. It is the program opend that is execed by the client in Program 15.13. First we have the opend.h header (Program 15.14) that includes the system headers and declares the global variables and function prototypes.

```
#include     <sys/types.h>
#include     <errno.h>
#include     "ourhdr.h"

#define CL_OPEN "open"                    /* client's request for server */

            /* declare global variables */
extern char  errmsg[];   /* error message string to return to client */
extern int   oflag;      /* open() flag: O_xxx ... */
extern char *pathname;   /* of file to open() for client */

            /* function prototypes */
int      cli_args(int, char **);
void     request(char *, int, int);
```

Program 15.14 The opend.h header.

```
#include     "opend.h"

            /* define global variables */
char     errmsg[MAXLINE];
int      oflag;
char     *pathname;

int
main(void)
{
    int     nread;
    char    buf[MAXLINE];

    for ( ; ; ) {   /* read arg buffer from client, process request */
        if ( (nread = read(STDIN_FILENO, buf, MAXLINE)) < 0)
            err_sys("read error on stream pipe");
        else if (nread == 0)
            break;       /* client has closed the stream pipe */

        request(buf, nread, STDOUT_FILENO);
    }
    exit(0);
}
```

Program 15.15 The main function.

The main function (Program 15.15) reads the requests from the client on the stream pipe (its standard input) and calls the function request.

The function request in Program 15.16 does all the work. It calls the function buf_args to break up the client's request into a standard argv-style argument list and calls the function cli_args to process the client's arguments. If all is OK, open is called to open the file, and then send_fd sends the descriptor back to the client across the stream pipe (its standard output). If an error is encountered, send_err is called to send back an error message, using the client–server protocol that we described earlier.

```
#include    "opend.h"
#include    <fcntl.h>

void
request(char *buf, int nread, int fd)
{
    int     newfd;

    if (buf[nread-1] != 0) {
        sprintf(errmsg, "request not null terminated: %*.*s\n"
                                    nread, nread, buf);
        send_err(fd, -1, errmsg);
        return;
    }

            /* parse the arguments, set options */
    if (buf_args(buf, cli_args) < 0) {
        send_err(fd, -1, errmsg);
        return;
    }

    if ( (newfd = open(pathname, oflag)) < 0) {
        sprintf(errmsg, "can't open %s: %s\n",
                                pathname, strerror(errno));
        send_err(fd, -1, errmsg);
        return;
    }

            /* send the descriptor */
    if (send_fd(fd, newfd) < 0)
        err_sys("send_fd error");
    close(newfd);         /* we're done with descriptor */
}
```

Program 15.16 The request function.

The client's request is a null terminated string of white-space separated arguments. The function buf_args in Program 15.17 breaks this string into a standard argv-style argument list and calls a user function to process the arguments. We'll use this function

later in this chapter and again in Chapter 18. We use the ANSI C function `strtok` to
tokenize the string into separate arguments.

```
#include    "ourhdr.h"

#define MAXARGC   50  /* max number of arguments in buf */
#define WHITE   " \t\n" /* white space for tokenizing arguments */

/* buf[] contains white-space separated arguments. We convert it
 * to an argv[] style array of pointers, and call the user's
 * function (*optfunc)() to process the argv[] array.
 * We return -1 to the caller if there's a problem parsing buf,
 * else we return whatever optfunc() returns. Note that user's
 * buf[] array is modified (nulls placed after each token). */

int
buf_args(char *buf, int (*optfunc)(int, char **))
{
    char    *ptr, *argv[MAXARGC];
    int     argc;

    if (strtok(buf, WHITE) == NULL)     /* an argv[0] is required */
        return(-1);
    argv[argc = 0] = buf;

    while ( (ptr = strtok(NULL, WHITE)) != NULL) {
        if (++argc >= MAXARGC-1)     /* -1 for room for NULL at end */
            return(-1);
        argv[argc] = ptr;
    }
    argv[++argc] = NULL;

    return( (*optfunc)(argc, argv) );
            /* Since argv[] pointers point into the user's buf[],
               user's function can just copy the pointers, even
               though argv[] array will disappear on return. */
}
```

Program 15.17 The `buf_args` function.

The server's function that is called by `buf_args` is `cli_args` (Program 15.18). It
verifies that the client sent the right number of arguments and stores the pathname and
open mode into global variables.

This completes the open server that is invoked by a `fork` and `exec` from the client.
A single stream pipe is created before the `fork` and used to communicate between the
client and server. With this arrangement we have one server per client.

After looking at client–server connections in the next section, we'll redo the open
server in Section 15.6 to use a single daemon server that is contacted by all clients.

```
#include     "opend.h"

/* This function is called by buf_args(), which is called by
 * request().  buf_args() has broken up the client's buffer
 * into an argv[] style array, which we now process. */

int
cli_args(int argc, char **argv)
{
    if (argc != 3 || strcmp(argv[0], CL_OPEN) != 0) {
        strcpy(errmsg, "usage: <pathname> <oflag>\n");
        return(-1);
    }

    pathname = argv[1];        /* save ptr to pathname to open */
    oflag = atoi(argv[2]);
    return(0);
}
```

Program 15.18 The `cli_args` function.

15.5   Client–Server Connection Functions

Stream pipes are useful for IPC between related processes, such as a parent and child.
The open server in the previous section was able to pass file descriptors from a child to
a parent using an unnamed stream pipe. But when we're dealing with unrelated processes (such as a server that is a daemon), a named stream pipe is required.

We can take an unnamed stream pipe (from the s_pipe function) and attach a
pathname in the filesystem to either end. A daemon server would create just one end of
a stream pipe and attach a name to that end. This way unrelated clients can rendezvous
with the daemon, sending messages to the server's end of the pipe. This is similar to
what we showed in Figure 14.12, where we used a well-known FIFO for the clients to
send their requests to.

An even better approach is to use a technique whereby the server creates one end of
a stream pipe with a well-known name, and clients *connect* to that end. Additionally,
each time a new client connects to the server's named stream pipe, a brand new stream
pipe is created between the client and server. This way the server is notified each time a
new client connects to the server, and when any client terminates. Both SVR4 and
4.3+BSD support this form of IPC. In this section we develop three functions that can
be used by a client–server to establish these per-client connections.

```
#include "ourhdr.h"

int serv_listen(const char *name);
```
                                                    Returns: file descriptor to listen on if OK, <0 on error

First a server has to announce its willingness to listen for client connections on a well-known name (some pathname in the filesystem) by calling `serv_listen`. *name* is the well-known name of the server. Clients will use this name when they want to connect to the server. The return value is the file descriptor for the server's end of the named stream pipe.

Once a server has called `serv_listen`, it calls `serv_accept` to wait for a client connection to arrive.

```
#include "ourhdr.h"

int serv_accept(int listenfd, uid_t *uidptr);
```
Returns: new file descriptor if OK, <0 on error

listenfd is a descriptor from `serv_listen`. This function doesn't return until a client connects to the server's well-known name. When the client does connect to the server, a brand new stream pipe is automatically created, and the new descriptor is returned as the value of the function. Additionally, the effective user ID of the client is stored through the pointer *uidptr*.

A client just calls `cli_conn` to connect to a server.

```
#include "ourhdr.h"

int cli_conn(const char *name);
```
Returns: file descriptor if OK, <0 on error

The *name* specified by the client must be the same name that was advertised by the server's call to `serv_listen`. The returned descriptor refers to a stream pipe that is connected to the server.

Using these three functions we can write server daemons that can manage any number of clients. The only limit is the number of descriptors available to a single process, since the server requires one descriptor for each client connection. Since these functions deal with normal file descriptors, the server can multiplex I/O requests among all its clients using either `select` or `poll`. Finally, since the client–server connections are all stream pipes, open descriptors can be passed across the connections.

In the next two sections we'll look at the implementations of these three functions under SVR4 and 4.3+BSD. Then in Section 15.6 we'll redo the open server from Section 15.4 using a single daemon server that uses these three functions. We'll also use these three functions in Chapter 18 when we develop a general connection server.

15.5.1 System V Release 4

SVR4 provides mounted streams and a streams processing module named `connld` that we can use to provide a named stream pipe with unique connections for the server.

> Mounted streams and the `connld` module were developed by Presotto and Ritchie [1990] for the Research Unix system. They were then picked up by SVR4.

First the server creates an unnamed stream pipe and pushes the streams processing module connld on one end. Figure 15.5 shows the resulting picture.

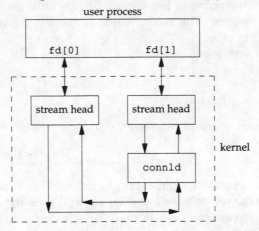

Figure 15.5 SVR4 pipe after pushing connld module onto one end.

We then attach a pathname to the end of the pipe that has the connld pushed onto it. SVR4 provides the fattach function to do this. Any process that opens this pathname (such as a client) is referring to the named end of the pipe.

Program 15.19 shows the dozen lines of code required to implement the serv_listen function.

When another process calls open for the named end of the pipe (the end with connld pushed onto it), the following occurs:

1. A new pipe is created.

2. One descriptor for the new pipe is passed back to the client as the return value from open.

3. The other descriptor is passed to the server on the other end of the named pipe (i.e., the end that does not have connld pushed onto it). The server receives this new descriptor using an ioctl of I_RECVFD.

Assume that the well-known name that the server fattaches to its pipe is /tmp/serv1. Figure 15.6 shows the resulting picture, after the client's call

```
fd = open("/tmp/serv1", O_RDWR);
```

has returned. The pipe between the client and server is created by the open, since the pathname being opened is really a named stream that has connld pushed onto it. The file descriptor in the client (fd) is returned by the open. The new file descriptor in the server (clifd1) is received by the server using an ioctl of I_RECVFD on the descriptor fd[0]. Once the server has pushed connld onto fd[1] and attached a name to fd[1], it never specifically uses fd[1] again.

```
#include      <sys/types.h>
#include      <sys/stat.h>
#include      <stropts.h>
#include      "ourhdr.h"

#define FIFO_MODE   (S_IRUSR|S_IWUSR|S_IRGRP|S_IWGRP|S_IROTH|S_IWOTH)
                        /* user rw, group rw, others rw */

int           /* returns fd if all OK, <0 on error */
serv_listen(const char *name)
{
    int       tempfd, fd[2], len;

                    /* create a file: mount point for fattach() */
    unlink(name);
    if ( (tempfd = creat(name, FIFO_MODE)) < 0)
        return(-1);
    if (close(tempfd) < 0)
        return(-2);

    if (pipe(fd) < 0)
        return(-3);
                            /* push connld & fattach() on fd[1] */
    if (ioctl(fd[1], I_PUSH, `"connld") < 0)
        return(-4);
    if (fattach(fd[1], name) < 0)
        return(-5);

    return(fd[0]);  /* fd[0] is where client connections arrive */
}
```

Program 15.19 The `serv_listen` function for SVR4.

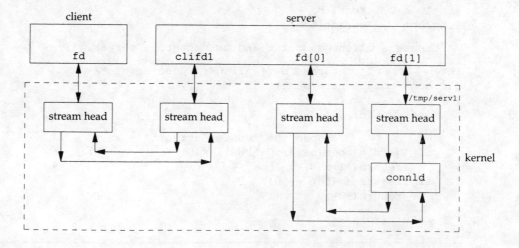

Figure 15.6 Client–server connection on a named stream pipe.

The server waits for a client connection to arrive by calling the `serv_accept` function shown in Program 15.20.

```
#include      <sys/types.h>
#include      <sys/stat.h>
#include      <stropts.h>
#include      "ourhdr.h"

/* Wait for a client connection to arrive, and accept it.
 * We also obtain the client's user ID. */

int            /* returns new fd if all OK, -1 on error */
serv_accept(int listenfd, uid_t *uidptr)
{
    struct strrecvfd   recvfd;

    if (ioctl(listenfd, I_RECVFD, &recvfd) < 0)
        return(-1);       /* could be EINTR if signal caught */

    if (uidptr != NULL)
        *uidptr = recvfd.uid;   /* effective uid of caller */

    return(recvfd.fd);  /* return the new descriptor */
}
```

Program 15.20 The `serv_accept` function for SVR4.

In Figure 15.6 the first argument to `serv_accept` would be the descriptor `fd[0]` and the return value from `serv_accept` would be the descriptor `clifd1`.

The client initiates the connection to the server by calling the `cli_conn` function in Program 15.21.

```
#include      <sys/types.h>
#include      <sys/stat.h>
#include      <fcntl.h>
#include      "ourhdr.h"

/* Create a client endpoint and connect to a server. */

int            /* returns fd if all OK, <0 on error */
cli_conn(const char *name)
{
    int     fd;

                /* open the mounted stream */
    if ( (fd = open(name, O_RDWR)) < 0)
        return(-1);
    if (isastream(fd) == 0)
        return(-2);

    return(fd);
}
```

Program 15.21 The `cli_conn` function for SVR4.

We double-check that the returned descriptor refers to a streams device, in case the server has not been started but the pathname still existed in the filesystem. (Under SVR4 there appears to be little reason to call cli_conn instead of just calling open directly. In the next section we'll see that the cli_conn function is more complicated under BSD systems.)

15.5.2   4.3+BSD

Under 4.3+BSD we have a different set of operations required to connect a client and server using Unix domain sockets. We won't go through all the details of the socket, bind, listen, accept, and connect functions that we use, since most of the details are for using these functions with other networking protocols. Refer to Chapter 6 of Stevens [1990] for these details.

> Since SVR4 also supports Unix domain sockets, the code shown in this section also works under SVR4.

Program 15.22 shows the serv_listen function. It is the first function called by the server.

```
#include      <sys/types.h>
#include      <sys/socket.h>
#include      <sys/un.h>
#include      "ourhdr.h"

/* Create a server endpoint of a connection. */

int           /* returns fd if all OK, <0 on error */
serv_listen(const char *name)
{
    int               fd, len;
    struct sockaddr_un  unix_addr;

                    /* create a Unix domain stream socket */
    if ( (fd = socket(AF_UNIX, SOCK_STREAM, 0)) < 0)
        return(-1);

    unlink(name);    /* in case it already exists */

                    /* fill in socket address structure */
    memset(&unix_addr, 0, sizeof(unix_addr));
    unix_addr.sun_family = AF_UNIX;
    strcpy(unix_addr.sun_path, name);
#ifdef  SCM_RIGHTS  /* 4.3BSD Reno and later */
    len = sizeof(unix_addr.sun_len) + sizeof(unix_addr.sun_family) +
        strlen(unix_addr.sun_path) + 1;
    unix_addr.sun_len = len;
#else               /* vanilla 4.3BSD */
    len = strlen(unix_addr.sun_path) + sizeof(unix_addr.sun_family);
#endif
```

```
                              /* bind the name to the descriptor */
    if (bind(fd, (struct sockaddr *) &unix_addr, len) < 0)
        return(-2);

    if (listen(fd, 5) < 0)   /* tell kernel we're a server */
        return(-3);

    return(fd);
}
```

Program 15.22 The serv_listen function for 4.3+BSD.

First a single Unix domain socket is created by socket. We then fill in a sockaddr_un structure with the well-known pathname to be assigned to the socket. This structure is the argument to bind. We then call listen to tell the kernel that we'll be a server awaiting connections from clients. (The second argument to listen, 5, is the maximum number of outstanding connection requests that the kernel will queue for this descriptor. Most implementations silently enforce an upper limit of 5 for this value.)

The client initiates the connection to the server by calling the cli_conn function (Program 15.23).

```
#include        <sys/types.h>
#include        <sys/socket.h>
#include        <sys/stat.h>
#include        <sys/un.h>
#include        "ourhdr.h"

/* Create a client endpoint and connect to a server. */

#define CLI_PATH        "/var/tmp/"        /* +5 for pid = 14 chars */
#define CLI_PERM        S_IRWXU            /* rwx for user only */

int             /* returns fd if all OK, <0 on error */
cli_conn(const char *name)
{
    int                 fd, len;
    struct sockaddr_un  unix_addr;

                    /* create a Unix domain stream socket */
    if ( (fd = socket(AF_UNIX, SOCK_STREAM, 0)) < 0)
        return(-1);

                    /* fill socket address structure w/our address */
    memset(&unix_addr, 0, sizeof(unix_addr));
    unix_addr.sun_family = AF_UNIX;
    sprintf(unix_addr.sun_path, "%s%05d", CLI_PATH, getpid());
#ifdef  SCM_RIGHTS  /* 4.3BSD Reno and later */
    len = sizeof(unix_addr.sun_len) + sizeof(unix_addr.sun_family) +
          strlen(unix_addr.sun_path) + 1;
    unix_addr.sun_len = len;
#else               /* vanilla 4.3BSD */
    len = strlen(unix_addr.sun_path) + sizeof(unix_addr.sun_family);
```

```
         if (len != 16)
             err_quit("length != 16");    /* hack */
#endif

         unlink(unix_addr.sun_path);        /* in case it already exists */
         if (bind(fd, (struct sockaddr *) &unix_addr, len) < 0)
             return(-2);
         if (chmod(unix_addr.sun_path, CLI_PERM) < 0)
             return(-3);

                      /* fill socket address structure w/server's addr */
         memset(&unix_addr, 0, sizeof(unix_addr));
         unix_addr.sun_family = AF_UNIX;
         strcpy(unix_addr.sun_path, name);
#ifdef   SCM_RIGHTS  /* 4.3BSD Reno and later */
         len = sizeof(unix_addr.sun_len) + sizeof(unix_addr.sun_family) +
             strlen(unix_addr.sun_path) + 1;
         unix_addr.sun_len = len;
#else                    /* vanilla 4.3BSD */
         len = strlen(unix_addr.sun_path) + sizeof(unix_addr.sun_family);
#endif

         if (connect(fd, (struct sockaddr *) &unix_addr, len) < 0)
             return(-4);

         return(fd);
}
```

Program 15.23 The `cli_conn` function for 4.3+BSD.

We call `socket` to create the client's end of a Unix domain socket. We then fill in a `sockaddr_un` structure with a client-specific name. The last five characters of the pathname are the process ID of the client. (We also verify that the size of this structure is exactly 14 characters to avoid some bugs in earlier implementations of Unix domain sockets.) `unlink` is called, just in case the pathname already exists. We call `bind` to assign a name to the client's socket, and this creates the pathname in the filesystem, and the file type is a socket. `chmod` is called to turn off all permissions other than user-read, user-write, and user-execute. In `serv_accept`, the server checks these permissions and the user ID of the socket to verify the client's identity.

We then have to fill in another `sockaddr_un` structure, this time with the well-known pathname of the server. Finally the `connect` function initiates the connection with the server.

The creation of a unique connection for each client is handled in the `serv_accept` function (Program 15.24) by the `accept` function.

```
#include        <sys/types.h>
#include        <sys/socket.h>
#include        <sys/stat.h>
#include        <sys/un.h>
#include        <stddef.h>
#include        <time.h>
```

```
#include    "ourhdr.h"

#define STALE  30 /* client's name can't be older than this (sec) */

/* Wait for a client connection to arrive, and accept it.
 * We also obtain the client's user ID from the pathname
 * that it must bind before calling us. */

int            /* returns new fd if all OK, <0 on error */
serv_accept(int listenfd, uid_t *uidptr)
{
    int             clifd, len;
    time_t          staletime;
    struct sockaddr_un  unix_addr;
    struct stat     statbuf;

    len = sizeof(unix_addr);
    if ( (clifd = accept(listenfd, (struct sockaddr *) &unix_addr, &len)) < 0)
        return(-1);       /* often errno=EINTR, if signal caught */

            /* obtain the client's uid from its calling address */
#ifdef  SCM_RIGHTS /* 4.3BSD Reno and later */
    len -= sizeof(unix_addr.sun_len) - sizeof(unix_addr.sun_family);
#else                  /* vanilla 4.3BSD */
    len -= sizeof(unix_addr.sun_family);     /* len of pathname */
#endif
    unix_addr.sun_path[len] = 0;              /* null terminate */

    if (stat(unix_addr.sun_path, &statbuf) < 0)
        return(-2);
#ifdef  S_ISSOCK     /* not defined for SVR4 */
    if (S_ISSOCK(statbuf.st_mode) == 0)
        return(-3);       /* not a socket */
#endif
    if ((statbuf.st_mode & (S_IRWXG | S_IRWXO)) ||
        (statbuf.st_mode & S_IRWXU) != S_IRWXU)
            return(-4);    /* is not rwx------ */

    staletime = time(NULL) - STALE;
    if (statbuf.st_atime < staletime ||
        statbuf.st_ctime < staletime ||
        statbuf.st_mtime < staletime)
            return(-5);    /* i-node is too old */

    if (uidptr != NULL)
        *uidptr = statbuf.st_uid;   /* return uid of caller */

    unlink(unix_addr.sun_path);     /* we're done with pathname now */

    return(clifd);
}
```

Program 15.24 The serv_accept function for 4.3+BSD.

The server blocks in the call to accept, waiting for a client to call cli_conn. When accept returns, its return value is a brand new descriptor that is connected to the client. (This is somewhat similar to what the connld module does under SVR4.) Additionally, the pathname that the client assigned to its socket (the name that contained the client's process ID) is also returned by accept, through the second argument (the pointer to the sockaddr_un structure). We null terminate this pathname and call stat. This lets us verify that the pathname is indeed a socket, and that the permissions allow only user-read, user-write, and user-execute. We also verify that the three times associated with the socket are no older than 30 seconds. (The time function returns the current time and date in seconds past the Unix Epoch.) If all these checks are OK, we assume that the identity of the client (its effective user ID) is the owner of the socket. While this check isn't perfect, it's the best we can do with current systems. (It would be better if the kernel returned the effective user ID to accept as the SVR4 I_RECVFD does.)

Figure 15.7 shows a picture of the connection, after the call to cli_conn has returned, assuming the server's well-known name is /tmp/serv1. Compare this with Figure 15.6.

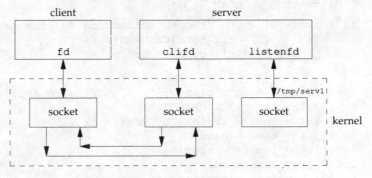

Figure 15.7 Client–server connection on a Unix domain socket.

15.6 An Open Server, Version 2

In Section 15.4 we developed an open server that was invoked by a fork and exec by the client. It demonstrated how we can pass file descriptors from a child to a parent. In this section we develop an open server as a daemon process. One server handles all clients. We expect this design to be more efficient, since a fork and exec are avoided. We still use a stream pipe between the client and server and demonstrate passing file descriptors between unrelated processes. We'll use the three functions serv_listen, serv_accept, and cli_conn from the previous section. This server also demonstrates how a single server can handle multiple clients, using both the select and poll functions from Section 12.5.

The client is similar to the client from Section 15.4. Indeed, the file main.c is identical (Program 15.12). We add the following line to the open.h header (Program 15.11)

    #define CS_OPEN "/home/stevens/open"   /* server's well-known name */

The file open.c does change from Program 15.13, since we now call cli_conn, instead of doing the fork and exec. This is shown in Program 15.25.

```
#include    "open.h"
#include    <sys/uio.h>        /* struct iovec */

/* Open the file by sending the "name" and "oflag" to the
 * connection server and reading a file descriptor back. */

int
csopen(char *name, int oflag)
{
    int          len;
    char         buf[10];
    struct iovec iov[3];
    static int   csfd = -1;

    if (csfd < 0) {      /* open connection to conn server */
        if ( (csfd = cli_conn(CS_OPEN)) < 0)
            err_sys("cli_conn error");
    }

    sprintf(buf, " %d", oflag);       /* oflag to ascii */
    iov[0].iov_base = CL_OPEN " ";
    iov[0].iov_len  = strlen(CL_OPEN) + 1;
    iov[1].iov_base = name;
    iov[1].iov_len  = strlen(name);
    iov[2].iov_base = buf;
    iov[2].iov_len  = strlen(buf) + 1;
                            /* null at end of buf always sent */
    len = iov[0].iov_len + iov[1].iov_len + iov[2].iov_len;
    if (writev(csfd, &iov[0], 3) != len)
        err_sys("writev error");

                    /* read back descriptor */
                    /* returned errors handled by write() */
    return( recv_fd(csfd, write) );
}
```

Program 15.25 The csopen function.

The protocol from the client to the server remains the same.

Let's look at the server. The header opend.h (Program 15.26) includes the standard headers, declares the global variables and the function prototypes.

Since this server handles all clients, it must maintain the state of each client connection. This is done with the client array defined in the opend.h header. Program 15.27 defines three functions that manipulate this array.

```
#include      <sys/types.h>
#include      <errno.h>
#include      "ourhdr.h"

#define CS_OPEN "/home/stevens/opend"  /* well-known name */
#define CL_OPEN "open"                 /* client's request for server */

            /* declare global variables */
extern int    debug;      /* nonzero if interactive (not daemon) */
extern char   errmsg[];   /* error message string to return to client */
extern int    oflag;      /* open flag: O_xxx ... */
extern char *pathname;    /* of file to open for client */

typedef struct {    /* one Client struct per connected client */
  int    fd;        /* fd, or -1 if available */
  uid_t uid;
} Client;

extern Client   *client;          /* ptr to malloc'ed array */
extern int       client_size;     /* # entries in client[] array */
                    /* (both manipulated by client_XXX() functions) */

            /* function prototypes */
int      cli_args(int, char **);
int      client_add(int, uid_t);
void     client_del(int);
void     loop(void);
void     request(char *, int, int, uid_t);
```

Program 15.26 The opend.h header.

```
#include      "opend.h"

#define NALLOC   10        /* #Client structs to alloc/realloc for */

static void
client_alloc(void)         /* alloc more entries in the client[] array */
{
    int     i;

    if (client == NULL)
        client = malloc(NALLOC * sizeof(Client));
    else
        client = realloc(client, (client_size + NALLOC) * sizeof(Client));
    if (client == NULL)
        err_sys("can't alloc for client array");

            /* have to initialize the new entries */
    for (i = client_size; i < client_size + NALLOC; i++)
        client[i].fd = -1;   /* fd of -1 means entry available */

    client_size += NALLOC;
}
```

```
/* Called by loop() when connection request from a new client arrives */
int
client_add(int fd, uid_t uid)
{
    int     i;

    if (client == NULL)        /* first time we're called */
        client_alloc();
again:
    for (i = 0; i < client_size; i++) {
        if (client[i].fd == -1) {    /* find an available entry */
            client[i].fd = fd;
            client[i].uid = uid;
            return(i);   /* return index in client[] array */
        }
    }
            /* client array full, time to realloc for more */
    client_alloc();
    goto again;        /* and search again (will work this time) */
}

/* Called by loop() when we're done with a client */
void
client_del(int fd)
{
    int     i;

    for (i = 0; i < client_size; i++) {
        if (client[i].fd == fd) {
            client[i].fd = -1;
            return;
        }
    }
    log_quit("can't find client entry for fd %d", fd);
}
```

Program 15.27 Functions to manipulate client array.

The first time client_add is called, it calls client_alloc, which calls malloc to allocate space for 10 entries in the array. After these 10 entries are all in use, a later call to client_add causes realloc to allocate additional space. By dynamically allocating space this way, we have not limited the size of the client array at compile time to some value that we guessed and put into a header.

These functions call the log_ functions (Appendix B) if an error occurs, since we assume that the server is a daemon.

The main function (Program 15.28) defines the global variables, processes the command-line options, and calls the function loop. If we invoke the server with the −d option, it runs interactively instead of as a daemon. This is used when testing the server.

```
#include    "opend.h"
#include    <syslog.h>

            /* define global variables */
int     debug;
char    errmsg[MAXLINE];
int     oflag;
char    *pathname;
Client  *client = NULL;
int     client_size;

int
main(int argc, char *argv[])
{
    int     c;

    log_open("open.serv", LOG_PID, LOG_USER);

    opterr = 0;     /* don't want getopt() writing to stderr */
    while ( (c = getopt(argc, argv, "d")) != EOF) {
        switch (c) {
        case 'd':       /* debug */
            debug = 1;
            break;

        case '?':
            err_quit("unrecognized option: -%c", optopt);
        }
    }

    if (debug == 0)
        daemon_init();

    loop();     /* never returns */
}
```

Program 15.28 The main function.

The function loop is the server's infinite loop. We'll show two versions of this function. Program 15.29 shows one that uses select (and works under both 4.3+BSD and SVR4), then we show one that uses poll (for SVR4).

```
#include    "opend.h"
#include    <sys/time.h>

void
loop(void)
{
    int     i, n, maxfd, maxi, listenfd, clifd, nread;
    char    buf[MAXLINE];
    uid_t   uid;
    fd_set  rset, allset;
```

```
        FD_ZERO(&allset);

                /* obtain fd to listen for client requests on */
        if ( (listenfd = serv_listen(CS_OPEN)) < 0)
            log_sys("serv_listen error");
        FD_SET(listenfd, &allset);
        maxfd = listenfd;
        maxi = -1;

        for ( ; ; ) {
            rset = allset;        /* rset gets modified each time around */
            if ( (n = select(maxfd + 1, &rset, NULL, NULL, NULL)) < 0)
                log_sys("select error");

            if (FD_ISSET(listenfd, &rset)) {
                    /* accept new client request */
                if ( (clifd = serv_accept(listenfd, &uid)) < 0)
                    log_sys("serv_accept error: %d", clifd);
                i = client_add(clifd, uid);
                FD_SET(clifd, &allset);
                if (clifd > maxfd)
                    maxfd = clifd;  /* max fd for select() */
                if (i > maxi)
                    maxi = i;       /* max index in client[] array */
                log_msg("new connection: uid %d, fd %d", uid, clifd);
                continue;
            }

            for (i = 0; i <= maxi; i++) {    /* go through client[] array */
                if ( (clifd = client[i].fd) < 0)
                    continue;
                if (FD_ISSET(clifd, &rset)) {
                        /* read argument buffer from client */
                    if ( (nread = read(clifd, buf, MAXLINE)) < 0)
                        log_sys("read error on fd %d", clifd);
                    else if (nread == 0) {
                        log_msg("closed: uid %d, fd %d",
                                            client[i].uid, clifd);
                        client_del(clifd);  /* client has closed conn */
                        FD_CLR(clifd, &allset);
                        close(clifd);
                    } else            /* process client's rquest */
                        request(buf, nread, clifd, client[i].uid);
                }
            }
        }
    }
```

Program 15.29 The loop function using select.

This function calls `serv_listen` to create the server's endpoint for the client connections. The remainder of the function is a loop that starts with a call to `select`. Two conditions can be true after `select` returns.

1. The descriptor `listenfd` can be ready for reading, which means a new client has called `cli_conn`. To handle this we call `serv_accept` and then update the `client` array and associated bookkeeping information for the new client. (We keep track of the highest descriptor number, for the first argument to `select`. We also keep track of the highest index in the `client` array that's in use.)

2. An existing client's connection can be ready for reading. This means one of two things: (a) the client has terminated, or (b) the client has sent a new request.

   We find out about a client termination by `read` returning 0 (end of file). If `read` returns greater than 0, there is a new request to process. We call `request` to handle the new client request.

We keep track of which descriptors are currently in use in the `allset` descriptor set. As new clients connect to the server, the appropriate bit is turned on in this descriptor set. The appropriate bit is turned off when the client terminates.

We always know when a client terminates, whether the termination is voluntary or not, since all the client's descriptors (including the connection to the server) are automatically closed by the kernel. This differs from the System V IPC mechanisms.

The `loop` function that uses the `poll` function is shown in Program 15.30.

```
#include     "opend.h"
#include     <poll.h>
#include     <stropts.h>

void
loop(void)
{
    int             i, maxi, listenfd, clifd, nread;
    char            buf[MAXLINE];
    uid_t           uid;
    struct pollfd   *pollfd;

    if ( (pollfd = malloc(open_max() * sizeof(struct pollfd))) == NULL)
        err_sys("malloc error");

                /* obtain fd to listen for client requests on */
    if ( (listenfd = serv_listen(CS_OPEN)) < 0)
        log_sys("serv_listen error");
    client_add(listenfd, 0);     /* we use [0] for listenfd */
    pollfd[0].fd = listenfd;
    pollfd[0].events = POLLIN;
    maxi = 0;
```

```
            for ( ; ; ) {
                if (poll(pollfd, maxi + 1, INFTIM) < 0)
                    log_sys("poll error");

                if (pollfd[0].revents & POLLIN) {
                        /* accept new client request */
                    if ( (clifd = serv_accept(listenfd, &uid)) < 0)
                        log_sys("serv_accept error: %d", clifd);
                    i = client_add(clifd, uid);
                    pollfd[i].fd = clifd;
                    pollfd[i].events = POLLIN;
                    if (i > maxi)
                        maxi = i;
                    log_msg("new connection: uid %d, fd %d", uid, clifd);
                }

                for (i = 1; i <= maxi; i++) {
                    if ( (clifd = client[i].fd) < 0)
                        continue;
                    if (pollfd[i].revents & POLLHUP)
                        goto hungup;
                    else if (pollfd[i].revents & POLLIN) {
                            /* read argument buffer from client */
                        if ( (nread = read(clifd, buf, MAXLINE)) < 0)
                            log_sys("read error on fd %d", clifd);
                        else if (nread == 0) {
hungup:
                            log_msg("closed: uid %d, fd %d",
                                                client[i].uid, clifd);
                            client_del(clifd);  /* client has closed conn */
                            pollfd[i].fd = -1;
                            close(clifd);
                        } else         /* process client's rquest */
                            request(buf, nread, clifd, client[i].uid);
                    }
                }
            }
        }
```

Program 15.30 The loop function using poll.

To allow for as many clients as there are open descriptors, we dynamically allocate space for the array of pollfd structures. (The function open_max was shown in Program 2.3.)

We use the zeroth entry of the client array for the listenfd descriptor. That way a client's index in the client array is the same index that we use in the pollfd array. The arrival of a new client connection is indicated by a POLLIN on the listenfd descriptor. As before, we call serv_accept to accept the connection.

For an existing client we have to handle two different events from poll: a client termination is indicated by POLLHUP and a new request from an existing client is indicated by POLLIN. Recall from Exercise 14.7 that the hangup message can arrive at the stream head while there is still data to be read from the stream. With a pipe we want to read all the data before processing the hangup. But with this server, when we receive the hangup from the client, we can close the connection (the stream) to the client, effectively throwing away any data still on the stream. This is because there is no reason to process any requests still on the stream, since we can't send any responses back.

As with the select version of this function, new requests from a client are handled by calling the request function (Program 15.31). This function is similar to the earlier version (Program 15.16). It calls the same function buf_args (Program 15.17) that calls cli_args (Program 15.18).

```
#include    "opend.h"
#include    <fcntl.h>

void
request(char *buf, int nread, int clifd, uid_t uid)
{
    int     newfd;

    if (buf[nread-1] != 0) {
        sprintf(errmsg, "request from uid %d not null terminated: %*.*s\n",
                            uid, nread, nread, buf);
        send_err(clifd, -1, errmsg);
        return;
    }
    log_msg("request: %s, from uid %d", buf, uid);

            /* parse the arguments, set options */
    if (buf_args(buf, cli_args) < 0) {
        send_err(clifd, -1, errmsg);
        log_msg(errmsg);
        return;
    }

    if ( (newfd = open(pathname, oflag)) < 0) {
        sprintf(errmsg, "can't open %s: %s\n",
                            pathname, strerror(errno));
        send_err(clifd, -1, errmsg);
        log_msg(errmsg);
        return;
    }

            /* send the descriptor */
    if (send_fd(clifd, newfd) < 0)
        log_sys("send_fd error");
    log_msg("sent fd %d over fd %d for %s", newfd, clifd, pathname);
    close(newfd);           /* we're done with descriptor */
}
```

Program 15.31 The request function.

This completes the open server, using a single daemon to handle all the client requests.

15.7 Summary

The key points in this chapter are the ability to pass file descriptors between processes and the ability of a server to accept unique connections from clients. We've seen how to do this under SVR4 and 4.3+BSD. These advanced IPC capabilities are provided by most current Unix systems. We'll use the functions that we developed in this chapter in Chapter 18 with our modem dialer.

We presented two versions of an open server. One version was invoked directly by the client, using fork and exec. The second was a daemon server that handled all client requests. Both versions used the file descriptor passing and receiving functions from Section 15.3. The final version also used the client–server connection functions from Section 15.5 and the I/O multiplexing functions from Section 12.5.

Exercises

15.1 Recode Program 15.1 to use the standard I/O library instead of read and write on the stream pipe.

15.2 Write the following program using the file descriptor passing functions from this chapter and the parent–child synchronization routines from Section 8.8. The program calls fork, the child opens an existing file and passes the open descriptor to the parent. The child then positions the file using lseek and notifies the parent. The parent reads the file's current offset and prints it for verification. If the file was passed from the child to the parent as we described, the parent and child should be sharing the same file table entry, so each time the child changes the file's current offset, that change should affect the parent's descriptor also. Have the child position the file to a different offset and notify the parent again.

15.3 In Programs 15.14 and 15.15 we differentiated between declaring and defining the global variables. What is the difference?

15.4 Recode the buf_args function (Program 15.17), removing the compile-time limit on the size of the argv array. Use dynamic memory allocation.

15.5 Describe ways to optimize the function loop in Program 15.29 and Program 15.30. Implement your optimizations.

16

A Database Library

16.1 Introduction

During the early 1980s Unix was considered a hostile environment for running a multi-user database system. (See Stonebraker [1981] and Weinberger [1982].) Earlier systems, such as Version 7, did indeed present large obstacles, since they did not provide any form of IPC (other than half-duplex pipes) and did not provide any form of record locking. Recent Unix systems, such as SVR4 and 4.3+BSD, provide a suitable environment for running a reliable, multiuser database system. Numerous commercial firms have offered these types of systems for years.

In this chapter we develop a simple, multiuser database library. It is a library of C functions that any program can call to fetch and store records in a database. This library of C functions is usually only one part of a complete database system. We do not develop the other pieces, such as a query language, leaving these items to the many textbooks on database systems. Our interest is the interface to Unix required by a database library and how that interface relates to the topics that we've already covered (such as record locking, in Section 12.3).

16.2 History

One popular library of database functions in Unix has been the dbm(3) library. This library was developed by Ken Thompson and uses a dynamic hashing scheme. It was originally provided with Version 7, appears in all Berkeley releases, and is also provided in the Berkeley compatibility library in SVR4. Seltzer and Yigit [1991] provide a detailed history of the dynamic hashing algorithm used by the dbm library, and other

515

implementations of this library. Unfortunately, a basic limitation of all these implementations is that none allows concurrent updating of the database by multiple processes. They provide no type of concurrency controls (such as record locking).

4.3+BSD provides a new db(3) library that supports three different forms of access: (a) record oriented, (b) hashing, and (c) a B-tree. Again, no form of concurrency is provided. (This fact is plainly stated in the BUGS section of the db(3) manual page.) Recent work by Seltzer and Olson [1992], however, indicates that a future release of this library will provide concurrency features similar to most commercial database systems.

Most commercial database libraries do provide the concurrency controls required for multiple processes to update a database simultaneously. These systems typically use advisory record locking, as we described in Section 12.3. These commercial systems usually implement their database using B+ trees [Comer 1979].

16.3 The Library

Let's first describe the C interface to the database library, then in the next section describe the actual implementation.

When we open a database we are returned a pointer to a DB structure. This is similar to fopen returning a pointer to a FILE structure (Section 5.2) and opendir returning a pointer to a DIR structure (Section 4.21). We'll pass this pointer to the remaining database functions.

```
#include "db.h"

DB *db_open(const char *pathname, int oflag, int mode);

                              Returns: pointer to DB structure if OK, NULL on error

void db_close(DB *db);
```

If db_open is successful, two files are created: *pathname.idx* is the index file and *pathname.dat* is the data file. The *oflag* argument is used as the second argument to open (Section 3.3) to specify how the files are to be opened (read-only, read–write, create file if it doesn't exist, etc.). *mode* is used as the third argument to open (the file access permissions) if the database files are created.

We call db_close when we're done with a database. It closes the index file and data file, and releases any memory that it allocated for internal buffers.

When we store a new record in the database we have to specify the key for the record and the data associated with the key. If the database contained personnel records, the key could be the employee ID and the data could be the employee's name, address, telephone number, date of hire, and the like. Our implementation requires that the key for each record be unique. (We can't have two different employee records with the same employee ID, for example.)

```
#include "db.h"

int db_store(DB *db, const char *key, const char *data, int flag);
```
                                    Returns: 0 if OK, nonzero on error (see following)

key and *data* are null-terminated character strings. The only restriction on these two strings is that neither can contain null bytes. They may contain, for example, newlines.

flag is either DB_INSERT (to insert a new record) or DB_REPLACE (to replace an existing record). These two constants are defined in the db.h header. If we specify DB_REPLACE and the record does not exist, the return value is −1. If we specify DB_INSERT and the record already exists, the return value is 1.

We can fetch any record from the database by just specifying its *key*.

```
#include "db.h"

char *db_fetch(DB *db, const char *key);
```
                                    Returns: pointer to data if OK, NULL if record not found

The return value is a pointer to the data that was stored with the *key*, if the record is found.

We can also delete a record from the database by specifying its *key*.

```
#include "db.h"

int db_delete(DB *db, const char *key);
```
                                    Returns: 0 if OK, −1 if record not found

In addition to fetching a record by specifying its key, we can also go through the entire database, reading each record in turn. To do this we first call db_rewind to rewind the database to the first record, and then call db_nextrec to read each sequential record.

```
#include "db.h"

void db_rewind(DB *db);

char *db_nextrec(DB *db, char *key);
```
                                    Returns: pointer to data if OK, NULL on end of file

If *key* is a nonnull pointer, db_nextrec stores the key starting at that location.

There is no order to the records returned by db_nextrec. All we're guaranteed is that we'll read each record in the database once. If we store three records with keys of

A, B, and C, in that order, we have no idea in which order db_nextrec will return the three records. It might return B, then A, then C, or some other (apparently random) order. The actual order depends on the implementation of the database.

These seven functions provide the interface to the database library. We now describe the actual implementation that we have chosen.

16.4   Implementation Overview

Most database access libraries use two files to store the information: an index file and a data file. The index file contains the actual index value (the key) and a pointer to the corresponding data record in the data file. Numerous techniques can be used to organize the index file so that it can be searched quickly and efficiently for any key—hashing and B+ trees are popular. We have chosen to use a fixed-size hash table with chaining for the index file. We mentioned in the description of db_open that we create two files—one with a suffix of .idx and a suffix of .dat for the other.

We store the key and index as null-terminated character strings—they cannot contain arbitrary binary data. Some database systems store numerical data in a binary format (one, two, or four bytes for an integer, for example) to save storage space. This complicates the functions and requires more work to make the database files portable between different systems. For example, if we have two systems on a network that use different formats for storing binary integers, we need to handle this if want both systems to access the database. (It is not at all uncommon today to have systems with different architectures sharing files on a network.) Storing all the records, both keys and data, as character strings simplifies everything. It does require additional disk space, but that is becoming less of a concern with the advances in disk technology.

db_store allows only one record to have a given key. Some database systems allow multiple records to have the same key, and then provide a way to access all the records associated with a given key. Additionally, we have only a single index file, meaning each data record can have only a single key. Some database systems allow each record to have multiple keys, and often use one index file per key. Each time a new record is inserted or deleted, each index file has to be updated accordingly. (An example of a file with multiple indexes is an employee file. We could have one index whose key is the employee ID and another whose key is the employee's Social Security number. Having an index whose key is the employee name could be a problem, as names need not be unique.)

Figure 16.1 shows a general picture of the database implementation. The index file consists of three portions: the free list pointer, the hash table, and the index records. All the fields in Figure 16.1 called *ptr* are just file offsets stored as an ASCII number.

To find a record in the database, given its key, db_fetch calculates the hash value of the key, which leads to one hash chain in the hash table. (The *chain ptr* field could be 0, indicating an empty chain.) We then follow this hash chain, which is a linked list of all the index records with this hash value. When we encounter a *chain ptr* value of 0, we've hit the end of the hash chain.

Let's look at an actual database file. Program 16.1 creates a new database and writes three records to it. Since we store all the fields in the database as ASCII

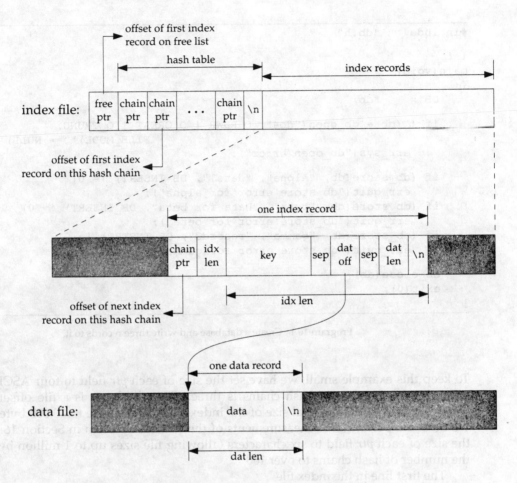

Figure 16.1 Arrangement of index file and data file.

characters, we can look at the actual index file and data file using any of the standard Unix tools.

```
$ ls -l db4.*
-rw-r--r--  1 stevens      28 Oct 30 06:42 db4.dat
-rw-r--r--  1 stevens      72 Oct 30 06:42 db4.idx
$ cat db4.idx
 0  53  35   0
 0  10Alpha:0:6
 0  10beta:6:14
17  11gamma:20:8
$ cat db4.dat
data1
Data for beta
record3
```

```
#include     "db.h"

int
main(void)
{
    DB        *db;

    if ( (db = db_open("db4", O_RDWR | O_CREAT | O_TRUNC,
                                        FILE_MODE)) == NULL)
        err_sys("db_open error");

    if (db_store(db, "Alpha", "data1", DB_INSERT) != 0)
        err_quit("db_store error for alpha");
    if (db_store(db, "beta", "Data for beta", DB_INSERT) != 0)
        err_quit("db_store error for beta");
    if (db_store(db, "gamma", "record3", DB_INSERT) != 0)
        err_quit("db_store error for gamma");

    db_close(db);
    exit(0);
}
```

Program 16.1 Create a database and write three records to it.

To keep this example small, we have set the size of each *ptr* field to four ASCII characters, and the number of hash chains is three. Since each *ptr* is a file offset, a four-character field limits the total size of the index file and data file to 10,000 bytes. When we do some performance measurements of the database system in Section 16.8, we set the size of each *ptr* field to six characters (allowing file sizes up to 1 million bytes), and the number of hash chains to over 100.

The first line in the index file

```
    0   53   35    0
```

is the free list pointer (0, the free list is empty), and the three hash chain pointers: 53, 35, and 0. The next line

```
    0   10Alpha:0:6
```

shows the format of each index record. The first field (0) is the four-character chain pointer. This record is the end of its hash chain. The next field (10) is the four-character *idx len*, the length of the remainder of this index record. We read each index record using two reads: one to read the two fixed-size fields (the *chain ptr* and *idx len*), then another to read the remaining (variable-length) portion. The remaining three fields, *key*, *dat off*, and *dat len*, are delimited by a separator character (a colon in this case). We need the separator character since each of these three fields is variable length. The separator character can't appear in the key. Finally, a newline terminates the index record. The newline isn't required, since *idx len* contains the length of the record. We store the newline to separate each index record so we can use the normal Unix tools, such as cat and more with the index file. The *key* is the value that we specified when we wrote the record to the database. The data offset (0) and data length (6) refer to the data file. We can see that the data record does start at offset 0 in the data file, and has a length of six bytes. (As with the index file, we automatically append a newline to each data record, so we can use the normal Unix tools with the file. This newline at the end is not returned to the caller by db_fetch.)

If we follow the three hash chains in this example, we see that the first record on the first hash chain is at offset 53 (gamma). The next record on this chain is at offset 17 (alpha), and this is the last record on the chain. The first record on the second hash chain is at offset 35 (beta), and it's the last record on the chain. The third hash chain is empty.

Notice that the order of the keys in the index file and the order of their corresponding records in the data file is the same as the order of the calls to db_store in Program 16.1. Since the O_TRUNC flag was specified for db_open, the index file and data file were both truncated and the database initialized from scratch. In this case db_store just appends the new index records and data records to the end of the corresponding file. We'll see later that db_store can also reuse portions of these two files that correspond to deleted records.

The choice of a fixed-size hash table for the index is a compromise. It allows fast access as long as each hash chain isn't too long. We want to be able to search for any key quickly, but we don't want to complicate the data structures by using either a B-tree or dynamic extensible hashing. Dynamic extensible hashing has the advantage that any data record can be located with only two disk accesses (see Seltzer and Yigit [1991] for details). B-trees have the advantage of traversing the database in key order (something that we can't do with the db_nextrec function, using a hash table.)

16.5 Centralized or Decentralized?

Given multiple processes accessing the same database, there are two ways we can implement the functions.

1. Centralized. Have a single process that is the database manager and have it be the only process that accesses the database. The functions contact this central process using some form of IPC.

2. Decentralized. Have each function apply the required concurrency controls (locking) and then issue its own I/O function calls.

Database systems have been built using each of these techniques. The trend in Unix systems, however, is the decentralized approach. Given adequate locking routines, the decentralized implementation is usually faster, because IPC is avoided. Figure 16.2 depicts the operation of the centralized approach.

We purposely show the IPC going through the kernel, as most forms of message passing under Unix operate this way. (Shared memory, as described in Section 14.9,

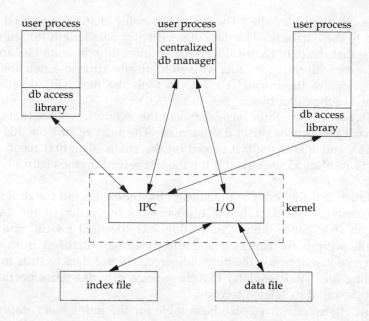

Figure 16.2 Centralized approach for database access.

avoids this copying of the data.) We see with the centralized approach that a record is read by the central process and then passed to the requesting process using IPC. This is a disadvantage of this design. Note that the centralized database manager is the only process that does I/O with the database files.

The centralized approach has the advantage that customer tuning of its operation may be possible. For example, we might be able to assign different priorities to different processes through the centralized process. This could affect the scheduling of I/O operations by the centralized process. With the decentralized approach this is harder to do. We are usually at the mercy of the kernel's disk I/O scheduling policy and locking policy (i.e., if three processes are waiting for a lock to become available, which process gets the lock next?).

The decentralized approach is shown in Figure 16.3. This is the design that we'll implement in this chapter. The user processes that call the functions in the database library to perform I/O are considered cooperating processes, since they use record locking to provide concurrent access.

16.6 Concurrency

We purposely chose a two-file implementation (an index file and a data file) because that's how most systems are implemented. It requires us to handle the locking interactions of both files. But there are numerous ways to handle the locking of these two files.

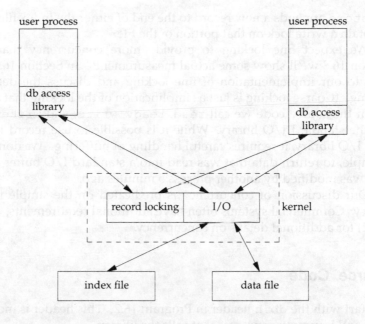

Figure 16.3 Decentralized approach for database access.

Coarse Locking

The simplest form of locking is to use one of the two files as a lock for the entire database and to require the caller to obtain this lock before operating on the database. We call this *coarse locking*. For example, we can say that the process with a read lock on byte 0 of the index file has read access to the entire database. A process with a write lock on byte 0 of the index file has write access to the entire database. We can use the normal Unix record locking semantics to allow any number of readers at one time, but only one writer at a time. (Recall Figure 12.2.) The functions db_fetch and db_nextrec require a read lock, and db_delete, db_store, and db_open all require a write lock. (The reason db_open requires a write lock is that if the file is being created it has to write the empty free list and hash chains at the front of the index file.)

The problem with coarse locking is that it doesn't allow the maximum amount of concurrency. If a process is adding a record to one hash chain, another process should be able to read a record on a different hash chain.

Fine Locking

We enhance coarse locking to allow more concurrency and call this *fine locking*. We first require a reader or writer to obtain a read lock or a write lock on the hash chain for a given record. We allow any number of readers at one time on any hash chain, but only a single writer on a hash chain. Next, a writer that needs to access the free list (either db_delete or db_store) must obtain a write lock on the free list. Finally, whenever db_store appends a new record to the end of either the index file or the data file, it has to obtain a write lock on that portion of the file.

We expect fine locking to provide more concurrency than coarse locking. In Section 16.8 we'll show some actual measurements. In Section 16.7 we show the source code to our implementation of fine locking and discuss the details of implementing locking. (Coarse locking is just a simplification of the locking that we show.)

In the source code we call read, readv, write, and writev directly. We do not use the standard I/O library. While it is possible to use record locking with the standard I/O library, it requires careful handling of buffering. We don't want an fgets, for example, to return data that was read into a standard I/O buffer 10 minutes ago, if the data was modified by another process 5 minutes ago.

Our discussion of concurrency is predicated on the simple needs of the database library. Commercial systems often have additional requirements. See Chapter 3 of Date [1982] for additional details on concurrency.

16.7 Source Code

We start with the db.h header in Program 16.2. This header is included by all the functions and by any user process that calls the library.

```
#include    <sys/types.h>
#include    <sys/stat.h>        /* open() & db_open() mode */
#include    <fcntl.h>           /* open() & db_open() flags */
#include    <stddef.h>          /* NULL */
#include    "ourhdr.h"

            /* flags for db_store() */
#define DB_INSERT   1           /* insert new record only */
#define DB_REPLACE  2           /* replace existing record */

            /* magic numbers */
#define IDXLEN_SZ   4           /* #ascii chars for length of index record */
#define IDXLEN_MIN  6           /* key, sep, start, sep, length, newline */
#define IDXLEN_MAX  1024        /* arbitrary */
#define SEP         ':'         /* separator character in index record */
#define DATLEN_MIN  2           /* data byte, newline */
#define DATLEN_MAX  1024        /* arbitrary */

            /* following definitions are for hash chains and free list chain
               in index file */
#define PTR_SZ      6           /* size of ptr field in hash chain */
#define PTR_MAX     999999      /* max offset (file size) = 10**PTR_SZ - 1 */
#define NHASH_DEF   137         /* default hash table size */
#define FREE_OFF    0           /* offset of ptr to free list in index file */
#define HASH_OFF    PTR_SZ      /* offset of hash table in index file */

typedef struct {    /* our internal structure */
  int  idxfd;  /* fd for index file */
  int  datfd;  /* fd for data file */
  int  oflag;  /* flags for open()/db_open(): O_xxx */
```

```
        char   *idxbuf;/* malloc'ed buffer for index record */
        char   *datbuf;/* malloc'ed buffer for data record*/
        char   *name;  /* name db was opened under */
        off_t idxoff; /* offset in index file of index record */
                      /* actual key is at (idxoff + PTR_SZ + IDXLEN_SZ) */
        size_t idxlen;/* length of index record */
                      /* excludes IDXLEN_SZ bytes at front of index record */
                      /* includes newline at end of index record */
        off_t datoff; /* offset in data file of data record */
        size_t datlen;/* length of data record */
                      /* includes newline at end */
        off_t ptrval; /* contents of chain ptr in index record */
        off_t ptroff; /* offset of chain ptr that points to this index record */
        off_t chainoff;/* offset of hash chain for this index record */
        off_t hashoff;/* offset in index file of hash table */
        int   nhash;  /* current hash table size */
        long  cnt_delok;  /* delete OK */
        long  cnt_delerr; /* delete error */
        long  cnt_fetchok;/* fetch OK */
        long  cnt_fetcherr;/* fetch error */
        long  cnt_nextrec;/* nextrec */
        long  cnt_stor1;  /* store: DB_INSERT, no empty, appended */
        long  cnt_stor2;  /* store: DB_INSERT, found empty, reused */
        long  cnt_stor3;  /* store: DB_REPLACE, diff data len, appended */
        long  cnt_stor4;  /* store: DB_REPLACE, same data len, overwrote */
        long  cnt_storerr;/* store error */
    } DB;

    typedef unsigned long  hash_t; /* hash values */

              /* user-callable functions */
    DB      *db_open(const char *, int, int);
    void     db_close(DB *);
    char    *db_fetch(DB *, const char *);
    int      db_store(DB *, const char *, const char *, int);
    int      db_delete(DB *, const char *);
    void     db_rewind(DB *);
    char    *db_nextrec(DB *, char *);
    void     db_stats(DB *);

              /* internal functions */
    DB      *_db_alloc(int);
    int      _db_checkfree(DB *);
    int      _db_dodelete(DB *);
    int      _db_emptykey(char *);
    int      _db_find(DB *, const char *, int);
    int      _db_findfree(DB *, int, int);
    int      _db_free(DB *);
    hash_t   _db_hash(DB *, const char *);
    char    *_db_nextkey(DB *);
    char    *_db_readdat(DB *);
    off_t    _db_readidx(DB *, off_t);
```

```
off_t       _db_readptr(DB *, off_t);
void        _db_writedat(DB *, const char *, off_t, int);
void        _db_writeidx(DB *, const char *, off_t, int, off_t);
void        _db_writeptr(DB *, off_t, off_t);
```

Program 16.2 The db.h header.

Here we define the fundamental limits of the implementation. These can be changed if desired, to support bigger databases. Some of the values that we have defined as constants could also be made variable, with some added complexity in the implementation. For example, we set the size of the hash table to 137 entries. A better technique would be to let the caller specify this as an argument to db_open, based on the expected size of the database. We would then have to store this size at the beginning of the index file.

The DB structure is where we keep all the information for each open database. The DB * pointer that is returned by db_open and used by all the other functions is just a pointer to one of these structures.

We have chosen to name all the user-callable functions starting with db_ and all the internal functions start with _db_.

In Program 16.3 we show db_open. It opens the index file and data file, initializing the index file if necessary. It calls _db_alloc to allocate a DB structure and initializes it.

```
#include    "db.h"

/* Open or create a database.  Same arguments as open(). */

DB *
db_open(const char *pathname, int oflag, int mode)
{
    DB          *db;
    int         i, len;
    char        asciiptr[PTR_SZ + 1],
                hash[(NHASH_DEF + 1) * PTR_SZ + 2];
                    /* +2 for newline and null */
    struct stat statbuff;

        /* Allocate a DB structure, and the buffers it needs */
    len = strlen(pathname);
    if ( (db = _db_alloc(len)) == NULL)
        err_dump("_db_alloc error for DB");

    db->oflag = oflag;      /* save a copy of the open flags */

        /* Open index file */
    strcpy(db->name, pathname);
    strcat(db->name, ".idx");
    if ( (db->idxfd = open(db->name, oflag, mode)) < 0) {
        _db_free(db);
        return(NULL);
    }
```

```
        /* Open data file */
    strcpy(db->name + len, ".dat");
    if ( (db->datfd = open(db->name, oflag, mode)) < 0) {
        _db_free(db);
        return(NULL);
    }

        /* If the database was created, we have to initialize it */
    if ((oflag & (O_CREAT | O_TRUNC)) == (O_CREAT | O_TRUNC)) {
            /* Write lock the entire file so that we can stat
               the file, check its size, and initialize it,
               as an atomic operation. */
        if (writew_lock(db->idxfd, 0, SEEK_SET, 0) < 0)
            err_dump("writew_lock error");

        if (fstat(db->idxfd, &statbuff) < 0)
            err_sys("fstat error");
        if (statbuff.st_size == 0) {
                /* We have to build a list of (NHASH_DEF + 1) chain
                   ptrs with a value of 0.  The +1 is for the free
                   list pointer that precedes the hash table. */
            sprintf(asciiptr, "%*d", PTR_SZ, 0);
            hash[0] = 0;
            for (i = 0; i < (NHASH_DEF + 1); i++)
                strcat(hash, asciiptr);
            strcat(hash, "\n");

            i = strlen(hash);
            if (write(db->idxfd, hash, i) != i)
                err_dump("write error initializing index file");
        }
        if (un_lock(db->idxfd, 0, SEEK_SET, 0) < 0)
            err_dump("un_lock error");
    }
    db->nhash   = NHASH_DEF;/* hash table size */
    db->hashoff = HASH_OFF; /* offset in index file of hash table */
                            /* free list ptr always at FREE_OFF */
    db_rewind(db);

    return(db);
}
```

Program 16.3 The db_open function.

We encounter locking if the database is being created. Consider two processes trying to create the same database at about the same time. Assume the first process calls fstat and is blocked by the kernel after fstat returns. The second process calls db_open, finds the length of the index file is 0, and initializes the free list and hash chain. The second process continues executing and writes one record to the database. At this point the second process is blocked and the first process continues executing right after the call to fstat. The first process finds the size of the index file to be 0 (since fstat was called before the second process initialized the index file) so the first process initializes the free list and hash chain, wiping out the record that the second process stored in the database. The way to prevent this is to use locking. We use the functions `readw_lock`, `writew_lock`, and `un_lock` from Section 12.3.

The function `_db_alloc` in Program 16.4 is called by `db_open` to allocate storage for the DB structure, an index buffer, and a data buffer.

```c
#include    "db.h"

/* Allocate & initialize a DB structure, and all the buffers it needs  */

DB *
_db_alloc(int namelen)
{
    DB      *db;

            /* Use calloc, to init structure to zero */
    if ( (db = calloc(1, sizeof(DB))) == NULL)
        err_dump("calloc error for DB");

    db->idxfd = db->datfd = -1;                /* descriptors */

        /* Allocate room for the name.
           +5 for ".idx" or ".dat" plus null at end. */

    if ( (db->name = malloc(namelen + 5)) == NULL)
        err_dump("malloc error for name");

        /* Allocate an index buffer and a data buffer.
           +2 for newline and null at end. */

    if ( (db->idxbuf = malloc(IDXLEN_MAX + 2)) == NULL)
        err_dump("malloc error for index buffer");
    if ( (db->datbuf = malloc(DATLEN_MAX + 2)) == NULL)
        err_dump("malloc error for data buffer");

    return(db);
}
```

Program 16.4 The `_db_alloc` function.

The sizes of the index buffer and data buffer are defined in the `db.h` header. An enhancement to the database library would be to allow these buffers to expand as required. We could keep track of the size of these two buffers and call `realloc` whenever we find we need a bigger buffer.

These dynamically allocated buffers are released, and the open files closed, by `_db_free` (Program 16.5). This function is called by `db_open` if an error occurs while opening the index file or data file. `_db_free` is also called by `db_close` (Program 16.6).

`db_fetch` (Program 16.7) reads a record, given its key. It calls `_db_find` to search the database for the index record and, if found, calls `_db_readdat` to read the corresponding data record.

```c
#include    "db.h"

/* Free up a DB structure, and all the malloc'ed buffers it
 * may point to.  Also close the file descriptors if still open. */

int
_db_free(DB *db)
{
    if (db->idxfd >= 0 && close(db->idxfd) < 0)
        err_dump("index close error");
    if (db->datfd >= 0 && close(db->datfd) < 0)
        err_dump("data close error");
    db->idxfd = db->datfd = -1;

    if (db->idxbuf != NULL)
        free(db->idxbuf);
    if (db->datbuf != NULL)
        free(db->datbuf);
    if (db->name != NULL)
        free(db->name);
    free(db);
    return(0);
}
```

Program 16.5 The _db_free function.

```c
#include    "db.h"

void
db_close(DB *db)
{
    _db_free(db);    /* closes fds, free buffers & struct */
}
```

Program 16.6 The db_close function.

```c
#include    "db.h"

/* Fetch a specified record.
 * We return a pointer to the null-terminated data. */

char *
db_fetch(DB *db, const char *key)
{
    char    *ptr;

    if (_db_find(db, key, 0) < 0) {
        ptr = NULL;                 /* error, record not found */
        db->cnt_fetcherr++;
    } else {
        ptr = _db_readdat(db);  /* return pointer to data */
        db->cnt_fetchok++;
    }
```

```
                    /* Unlock the hash chain that _db_find() locked */
        if (un_lock(db->idxfd, db->chainoff, SEEK_SET, 1) < 0)
            err_dump("un_lock error");
        return(ptr);
}
```

Program 16.7 The db_fetch function.

Program 16.8 shows _db_find, the function that traverses a hash chain. It's called by all the functions that look up a record given a key: db_fetch, db_delete, and db_store.

```
#include    "db.h"

/* Find the specified record.
 * Called by db_delete(), db_fetch(), and db_store(). */

int
_db_find(DB *db, const char *key, int writelock)
{
    off_t    offset, nextoffset;

        /* Calculate hash value for this key, then calculate byte
           offset of corresponding chain ptr in hash table.
           This is where our search starts. */

            /* calc offset in hash table for this key */
    db->chainoff = (_db_hash(db, key) * PTR_SZ) + db->hashoff;
    db->ptroff = db->chainoff;

            /* Here's where we lock this hash chain.  It's the
               caller's responsibility to unlock it when done.
               Note we lock and unlock only the first byte. */
    if (writelock) {
        if (writew_lock(db->idxfd, db->chainoff, SEEK_SET, 1) < 0)
            err_dump("writew_lock error");
    } else {
        if (readw_lock(db->idxfd, db->chainoff, SEEK_SET, 1) < 0)
            err_dump("readw_lock error");
    }
            /* Get the offset in the index file of first record
               on the hash chain (can be 0) */
    offset = _db_readptr(db, db->ptroff);

    while (offset != 0) {
        nextoffset = _db_readidx(db, offset);
        if (strcmp(db->idxbuf, key) == 0)
            break;       /* found a match */

        db->ptroff = offset;   /* offset of this (unequal) record */
        offset = nextoffset;   /* next one to compare */
    }
```

```
        if (offset == 0)
            return(-1);        /* error, record not found */

        /* We have a match.  We're guaranteed that db->ptroff contains
           the offset of the chain ptr that points to this matching
           index record.  _db_dodelete() uses this fact.  (The chain
           ptr that points to this matching record could be in an
           index record or in the hash table.) */
    return(0);
}
```

Program 16.8 The _db_find function.

The last argument to _db_find specifies if we want a read lock (0) or a write lock (1). We saw that db_fetch requires a read lock, while db_delete and db_store both require a write lock. _db_find waits for the given lock before going through the hash chain.

The while loop in _db_find is where we go through each index record on the hash chain, comparing keys. The function _db_readidx is called to read each index record.

Note the final comment in _db_find. As we make our way through the hash chain, we keep track of the previous index record that points to the current index record. We'll use this when we delete a record, since we have to modify the chain pointer of the previous record when we delete the current record.

Let's start with the easy functions that are called by _db_find first. _db_hash (Program 16.9) calculates the hash value for a given key. It just multiplies each ASCII character times its 1-based index and divides the result by the number of hash table entries. The remainder from this division is the hash value for this key.

```
#include    "db.h"

/* Calculate the hash value for a key. */

hash_t
_db_hash(DB *db, const char *key)
{
    hash_t      hval;
    const char  *ptr;
    char        c;
    int         i;

    hval = 0;
    for (ptr = key, i = 1; c = *ptr++; i++)
        hval += c * i;      /* ascii char times its 1-based index */

    return(hval % db->nhash);
}
```

Program 16.9 The _db_hash function.

The next function called by `_db_find` is `_db_readptr` (Program 16.10). It reads any one of three different chain pointers: (1) the pointer at the beginning of the index file that points to the first index record on the free list, (2) the pointers in the hash table that point to the first index record on each hash chain, and (3) the pointers that are stored at the beginning of each index record (whether the index record is part of a hash chain or on the free list). No locking is done by this function—that is up to the caller.

```
#include    "db.h"

/* Read a chain ptr field from anywhere in the index file:
 * the free list pointer, a hash table chain ptr, or an
 * index record chain ptr. */

off_t
_db_readptr(DB *db, off_t offset)
{
    char    asciiptr[PTR_SZ + 1];

    if (lseek(db->idxfd, offset, SEEK_SET) == -1)
        err_dump("lseek error to ptr field");
    if (read(db->idxfd, asciiptr, PTR_SZ) != PTR_SZ)
        err_dump("read error of ptr field");

    asciiptr[PTR_SZ] = 0;                   /* null terminate */
    return(atol(asciiptr));
}
```

Program 16.10 The `_db_readptr` function.

The while loop in `_db_find` calls `_db_readidx` to read each index record. This is a larger function (Program 16.11) that reads the index record and divides it into the appropriate fields.

```
#include    "db.h"
#include    <sys/uio.h>        /* struct iovec */

/* Read the next index record. We start at the specified offset in
 * the index file. We read the index record into db->idxbuf and
 * replace the separators with null bytes. If all is OK we set
 * db->datoff and db->datlen to the offset and length of the
 * corresponding data record in the data file. */

off_t
_db_readidx(DB *db, off_t offset)
{
    int            i;
    char           *ptr1, *ptr2;
    char           asciiptr[PTR_SZ + 1], asciilen[IDXLEN_SZ + 1];
    struct iovec   iov[2];

        /* Position index file and record the offset. db_nextrec()
           calls us with offset==0, meaning read from current offset.
           We still need to call lseek() to record the current offset. */
```

```
    if ( (db->idxoff = lseek(db->idxfd, offset,
                            offset == 0 ? SEEK_CUR : SEEK_SET)) == -1)
        err_dump("lseek error");

        /* Read the ascii chain ptr and the ascii length at
           the front of the index record.  This tells us the
           remaining size of the index record. */
    iov[0].iov_base = asciiptr;
    iov[0].iov_len  = PTR_SZ;
    iov[1].iov_base = asciilen;
    iov[1].iov_len  = IDXLEN_SZ;
    if ( (i = readv(db->idxfd, &iov[0], 2)) != PTR_SZ + IDXLEN_SZ) {
        if (i == 0 && offset == 0)
            return(-1);         /* EOF for db_nextrec() */
        err_dump("readv error of index record");
    }

    asciiptr[PTR_SZ] = 0;               /* null terminate */
    db->ptrval = atol(asciiptr);    /* offset of next key in chain */
                        /* this is our return value; always >= 0 */
    asciilen[IDXLEN_SZ] = 0;            /* null terminate */
    if ( (db->idxlen = atoi(asciilen)) < IDXLEN_MIN ||
                        db->idxlen > IDXLEN_MAX)
        err_dump("invalid length");

        /* Now read the actual index record.  We read it into the key
           buffer that we malloced when we opened the database. */
    if ( (i = read(db->idxfd, db->idxbuf, db->idxlen)) != db->idxlen)
        err_dump("read error of index record");
    if (db->idxbuf[db->idxlen-1] != '\n')
        err_dump("missing newline");    /* sanity checks */
    db->idxbuf[db->idxlen-1] = 0;           /* replace newline with null */

        /* Find the separators in the index record */
    if ( (ptr1 = strchr(db->idxbuf, SEP)) == NULL)
        err_dump("missing first separator");
    *ptr1++ = 0;                        /* replace SEP with null */

    if ( (ptr2 = strchr(ptr1, SEP)) == NULL)
        err_dump("missing second separator");
    *ptr2++ = 0;                        /* replace SEP with null */

    if (strchr(ptr2, SEP) != NULL)
        err_dump("too many separators");

        /* Get the starting offset and length of the data record */
    if ( (db->datoff = atol(ptr1)) < 0)
        err_dump("starting offset < 0");
    if ( (db->datlen = atol(ptr2)) <= 0 || db->datlen > DATLEN_MAX)
        err_dump("invalid length");
    return(db->ptrval);     /* return offset of next key in chain */
}
```

Program 16.11 The _db_readidx function.

We call readv to read the two fixed-length fields at the beginning of the index record: the chain pointer to the next index record and the size of the variable-length index record that follows. Once these two fields are read, the variable-length index record is read, and the three remaining fields are separated: the key, the offset of the corresponding data record, and the length of the data record. Note that the data record is not read. That is left to the caller. In db_fetch, for example, we don't read the data record until _db_find has read the index record that matches the key that we're looking for.

We now return to db_fetch. If _db_find locates the index record with the matching key, we call _db_readdat to read the corresponding data record. This is a simple function (Program 16.12).

```
#include    "db.h"

/* Read the current data record into the data buffer.
 * Return a pointer to the null-terminated data buffer. */

char *
_db_readdat(DB *db)
{
    if (lseek(db->datfd, db->datoff, SEEK_SET) == -1)
        err_dump("lseek error");

    if (read(db->datfd, db->datbuf, db->datlen) != db->datlen)
        err_dump("read error");
    if (db->datbuf[db->datlen - 1] != '\n')       /* sanity check */
        err_dump("missing newline");
    db->datbuf[db->datlen - 1] = 0;        /* replace newline with null */

    return(db->datbuf);     /* return pointer to data record */
}
```

Program 16.12 The _db_readdat function.

We started at db_fetch and have finally read both the index record and corresponding data record. Note that the only locking that has been done has been the read lock applied by _db_find. Since we have the hash chain read locked, we're guaranteed that no other process is proceeding down the same hash chain modifying anything.

Now let's examine the db_delete function (Program 16.13). It starts the same as db_fetch, calling _db_find to locate the record. But this time the final argument to _db_find is 1, indicating that we need the hash chain write locked.

db_delete calls _db_dodelete (Program 16.14) to do all the work. (We'll see later that db_store also calls _db_dodelete.) Most of the function just updates two linked lists, the free list and the hash chain for this key.

When a record is deleted we set its key and data record to blanks. This fact is used by db_nextrec, which we'll examine later in this section.

_db_dodelete write locks the free list. This is to prevent two processes that are deleting records at the same time, on two different hash chains, from interfering with each other. Since we'll add the deleted record to the free list, which changes the free list pointer, only one process at a time can be doing this.

```
#include     "db.h"

/* Delete the specified record */

int
db_delete(DB *db, const char *key)
{
    int     rc;

    if (_db_find(db, key, 1) == 0) {
        rc = _db_dodelete(db);    /* record found */
        db->cnt_delok++;
    } else {
        rc = -1;                  /* not found */
        db->cnt_delerr++;
    }

    if (un_lock(db->idxfd, db->chainoff, SEEK_SET, 1) < 0)
        err_dump("un_lock error");
    return(rc);
}
```

Program 16.13 The db_delete function.

```
#include     "db.h"

/* Delete the current record specified by the DB structure.
 * This function is called by db_delete() and db_store(),
 * after the record has been located by _db_find(). */

int
_db_dodelete(DB *db)
{
    int     i;
    char    *ptr;
    off_t   freeptr, saveptr;

        /* Set data buffer to all blanks */
    for (ptr = db->datbuf, i = 0; i < db->datlen - 1; i++)
        *ptr++ = ' ';
    *ptr = 0;    /* null terminate for _db_writedat() */

        /* Set key to blanks */
    ptr = db->idxbuf;
    while (*ptr)
        *ptr++ = ' ';

        /* We have to lock the free list */
    if (writew_lock(db->idxfd, FREE_OFF, SEEK_SET, 1) < 0)
        err_dump("writew_lock error");
```

```
                /* Write the data record with all blanks */
        _db_writedat(db, db->datbuf, db->datoff, SEEK_SET);

                /* Read the free list pointer.  Its value becomes the
                   chain ptr field of the deleted index record.  This means
                   the deleted record becomes the head of the free list. */
        freeptr = _db_readptr(db, FREE_OFF);

                /* Save the contents of index record chain ptr,
                   before it's rewritten by _db_writeidx(). */
        saveptr = db->ptrval;

                /* Rewrite the index record.  This also rewrites the length
                   of the index record, the data offset, and the data length,
                   none of which has changed, but that's OK. */
        _db_writeidx(db, db->idxbuf, db->idxoff, SEEK_SET, freeptr);

                /* Write the new free list pointer */
        _db_writeptr(db, FREE_OFF, db->idxoff);

                /* Rewrite the chain ptr that pointed to this record
                   being deleted.  Recall that _db_find() sets db->ptroff
                   to point to this chain ptr.  We set this chain ptr
                   to the contents of the deleted record's chain ptr,
                   saveptr, which can be either zero or nonzero. */
        _db_writeptr(db, db->ptroff, saveptr);

        if (un_lock(db->idxfd, FREE_OFF, SEEK_SET, 1) < 0)
                err_dump("un_lock error");

        return(0);
}
```

Program 16.14 The _db_dodelete function.

_db_dodelete writes the all-blank data record by calling _db_writedat
(Program 16.15). Notice that the data file is not locked by _db_writedat. Since
db_delete has write locked the hash chain for this record, we know that no other process is reading or writing this particular data record. When we cover db_store later in
this section, we'll encounter the case where _db_writedat is appending to the data
file and has to lock it.

_db_writedat calls writev to write the data record and newline. We can't
assume that the caller's buffer has room at the end for us to append the newline to it.
Recall Section 12.7, where we determined that a single writev is faster than two
writes.

Then _db_dodelete rewrites the index record, after changing the chain pointer in
the index record to point to the first record on the free list. (If the free list was empty,
this new chain pointer is 0.) The free list pointer is then rewritten, to point to the index
record that we just wrote (the deleted record). This means that the free list is handled
on a first-in, first-out basis—deleted records are added to the front of the free list.

```
#include    "db.h"
#include    <sys/uio.h>        /* struct iovec */

/* Write a data record. Called by _db_dodelete() (to write
   the record with blanks) and db_store(). */

void
_db_writedat(DB *db, const char *data, off_t offset, int whence)
{
    struct iovec    iov[2];
    static char     newline = '\n';

        /* If we're appending, we have to lock before doing the lseek()
           and write() to make the two an atomic operation.  If we're
           overwriting an existing record, we don't have to lock. */
    if (whence == SEEK_END)       /* we're appending, lock entire file */
        if (writew_lock(db->datfd, 0, SEEK_SET, 0) < 0)
            err_dump("writew_lock error");

    if ( (db->datoff = lseek(db->datfd, offset, whence)) == -1)
        err_dump("lseek error");
    db->datlen = strlen(data) + 1;   /* datlen includes newline */

    iov[0].iov_base = (char *) data;
    iov[0].iov_len  = db->datlen - 1;
    iov[1].iov_base = &newline;
    iov[1].iov_len  = 1;
    if (writev(db->datfd, &iov[0], 2) != db->datlen)
        err_dump("writev error of data record");

    if (whence == SEEK_END)
        if (un_lock(db->datfd, 0, SEEK_SET, 0) < 0)
            err_dump("un_lock error");
}
```

Program 16.15 The `_db_writedat` function.

Notice that we don't have a separate free list for the index file and data file. When the record is deleted, the index record is added to the free list, and this index record points to the deleted data record. There are better ways to handle record deletion, in exchange for added code complexity.

Program 16.16 shows `_db_writeidx`, the function called by `_db_dodelete` to write an index record. As with `_db_writedat`, this function deals with locking only when a new index record is being appended to the index file. When `_db_dodelete` calls this function, we're rewriting an existing index record. We know in this case that the caller has write locked the hash chain, so no additional locking is required.

```
#include    "db.h"
#include    <sys/uio.h>        /* struct iovec */

/* Write an index record.
 * _db_writedat() is called before this function, to set the fields
 * datoff and datlen in the DB structure, which we need to write
 * the index record. */

void
_db_writeidx(DB *db, const char *key,
                    off_t offset, int whence, off_t ptrval)
{
    struct iovec    iov[2];
    char            asciiptrlen[PTR_SZ + IDXLEN_SZ +1];
    int             len;

    if ( (db->ptrval = ptrval) < 0 || ptrval > PTR_MAX)
        err_quit("invalid ptr: %d", ptrval);

    sprintf(db->idxbuf, "%s%c%d%c%d\n",
                key, SEP, db->datoff, SEP, db->datlen);
    if ( (len = strlen(db->idxbuf)) < IDXLEN_MIN || len > IDXLEN_MAX)
        err_dump("invalid length");
    sprintf(asciiptrlen, "%*d%*d", PTR_SZ, ptrval, IDXLEN_SZ, len);

        /* If we're appending, we have to lock before doing the lseek()
            and write() to make the two an atomic operation.  If we're
            overwriting an existing record, we don't have to lock. */
    if (whence == SEEK_END)      /* we're appending */
        if (writew_lock(db->idxfd, ((db->nhash+1)*PTR_SZ)+1,
                                                SEEK_SET, 0) < 0)
            err_dump("writew_lock error");

        /* Position the index file and record the offset */
    if ( (db->idxoff = lseek(db->idxfd, offset, whence)) == -1)
        err_dump("lseek error");

    iov[0].iov_base = asciiptrlen;
    iov[0].iov_len  = PTR_SZ + IDXLEN_SZ;
    iov[1].iov_base = db->idxbuf;
    iov[1].iov_len  = len;
    if (writev(db->idxfd, &iov[0], 2) != PTR_SZ + IDXLEN_SZ + len)
        err_dump("writev error of index record");

    if (whence == SEEK_END)
        if (un_lock(db->idxfd, ((db->nhash+1)*PTR_SZ)+1, SEEK_SET, 0) < 0)
            err_dump("un_lock error");
}
```

Program 16.16 The _db_writeidx function.

The final function that _db_dodelete calls is _db_writeptr (Program 16.17). It is called twice—once to rewrite the free list pointer and once to rewrite the hash chain pointer (that pointed to the deleted record).

```
#include     "db.h"

/* Write a chain ptr field somewhere in the index file:
 * the free list, the hash table, or in an index record. */

void
_db_writeptr(DB *db, off_t offset, off_t ptrval)
{
    char     asciiptr[PTR_SZ + 1];

    if (ptrval < 0 || ptrval > PTR_MAX)
        err_quit("invalid ptr: %d", ptrval);
    sprintf(asciiptr, "%*d", PTR_SZ, ptrval);

    if (lseek(db->idxfd, offset, SEEK_SET) == -1)
        err_dump("lseek error to ptr field");
    if (write(db->idxfd, asciiptr, PTR_SZ) != PTR_SZ)
        err_dump("write error of ptr field");
}
```

Program 16.17 The _db_writeptr function.

In Program 16.18 we cover the largest of the database functions, db_store. It starts by calling _db_find to see if the record already exists. It is OK if the record already exists and DB_REPLACE is specified or if the record doesn't exist and DB_INSERT is specified. If we're replacing an existing record, that implies that the keys are identical but the data records probably differ.

Note that the final argument to _db_find specifies that the hash chain must be write locked, as we will probably be modifying this hash chain.

If we are inserting a new record into the database, we call _db_findfree (Program 16.19) to search the free list for a deleted record with the same size key and the same size data.

The while loop in _db_findfree goes through the free list, looking for a record with a matching key size and matching data size. In this simple implementation we reuse a deleted record only if the key length and data length equal the lengths for the new record being inserted. There are a variety of better ways to reuse this deleted space, in exchange for added complexity.

_db_findfree needs to write lock the free list to avoid interfering with any other processes using the free list. Once the record has been removed from the free list, the write lock can be released. Recall that _db_dodelete also modified the free list.

```
#include     "db.h"

/* Store a record in the database.
 * Return 0 if OK, 1 if record exists and DB_INSERT specified,
 * -1 if record doesn't exist and DB_REPLACE specified. */

int
db_store(DB *db, const char *key, const char *data, int flag)
{
    int     rc, keylen, datlen;
    off_t   ptrval;

    keylen = strlen(key);
    datlen = strlen(data) + 1;        /* +1 for newline at end */
    if (datlen < DATLEN_MIN || datlen > DATLEN_MAX)
        err_dump("invalid data length");

        /* _db_find() calculates which hash table this new record
           goes into (db->chainoff), regardless whether it already
           exists or not.  The calls to _db_writeptr() below
           change the hash table entry for this chain to point to
           the new record.  This means the new record is added to
           the front of the hash chain. */

    if (_db_find(db, key, 1) < 0) {      /* record not found */
        if (flag & DB_REPLACE) {
            rc = -1;
            db->cnt_storerr++;
            goto doreturn;       /* error, record does not exist */
        }

            /* _db_find() locked the hash chain for us; read the
               chain ptr to the first index record on hash chain */
        ptrval = _db_readptr(db, db->chainoff);

        if (_db_findfree(db, keylen, datlen) < 0) {
                /* An empty record of the correct size was not found.
                   We have to append the new record to the ends of
                   the index and data files */
            _db_writedat(db, data, 0, SEEK_END);
            _db_writeidx(db, key, 0, SEEK_END, ptrval);
                /* db->idxoff was set by _db_writeidx().  The new
                   record goes to the front of the hash chain. */
            _db_writeptr(db, db->chainoff, db->idxoff);
            db->cnt_stor1++;
        } else {
```

```
                    /* We can reuse an empty record.
                       _db_findfree() removed the record from the free
                       list and set both db->datoff and db->idxoff. */
                _db_writedat(db, data, db->datoff, SEEK_SET);
                _db_writeidx(db, key, db->idxoff, SEEK_SET, ptrval);
                    /* reused record goes to the front of the hash chain. */
                _db_writeptr(db, db->chainoff, db->idxoff);
                db->cnt_stor2++;
        }

    } else {                             /* record found */
        if (flag & DB_INSERT) {
            rc = 1;
            db->cnt_storerr++;
            goto doreturn;        /* error, record already in db */
        }

            /* We are replacing an existing record.  We know the new
               key equals the existing key, but we need to check if
               the data records are the same size. */
        if (datlen != db->datlen) {
            _db_dodelete(db);     /* delete the existing record */

                /* Reread the chain ptr in the hash table
                   (it may change with the deletion). */
            ptrval = _db_readptr(db, db->chainoff);

                /* append new index and data records to end of files */
            _db_writedat(db, data, 0, SEEK_END);
            _db_writeidx(db, key, 0, SEEK_END, ptrval);
                /* new record goes to the front of the hash chain. */
            _db_writeptr(db, db->chainoff, db->idxoff);
            db->cnt_stor3++;

        } else {
                /* same size data, just replace data record */
            _db_writedat(db, data, db->datoff, SEEK_SET);
            db->cnt_stor4++;
        }
    }
    rc = 0;         /* OK */
doreturn:   /* unlock the hash chain that _db_find() locked */
    if (un_lock(db->idxfd, db->chainoff, SEEK_SET, 1) < 0)
        err_dump("un_lock error");
    return(rc);
}
```

Program 16.18 The db_store function.

```
#include    "db.h"

/* Try to find a free index record and accompanying data record
 * of the correct sizes.  We're only called by db_store(). */

int
_db_findfree(DB *db, int keylen, int datlen)
{
    int     rc;
    off_t   offset, nextoffset, saveoffset;

        /* Lock the free list */
    if (writew_lock(db->idxfd, FREE_OFF, SEEK_SET, 1) < 0)
        err_dump("writew_lock error");

        /* Read the free list pointer */
    saveoffset = FREE_OFF;
    offset = _db_readptr(db, saveoffset);

    while (offset != 0) {
        nextoffset = _db_readidx(db, offset);
        if (strlen(db->idxbuf) == keylen && db->datlen == datlen)
            break;          /* found a match */

        saveoffset = offset;
        offset = nextoffset;
    }

    if (offset == 0)
        rc = -1;      /* no match found */
    else {
            /* Found a free record with matching sizes.
               The index record was read in by _db_readidx() above,
               which sets db->ptrval.  Also, saveoffset points to
               the chain ptr that pointed to this empty record on
               the free list.  We set this chain ptr to db->ptrval,
               which removes the empty record from the free list. */

        _db_writeptr(db, saveoffset, db->ptrval);
        rc = 0;

            /* Notice also that _db_readidx() set both db->idxoff
               and db->datoff.  This is used by the caller, db_store(),
               to write the new index record and data record. */
    }
        /* Unlock the free list */
    if (un_lock(db->idxfd, FREE_OFF, SEEK_SET, 1) < 0)
        err_dump("un_lock error");
    return(rc);
}
```

Program 16.19 The _db_findfree function.

Returning to db_store, after the call to _db_find, the code divides into four cases.

1. A new record is being inserted and an empty record with the correct sizes was not found by _db_findfree. This means we have to append the new record to the ends of the index file and data file. The new record is added to the front of the hash chain by calling _db_writeptr.

2. A new record is being added and an empty record with the correct sizes was found by _db_findfree. The empty record is removed from the free list by _db_findfree, and the new data record and index record are rewritten. The new record is added to the front of the hash chain by calling _db_writeptr.

3. An existing record is being replaced and the length of the new data record differs from the length of the existing data record. We call _db_dodelete to delete the existing record and then append the new record to the ends of the index file and data file. (There are other ways to handle this case. We could try to find a deleted record that has the correct data size.) The new record is added to the front of the hash chain by calling _db_writeptr.

4. An existing record is being replaced and the length of the new data record equals the length of the existing data record. This is the easiest case—we just rewrite the data record.

We need to describe the locking when new index records or data records are appended to the end of the file. (Recall the problems we encountered in Program 12.6 with locking relative to the end of file.) In cases 1 and 3, db_store calls both _db_writeidx and _db_writedat with a third argument of 0 and a fourth argument of SEEK_END. This fourth argument is the flag to these two functions that the new record is being appended to the file. The technique used by _db_writeidx is to write lock the index file, from the end of the hash chain to the end of file. This won't interfere with any other readers or writers of the database (since they will lock a hash chain) but it does prevent other callers of db_store from trying to append at the same time. The technique used by _db_writedat is to write lock the entire data file. Again, this won't interfere with other readers or writers of the database (since they don't even try to lock the data file), but it does prevent other callers of db_store from trying to append to the data file at the same time. (See Exercise 16.3.)

We complete the tour of the source code with db_nextrec and db_rewind, the functions used to read all the records in the database. The normal use of these functions is in a loop of the form

```
db_rewind(db);
while ( (ptr = db_nextrec(db, key)) != NULL) {
    /* process record */
}
```

As we warned earlier, there is no order to the returned records—they are not in key order.

The technique for db_rewind (Program 16.20) is to position the index file to the first index record (immediately following the hash table).

```
#include    "db.h"

/* Rewind the index file for db_nextrec().
 * Automatically called by db_open().
 * Must be called before first db_nextrec().
 */

void
db_rewind(DB *db)
{
    off_t   offset;

    offset = (db->nhash + 1) * PTR_SZ;          /* +1 for free list ptr */

        /* We're just setting the file offset for this process
            to the start of the index records; no need to lock.
            +1 below for newline at end of hash table. */

    if ( (db->idxoff = lseek(db->idxfd, offset+1, SEEK_SET)) == -1)
        err_dump("lseek error");
}
```

Program 16.20 The db_rewind function.

Once db_rewind has positioned the index file, db_nextrec just sequentially reads all the index records. As we see in Program 16.21, db_nextrec does not use the hash chains. Since db_nextrec reads all the deleted records along with the records on a hash chain, it has to check if a record has been deleted (its key is all blank) and ignore these deleted records.

If the database is being modified while db_nextrec is called from a loop, the records returned by db_nextrec are just a snapshot of a changing database at some point in time. db_nextrec always returns a "correct" record when it is called; that is, it won't return a record that was deleted. But it is possible for a record returned by db_nextrec to be deleted immediately after db_nextrec returns. Similarly, if a deleted record is reused right after db_nextrec skips over the deleted record, we won't see that new record unless we rewind the database and go through it again. If it's important to obtain an accurate "frozen" snapshot of the database using db_nextrec, there must be no insertions or deletions going on at the same time.

Look at the locking employed by db_nextrec. We're not going through any hash chain, and we can't determine the hash chain that a record belongs on. Therefore, it is possible for an index record to be in the process of being deleted when db_nextrec is reading the record. To prevent this, db_nextrec read locks the free list, to avoid any interactions with _db_dodelete and _db_findfree.

```
#include    "db.h"

/* Return the next sequential record.
 * We just step our way through the index file, ignoring deleted
 * records.  db_rewind() must be called before this function is
 * called the first time.
 */

char *
db_nextrec(DB *db, char *key)
{
    char    c, *ptr;

        /* We read lock the free list so that we don't read
           a record in the middle of its being deleted. */
    if (readw_lock(db->idxfd, FREE_OFF, SEEK_SET, 1) < 0)
        err_dump("readw_lock error");

    do {
            /* read next sequential index record */
        if (_db_readidx(db, 0) < 0) {
            ptr = NULL;     /* end of index file, EOF */
            goto doreturn;
        }
            /* check if key is all blank (empty record) */
        ptr = db->idxbuf;
        while ( (c = *ptr++) != 0  &&  c == ' ')
            ;    /* skip until null byte or nonblank */
    } while (c == 0);    /* loop until a nonblank key is found */

    if (key != NULL)
        strcpy(key, db->idxbuf);    /* return key */
    ptr = _db_readdat(db);  /* return pointer to data buffer */

    db->cnt_nextrec++;
doreturn:
    if (un_lock(db->idxfd, FREE_OFF, SEEK_SET, 1) < 0)
        err_dump("un_lock error");

    return(ptr);
}
```

Program 16.21 The db_nextrec function.

16.8 Performance

To test the database library and to obtain some timing measurements, a test program
was written. This program takes two command-line arguments: the number of children
to create and the number of database records (*nrec*) for each child to write to the
database. The program then creates an empty database (by calling db_open), forks

the number of child processes, and waits for all the children to terminate. Each child performs the following steps:

- Write *nrec* records to the database.

- Read the *nrec* records back by key value.

- Perform the following loop *nrec* × 5 times.

  - Read a random record.

  - Every 37 times through the loop, delete a random record.

  - Every 11 times through the loop, insert a new record and read the record back.

  - Every 17 times through the loop, replace a random record with a new record. Every other one of these replacements is a record with the same size data and the alternate is a record with a longer data portion.

- Delete all the records that this child wrote. Every time a record is deleted, 10 random records are looked up.

The actual number of operations performed on the database is counted by the cnt_xxx variables in the DB structure, which were incremented in the functions. The number of operations differs from one child to the next, since the random number generator used to select records is initialized in each child to the child's process ID. A typical count of the operations performed in each child, when *nrec* is 500, is shown in Figure 16.4.

Operation	Count
db_store, DB_INSERT, no empty record, appended	675
db_store, DB_INSERT, empty record reused	170
db_store, DB_REPLACE, different data length, appended	100
db_store, DB_REPLACE, equal data length	100
db_store, record not found	20
db_fetch, record found	8300
db_fetch, record not found	750
db_delete, record found	840
db_delete, record not found	100

Figure 16.4 Typical count of operations performed by each child when *nrec* is 500.

We performed about 10 times more fetches than stores or deletions, which is probably typical of many database applications.

Each child is doing these operations (fetching, storing, and deleting), only with the records that the child wrote. All the concurrency controls are being exercised because all the children are operating on the same database (albeit different records in the same database). The total number of records in the database increases in proportion to the number of children. (With one child, *nrec* records are originally written to the database. With two children, *nrec* × 2 records are originally written, and so on.)

To test the concurrency provided by coarse locking versus fine locking and to compare the three different types of locking (no locking, advisory locking, and mandatory locking), we ran three versions of the test program. The first version used the source code shown in Section 16.7, which we've called fine locking. The second version changed the locking calls to implement coarse locking, as described in Section 16.6. The third version had all locking calls removed, so we could measure the overhead involved in locking. We can run the first and second versions (fine locking and coarse locking) using either advisory or mandatory locking, by changing the permission bits on the database files. (In all the tests reported in this section, we measured the times for mandatory locking using only the implementation of fine locking.)

All the timing tests in this sections were done on an 80386 system running SVR4.

Single-Process Results

Figure 16.5 shows the results when only a single child process ran, with an *nrec* of 500, 1000, and 2000.

| | No locking | | | Advisory locking | | | | | | Mandatory locking | | |
| | | | | Coarse locking | | | Fine locking | | | Fine locking | | |
nrec	User	Sys	Clock	User	Sys	Clock	User	Sys	Clock	User	Sys	Clock
500	15	68	84	16	78	94	15	79	94	16	92	109
1000	61	340	402	63	360	425	63	366	430	71	412	488
2000	157	906	1068	158	936	1096	158	934	1097	159	1081	1253

Figure 16.5 Single child, varying *nrec*, different locking techniques.

The last 12 columns give the corresponding times in seconds. In all cases the user CPU time plus the system CPU time approximately equals the clock time. This set of tests was CPU limited and not disk limited.

The middle six columns (advisory locking, coarse and fine) are almost equal for each row. This makes sense—for a single process there is no difference between coarse locking and fine locking.

Comparing no locking versus advisory locking, we see that adding the locking calls adds between 3% and 15% to the system CPU time. Even though the locks are never used (since only a single process is running), the system call overhead in the calls to fcntl adds time. Also note that the user CPU time is about the same for all four versions of locking. Since the user code is almost equivalent (except for the number of calls to fcntl) this makes sense.

The final point to note from Figure 16.5 is that mandatory locking adds about 15% to the system CPU time, compared to advisory locking. Since the number of locking calls are the same for advisory fine locking and mandatory fine locking, the additional system call overhead must be in the reads and writes.

The final test that was run was to try the no-locking program with multiple children. The results, as expected, were random errors. Normally, records that were added to the database couldn't be found, and the test program aborted. Every time the test program was run, different errors occurred. This is a classic race condition—having multiple processes updating the same file without using any form of locking.

Multiple-Process Results

The next set of measurements looks mainly at the differences between coarse locking and fine locking. As we said earlier, intuitively we expect fine locking to provide additional concurrency, since there is less time that portions of the database are locked from other processes. Figure 16.6 shows the results, for an *nrec* of 500, varying the number of children from 1 to 12.

	Advisory locking							Mandatory locking			
	Coarse locking			Fine locking			Δ	Fine locking			Δ
#Proc	User	Sys	Clock	User	Sys	Clock	Clock	User	Sys	Clock	Percent
1	16	79	96	16	83	99	3	16	96	112	16
2	42	230	273	43	237	281	8	43	271	315	14
3	79	454	536	81	464	547	11	78	545	626	18
4	128	753	884	132	757	892	8	123	888	1015	17
5	185	1123	1315	196	1173	1376	61	189	1366	1560	16
6	262	1601	1870	270	1611	1888	18	264	1931	2205	20
7	351	2164	2526	354	2174	2537	11	341	2527	2877	16
8	451	2801	3264	454	2766	3230	−34	438	3298	3750	19
9	565	3513	4092	569	3483	4067	−25	548	4148	4712	19
10	684	4293	5000	688	4215	4925	−75	658	5048	5732	20
11	812	5151	5987	811	5043	5876	−111	797	6198	7020	23
12	958	6075	7058	960	5992	6980	−78	937	7298	8265	22

Figure 16.6 Comparison of different locking techniques, *nrec* = 500.

All the user, system, and clock times are in seconds. All these times are the total for the parent and all its children. There are many items to consider from this data.

The eighth column, labeled "Δ clock," is the difference in seconds between the clock times from advisory-coarse locking to advisory-fine locking. This is the measurement of how much concurrency we obtain by going from coarse locking to fine locking. On the system used for these tests, coarse locking is faster, until we have more than seven processes. Even after seven processes, the decrease in clock time using fine locking isn't that great (around 1%), which makes us wonder if the additional code required to implement fine locking is worth the effort.

We would like the clock time to decrease, from coarse to fine locking, as it eventually does, but we expect the system time to remain higher for fine locking, for any number of processes. The reason we expect this is because with fine locking we are issuing more fcntl calls than with coarse locking. If we total the number of fcntl calls in Figure 16.4 for coarse locking and fine locking, we have an average of 22,110 for coarse locking and 25,680 for fine locking. (To get these numbers, realize that each of the operations in Figure 16.4 requires two calls to fcntl for coarse locking, and the first three calls to db_store along with record deletion (record found) each requires four calls to fcntl for fine locking.) We expect this increase of 16% in the number of calls to fcntl to result in an increased system time for fine locking. Therefore the slight decrease in system time for fine locking, when the number of processes exceeds seven, is puzzling.

The final column, labeled "Δ percent," is the percentage increase in the system CPU time from advisory-fine locking to mandatory-fine locking. These percentages verify what we saw in Figure 16.5, that mandatory locking adds around 15–20% to the system time.

Since the user code for all these tests is almost identical (there are some additional `fcntl` calls for both advisory-fine and mandatory-fine locking), we expect the user CPU times to be the same across any row. But the user CPU times always increase 1–3% from advisory-coarse locking to advisory-fine locking. The user CPU times always decrease 1–3% from advisory-fine locking to mandatory-fine locking. There is no apparent explanation for these differences.

The values in the first row of Figure 16.6 are similar to those for an *nrec* of 500 in Figure 16.5. We expect this.

Figure 16.7 is a graph of the data from Figure 16.6, for advisory fine locking. We plot the clock time as the number of processes goes from one to nine. (We don't plot the values for 10, 11, and 12, to avoid expanding the graph in the vertical direction.) We also plot the user CPU time divided by the number of processes and the system CPU time divided by the number of processes.

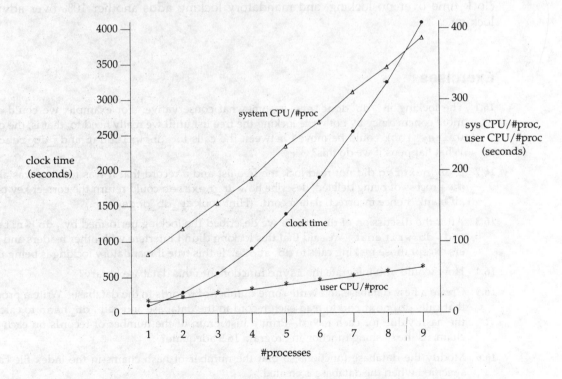

Figure 16.7 Values from Figure 16.6 for advisory-fine locking.

Note that both CPU times, divided by the number of processes, are linear, but the plot of the clock time is nonlinear. If we sum the user CPU time and system CPU time from Figure 16.6 and compare it to the clock time for a given row, the difference between the two increases as the number of processes increases. The probable reason is the added amount of CPU time used by the operating system as the number of processes increases. This operating system overhead would show up as an increased clock time, but shouldn't affect the CPU times of the individual processes.

The reason the user CPU time increases with the number of processes is because there are more records in the database. Each hash chain is getting longer, so it takes the _db_find function longer, on the average, to find a record.

16.9 Summary

This chapter has taken a long look at the design and implementation of a database library. Although we've kept the library small and simple, for presentation purposes, it contains the record locking required to allow concurrent access by multiple processes.

We've also looked at the performance of this library, with various number of processes, using four different types of locking: no locking, advisory locking (fine and coarse), and mandatory locking. We saw that advisory locking adds about 10% to the clock time over no locking, and mandatory locking adds another 10% over advisory locking.

Exercises

16.1 The locking in _db_dodelete is somewhat conservative. For example, we could allow more concurrency by not write locking the free list until we really need to; that is, the call to writew_lock could be moved between the calls to _db_writedat and _db_readptr. What happens if we do this?

16.2 If db_nextrec did not read lock the free list and a record that it was reading was also in the process of being deleted, describe how db_nextrec could return the correct key but an all-blank (hence incorrect) data record. (Hint: look at _db_dodelete.)

16.3 After the discussion of db_store we described the locking performed by _db_writeidx and _db_writedat. We said that this locking didn't interfere with other readers and writers except those making calls to db_store. Is this true if mandatory locking is being used?

16.4 How would you integrate the fsync function into this database library?

16.5 Create a new database and write some number of records to the database. Write a program that calls db_nextrec to read each record in the database and call _db_hash to calculate the hash value for each record. Print a histogram of the number of records on each hash chain. Is the hashing function in Program 16.9 adequate?

16.6 Modify the database functions so that the number of hash chains in the index file can be specified when the database is created.

16.7 If your systems support a network filesystem, such as Sun's Network File System (NFS) or AT&T's Remote File Sharing (RFS), compare the performance of the database functions when the database is (a) on the same host as the test program and (b) on a different host. Does the record locking provided by the database library still work?

17

Communicating with a PostScript Printer

17.1 Introduction

We now develop a program that can communicate with a PostScript printer. PostScript printers are popular today and normally communicate with a host using an RS-232 serial interface. This gives us a chance to use some of the terminal I/O functions from Chapter 11. Also, communication with a PostScript printer is full duplex, meaning that as we send data to the printer we also have to be prepared to read status information from the printer. This gives us a chance to use the I/O multiplexing functions from Section 12.5: select and poll. The program that we develop is based on the lprps program written by James Clark. This program and others, making up the lprps package, was posted to the comp.sources.misc Usenet news group, Volume 21 (July 1991).

17.2 PostScript Communication Dynamics

The first thing to realize about printing on a PostScript printer is that we don't send a file to the printer to be printed—we send a PostScript program to the printer for it to execute. There is normally a PostScript interpreter within the printer that executes the program, generating one or more pages of printed output. If the PostScript program contains errors, the printer (actually the PostScript interpreter) returns an error message and may or may not generate any output.

The following PostScript program causes the familiar string to be printed on a page. (We won't describe PostScript programming in this text, see Adobe Systems [1985 and 1986] for these details. Our interest is in communicating with a PostScript printer.)

```
%!
/Times-Roman findfont
15 scalefont              % point size of 15
setfont                   % establish current font
300 350 moveto            % x=300, y=350 (position on page)
(hello, world) show       % output the string to current page
showpage                  % and output page to output device
```

If we change the word setfont to ssetfont in the PostScript program and send it to the printer, nothing is printed. Instead we get the following messages back from the printer

```
%%[ Error: undefined; OffendingCommand: ssetfont ]%%
%%[ Flushing: rest of job (to end-of-file) will be ignored ]%%
```

These error messages, which can arrive from the printer at any time, are what complicate the handling of a PostScript printer. We can't just send the entire PostScript program to the printer and forget about it—we must handle these potential error messages intelligently. (Throughout this chapter we'll usually say "printer" when technically we mean the PostScript interpreter.)

PostScript printers are usually attached to a host computer using an RS-232 serial connection. This looks to the host like a terminal connection. Everything that we said about terminal I/O in Chapter 11 applies here. (There are other ways to connect PostScript printers to a host: network interfaces are becoming popular. The predominant interface these days is a serial connection.) Figure 17.2 shows the typical arrangement. A PostScript program can generate two forms of output—output on the printed page from the showpage operator and output to its standard output (the serial link to the host in this case) from the print operator.

The PostScript interpreter sends and receives seven-bit ASCII characters. A PostScript program consists entirely of printable ASCII characters. Some of the nonprinting ASCII characters have special meaning, as listed in Figure 17.1.

Character	Octal value	Description
Control-C	003	Interrupt. Causes the PostScript interrupt operator to be executed. Normally this terminates the PostScript program being interpreted.
Control-D	004	End of file.
Line feed	012	End of line, the PostScript newline character. If a return and line feed are received in sequence, only a single newline character is passed to the interpreter.
Return	015	End of line. Translated to the PostScript newline character.
Control-Q	021	Start output (XON flow control).
Control-S	023	Stop output (XOFF flow control).
Control-T	024	Status query. The PostScript interpreter responds with a one-line status message.

Figure 17.1 Special characters sent from computer to PostScript interpreter.

The PostScript end-of-file character (Control-D) is used to synchronize the printer with the host. We send a PostScript program to the printer and then send an EOF to the

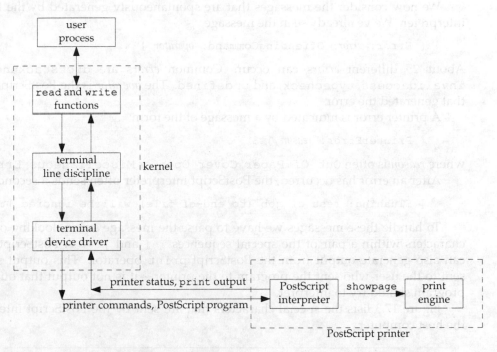

Figure 17.2 Communicating with a PostScript printer using a serial connection.

printer. When the printer has finished executing the PostScript program, it sends an EOF back.

While the interpreter is executing a PostScript program we can send it an interrupt (Control-C). This normally causes the program being executed by the printer to terminate.

The status query message (Control-T) causes a one-line status message to be returned by the printer. All messages received from the printer have the following format:

```
%%[ key: val ]%%
```

Any number of *key: val* pairs can appear in a message, separated by semicolons. Recall the messages returned in the earlier example:

```
%%[ Error: undefined; OffendingCommand: ssetfont ]%%
%%[ Flushing: rest cf job (to end-of-file) will be ignored ]%%
```

The status messages have the form

```
%%[ status: idle ]%%
```

Other status indications, besides `idle` (no job in progress), are `busy` (executing a Post-Script program), `waiting` (waiting for more of the PostScript program to execute), `printing` (paper in motion), `initializing`, and `printing test page`.

We now consider the messages that are spontaneously generated by the PostScript interpreter. We've already seen the message

```
%%[ Error:· error; OffendingCommand: operator ]%%
```

About 25 different *error*s can occur. Common *error*s are `dictstackunderflow`, `invalidaccess`, `typecheck`, and `undefined`. The *operator* is the PostScript operator that generated the error.

A printer error is indicated by a message of the form

```
%%[ PrinterError: reason ]%%
```

where *reason* is often `Out Of Paper`, `Cover Open`, or `Miscellaneous Error`.

After an error has occurred, the PostScript interpreter often sends a second message

```
%%[ Flushing: rest of job (to end-of-file) will be ignored ]%%
```

To handle these messages we have to parse the message string, looking only at the characters within a pair of the special sequences `%%[` and `]%%`. A PostScript program can also generate output from the PostScript `print` operator. This output should be sent to the user who sent the program to the printer—it is not output that our printing program should try to interpret.

Figure 17.3 lists the special characters that are sent by the PostScript interpreter to the host computer.

Character	Octal value	Description
Control-D	004	End of file.
Line feed	012	Newline. When a newline is written to the interpreter's standard output, it is translated to a return followed by a line feed.
Control-Q	021	Start output (XON flow control).
Control-S	023	Stop output (XOFF flow control).

Figure 17.3 Special characters sent from PostScript interpreter to computer.

17.3 Printer Spooling

The program that we develop in this chapter sends a PostScript program to a PostScript printer in either stand-alone mode or through the BSD line printer spooling system. Normal usage is within a spooling system, but it is useful to provide a stand-alone (debug) mode, for testing.

SVR4 also provides a spooling system, albeit more complicated than the BSD system. Details of this spooling system can be found in all the manual pages that begin with `lp` in Section 1 of AT&T [1991]. Chapter 13 of Stevens [1990] provides details on the BSD spooling system and the pre-SVR4 System V spooling system. Our interest in this chapter is not in these spooling systems per se, but in communicating with a PostScript printer.

In the BSD spooling system we print a file with a command of the form

```
lpr -pps main.c
```

This sends the file `main.c` to the printer whose name is `ps`. If we didn't specify `-pps` the output would be sent to either the printer specified by the `PRINTER` environment variable or to the default printer `lp`. The printer is looked up in the file `/etc/printcap`. Figure 17.4 shows an entry for our PostScript printer.

```
lp|ps:\
     :br#19200:lp=/dev/ttyb:\
     :sf:sh:rw:\
     :fc#0000374:fs#0000003:xc#0:xs#0040040:\
     :af=/var/adm/psacct:lf=/var/adm/pslog:sd=/var/spool/pslpd:\
     :if=/usr/local/lib/psif:
```

Figure 17.4 The `printcap` entry for the PostScript printer.

The first line gives the name of this entry as either `ps` or `lp`. The `br` value specifies the baud rate as 19200. `lp` specifies the pathname of the special device file for the printer. `sf` says to suppress form feeds, and `sh` says to suppress printing a burst page header at the beginning of each job. `rw` specifies that the device is to be opened for reading and writing. This is required for a PostScript printer, as described in Section 17.2.

The next four fields specify bits to turn off and turn on in the old BSD-style `sgtty` structure. (We describe these here because most BSD systems that use this form of `printcap` file support this older style of setting terminal parameters. In the source code later in this chapter we'll see how to set all the terminal parameters with the POSIX.1 functions from Chapter 11.) First the `fc` mask clears the following bits in the `sg_flags` element: `EVENP` and `ODDP` (turns off parity checking and generation), `RAW` (turns off raw mode), `CRMOD` (turns off CR/LF mapping on input and output), `ECHO` (turns off echo), and `LCASE` (turns off uppercase/lowercase mapping on input and output). Then the `fs` mask turns on the following bits: `CBREAK` (one character-at-a-time input), and `TANDEM` (host generates Control-S, Control-Q flow control). Next, the `xc` value clears bits in the local mode word. In this example the value of 0 does nothing. Finally, the `xs` value sets bits in the local mode word: `LDECCTQ` (only Control-Q restarts output that was stopped by a Control-S), and `LLITOUT` (suppress output translations).

The `af` and `lf` strings specify the accounting file and log file, respectively. `sd` specifies the spooling directory, and `if` specifies the input filter.

The input filter is invoked for every file to be printed. It is invoked as

filter −n *loginname* −h *hostname* *acctfile*

There are several optional arguments that can also appear, which can be safely ignored for a PostScript printer. The file to be printed is on the standard input, and the printer device (from the `lp` entry in the `printcap` file) is open on the standard output. The standard input can be a pipe.

With a PostScript printer, the input filter should look at the first two bytes of the input file and determine if the file is an ASCII text file or a PostScript program. The normal convention is that the two-character sequence %! at the beginning of a file designates a PostScript program. If the file is a PostScript program, the lprps program (detailed later in this chapter) can send it to the printer. But if the file is an ASCII text file, a program is required to convert this into a PostScript program that prints the text file.

The filter psif, mentioned in the printcap file, is supplied with the lprps package. The program textps in this package converts an ASCII text file into a PostScript program that prints the file. Figure 17.5 outlines all these programs.

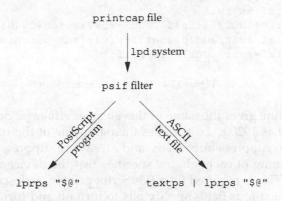

Figure 17.5 Overview of lprps system.

There is another program not shown in this figure, psrev, that reverses the pages of output generated by a PostScript program. This can be used if the PostScript printer generates its output face up instead of face down.

Having covered all these preliminaries, we can now look at the design and source code of the lprps program.

17.4 Source Code

Let's start with an overview of the functions called by main and how they interact with the printer. Figure 17.6 details this interaction. The second column, labeled "Int?", specifies if the function is interruptible with a SIGINT signal. The third column specifies the time-out value (in seconds) set by the function. Notice that when we're sending the user's PostScript program to the printer, there is no time out. This is because a PostScript program can take any amount of time to execute. The reference to "our PostScript program" for the get_page function refers to the small PostScript program in Program 17.9 that fetches the current page counter.

Program 17.1 lists the header lprps.h. It is included by all the source files. This header includes the system headers that most files require, defines some constants, and declares the global variables and function prototypes for the global functions.

Function	Int?	Timeout?	Send to printer	Receive from printer
get_status	no	5	Control-T	%%[status: idle]%%
get_page	no	30	our PostScript program EOF	%%[pagecount: *n*]%% EOF
send_file	yes	none	user's PostScript program EOF	EOF
get_page .	no	30	our PostScript program EOF	%%[pagecount: *n*]%% EOF

Figure 17.6 Functions called by main.

```
#include     <sys/types.h>
#include     <sys/time.h>
#include     <errno.h>
#include     <signal.h>
#include     <syslog.h>        /* since we're a daemon */
#include     "ourhdr.h"

#define EXIT_SUCCESS      0    /* defined by BSD spooling system */
#define EXIT_REPRINT      1
#define EXIT_THROW_AWAY 2

#define DEF_DEVICE   "/dev/ttyb" /* defaults for debug mode */
#define DEF_BAUD     B19200

                         /* modify following as appropriate */
#define MAILCMD      "mail -s \"printer job\" %s@%s < %s"

#define OBSIZE  1024    /* output buffer */
#define IBSIZE  1024    /* input buffer */
#define MBSIZE  1024    /* message buffer */

              /* declare global variables */
extern char *loginname;
extern char *hostname;
extern char *acct_file;
extern char  eofc;       /* PS end-of-file (004) */
extern int   debug;      /* true if interactive (not a daemon) */
extern int   in_job;     /* true if sending user's PS job to printer */
extern int   psfd;       /* file descriptor for PostScript printer */
extern int   start_page;/* starting page# */
extern int   end_page;  /* ending page# */
```

```
extern volatile sig_atomic_t    intr_flag; /* set if SIGINT is caught */
extern volatile sig_atomic_t    alrm_flag; /* set if SIGALRM goes off */

extern enum status {     /* printer status */
    INVALID, UNKNOWN, IDLE, BUSY, WAITING
} status;

                 /* global function prototypes */
void    do_acct(void);                  /* acct.c */

void    clear_alrm(void);               /* alarm.c */
void    handle_alrm(void);
void    set_alrm(unsigned int);

void    get_status(void);               /* getstatus.c */

void    init_input(int);                /* input.c */
void    proc_input_char(int);
void    proc_some_input(void);
void    proc_upto_eof(int);

void    clear_intr(void);               /* interrupt.c */
void    handle_intr(void);
void    set_intr(void);

void    close_mailfp(void);             /* mail.c */
void    mail_char(int);
void    mail_line(const char *, const char *);

void    msg_init(void);                 /* message.c */
void    msg_char(int);
void    proc_msg(void);

void    out_char(int);                  /* output.c */

void    get_page(int *);                /* pagecount.c */

void    send_file(void);                /* sendfile.c */

void    block_write(const char *, int); /* tty.c */
void    tty_flush(void);
void    set_block(void);
void    set_nonblock(void);
void    tty_open(void);
```

Program 17.1 The lprps.h header.

The file vars.c (Program 17.2) defines the global variables.

Execution starts at the main function, shown in Program 17.3. The main function calls the log_open function (shown in Appendix B) since this program normally runs as a daemon. We cannot write error messages to the standard error—instead we use the syslog facility described in Section 13.4.2.

```
#include    "lprps.h"

char    *loginname;
char    *hostname;
char    *acct_file;
char    eofc = '\004';                    /* Control-D = PostScript EOF */

int     psfd = STDOUT_FILENO;
int     start_page = -1;
int     end_page = -1;
int     debug;
int     in_job;

volatile sig_atomic_t    intr_flag;
volatile sig_atomic_t    alrm_flag;

enum status       status = INVALID;
```

Program 17.2 Declare the global variables.

```
#include    "lprps.h"

static void usage(void);

int
main(int argc, char *argv[])
{
    int         c;

    log_open("lprps", LOG_PID, LOG_LPR);

    opterr = 0;      /* don't want getopt() writing to stderr */
    while ( (c = getopt(argc, argv, "cdh:i:l:n:x:y:w:")) != EOF) {
        switch (c) {
        case 'c':           /* control chars to be passed */
        case 'x':           /* horizontal page size */
        case 'y':           /* vertical page size */
        case 'w':           /* width */
        case 'l':           /* length */
        case 'i':           /* indent */
            break;  /* not interested in these */

        case 'd':           /* debug (interactive) */
            debug = 1;
            break;
        case 'n':           /* login name of user */
            loginname = optarg;
            break;
        case 'h':           /* host name of user */
            hostname = optarg;
            break;
```

```
                case '?':
                    log_msg("unrecognized option: -%c", optopt);
                    usage();
                }
        }

        if (hostname == NULL || loginname == NULL)
            usage();      /* require both hostname and loginname */

        if (optind < argc)
            acct_file = argv[optind];    /* remaining arg = acct file */

        if (debug)
            tty_open();

        if (atexit(close_mailfp) < 0)    /* register func for exit() */
            log_sys("main: atexit error");

        get_status();

        get_page(&start_page);

        send_file();                 /* copies stdin to printer */

        get_page(&end_page);

        do_acct();

        exit(EXIT_SUCCESS);
    }

    static void
    usage(void)
    {
        log_msg("lprps: invalid arguments");
        exit(EXIT_THROW_AWAY);
    }
```

Program 17.3 The main function.

The command-line arguments are then processed, most of which can be ignored for
a PostScript printer. We use the −d flag to indicate that the program is being run interactively, not as a daemon. If this flag is set, we need to initialize the terminal mode
(tty_open). We describe the function close_mailfp, which we establish as an exit
handler, later.

We then call the functions that we mentioned in Figure 17.6: fetch the printer status
to assure it is ready (get_status), get the printer's starting page count (get_page),
send the file (the PostScript program) to the printer (send_file), get the printer's ending page count (get_page), write an accounting record (do_acct), and terminate.

The file acct.c defines the function do_acct (Program 17.4). It is called at the
end of main to write an accounting record. The name of the accounting file is taken
from the printcap entry (Figure 17.4) and passed as the final command-line argument.

```
#include    "lprps.h"

/* Write the number of pages, hostname, and loginname to the
 * accounting file.  This function is called by main() at the end
 * if all was OK, by printer_flushing(), and by handle_intr() if
 * an interrupt is received. */

void
do_acct(void)
{
    FILE    *fp;

    if (end_page > start_page &&
        acct_file != NULL &&
        (fp = fopen(acct_file, "a")) != NULL) {
            fprintf(fp, "%7.2f %s:%s\n",
                        (double)(end_page - start_page),
                        hostname, loginname);
            if (fclose(fp) == EOF)
                log_sys("do_acct: fclose error");
    }
}
```

Program 17.4 The do_acct function.

Historically all BSD print filters write the number of pages output to the accounting file with the %7.2f printf format. This allows raster devices to report output in feet (and fractions thereof), instead of pages.

The next file, tty.c (Program 17.5), contains all the terminal I/O functions. These call the functions we described in Chapter 3 (fcntl, write, and open), and the POSIX.1 terminal functions from Chapter 11 (tcflush, tcgetattr, tcsetattr, cfsetispeed, and cfsetospeed). There are times when we don't care if a write blocks, and we'll call block_write for these cases. But if we don't want to block, we call set_nonblock and then call read or write ourself. Since a PostScript printer is a full-duplex device, we don't want to block on a write if there is a chance that the printer might want to send data to us (such as an error message). If the printer sends us an error message while we're blocked trying to send it data, we can encounter a dead-lock.

The kernel normally buffers terminal input and output, so if an error condition is encountered we call tty_flush to flush both the input and output queue.

The function tty_open is called from main if we're running interactively (not as a daemon). We need to set the terminal mode to noncanonical, set the baud rates, and set any other terminal flags. Be aware that these settings are not the same for all PostScript printers. Check your printer manuals for its settings. (The number of bits of data, seven-bit or eight-bit, the number of start and stop bits, and the parity, are most likely to change between printers.)

```
#include      "lprps.h"
#include      <fcntl.h>
#include      <termios.h>

static int      block_flag = 1;         /* default is blocking I/O */

void
set_block(void)       /* turn off nonblocking flag */
{                     /* called only by block_write() below */
    int      val;

    if (block_flag == 0) {
        if ( (val = fcntl(psfd, F_GETFL, 0)) < 0)
            log_sys("set_block: fcntl F_GETFL error");
        val &= ~O_NONBLOCK;
        if (fcntl(psfd, F_SETFL, val) < 0)
            log_sys("set_block: fcntl F_SETFL error");

        block_flag = 1;
    }
}

void
set_nonblock(void)   /* set descriptor nonblocking */
{
    int      val;

    if (block_flag) {
        if ( (val = fcntl(psfd, F_GETFL, 0)) < 0)
            log_sys("set_nonblock: fcntl F_GETFL error");
        val |= O_NONBLOCK;
        if (fcntl(psfd, F_SETFL, val) < 0)
            log_sys("set_nonblock: fcntl F_SETFL error");

        block_flag = 0;
    }
}

void
block_write(const char *buf, int n)
{
    set_block();
    if (write(psfd, buf, n) != n)
        log_sys("block_write: write error");
}

void
tty_flush(void)       /* flush (empty) tty input and output queues */
{
    if (tcflush(psfd, TCIOFLUSH) < 0)
        log_sys("tty_flush: tcflush error");
}
```

```
void
tty_open(void)
{
    struct termios  term;

    if ( (psfd = open(DEF_DEVICE, O_RDWR)) < 0)
        log_sys("tty_open: open error");

    if (tcgetattr(psfd, &term) < 0)      /* fetch attributes */
        log_sys("tty_open: tcgetattr error");
    term.c_cflag  = CS8 |                 /* 8-bit data */
                    CREAD |               /* enable receiver */
                    CLOCAL;               /* ignore modem status lines */
                                          /* no parity, 1 stop bit */
    term.c_oflag &= ~OPOST;               /* turn off post processing */
    term.c_iflag  = IXON | IXOFF |        /* Xon/Xoff flow control */
                    IGNBRK |              /* ignore breaks */
                    ISTRIP |              /* strip input to 7 bits */
                    IGNCR;                /* ignore received CR */
    term.c_lflag  = 0;          /* everything off in local flag:
                                   disables canonical mode, disables
                                   signal generation, disables echo */
    term.c_cc[VMIN]  = 1;       /* 1 byte at a time, no timer */
    term.c_cc[VTIME] = 0;
    cfsetispeed(&term, DEF_BAUD);
    cfsetospeed(&term, DEF_BAUD);
    if (tcsetattr(psfd, TCSANOW, &term) < 0)      /* set attributes */
        log_sys("tty_open: tcsetattr error");
}
```

Program 17.5 Terminal functions.

The program handles two signals: SIGINT and SIGALRM. Handling SIGINT is a requirement for any filter invoked by the BSD spooling system. This signal is sent to the filter if the printer job is removed by the lprm(1) command. We use SIGALRM for setting time outs. Both signals are handled in a similar fashion: we provide a set_XXX function to establish the signal handler, and a clear_XXX function to disable the signal handler. If the signal is delivered to the process the signal handler just sets a global flag, intr_flag and alrm_flag, and returns. It is up to the rest of the program to test these flags at the appropriate times, to see if the signal has been caught. One obvious time is after an I/O function returns an error of EINTR. The program then calls either handle_intr or handle_alrm to handle the condition. We call the signal_intr function (Program 10.13) so that either signal interrupts a slow system call. Program 17.6 shows the file interrupt.c that handles SIGINT.

When an interrupt occurs we have to send the PostScript interrupt character (Control-C) to the printer, followed by an EOF. This normally causes the PostScript interpreter to abort the program that it's interpreting. We then wait for an EOF back from the printer. (We describe the function proc_upto_eof later.) We finish up by reading the ending page count, writing an accounting record, and terminating.

```
#include    "lprps.h"

static void
sig_int(int signo)      /* SIGINT handler */
{
    intr_flag = ·1;
    return;
}

/* This function is called after SIGINT has been delivered,
 * and the main loop has recognized it.  (It not called as
 * a signal handler, set_intr() above is the handler.) */

void
handle_intr(void)
{
    char    c;

    intr_flag = 0;
    clear_intr();               /* turn signal off */

    set_alrm(30);           /* 30 second timeout to interrupt printer */

    tty_flush();            /* discard any queued output */
    c = '\003';
    block_write(&c, 1);     /* Control-C interrupts the PS job */
    block_write(&eofc, 1);  /* followed by EOF */
    proc_upto_eof(1);       /* read & ignore up through EOF */

    clear_alrm();

    get_page(&end_page);
    do_acct();
    exit(EXIT_SUCCESS);     /* success since user lprm'ed the job */
}

void
set_intr(void)      /* enable signal handler */
{
    if (signal_intr(SIGINT, sig_int) == SIG_ERR)
        log_sys("set_intr: signal_intr error");
}

void
clear_intr(void)    /* ignore signal */
{
    if (signal(SIGINT, SIG_IGN) == SIG_ERR)
        log_sys("clear_intr: signal error");
}
```

Program 17.6 The interrupt.c file to handle interrupt signals.

Figure 17.6 noted which functions set time outs. We set a time out only when we request the printer status (get_status), when we read the printer's page count (get_page), or when we're interrupting the printer (handle_intr). If a time out does occur, we just log an error, wait for a while, and terminate. Program 17.7 shows the file alarm.c.

```
#include    "lprps.h"

static void
sig_alrm(int signo)              /* SIGALRM handler */
{
    alrm_flag = 1;
    return;
}

void
handle_alrm(void)
{
    log_ret("printer not responding");
    sleep(60);        /* it will take at least this long to warm up */

    exit(EXIT_REPRINT);
}

void         /* Establish the signal handler and set the alarm. */
set_alrm(unsigned int nsec) `
{
    alrm_flag = 0;
    if (signal_intr(SIGALRM, sig_alrm) == SIG_ERR)
        log_sys("set_alrm: signal_intr error");
    alarm(nsec);
}

void
clear_alrm(void)
{
    alarm(0);
    if (signal(SIGALRM, SIG_IGN) == SIG_ERR)
        log_sys("clear_alrm: signal error");
    alrm_flag = 0;
}
```

Program 17.7 The alarm.c file to handle time outs.

Program 17.8 shows the function get_status, which we called from main. It fetches the status by sending a Control-T to the printer. The printer should respond with a one-line message. The message that we're looking for is

```
%%[ status: idle ]%%
```

which means the printer is ready for a new job. This message is read and processed by proc_some_input, which we look at later.

```
#include    "lprps.h"

/* Called by main() before printing job.
 * We send a Control-T to the printer to fetch its status.
 * If we timeout before reading the printer's status, something
 * is wrong. */

void
get_status(void)
{
    char    c;

    set_alrm(5);                /* 5 second timeout to fetch status */

    tty_flush();
    c = '\024';
    block_write(&c, 1);         /* send Control-T to printer */

    init_input(0);
    while (status == INVALID)
        proc_some_input();   /* wait for something back */

    switch (status) {
    case IDLE:         /* this is what we're looking for ... */
        clear_alrm();
        return;

    case WAITING:    /* printer thinks it's in the middle of a job */
        block_write(&eofc, 1);   /* send EOF to printer */
        sleep(5);
        exit(EXIT_REPRINT);

    case BUSY:
    case UNKNOWN:
        sleep(15);
        exit(EXIT_REPRINT);
    }
}
```

Program 17.8 The get_status function.

If we receive the message

```
%%[ status: waiting ]%%
```

it means the printer is waiting for us to send it more data for a job that it is currently printing. This means something funny happened to the previous job. To clear this state we send the printer an EOF, then terminate.

PostScript printers maintain a page counter. It is incremented each time a page is printed and is maintained even when the power is turned off. To read this counter requires us to send the printer a PostScript program. The file pagecount.c (Program 17.9) contains this small PostScript program (about a dozen PostScript operators) and the function get_page that sends this program to the printer.

```
#include      "lprps.h"

/* PostScript program to fetch the printer's pagecount.
 * Notice that the string returned by the printer:
 *       %%[ pagecount: N ]%%
 * will be parsed by proc_msg(). */

static char pagecount_string[] =
    "(%%[ pagecount: ) print "   /* print writes to current output file */
    "statusdict begin pagecount end "    /* push pagecount onto stack */
    "20 string "          /* creates a string of length 20 */
    "cvs "                /* convert to string */
    "print "              /* write to current output file */
    "( ]%%) print "
    "flush\n";            /* flush current output file */

/* Read the starting or ending pagecount from the printer.
 * The argument is either &start_page or &end_page. */

void
get_page(int *ptrcount)
{
    set_alrm(30);                 /* 30 second timeout to read pagecount */

    tty_flush();
    block_write(pagecount_string, sizeof(pagecount_string) - 1);
                                  /* send query to printer */
    init_input(0);
    *ptrcount = -1;
    while (*ptrcount < 0)
        proc_some_input();   /* read results from printer */

    block_write(&eofc, 1);   /* send EOF to printer */
    proc_upto_eof(0);        /* wait for EOF from printer */

    clear_alrm();
}
```

Program 17.9 The pagecount.c file—fetch the printer's page count.

The array pagecount_string contains the small PostScript program. Although we could fetch the page count and print it using just

    statusdict begin pagecount end = flush

we purposely format the output to look like a status message returned by the printer:

    %%[pagecount: N]%%

By doing this the function proc_some_input handles the message similar to any printer status message.

The function send_file in Program 17.10 is called by main to send the user's PostScript program to the printer.

```
#include    "lprps.h"

void
send_file(void)      /* called by main() to copy stdin to printer */
{
    int     c;

    init_input(1);
    set_intr();                 /* we catch SIGINT */

    while ( (c = getchar()) != EOF)    /* main loop of program */
        out_char(c);            /* output each character */
    out_char(EOF);              /* output final buffer */

    block_write(&eofc, 1);      /* send EOF to printer */
    proc_upto_eof(0);           /* wait for printer to send EOF back */
}
```

Program 17.10 The send_file function.

This function is just a while loop that reads from the standard input (getchar) and
calls the function out_char to output each character to the printer. When the end of
file is encountered on the standard input, an EOF is sent to the printer (indicating the
end of job), and we wait for an end of file back from the printer (proc_upto_eof).

Recall from Figure 17.2 that the output from the PostScript interpreter on the serial
port can be either printer status messages or output from the PostScript print operator.
It is possible for what we think of as a "file to be printed" to generate no printed pages
at all! This file can be a PostScript program that executes and sends its results back to
the host computer. PostScript is not a language that many want to program in. Nevertheless, there are times when we want to send a PostScript program to the printer and
have all its output sent back to the host, not printed on a page. One example is a Post-
Script program to fetch the page count every day, to track printer usage.

```
%!
statusdict begin pagecount end =
```

We want any output returned to the host by the PostScript interpreter, which is not a
status message, to be sent as e-mail to the user. The file mail.c, shown in
Program 17.11, handles this.

```
#include    "lprps.h"

static FILE *mailfp;
static char temp_file[L_tmpnam];
static void open_mailfp(void);

/* Called by proc_input_char() when it encounters characters
 * that are not message characters.  We have to send these
 * characters back to the user. */
void
mail_char(int c)
{
```

```
        static int  done_intro = 0;
        if (in_job && (done_intro || c != '\n')) {
            open_mailfp();
            if (done_intro == 0) {
                fputs("Your PostScript printer job "
                        "produced the following output:\n", mailfp);
                done_intro = 1;
            }
            putc(c, mailfp);
        }
    }

    /* Called by proc_msg() when an "Error" or "OffendingCommand" key
     * is returned by the PostScript interpreter.  Send the key and
     * val to the user. */

    void
    mail_line(const char *msg, const char *val)
    {
        if (in_job) {
            open_mailfp();
            fprintf(mailfp, msg, val);
        }
    }

    /* Create and open a temporary mail file, if not already open.
     * Called by mail_char() and mail_line() above. */

    static void
    open_mailfp(void)
    {
        if (mailfp == NULL) {
            if ( (mailfp = fopen(tmpnam(temp_file), "w")) == NULL)
                log_sys("open_mailfp: fopen error");
        }
    }

    /* Close the temporary mail file and send it to the user.
     * Registered to be called on exit() by atexit() in main(). */

    void
    close_mailfp(void)
    {
        char    command[1024];

        if (mailfp != NULL) {
            if (fclose(mailfp) == EOF)
                log_sys("close_mailfp: fclose error");
            sprintf(command, MAILCMD, loginname, hostname, temp_file);
            system(command);
            unlink(temp_file);
        }
    }
```

Program 17.11 The mail.c file.

The function mail_char is called each time a character is returned by the printer to the host, if the character is not part of a status message. (Later in this section we look at the function proc_input_char that calls mail_char.) The variable in_job is set only while the function send_file is sending a file to the printer. It is not set at other times, such as when we're fetching the printer's status or the printer's page count. The function mail_line is called to write a line to the mail file.

The first time the function open_mailfp is called, it creates a temporary file, and opens it. The function close_mailfp is set by main as an exit handler, to be called whenever exit is called. If the temporary mail file was created, it is closed and mailed to the user.

If we send the one-line PostScript program

```
%!
statusdict begin pagecount end =
```

to fetch the printer's page count, the mail message returned to us is

```
Your PostScript printer job produced the following output:
11185
```

The file output.c (Program 17.12) contains the function out_char that was called by send_file to output each character to the printer.

```
#include    "lprps.h"

static char outbuf[OBSIZE];
static int  outcnt = OBSIZE;     /* #bytes remaining */
static char *outptr = outbuf;

static void out_buf(void);

/* Output a single character.
 * Called by main loop in send_file(). */

void
out_char(int c)
{
    if (c == EOF) {
        out_buf();         /* flag that we're all done */
        return;
    }

    if (outcnt <= 0)
        out_buf();         /* buffer is full, write it first */

    *outptr++ = c;         /* just store in buffer */
    outcnt--;
}

/* Output the buffer that out_char() has been storing into.
 * We have our own output function, so that we never block on a write
 * to the printer.  Each time we output our buffer to the printer,
 * we also see if the printer has something to send us.  If so,
 * we call proc_input_char() to process each character. */
```

```
      static void
      out_buf(void)
      {
           char    *wptr, *rptr, ibuf[IBSIZE];
           int     wcnt, nread, nwritten;
           fd_set  rfds, wfds;

           FD_ZERO(&wfds);
           FD_ZERO(&rfds);
           set_nonblock();              /* don't want the write() to block */
           wptr = outbuf;               /* ptr to first char to output */
           wcnt = outptr - wptr;        /* #bytes to output */
           while (wcnt > 0) {
               FD_SET(psfd, &wfds);
               FD_SET(psfd, &rfds);
               if (intr_flag)
                   handle_intr();
               while (select(psfd + 1, &rfds, &wfds, NULL, NULL) < 0) {
                   if (errno == EINTR) {
                       if (intr_flag)
                           handle_intr();      /* no return */
                   } else
                       log_sys("out_buf: select error");
               }
               if (FD_ISSET(psfd, &rfds)) {            /* printer is readable */
                   if ( (nread = read(psfd, ibuf, IBSIZE)) < 0)
                       log_sys("out_buf: read error");
                   rptr = ibuf;
                   while (--nread >= 0)
                       proc_input_char(*rptr++);
               }
               if (FD_ISSET(psfd, &wfds)) {            /* printer is writeable */
                   if ( (nwritten = write(psfd, wptr, wcnt)) < 0)
                       log_sys("out_buf: write error");
                   wcnt -= nwritten;
                   wptr += nwritten;
               }
           }
           outptr = outbuf;     /* reset buffer pointer and count */
           outcnt = OBSIZE;
      }
```

Program 17.12 The output.c file.

When the argument to out_char is EOF, that's a signal that the end of the input has been reached, and the final output buffer should be sent to the printer.

The function out_char places each character in the output buffer, calling out_buf when the buffer is full. We have to be careful writing out_buf: in addition to sending output to the printer, the printer can be sending us data also. To avoid blocking on a write, we must set the descriptor nonblocking. (Recall the example, Program 12.1.)

We use the select function to multiplex the two I/O directions: **input and output. We** set the same descriptor in the read set and the write set. There is **also a chance that the** select can be interrupted by a caught signal (SIGINT), so we **have to check for this on** any error return.

If we receive asynchronous input from the printer, we call **proc_input_char to** process each character. This input could be either a status **message from the printer or** output to be mailed to the user.

When we write to the printer we have to handle the case of **the write returning a** count less than the requested amount. Again, recall the example **in Program 12.1, where** we saw that a terminal device can accept any amount of data **on each write.**

The file input.c, shown in Program 17.13, defines the functions **that handle all the** input from the printer. This can be either printer status messages **or output for the user.**

```c
#include    "lprps.h"

static int  eof_count;
static int  ignore_input,
static enum parse_state {    /* state of parsing input from printer */
    NORMAL,
    HAD_ONE_PERCENT,
    HAD_TWO_PERCENT,
    IN_MESSAGE,
    HAD_RIGHT_BRACKET,
    HAD_RIGHT_BRACKET_AND_PERCENT
} parse_state;

/* Initialize our input machine. */

void
init_input(int job)
{
    in_job = job;        /* only true when send_file() calls us */
    parse_state = NORMAL;
    ignore_input = 0;
}

/* Read from the printer until we encounter an EOF.
 * Whether or not the input is processed depends on "ignore". */

void
proc_upto_eof(int ignore)
{
    int     ec;

    ignore_input = ignore;
    ec = eof_count;      /* proc_input_char() increments eof_count */
    while (ec == eof_count)
        proc_some_input();
}

/* Wait for some data then read it.
 * Call proc_input_char() for every character read. */
```

```
void
proc_some_input(void)
{
    char    ibuf[IBSIZE];
    char    *ptr;
    int     nread;
    fd_set  rfds;

    FD_ZERO(&rfds);
    FD_SET(psfd, &rfds);
    set_nonblock();
    if (intr_flag)
        handle_intr();
    if (alrm_flag)
        handle_alrm();
    while (select(psfd + 1, &rfds, NULL, NULL, NULL) < 0) {
        if (errno == EINTR) {
            if (alrm_flag)
                handle_alrm();          /* doesn't return */
            else if (intr_flag)
                handle_intr();          /* doesn't return */
        } else
            log_sys("proc_some_input: select error");
    }
    if ( (nread = read(psfd, ibuf, IBSIZE)) < 0)
        log_sys("proc_some_input: read error");
    else if (nread == 0)
        log_sys("proc_some_input: read returned 0");

    ptr = ibuf;
    while (--nread >= 0)
        proc_input_char(*ptr++);    /* process each character */
}

/* Called by proc_some_input() above after some input has been read.
 * Also called by out_buf() whenever asynchronous input appears. */

void
proc_input_char(int c)
{
    if (c == '\004') {
        eof_count++;    /* just count the EOFs */
        return;
    } else if (ignore_input)
        return;              /* ignore everything except EOFs */

    switch (parse_state) {       /* parse the input */
    case NORMAL:
        if (c == '%')
            parse_state = HAD_ONE_PERCENT;
        else
            mail_char(c);
        break;
```

```
    case HAD_ONE_PERCENT:
        if (c == '%')
            parse_state = HAD_TWO_PERCENT;
        else {
            mail_char('%'); mail_char(c);
            parse_state = NORMAL;.
        }
        break;
    case HAD_TWO_PERCENT:
        if (c == '[') {
            msg_init();        /* message starting; init buffer */
            parse_state = IN_MESSAGE;
        } else {
            mail_char('%'); mail_char('%'); mail_char(c);
            parse_state = NORMAL;
        }
        break;
    case IN_MESSAGE:
        if (c == ']')
            parse_state = HAD_RIGHT_BRACKET;
        else
            msg_char(c);
        break;
    case HAD_RIGHT_BRACKET:
        if (c == '%')
            parse_state = HAD_RIGHT_BRACKET_AND_PERCENT;
        else {
            msg_char(']'); msg_char(c);
            parse_state = IN_MESSAGE;
        }
        break;
    case HAD_RIGHT_BRACKET_AND_PERCENT:
        if (c == '%') {
            parse_state = NORMAL;
            proc_msg();        /* we have a message; process it */
        } else {
            msg_char(']'); msg_char('%'); msg_char(c);
            parse_state = IN_MESSAGE;
        }
        break;
    default:
        abort();
    }
}
```

Program 17.13 The input.c file—read and process input from the printer.

The function `proc_upto_eof` is called whenever we are waiting for an EOF from the printer.

The function `proc_some_input` reads from the serial port. Note that we call `select` to determine when the descriptor is readable. This is because `select` is normally interrupted by a caught signal—it is not automatically restarted. Since the `select` can be interrupted by either `SIGALRM` or `SIGINT`, we don't want it restarted. Recall the discussion of `select` normally being interrupted in Section 12.5. Also recall from Section 10.5 that we can set `SA_RESTART` to specify that I/O functions should be automatically restarted when a certain signal occurs, but there is not always a complementary flag that lets us specify that I/O functions should not be restarted. If we don't set `SA_RESTART` then we are at the mercy of the system default, which could be to restart interrupted I/O function calls automatically. When input does arrive from the printer we `read` it in a nonblocking mode, taking whatever the printer has ready for us. The function `proc_input_char` is called to process each character.

The dirty work of processing the messages that the printer can send us is handled by `proc_input_char`. We have to look at every character and remember what state we're in. The variable `parse_state` keeps track of the state. All the characters after the sequence `%%[` are stored in the message buffer by calling `msg_char`. When we encounter the ending `]%%` we call `proc_msg` to process the message. Any characters other than the beginning `%%[`, the ending `]%%`, and the message in between are assumed to be the user's output and are mailed back to the user (by calling `mail_char`).

We now look at the functions that process the message that was accumulated by the input functions above. Program 17.14 shows the file `message.c`.

The function `msg_init` is called after the sequence `%%[` has been seen, and it just initializes the buffer counter. `msg_char` is then called for every character of the message.

The function `proc_msg` breaks up the message into separate *key: val* pairs, and looks at each *key*. The ANSI C function `strtok` is called to break the message into tokens, each *key: val* token separated by a semicolon.

A message of the form

```
%%[ Flushing: rest of job (to end-of-file) will be ignored ]%%
```

causes the function `printer_flushing` to be called. It flushes the terminal buffers, sends an EOF to the printer, and waits for an EOF back from the printer.

If a message of the form

```
%%[ PrinterError: reason ]%%
```

is received, `log_msg` is called to log the error. Other errors with a *key* of `Error` are mailed back to the user. These usually indicate an error in the PostScript program.

If a status message is returned, denoted with a *key* of `status`, it is probably because the function `get_status` sent the printer a status request (Control-T). We look at the *val* and set the variable `status` accordingly.

```
#include    "lprps.h"
#include    <ctype.h>

static char msgbuf[MBSIZE];
static int  msgcnt;
static void printer_flushing(void);

/* Called by proc_input_char() after it's seen the "%%[" that
 * starts a message. */

void
msg_init(void)
{
    msgcnt = 0;      /* count of chars in message buffer */
}

/* All characters received from the printer between the starting
 * %%[ and the terminating ]%% are placed into the message buffer
 * by proc_some_input().  This message will be examined by
 * proc_msg() below. */

void
msg_char(int c)
{
    if (c != '\0' && msgcnt < MBSIZE - 1)
        msgbuf[msgcnt++] = c;
}

/* This function is called by proc_input_char() only after the final
 * percent in a "%%[ <message> ]%%" has been seen.  It parses the
 * <message>, which consists of one or more "key: val" pairs.
 * If there are multiple pairs, "val" can end in a semicolon. */

void
proc_msg(void)
{
    char    *ptr, *key, *val;
    int     n;

    msgbuf[msgcnt] = 0;      /* null terminate message */
    for (ptr = strtok(msgbuf, ";"); ptr != NULL;
                                    ptr = strtok(NULL, ";")) {
        while (isspace(*ptr))
            ptr++;           /* skip leading spaces in key */
        key = ptr;

        if ( (ptr = strchr(ptr, ':')) == NULL)
            continue;  /* missing colon, something wrong, ignore */
        *ptr++ = '\0';  /* null terminate key (overwrite colon) */

        while (isspace(*ptr))
            ptr++;           /* skip leading spaces in val */
        val = ptr;
                             /* remove trailing spaces in val */
        ptr = strchr(val, '\0');
        while (ptr > val && isspace(ptr[-1]))
```

```
                --ptr;
            *ptr = '\0';

        if (strcmp(key, "Flushing") == 0) {
            printer_flushing();        /* never returns */
        } else if (strcmp(key, "PrinterError") == 0) {
            log_msg("proc_msg: printer error: %s", val);
        } else if (strcmp(key, "Error") == 0) {
            mail_line("Your PostScript printer job "
                      "produced the error '%s'.\n", val);
        } else if (strcmp(key, "status") == 0) {
            if (strcmp(val, "idle") == 0)
                status = IDLE;
            else if (strcmp(val, "busy") == 0)
                status = BUSY;
            else if (strcmp(val, "waiting") == 0)
                status = WAITING;
            else
                status = UNKNOWN;    /* "printing", "PrinterError",
                        "initializing", or "printing test page". */
        } else if (strcmp(key, "OffendingCommand") == 0) {
            mail_line("The offending command was '%s'.\n", val);
        } else if (strcmp(key, "pagecount") == 0) {
            if (sscanf(val, "%d", &n) == 1 && n >= 0) {
                if (start_page < 0)
                    start_page = n;
                else
                    end_page = n;
            }
        }
    }
}

/* Called only by proc_msg() when the "Flushing" message
 * is received from the printer.  We exit..*/

static void
printer_flushing(void)
{
    clear_intr();               /* don't catch SIGINT */

    tty_flush();                /* empty tty input and output queues */
    block_write(&eofc, 1);      /* send an EOF to the printer */

    proc_upto_eof(1);           /* this call won't be recursive,
                                   since we specify to ignore input */
    get_page(&end_page);
    do_acct();
    exit(EXIT_SUCCESS);
}
```

Program 17.14 The message.c file, process messages returned from the printer.

A *key* of OffendingCommand usually appears with other *key: val* pairs, as in

```
%%[ Error: stackunderflow; OffendingCommand: pop ]%%
```

We add another line to the mail message that is sent back to the user.

Finally, a *key* of pagecount is generated by the PostScript program in the get_page function (Program 17.9). We call sscanf to convert *val* to binary, and set either the starting or ending page count variable. The while loop in the function get_page is waiting for this variable to become nonnegative.

17.5 Summary

This chapter has examined in detail a complete program—one that sends a PostScript program to a PostScript printer over an RS-232 serial connection. It has given us a chance to see lots of functions that we described in earlier chapters used in a real program: I/O multiplexing, nonblocking I/O, terminal I/O, and signals.

Exercises

17.1 We said that the file to be printed by lprps is on its standard input and could be a pipe. How would you write the psif program (Figure 17.5) to handle this condition, since psif has to look at the first two bytes of the file?

17.2 Implement the psif filter, handling the case outlined in the previous exercise.

17.3 Read Section 12.5 of Adobe Systems [1988] about the handling of font requests in a Post-Script program. Modify the lprps program in this chapter to handle font requests.

18

A Modem Dialer

18.1 Introduction

Programs that deal with modems have always had a hard time coping with the wide variety of modems that are available. On most Unix systems there are two programs that handle modems. The first is a remote login program that lets us dial some other computer, log in, and use that system. In the System V world this program is called cu, while Berkeley systems call it tip. Both programs do similar things, and both have knowledge of many different types of modems. The other program that uses a modem is uucico, part of the UUCP package. The problem is that knowledge that a modem is being used is often built into these programs, and if we want to write some other program that needs a modem, we have to perform many of the same tasks. Also, if we want to change these programs to use some form of communication instead of a modem (such as a network connection), major changes are often required.

In this chapter we develop a separate program that handles all the details of modem handling. This lets us isolate all these details into a single program, instead of having it spread through multiple programs. (This program was motivated by the connection server described in Presotto and Ritchie [1990].) To use this program we have to be able to invoke it and have it pass back a file descriptor, as we described in Section 15.3. We then use this program in developing a remote login program (similar to cu and tip).

18.2 History

The cu(1) command (which stands for "call Unix") appeared in Version 7. But it handled only one particular ACU (automatic call unit). Bill Shannon at Berkeley modified cu, and it appeared in 4.2BSD as the tip(1) program. The biggest change was the use of a text file (/etc/remote) to contain all the information for various systems (phone

579

number, preferred dialer, baud rate, parity, flow control, etc.). This version of tip supported about six different call units and modems, but to add support for some other type of modem required source code changes.

Along with cu and tip, the UUCP system also accessed modems and automatic call units. UUCP managed locks on different modems, so that multiple instances of UUCP could be running at the same time. The tip and cu programs had to honor the UUCP locking protocol, to avoid interfering with UUCP. On the BSD systems UUCP developed its own set of dialer functions. These functions were link edited into the UUCP executable, which meant the addition of a new modem type required source code changes.

SVR2 provided a dial(3) function that attempted to isolate the unique features of modem dialing into a single library function. It was used by cu, but not by UUCP. This function was in the standard C library, so it was available to any program.

The Honey DanBer UUCP system [Redman 1989] took the modem commands out of the C source files and put them into a Dialers file. This allowed the addition of new modem types without having to modify the source code. But the functions used by cu and UUCP to access the Dialers file were not generally available. This means that without redeveloping all the code to process the dialing information in the Dialers file, programs other than cu and UUCP couldn't use this file.

Throughout all these versions of cu, tip, and UUCP, locking was required to assure only a single program accessed a single device at a time. Since all these programs worked across many different systems, earlier versions of which provided no record locking, a rudimentary form of file locking was used. This could lead to lock files being left around after a program crashed, and ad hoc techniques were developed to handle this. (We can't use record locking on special device files, so record locking by itself isn't the final solution.)

18.3 Program Design

Let's detail the features that we want the modem dialer to have.

1. It must be possible to add new modem types without requiring source code changes.

   To obtain this feature, we'll use the Honey DanBer Dialers file. We'll put all the code that uses this file to dial the modem into a daemon server, so any program can access it using the client–server functions from Section 15.5.

2. Some form of locking must be used so that the abnormal termination of a program holding a lock automatically releases the lock. Ad hoc techniques, such as those still used by most versions of cu and UUCP, should finally be discarded, since better methods exist.

   We'll let the server daemon handle all the device locking. Since the client–server functions from Section 15.5 automatically notify the server when a client terminates, the daemon can release any locks that the process had.

3. New programs must be able to use all the features that we develop. A new program that deals with a modem should not have to reinvent the wheel. Dialing any type of modem should be as simple as a function call.

   For this feature, we'll let the central server daemon do all the dialing, passing back a file descriptor.

4. Client programs, such as cu and tip, shouldn't need special privileges. They should not be set-user-ID programs.

   We'll give the special privileges to the server daemon, allowing its clients to run without any special privileges.

Obviously we can't change the existing cu, tip, and UUCP programs, but we should make it easier for others to build on this work. Also, we should take the best features of the existing Unix dialing programs.

Figure 18.1 shows the arrangement of the client and server.

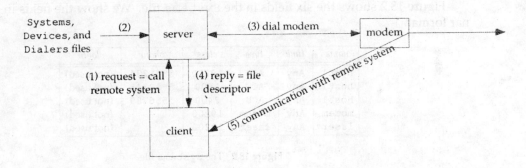

Figure 18.1 Overview of client and server.

The steps involved in establishing communications with a remote system are as follows:

0. The server is started.

1. The client is started and opens a connection to the server, using the cli_conn function (Section 15.5). The client sends a request for the server to call the remote system.

2. The server reads the Systems, Devices, and Dialers files to determine how to call the remote system. (We describe these files in the next section.) If a modem is being used, the Dialers file contains all the modem-specific commands to dial the modem.

3. The server opens the modem device and dials the modem. This can take a while (typically around 15–30 seconds). The server handles all locking of this device, to avoid interfering with other users of this device.

4. If the dialing was successful, the server passes back the open file descriptor for the modem device to the client. Our functions from Section 15.3 send and receive the descriptor.

5. The client communicates directly with the remote system. The server is not involved in this communication—the client reads and writes the file descriptor returned in step 4.

The communication between the client and server (steps 1 and 4) is across a stream pipe. When the client is finished communicating with the remote system it closes this stream pipe (normally just by terminating). The server notices this close and releases the lock on the modem device.

18.4 Data Files

In this section we describe the three files used by the Honey DanBer UUCP system: Systems, Devices, and Dialers. There are many fields in these files that are used by the UUCP system. We don't describe these additional fields (or the UUCP system) in detail. Refer to Redman [1989] for additional details.

Figure 18.2 shows the six fields in the Systems file. We show the fields in a columnar format.

name	time	type	class	phone	login
host1	Any	ACU	19200	5551234	(not used)
host1	Any	ACU	9600	5552345	(not used)
host1	Any	ACU	2400	5556789	(not used)
modem	Any	modem	19200	–	(not used)
laser	Any	laser	19200	–	(not used)

Figure 18.2 The Systems file.

The *name* is the name of the remote system. We use this in commands of the form cu host1, for example. Note that we can have multiple entries for the same remote system. These entries are tried in order. The entries named modem and laser are for connecting directly to a modem and a laser printer. We don't need to dial a modem to connect to these devices, but we still need to open the appropriate terminal line, and handle the appropriate locks.

time specifies the time-of-day and days of the week to call this host. This is a UUCP field. The *type* field specifies which entry in the Devices file is to be used for this *name*. The *class* field is really the line speed to be used (baud rate). *phone* specifies the phone number for entries with a *type* of ACU. For other entries the phone field is just a hyphen. The final field, *login*, is the remainder of the line. It is a series of strings used by UUCP to log in to the remote system. We don't need this field.

The Devices file contains information on the modems and directly connected hosts. Figure 18.3 shows the five fields in this file. The *type* field matches an entry in the Systems file with an entry in the Devices file. The *class* field must also match the corresponding field in the Systems file. It normally specifies the line speed.

The actual name of a device is obtained by prefixing the *line* field with /dev/. In this example the actual devices are /dev/cua0, /dev/ttya, and /dev/ttyb. The next field, *line2*, is not used.

type	line	line2	class	dialer
ACU	cua0	–	19200	tbfast
ACU	cua0	–	9600	tb9600
ACU	cua0	–	2400	tb2400
ACU	cua0	–	1200	tb1200
modem	ttya	–	19200	direct
laser	ttyb	–	19200	direct

Figure 18.3 The Devices file.

The final field, *dialer*, matches the corresponding entry in the Dialers file. For the directly connected entries this field is direct.

Figure 18.4 shows the format of the Dialers file. This is the file that contains all the modem-specific dialing commands.

dialer	sub	handshake
tb9600	=W,-	"" \dA\pA\pA\pTQ0S2=255S12=255s50=6s58=2s68=255\r\c OK\r \EATDT\T\r\c CONNECT\s9600 \r\c ""
tbfast	=W,-	"" \dA\pA\pA\pTQ0S2=255S12=255s50=255s58=2s68=255s110=1s111=30\r\c OK\r \EATDT\T\r\c CONNECT\sFAST

Figure 18.4 The Dialers file.

We show only two entries for this file—we don't show the entries for tb1200 and tb2400 that were referenced in the Devices file. The *handshake* field is contained on a single line. We have broken it into two lines to fit on the page.

The *dialer* field is used to locate the matching entry from the Devices file. The *sub* field specifies substitutions to be performed for an equals sign and a minus sign that appear in a phone number. In the two entries in Figure 18.4 this field says to substitute a W for an equals sign, and a comma for a minus sign. This allows the phone numbers in the Systems file to contain an equals sign (meaning "wait for dialtone") and a minus sign (meaning "pause"). The translation of these two characters to whatever each particular modem requires is specified by the Dialers file.

The final field, *handshake*, contains the actual dialing instructions. It is a sequence of blank-separated strings called expect–send strings. We expect (i.e., read until we match) the first string and then send (i.e., write) the next string. Let's look at the tbfast entry as an example. This entry is for a Telebit Trailblazer modem in its PEP mode (packetized ensemble protocol).

1. The first expect string is empty, meaning "expect nothing." We always successfully match this empty string.

2. We send the next string. Special send sequences are specified with the backslash character. \d causes a delay for 2 seconds. We then send an A. We pause for one-half second (\p), send another A, pause, send another A, and pause again. We then send the remaining characters in the string, starting with T. These

commands all set parameters in the modem. The \r sends a carriage return and the final \c says not to write the normal newline at the end of the send string.

3. We read from the modem until we receive the string OK\r. (Again, the sequence \r means a carriage return.)

4. The next send string begins with \E. This enables echo checking: each time we send a character to the modem, we read back until the character is echoed. We then send the four characters ATDT. The next special character, \T, causes the phone number to be substituted. This is followed by a carriage return and the normal newline at the end of the send string is not sent.

5. The final expect string waits for CONNECT FAST to be returned by the modem. (The sequence \s means a single space.)

When this final expect string is received, the dialing is complete. (There are many more special sequences that can appear in the *handshake* string that we don't cover.)

Let's summarize the actions that we have to perform with these three files.

1. Using the name of the remote system, find the first entry in the Systems file with the same *name*.

2. Find the matching entry in the Devices file with a *type* and *class* that match the corresponding entries in the Systems file entry.

3. Find the entry in the Dialers file that matches the *dialer* field in the Devices file.

4. Dial the modem.

There are two reasons why this can fail: (1) the device corresponding to the *line* field in the Devices file is already in use by someone else or (2) the dialing is unsuccessful (e.g., the phone on the remote system is busy, or the remote system is down and is not answering the phone). The second case is often detected by a time out occurring when we're reading from the modem, trying to match an expect string (see Exercise 18.10). In either case, we want to go back to step 1 and search for the next entry for the same remote system. As we saw in Figure 18.2, a given host can have multiple entries, each with a different phone number (and each phone number could correspond to a different device).

There are other files in the Honey DanBer system that we don't use in the example in this chapter. The file Dialcodes specifies dialcode abbreviations for phone numbers in the Systems file. The file Sysfiles allows the specification of alternate copies of the three files Systems, Devices, and Dialers.

18.5 Server Design

We'll start with a description of the server. Two factors affect the design of the server:

1. Dialing can take a while (15–30 seconds), so the server has to fork a child process to do the actual dialing.

2. The daemon server (the parent) has to be the one process that manages all the locks.

Figure 18.5 shows the arrangement of the processes.

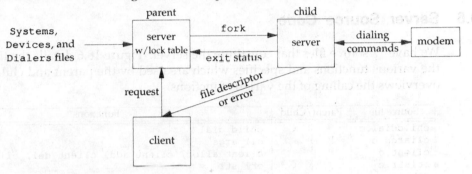

Figure 18.5 Arrangement of processes in modem dialer.

The steps performed by the server are the following:

1. The parent receives the request from the client at the server's well-known name. As we described in Section 15.5, this creates a unique stream pipe between the client and server. This parent process has to handle multiple clients at the same time, like the open server in Section 15.6.

2. Based on the name of the remote system that the client wants to contact, the parent goes through the Systems file and Devices file, to find a match. The parent also keeps a lock table of which devices are currently in use, so it can skip those entries in the Devices file that are in use.

3. If a match is found, a child is forked to do the actual dialing. (The parent can handle other clients at this point.) If successful the child sends the file descriptor for the modem back to the client on the client-specific stream pipe (which got duplicated across the fork) and calls exit(0). If an error occurs (phone line busy, no answer, etc.) the child calls exit(1).

4. The parent is notified of the child termination by SIGCHLD and fetches its termination status (waitpid).

   If the child was successful there is nothing more for the parent to do. The lock must be held until the client is finished with the modem device. The client-specific stream pipe between the client and parent is left open. This way, when the client does terminate, the parent is notified, and the parent releases the lock.

   If the child was not successful, the parent picks up in the Systems file where it left off for this client and tries to find another match. If another entry is found for the remote system, the parent goes back to step 3 and forks a new child to do the actual dialing. If no more entries exist for the remote system, the parent calls send_err (Program 15.4) and closes the client-specific stream pipe.

Having a unique connection to each client allows the child to send debug output back to the client, if desired. Often the client wants to see the progress of the actual dialing, if problems occur. Even though the dialing is being done by the child of an unrelated server, the unique connection allows the child to send output directly back to its client.

18.6 Server Source Code

We have 17 source files that constitute the server. Figure 18.6 details the files containing the various functions and specifies which are used by the parent and child. Figure 18.7 overviews the calling of the various functions.

Source file	Parent/Child		Functions
childdial.c		C	child_dial
cliargs.c	P		cli_args
client.c	P		client_alloc, client_add, client_del, client_sigchld
ctlstr.c		C	ctl_str
debug.c		C	DEBUG, DEBUG_NONL
devfile.c	P		dev_next, dev_rew, dev_find
dialfile.c		C	dial_next, dial_rew, dial_find
expectstr.c		C	expect_str, exp_read, sig_alrm
lock.c	P		find_line, lock_set, lock_rel, is_locked
loop.c	P		loop, cli_done, child_done
main.c	P		main
request.c	P		request
sendstr.c		C	send_str
sigchld.c	P		sig_chld
sysfile.c	P		sys_next, sys_rew, sys_posn
ttydial.c		C	tty_dial
ttyopen.c		C	tty_open

Figure 18.6 Source files for server.

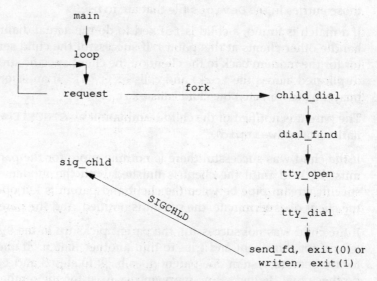

Figure 18.7 Overview of function calling in server.

Program 18.1 shows the calld.h header, which is included by all the source files. It includes the standard system headers, defines some basic constants, and declares the global variables.

```c
#include     <sys/types.h>
#include     <errno.h>
#include     <signal.h>
#include     "ourhdr.h"

#define CS_CALL "/home/stevens/calld"     /* well-known name */
#define CL_CALL "call"
#define MAXSYSNAME  256
#define MAXSPEEDSTR 256
#define NALLOC  10                        /* #structs to alloc/realloc for */
                 /* Client structs (client.c), Lock structs (lock.c) */
#define WHITE        " \t\n"              /* for separating tokens */
#define SYSTEMS      "./Systems"          /* my own copies for now */
#define DEVICES      "./Devices"
#define DIALERS      "./Dialers"

                /* declare global variables */
extern int       clifd;
extern int       debug;        /* nonzero if interactive (not daemon) */
extern int       Debug;        /* nonzero for dialing debug output */
extern char      errmsg[];     /* error message string to return to client */
extern char      *speed;       /* speed (actually "class") to use */
extern char      *sysname;     /* name of system to call */
extern uid_t     uid;          /* client's uid */
extern volatile sig_atomic_t         chld_flag;  /* when SIGCHLD occurs */
extern enum parity { NONE, EVEN, ODD } parity;  /* specified by client */

typedef struct {          /* one Client struct per connected client */
  int    fd;          /* fd, or -1 if available */
  pid_t pid;          /* child pid while dialing */
  uid_t uid;          /* client's user ID */
  int    childdone;   /* nonzero when SIGCHLD from dialing child recvd:
                          1 means exit(0), 2 means exit(1) */
  long  sysftell;     /* next line to read in Systems file */
  long  foundone;     /* true if we find a matching sysfile entry */
  int   Debug;                /* option from client */
  enum parity parity;         /* option from client */
  char  speed[MAXSPEEDSTR];   /* option from client */
  char  sysname[MAXSYSNAME];  /* option from client */
} Client;

extern Client    *client;     /* ptr to malloc'ed array of Client structs */
extern int       client_size;/* # entries in client[] array */
                 /* (both manipulated by client_XXX() functions) */

typedef struct {          /* everything for one entry in Systems file */
  char *name;         /* system name */
  char *time;         /* (e.g., "Any") time to call (ignored) */
```

```
   char   *type;       /* (e.g., "ACU") or system name if direct connect */
   char   *class;      /* (e.g., "9600") speed */
   char   *phone;      /* phone number or "-" if direct connect */
   char   *login;      /* uucp login chat (ignored) */
} Systems;

typedef struct {         /* everything for one entry in Devices file */
   char   *type;       /* (e.g., "ACU") matched by type in Systems */
   char   *line;       /* (e.g., "cua0") without preceding "/dev/" */
   char   *line2;      /* (ignored) */
   char   *class;      /* matched by class in Systems */
   char   *dialer;     /* name of dialer in Dialers */
} Devices;

typedef struct {         /* everything for one entry in Dialers file */
   char   *dialer;     /* matched by dialer in Devices */
   char   *sub;        /* phone number substitution string (ignored) */
   char   *expsend;    /* expect/send chat */
} Dialers;

extern Systems  systems;    /* filled in by sys_next() */
extern Devices  devices;    /* filled in by dev_next() */
extern Dialers  dialers;    /* filled in by dial_next() */

                /* our function prototypes */
void     child_dial(Client *);                  /* childdial.c */

int      cli_args(int, char **);                /* cliargs.c */

int      client_add(int, uid_t);                /* client.c */
void     client_del(int);
void     client_sigchld(pid_t, int);

void     loop(void);                            /* loop.c */

char     *ctl_str(char);                         /* ctlstr.c */

int      dev_find(Devices *, const Systems *);  /* devfile.c */
int      dev_next(Devices *);
void     dev_rew(void);

int      dial_find(Dialers *, const Devices *); /* dialfile.c */
int      dial_next(Dialers *);
void     dial_rew(void);

int      expect_str(int, char *);               /* expectstr.c */

int      request(Client *);                     /* request.c */

int      send_str(int, char *, char *, int);    /* sendstr.c */

void     sig_chld(int);                         /* sigchld.c */

long     sys_next(Systems *);                   /* sysfile.c */
void     sys_posn(long);
```

```
void      sys_rew(void);

int       tty_open(char *, char *, enum parity, int);    /* ttyopen.c */

int       tty_dial(int, char *, char *, char *, char *); /* ttydial.c */

pid_t     is_locked(char *);                       /* lock.c */
void      lock_set(char *, pid_t);
void      lock_rel(pid_t);

void      DEBUG(char *, ...);                      /* debug.c */
void      DEBUG_NONL(char *, ...);
```

Program 18.1 The `calld.h` header.

We define a `Client` structure that contains all the information for each client. This is an expansion of the similar structure in Program 15.26. In the time between forking a child to dial for a client and that child terminating, we can handle any number of other clients. This structure contains all the information that we need to try to find another `Systems` file entry for that client, and try dialing again.

We also define one structure for all the information for a single entry in the `Systems`, `Devices`, and `Dialers` files.

Program 18.2 shows the `main` function for the server. Since this program is normally run as a daemon server, we provide a −d command line option that lets us run the program interactively.

```
#include      "calld.h"
#include      <syslog.h>

              /* define global variables */
int           clifd;
int           debug;   /* daemon's command line flag */
int           Debug;   /* Debug controlled by client, not cmd line */
char          errmsg[MAXLINE];
char          *speed;
char          *sysname;
uid_t         uid;
Client        *client = NULL;
int           client_size;
Systems       systems;
Devices       devices;
Dialers       dialers;
volatile sig_atomic_t chld_flag;
enum parity parity = NONE;

int
main(int argc, char *argv[])
{
    int       c;

    log_open("calld", LOG_PID, LOG_USER);
```

```
    opterr = 0;      /* don't want getopt() writing to stderr */
    while ( (c = getopt(argc, argv, "d")) != EOF) {
        switch (c) {
        case 'd':         /* debug */
            debug = 1;
            break;

        case '?':
            log_quit("unrecognized option: -%c", optopt);
        }
    }

    if (debug == 0)
        daemon_init();

    loop();      /* never returns */
}
```

Program 18.2 The main function.

When the −d option is set, all the calls to the log_XXX functions (Appendix B) are sent
to standard error. Otherwise they are logged using syslog.

The function loop is the main loop of the server (Program 18.3). It multiplexes the
various descriptors with the select function.

```
#include      "calld.h"
#include      <sys/time.h>
#include      <errno.h>

static void cli_done(int);
static void child_done(int);

static fd_set   allset; /* one bit per client conn, plus one for listenfd
                        /* modified by loop() and cli_done() */

void
loop(void)
{
    int       i, n, maxfd, maxi, listenfd, nread;
    char      buf[MAXLINE];
    Client    *cliptr;
    uid_t     uid;
    fd_set    rset;

    if (signal_intr(SIGCHLD, sig_chld) == SIG_ERR)
        log_sys("signal error");

                /* obtain descriptor to listen for client requests on */
    if ( (listenfd = serv_listen(CS_CALL)) < 0)
        log_sys("serv_listen error");

    FD_ZERO(&allset);
    FD_SET(listenfd, &allset);
```

```
            maxfd = listenfd;
            maxi = -1;

            for ( ; ; ) {
                if (chld_flag)
                    child_done(maxi);
                rset = allset;          /* rset gets modified each time around */
                if ( (n = select(maxfd + 1, &rset, NULL, NULL, NULL)) < 0) {
                    if (errno == EINTR) {
                            /* caught SIGCHLD, find entry with childdone set */
                        child_done(maxi);
                        continue;           /* issue the select again */
                    } else
                        log_sys("select error");
                }

                if (FD_ISSET(listenfd, &rset)) {
                            /* accept new client request */
                    if ( (clifd = serv_accept(listenfd, &uid)) < 0)
                        log_sys("serv_accept error: %d", clifd);

                    i = client_add(clifd, uid);
                    FD_SET(clifd, &allset);
                    if (clifd > maxfd)
                        maxfd = clifd;  /* max fd for select() */
                    if (i > maxi)
                        maxi = i;           /* max index in client[] array */
                    log_msg("new connection: uid %d, fd %d", uid, clifd);
                    continue;
                }

                /* Go through client[] array.
                   Read any client data that has arrived. */

                for (cliptr = &client[0]; cliptr <= &client[maxi]; cliptr++) {
                    if ( (clifd = cliptr->fd) < 0)
                        continue;
                    if (FD_ISSET(clifd, &rset)) {
                            /* read argument buffer from client */
                        if ( (nread = read(clifd, buf, MAXLINE)) < 0)
                            log_sys("read error on fd %d", clifd);

                        else if (nread == 0) {
                            /* The client has terminated or closed the stream
                               pipe.  Now we can release its device lock. */

                            log_msg("closed: uid %d, fd %d",
                                                cliptr->uid, clifd);
                            lock_rel(cliptr->pid);
                            cli_done(clifd);
                            continue;
                        }
```

```
                    /*· Data has arrived from the client.  Process the
                       client's request. */

                    if (buf[nread-1] != 0) {
                        log_quit("request from uid %d not null terminated:"
                                 " %*.*s", uid, nread, nread, buf);
                        cli_done(clifd);
                        continue;
                    }
                    log_msg("starting: %s, from uid %d", buf, uid);

                            /* Parse the arguments, set options.  Since
                               we may need to try calling again for this
                               client, save options in client[] array. */
                    if (buf_args(buf, cli_args) < 0)
                        log_quit("command line error: %s", buf);
                    cliptr->Debug = Debug;
                    cliptr->parity = parity;
                    strcpy(cliptr->sysname, sysname);
                    strcpy(cliptr->speed, (speed == NULL) ? "" : speed);
                    cliptr->childdone = 0;
                    cliptr->sysftell = 0;
                    cliptr->foundone = 0;

                    if (request(cliptr) < 0) {
                            /* system not found, or unable to connect */
                        if (send_err(cliptr->fd, -1, errmsg) < 0)
                            log_sys("send_err error");
                        cli_done(clifd);
                        continue;
                    }
                    /* At this point request() has forked a child that is
                       trying to dial the remote system.  We'll find
                       out the child's status when it terminates. */
                }
            }
        }
}

/* Go through the client[] array looking for clients whose dialing
   children have terminated.  This function is called by loop() when
   chld_flag (the flag set by the SIGCHLD handler) is nonzero. */

static void
child_done(int maxi)
{
    Client  *cliptr;

again:
    chld_flag = 0;  /* to check when done with loop for more SIGCHLDs */
```

```
                    for (cliptr = &client[0]; cliptr <= &client[maxi]; cliptr++) {
                        if ( (clifd = cliptr->fd) < 0)
                            continue;
                        if (cliptr->childdone) {
                            log_msg("child done: pid %d, status %d",
                                            cliptr->pid, cliptr->childdone-1);

                            /* If the child was successful (exit(0)), just clear
                               the flag.  When the client terminates, we'll read
                               the EOF on the stream pipe above and release
                               the device lock. */

                            if (cliptr->childdone == 1) {    /* child did exit(0) */
                                cliptr->childdone = 0;
                                continue;
                            }

                            /* Unsuccessful: child did exit(1).  Release the device
                               lock and try again from where we left off. */

                            cliptr->childdone = 0;
                            lock_rel(cliptr->pid);   /* unlock the device entry */
                            if (request(cliptr) < 0) {
                                        /* still unable, time to give up */
                                if (send_err(cliptr->fd, -1, errmsg) < 0)
                                    log_sys("send_err error");
                                cli_done(clifd);
                                continue;
                            }
                            /* request() has forked another child for this client */
                        }
                    }
                    if (chld_flag)  /* additional SIGCHLDs have been caught */
                        goto again; /* need to check all childdone flags again */
                }

                /* Clean up when we're done with a client. */

                static void
                cli_done(int clifd)
                {
                    client_del(clifd);         /* delete entry in client[] array */
                    FD_CLR(clifd, &allset); /* turn off bit in select() set */
                    close(clifd);              /* close our end of stream pipe */
                }
```

Program 18.3 The loop.c file.

This function initializes the client array and establishes a signal handler for SIGCHLD. We call signal_intr instead of signal so that any slow system call is interrupted when our signal handler returns. The `loop` function then calls `serv_listen` (Programs 15.19 and 15.22). The rest of the function is an infinite loop based on the `select` function, that tests for the following two conditions:

1. If a new client connection arrives, we call `serv_accept` (Programs 15.20 and 15.24). The function `client_add` creates an entry in the `client` array for the new client.

2. We then go through the `client` array, to see if (a) any client has terminated, or (b) any client requests have arrived.

   When a client terminates (whether voluntarily or not) its client-specific stream pipe to the server is closed, and we read an end of file from our end of the pipe. At this point we can release any device locks that the client owned and release the entry in the `client` array.

   When a request arrives from a client, we set things up and call `request`. (We showed the function `buf_args` in Program 15.17.) If the name of the remote system is valid and if an available device entry is located, `request` forks a child process and returns.

One external event that can happen at any time in this function is the termination of a child. If we're blocked in the `select` function, it returns an error of `EINTR`. Since the signal can also happen at other points in the `loop` function, we test the flag `chld_flag` each time through the loop before calling `select`. If the signal has occurred, we call the function `child_done` to process the termination.

This function goes through the `client` array, examining the `childdone` flag for each valid entry. If the child was successful, there's nothing else to do at this point. But if the child terminated with an `exit` status of 1, we call `request` to try to find another `Systems` file entry for this client.

Program 18.4 shows the function `cli_args` that is called by `buf_args` in the `loop` function, when a client request arrives. It processes the command-line arguments from the client. Note that this function sets global variables based on the command-line arguments, which `loop` then copies into the appropriate entry in the `client` array, since these options affect only a single client's request.

Program 18.5 shows the file `client.c`, which defines the functions that manipulate the `client` array. The only difference between Program 18.5 and Program 15.27 is that we now have to look up an entry based on the process ID (the function `client_sigchld`).

Program 18.6 is the file `lock.c`. These functions manage the `lock` array for the parent. As with the `client` functions, we call `realloc` to allocate space dynamically for the `lock` array, to avoid compile time limits.

```
#include    "calld.h"
/* This function is called by buf_args(), which is called by loop().
 * buf_args() has broken up the client's buffer into an argv[] style
 * array, which is now processed. */
int
cli_args(int argc, char **argv)
{
    int     c;

    if (argc < 2 || strcmp(argv[0], CL_CALL) != 0) {
        strcpy(errmsg, "usage: call <options> <hostname>");
        return(-1);
    }
    Debug = 0;       /* option defaults */
    parity = NONE;
    speed = NULL;
    opterr = 0;      /* don't want getopt() writing to stderr */
    optind = 1;      /* since we call getopt() multiple times */
    while ( (c = getopt(argc, argv, "des:o")) != EOF) {
        switch (c) {
        case 'd':
            Debug = 1;   /* client wants DEBUG() output */
            break;

        case 'e':          /* even parity */
            parity = EVEN;
            break;

        case 'o':          /* odd parity */
            parity = ODD;
            break;

        case 's':          /* speed */
            speed = optarg;
            break;

        case '?':
            sprintf(errmsg, "unrecognized option: -%c\n", optopt);
            return(-1);
        }
    }
    if (optind < argc)
        sysname = argv[optind];        /* name of host to call */
    else {
        sprintf(errmsg, "missing <hostname> to call\n");
        return(-1);
    }
    return(0);
}
```

Program 18.4 The cli_args function.

```c
#include    "calld.h"

static void
client_alloc(void)          /* alloc more entries in the client[] array */
{
    int     i;

    if (client == NULL)
        client = malloc(NALLOC * sizeof(Client));
    else
        client = realloc(client, (client_size + NALLOC) * sizeof(Client));
    if (client == NULL)
        err_sys("can't alloc for client array");

            /* have to initialize the new entries */
    for (i = client_size; i < client_size + NALLOC; i++)
        client[i].fd = -1;  /* fd of -1 means entry available */

    client_size += NALLOC;
}

/* Called by loop() when connection request from a new client arrives */

int
client_add(int fd, uid_t uid)
{
    int     i;

    if (client == NULL)     /* first time we're called */
        client_alloc();
again:
    for (i = 0; i < client_size; i++) {
        if (client[i].fd == -1) {   /* find an available entry */
            client[i].fd = fd;
            client[i].uid = uid;
            return(i);  /* return index in client[] array */
        }
    }
            /* client array full, time to realloc for more */
    client_alloc();
    goto again;     /* and search again (will work this time) */
}

/* Called by loop() when we're done with a client */

void
client_del(int fd)
{
    int     i;

    for (i = 0; i < client_size; i++) {
        if (client[i].fd == fd) {
            client[i].fd = -1;
            return;
```

```
                }
            }
        log_quit("can't find client entry for fd %d", fd);
}

/* Find the client entry corresponding to a process ID.
 * This function is called by the sig_chld() signal
 * handler only after a child has terminated. */

void
client_sigchld(pid_t pid, int stat)
{
    int      i;

    for (i = 0; i < client_size; i++) {
        if (client[i].pid == pid) {
            client[i].childdone = stat; /* child's exit() status +1 */
            return;
        }
    }
    log_quit("can't find client entry for pid %d", pid);
}
```

Program 18.5 The client.c file.

```
#include    "calld.h"

typedef struct {
  char  *line;   /* points to malloc()ed area */
                 /* we lock by line (device name) */
  pid_t pid;     /* but unlock by process ID */
                 /* pid of 0 means available */
} Lock;
static Lock *lock = NULL;   /* the malloc'ed/realloc'ed array */
static int   lock_size;     /* #entries in lock[] */
static int   nlocks;        /* #entries currently used in lock[] */

/* Find the entry in lock[] for the specified device (line)
 * If we don't find it, create a new entry at the end of tne
 * lock[] array for the new device.  This is how all the possible
 * devices get added to the lock[] array over time. */

static Lock *
find_line(char *line)
{
    int      i;
    Lock     *lptr;

    for (i = 0; i < nlocks; i++) {
        if (strcmp(line, lock[i].line) == 0)
            return(&lock[i]);   /* found entry for device */
    }
```

```
    /* Entry not found.  This device has never been locked before.
       Add a new entry to lock[] array. */

    if (nlocks >= lock_size) {   /* lock[] array is full */
        if (lock == NULL)         /* first time through */
            lock = malloc(NALLOC * sizeof(Lock));
        else
            lock = realloc(lock, (lock_size + NALLOC) * sizeof(Lock));
        if (lock == NULL)
            err_sys("can't alloc for lock array");

        lock_size += NALLOC;
    }

    lptr = &lock[nlocks++];
    if ( (lptr->line = malloc(strlen(line) + 1)) == NULL)
        log_sys("malloc error");
    strcpy(lptr->line, line);   /* copy caller's line name */
    lptr->pid  = 0;
    return(lptr);
}

void
lock_set(char *line, pid_t pid)
{
    Lock    *lptr;

    log_msg("locking %s for pid %d", line, pid);
    lptr = find_line(line);
    lptr->pid  = pid;
}

void
lock_rel(pid_t pid)
{
    Lock    *lptr;

    for (lptr = &lock[0]; lptr < &lock[nlocks]; lptr++) {
        if (lptr->pid == pid) {
            log_msg("unlocking %s for pid %d", lptr->line, pid);
            lptr->pid  = 0;
            return;
        }
    }
    log_msg("can't find lock for pid = %d", pid);
}

pid_t
is_locked(char *line)
{
    return( find_line(line)->pid ); /* nonzero pid means locked */
}
```

Program 18.6 Functions for managing client device locks.

Each entry in the lock array is associated with a single *line* (the second field in the Devices file). Since these locking functions don't know all the different *line* values in this data file, new entries in the lock array are created whenever a new *line* is locked the first time. The function find_line handles this.

The next three source files handle the three data files: Systems, Devices, and Dialers. Each file has a XXX_next function that reads the next line of the file and breaks it up into fields. The ANSI C function strtok is called to break the lines into fields. Program 18.7 handles the Systems file.

```c
#include    "calld.h"

static FILE *fpsys = NULL;
static int   syslineno;           /* for error messages */
static char  sysline[MAXLINE];
        /* can't be automatic; sys_next() returns pointers into here */

/* Read and break apart a line in the Systems file. */

long                            /* return >0 if OK, -1 on EOF */
sys_next(Systems *sysptr)    /* structure is filled in with pointers */
{
    if (fpsys == NULL) {
        if ( (fpsys = fopen(SYSTEMS, "r")) == NULL)
            log_sys("can't open %s", SYSTEMS);
        syslineno = 0;
    }

again:
    if (fgets(sysline, MAXLINE, fpsys) == NULL)
        return(-1);       /* EOF */
    syslineno++;

    if ( (sysptr->name = strtok(sysline, WHITE)) == NULL) {
        if (sysline[0] == '\n')
            goto again;       /* ignore empty line */
        log_quit("missing `name' in Systems file, line %d", syslineno);
    }
    if (sysptr->name[0] == '#')
        goto again;               /* ignore comment line */

    if ( (sysptr->time = strtok(NULL, WHITE)) == NULL)
        log_quit("missing `time' in Systems file, line %d", syslineno);

    if ( (sysptr->type = strtok(NULL, WHITE)) == NULL)
        log_quit("missing `type' in Systems file, line %d", syslineno);

    if ( (sysptr->class = strtok(NULL, WHITE)) == NULL)
        log_quit("missing `class' in Systems file, line %d", syslineno);

    if ( (sysptr->phone = strtok(NULL, WHITE)) == NULL)
        log_quit("missing `phone' in Systems file, line %d", syslineno);

    if ( (sysptr->login = strtok(NULL, "\n")) == NULL)
        log_quit("missing `login' in Systems file, line %d", syslineno);
```

```
        return(ftell(fpsys));    /* return the position in Systems file */
}

void
sys_rew(void)
{
    if (fpsys != NULL)
        rewind(fpsys);
    syslineno = 0;
}

void
sys_posn(long posn)        /* position Systems file */
{
    if (posn == 0)
        sys_rew();
    else if (fseek(fpsys, posn, SEEK_SET) != 0)
        log_sys("fseek error");
}
```

Program 18.7 Functions to read Systems file.

The function sys_next is called by request to read the next entry in the file.

We have to remember our position in this file for each client (the sysftell member of the Client structure). This is so that if a child fails to dial the remote system, we can pick up where we left off in the Systems file (for that client), to try to find another entry for the remote system. The position is obtained by calling the standard I/O function ftell and reset using fseek.

Program 18.8 contains the functions for reading the Devices file.

```
#include    "calld.h"

static FILE *fpdev = NULL;
static int  devlineno;              /* for error messages */
static char devline[MAXLINE];
        /* can't be automatic; dev_next() returns pointers into here */

/* Read and break apart a line in the Devices file. */

int
dev_next(Devices *devptr)          /* pointers in structure are filled in */
{
    if (fpdev == NULL) {
        if ( (fpdev = fopen(DEVICES, "r")) == NULL)
            log_sys("can't open %s", DEVICES);
        devlineno = 0;
    }

again:
    if (fgets(devline, MAXLINE, fpdev) == NULL)
        return(-1);       /* EOF */
    devlineno++;
```

```
        if ( (devptr->type = strtok(devline, WHITE)) == NULL) {
            if (devline[0] == '\n')
                goto again;       /* ignore empty line */
            log_quit("missing 'type' in Devices file, line %d", devlineno);
        }
        if (devptr->type[0] == '#')
            goto again;           /* ignore comment line */

        if ( (devptr->line = strtok(NULL, WHITE)) == NULL)
            log_quit("missing 'line' in Devices file, line %d", devlineno);

        if ( (devptr->line2 = strtok(NULL, WHITE)) == NULL)
            log_quit("missing 'line2' in Devices file, line %d", devlineno);

        if ( (devptr->class = strtok(NULL, WHITE)) == NULL)
            log_quit("missing 'class' in Devices file, line %d", devlineno);

        if ( (devptr->dialer = strtok(NULL, WHITE)) == NULL)
            log_quit("missing 'dialer' in Devices file, line %d", devlineno);

        return(0);
    }

    void
    dev_rew(void)
    {
        if (fpdev != NULL)
            rewind(fpdev);
        devlineno = 0;
    }

    /* Find a match of type and class */

    int
    dev_find(Devices *devptr, const Systems *sysptr)
    {
        dev_rew();
        while (dev_next(devptr) >= 0) {
            if (strcmp(sysptr->type, devptr->type) == 0 &&
                strcmp(sysptr->class, devptr->class) == 0)
                    return(0);        /* found a device match */
        }
        sprintf(errmsg, "device '%s'/'%s' not found\n",
                                sysptr->type, sysptr->class);
        return(-1);
    }
```

Program 18.8 Functions for reading Devices file.

We'll see that the request function calls dev_find to locate an entry with *type* and *class* fields that match an entry in the Systems file.

Program 18.9 contains the functions for reading the Dialers file.

```
#include    "calld.h"

static FILE *fpdial = NULL;
static int  diallineno;              /* for error messages */
static char dialline[MAXLINE];
        /* can't be automatic; dial_next() returns pointers into here */

/* Read and break apart a line in the Dialers file. */

int
dial_next(Dialers *dialptr) /* pointers in structure are filled in */
{
    if (fpdial == NULL) {
        if ( (fpdial = fopen(DIALERS, "r")) == NULL)
            log_sys("can't open %s", DIALERS);
        diallineno = 0;
    }

again:
    if (fgets(dialline, MAXLINE, fpdial) == NULL)
        return(-1);        /* EOF */
    diallineno++;

    if ( (dialptr->dialer = strtok(dialline, WHITE)) == NULL) {
        if (dialline[0] == '\n')
            goto again;       /* ignore empty line */
        log_quit("missing 'dialer' in Dialers file, line %d", diallineno);
    }
    if (dialptr->dialer[0] == '#')
        goto again;            /* ignore comment line */

    if ( (dialptr->sub = strtok(NULL, WHITE)) == NULL)
        log_quit("missing 'sub' in Dialers file, line %d", diallineno);

    if ( (dialptr->expsend = strtok(NULL, "\n")) == NULL)
        log_quit("missing 'expsend' in Dialers file, line %d", diallineno);

    return(0);
}

void
dial_rew(void)
{
    if (fpdial != NULL)
        rewind(fpdial);
    diallineno = 0;
}

/* Find a dialer match */

int
dial_find(Dialers *dialptr, const Devices *devptr)
{
```

```
        dial_rew();
        while (dial_next(dialptr) >= 0) {
            if (strcmp(dialptr->dialer, devptr->dialer) == 0)
                return(0);           /* found a dialer match */
        }
        sprintf(errmsg, "dialer '%s' not found\n", dialptr->dialer);
        return(-1);
}
```

Program 18.9 Functions for reading Dialers file.

We'll see that the child_dial function calls dial_find to find an entry with a *dialer* field that matches a particular device.

Notice from Figure 18.6 that the Systems and Devices files are handled by the parent, while the Dialers file is handled by the child. This was one of the design goals—the parent finds a matching device that is not locked and forks a child to do the actual dialing.

We look at the request function in Program 18.10. It was called by the loop function to try to locate an unlocked device for the specified remote host. To do this it goes through the Systems file, then the Devices file. If a match is found, a child is forked. We allow the client to specify a speed, in addition to the name of the remote system. For example, with the Systems file in Figure 18.2, the client's request can look like

```
call -s 9600 host1
```

which causes us to ignore the other two entries for host1 in Figure 18.2.

Notice that we can't record the device lock using lock_set until we know the process ID of the child (i.e., after the fork), but we have to test whether the device is locked before the fork. Since we don't want the child starting until we have set the lock, we use the TELL_WAIT functions (Program 10.17) to synchronize the parent and child. Also note that although the test is_locked and the actual setting of the lock by set_lock are two separate operations (i.e., not a single atomic operation) we do not have a race condition. This is because request is called only by the single parent server daemon—it is not called by multiple processes.

If request returns 0, a child was forked to start the dial, otherwise it returns −1 to indicate that either the name of the remote system wasn't valid or all the possible devices for the remote system were locked.

```
#include     "calld.h"

int                             /* return 0 if OK, -1 on error */
request(Client *cliptr)
{
    pid_t   pid;

    errmsg[0] = 0;
        /* position where this client left off last (or rewind) */
    sys_posn(cliptr->sysftell);
```

```
    while ( (cliptr->sysftell = sys_next(&systems)) >= 0) {
        if (strcmp(cliptr->sysname, systems.name) == 0) {
                /* system match */
            /* if client specified a speed, it must match too */
            if (cliptr->speed[0] != 0 &&
                strcmp(cliptr->speed, systems.class) != 0)
                    continue;   /* speeds don't match */

            DEBUG("trying sys: %s, %s, %s, %s", systems.name,
                    systems.type, systems.class, systems.phone);
            cliptr->foundone++;

            if (dev_find(&devices, &systems) < 0)
                break;
            DEBUG("trying dev: %s, %s, %s, %s", devices.type,
                    devices.line, devices.class, devices.dialer);
            if ( (pid = is_locked(devices.line)) != 0) {
                sprintf(errmsg, "device '%s' already locked by pid %d\n",
                                                devices.line, pid);
                continue;   /* look for another entry in Systems file */
            }

                /* We've found a device that's not locked.
                   fork() a child to to the actual dialing. */
            TELL_WAIT();
            if ( (cliptr->pid = fork()) < 0)
                log_sys("fork error");
            else if (cliptr->pid == 0) {    /* child */
                WAIT_PARENT();      /* let parent set lock */
                child_dial(cliptr); /* never returns */
            }
            /* parent */
            lock_set(devices.line, cliptr->pid);
                /* let child resume, now that lock is set */
            TELL_CHILD(cliptr->pid);
            return(0);  /* we've started a child */
        }
    }
    /* reached EOF on Systems file */
    if (cliptr->foundone == 0)
        sprintf(errmsg, "system '%s' not found\n", cliptr->sysname);
    else if (errmsg[0] == 0)
        sprintf(errmsg, "unable to connect to system '%s'\n",
                                                cliptr->sysname);
    return(-1);     /* also, cliptr->sysftell is -1 */
}
```

Program 18.10 The request function.

The last of the parent-specific functions is sig_chld, the signal handler for the
SIGCHLD signal. This is shown in Program 18.11.

```
#include    "calld.h"
#include    <sys/wait.h>

/* SIGCHLD handler, invoked when a child terminates. */

void
sig_chld(int signo)
{
    int     stat, errno_save;
    pid_t   pid;

    errno_save = errno;        /* log_msg() might change errno */
    chld_flag = 1;
    if ( (pid = waitpid(-1, &stat, 0)) <= 0)
        log_sys("waitpid error");

    if (WIFEXITED(stat) != 0)
                    /* set client's childdone status for loop() */
        client_sigchld(pid, WEXITSTATUS(stat)+1):
    else
        log_msg("child %d terminated abnormally: %04x", pid, stat);

    errno = errno_save;
    return;       /* probably interrupts accept() in serv_accept() */
```

Program 18.11 The sig_chld signal handler.

When a child terminates we must record its termination status and process ID in the appropriate entry in the client array. We call the function client_sigchld (Program 18.5) to do this.

Note that we are violating one of our earlier rules from Chapter 10—a signal handler should only set a global variable and nothing else. Here we call waitpid and the function client_sigchld (Program 18.5). This latter function is signal safe. All it does is record information in an entry in the client array—it doesn't create or delete entries (which would be nonreentrant) and it doesn't call any system functions.

waitpid is defined by POSIX.1 to be signal safe (Figure 10.3). If we didn't call waitpid from the signal handler, the parent would have to call it when the flag chld_flag was nonzero. But since numerous children can terminate before the main loop gets a chance to look at chld_flag, we would either need to increment chld_flag each time a child terminated (so the main loop would know how many times to call waitpid) or call waitpid in a loop, with the WNOHANG flag (Figure 8.3). The simplest solution is to call waitpid from the signal handler, and record the information in the client array.

We now proceed to the functions that are called by the child as part of its attempt to dial the remote system. Everything starts for the child after the fork when request calls child_dial (Program 18.12).

```
#include    "calld.h"

/* The child does the actual dialing and sends the fd back to
 * the client.  This function can't return to caller, must exit.
 * If successful, exit(0), else exit(1).
 * The child uses the following global variables, which are just
 * in the copy of the data space from the parent:
 *      cliptr->fd (to send DEBUG() output and fd back to client),
 *      cliptr->Debug (for all DEBUG() output), cliptr->parity,
 *      systems, devices, dialers. */

void
child_dial(Client *cliptr)
{
    int     fd, n;

    Debug = cliptr->Debug;
    DEBUG("child, pid %d", getpid());

    if (strcmp(devices.dialer, "direct") == 0) { /* direct tty line */
        fd = tty_open(systems.class, devices.line, cliptr->parity, 0);
        if (fd < 0)
            goto die;
    } else {                        /* else assume dialing is needed */
        if (dial_find(&dialers, &devices) < 0)
            goto die;
        fd = tty_open(systems.class, devices.line, cliptr->parity, 1);
        if (fd < 0)
            goto die;
        if (tty_dial(fd, systems.phone, dialers.dialer,
                            dialers.sub, dialers.expsend) < 0)
            goto die;
    }

    DEBUG("done");
            /* send the open descriptor to client */
    if (send_fd(cliptr->fd, fd) < 0)
        log_sys("send_fd error");
    exit(0);    /* parent will see this */

die:
    /* The child can't call send_err() as that would send the final
       2-byte protocol to the client.  We just send our error message
       back to the client.  If the parent finally gives up, it'll
       call send_err(). */

    n = strlen(errmsg);
    if (writen(cliptr->fd, errmsg, n) != n) /* send error to client */
        log_sys("writen error");
    exit(1);    /* parent will see this, release lock, and try again */
}
```

Program 18.12 The child_dial function.

If the device being used is directly connected, just the function `tty_open` is called to open the terminal device and set all the appropriate terminal parameters. But if the device is a modem, three functions are called: `dial_find` (to locate the appropriate entry in the `Dialers` file), `tty_open`, and `tty_dial` (to do the actual dialing).

If `child_dial` is successful, it returns the file descriptor to the client by calling `send_fd` (Programs 15.5 and 15.9) and calls `exit(0)`. Otherwise it sends an error message back to the client across the stream pipe and calls `exit(1)`. The client-specific stream pipe is duplicated across the `fork`, so the child can send either the descriptor or error message directly back to the client.

```
#include    "calld.h"
#include    <stdarg.h>

/* Note that all debug output goes back to the client. */

void
DEBUG(char *fmt, ...)          /* debug output, newline at end */
{
    va_list args;
    char    line[MAXLINE];
    int     n;

    if (Debug == 0)
        return;
    va_start(args, fmt);
    vsprintf(line, fmt, args);
    strcat(line, "\n");
    va_end(args);

    n = strlen(line);
    if (writen(clifd, line, n) != n)
        log_sys("writen error");
}

void
DEBUG_NONL(char *fmt, ...)  /* debug output, NO newline at end */
{
    va_list args;
    char    line[MAXLINE];
    int     n;

    if (Debug == 0)
        return;
    va_start(args, fmt);
    vsprintf(line, fmt, args);
    va_end(args);

    n = strlen(line);
    if (writen(clifd, line, n) != n)
        log_sys("writen error");
}
```

Program 18.13 Debugging functions.

The client can send a −d option in its command to the server, and this sets the client-specific variable Debug. This flag is used in Program 18.13 by the two functions DEBUG and DEBUG_NONL to send debugging information back to the client. This information is useful when dialing problems are encountered for a particular system. These two functions are called predominantly by the child, although the parent also called them from the request function (Program 18.10).

Program 18.14 shows the tty_open function. It is called for both modem devices and direct connect devices, to open the terminal and set its modes. The *class* field of the Systems and Devices file specified the line speed, and the client can specify the parity.

```
#include    "calld.h"
#include    <fcntl.h>
#include    <termios.h>

/* Open the terminal line */

int
tty_open(char *class, char *line, enum parity parity, int modem)
{
    int             fd, baud;
    char            devname[100];
    struct termios  term;

            /* first open the device */
    strcpy(devname, "/dev/");
    strcat(devname, line);
    if ( (fd = open(devname, O_RDWR | O_NONBLOCK)) < 0) {
        sprintf(errmsg, "can't open %s: %s\n",
                                    devname, strerror(errno));
        return(-1);
    }
    if (isatty(fd) == 0) {
        sprintf(errmsg, "%s is not a tty\n", devname);
        return(-1);
    }

            /* fetch then set modem's terminal status */
    if (tcgetattr(fd, &term) < 0)
        log_sys("tcgetattr error");

    if (parity == NONE)
        term.c_cflag = CS8;
    else if (parity == EVEN)
        term.c_cflag = CS7 | PARENB;
    else if (parity == ODD)
        term.c_cflag = CS7 | PARENB | PARODD;
    else
        log_quit("unknown parity");
    term.c_cflag |= CREAD |         /* enable receiver */
                    HUPCL;          /* lower modem lines on last close */
                                    /* 1 stop bit (since CSTOPB off) */
```

```
        if (modem == 0)
            term.c_cflag |= CLOCAL;      /* ignore modem status lines */

        term.c_oflag  = 0;               /* turn off all output processing */
        term.c_iflag  = IXON | IXOFF |   /* Xon/Xoff flow control (default) */
                        IGNBRK |         /* ignore breaks */
                        ISTRIP |         /* strip input to 7 bits */
                        IGNPAR;          /* ignore input parity errors */
        term.c_lflag  = 0;          /* everything off in local flag:
                                       disables canonical mode, disables
                                       signal generation, disables echo */
        term.c_cc[VMIN]  = 1;       /* 1 byte at a time, no timer */
        term.c_cc[VTIME] = 0;       /* (See Figure 18.10) */
        if      (strcmp(class, "38400") == 0)   baud = B38400;
        else if (strcmp(class, "19200") == 0)   baud = B19200;
        else if (strcmp(class, "9600") == 0)    baud = B9600;
        else if (strcmp(class, "4800") == 0)    baud = B4800;
        else if (strcmp(class, "2400") == 0)    baud = B2400;
        else if (strcmp(class, "1800") == 0)    baud = B1800;
        else if (strcmp(class, "1200") == 0)    baud = B1200;
        else if (strcmp(class, "600") == 0)     baud = B600;
        else if (strcmp(class, "300") == 0)     baud = B300;
        else if (strcmp(class, "200") == 0)     baud = B200;
        else if (strcmp(class, "150") == 0)     baud = B150;
        else if (strcmp(class, "134") == 0)     baud = B134;
        else if (strcmp(class, "110") == 0)     baud = B110;
        else if (strcmp(class, "75") == 0)      baud = B75;
        else if (strcmp(class, "50") == 0)      baud = B50;
        else {
            sprintf(errmsg, "invalid baud rate: %s\n", class);
            return(-1);
        }
        cfsetispeed(&term, baud);
        cfsetospeed(&term, baud);

        if (tcsetattr(fd, TCSANOW, &term) < 0)   /* set attributes */
            log_sys("tcsetattr error");

        DEBUG("tty open");
        clr_fl(fd, O_NONBLOCK);         /* turn off nonblocking */
        return(fd);
}
```

Program 18.14 The tty_open function.

We open the terminal device with the nonblocking flag, as sometimes the open of a terminal connected to a modem doesn't return until the modem's carrier is present. Since we are dialing out and not dialing in, we don't want to wait. At the end of the function we call the clr_fl function to clear the nonblocking mode. The only difference between a modem and a direct connect line in the tty_open function is for a direct connect line we set the CLOCAL bit.

The details of dialing a modem takes place in the `tty_dial` function (Program 18.15). This function is only called for modem lines, not for direct connect lines.

```
#include    "calld.h"

int
tty_dial(int fd, char *phone, char *dialer, char *sub, char *expsend)
{
    char    *ptr;

    ptr = strtok(expsend, WHITE);   /* first expect string */
    for ( ; ; ) {
        DEBUG_NONL("expect = %s\nread: ", ptr);
        if (expect_str(fd, ptr) < 0)
            return(-1);

        if ( (ptr = strtok(NULL, WHITE)) == NULL)
            return(0);        /* at the end of the expect/send */
        DEBUG_NONL("send = %s\nwrite: ", ptr);
        if (send_str(fd, ptr, phone, 0) < 0)
            return(-1);

        if ( (ptr = strtok(NULL, WHITE)) == NULL)
            return(0);        /* at the end of the expect/send */
    }
}
```

Program 18.15 The `tty_dial` function.

The function just calls one function to handle the expect string and another to handle the send string. We are done when there are no more send or expect strings. (Note that we do not handle the *sub* string from Figure 18.4.)

Program 18.16 shows the function `send_str` that outputs the send strings. To keep the size of this example manageable, we have not implemented every special escape sequence—we have implemented enough to use the program with the `Dialers` files shown in Figure 18.4.

```
#include    "calld.h"

int
send_str(int fd, char *ptr, char *phone, int echocheck)
{
    char    c, tempc;

        /* go though send string, converting escape sequences on the fly */
    while ( (c = *ptr++) != 0) {
        if (c == '\\') {
            if (*ptr == 0) {
                sprintf(errmsg, "backslash at end of send string\n");
                return(-1);
            }
```

```
                c = *ptr++;        /* char following backslash */

            switch (c) {
            case 'c':          /* no CR, if at end of string */
                if (*ptr == 0)
                    goto returnok;
                continue;      /* ignore if not at end of string */

            case 'd':          /* 2 second delay */
                DEBUG_NONL("<delay>");
                sleep(2);
                continue;

            case 'p':          /* 0.25 second pause */
                DEBUG_NONL("<pause>");
                sleep_us(250000);    /* Exercise 12.6 */
                continue;

            case 'e':
                DEBUG_NONL("<echo check off>");
                echocheck = 0;
                continue;

            case 'E':
                DEBUG_NONL("<echo check on>");
                echocheck = 1;
                continue;

            case 'T':          /* output phone number */
                send_str(fd, phone, phone, echocheck);  /* recursive */
                continue;

            case 'r':
                c = '\r';
                break;

            case 's':
                c = ' ';
                break;


                /* room for lots more case statements ... */


            default:
                sprintf(errmsg, "unknown send escape char: \\%s\n",
                                                    ctl_str(c));
                return(-1);
            }
        }

        DEBUG_NONL("%s", ctl_str(c));
        if (write(fd, &c, 1) != 1)
            log_sys("write error");
```

```
        if (echocheck) {           /* wait for char to be echoed */
            do {
                if (read(fd, &tempc, 1) != 1)
                    log_sys("read error");
                DEBUG_NONL("{%s}", ctl_str(tempc));
            } while (tempc != c);
        }
    }
    c = '\r';    /* if no \c at end of string, CR written at end */
    DEBUG_NONL("%s", ctl_str(c));
    if (write(fd, &c, 1) != 1)
        log_sys("write error");
returnok:
    DEBUG("");
    return(0);
}
```

Program 18.16 The send_str function.

send_str calls the function ctl_str to convert ASCII control characters into a printable version. Program 18.17 shows the ctl_str function.

```
#include    "calld.h"

/* Make a printable string of the character "c", which may be a
 * control character.  Works only with ASCII. */

char *
ctl_str(char c)
{
    static char tempstr[6];      /* biggest is "\177" + null */

    c &= 255;
    if (c == 0)
        return("\\0");                /* really shouldn't see a null */
    else if (c < 040)
        sprintf(tempstr, "^%c", c + 'A' - 1);
    else if (c == 0177)
        return("DEL");
    else if (c > 0177)
        sprintf(tempstr, "\\%03o", c);
    else
        sprintf(tempstr, "%c", c);
    return(tempstr);
}
```

Program 18.17 The ctl_str function.

The hardest part of dialing the modem is recognizing the expect strings. Program 18.18 shows the function expect_str that does this. (As with the send strings, we have implemented only a subset of all the possible features provided by the Dialers file.)

```
#include    "calld.h"

#define EXPALRM    45            /* alarm time to read expect string */

static int        expalarm = EXPALRM;
static void       sig_alrm(int);
static volatile sig_atomic_t    caught_alrm;

static size_t    exp_read(int, char *);

int                        /* return 0 if got it, -1 if not */
expect_str(int fd, char *ptr)
{
    char    expstr[MAXLINE], inbuf[MAXLINE];
    char    c, *src, *dst, *inptr, *cmpptr;
    int     i, matchlen;

    if (strcmp(ptr, "\"\"") == 0)
        goto returnok;       /* special case of "" (expect nothing) */

            /* copy expect string, converting escape sequences */
    for (src = ptr, dst = expstr; (c = *src++) != 0; ) {
        if (c == '\\') {
            if (*src == 0) {
                sprintf(errmsg, "invalid expect string: %s\n", ptr);
                return(-1);
            }
            c = *src++;      /* char following backslash */
            switch (c) {
            case 'r':    c = '\r'; break;
            case 's':    c = ' '; break;
                /* room for lots more case statements ... */
            default:
                sprintf(errmsg, "unknown expect escape char: \\%s\n",
                                                    ctl_str(c));
                return(-1);
            }
        }
        *dst++ = c;
    }
    *dst = 0;
    matchlen = strlen(expstr);

    if (signal(SIGALRM, sig_alrm) == SIG_ERR)
        log_quit("signal error");
    caught_alrm = 0;
    alarm(expalarm);

    do {
        if (exp_read(fd, &c) < 0)
            return(-1);
    } while (c != expstr[0]);   /* skip until first chars equal */
```

```
        cmpptr = inptr = inbuf;
        *inptr = c;

        for (i = 1; i < matchlen; i++) {    /* read matchlen chars */
            inptr++;
            if (exp_read(fd, inptr) < 0)
                return(-1);
        }

        for ( ; ; ) {          /* keep reading until we have a match */
            if (strncmp(cmpptr, expstr, matchlen) == 0)
                break;         /* have a match */
            inptr++;
            if (exp_read(fd, inptr) < 0)
                return(-1);
            cmpptr++;
        }
returnok:
    alarm(0);
    DEBUG("\nexpect: got it");
    return(0);
}

size_t              /* read one byte, handle timeout errors & DEBUG */
exp_read(int fd, char *buf)
{
    if (caught_alrm) {  /* test flag before blocking in read */
        DEBUG("\nread timeout");
        return(-1);
    }
    if (read(fd, buf, 1) == 1) {
        DEBUG_NONL("%s", ctl_str(*buf));
        return(1);
    }
    if (errno == EINTR && caught_alrm) {
        DEBUG("\nread timeout");
        return(-1);
    }
    log_sys("read error");
}

static void
sig_alrm(int signo)
{
    caught_alrm = 1;
    return;
}
```

Program 18.18 Functions to read and recognize expect strings.

We first copy the expect string, converting the special characters. Our matching technique is to read characters from the modem until the character matches the first character of the expect string. We then read enough characters to equal the number of characters in the expect string. From that point we continually read characters from the modem into the buffer, comparing them against the expect string, until we have a match or until the alarm goes off. (There are better algorithms for string matching—ours was chosen to simplify the coding. The number of characters returned by the modem that are compared to the expect string is usually on the order of 50, and the size of the expect string is often around 10−20 characters.)

Note that we have to set an alarm each time we try to match an expect string, as the alarm is the only way we can determine that we didn't receive what we were waiting for.

This completes the server daemon. All it does is open a terminal device and dial a modem. What happens with the terminal device after it is opened depends on the client. We'll now examine a client that provides an interface similar to cu and tip, allowing us to dial a remote system and log in.

18.7 Client Design

The interface between the client and server is only about a dozen lines of code. The client formats a command line, sends it to the server, and receives back either a file descriptor or an error indication. The rest of the client design depends on what the client wants to do with the returned descriptor. In this section we'll outline the design of the call client that works like the familiar cu and tip programs. It allows us to call a remote system and log in to it. The remote system need not be a Unix system—we can use it to communicate with any system or device that's connected to the host with an RS-232 serial connection.

Terminal Line Disciplines

In Figures 12.11 and 12.12 we gave an overview of the modem dialer. Figure 18.8 is an expansion of Figure 12.11, recognizing the fact that there are two line disciplines between the user and the modem and assuming that we're using the program to dial into a remote Unix host. (Recall from the output of Program 12.10 that for a streams-based terminal system, Figure 18.8 is a simplification. There may be multiple streams modules making up the line discipline and multiple modules making up the terminal device driver. We also don't explicitly show the stream head.)

The two dashed boxes in Figure 18.8 above the modem on the local system were established by the server's tty_open function (Program 18.14). That function set the dashed terminal line discipline module to noncanonical (i.e., raw) mode. The modem on the local system was dialed by the server's tty_dial function (Program 18.15). The two arrows between the dashed terminal line discipline box and the call process correspond to the descriptor returned by the server. (We show the single descriptor as two arrows, to reiterate the fact that it's a full-duplex descriptor.)

The line discipline box beneath the shell on the remote system is set by the login process on that system to be in the canonical mode. After we have dialed the remote

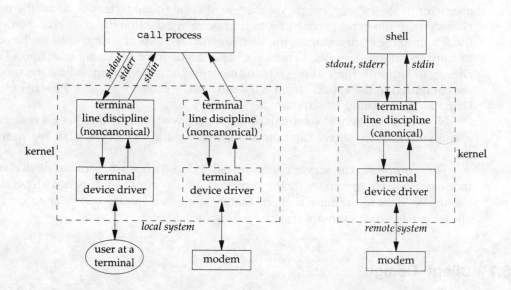

Figure 18.8 Overview of modem dialer process to log in to remote Unix host.

system we want the special terminal input characters (end of file, erase line, etc. from Section 11.3) recognized by the line discipline module on the remote host. That means we have to set the mode of the line discipline module above the terminal (standard input, standard output, and standard error of the `call` process) to noncanonical mode.

One Process or Two?

In Figure 18.8 we show the `call` process as a single process. Doing so requires support for an I/O multiplexing function such as `select` or `poll`, since two descriptors are being read from and two descriptors are being written to. We could also design the client as two processes, a parent and a child, as we showed in Figure 12.12. Figure 18.9 shows only these two processes and the line disciplines beneath them. Historically, `cu` and `tip` have always been two processes, as in Figure 18.9. This is because early Unix systems didn't support an I/O multiplexing function.

We choose to use a single process for the following two reasons.

1. Having two processes complicates the termination of the client. If we terminate the connection by entering ˜ . (a tilde followed by a period) at the beginning of a line, the child recognizes this and terminates. The parent then has to catch the `SIGCHLD` signal so that the parent can terminate too.

    If the connection is terminated by the remote system or if the line is dropped, the parent will detect this by reading an end of file from the modem descriptor. The parent then has to notify the child, so that the child can also terminate.

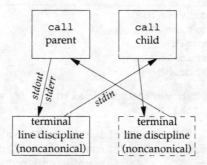

Figure 18.9 The call client as two processes.

Using a single process obviates the need for one process notifying the other when it terminates.

2. We are going to implement a file transfer function in the client, similar to the put and take commands of cu and tip. We enter these commands on the standard input, on a line that begins with a tilde (the default escape character). These commands are recognized by the child if two processes are being used (Figure 18.9). But the file that's received by the client, in the case of a take command, comes across the modem descriptor, which is being read by the parent. This means, to implement the take command, the child has to notify the parent so that the parent stops reading from the modem. The parent is probably blocked in a read on this descriptor, so a signal is required to interrupt the parent's read. When the child is done, another notification is required to tell the parent to resume reading from the modem. While possible, this scenario quickly becomes messy.

A single process simplifies the entire client. By using a single process, however, we lose the ability to job-control stop just the child. The BSD tip program supports this feature. It allows us to stop the child while the parent continues running. This means all the terminal input is directed back to our shell instead of the child, letting us work on the local system, but we'll still see any output generated by the remote system. This is handy if we start a long running job on the remote system and want to see any output that it generates, while working on the local system.

We now look at the source code to implement the client.

18.8 Client Source Code

The client is smaller than the server, since the client doesn't handle all the details of connecting the remote system—the server from Section 18.6 handles this. About one-half of the client is to handle commands such as take and put.

Program 18.19 shows the call.h header that is included by all the source files.

```
#include    <sys/types.h>
#include    <sys/time.h>
#include    <errno.h>
#include    <termios.h>
#include    "ourhdr.h"

#define CS_CALL "/home/stevens/calld"    /* well-known server name */
#define CL_CALL "call"                   /* command for server */

               /* declare global variables */
extern char  escapec;    /* tilde for local commands */
extern char *src;         /* for take and put commands */
extern char *dst;         /* for take and put commands */

               /* function prototypes */
int     call(const char *);
int     doescape(int);
void    loop(int);
int     prompt_read(char *, int (*)(int, char **));
void    put(int);
void    take(int);
int     take_put_args(int, char **);
```

Program 18.19 The call.h header.

The command for the server and the server's well-known name have to correspond to the values in Program 18.1.

Program 18.20 shows the main function.

```
#include    "call.h"

               /* define global variables */
char    escapec = '~';
char   *src;
char   *dst;

static void usage(char *);

int
main(int argc, char *argv[])
{
    int        c, remfd, debug;
    char       args[MAXLINE];

    args[0] = 0;    /* build arg list for conn server here */
    opterr = 0;     /* don't want getopt() writing to stderr */
    while ( (c = getopt(argc, argv, "des:o")) != EOF) {
        switch (c) {
        case 'd':         /* debug */
            debug = 1;
            strcat(args, "-d ");
            break;
```

```
            case 'e':              /* even parity */
                strcat(args, "-e ");
                break;

        case 'o':              /* odd parity */
            strcat(args, "-o ");
            break;

        case 's':              /* speed */
            strcat(args, " s ");
            strcat(args, optarg);
            strcat(args, " ");
            break;

        case '?':
            usage("unrecognized option");
        }
    }
    if (optind < argc)
        strcat(args, argv[optind]); /* name of host to call */
    else
        usage("missing <hostname> to call");

    if ( (remfd = call(args)) < 0)   /* place the call */
        exit(1);         /* call() prints reason for failure */
    printf("Connected\n");

    if (tty_raw(STDIN_FILENO) < 0)   /* user's tty to raw mode */
        err_sys("tty_raw error");
    if (atexit(tty_atexit) < 0)       /* reset user's tty on exit */
        err_sys("atexit error");

    loop(remfd);                      /* and do it */

    printf("Disconnected\n\r");
    exit(0);
}

static void
usage(char *msg)
{
    err_quit("%s\nusage: call -d -e -o -s<speed> <hostname>", msg);
}
```

Program 18.20 The main function.

It processes the command-line arguments, saving them in the array args, which is sent to the server. The function call contacts the server and returns the file descriptor to the remote system.

The line discipline module above the terminal (Figure 18.8) is set to noncanonical mode using the tty_raw function (Program 11.10). To reset the terminal when we're done we establish the function tty_atexit as an exit handler.

The function `loop` is then called to copy everything that we enter to the modem and everything from the modem to the terminal.

The `call` function in Program 18.21 contacts the server to obtain a file descriptor for the modem. As we said earlier, it takes only a dozen lines of code to contact the server to obtain the descriptor.

```
#include     "call.h"
#include     <sys/uio.h>        /* struct iovec */

/* Place the call by sending the "args" to the calling server,
 * and reading a file descriptor back. */

int
call(const char *args)
{
    int          csfd, len;
    struct iovec iov[2];

                        /* create connection to conn server */
    if ( (csfd = cli_conn(CS_CALL)) < 0)
        err_sys("cli_conn error");

    iov[0].iov_base = CL_CALL " ";
    iov[0].iov_len  = strlen(CL_CALL) + 1;
    iov[1].iov_base = (char *) args;
    iov[1].iov_len  = strlen(args) + 1;
                            /* null at end of args always sent */
    len = iov[0].iov_len + iov[1].iov_len;
    if (writev(csfd, &iov[0], 2) != len)
        err_sys("writev error");

                    /* read back descriptor */
                    /* returned errors handled by write() */
    return( recv_fd(csfd, write) );
}
```

Program 18.21 The `call` function.

The function `loop` handles the I/O multiplexing between the two input streams and the two output streams. We can use either `poll` or `select`, depending what the local system provides. Program 18.22 shows an implementation using `poll`.

```
#include     "call.h"
#include     <poll.h>
#include     <stropts.h>

/* Copy everything from stdin to "remfd",
 * and everything from "remfd" to stdout. */

#define BUFFSIZE     512

void
loop(int remfd)
```

```
{
    int         bol, n, nread;
    char        c, buff[BUFFSIZE];
    struct pollfd  fds[2];

    setbuf(stdout, NULL);           /* set stdout unbuffered */
                                    /* (for printfs in take() and put() */
    fds[0].fd = STDIN_FILENO;       /* user's terminal input */
    fds[0].events = POLLIN;
    fds[1].fd = remfd;              /* input from remote (modem) */
    fds[1].events = POLLIN;

    for ( ; ; ) {
        if (poll(fds, 2, INFTIM) <= 0)
            err_sys("poll error");

        if (fds[0].revents & POLLIN) {  /* data to read on stdin */
            if (read(STDIN_FILENO, &c, 1) != 1)
                err_sys("read error from stdin");

            if (c == escapec && bol) {
                if ( (n = doescape(remfd)) < 0)
                    break;          /* user wants to terminate */
                else if (n == 0)
                    continue;   /* escape seq has been processed */

                /* else, char following escape was not special,
                   so it's returned and echoed below */
                c = n;
            }
            if (c == '\r' || c == '\n')
                bol = 1;
            else
                bol = 0;

            if (write(remfd, &c, 1) != 1)
                err_sys("write error");
        }
        if (fds[0].revents & POLLHUP)
            break;          /* stdin hangup -> done */

        if (fds[1].revents & POLLIN) {  /* data to read from remote */
            if ( (nread = read(remfd, buff, BUFFSIZE)) <= 0)
                break;          /* error or EOF, terminate */

            if (writen(STDOUT_FILENO, buff, nread) != nread)
                err_sys("writen error to stdout");
        }
        if (fds[1].revents & POLLHUP)
            break;          /* modem hangup -> done */
    }
}
```

Program 18.22 The loop function using the poll function.

The basic loop of this function just waits for data to appear from either the terminal or the modem. When data is read from the terminal, it's just copied to the modem and vice versa. The only complication is to recognize the escape character (the tilde) as the first character of a line.

Note that we read one character at a time from the terminal (standard input), but up to one buffer at a time from the modem. One reason for the single character at a time from the terminal is because we have to look at every character to know when a new line begins, to recognize the special commands. Although this character-at-a-time I/O is expensive in terms of CPU time (recall Figure 3.1), there is usually far less input from the terminal than from the remote system. (In remote login sessions using this program measured by the author, there are around 100 characters output by the remote host for every character input.)

When the escape character is seen, doescape is called to process the command (Program 18.23). We support only five commands. Simple commands are handled directly in this function, while the more complicated take and put commands are handled by separate functions (take and put).

- A period terminates the client. For some devices, such as a laser printer, this is the only way to terminate the client. When we're logged into a remote system, such as in Figure 18.8, logging out from that system usually causes the remote modem to drop the phone line, causing a hangup to be received on the modem descriptor by the loop function.

- If the system supports job control we recognize the job-control suspend character and suspend the client. Note that it is simpler for us to recognize this character directly and stop ourselves than to have the line discipline recognize the character and generate the SIGSTOP signal (compare with Program 10.22). We have to reset the terminal mode before stopping ourselves, and reset it when we're continued.

- A pound sign generates a BREAK on the modem descriptor. We use the POSIX.1 tcsendbreak function to do this (Section 11.8). The BREAK condition often causes the remote system's getty or ttymon program to switch line speeds (Section 9.2).

- The take and put commands require separate functions to be called. The way to distinguish between the two commands is to remember that the command describes what the client is doing on the local system: taking a file from the remote system or putting a file to the remote system.

Program 18.24 shows the code required to handle the take command. The function take first calls prompt_read (which we show in Program 18.25) to echo ~[take]. in response to the ~t command. The prompt_read function then reads a line of input from the terminal, containing the source pathname (the file on the remote host) and the destination pathname (the file on the local host). The results are stored in the global variables src and dst.

```c
#include    "call.h"
#include    <signal.h>

/* Called when first character of a line is the escape character
 * (tilde).  Read the next character and process.  Return -1
 * if next character is "terminate" character, 0 if next character
 * is valid command character (that's been processed), or next
 * character itself (if the next character is not special). */

int
doescape(int remfd)
{
    char    c;

    if (read(STDIN_FILENO, &c, 1) != 1)        /* next input char */
        err_sys("read error from stdin");

    if (c == escapec)           /* two in a row -> process as one */
        return(escapec);

    else if (c == '.') {        /* terminate */
        write(STDOUT_FILENO, "~.\n\r", 4);
        return(-1);

#ifdef  VSUSP
    } else if (c == tty_termios()->c_cc[VSUSP]) { /* suspend client */
        tty_reset(STDIN_FILENO);    /* restore tty mode */
        kill(getpid(), SIGTSTP);    /* suspend ourself */

        tty_raw(STDIN_FILENO);          /* and reset tty to raw */
        return(0);
#endif

    } else if (c == '#') {  /* generate break */
        tcsendbreak(remfd, 0);
        return(0);

    } else if (c == 't') {  /* take a file from remote host */
        take(remfd);
        return(0);

    } else if (c == 'p') {  /* put a file to remote host */
        put(remfd);
        return(0);
    }

    return(c);              /* not a special character */
}
```

Program 18.23 The escape function.

```
#include    "call.h"

#define CTRLA   001     /* eof designator for take */

static int      rem_read(int);
static char     rem_buf[MAXLINE];
static char     *rem_ptr;
static int      rem_cnt = 0;

/* Copy a file from remote to local. */

void
take(int remfd)
{
    int     n, linecnt;
    char    c, cmd[MAXLINE];
    FILE    *fpout;

    if (prompt_read("~[take] ", take_put_args) < 0) {
        printf("usage: [take] <sourcefile> <destfile>\n\r");
        return;
    }

            /* open local output file */
    if ( (fpout = fopen(dst, "w")) == NULL) {
        err_ret("can't open %s for writing", dst);
        putc('\r', stderr);
        fflush(stderr);
        return;
    }

            /* send cat/echo command to remote host */
    sprintf(cmd, "cat %s; echo %c\r", src, CTRLA);
    n = strlen(cmd);
    if (write(remfd, cmd, n) != n)
        err_sys("write error");

            /* read echo of cat/echo command line from remote host */
    rem_cnt = 0;        /* initialize rem_read() */
    for ( ; ; ) {
        if ( (c = rem_read(remfd)) == 0)
            return;     /* line has dropped */
        if (c == '\n')
            break;      /* end of echo line */
    }

            /* read file from remote host */
    linecnt = 0;
    for ( ; ; ) {
        if ( (c = rem_read(remfd)) == 0)
            break;          /* line has dropped */
        if (c == CTRLA)
            break;          /* all done */
```

```
            if (c == '\r')
                continue;           /* ignore returns */
            if (c == '\n')          /* but newlines are written to file */
                printf("\r%d", ++linecnt);
            if (putc(c, fpout) == EOF)
                break;              /* output error */
        }
        if (ferror(fpout) || fclose(fpout) == EOF) {
            err_msg("output error to local file");
            putc('\r', stderr);
            fflush(stderr);
        }
        c = '\n';
        write(remfd, &c, 1);
    }

/* Read from remote.  Read up to MAXLINE, but parcel out one
 * character at a time. */

int
rem_read(int remfd)
{
    if (rem_cnt <= 0) {
        if ( (rem_cnt = read(remfd, rem_buf, MAXLINE)) < 0)
            err_sys("read error");
        else if (rem_cnt == 0)
            return(0);
        rem_ptr = rem_buf;
    }
    rem_cnt--;
    return(*rem_ptr++ & 0177);
}
```

Program 18.24 Processing the take command.

After the `take` function opens the local file for writing it sends the following command to the remote host:

cat *sourcefile* ; echo ^A

This causes the remote host to execute the `cat` command, followed by an echo of the ASCII Control-A character. We look for this Control-A in all the characters that are returned by the remote host, and when we encounter it, we know the file transfer is complete. Note that we also have to read back the echo of the command line that we send to the remote host. Only after that echo do we start receiving the output of the `cat` command.

While we're reading the remote file we look for newline characters and count the lines returned. We display these at the left margin, overwriting each line number with the next (since we terminate the line in the `printf` with a carriage return only and not a newline). This provides a visual display on the terminal of the progress of the file transfer and a final line count at the end.

This source file also contains the function rem_read, which is called to read each character from the remote host. We read up to one buffer at a time, but return only one character at a time to the caller.

Originally the take command was written to read one character at a time, similar to what cu and tip have historically done. Ten years ago, when 1200 baud modems were considered fast, this was OK. But with today's much faster modems, delivering characters to the terminal device driver at 9600 baud and above, characters get lost, even on the faster CPUs found today. The author encountered this with both cu and tip, using a Telebit T2500 modem in PEP mode, even when both the local host and remote host use flow control. When transferring a large text file (about 75,000 bytes) about half the time characters were lost, requiring the transfer to be done again.

The solution was just to code the rem_read function to read up to a buffer at a time. Doing this reduced the system CPU time by a factor of three (from 16 seconds to 5 seconds, to transfer the 75,000 byte file) and provided a reliable transfer every time. A counter was temporarily added to the rem_read function, to see how many bytes were returned by each call to read. Figure 18.10 shows the results.

#bytes	Count	#bytes	Count	#bytes	Count	#bytes	Count
1	1	28	2	39	1	55	1
13	1	29	1	40	1	56	9
16	1	32	1	46	1	57	751
17	1	33	1	48	2	58	530
22	1	34	1	51	2	59	2
24	1	35	1	52	2	114	1
25	4	37	1	53	1	115	1
26	3	38	1	54	1	194	1

Figure 18.10 Number of bytes returned by read during file transfer.

Only once was a single byte returned; 99% of the time either 57 or 58 bytes were returned by read. Making this small change reduced the number of reads from more than 75,000 to 1,329.

Note that the number of bytes returned by read in Figure 18.10 occurred even though the line discipline module for the modem had its MIN set to 1 and TIME set to 0 by the tty_open function (Program 18.14). This is case B from Section 11.11. This reiterates the fact that MIN is only a minimum. If we ask for more than the minimum, and the bytes are ready to be read, they're returned. We are not restricted to character-at-a-time input when we set MIN to 1.

Program 18.25 shows the two ancillary functions take_put_args and prompt_read. The latter is called from both the take and put functions, with the former as an argument (that is then called by the buf_args function, Program 15.17).

```
#include    "call.h"

/* Process the argv-style arguments for take or put commands. */

int
take_put_args(int argc, char **argv)
```

```
    {
        if (argc == 1) {
            src = dst = argv[0];
            return(0);
        } else if (argc == 2) {
            src = argv[0];
            dst = argv[1];
            return(0);
        }
        return(-1);
    }

    static char cmdargs[MAXLINE];
                /* can't be automatic; src/dst point into here */

    /* Read a line from the user.  Call our buf_args() function to
     * break it into an argv-style array, and call userfunc() to
     * process the arguments. */

    int
    prompt_read(char *prompt, int (*userfunc)(int, char **))
    {
        int     n;
        char    c, *ptr;

        tty_reset(STDIN_FILENO);     /* allow user's editing chars */

        n = strlen(prompt);
        if (write(STDOUT_FILENO, prompt, n) != n)
            err_sys("write error");

        ptr = cmdargs;
        for ( ; ; ) {
            if ( (n = read(STDIN_FILENO, &c, 1)) < 0)
                err_sys("read error");
            else if (n == 0)
                break;
            if (c == '\n')
                break;
            if (ptr < &cmdargs[MAXLINE-2])
                *ptr++ = c;
        }
        *ptr = 0;          /* null terminate */

        tty_raw(STDIN_FILENO);        /* reset tty mode to raw */

        return( buf_args(cmdargs, userfunc) );
                    /* return whatever userfunc() returns */
    }
```

Program 18.25 The take_put_args and prompt_read functions.

The function `prompt_read` reads a line of input from the terminal, and then calls `buf_args` to split the line into a standard argument list that is processed by `take_put_args`. Note that the terminal is reset to canonical mode to read the arguments, allowing the use of the standard editing characters while entering the line.

The final client function is put, shown in Program 18.26. It is called to copy a local file to the remote host.

```c
#include     "call.h"

/* Copy a file from local to remote. */

void
put(int remfd)
{
    int      i, n, linecnt;
    char     c, cmd[MAXLINE];
    FILE     *fpin;

    if (prompt_read("~[put] ", take_put_args) < 0) {  .
        printf("usage: [put] <sourcefile> <destfile>\n\r");
        return;
    }

            /* open local input file */
    if ( (fpin = fopen(src, "r")) == NULL) {
        err_ret("can't open %s for reading", src);
        putc('\r', stderr);
        fflush(stderr);
        return;
    }

            /* send stty/cat/stty command to remote host */
    sprintf(cmd, "stty -echo; cat >%s; stty echo\r", dst);
    n = strlen(cmd);
    if (write(remfd, cmd, n) != n)
        err_sys("write error");
    tcdrain(remfd);       /* wait for our output to be sent */
    sleep(4);             /* and let stty take effect */

            /* send file to remote host */
    linecnt = 0;
    for ( ; ; ) {
        if ( (i = getc(fpin)) == EOF)
            break;          /* all done */
        c = i;
        if (write(remfd, &c, 1) != 1)
            break;          /* line has probably dropped */
        if (c == '\n')      /* increment and display line counter */
            printf("\r%d", ++linecnt);
    }
```

```
                    /* send EOF to remote, to terminate cat */
    c = tty_termios()->c_cc[VEOF];
    write(remfd, &c, 1);
    tcdrain(remfd);                    /* wait for our output to be sent */
    sleep(2);
    tcflush(remfd, TCIOFLUSH);    /* flush echo of stty/cat/stty */
    c = '\n';
    write(remfd, &c, 1);

    if (ferror(fpin)) {
        err_msg("read error of local file");
        putc('\r', stderr);
        fflush(stderr);
    }
    fclose(fpin);
}
```

Program 18.26 The put function.

As with the take command, we send a command string to the remote system. This time the command is

stty —echo; cat > *destfile* ; stty echo

We have to turn echo off, otherwise the entire file would also be sent back to us. To terminate the cat command we send the end-of-file character (often Control-D). This requires that the same end-of-file character be used on both the local system and the remote system. Additionally, the file cannot contain the ERASE or KILL characters in use on the remote system.

18.9 Summary

In this chapter we've looked at two different programs: a daemon server that dials a modem and a remote login program that uses the server to contact a remote system that's connected through a terminal port. The server can be used by other programs that need to contact remote systems or hardware devices connected through asynchronous terminal ports.

The design of the server was similar to the open server in Section 15.6 and required the use of stream pipes, unique per-client connections to the server, and the passing of file descriptors. These advanced IPC features allow us to build client–server applications with many desirable features, as described in Section 18.3.

The client is similar to the cu and tip programs provided by many Unix systems, but in our example we didn't have to worry about dialing a modem, interfering with UUCP lock files, setting the characteristics of the modem's line discipline module, and the like. The server handles all these details. It let us concentrate on the real issues of the client, such as providing a reliable file transfer mechanism.

Exercises

18.1 How can we avoid step 0 (starting the server by hand) in Section 18.3?

18.2 What happens if we don't set optind to 1 in Program 18.4?

18.3 What happens if someone edits the Systems file between the time request (Program 18.10) forks a child and the time the child terminates with a status of 1?

18.4 In Section 7.8 we said to be careful any time we use pointers into a region that gets realloced, since the region can move around in memory on each call to realloc. Why can we use the pointer cliptr in Program 18.3 when the client array is manipulated by realloc?

18.5 What happens if either of the pathname arguments to the take and put commands contain a semicolon?

18.6 Modify the server to read its three data files once when it starts, storing them in memory. If the files are modified, how should the server handle this?

18.7 In Program 18.21 why do we cast the argument args when filling in the structure for writev?

18.8 Implement Program 18.22 using select instead of poll.

18.9 How can you verify that the file being sent with the put command does not contain characters that will be interpreted by the line discipline on the remote system?

18.10 The faster the dialing function recognizes that a dial has failed, the faster it can proceed to the next possible entry in the Systems file. For example, if we can determine that the remote phone is busy and terminate before the timer in expect_str expires, we can save 15 or 20 seconds. To handle these types of errors, the 4.3BSD UUCP expect–send strings allow an expect string of ABORT, followed by a string that if matched, aborts the current dial. For example, right before the final expect string CONNECT\sFAST in Figure 18.4 we would like to add

```
ABORT BUSY
```

Implement this feature.

19

Pseudo Terminals

19.1   Introduction

In Chapter 9 we saw that terminal logins come in through a terminal device, automatically providing terminal semantics. There is a terminal line discipline (Figure 11.2) between the terminal and the programs that we run, so we can set the terminal's special characters (backspace, line erase, interrupt, etc.) and the like. When a login arrives on a network connection, however, a terminal line discipline is not automatically provided between the incoming network connection and the login shell. Figure 9.5 showed that a *pseudo-terminal* device driver is used to provide terminal semantics.

In addition to network logins, pseudo terminals have other uses that we explore in this chapter. We start by providing functions to create pseudo terminals under SVR4 and 4.3+BSD and then use these functions to write a program that we call pty. We'll show various uses of this program: making a transcript of all the character input and output on the terminal (the BSD script program) and running coprocesses to avoid the buffering problems we encountered in Program 14.10.

19.2   Overview

The term *pseudo terminal* implies that it looks like a terminal to an application program, but it's not a real terminal. Figure 19.1 shows the typical arrangement of the processes involved when a pseudo terminal is being used. The key points in this figure are the following.

1. Normally a process opens the pseudo-terminal master and then calls fork. The child establishes a new session, opens the corresponding pseudo-terminal slave, duplicates it to be standard input, standard output, and standard error, and then

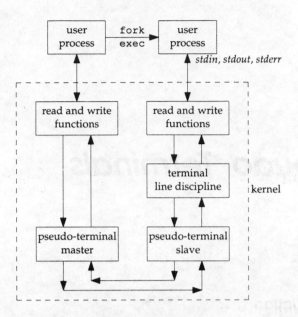

Figure 19.1 Typical arrangement of processes using a pseudo terminal.

calls `exec`. The pseudo-terminal slave becomes the controlling terminal for the child process.

2. It appears to the user process above the slave that its standard input, standard output, and standard error are a terminal device. It can issue all the terminal I/O functions from Chapter 11 on these descriptors. But since there is not an actual terminal device beneath the slave, functions that don't make sense (change the baud rate, send a break character, set odd parity, etc.) are just ignored.

3. Anything written to the master appears as input to the slave and vice versa. Indeed all the input to the slave comes from the user process above the pseudo-terminal master. This looks like a stream pipe (Figure 15.3) but with the terminal line discipline module above the slave we have additional capabilities over a plain pipe.

Figure 19.1 shows what a pseudo terminal looks like on a BSD system. In Section 19.3.2 we show how to open these devices.

Under SVR4 a pseudo terminal is built using the streams system (Section 12.4). Figure 19.2 details the arrangement of the pseudo-terminal streams modules under SVR4. The two streams modules that are shown as dashed boxes are optional. Note that the three streams modules above the slave are the same as the output from Program 12.10 for a network login. In Section 19.3.1 we show how to build this arrangement of streams modules.

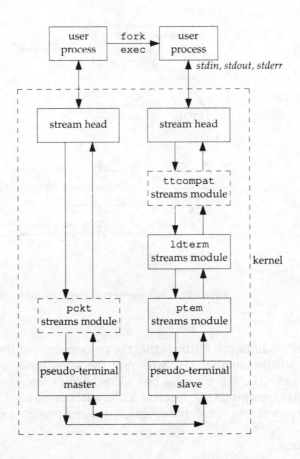

Figure 19.2 Arrangement of pseudo terminals under SVR4.

From this point on we'll simplify the figures by not showing the "read and write functions" from Figure 19.1 or the "stream head" from Figure 19.2. We'll also use the abbreviation "pty" for pseudo terminal and lump all the streams modules above the slave pty in Figure 19.2 into a box called "terminal line discipline" as in Figure 19.1.

We'll now examine some of the typical uses of pseudo terminals.

Network Login Servers

Pseudo terminals are built into servers that provide network logins. The typical examples are the `telnetd` and `rlogind` servers. Chapter 15 of Stevens [1990] details the steps involved in the `rlogin` service. Once the login shell is running on the remote host we have the arrangement shown in Figure 19.3. A similar arrangement is used by the `telnetd` server.

We show two calls to `exec` between the `rlogind` server and the login shell, because the `login` program is usually between the two to validate the user.

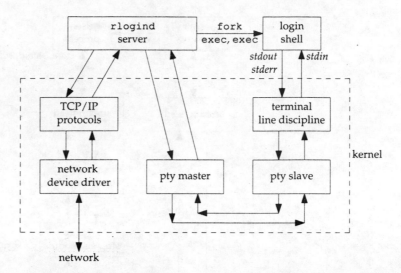

Figure 19.3 Arrangement of processes for `rlogind` server.

A key point in this figure is that the process driving the pty master is normally reading and writing another I/O stream at the same time. In this example the other I/O
stream is the TCP/IP protocol box. This implies that the process must be using some
form of I/O multiplexing (Section 12.5), such as `select` or `poll` or must be divided
into two processes. Recall the discussion of one process versus two in Section 18.7.

`script` Program

The `script`(1) program that is supplied with SVR4 and 4.3+BSD makes a copy in a file
of everything that is input and output during a terminal session. It does this by placing
itself between the terminal and a new invocation of our login shell. Figure 19.4 details
the interactions involved in the `script` program. Here we specifically show that the
`script` program is normally run from a login shell, which then waits for `script` to
terminate.

While `script` is running, everything output by the terminal line discipline above
the pty slave is copied to the script file (usually called `typescript`). Since our
keystrokes are normally echoed by that line discipline module, the script file also contains our input. The script file won't contain any passwords that we enter, however,
since passwords aren't echoed.

> All the examples in this text that consist of running a program and displaying its output were
> generated with the `script` program. This avoids typographical errors that could occur when
> copying program output by hand.

After developing the general `pty` program in Section 19.5 we'll see that a trivial
shell script turns it into a version of the `script` program.

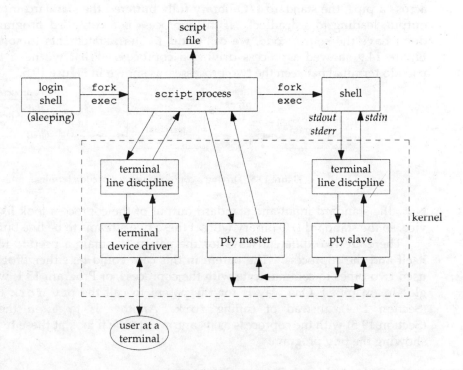

Figure 19.4 The script program.

expect **Program**

Pseudo terminals can be used to drive interactive programs in noninteractive modes. Numerous programs are hardwired to require a terminal to run. The call process in Section 18.7 is an example. It assumes that standard input is a terminal and sets it to raw mode when it starts up (Program 18.20). This program cannot be run from a shell script to automatically dial a remote system, log in, fetch some information, and log out.

Rather than modify all the interactive programs to support a batch mode of operation, a better solution is to provide a way to drive any interactive program from a script. The expect program [Libes 1990; 1991] provides a way to do this. It uses pseudo terminals to run other programs, similar to the pty program in Section 19.5. But expect also provides a programming language to examine the output of the program being run to make decisions about what to send the program as input. When an interactive program is being run from a script, we can't just copy everything from the script to the program and vice versa. Instead we have to send the program some input, look at its output, and decide what to send it next.

Running Coprocesses

In the coprocess example in Program 14.10 we couldn't invoke a coprocess that used the standard I/O library for its input and output, because when we talked to the coprocess across a pipe, the standard I/O library fully buffered the standard input and standard output, leading to a deadlock. If the coprocess is a compiled program for which we don't have the source code, we can't add `fflush` statements to solve this problem. Figure 14.9 showed a process driving a coprocess. What we need to do is place a pseudo terminal between the two processes, as shown in Figure 19.5.

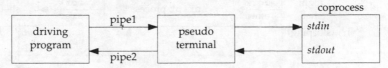

Figure 19.5 Driving a coprocess using a pseudo terminal.

Now the standard input and standard output of the coprocess look like a terminal device, so the standard I/O library will set these two streams to be line buffered.

There are two different ways for the parent to obtain a pseudo terminal between itself and the coprocess. (The parent in this case could be either Program 14.9, which used two pipes to communicate with the coprocess, or Program 15.1, which used a single stream pipe.) One way is for the parent to call the `pty_fork` function directly (Section 19.4), instead of calling `fork`. Another is to `exec` the `pty` program (Section 19.5) with the coprocess as its argument. We'll look at these two solutions after showing the `pty` program.

Watching the Output of Long Running Programs

If we have a program that runs for a long time we can easily run it in the background using any of the standard shells. But if we redirect its standard output to a file, and if it doesn't generate much output, we can't easily monitor its progress because the standard I/O library will fully buffer its standard output. All that we'll see are blocks of output written by the standard I/O library to the output file, possibly in chunks as large as 8192 bytes.

If we have the source code we can insert calls to `fflush`. Alternatively, we can run the program under the `pty` program, making its standard I/O library think that its standard output is a terminal. Figure 19.6 shows this arrangement, where we have called the slow output program `slowout`. The `fork/exec` arrow from the login shell to the `pty` process is shown as a dashed arrow to reiterate that the `pty` process is running as a background job.

19.3 Opening Pseudo-Terminal Devices

Opening a pseudo-terminal device differs between SVR4 and 4.3+BSD. We provide two functions that handle all the details: `ptym_open` to open the next available pty master device and `ptys_open` to open the corresponding slave device.

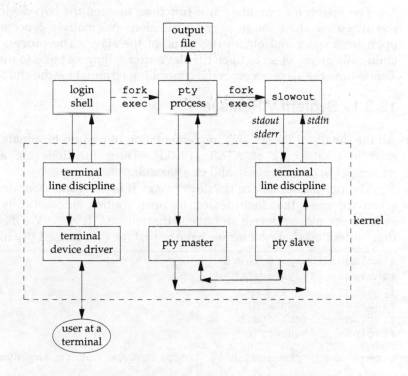

Figure 19.6 Running a slow output program using a pseudo terminal.

```
#include "ourhdr.h"

int ptym_open(char *pts_name);
```
Returns: file descriptor of pty master if OK, −1 on error

```
int ptys_open(int fdm, char *pts_name);
```
Returns: file descriptor of pty slave if OK, −1 on error

Normally we don't call these two functions directly—the function `pty_fork` (Section 19.4) calls them and also `fork`s a child process.

`ptym_open` determines the next available pty master and `open`s the device. The caller must allocate an array to hold the name of either the master or slave, and if the call succeeds the name of the corresponding slave is returned through *pts_name*. This name and the file descriptor returned by `ptym_open` are then passed to `ptys_open`, which `open`s the slave device.

The reason for providing two functions to open the two devices will become obvious when we show the `pty_fork` function. Normally a process calls `ptym_open` to open the master and obtain the name of the slave. The process then `forks` and the child calls `ptys_open` to open the slave after calling `setsid` to establish a new session. This is how the slave becomes the controlling terminal for the child.

19.3.1 System V Release 4

All the details of the streams implementation of pseudo terminals under SVR4 are covered in Chapter 12 of AT&T [1990d]. Three functions are also described there: `grantpt(3)`, `unlockpt(3)`, and `ptsname(3)`.

The pty master device is `/dev/ptmx`. It is a streams *clone device*. This means that when we open the clone device, its open routine automatically determines the first unused pty master device and opens that unused device. (We'll see in the next section that under Berkeley systems we have to find the first unused pty master ourselves.)

```
#include     <sys/types.h>
#include     <sys/stat.h>
#include     <errno.h>
#include     <fcntl.h>
#include     <stropts.h>
#include     "ourhdr.h"

extern char *ptsname(int);  /* prototype not in any system header */

int
ptym_open(char *pts_name)
{
    char      *ptr;
    int       fdm;

    strcpy(pts_name, "/dev/ptmx");  /* in case open fails */
    if ( (fdm = open(pts_name, O_RDWR)) < 0)
        return(-1);

    if (grantpt(fdm) < 0) {      /* grant access to slave */
        close(fdm);
        return(-2);
    }
    if (unlockpt(fdm) < 0) {     /* clear slave's lock flag */
        close(fdm);
        return(-3);
    }
    if ( (ptr = ptsname(fdm)) == NULL) {    /* get slave's name */
        close(fdm);
        return(-4);
    }

    strcpy(pts_name, ptr);  /* return name of slave */
    return(fdm);            /* return fd of master */
}
```

```
int
ptys_open(int fdm, char *pts_name)
{
    int       fds;

            /* following should allocate controlling terminal */
    if ( (fds = open(pts_name, O_RDWR)) < 0) {
        close(fdm);
        return(-5);
    }
    if (ioctl(fds, I_PUSH, "ptem") < 0) {
        close(fdm);
        close(fds);
        return(-6);
    }
    if (ioctl(fds, I_PUSH, "ldterm") < 0) {
        close(fdm);
        close(fds);
        return(-7);
    }
    if (ioctl(fds, I_PUSH, "ttcompat") < 0) {
        close(fdm);
        close(fds);
        return(-8);
    }

    return(fds);
}
```

Program 19.1 Pseudo-terminal open functions for SVR4.

We first open the clone device /dev/ptmx and obtain the file descriptor for the pty master. Opening this master device automatically locks out the corresponding slave device.

We then call grantpt to change permissions of the slave device. It does the following: (a) changes the ownership of the slave to the effective user ID, (b) changes the group ownership to the group tty, and (c) changes the permissions to allow only user-read, user-write, and group-write. The reason for setting the group ownership to tty and enabling group-write permission is that the programs wall(1) and write(1) are set-group-ID to the group tty. Calling the grantpt function executes the program /usr/lib/pt_chmod. This program is set-user-ID to root so that it can modify the ownership and permissions of the slave.

The function unlockpt is called to clear an internal lock on the slave device. We have to do this before we can open the slave. Additionally we must call ptsname to obtain the name of the slave device. This name is of the form /dev/pts/NNN.

The next function in the file is ptys_open, which does the actual open of the slave device. Under SVR4, if the caller is a session leader that does not already have a controlling terminal, this open allocates the pty slave as the controlling terminal. If we didn't want this to happen, we could specify the O_NOCTTY flag for open.

After opening the slave device we push three streams modules onto the slave's stream. ptem stands for "pseudo-terminal emulation module" and ldterm is the terminal line discipline module. Together these two modules act like a real terminal. ttcompat provides compatibility for older V7, 4BSD, and Xenix ioctl calls. It's an optional module but since it's automatically pushed for console logins and network logins (see the output from Program 12.10), we push it onto the slave's stream.

The result of calling these two functions is a file descriptor for the master and a file descriptor for the slave.

19.3.2   4.3+BSD

Under 4.3+BSD we have to determine the first available pty master device ourself. To do this we start at /dev/ptyp0 and keep trying until we successfully open a pty master or until we run out of devices. We can get two different errors from open: EIO means that the device is already in use, while ENOENT means that the device doesn't exist. In the latter case we can terminate the search as all pseudo terminals are in use. Once we are able to open a pty master, say /dev/ptyMN, the name of the corresponding slave is /dev/ttyMN.

The function ptys_open in Program 19.2 opens the slave device. We call chown and chmod but realize that these two functions won't work unless the calling process has superuser permissions. If it is important that the ownership and protection be changed, these two function calls need to be placed into a set-user-ID root executable, similar to the SVR4 grantpt function.

The open of the slave pty under 4.3+BSD does not have the side effect of allocating the device as the controlling terminal. We'll see in the next section how to allocate the controlling terminal under 4.3+BSD.

This function tries 16 different groups of 16 pty master devices: /dev/ptyp0 through /dev/ptyTf. The actual number of pty devices available depends on two factors: (a) the number configured into the kernel, and (b) the number of special device files that have been created in the /dev directory. The number available to any program is the lesser of (a) or (b). Also, even if the lesser of (a) or (b) is greater than 64, many existing BSD applications (telnetd, rlogind, etc.) search in the first for loop in Program 19.2 only through "pqrs".

```
#include      <sys/types.h>
#include      <sys/stat.h>
#include      <errno.h>
#include      <fcntl.h>
#include      <grp.h>
#include      "ourhdr.h"

int
ptym_open(char *pts_name)
{
    int      fdm;
    char     *ptr1, *ptr2;

    strcpy(pts_name, "/dev/ptyXY");
      /* array index: 0123456789 (for references in following code) *
```

```
                 for (ptr1 = "pqrstuvwxyzPQRST"; *ptr1 != 0; ptr1++) {
                     pts_name[8] = *ptr1;
                     for (ptr2 = "0123456789abcdef"; *ptr2 != 0; ptr2++) {
                         pts_name[9] = *ptr2;

                                    /* try to open master */
                         if ( (fdm = open(pts_name, O_RDWR)) < 0) {
                             if (errno == ENOENT)    /* different from EIO */
                                 return(-1);         /* out of pty devices */
                             else
                                 continue;           /* try next pty device */
                         }

                         pts_name[5] = 't';  /* change "pty" to "tty" */
                         return(fdm);              /* got it, return fd of master */
                     }
                 }
                 return(-1);       /* out of pty devices */
             }

             int
             ptys_open(int fdm, char *pts_name)
             {
                 struct group    *grptr;
                 int             gid, fds;

                 if ( (grptr = getgrnam("tty")) != NULL)
                     gid = grptr->gr_gid;
                 else
                     gid = -1;         /* group tty is not in the group file */

                         /* following two functions don't work unless we're root */
                 chown(pts_name, getuid(), gid);
                 chmod(pts_name, S_IRUSR | S_IWUSR | S_IWGRP);

                 if ( (fds = open(pts_name, O_RDWR)) < 0) {
                     close(fdm);
                     return(-1);
                 }
                 return(fds);
             }
```

Program 19.2 Pseudo-terminal open functions for 4.3+BSD.

19.4   pty_fork **Function**

We now use the two functions from the previous section, ptym_open and ptys_open,
to write a new function that we call pty_fork. This new function combines the opening of the master and slave with a call to fork, establishing the child as a session leader
with a controlling terminal.

```
#include <sys/types.h>
#include <termios.h>
#include <sys/ioctl.h> /* 4.3+BSD defines struct winsize here */
#include "ourhdr.h"

pid_t pty_fork(int *ptrfdm, char *slave_name,
               const struct termios *slave_termios,
               const struct winsize *slave_winsize);
```

Returns: 0 in child, process ID of child in parent, −1 on error

The file descriptor of the pty master is returned through the *ptrfdm* pointer.

If *slave_name* is nonnull, the name of the slave device is stored at that location. The caller has to allocate the storage pointed to by this argument.

If the pointer *slave_termios* is nonnull, the referenced structure initializes the terminal line discipline of the slave. If this pointer is null, the system initializes the slave's `termios` structure to an implementation-defined initial state. Similarly, if the *slave_winsize* pointer is nonnull, the referenced structure initializes the slave's window size. If this pointer is null, the `winsize` structure is normally initialized to 0.

Program 19.3 shows the code for this function. This function works under both SVR4 and 4.3+BSD, calling the appropriate `ptym_open` and `ptys_open` functions.

After opening the pty master, `fork` is called. As we mentioned before, we want to wait to call `ptys_open` until in the child, and after calling `setsid` to establish a new session. When it calls `setsid` the child is not a process group leader (why?) so the three steps listed in Section 9.5 occur: (a) a new session is created with the child as the session leader, (b) a new process group is created for the child, and (c) the child has no controlling terminal. Under SVR4 the slave becomes the controlling terminal of this new session when `ptys_open` is called. Under 4.3+BSD we have to call `ioctl` with an argument of `TIOCSCTTY` to allocate the controlling terminal. The two structures `termios` and `winsize` are then initialized in the child. Finally the slave file descriptor is duplicated onto standard input, standard output, and standard error in the child. This means that whatever process the caller `execs` from the child will have these three descriptors connected to the slave pty (its controlling terminal).

After the call to `fork` the parent just returns the pty master descriptor and returns. In the next section we use the `pty_fork` function in the `pty` program.

```
#include     <sys/types.h>
#include     <termios.h>
#ifndef TIOCGWINSZ
#include     <sys/ioctl.h>    /* 4.3+BSD requires this too */
#endif
#include     "ourhdr.h"

pid_t
pty_fork(int *ptrfdm, char *slave_name,
        const struct termios *slave_termios,
        const struct winsize *slave_winsize)
{
```

```
            int     fdm, fds;
            pid_t   pid;
            char    pts_name[20];

            if ( (fdm = ptym_open(pts_name)) < 0)
                err_sys("can't open master pty: %s", pts_name);

            if (slave_name != NULL)
                strcpy(slave_name, pts_name);    /* return name of slave */

            if ( (pid = fork()) < 0)
                return(-1);

            else if (pid == 0) {              /* child */
                if (setsid() < 0)
                    err_sys("setsid error");

                        /* SVR4 acquires controlling terminal on open() */
                if ( (fds = ptys_open(fdm, pts_name)) < 0)
                    err_sys("can't open slave pty");
                close(fdm);     /* all done with master in child */
#if defined(TIOCSCTTY) && !defined(CIBAUD)
                        /* 4.3+BSD way to acquire controlling terminal */
                        /* !CIBAUD to avoid doing this under SunOS */
                if (ioctl(fds, TIOCSCTTY, (char *) 0) < 0)
                    err_sys("TIOCSCTTY error");
#endif
                        /* set slave's termios and window size */
                if (slave_termios != NULL) {
                    if (tcsetattr(fds, TCSANOW, slave_termios) < 0)
                        err_sys("tcsetattr error on slave pty");
                }
                if (slave_winsize != NULL) {
                    if (ioctl(fds, TIOCSWINSZ, slave_winsize) < 0)
                        err_sys("TIOCSWINSZ error on slave pty");
                }
                        /* slave becomes stdin/stdout/stderr of child */
                if (dup2(fds, STDIN_FILENO) != STDIN_FILENO)
                    err_sys("dup2 error to stdin");
                if (dup2(fds, STDOUT_FILENO) != STDOUT_FILENO)
                    err_sys("dup2 error to stdout");
                if (dup2(fds, STDERR_FILENO) != STDERR_FILENO)
                    err_sys("dup2 error to stderr");
                if (fds > STDERR_FILENO)
                    close(fds);
                return(0);      /* child returns 0 just like fork() */

            } else {                          /* parent */
                *ptrfdm = fdm;  /* return fd of master */
                return(pid);    /* parent returns pid of child */
            }
        }
```

Program 19.3 The pty_fork function.

19.5 `pty` Program

The goal in writing the `pty` program is to be able to type

```
pty prog arg1 arg2
```

instead of

```
prog arg1 arg2
```

When we use `pty` to execute another program, that program is executed in a session of its own, connected to a pseudo terminal.

Let's look at the source code for the `pty` program. The first file (Program 19.4) contains the `main` function. It calls the `pty_fork` function from the previous section.

```c
#include     <sys/types.h>
#include     <termios.h>
#ifndef TIOCGWINSZ
#include     <sys/ioctl.h>    /* 4.3+BSD requires this too */
#endif
#include     "ourhdr.h"

static void set_noecho(int);    /* at the end of this file */
void        do_driver(char *);  /* in the file driver.c */
void        loop(int, int);     /* in the file loop.c */

int
main(int argc, char *argv[])
{
    int            fdm, c, ignoreeof, interactive, noecho, verbose;
    pid_t          pid;
    char           *driver, slave_name[20];
    struct termios orig_termios;
    struct winsize size;

    interactive = isatty(STDIN_FILENO);
    ignoreeof = 0;
    noecho = 0;
    verbose = 0;
    driver = NULL;

    opterr = 0;      /* don't want getopt() writing to stderr */
    while ( (c = getopt(argc, argv, "d:einv")) != EOF) {
        switch (c) {
        case 'd':        /* driver for stdin/stdout */
            driver = optarg;
            break;

        case 'e':        /* noecho for slave pty's line discipline */
            noecho = 1;
            break;

        case 'i':        /* ignore EOF on standard input */
            ignoreeof = 1;
            break;
```

```
            case 'n':         /* not interactive */
                interactive = 0;
                break;

            case 'v':         /* verbose */
                verbose = 1;
                break;

            case '?':
                err_quit("unrecognized option: -%c", optopt);
            }
        }
        if (optind >= argc)
            err_quit("usage: pty [ -d driver -einv ] program [ arg ... ]");

        if (interactive) {   /* fetch current termios and window size */
            if (tcgetattr(STDIN_FILENO, &orig_termios) < 0)
                err_sys("tcgetattr error on stdin");
            if (ioctl(STDIN_FILENO, TIOCGWINSZ, (char *) &size) < 0)
                err_sys("TIOCGWINSZ error");
            pid = pty_fork(&fdm, slave_name, &orig_termios, &size);

        } else
            pid = pty_fork(&fdm, slave_name, NULL, NULL);

        if (pid < 0)
            err_sys("fork error");

        else if (pid == 0) {            /* child */
            if (noecho)
                set_noecho(STDIN_FILENO);   /* stdin is slave pty */

            if (execvp(argv[optind], &argv[optind]) < 0)
                err_sys("can't execute: %s", argv[optind]);
        }

        if (verbose) {
            fprintf(stderr, "slave name = %s\n", slave_name);
            if (driver != NULL)
                fprintf(stderr, "driver = %s\n", driver);
        }

        if (interactive && driver == NULL) {
            if (tty_raw(STDIN_FILENO) < 0)  /* user's tty to raw mode */
                err_sys("tty_raw error");
            if (atexit(tty_atexit) < 0)     /* reset user's tty on exit */
                err_sys("atexit error");
        }

        if (driver)
            do_driver(driver);  /* changes our stdin/stdout */

        loop(fdm, ignoreeof);   /* copies stdin -> ptym, ptym -> stdout */

        exit(0);
    }
```

```
static void
set_noecho(int fd)            /* turn off echo (for slave pty) */
{
    struct termios  stermios;

    if (tcgetattr(fd, &stermios) < 0)
        err_sys("tcgetattr error");

    stermios.c_lflag &= ~(ECHO | ECHOE | ECHOK | ECHONL);
    stermios.c_oflag &= ~(ONLCR);
            /* also turn off NL to CR/NL mapping on output */

    if (tcsetattr(fd, TCSANOW, &stermios) < 0)
        err_sys("tcsetattr error");
}
```

Program 19.4 The main function for the pty program.

We'll look at the various command-line options when we examine different uses of the pty program in the next section.

Before calling pty_fork we fetch the current values for the termios and winsize structures, passing these as arguments to pty_fork. This way the pty slave assumes the same initial state as the current terminal.

After returning from pty_fork the child optionally turns off echoing for the slave pty and then calls execvp to execute the program specified on the command line. All remaining command-line arguments are passed as arguments to this program.

The parent optionally sets the user's terminal to raw mode setting an exit handler to reset the terminal state when exit is called. We describe the do_driver function in the next section.

The function loop (Program 19.5) is then called by the parent. It just copies everything received from the standard input to the pty master and everything from the pty master to standard output. We have the same decision as we had in Section 18.7—one process or two? For variety we have coded it in two processes this time, although a single process using either select or poll would also work.

```
#include    <sys/types.h>
#include    <signal.h>
#include    "ourhdr.h"

#define BUFFSIZE    512

static void sig_term(int);
static volatile sig_atomic_t    sigcaught;  /* set by signal handler */

void
loop(int ptym, int ignoreeof)
{
    pid_t   child;
    int     nread;
    char    buff[BUFFSIZE];
```

```
        if ( (child = fork()) < 0) {
            err_sys("fork error");

        } else if (child == 0) {     /  child copies stdin to ptym */
            for ( ; ; ) {
                if ( (nread = read(STDIN_FILENO, buff, BUFFSIZE)) < 0)
                    err_sys("read error from stdin");
                else if (nread == 0)
                    break;        /* EOF on stdin means we're done */

                if (writen(ptym, buff, nread) != nread)
                    err_sys("writen error to master pty");
            }

                /* We always terminate when we encounter an EOF on stdin,
                    but we only notify the parent if ignoreeof is 0. */
            if (ignoreeof == 0)
                kill(getppid(), SIGTERM);   /* notify parent */
            exit(0);    /* and terminate; child can't return */
        }

            /* parent copies ptym to stdout */
        if (signal_intr(SIGTERM, sig_term) == SIG_ERR)
            err_sys("signal_intr error for SIGTERM");

        for ( ; ; ) {
            if ( (nread = read(ptym, buff, BUFFSIZE)) <= 0)
                break;        /* signal caught, error, or EOF */

            if (writen(STDOUT_FILENO, buff, nread) != nread)
                err_sys("writen error to stdout");
        }

        /* There are three ways to get here: sig_term() below caught the
         * SIGTERM from the child, we read an EOF on the pty master (which
         * means we have to signal the child to stop), or an error. */

        if (sigcaught == 0) /* tell child if it didn't send us the signal */
            kill(child, SIGTERM);
        return;        /* parent returns to caller */
    }

/* The child sends us a SIGTERM when it receives an EOF on
 * the pty slave or encounters a read() error. */
static void
sig_term(int signo)
{
    sigcaught = 1;        /* just set flag and return */
    return;                /* probably interrupts read() of ptym */
}
```

Program 19.5 The loop function.

Note that, with two processes, when one terminates it has to notify the other. We use the SIGTERM signal for this notification.

19.6 Using the pty Program

We'll now look at various examples with the pty program, seeing the need for the various command-line options.

If our shell is the KornShell we can execute

```
pty ksh
```

and get a brand new invocation of the shell, running under a pseudo terminal.

If the file ttyname is the program we showed in Program 11.7, then we can run the pty program as follows:

```
$ who
stevens   console Feb  6 10:43
stevens   ttyp0   Feb  6 15:00
stevens   ttyp1   Feb  6 15:00
stevens   ttyp2   Feb  6 15:00
stevens   ttyp3   Feb  6 15:48
stevens   ttyp4   Feb  7 14:28       ttyp4 is the highest pty currently in use
$ pty ttyname                        run Program 11.7 from pty
fd 0: /dev/ttyp5                     ttyp5 is the next available pty
fd 1: /dev/ttyp5
fd 2: /dev/ttyp5
```

utmp File

In Section 6.7 we described the utmp file that records all users currently logged into a Unix system. The question is whether a user running a program on a pseudo terminal is considered logged in or not. In the case of remote logins, telnetd and rlogind, obviously an entry should be made in the utmp file for the user logged in on the pseudo terminal. There is little agreement, however, whether users running a shell on a pseudo terminal, from a window system or from a program such as script, should have entries made in the utmp file. Some systems record these and some don't. If a system doesn't record these in the utmp file, the who(1) program normally won't show the corresponding pseudo terminals as being used.

Unless the utmp file has other-write permission enabled, random programs that use pseudo terminals won't be able to write to this file. Some systems, however, deliver the utmp file with all write permissions enabled.

Job-Control Interaction

If we run a job-control shell under pty it works normally. For example,

```
pty ksh
```

runs the KornShell under pty. We can run programs under this new shell and use job control just as our login shell. But if we run an interactive program other than a job-control shell under pty, as in

    pty cat

everything is fine until we type our job-control suspend character. At that point under SVR4 and 4.3+BSD the job-control character is echoed as ^Z and is ignored. Under SunOS 4.1.2 the cat process terminates, the pty process terminates, and we're back to our original shell.

To understand what's going on here we need to examine all the processes involved, their process groups, and sessions. Figure 19.7 shows the arrangement when pty cat is running.

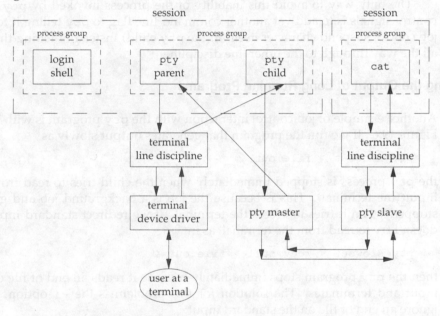

Figure 19.7 Process groups and sessions for pty cat.

When we type the suspend character (Control-Z) it is recognized by the line discipline module beneath the cat process, since pty puts the terminal (beneath the pty parent) into a raw mode. But the kernel won't stop the cat process because it belongs to an orphaned process group (Section 9.10). The parent of cat is the pty parent, and it belongs to another session.

Different systems handle this condition differently. POSIX.1 just says that the SIGTSTP signal can't be delivered to the process. Earlier Berkeley-derived systems deliver SIGKILL instead, which the process can't even catch. This is what we see under SunOS 4.1.2. (The POSIX.1 Rationale suggests SIGHUP as a better alternative, since the process can at least catch it.) Enabling process accounting and looking at the termination status of the cat process with Program 8.17 shows that it is indeed terminated by a SIGKILL signal.

Under SVR4 and 4.3+BSD we use a modification to Program 10.22 to see what's going on. The modification has the signal handler for `SIGTSTP` print when the signal is caught and print again when the `SIGCONT` signal is sent and the process resumes. Doing this shows that `SIGTSTP` is caught by the process but when the process tries to send that signal to itself using `kill` (to really suspend itself), the kernel immediately sends `SIGCONT` to resume the process. The kernel will not let the process be job-control stopped. This handling of the signal by SVR4 and 4.3+BSD is less drastic than sending `SIGKILL`.

When we use `pty` to run a job-control shell, the jobs invoked by this new shell are never members of an orphaned process group because the job-control shell always belongs to the same session. In that case the Control-Z that we type is sent to the process invoked by the shell, not to the shell itself.

The only way to avoid this inability of the process invoked by `pty` to handle job-control signals is to add yet another command-line flag to `pty` telling it to recognize the job control suspend character itself (in the `pty` child) instead of letting the character get all the way through to the other line discipline.

Watching the Output of Long Running Programs

Another example of job-control interaction with the `pty` program is with the example in Figure 19.6. If we run the program that generates output slowly as

```
pty slowout > file.out &
```

the `pty` process is stopped immediately when the child tries to read from its standard input (the terminal). This is because the job is a background job and gets job-control stopped when it tries to access the terminal. If we redirect standard input so that `pty` doesn't try to read from the terminal, as in

```
pty slowout < /dev/null > file.out &
```

then the `pty` program stops immediately because it reads an end of file on its standard input and terminates. The solution for this problem is the `-i` option, which says to ignore an end of file on the standard input:

```
pty -i slowout < /dev/null > file.out &
```

This flag causes the `pty` child in Program 19.5 to terminate when the end of file is encountered, but the child doesn't tell the parent to terminate. Instead the parent continues copying the pty slave output to standard output (the file `file.out` in the example).

`script` Program

Using the `pty` program we can implement the BSD `script(1)` program as the following shell script.

```
#!/bin/sh

pty "${SHELL:-/bin/sh}" | tee typescript
```

Once we run this shell script we can execute the ps command to see all the process relationships. Figure 19.8 details these relationships.

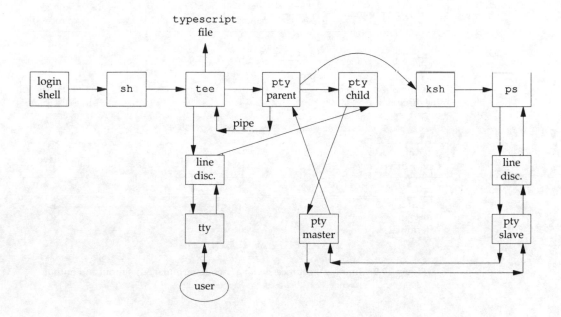

Figure 19.8 Arrangement of process for script shell script.

In this example we assume that the SHELL variable is the KornShell (probably /bin/ksh). As we mentioned earlier, script only copies what is output by the new shell (and any processes that it invokes) but since the line discipline module above the pty slave normally has echo enabled, most of what we type also gets written to the typescript file.

Running Coprocesses

In Program 14.9 we couldn't have the coprocess use the standard I/O functions because they set the standard input and standard output fully buffered, since the two descriptors do not refer to a terminal. If we run the coprocess under pty by replacing the line

```
if (execl("./add2", "add2", (char *) 0) < 0)
```

with

```
if (execl("./pty", "pty", "-e", "add2", (char *) 0) < 0)
```

the program now works, even if the coprocess uses standard I/O.

Figure 19.9 shows the arrangement of processes when we run the coprocess with a pseudo terminal as its input and output. The box labeled "driving program" is Program 14.9 with the execl changed as described previously. This figure is an expansion of Figure 19.5 showing all the process connections and data flow.

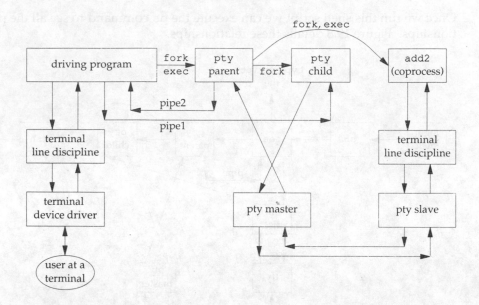

Figure 19.9 Running a coprocess with a pseudo terminal as its input and output.

This example shows the need for the −e (no echo) option for the pty program. pty is not running interactively because its standard input is not connected to a terminal. In Program 19.4 the interactive flag defaults to false since the call to isatty returns false. This means that the line discipline above the actual terminal remains in a canonical mode with echo enabled. By specifying the −e option we turn off echo in the line discipline module above the pty slave. If we don't do this, everything we type is echoed twice—by both line discipline modules.

We also have the −e option turn off the ONLCR flag in the termios structure to prevent all the output from the coprocess from being terminated with a carriage return and a newline.

Testing this example on different systems showed another problem that we alluded to in Section 12.8 when we described the readn and writen functions. The amount of data returned by a read, when the descriptor refers to something other than an ordinary disk file, can differ between implementations. This coprocess example using pty gave unexpected results that were tracked down to the read function on the pipe in Program 14.9 returning less than a line. The solution was to not use Program 14.9 but to use the version of this program from Exercise 14.5 that was modified to use the standard I/O library, with the standard I/O streams for the both pipes set to line buffering. By doing this the fgets function does as many reads as required to obtain a complete line. The while loop in Program 14.9 assumes that each line sent to the coprocess causes one line to be returned.

Driving Interactive Programs Noninteractively

Although it's tempting to think that pty can run any coprocess, even a coprocess that is interactive, it doesn't work. The problem is that pty just copies everything on its standard input to the pty and everything from the pty to its standard output. It never looks at what it sends or what it gets back.

As an example, we can run the call client from Section 18.7 under pty talking directly to the modem.

```
pty call t2500
```

Doing this provides no benefit over just typing call t2500, but we would like to run the call program from a script, perhaps to fetch the contents of the modem's internal registers. If the file t2500.cmd contains the two lines

```
aatn?
```

the first line prints all the modem's registers and the second line terminates the call program. But if we run this script as

```
pty -i < t2500.cmd call t2500
```

the output isn't what we want. What happens is that the contents of the file t2500.cmd are sent to the modem before it has a chance to say that it's ready. When we run the call program interactively we wait for the modem to say Connected, but the pty program doesn't know to do this. This is why it takes a more sophisticated program than pty, such as expect, to drive an interactive program from a script file.

Even running pty from Program 14.9 as we showed earlier doesn't help, because Program 14.9 assumes that each line that it writes to the pipe generates exactly one line on the other pipe. With an interactive program one line of input may generate many lines of output. Furthermore Program 14.9 always sent a line to the coprocess before reading from it. In the case of the preceding modem example, we want to read from the coprocess (the call program) to receive the line Connected before sending it anything.

There are a few ways to proceed from here to be able to drive an interactive program from a script. We could add a command language and interpreter to pty, but a reasonable command language would probably be 10 times larger than the pty program. Another option is to take a command language and use the pty_fork function to invoke interactive programs. This is what the expect program does.

We'll take a different path and just provide an option (-d) to allow pty to be connected to a driver process for its input and output. The standard output of the driver is pty's standard input and vice versa. This is similar to a coprocess, but on "the other side" of pty. The resulting arrangement of processes is almost identical to Figure 19.9 but in the current scenario pty does the fork and exec of the driver process. Also we'll use a single stream pipe between pty and the driver process, instead of two half-duplex pipes.

Program 19.6 shows the source for the do_driver function that is called by the main function of pty (Program 19.4) when the -d option is specified.

```c
#include     <sys/types.h>
#include     <signal.h>
#include     "ourhdr.h"

void
do_driver(char *driver)
{
    pid_t   child;
    int     pipe[2];

        /* create a stream pipe to communicate with the driver */
    if (s_pipe(pipe) < 0)
        err_sys("can't create stream pipe");

    if ( (child = fork()) < 0)
        err_sys("fork error");

    else if (child == 0) {              /* child */
        close(pipe[1]);

                /* stdin for driver */
        if (dup2(pipe[0], STDIN_FILENO) != STDIN_FILENO)
            err_sys("dup2 error to stdin");

                /* stdout for driver */
        if (dup2(pipe[0], STDOUT_FILENO) != STDOUT_FILENO)
            err_sys("dup2 error to stdout");
        close(pipe[0]);

                /* leave stderr for driver alone */

        execlp(driver, driver, (char *) 0);
        err_sys("execlp error for: %s", driver);
    }

    close(pipe[0]);     /* parent */

    if (dup2(pipe[1], STDIN_FILENO) != STDIN_FILENO)
        err_sys("dup2 error to stdin");

    if (dup2(pipe[1], STDOUT_FILENO) != STDOUT_FILENO)
        err_sys("dup2 error to stdout");
    close(pipe[1]);

    /* Parent returns, but with stdin and stdout connected
       to the driver. */
}
```

Program 19.6 The do_driver function for the pty program.

By writing our own driver program that is invoked by pty we can drive interactive programs in any way desired. Even though the driver process has its standard input and standard output connected to pty, it can still interact with the user by reading and writing /dev/tty. This solution still isn't as general as the expect program, but it provides a useful option to pty for less than 50 lines of code.

19.7 Advanced Features

Pseudo terminals have some additional capabilities that we briefly mention here. These are further documented in AT&T [1990d] and the 4.3+BSD pty(4) manual page.

Packet Mode

Packet mode lets the pty master learn of state changes in the pty slave. Under SVR4 this mode is enabled by pushing the streams module pckt onto the pty master side. We showed this optional module in Figure 19.2. Under 4.3+BSD this mode is enabled with an ioctl of TIOCPKT.

The details of packet mode differ between SVR4 and 4.3+BSD. Under SVR4 the process reading the pty master has to call getmsg to fetch the messages from the stream head, because the pckt module converts certain events into non-data streams messages. With 4.3+BSD each read from the pty master returns a status byte followed by optional data.

Regardless of the implementation details, the purpose of packet mode is to inform the process reading the pty master when the following events occur at the line discipline module above the pty slave: when the read queue is flushed, when the write queue is flushed, whenever output is stopped (e.g., Control-S), whenever output is restarted, whenever XON/XOFF flow control is enabled after being disabled, and whenever XON/XOFF flow control is disabled after being enabled. These events are used, for example, by the rlogin client and rlogind server.

Remote Mode

A pty master can set the pty slave into remote mode by issuing an ioctl of TIOCREMOTE. Although both SVR4 and 4.3+BSD use the same command to enable and disable this feature, under SVR4 the third argument to ioctl is an integer while with 4.3+BSD it is a pointer to an integer.

When the pty master sets this mode it is telling the pty slave's line discipline module not to perform any processing of the data that it receives from the pty master, regardless of the canonical/noncanonical flag in the slave's termios structure. Remote mode is intended for an application such as a window manager that does its own line editing.

Window Size Changes

The process above the pty master can issue the ioctl of TIOCSWINSZ to set the window size of the slave. If the new size differs from the current size, a SIGWINCH signal is sent to the foreground process group of the pty slave.

Signal Generation

The process reading and writing the pty master can send signals to the process group of the pty slave. Under SVR4 this is done with an ioctl of TIOCSIGNAL with the third argument being the actual signal number. With 4.3+BSD the ioctl is TIOCSIG and the third argument is a pointer to the integer signal number.

19.8 Summary

We started this chapter by examining the code required to open a pseudo terminal under both SVR4 and 4.3+BSD. We then used this code to provide the generic pty_fork function that can be used by many different applications. We used this function as the basis for a small program (pty), which we then used to explore many of the properties of pseudo terminals.

Pseudo terminals are used daily on most Unix systems to provide network logins. We've examined other uses for pseudo terminals, from the script program to driving interactive programs from a batch script.

Exercises

19.1 When we remotely log in to a BSD system using either telnet or rlogin, the ownership of the pty slave and its permissions are set, as we described in Section 19.3.2. How does this happen?

19.2 Modify the 4.3+BSD function ptys_open to invoke a set-user-ID program to change the ownership and protection of the pty slave device (similar to what the SVR4 grantpt function does).

19.3 Use the pty program to determine the values used by your system to initialize a slave pty's termios structure and winsize structure.

19.4 Recode the loop function (Program 19.5) as a single process using either select or poll.

19.5 In the child process after pty_fork returns, standard input, standard output, and standard error are all open for read–write. Can you change standard input to be read-only and the other two to be write-only?

19.6 In Figure 19.7 identify which process groups are foreground and which are background, and identify the session leaders.

19.7 In Figure 19.7 in what order do the processes terminate when we type our end-of-file character? Verify this with process accounting, if possible.

19.8 The script(1) program normally adds a line to the beginning of the output file with the starting time, and another line at the end of the output file with the ending time. Add these features to the simple shell script that we showed.

19.9 Explain why the contents of the file data are output to the terminal in the following example, when the program ttyname only generates output and never reads its input.

```
$ cat data                    a file with two lines
hello,
world
$ pty -i < data ttyname       -i says ignore eof on stdin
hello,                        where did these two lines come from?
world
fd 0: /dev/ttyp5
fd 1: /dev/ttyp5              we expect these three lines from ttyname
fd 2: /dev/ttyp5
```

19.10 Write a program that calls pty_fork and have the child exec another program that you must write. The new program that the child execs must catch SIGTERM and SIGWINCH. When it catches a signal it should print that it did, and for the latter signal it should also print the terminal's window size. Then have the parent process send the SIGTERM signal to the process group of the pty slave with the ioctl we described in Section 19.7. Read back from the slave to verify that the signal was caught. Follow this with the parent setting the window size of the pty slave and read back the slave's output again. Have the parent exit and determine if the slave process also terminates, and if so, how does it terminate?

Appendix A

Function Prototypes

This appendix contains the function prototypes for the standard Unix, POSIX, and ANSI C functions described in the text. Often we want to see just the arguments to a function ("which argument is the file pointer for `fgets`?") or just the return value ("does `sprintf` return a pointer or a count?).

These prototypes also show which headers need to be included to obtain the definitions of any special constants, and to obtain the ANSI C function prototype to help detect any compile-time errors.

The page number reference with each prototype gives the page containing the actual prototype for the function. That page should be consulted for additional information on the function.

```
void     _exit(int status);
                    <unistd.h>                    p. 162
                    This function never returns

void     abort(void);
                    <stdlib.h>                    p. 309
                    This function never returns

int      access(const char *pathname, int mode);
                    <unistd.h>                    p. 82
                    mode: R_OK, W_OK, X_OK, F_OK
                    Returns: 0 if OK, −1 on error

unsigned
int      alarm(unsigned int seconds);
                    <unistd.h>                    p. 285
                    Returns: 0 or #seconds until previously set alarm
```

```
char    *asctime(const struct tm *tmptr);
                        <time.h>                        p. 157
                        Returns: pointer to null terminated string

int     atexit(void (*func)(void));
                        <stdlib.h>                      p. 163
                        Returns: 0 if OK, nonzero on error

void    *calloc(size_t nobj, size_t size);
                        <stdlib.h>                      p. 170
                        Returns: nonnull pointer if OK, NULL on error

speed_t cfgetispeed(const struct termios *termptr);
                        <termios.h>                     p. 343
                        Returns: baud rate value

speed_t cfgetospeed(const struct termios *termptr);
                        <termios.h>                     p. 343
                        Returns: baud rate value

int     cfsetispeed(struct termios *termptr, speed_t speed);
                        <termios.h>                     p. 343
                        Returns: 0 if OK, −1 on error

int     cfsetospeed(struct termios *termptr, speed_t speed);
                        <termios.h>                     p. 343
                        Returns: 0 if OK, −1 on error

int     chdir(const char *pathname);
                        <unistd.h>                      p. 112
                        Returns: 0 if OK, −1 on error

int     chmod(const char *pathname, mode_t mode);
                        <sys/types.h>                   p. 85
                        <sys/stat.h>
                        mode: S_IS[UG]ID, S_ISVTX, S_I[RWX](USR|GRP|OTH)
                        Returns: 0 if OK, −1 on error

int     chown(const char *pathname, uid_t owner, gid_t group);
                        <sys/types.h>                   p. 89
                        <unistd.h>
                        Returns: 0 if OK, −1 on error

void    clearerr(FILE *fp);
                        <stdio.h>                       p. 129

int     close(int filedes);
                        <unistd.h>                      p. 51
                        Returns: 0 if OK, −1 on error

int     closedir(DIR *dp);
                        <sys/types.h>                   p. 107
                        <dirent.h>
                        Returns: 0 if OK, −1 on error

void    closelog(void);
                        <syslog.h>                      p. 422
```

```
int      creat(const char *pathname, mode_t mode);
                      <sys/types.h>                     p. 50
                      <sys/stat.h>
                      <fcntl.h>
                      mode: S_IS[UG]ID, S_ISVTX, S_I[RWX](USR|GRP|OTH)
                      Returns: file descriptor opened for write-only if OK, –1 on error

char     *ctermid(char *ptr);
                      <stdio.h>                         p. 345
                      Returns: pathname of controlling terminal

char     *ctime(const time_t *calptr);
                      <time.h>                          p. 157
                      Returns: pointer to null terminated string

int      dup(int filedes);
                      <unistd.h>                        p. 61
                      Returns: new file descriptor if OK, –1 on error

int      dup2(int filedes, int filedes2);
                      <unistd.h>                        p. 61
                      Returns: new file descriptor if OK, –1 on error

void     endgrent(void);
                      <sys/types.h>                     p. 150
                      <grp.h>

void     endpwent(void);
                      <sys/types.h>                     p. 147
                      <pwd.h>

int      execl(const char *pathname, const char *arg0, ... /* (char *) 0 */ );
                      <unistd.h>                        p. 207
                      Returns: –1 on error, no return on success

int      execle(const char *pathname, const char *arg0, ... /* (char *) 0,
              char *const envp[] */ );
                      <unistd.h>                        p. 207
                      Returns: –1 on error, no return on success

int      execlp(const char *filename, const char *arg0, ... /* (char *) 0 */ );
                      <unistd.h>                        p. 207
                      Returns: –1 on error, no return on success

int      execv(const char *pathname, char *const argv[]);
                      <unistd.h>                        p. 207
                      Returns: –1 on error, no return on success

int      execve(const char *pathname, char *const argv[], char *const envp[]);
                      <unistd.h>                        p. 207
                      Returns: –1 on error, no return on success

int      execvp(const char *filename, char *const argv[]);
                      <unistd.h>                        p. 207
                      Returns: –1 on error, no return on success
```

```
void     exit(int status);
                    <stdlib.h>                        p. 162
                    This function never returns

int      fchdir(int filedes);
                    <unistd.h>                        p. 112
                    Returns: 0 if OK, −1 on error

int      fchmod(int filedes, mode_t mode);
                    <sys/types.h>                     p. 85
                    <sys/stat.h>
                    mode: S_IS[UG]ID, S_ISVTX, S_I[RWX](USR|GRP|OTH)
                    Returns: 0 if OK, −1 on error

int      fchown(int filedes, uid_t owner, gid_t group);
                    <sys/types.h>                     p. 89
                    <unistd.h>
                    Returns: 0 if OK, −1 on error

int      fclose(FILE *fp);
                    <stdio.h>                         p. 127
                    Returns: 0 if OK, EOF on error

int      fcntl(int filedes, int cmd, ... /* int arg */ );
                    <sys/types.h>                     p. 63
                    <unistd.h>
                    <fcntl.h>
                    cmd: F_DUPFD, F_GETFD, F_SETFD, F_GETFL, F_SETFL
                    Returns: depends on cmd if OK, −1 on error

FILE     *fdopen(int filedes, const char *type);
                    <stdio.h>                         p. 125
                    type: "r", "w", "a", "r+", "w+", "a+",
                    Returns: file pointer if OK, NULL on error

int      feof(FILE *fp);
                    <stdio.h>                         p. 129
                    Returns: nonzero (true) if end of file on stream, 0 (false) otherwise

int      ferror(FILE *fp);
                    <stdio.h>                         p. 129
                    Returns: nonzero (true) if error on stream, 0 (false) otherwise

int      fflush(FILE *fp);
                    <stdio.h>                         p. 125
                    Returns: 0 if OK, EOF on error

int      fgetc(FILE *fp);
                    <stdio.h>                         p. 128
                    Returns: next character if OK, EOF on end of file or error

int      fgetpos(FILE *fp, fpos_t *pos);
                    <stdio.h>                         p. 136
                    Returns: 0 if OK, nonzero on error
```

```
char     *fgets(char *buf, int n, FILE *fp);
                    <stdio.h>                          p. 130
                    Returns: buf if OK, NULL on end of file or error


int      fileno(FILE *fp);
                    <stdio.h>                          p. 138
                    Returns: file descriptor associated with the stream


FILE     *fopen(const char *pathname, const char *type);
                    <stdio.h>                          p. 125
                    type: "r", "w", "a", "r+", "w+", "a+",
                    Returns: file pointer if OK, NULL on error


pid_t    fork(void);
                    <sys/types.h>                      p. 188
                    <unistd.h>
                    Returns: 0 in child, process ID of child in parent, −1 on error


long     fpathconf(int filedes, int name);
                    <unistd.h>                         p. 35
                    name: _PC_CHOWN_RESTRICTED, _PC_LINK_MAX, _PC_MAX_CANON,
                          _PC_MAX_INPUT, _PC_NAME_MAX, _PC_NO_TRUNC,
                          _PC_PATH_MAX, _PC_PIPE_BUF, _PC_VDISABLE
                    Returns: corresponding value if OK, −1 on error


int      fprintf(FILE *fp, const char *format, ...);
                    <stdio.h>                          p. 136
                    Returns: #characters output if OK, negative value if output error


int      fputc(int c, FILE *fp);
                    <stdio.h>                          p. 130
                    Returns: c if OK, EOF on error


int      fputs(const char *str, FILE *fp);
                    <stdio.h>                          p. 131
                    Returns: nonnegative value if OK, EOF on error


size_t   fread(void *ptr, size_t size, size_t nobj, FILE *fp);
                    <stdio.h>                          p. 134
                    Returns: number of objects read


void     free(void *ptr);
                    <stdlib.h>                         p. 170


FILE     *freopen(const char *pathname, const char *type, FILE *fp);
                    <stdio.h>                          p. 125
                    type: "r", "w", "a", "r+", "w+", "a+",
                    Returns: file pointer if OK, NULL on error


int      fscanf(FILE *fp, const char *format, ...);
                    <stdio.h>                          p. 137
                    Returns: #input items assigned, EOF if input error or EOF before any conversion


int      fseek(FILE *fp, long offset, int whence);
                    <stdio.h>                          p. 135
                    whence: SEEK_SET, SEEK_CUR, SEEK_END
                    Returns: 0 if OK, nonzero on error
```

```
int        fsetpos(FILE *fp, const fpos_t *pos);
                        <stdio.h>                              p. 136
                        Returns: 0 if OK, nonzero on error

int        fstat(int filedes, struct stat *buf);
                        <sys/types.h>                          p. 73
                        <sys/stat.h>
                        Returns: 0 if OK, −1 on error

int        fsync(int filedes);
                        <unistd.h>                             p. 116
                        Returns: 0 if OK, −1 on error

long       ftell(FILE *fp);
                        <stdio.h>                              p. 135
                        Returns: current file position indicator if OK, −1L on error

int        ftruncate(int filedes, off_t length);
                        <sys/types.h>                          p. 92
                        <unistd.h>
                        Returns: 0 if OK, −1 on error

size_t     fwrite(const void *ptr, size_t size, size_t nobj, FILE *fp);
                        <stdio.h>                              p. 134
                        Returns: number of objects written

int        getc(FILE *fp);
                        <stdio.h>                              p. 128
                        Returns: next character if OK, EOF on end of file or error

int        getchar(void);
                        <stdio.h>                              p. 128
                        Returns: next character if OK, EOF on end of file or error

char       *getcwd(char *buf, size_t size);
                        <unistd.h>                             p. 113
                        Returns: buf if OK, NULL on error

gid_t      getegid(void);
                        <sys/types.h>                          p. 188
                        <unistd.h>
                        Returns: effective group ID of calling process

char       *getenv(const char *name);
                        <stdlib.h>                             p. 172
                        Returns: pointer to value associated with name, NULL if not found

uid_t      geteuid(void);
                        <sys/types.h>                          p. 188
                        <unistd.h>
                        Returns: effective user ID of calling process

gid_t      getgid(void);
                        <sys/types.h>                          p. 188
                        <unistd.h>
                        Returns: real group ID of calling process
```

```
struct
group    *getgrent(void);
                          <sys/types.h>                              p. 150
                          <grp.h>
                          Returns: pointer if OK, NULL on error or end of file


struct
group    *getgrgid(gid_t gid);
                          <sys/types.h>                              p. 150
                          <grp.h>
                          Returns: pointer if OK, NULL on error


struct
group    *getgrnam(const char *name);
                          <sys/types.h>                              p. 150
                          <grp.h>
                          Returns: pointer if OK, NULL on error


int       getgroups(int gidsetsize, gid_t grouplist[]);
                          <sys/types.h>                              p. 151
                          <unistd.h>
                          Returns: number of supplementary group IDs if OK, −1 on error


int       gethostname(char *name, int namelen);
                          <unistd.h>                                 p. 154
                          Returns: 0 if OK, −1 on error


char     *getlogin(void);
                          <unistd.h>                                 p. 232
                          Returns: pointer to string giving login name if OK, NULL on error


int       getmsg(int filedes, struct strbuf *ctlptr, struct strbuf *dataptr, int *flagptr);
                          <stropts.h>                                p. 392
                          *flagptr: 0, RS_HIPRI
                          Returns: nonnegative value if OK, −1 on error


pid_t     getpgrp(void);
                          <sys/types.h>                              p. 243
                          <unistd.h>
                          Returns: process group ID of calling process


pid_t     getpid(void);
                          <sys/types.h>                              p. 188
                          <unistd.h>
                          Returns: process ID of calling process


int       getpmsg(int filedes, struct strbuf *ctlptr, struct strbuf *dataptr, int *bandptr,
             int *flagptr);
                          <stropts.h>                                p. 392
                          *flagptr: 0, MSG_HIPRI, MSG_BAND, MSG_ANY
                          Returns: nonnegative value if OK, −1 on error


pid_t     getppid(void);
                          <sys/types.h>                              p. 188
                          <unistd.h>
                          Returns: parent process ID of calling process
```

```
struct
passwd  *getpwent(void);
                    <sys/types.h>                      p. 147
                    <pwd.h>
                    Returns: pointer if OK, NULL on error or end of file

struct
passwd  *getpwnam(const char *name);
                    <sys/types.h>                      p. 147
                    <pwd.h>
                    Returns: pointer if OK, NULL on error

struct
passwd  *getpwuid(uid_t uid);
                    <sys/types.h>                      p. 147
                    <pwd.h>
                    Returns: pointer if OK, NULL on error

int     getrlimit(int resource, struct rlimit *rlptr);
                    <sys/time.h>                       p. 180
                    <sys/resource.h>
                    Returns: 0 if OK, nonzero on error

char    *gets(char *buf);
                    <stdio.h>                          p. 130
                    Returns: buf if OK, NULL on end of file or error

uid_t   getuid(void);
                    <sys/types.h>                      p. 188
                    <unistd.h>
                    Returns: real user ID of calling process

struct
tm      *gmtime(const time_t *calptr);
                    <time.h>                           p. 156
                    Returns: pointer to broken-down time

int     initgroups(const char *username, gid_t basegid);
                    <sys/types.h>                      p. 151
                    <unistd.h>
                    Returns: 0 if OK, -1 on error

int     ioctl(int filedes, int request, ...);
                    <unistd.h>      /* SVR4 */         p. 68
                    <sys/ioctl.h>   /* 4.3+BSD */
                    Returns: -1 on error, something else if OK

int     isastream(int filedes);                        p. 388
                    Returns: 1 (true) if streams device, 0 (false) otherwise

int     isatty(int filedes);
                    <unistd.h>                         p. 346
                    Returns: 1 (true) if terminal device, 0 (false) otherwise
```

```
int      kill(pid_t pid, int signo);
                       <sys/types.h>                    p. 284
                       <signal.h>
                       Returns: 0 if OK, −1 on error

int      lchown(const char *pathname, uid_t owner, gid_t group);
                       <sys/types.h>                    p. 89
                       <unistd.h>
                       Returns: 0 if OK, −1 on error

int      link(const char *existingpath, const char *newpath);
                       <unistd.h>                       p. 95
                       Returns: 0 if OK, −1 on error

struct
tm       *localtime(const time_t *calptr);
                       <time.h>                         p. 156
                       Returns: pointer to broken-down time

void     longjmp(jmp_buf env, int val);
                       <setjmp.h>                       p. 176
                       This function never returns

off_t    lseek(int filedes, off_t offset, int whence);
                       <sys/types.h>                    p. 51
                       <unistd.h>
                       whence: SEEK_SET, SEEK_CUR, SEEK_END
                       Returns: new file offset if OK, −1 on error

int      lstat(const char *pathname, struct stat *buf);
                       <sys/types.h>                    p. 73
                       <sys/stat.h>
                       Returns: 0 if OK, −1 on error

void     *malloc(size_t size);
                       <stdlib.h>                       p. 170
                       Returns: nonnull pointer if OK, NULL on error

int      mkdir(const char *pathname, mode_t mode);
                       <sys/types.h>                    p. 106
                       <sys/stat.h>
                       mode: S_IS[UG]ID, S_ISVTX, S_I[RWX](USR|GRP|OTH)
                       Returns: 0 if OK, −1 on error

int      mkfifo(const char *pathname, mode_t mode);
                       <sys/types.h>                    p. 445
                       <sys/stat.h>
                       mode: S_IS[UG]ID, S_ISVTX, S_I[RWX](USR|GRP|OTH)
                       Returns: 0 if OK, −1 on error

time_t   mktime(struct tm *tmptr);
                       <time.h>                         p. 157
                       Returns: calendar time if OK, −1 on error
```

```
caddr_t   mmap(caddr_t addr, size_t len, int prot, int flag, int filedes, off_t off);
                    <sys/types.h>                        p. 407
                    ·sys/mman.h>
                    prot: PROT_READ, PROT_WRITE, PROT_EXEC, PROT_NONE
                    flag: MAP_FIXED, MAP_SHARED, MAP_PRIVATE
                    Returns: starting address of mapped region if OK, −1 on error

int       msgctl(int msqid, int cmd, struct msqid_ds *buf);
                    <sys/types.h>                        p. 454
                    <sys/ipc.h>
                    <sys/msg.h>
                    cmd: IPC_STAT, IPC_SET, IPC_RMID
                    Returns: 0 if OK, −1 on error

int       msgget(key_t key, int flag);
                    <sys/types.h>                        p. 454
                    <sys/ipc.h>
                    <sys/msg.h>
                    flag: 0, IPC_CREAT, IPC_EXCL
                    Returns: message queue ID if OK, −1 on error

int       msgrcv(int msqid, void *ptr, size_t nbytes, long type, int flag);
                    <sys/types.h>                        p. 456
                    <sys/ipc.h>
                    <sys/msg.h>
                    flag: 0, IPC_NOWAIT, MSG_NOERROR
                    Returns: size of data portion of message if OK, −1 on error

int       msgsnd(int msqid, const void *ptr, size_t nbytes, int flag);
                    <sys/types.h>                        p. 455
                    <sys/ipc.h>
                    <sys/msg.h>
                    flag: 0, IPC_NOWAIT
                    Returns: 0 if OK, −1 on error

int       munmap(caddr_t addr, size_t len);
                    <sys/types.h>                        p. 411
                    <sys/mman.h>
                    Returns: 0 if OK, −1 on error

int       open(const char *pathname, int oflag, ... /* , mode_t mode */ );
                    <sys/types.h>                        p. 48
                    <sys/stat.h>
                    <fcntl.h>
                    oflag: O_RDONLY, O_WRONLY, O_RDWR;
                           O_APPEND, O_CREAT, O_EXCL, O_TRUNC,
                           O_NOCTTY, O_NONBLOCK, O_SYNC
                    mode: S_IS[UG]ID, S_ISVTX, S_I[RWX](USR|GRP|OTH)
                    Returns: file descriptor if OK, −1 on error

DIR       *opendir(const char *pathname);
                    <sys/types.h>                        p. 107
                    <dirent.h>
                    Returns: pointer if OK, NULL on error
```

```
void       openlog(char *ident, int option, int facility);
                        <syslog.h>                          p. 422
                        option: LOG_CONS, LOG_NDELAY, LOG_PERROR, LOG_PID
                        facility: LOG_AUTH, LOG_CRON, LOG_DAEMON, LOG_KERN,
                                LOG_LOCAL[0-7], LOG_LPR, LOG_MAIL, LOG_NEWS,
                                LOG_SYSLOG, LOG_USER, LOG_UUCP

long       pathconf(const char *pathname, int name);
                        <unistd.h>                          p. 35
                        name: _PC_CHOWN_RESTRICTED, _PC_LINK_MAX, _PC_MAX_CANON,
                                _PC_MAX_INPUT, _PC_NAME_MAX, _PC_NO_TRUNC,
                                _PC_PATH_MAX, _PC_PIPE_BUF, _PC_VDISABLE
                        Returns: corresponding value if OK, -1 on error

int        pause(void);
                        <unistd.h>                          p. 285
                        Returns: -1 with errno set to EINTR

int        pclose(FILE *fp);
                        <stdio.h>                           p. 435
                        Returns: termination status of cmdstring, or -1 on error

void       perror(const char *msg);
                        <stdio.h>                           p. 15

int        pipe(int filedes[2]);
                        <unistd.h>                          p. 428
                        Returns: 0 if OK, -1 on error

int        poll(struct pollfd fdarray[], unsigned long nfds, int timeout);
                        <stropts.h>                         p. 400
                        <poll.h>
                        Returns: count of ready descriptors, 0 on timeout, -1 on error

FILE       *popen(const char *cmdstring, const char *type);
                        <stdio.h>                           p. 435
                        type: "r", "w"
                        Returns: file pointer if OK, NULL on error

int        printf(const char *format, ...);
                        <stdio.h>                           p. 136
                        Returns: # characters output if OK, negative value if output error

void       psignal(int signo, const char *msg);
                        <signal.h>                          p. 322

int        putc(int c, FILE *fp);
                        <stdio.h>                           p. 130
                        Returns: c if OK, EOF on error

int        putchar(int c);
                        <stdio.h>                           p. 130
                        Returns: c if OK, EOF on error

int        putenv(const char *str);
                        <stdlib.h>                          p. 173
                        Returns: 0 if OK, nonzero on error
```

```
int       putmsg(int filedes, const struct strbuf *ctlptr, const struct strbuf *dataptr,
              int flag);
                      <stropts.h>                      p. 386
                      flag: 0, RS_HIPRI
                      Returns: 0 if OK, −1 on error

int       putpmsg(int filedes, const struct strbuf *ctlptr, const struct strbuf *dataptr,
              int band, int flag);
                      <stropts.h>                      p. 386
                      flag: 0, MSG_HIPRI, MSG_BAND
                      Returns: 0 if OK, −1 on error

int       puts(const char *str);
                      <stdio.h>                        p. 131
                      Returns: nonnegative value if OK, EOF on error

int       raise(int signo);
                      <sys/types.h>                    p. 284
                      <signal.h>
                      Returns: 0 if OK, −1 on error

ssize_t   read(int filedes, void *buff, size_t nbytes);
                      <unistd.h>                       p. 54
                      Returns: #bytes read if OK, 0 if end of file, −1 on error

struct
dirent   *readdir(DIR *dp);
                      <sys/types.h>                    p. 107
                      <dirent.h>
                      Returns: pointer if OK, NULL at end of directory or error

int       readlink(const char *pathname, char *buf, int bufsize);
                      <unistd.h>                       p. 102
                      Returns: #bytes read if OK, −1 on error

ssize_t   readv(int filedes, const struct iovec iov[], int iovcnt);
                      <sys/types.h>                    p. 404
                      <sys/uio.h>
                      Returns: #bytes read if OK, −1 on error

void     *realloc(void *ptr, size_t newsize);
                      <stdlib.h>                       p. 170
                      Returns: nonnull pointer if OK, NULL on error

int       remove(const char *pathname);
                      <stdio.h>                        p. 98
                      Returns: 0 if OK, −1 on error

int       rename(const char *oldname, const char *newname);
                      <stdio.h>                        p. 98
                      Returns: 0 if OK, −1 on error

void      rewind(FILE *fp);
                      <stdio.h>                        p. 135
```

```
void      rewinddir(DIR *dp);
                     <sys/types.h>                    p. 107
                     <dirent.h>

int       rmdir(const char *pathname);
                     <unistd.h>                       p. 107
                     Returns: 0 if OK, -1 on error

int       scanf(const char *format, ...);
                     <stdio.h>                         p. 137
                     Returns: #input items assigned, EOF if input error or EOF before any conversion

int       select(int maxfdp1, fd_set *readfds, fd_set *writefds, fd_set *exceptfds,
                 struct timeval *tvptr);
                     <sys/types.h>                    p. 397
                     <sys/time.h>
                     <unistd.h>
                     Returns: count of ready descriptors, 0 on timeout, -1 on error
                     FD_ZERO(fd_set *fdset);
                     FD_SET(int filedes, fd_set *fdset);
                     FD_CLR(int filedes, fd_set *fdset);
                     FD_ISSET(int filedes, fd_set *fdset);

int       semctl(int semid, int semnum, int cmd, union semun arg);
                     <sys/types.h>                    p. 459
                     <sys/ipc.h>
                     <sys/sem.h>
                     cmd: IPC_STAT, IPC_SET, IPC_RMID, GETPID, GETNCNT, GETZCNT,
                          GETVAL, SETVAL, GETALL, SETALL
                     Returns: (depends on command)

int       semget(key_t key, int nsems, int flag);
                     <sys/types.h>                    p. 459
                     <sys/ipc.h>
                     <sys/sem.h>
                     flag: 0, IPC_CREAT, IPC_EXCL
                     Returns: semaphore ID if OK, -1 on error

int       semop(int semid, struct sembuf semoparray[], size_t nops);
                     <sys/types.h>                    p. 461
                     <sys/ipc.h>
                     <sys/sem.h>
                     Returns: 0 if OK, -1 on error

void      setbuf(FILE *fp, char *buf);
                     <stdio.h>                         p. 124

int       setegid(gid_t gid);
                     <sys/types.h>                    p. 216
                     <unistd.h>
                     Returns: 0 if OK, -1 on error

int       setenv(const char *name, const char *value, int rewrite);
                     <stdlib.h>                        p. 173
                     Returns: 0 if OK, nonzero on error
```

```
int      seteuid(uid_t uid);
                         <sys/types.h>                    p. 216
                         <unistd.h>
                         Returns: 0 if OK, -1 on error

int      setgid(gid_t gid);
                         <sys/types.h>                    p. 213
                         <unistd.h>
                         Returns: 0 if OK, -1 on error

void     setgrent(void);
                         <sys/types.h>                    p. 150
                         <grp.h>

int      setgroups(int ngroups, const gid_t grouplist[]);
                         <sys/types.h>                    p. 151
                         <unistd.h>
                         Returns: 0 if OK, -1 on error

int      setjmp(jmp_buf env);
                         <setjmp.h>                       p. 176
                         Returns: 0 if called directly, nonzero if returning from a call to longjmp

int      setpgid(pid_t pid, pid_t pgid);
                         <sys/types.h>                    p. 244
                         <unistd.h>
                         Returns: 0 if OK, -1 on error

void     setpwent(void);
                         <sys/types.h>                    p. 147
                         <pwd.h>

int      setregid(gid_t rgid, gid_t egid);
                         <sys/types.h>                    p. 215
                         <unistd.h>
                         Returns: 0 if OK, -1 on error

int      setreuid(uid_t ruid, uid_t euid);
                         <sys/types.h>                    p. 215
                         <unistd.h>
                         Returns: 0 if OK, -1 on error

int      setrlimit(int resource, const struct rlimit *rlptr);
                         <sys/time.h>                     p. 180
                         <sys/resource.h>
                         Returns: 0 if OK, nonzero on error

pid_t    setsid(void);
                         <sys/types.h>                    p. 245
                         <unistd.h>
                         Returns: process group ID if OK, -1 on error

int      setuid(uid_t uid);
                         <sys/types.h>                    p. 213
                         <unistd.h>
                         Returns: 0 if OK, -1 on error
```

```
int        setvbuf(FILE *fp, char *buf, int mode, size_t size);
                    <stdio.h>                              p. 124
                    mode: _IOFBF, _IOLBF, _IONBF
                    Returns: 0 if OK, nonzero on error

void      *shmat(int shmid, void *addr, int flag);
                    <sys/types.h>                          p. 465
                    <sys/ipc.h>
                    <sys/shm.h>
                    flag: 0, SHM_RND, SHM_RDONLY
                    Returns: pointer to shared memory segment if OK, -1 on error

int        shmctl(int shmid, int cmd, struct shmid_ds *buf);
                    <sys/types.h>                          p. 465
                    <sys/ipc.h>
                    <sys/shm.h>
                    cmd: IPC_STAT, IPC_SET, IPC_RMID,
                         SHM_LOCK, SHM_UNLOCK
                    Returns: 0 if OK, -1 on error

int        shmdt(void *addr);
                    <sys/types.h>                          p. 466
                    <sys/ipc.h>
                    <sys/shm.h>
                    Returns: 0 if OK, -1 on error

int        shmget(key_t key, int size, int flag);
                    <sys/types.h>                          p. 464
                    <sys/ipc.h>
                    <sys/shm.h>
                    flag: 0, IPC_CREAT, IPC_EXCL
                    Returns: shared memory ID if OK, -1 on error

int        sigaction(int signo, const struct sigaction *act, struct sigaction *oact);
                    <signal.h>                             p. 296
                    Returns: 0 if OK, -1 on error

int        sigaddset(sigset_t *set, int signo);
                    <signal.h>                             p. 291
                    Returns: 0 if OK, -1 on error

int        sigdelset(sigset_t *set, int signo);
                    <signal.h>                             p. 291
                    Returns: 0 if OK, -1 on error

int        sigemptyset(sigset_t *set);
                    <signal.h>                             p. 291
                    Returns: 0 if OK, -1 on error

int        sigfillset(sigset_t *set);
                    <signal.h>                             p. 291
                    Returns: 0 if OK, -1 on error

int        sigismember(const sigset_t *set, int signo);
                    <signal.h>                             p. 291
                    Returns: 1 if true, 0 if false
```

```
void       siglongjmp(sigjmp_buf env, int val);
                    <setjmp.h>                            p. 300
                    This function never returns

void       (*signal(int signo, void (*func)(int)))(int);
                    <signal.h>                            p. 270
                    Returns: previous disposition of signal, SIG_ERR on error

int        sigpending(sigset_t *set);
                    <signal.h>                            p. 293
                    Returns: 0 if OK, -1 on error

int        sigprocmask(int how, const sigset_t *set, sigset_t *oset);
                    <signal.h>                            p. 293
                    how: SIG_BLOCK, SIG_UNBLOCK, SIG_SETMASK
                    Returns: 0 if OK, -1 on error

int        sigsetjmp(sigjmp_buf env, int savemask);
                    <setjmp.h>                            p. 300
                    Returns: 0 if called directly, nonzero if returning from a call to siglongjmp

int        sigsuspend(const sigset_t *sigmask);
                    <signal.h>                            p. 303
                    Returns: -1 with errno set to EINTR

unsigned
int        sleep(unsigned int seconds);
                    <unistd.h>                            p. 317
                    Returns: 0 or number of unslept seconds

int        sprintf(char *buf, const char *format, ...);
                    <stdio.h>                             p. 136
                    Returns: #characters stored in array

int        sscanf(const char *buf, const char *format, ...);
                    <stdio.h>                             p. 137
                    Returns: #input items assigned, EOF if input error or EOF before any conversion

int        stat(const char *pathname, struct stat *buf);
                    <sys/types.h>                         p. 73
                    <sys/stat.h>
                    Returns: 0 if OK, -1 on error

char       *strerror(int errnum);
                    <string.h>                            p. 14
                    Returns: pointer to message string

size_t     strftime(char *buf, size_t maxsize, const char *format, const struct tm *tmptr);
                    <time.h>                              p. 157
                    Returns: #characters stored in array if room, else 0

int        symlink(const char *actualpath, const char *sympath);
                    <unistd.h>                            p. 102
                    Returns: 0 if OK, -1 on error

void       sync(void);
                    <unistd.h>                            p. 116
```

long   **sysconf**(int *name*);
                                <unistd.h>   p. 35
                                name: _SC_ARG_MAX, _SC_CHILD_MAX, _SC_CLK_TCK,
                                                _SC_NGROUPS_MAX, _SC_OPEN_MAX, _SC_PASS_MAX,
                                                _SC_STREAM_MAX, _SC_TZNAME_MAX, _SC_JOB_CONTROL,
                                                _SC_SAVED_IDS, _SC_VERSION, _SC_XOPEN_VERSION
                                Returns: corresponding value if OK, −1 on error

void   **syslog**(int *priority*, char **format*, ...);
                                <syslog.h>   p. 422

int   **system**(const char **cmdstring*);
                                <stdlib.h>   p. 222
                                Returns: termination status of shell

int   **tcdrain**(int *filedes*);
                                  <termios.h>   p. 344
                                Returns: 0 if OK, −1 on error

int   **tcflow**(int *filedes*, int *action*);
                                  <termios.h>   p. 344
                                action: TCOOFF, TCOON, TCIOFF, TCION
                                Returns: 0 if OK, −1 on error

int   **tcflush**(int *filedes*, int *queue*);
                                  <termios.h>   p. 344
                                queue: TCIFLUSH, TCOFLUSH, TCIOFLUSH
                                Returns: 0 if OK, −1 on error

int   **tcgetattr**(int *filedes*, struct termios **termptr*);
                                  <termios.h>   p. 336
                                Returns: 0 if OK, −1 on error

pid_t   **tcgetpgrp**(int *filedes*);
                                  <sys/types.h>   p. 248
                                  <unistd.h>
                                Returns: process group ID of foreground process group if OK, −1 on error

int   **tcsendbreak**(int *filedes*, int *duration*);
                                <termios.h>   p. 344
                                Returns: 0 if OK, −1 on error

int   **tcsetattr**(int *filedes*, int *opt*, const struct termios **termptr*);
                                  <termios.h>   p. 336
                                opt: TCSANOW, TCSADRAIN, TCSAFLUSH
                                Returns: 0 if OK, −1 on error

int   **tcsetpgrp**(int *filedes*, pid_t *pgrpid*);
                                  <sys/types.h>   p. 248
                                  <unistd.h>
                                Returns: 0 if OK, −1 on error

char   ***tempnam**(const char **directory*, const char **prefix*);
                                  <stdio.h>   p. 141
                                Returns: pointer to unique pathname

time_t   **time**(time_t *calptr*);
                                  <time.h>   p. 155
                                  Returns: value of time if OK, −1 on error

clock_t   **times**(struct tms *buf*);
                                  <sys/times.h>   p. 232
                                  Returns: elapsed wall clock time in clock ticks if OK, −1 on error

FILE   ***tmpfile**(void);
                                  <stdio.h>   p. 140
                                  Returns: file pointer if OK, NULL on error

char   ***tmpnam**(char *ptr*);
                                  <stdio.h>   p. 140
                                  Returns: pointer to unique pathname

int   **truncate**(const char *pathname*, off_t *length*);
                                  <sys/types.h>   p. 92
                                  <unistd.h>
                                  Returns: 0 if OK, −1 on error

char   ***ttyname**(int *filedes*);
                                  <unistd.h>   p. 346
                                  Returns: pointer to pathname of terminal, NULL on error

mode_t   **umask**(mode_t *cmask*);
                                  <sys/types.h>   p. 84
                                  <sys/stat.h>
                                  Returns: previous file mode creation mask

int   **uname**(struct utsname *name*);
                                  <sys/utsname.h>   p. 154
                                  Returns: nonnegative value if OK, −1 on error

int   **ungetc**(int *c*, FILE *fp*);
                                  <stdio.h>   p. 129
                                  Returns: *c* if OK, EOF on error

int   **unlink**(const char *pathname*);
                                  <unistd.h>   p. 96
                                  Returns: 0 if OK, −1 on error

void   **unsetenv**(const char *name*);
                                  <stdlib.h>   p. 173

int   **utime**(const char *pathname*, const struct utimbuf *times*);
                                  <sys/types.h>   p. 103
                                  <utime.h>
                                  Returns: 0 if OK, −1 on error

int   **vfprintf**(FILE *fp*, const char *format*, va_list *arg*);
                                  <stdarg.h>   p. 137
                                  <stdio.h>
                                  Returns: #characters output if OK, negative value if output error

int   **vprintf**(const char *_format_, va_list _arg_);
                    <stdarg.h>   p. 137
                    <stdio.h>
                    Returns: #characters output if OK, negative value if output error

int   **vsprintf**(char *_buf_, const char *_format_, va_list _arg_);
                    <stdarg.h>   p. 137
                    <stdio.h>
                    Returns: #characters stored in array

pid_t   **wait**(int *_statloc_);
                    <sys/types.h>   p. 197
                    <sys/wait.h>
                    Returns: process ID if OK, 0, or –1 on error

pid_t   **wait3**(int *_statloc_, int _options_, struct rusage *_rusage_);
                    <sys/types.h>   p. 203
                    <sys/wait.h>
                    <sys/time.h>
                    <sys/resource.h>
                    options: 0, WNOHANG, WUNTRACED
                    Returns: process ID if OK, 0, or –1 on error

pid_t   **wait4**(pid_t _pid_, int *_statloc_, int _options_, struct rusage *_rusage_);
                    <sys/types.h>   p. 203
                    <sys/wait.h>
                    <sys/time.h>
                    <sys/resource.h>
                    options: 0, WNOHANG, WUNTRACED
                    Returns: process ID if OK, 0, or –1 on error

pid_t   **waitpid**(pid_t _pid_, int *_statloc_, int _options_);
                    <sys/types.h>   p. 197
                    <sys/wait.h>
                    options: 0, WNOHANG, WUNTRACED
                    Returns: process ID if OK, 0, or –1 on error

ssize_t   **write**(int _filedes_, const void *_buff_, size_t _nbytes_);
                    <unistd.h>   p. 55
                    Returns: #bytes written if OK, –1 on error

ssize_t   **writev**(int _filedes_, const struct iovec _iov_[], int _iovcnt_);
                    <sys/types.h>   p. 404
                    <sys/uio.h>
                    Returns: #bytes written if OK, –1 on error

Appendix B

Miscellaneous Source Code

B.1 Our Header File

Most programs in the text include the header ourhdr.h, shown in Program B.1. It defines constants (such as MAXLINE) and prototypes for our own functions.

Since most programs need to include the following headers: <stdio.h>, <stdlib.h> (for the exit function prototype), and <unistd.h> (for all the standard Unix function prototypes), our header automatically includes these system headers, along with <string.h>. This also reduces the size of all the program listings in the text.

```
/* Our own header, to be included *after* all standard system headers */

#ifndef __ourhdr_h
#define __ourhdr_h

#include     <sys/types.h>    /* required for some of our prototypes */
#include     <stdio.h>        /* for convenience */
#include     <stdlib.h>       /* for convenience */
#include     <string.h>       /* for convenience */
#include     <unistd.h>       /* for convenience */

#define MAXLINE 4096               /* max line length */

#define FILE_MODE    (S_IRUSR | S_IWUSR | S_IRGRP | S_IROTH)
                     /* default file access permissions for new files */
#define DIR_MODE     (FILE_MODE | S_IXUSR | S_IXGRP | S_IXOTH)
                     /* default permissions for new directories */

typedef void    Sigfunc(int);    /* for signal handlers */
```

```
                          /* 4.3BSD Reno <signal.h> doesn't define SIG_ERR */
#if defined(SIG_IGN) && !defined(SIG_ERR)
#define SIG_ERR ((Sigfunc *)-1)
#endif

#define min(a,b)     ((a) < (b) ? (a) : (b))
#define max(a,b)     ((a) > (b) ? (a) : (b))

                         /* prototypes for our own functions */
char     *path_alloc(int *);           /* Program 2.2 */
int       open_max(void);              /* Program 2.3 */
void      clr_fl(int, int);            /* Program 3.5 */
void      set_fl(int, int);            /* Program 3.5 */
void      pr_exit(int);                /* Program 8.3 */
void      pr_mask(const char *);       /* Program 10.10 */
Sigfunc *signal_intr(int, Sigfunc *);/* Program 10.13 */

int       tty_cbreak(int);             /* Program 11.10 */
int       tty_raw(int);                /* Program 11.10 */
int       tty_reset(int);              /* Program 11.10 */
void      tty_atexit(void);            /* Program 11.10 */
#ifdef  ECHO    /* only if <termios.h> has been included */
struct termios  *tty_termios(void); /* Program 11.10 */
#endif

void      sleep_us(unsigned int);      /* Exercise 12.6 */
ssize_t  readn(int, void *, size_t);/* Program 12.13 */
ssize_t  writen(int, const void *, size_t);/* Program 12.12 */
int       daemon_init(void);           /* Program 13.1 */

int       s_pipe(int *);               /* Programs 15.2 and 15.3 */
int       recv_fd(int, ssize_t (*func)(int, const void *, size_t));
                                       /* Programs 15.6 and 15.8 */
int       send_fd(int, int);           /* Programs 15.5 and 15.7 */
int       send_err(int, int, const char *);/* Program 15.4 */
int       serv_listen(const char *); /* Programs 15.19 and 15.22 */
int       serv_accept(int, uid_t *); /* Programs 15.20 and 15.24 */
int       cli_conn(const char *);    /* Programs 15.21 and 15.23 */
int       buf_args(char *, int (*func)(int, char **));
                                       /* Program 15.17 */

int       ptym_open(char *);           /* Programs 19.1 and 19.2 */
int       ptys_open(int, char *);    /* Programs 19.1 and 19.2 */
#ifdef  TIOCGWINSZ
pid_t    pty_fork(int *, char *, const struct termios *,
                  const struct winsize *);  /* Program 19.3 */
#endif

int       lock_reg(int, int, int, off_t, int, off_t);
                                       /* Program 12.2 */
#define read_lock(fd, offset, whence, len) \
            lock_reg(fd, F_SETLK, F_RDLCK, offset, whence, len)
#define readw_lock(fd, offset, whence, len) \
```

```
                lock_reg(fd, F_SETLKW, F_RDLCK, offset, whence, len)
#define write_lock(fd, offset, whence, len) \
                lock_reg(fd, F_SETLK, F_WRLCK, offset, whence, len)
#define writew_lock(fd, offset, whence, len) \
                lock_reg(fd, F_SETLKW, F_WRLCK, offset, whence, len)
#define un_lock(fd, offset, whence, len) \
                lock_reg(fd, F_SETLK, F_UNLCK, offset, whence, len)

pid_t   lock_test(int, int, off_t, int, off_t);
                                        /* Program 12.3 */

#define is_readlock(fd, offset, whence, len) \
                lock_test(fd, F_RDLCK, offset, whence, len)
#define is_writelock(fd, offset, whence, len) \
                lock_test(fd, F_WRLCK, offset, whence, len)

void    err_dump(const char *, ...);    /* Appendix B */
void    err_msg(const char *, ...);
void    err_quit(const char *, ...);
void    err_ret(const char *, ...);
void    err_sys(const char *, ...);

void    log_msg(const char *, ...);     /* Appendix B */
void    log_open(const char *, int, int);
void    log_quit(const char *, ...);
void    log_ret(const char *, ...);
void    log_sys(const char *, ...);

void    TELL_WAIT(void);                /* parent/child from Section 8.8 */
void    TELL_PARENT(pid_t);
void    TELL_CHILD(pid_t);
void    WAIT_PARENT(void);
void    WAIT_CHILD(void);

#endif  /* __ourhdr_h */
```

Program B.1 Our header ourhdr.h.

The reason we include our header after all the normal system headers is to fix up any system differences (such as the missing SIG_ERR from 4.3BSD Reno) and to define some of our prototypes, needed only if certain headers have been included. Some ANSI C compilers complain if they encounter references to structures in prototypes, when the structure has not been defined.

B.2   Standard Error Routines

We have two sets of error functions that are used in most of the examples throughout the text to handle error conditions. One set begins with err_ and outputs an error message to standard error. The other set begins with log_ and is for daemon processes (Chapter 13) that probably have no controlling terminal.

The reason for our own error functions is to let us write our error handling with a single line of C code, as in

```
if (error condition)
        err_dump (printf format with any number of arguments);
```

instead of

```
if (error condition) {
        char buff[200];
        sprintf(buff, printf format with any number of arguments);
        perror(buff);
        abort();
}
```

Our error functions use the variable-length argument list facility from ANSI C. See Section 7.3 of Kernighan and Ritchie [1988] for additional details. Be aware that this ANSI C facility differs from the varargs facility provided by earlier systems (such as SVR3 and 4.3BSD). The names of the macros are the same, but the arguments to some of the macros have changed.

Figure B.1 details the differences between the various error functions.

Function	strerror(errno) ?	Terminate ?
err_ret	yes	return;
err_sys	yes	exit(1);
err_dump	yes	abort();
err_msg	no	return;
err_quit	no	exit(1);
log_ret	yes	return;
log_sys	yes	exit(2);
log_msg	no	return;
log_quit	no	exit(2);

Figure B.1 Our standard error functions.

Program B.2 shows the error functions that output to standard error.

```
#include     <errno.h>        /* for definition of errno */
#include     <stdarg.h>       /* ANSI C header file */
#include     "ourhdr.h"

static void err_doit(int, const char *, va_list);

char     *pname = NULL;       /* caller can set this from argv[0] */

/* Nonfatal error related to a system call.
 * Print a message and return. */

void
err_ret(const char *fmt, ...)
{
    va_list     ap;
```

```
        va_start(ap, fmt);
        err_doit(1, fmt, ap);
        va_end(ap);
        return;
}

/* Fatal error related to a system call.
 * Print a message and terminate. */

void
err_sys(const char *fmt, ...)
{
        va_list        ap;

        va_start(ap, fmt);
        err_doit(1, fmt, ap);
        va_end(ap);
        exit(1);
}

/* Fatal error related to a system call.
 * Print a message, dump core, and terminate. */

void
err_dump(const char *fmt, ...)
{
        va_list        ap;

        va_start(ap, fmt);
        err_doit(1, fmt, ap);
        va_end(ap);
        abort();              /* dump core and terminate */
        exit(1);              /* shouldn't get here */
}

/* Nonfatal error unrelated to a system call.
 * Print a message and return. */

void
err_msg(const char *fmt, ...)
{
        va_list        ap;

        va_start(ap, fmt);
        err_doit(0, fmt, ap);
        va_end(ap);
        return;
}

/* Fatal error unrelated to a system call.
 * Print a message and terminate. */

void
err_quit(const char *fmt, ...)
```

```
{
    va_list      ap;

    va_start(ap, fmt);
    err_doit(0, fmt, ap);
    va_end(ap);
    exit(1);
}

/* Print a message and return to caller.
 * Caller specifies "errnoflag". */

static void
err_doit(int errnoflag, const char *fmt, va_list ap)
{
    int       errno_save;
    char      buf[MAXLINE];

    errno_save = errno;       /* value caller might want printed */
    vsprintf(buf, fmt, ap);
    if (errnoflag)
        sprintf(buf+strlen(buf), ": %s", strerror(errno_save));
    strcat(buf, "\n");
    fflush(stdout);       /* in case stdout and stderr are the same */
    fputs(buf, stderr);
    fflush(NULL);         /* flushes all stdio output streams */
    return;
}
```

Program B.2 Error functions that output to standard error.

Program B.3 shows the log_XXX error functions. These require the caller to define the variable debug and set it nonzero if the process is not running as a daemon. In this case the error messages are sent to standard error. If the debug flag is 0, the syslog facility (Section 13.4.2) is used.

```
/* Error routines for programs that can run as a daemon. */

#include    <errno.h>         /* for definition of errno */
#include    <stdarg.h>        /* ANSI C header file */
#include    <syslog.h>
#include    "ourhdr.h"

static void log_doit(int, int, const char *, va_list ap);

extern int  debug;        /* caller must define and set this:
                             nonzero if interactive, zero if daemon */

/* Initialize syslog(), if running as daemon. */

void
log_open(const char *ident, int option, int facility)
{
```

```
        if (debug == 0)
            openlog(ident, option, facility);
}

/* Nonfatal error related to a system call.
 * Print a message with the system's errno value and return. */

void
log_ret(const char *fmt, ...)
{
    va_list      ap;

    va_start(ap, fmt);
    log_doit(1, LOG_ERR, fmt, ap);
    va_end(ap);
    return;
}

/* Fatal error related to a system call.
 * Print a message and terminate. */

void
log_sys(const char *fmt, ...)
{
    va_list      ap;

    va_start(ap, fmt);
    log_doit(1, LOG_ERR, fmt, ap);
    va_end(ap);
    exit(2);
}

/* Nonfatal error unrelated to a system call.
 * Print a message and return. */

void
log_msg(const char *fmt, ...)
{
    va_list      ap;

    va_start(ap, fmt);
    log_doit(0, LOG_ERR, fmt, ap);
    va_end(ap);
    return;
}

/* Fatal error unrelated to a system call.
 * Print a message and terminate. */

void
log_quit(const char *fmt, ...)
{
    va_list      ap;
```

```
        va_start(ap, fmt);
        log_doit(0, LOG_ERR, fmt, ap);
        va_end(ap);
        exit(2);
}

/* Print a message and return to caller.
 * Caller specifies "errnoflag" and "priority". */

static void
log_doit(int errnoflag, int priority, const char *fmt, va_list ap)
{
    int     errno_save;
    char    buf[MAXLINE];

    errno_save = errno;         /* value caller might want printed */
    vsprintf(buf, fmt, ap);
    if (errnoflag)
        sprintf(buf+strlen(buf), ": %s", strerror(errno_save));
    strcat(buf, "\n");
    if (debug) {
        fflush(stdout);
        fputs(buf, stderr);
        fflush(stderr);
    } else
        syslog(priority, buf);
    return;
}
```

Program B.3 Error functions for daemons.

Appendix C

Solutions to Selected Exercises

Chapter 1

1.1 For this exercise we use the following two arguments for the ls(1) command: -i prints the i-node number of the file or directory (we say more about i-nodes in Section 4.14), and -d which outputs information about a directory, instead of information on all the files in the directory.

Execute the following

```
$ ls -ldi /etc/. /etc/..              -i says print i-node number
  3077 drwxr-sr-x  7 bin    2048 Aug  5 20:12 /etc/./
     2 drwxr-xr-x 13 root    512 Aug  5 20:11 /etc/../
$ ls -ldi /. /..                      both . and .. have i-node number 2
     2 drwxr-xr-x 13 root    512 Aug  5 20:11 /./
     2 drwxr-xr-x 13 root    512 Aug  5 20:11 /../
```

1.2 Unix is a multiprogramming or multitasking system. Other processes were running at the time this program was run.

1.3 Since the *ptr* argument to perror is a pointer, perror could modify the string that *ptr* points to. The qualifier const, however, says that perror does not modify what the pointer points to. The error number argument to strerror, however, is an integer, and since C passes all arguments by value, the strerror function couldn't modify this value even if it wanted to. (If the handling of function arguments in C is not clear, you should review Section 5.2 of Kernighan and Ritchie [1988].)

1.4   It is possible for the calls to `fflush`, `fprintf`, and `vprintf` to modify `errno`. If they did modify its value and we didn't save it, the error message finally printed would be incorrect.

This specific problem has shown up in many historical programs that didn't save `errno` as we have done. The classic error message often printed was "Not a type-writer." In Section 5.4 we'll see that the standard I/O library changes the buffering of some standard I/O streams, based on whether the stream refers to a terminal device or not. The function `isatty` (Section 11.9) is usually called to determine if the stream refers to a terminal device. If the stream doesn't refer to a terminal device, `errno` can be set to `ENOTTY`, causing this error. Program C.1 shows this feature.

```
#include     <stdio.h>

/*
 * The following prints errno=25 (ENOTTY) under 4.3BSD and SVR2,
 * when stdout is redirected to a file.
 * Under SVR4 and 4.3+BSD it works OK.
 */

int
main()
{
    int         fd;
    extern int  errno;

    if ( (fd = open("/no/such/file", 0)) < 0) {
        printf("open error: ");
        printf("errno = %d\n", errno);
    }
    exit(0);
}
```

Program C.1   Show `errno` interaction with `printf`.

Running this program we have

```
$ grep BSD /etc/motd
4.3 BSD UNIX #29: Thu Mar 29 11:14:13 MST 1990
$ a.out
open error: errno = 2     works correctly because stdout is a terminal device
$ a.out > temp.foo
$ cat temp.foo
open error: errno = 25    wrong
```

1.5   During the year 2038. (Actually, a more important date is January 1, 2000, when many computer programs across the world could break.)

1.6   Approximately 248 days.

Chapter 2

2.1   The following technique is used by 4.3+BSD. The primitive data types that can appear in multiple headers are defined with an uppercase name in the header `<machine/ansi.h>`. For example,

```
#ifndef _ANSI_H_
#define _ANSI_H_

#define _CLOCK_T_  unsigned long
#define _SIZE_T_   unsigned int
...

#endif  /* _ANSI_H_ */
```

In each of the six headers that can define the `size_t` primitive system data type, we have the sequence

```
#ifdef  _SIZE_T_
typedef _SIZE_T_  size_t;
#undef  _SIZE_T_
#endif
```

This way the actual `typedef` is only executed once.

Chapter 3

3.1   All disk I/O goes through the kernel's block buffers (also called the kernel's buffer cache). The exception to this is I/O on a raw disk device, which we aren't considering. Chapter 3 of Bach [1986] describes the operation of this buffer cache. Since the data that we `read` or `write` is buffered by the kernel, the term "unbuffered I/O" refers to the fact that there is no automatic buffering in the user process with these two functions. Each `read` or `write` invokes a single system call.

3.3   Each call to open gives us a new file table entry. But since both opens reference the same file, both file table entries point to the same v-node table entry. The call to dup references the existing file table entry. We show this in Figure C.1. An `F_SETFD` on `fd1` affects only the file descriptor flags for `fd1`. But an `F_SETFL` on `fd1` affects the file table entry that both `fd1` and `fd2` point to.

3.4   If `fd` is 1, then the `dup2(fd, 1)` returns 1 without closing descriptor 1. (Remember our discussion of this in Section 3.12.) After the three calls to dup2 all three descriptors point to the same file table entry. Nothing needs to be closed.

If `fd` is 3, however, after the three calls to dup2 there are four descriptors pointing to the same file table entry. In this case we need to close descriptor 3.

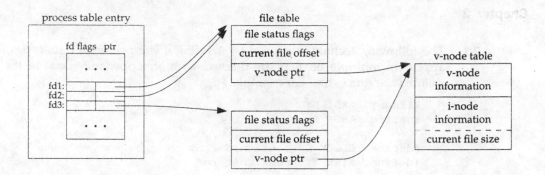

Figure C.1 Result of dup and open.

3.5 Since the shells process their command line from left to right, the command

```
a.out > outfile 2>&1
```

first sets standard output to `outfile` and then dups standard output onto descriptor 2 (standard error). The result is that standard output and standard error are set to the same file. Descriptors 1 and 2 both point to the same file table entry. With

```
a.out 2>&1 > outfile
```

however, the dup is executed first, causing descriptor 2 to be the terminal (assuming the command is run interactively). Then standard output is redirected to the file `outfile`. The result is that descriptor 1 points to the file table entry for `outfile` and descriptor 2 points to the file table entry for the terminal.

3.6 You can still `lseek` and `read` anywhere in the file, but a `write` automatically resets the file offset to the end of file before the data is actually written. This makes it impossible to `write` anywhere other than at the end of file.

Chapter 4

4.1 If `stat` is called, it always tries to follow a symbolic link (Figure 4.10), so the program will never print a file type of "symbolic link." For the example shown in the text, where `/bin` is a symbolic link to `/usr/bin`, `stat` reports that `/bin` is a directory, not a symbolic link. If the symbolic link points to a nonexistent file, `stat` returns an error.

4.2 The following lines can be added to `ourhdr.h`.

```
#if defined(S_IFLNK) && !defined(S_ISLNK)
#define S_ISLNK(mode)   (((mode) & S_IFMT) == S_IFLNK)
#endif
```

This is an example of how our own header can mask certain system differences.

4.3   All permissions are turned off.

```
$ umask 777
$ date > temp.foo
$ ls -l temp.foo
---------- 1 stevens      29 Jan 14 06:39 temp.foo
```

4.4   The following shows what happens when user-read permission is turned off.

```
$ date > foo
$ chmod u-r foo                         turn off user-read permission
$ ls -l foo                             verify the file's permissions
--w-rw-r-- 1 stevens      29 Jul 31 09:00 foo
$ cat foo                               and try to read it
cat: foo: Permission denied
```

4.5   If we try to create a file that already exists, using either open or creat, the file's access permission bits are not changed. We can verify this by running Program 4.3.

```
$ rm foo bar                            delete the files in case they already exist
$ date > foo                            create them with some data
$ date > bar
$ chmod a-r foo bar                     turn off all read permissions
$ ls -l foo bar                         verify their permissions
--w--w---- 1 stevens      29 Jul 31 10:47 bar
--w--w---- 1 stevens      29 Jul 31 10:47 foo
$ a.out                                 run Program 4.3
$ ls -l foo bar                         check permissions and sizes
--w--w---- 1 stevens       0 Jul 31 10:47 bar
--w--w---- 1 stevens       0 Jul 31 10:47 foo
```

Notice that the permissions didn't change but the files were truncated.

4.6   The size of a directory should never be 0 since there should always be entries for dot and dot-dot. The size of a symbolic link is the number of characters in the pathname contained in the symbolic link, and this pathname must always contain at least one character.

4.8   The kernel has a default setting for the file access permission bits when it creates a new core file. In this example it was rw-r--r--. This default value may or may not be modified by the umask value. The shell also has a default setting for the file access permission bits when it creates a new file for redirection. In this example it was rw-rw-rw- and this value is always modified by our current umask. In this example our umask was 02.

4.9   We can't use du because it requires either the name of the file, as in

```
du tempfile
```

or a directory name, as in

```
du .
```

But when the unlink function returns, the directory entry for tempfile is gone. The du . command just shown would not account for the space still taken by tempfile. We have to use the df command in this example, to see the actual amount of free space on the filesystem.

4.10 If the link being removed is not the last link to the file, the file is not removed. In this case the changed-status time of the file is updated. But if the link being removed is the last link to the file, it makes no sense to update this time, because all the information about the file (the i-node) is removed with the file.

4.11 We recursively call our function dopath after opening a directory with opendir. Assuming that opendir uses a single file descriptor this means that each time we descend one level we use another descriptor. (We assume the descriptor isn't closed until we're finished with a directory and call closedir.) This limits the depth of the filesystem tree that we can traverse to the maximum number of open descriptors for the process. Notice that the SVR4 function ftw allows the caller to specify the number of descriptors to use, implying that this implementation can close and reuse descriptors.

4.13 The chroot function is used by the Internet File Transfer Program (FTP) to aid in security. Users without accounts on a system (termed "anonymous FTP") are placed in a separate directory and a chroot is done to that directory. This prevents the user from accessing any file outside this new root directory.

chroot can also be used to build a copy of a filesystem hierarchy at a new location and then modify this new copy without changing the original filesystem. This could be used, for example, to test the installation of new software packages.

chroot can be executed only by the superuser, and once you change the root of a process, it (and all its descendants) can never get back to the original root.

4.14 First call stat to fetch the three times for the file, then call utime to set the desired value. The value that we don't want to change in the call to utime should be the corresponding value from stat.

4.15 finger(1) calls stat on the mailbox. The last-modification time is the time that mail was last received, and the last-access time is when the mail was last read.

4.16 Both cpio and tar store only the modification time (st_mtime) on the archive. The access time isn't stored because its value corresponds to the time the archive was created, since the file has to be read to be archived. The -a option to cpio has it reset the access time of each input file after the file has been read. This way the creation of the archive doesn't change the access time. (Resetting the access time, however, does modify the changed-status time.) The changed-status time isn't stored on the archive because we can't set this value on extraction even if it was archived. (The utime function can change only the access time and the modification time.)

When the archive is read back (extracted), tar, by default, restores the modification time to the value on the archive. The m option to tar tells it to not restore the modification time from the archive—instead the modification time is set to the time of extraction. In all cases with tar, the access time after extraction will be the time of extraction.

On the other hand, cpio sets the access time and the modification time to the time of extraction. By default it doesn't try to set the modification time to the value on the archive. The −m option to cpio has it set both the access time and the modification time to the value that was archived.

4.17 Some versions of file(1) call utime to reset the file's access time, trying to undo the fact that read updates the access time. Doing this, however, updates the changed-status time.

4.18 The kernel has no inherent limit on the depth of a directory tree. But many commands will fail on pathnames that exceed PATH_MAX. Program C.2 creates a directory tree that is 100 levels deep, with each level being a 45-character name. We are able to create this structure and obtain the absolute pathname of the directory at the 100th level using getcwd. (We have to call realloc numerous times to obtain a buffer that is large enough.) Running this program gives us

```
$ a.out
getcwd failed, size = 1025: Result too large
getcwd failed, size = 1125: Result too large
...                        33 more lines
getcwd failed, size = 4525: Result too large
length = 4613
                    the 4613-byte pathname is printed here
```

We are not able to archive this directory, however, using either tar or cpio. Both complain of a filename that is too long. (With cpio it is the find(1) program that complains.) The command rm −r also fails because of the long pathname. (How can you delete the directory tree?)

4.19 The /dev directory has all write permissions turned off to prevent a normal user from removing the filenames in the directory. This means the unlink fails.

Chapter 5

5.2 fgets reads up through and including the next newline *or* until the buffer is full (leaving room, of course, for the terminating null). Also, fputs writes everything in the buffer until it hits a null byte—it doesn't care if there is a newline in the buffer or not. So, if MAXLINE is too small, both functions still work, they're just called more often than they would be if the buffer were larger.

If either of these functions removed or added the newline (as gets and puts do) then we would have to assure that our buffer was big enough for the largest line.

5.3 The function call

```
printf("");
```

returns 0 since no characters are output.

```c
#include        <sys/types.h>
#include        <sys/stat.h>
#include        <fcntl.h>
#include        "ourhdr.h"

#define DEPTH   100             /* directory depth */
#define MYHOME  "/home/stevens"
#define NAME    "alonglonglonglonglonglonglonglonglonglongname"

int
main(void)
{
    int     i, size;
    char    *path;

    if (chdir(MYHOME) < 0)
        err_sys("chdir error");

    for (i = 0; i < DEPTH; i++) {
        if (mkdir(NAME, DIR_MODE) < 0)
            err_sys("mkdir failed, i = %d", i);
        if (chdir(NAME) < 0)
            err_sys("chdir failed, i = %d", i);
    }
    if (creat("afile", FILE_MODE) < 0)
        err_sys("creat error");

    /*
     * The deep directory is created, with a file at the leaf.
     * Now let's try and obtain its pathname.
     */

    path = path_alloc(&size);
    for ( ; ; ) {
        if (getcwd(path, size) != NULL)
            break;
        else {
            err_ret("getcwd failed, size = %d", size);
            size += 100;
            if ( (path = realloc(path, size)) == NULL)
                err_sys("realloc error");
        }
    }
    printf("length = %d\n%s\n", strlen(path), path);

    exit(0);
}
```

Program C.2 Create a deep directory tree.

5.4 This is a common error with the standard I/O library. The return value from getc (and hence getchar) is an integer, not a character. Since EOF is often defined to be –1, if the system uses signed characters, the code normally works. But if the system uses unsigned characters, after the EOF returned by getchar is stored as an unsigned character, it no longer equals –1, so the loop never terminates.

5.5 A 5-character prefix, a 4-character per-process unique identifier, and a 5-character per-system unique identifier (the process ID) equals 14 characters, the traditional Unix limit on a filename.

5.6 Call fsync after each call to fflush. The argument to fsync is obtained with the fileno function. Calling fsync without calling fflush might do nothing, if all the data were still in memory buffers.

5.7 Standard input and standard output are both line buffered when the programs are run interactively. When fgets is called, standard output is automatically flushed.

Chapter 6

6.1 Under SVR4 the functions to access the shadow password file are documented in the getspent(3) manual page. To compare an encrypted password we can't use the value returned in the pw_passwd field by the functions described in Section 6.2, since that field is not the encrypted password. Instead we need to find the user's entry in the shadow file and use the field in the shadow file that contains the encrypted password.

With 4.3+BSD the shadowing of the password file is done automatically. When the passwd structure is returned by either getpwnam or getpwuid, the field pw_passwd is filled in with the encrypted password only if the caller's **effective** user ID is 0.

6.2 Under SVR4 Program C.3 prints the encrypted password. Unless this program is run with superuser permissions, the call to getspnam fails with an error of EACCES. Under 4.3+BSD Program C.4 prints the encrypted password, if the program is run with superuser permissions. Otherwise the value returned in pw_passwd is an asterisk.

6.4 Program C.5 prints the date in a format similar to date. Running this program gives us

```
$ echo $TZ                            author's default
MST7
$ a.out
Wed Jan 15 06:48:57 MST 1992
$ TZ=EST5EDT a.out                    U.S. East Coast
Wed Jan 15 08:49:06 EST 1992
$ TZ=JST-9 a.out                      Japan
Wed Jan 15 22:49:12 JST 1992
```

```
#include        <sys/types.h>
#include        <shadow.h>
#include        "ourhdr.h"

int
main(void)          /* SVR4 version */
{
    struct spwd *ptr;

    if ( (ptr = getspnam("stevens")) == NULL)
        err_sys("getspnam error");

    printf("sp_pwdp = %s\n",
                ptr->sp_pwdp == NULL || ptr->sp_pwdp[0] == 0 ?
                "(null)" : ptr->sp_pwdp);
    exit(0);
}
```

Program C.3 Print encrypted password under SVR4

```
#include        <sys/types.h>
#include        <pwd.h>
#include        "ourhdr.h"

int
main(void)          /* 4.3+BSD version */
{
    struct passwd    *ptr;

    if ( (ptr = getpwnam("stevens")) == NULL)
        err_sys("getpwnam error");

    printf("pw_passwd = %s\n",
                ptr->pw_passwd == NULL || ptr->pw_passwd[0] == 0 ?
                "(null)" : ptr->pw_passwd);
    exit(0);
}
```

Program C.4 Print encrypted password under 4.3+BSD

Chapter 7

7.1   It appears that the return value from `printf` (the number of characters output)
       becomes the return value of `main`. Not all systems exhibit this property.

7.2   When the program is run interactively, standard output is usually line buffered, so
       the actual output occurs when each newline is output. If standard output were

```
#include     <time.h>
#include     "ourhdr.h"

int
main(void)
{
    time_t       caltime;
    struct tm    *tm;
    char         line[MAXLINE];

    if ( (caltime = time(NULL)) == -1)
        err_sys("time error");
    if ( (tm = localtime(&caltime)) == NULL)
        err_sys("localtime error");

    if (strftime(line, MAXLINE, "%a %b %d %X %Z %Y\n", tm) == 0)
        err_sys("strftime error");
    fputs(line, stdout);

    exit(0);
}
```

Program C.5 Print the time and date in a format similar to date(1).

directed to a file, however, it would probably be fully buffered, and the actual output wouldn't occur until the standard I/O cleanup is performed.

7.3   On most Unix systems there is no way to do this. Copies of argc and argv are not kept in global variables like environ.

7.4   This provides a way to terminate the process when it tries to dereference a null pointer, a common C programming error.

7.5   The definitions are:

```
typedef void     Exitfunc(void);

int atexit(Exitfunc *func);
```

7.6   calloc initializes the memory that it allocates to all zero bits. ANSI C does not guarantee that this is the same as either a floating point 0 or a null pointer.

7.7   The heap and stack aren't allocated until a program is executed by one of the exec functions (described in Section 8.9).

7.8   The executable file (a.out) contains symbol table information that can be helpful in debugging a core file. To remove this information the strip(1) command is used. Executing this command on the two a.out files reduces their size to 98304 and 16384.

7.9   When shared libraries are not used, a large portion of the executable file is occupied by the standard I/O library.

7.10   The code is incorrect since it references the automatic integer `val` through a pointer after the automatic variable is no longer in existence. Automatic variables declared after the left brace that starts a compound statement disappear after the matching right brace.

Chapter 8

8.1   Replace the call to `printf` with the lines

```
i = printf("pid = %d, glob = %d, var = %d\n",
                                   getpid(), glob, var);
sprintf(buf, "%d\n", i);
write(STDOUT_FILENO, buf, strlen(buf));
```

You need to define the variables `i` and `buf` also.

This assumes the standard I/O stream `stdout` is closed when the child calls `exit`, not the file descriptor `STDOUT_FILENO`. Some versions of the standard I/O library close the file descriptor associated with standard output, which would cause the `write` to standard output to also fail. In this case, `dup` standard output to another descriptor and use this new descriptor for the `write`.

8.2   Consider Program C.6. When `vfork` is called, the parent's stack pointer points to the stack frame for the `f1` function that calls `vfork`. Figure C.2 shows this.

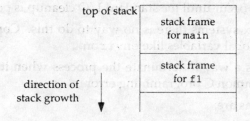

Figure C.2   Stack frames when `vfork` is called.

`vfork` causes the child to execute first and the child returns from `f1`. The child then calls `f2` and its stack frame overwrites the previous stack frame for `f1`. The child then zeroes out the automatic variable `buf`, setting 1000 bytes of the stack frame to 0. The child returns from `f2`, and then calls `_exit`, but the contents of the stack beneath the stack frame for `main` have been changed. The parent then resumes after the call to `vfork` and does a return from `f1`. The return information is often stored in the stack frame, and that information has probably been modified by the child. What happens with this example, after the parent resumes, depends on many implementation features of your Unix system (where in the stack frame the return information is stored, what information in the stack frame

```
#include      <sys/types.h>
#include      "ourhdr.h"

static void f1(void), f2(void);

int
main(void)
{
    f1();
    f2();
    _exit(0);
}

static void
f1(void)
{
    pid_t    pid;

    if ( (pid = vfork()) < 0)
        err_sys("vfork error");
    /* child and parent both return */
}

static void
f2(void)
{
    char    buf[1000];        /* automatic variables */
    int     i;

    for (i = 0; i < sizeof(buf); i++)
        buf[i] = 0;
}
```

Program C.6 Incorrect use of vfork.

is wiped out when the automatic variables are modified, and so on). The normal result is a core file, but your results may differ.

8.3 In Program 8.7 we have the parent output first. When the parent is done the child writes its output, but we let the parent terminate. Whether the parent terminates or whether the child finishes its output first depends on the kernel's scheduling of the two processes (another race condition). When the parent terminates, the shell starts up the next program and this next program can interfere with the output from the previous child.

We can prevent this from happening by not letting the parent terminate until the child has also finished its output. Replace the code following the fork with the following:

```
    else if (pid == 0) {
        WAIT_PARENT();                /* parent goes first */
        charatatime("output from child\n");
        TELL_PARENT(getppid()); /* tell parent we're done */
    } else {
        charatatime("output from parent\n");
        TELL_CHILD(pid);              /* tell child we're done */
        WAIT_CHILD();                 /* wait for child to finish */
    }
```

We won't see this happen if we let the child go first, since the shell doesn't start the next program until the parent terminates.

8.4 The same value (/home/stevens/bin/testinterp) is printed for argv[2]. The reason is that execlp ends up calling execve with the same *pathname* as when we call execl directly. Recall Figure 8.6.

8.5 A function is not provided to return the saved set-user-ID. Instead, we must save the effective user ID when the process is started.

8.6 Program C.7 creates a zombie.

```
#include    "ourhdr.h"

int
main(void)
{
    pid_t   pid;

    if ( (pid = fork()) < 0)
        err_sys("fork error");
    else if (pid == 0)        /* child */
        exit(0);

    /* parent */
    sleep(4);

    system("ps");

    exit(0);
}
```

Program C.7 Create a zombie and look at it's status with ps.

Zombies are usually designated by ps(1) with a status of "Z".

```
$ a.out
  PID TT STAT  TIME COMMAND
 5940 p3 S    0:00 a.out
 5941 p3 Z    0:00 <defunct>        the zombie
 5942 p3 S    0:00 sh -c ps
 5943 p3 R    0:00 ps
```

Chapter 9

9.1 init is the process that learns when a terminal user logs out, because init is the parent of the login shell and receives the SIGCHLD signal when the login shell terminates.

For a network login, however, init is not involved. Instead the login entries in the utmp and wtmp files, and their corresponding logout entries are usually written by the process that handles the login and detects the logout (telnetd in our example).

Chapter 10

10.1 The program terminates the first time we send it a signal. This is because the pause function returns whenever a signal is caught.

10.2 Program C.8 implements the raise function.

```
#include    <sys/types.h>
#include    <signal.h>
#include    <unistd.h>

int
raise(int signo)
{
    return( kill(getpid(), signo) );
}
```

Program C.8 Implementation of raise function.

10.3 Figure C.3 shows the stack frames.

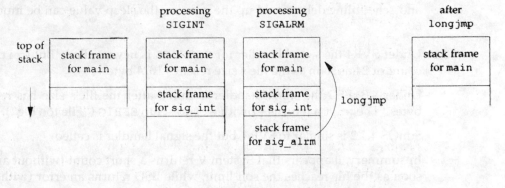

Figure C.3 Stack frames before and after longjmp.

The longjmp from sig_alrm back to main effectively aborts the call to sig_int.

10.4 We again have a race condition, this time between the first call to `alarm` and the call to `setjmp`. If the process is blocked by the kernel between these two function calls, the alarm will go off, the signal handler is called, and `longjmp` is called. But since `setjmp` was never called, the buffer `env_alrm` is not set. The operation of `longjmp` is undefined if its jump buffer has not been initialized by `setjmp`.

10.5 See "Implementing Software Timers" by Don Libes (*C Users Journal*, Vol. 8, no. 11, Nov. 1990) for an example.

10.7 If we just called `_exit` the termination status of the process would not show that it was terminated by the `SIGABRT` signal.

10.8 If the signal was sent by a process owned by some other user, the process has to be set-user-ID to either root or to the owner of the receiving process or the `kill` won't work. Therefore, the real user ID provides more information to the receiver of the signal.

10.10 On one system used by the author the value for the number of seconds increased by one about every 60–90 minutes. This skew is because each call to `sleep` schedules an event for a time in the future, but we're not awakened exactly when that event occurs (because of CPU scheduling). Plus there is a finite amount of time required for our process to start running and call `sleep` again.

A program such as the BSD `cron` has to fetch the current time every minute. It also has to set its first sleep period so that it wakes up at the beginning of the next minute. (Convert the current time to the local time and look at the `tm_sec` value.) Every minute, it sets the next sleep period so that it'll wake up at the next minute. Most of the calls will probably be `sleep(60)`, with an occasional `sleep(59)` to resynchronize with the next minute. But if at some point the process takes a long time executing commands or if the system gets heavily loaded and scheduling delays hold up the process, the sleep value can be much less than 60.

10.11 Under SVR4 the signal handler for `SIGXFSZ` is never called. But `write` returns a count of 24 as soon as the file's size reaches 1024 bytes.

Under 4.3+BSD the signal handler is called after the file's size has reached 1500 bytes. The `write` returns −1 with `errno` set to `EFBIG` ("File too big").

SunOS 4.1.2 is similar to SVR4, but the signal handler is called.

In summary, it appears that System V returns a short count (without any error) as soon as the file reaches the soft limit, while BSD returns an error (without writing any data) when it determines the limit has been passed.

10.12 The results depend on the implementation of the standard I/O library—how the `fwrite` function handles an interrupted `write`.

Chapter 11

11.1 Note that you have to terminate the reset command with a linefeed character, not a return, since the terminal is in noncanonical mode.

11.2 It builds a table for each of the 128 characters and sets the high-order bit (the parity bit) according to the user's specification. It then uses eight-bit I/O, handling the parity generation itself.

11.3 Under SVR4 execute stty -a with standard input redirected to the terminal running vi. This shows that vi sets MIN to 1 and TIME to 1. The reads wait for at least one character to be typed, but after that character is entered, read waits only one-tenth of a second for additional characters before returning.

11.4 Under SVR4 the extended general terminal interface is used. This is documented in the termiox(7) manual page in AT&T [1991]. Under 4.3+BSD the flags CCTS_OFLOW and CRTS_IFLOW in the c_cflag field are used (Figure 11.3).

Chapter 12

12.1 The program works fine (it doesn't get the ENOLCK error). The first time through the loop we call writew_lock, write, and un_lock. The call to un_lock releases the lock from the current end of file through any future end of file, as before, leaving just the first byte locked. We then go through the loop again, but this time the call to writew_lock causes this new lock that we've specified to be merged with the existing lock on the first byte. Figure C.4 shows the state of the file after the second time through the loop.

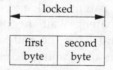

Figure C.4 State of record lock after second time through loop.

Each time through the loop we extend this single lock by an additional byte. Since the kernel merges each lock with the existing lock, only a single lock is maintained by the kernel, and it never runs out of lock structures.

12.2 Both SVR4 and 4.3+BSD define the fd_set data type to be a structure that contains a single member: an array of long integers. One bit in this array corresponds to each descriptor. The four FD_ macros then manipulate this array of longs, turning specific bits on and off and testing specific bits.

One reason that the data type is defined to be a structure containing an array and not just an array is to allow variables of type fd_set to be assigned to one another with the C assignment statement.

12.3 SVR4 and 4.3+BSD allow us to define the constant `FD_SETSIZE` before including the header `<sys/types.h>`. For example, we can write

```
#define FD_SETSIZE  2048
#include     <sys/types.h>
```

to define the `fd_set` data type to accommodate 2048 descriptors.

12.4 The following table lists the functions that do similar things.

FD_ZERO	sigemptyset
FD_SET	sigaddset
FD_CLR	sigdelset
FD_ISSET	sigismember

There is not an `FD_xxx` function that corresponds to `sigfillset`. With signal sets the pointer to the set is always the first argument and the signal number is the second argument. With descriptor sets the descriptor number is the first argument and the pointer to the set is the next argument.

12.5 Up to five different types of information are returned by `getmsg`: the data itself, the length of the data, the control information, the length of the control information, and the flags.

12.6 Program C.9 shows an implementation using `select`. As the BSD `usleep`(3) manual page states, `usleep` utilizes the `setitimer` interval timer and performs eight system calls each time it's called. It correctly interacts with other timers set by the calling process, and it is not interrupted if a signal is caught.

Program C.10 shows an implementation using `poll`.

12.7 No. What we would like to do is have `TELL_WAIT` create a temporary file and use one byte for the parent's lock and one byte for the child's lock. `WAIT_CHILD` would have the parent wait to obtain a lock on the child's byte, and `TELL_PARENT` would have the child release the lock on the child's byte. The problem, however, is that calling `fork` releases all the locks in the child, so the child can't start off with any locks of its own.

12.8 A solution using `select` is shown in Program C.11. The same technique can be used with `poll`.

Under SVR4 and SunOS 4.1.1 the values calculated using both `select` and `poll` equal the values from Figure 2.6. Under 4.3+BSD the value calculated using `select` is 3073.

12.9 Under SVR4, 4.3+BSD, and SunOS 4.1.2 Program 12.14 does update the last-access time for the input file.

Chapter 13

13.1 If the process calls `chroot` it will not be able to open `/dev/log`. The solution is for the daemon to call `openlog` with an *option* of `LOG_NDELAY`, before calling

```
#include        <sys/types.h>
#include        <sys/time.h>
#include        <stddef.h>
#include        "ourhdr.h"

void
sleep_us(unsigned int nusecs)
{
    struct timeval  tval;

    tval.tv_sec = nusecs / 1000000;
    tval.tv_usec = nusecs % 1000000;
    select(0, NULL, NULL, NULL, &tval);
}
```

Program C.9 Implementation of sleep_us using select.

```
#include        <sys/types.h>
#include        <poll.h>
#include        <stropts.h>
#include        "ourhdr.h"

void
sleep_us(unsigned int nusecs)
{
    struct pollfd   dummy;
    int             timeout;

    if ( (timeout = nusecs / 1000) <= 0)
        timeout = 1;
    poll(&dummy, 0, timeout);
}
```

Program C.10 Implementation of sleep_us using poll.

chroot. This opens the special device file (the Unix domain datagram socket), yielding a descriptor that is still valid, even after a call to chroot. This scenario is encountered in daemons such as tftpd (the Trivial File Transfer Daemon) that specifically call chroot for security reasons, but still need to call syslog to log error conditions.

13.3 Program C.12 shows a solution. The results depend on the implementation and whether we close file descriptors 0, 1, and 2. The reason closing the descriptors affects the outcome is that when the program is started they are connected to the controlling terminal. Closing the three descriptors after calling daemon_init means getlogin won't have a controlling terminal, so it won't be able to look in the utmp file for our login entry.

```
#include        <sys/types.h>
#include        <sys/time.h>
#include        "ourhdr.h"

int
main(void)
{
    int             i, n, fd[2];
    fd_set          writeset;
    struct timeval  tv;

    if (pipe(fd) < 0)
        err_sys("pipe error");
    FD_ZERO(&writeset);

    for (n = 0; ; n++) { /* write 1 byte at a time until pipe is full */
        FD_SET(fd[1], &writeset);
        tv.tv_sec = tv.tv_usec = 0;      /* don't wait at all */
        if ( (i = select(fd[1]+1, NULL, &writeset, NULL, &tv)) < 0)
            err_sys("select error");
        else if (i == 0)
            break;
        if (write(fd[1], "a", 1) != 1)
            err_sys("write error");
    }
    printf("pipe capacity = %d\n", n);
    exit(0);
}
```

Program C.11 Calculation of pipe capacity using select.

```
#include        "ourhdr.h"

int
main(void)
{
    char    *ptr, buff[MAXLINE];

    daemon_init();

    close(0);
    close(1);
    close(2);

    ptr = getlogin();
    sprintf(buff, "login name: %s\n",
                    (ptr == NULL) ? "(empty)" : ptr);
    write(3, buff, strlen(buff));
    exit(0);
}
```

Program C.12 Call daemon_init and then obtain login name.

Under 4.3+BSD, however, the login name is maintained in the process table and copied across a fork. This means the process can always get the login name, unless the parent didn't have a login name (such as init when the system is bootstrapped).

Chapter 14

14.1 If the write end of the pipe is never closed, the reader never sees an end of file. The pager program blocks forever reading from its standard input.

14.2 The parent terminates right after writing the last line to the pipe. The read end of the pipe is automatically closed when the parent terminates. But the parent is probably running ahead of the child by one pipe buffer, since the child (the pager program) is waiting for us to look at a page of output. If we're running a shell such as the KornShell with interactive command-line editing enabled, the shell probably changes the terminal mode when our parent terminates and the shell prints a prompt. This undoubtably interferes with the pager program, which has also modified the terminal mode. (Most pager programs set the terminal to non-canonical mode when awaiting input to proceed to the next page.)

14.3 popen returns a file pointer, because the shell is executed. But the shell can't execute the nonexistent command so it prints

```
sh: a.out: not found
```

on the standard error and terminates with an exit status of 1. pclose returns this exit status of 1.

14.4 When the parent terminates, look at its termination status with the shell. For the Bourne shell and KornShell the command is echo $?. The number printed is 128 plus the signal number.

14.5 First add the declaration

```
FILE    *fpin, *fpout;
```

Then use fdopen to associate the pipe descriptors with a standard I/O stream and set the streams to be line buffered. Do this before the while loop that reads from standard input:

```
if ( (fpin = fdopen(fd2[0], "r")) == NULL)
    err_sys("fdopen error");
if ( (fpout = fdopen(fd1[1], "w")) == NULL)
    err_sys("fdopen error");
if (setvbuf(fpin, NULL, _IOLBF, 0) < 0)
    err_sys("setvbuf error");
if (setvbuf(fpout, NULL, _IOLBF, 0) < 0)
    err_sys("setvbuf error");
```

The write and read in the while loop are replaced with

```
    if (fputs(line, fpout) == EOF)
        err_sys("fputs error to pipe");
    if (fgets(line, MAXLINE, fpin) == NULL) {
        err_msg("child closed pipe");
        break;
    }
```

14.6 The `system` function calls `wait` and the first child to terminate is the child generated by `popen`. Since that's not the child that `system` created, it calls `wait` again,
and blocks until the `sleep` is done. `system` then returns. When `pclose` calls
`wait`, an error is returned since there are no more children to `wait` for. `pclose`
returns an error.

14.7 `select` indicates that the descriptor is readable. When we call `read`, after all the
data has been read, it returns 0 to indicate the end of file. But with `poll` (assuming the pipe is a streams device), the `POLLHUP` event is returned, and this event
may be returned while there is still data to be read. Once we have read all the
data, however, `read` returns 0 to indicate the end of file. After all the data has
been read, the `POLLIN` event is not returned, even though we need to issue a
`read` to receive the end of file notification (the return of 0).

With an output descriptor that refers to a pipe that has been closed by the reader,
`select` indicates that the descriptor is writable. But when we call `write` the
`SIGPIPE` signal is generated. If we either ignore this signal or return from its signal handler, `write` returns an error of `EPIPE`. With `poll`, however, if the pipe is
a streams device, `poll` returns with an indication of `POLLHUP` for the descriptor.

14.8 Anything written by the child to standard error appears wherever the parent's
standard error would appear. To send standard error back to the parent, include
the shell redirection `2>&1` in the *cmdstring*.

14.9 `popen` `forks` a child, and the child `execs` the Bourne shell. The shell in turn calls
`fork`, and the child of the shell `execs` the command string. When *cmdstring* terminates, the shell is waiting for this to happen. The shell then `exits`, which is
what the `waitpid` in `pclose` is waiting for.

14.10 The trick is to open the FIFO twice—once for reading and once for writing. We
never use the descriptor that is opened for writing, but leaving that descriptor
open prevents and end of file from being generated when the number of clients
goes from 1 to 0. Opening the FIFO twice requires some care, as a nonblocking
open is required. We have to do a nonblocking, read-only open first, followed by
a blocking open for write-only. (If we tried a nonblocking open for write-only
first, it would return an error.) We then turn off nonblocking for the read descriptor. Program C.13 shows the code for this.

14.11 Randomly reading a message from an active queue would interfere with the
client–server protocol, as either a client request or a server's response would be
lost. To read the queue, all the process needs to know is the identifier for the
queue, and for the queue to allow world-read.

```
#include     <sys/types.h>
#include     <sys/stat.h>
#include     <fcntl.h>
#include     "ourhdr.h"

#define FIFO    "temp.fifo"

int
main(void)
{
    int     fdread, fdwrite;

    unlink(FIFO);
    if (mkfifo(FIFO, FILE_MODE) < 0)
        err_sys("mkfifo error");

    if ( (fdread = open(FIFO, O_RDONLY | O_NONBLOCK)) < 0)
        err_sys("open error for reading");
    if ( (fdwrite = open(FIFO, O_WRONLY)) < 0)
        err_sys("open error for writing");

    clr_fl(fdread, O_NONBLOCK);

    exit(0);
}
```

Program C.13 Opening a FIFO for reading and writing, without blocking.

14.13 We never store actual addresses in a shared memory segment, since it's possible for the server and all the clients to attach the segment at different addresses. Instead, when a linked list is built in a shared memory segment, the list pointers should be stored as offsets to other objects in the shared memory segment. These offsets are formed by subtracting the start of the shared memory segment from the actual address of the object.

14.14 Figure C.5 shows the relevant events.

Chapter 15

15.3 A *declaration* specifies the attributes (such as the data type) of a set of identifiers. If the declaration also causes storage to be allocated, it is called a *definition*.

In the opend.h header we declare the three global variables with the extern storage class. These declarations do not cause storage to be allocated for the variables. In the main.c file we define the three global variables. Sometimes we'll also initialize a global variable when we define it, but typically we let the C default apply.

Parent i set to	Child i set to	Shared value set to	update returns	Comment
		0		initialized by mmap
	1			child runs first, then is blocked
0				parent runs
		1		
			0	then parent is blocked
		2		child resumes
			1	
	3			then child is blocked
2				parent resumes
		3		
			2	then parent is blocked
		4		
			3	
	5			then child is blocked
4				parent resumes

Figure C.5 Alternation between parent and child in Program 14.12.

15.5 Both select and poll return the number of ready descriptors as the value of the function. The loop that goes through the client array can terminate when the number of ready descriptors have been processed.

Chapter 16

16.1 Our conservative locking in _db_dodelete is to avoid race conditions with db_nextrec. If the call to _db_writedat were not protected with a write lock, it would be possible to erase the data record while db_nextrec was reading that data record: db_nextrec would read an index record, determine it was not all blank, and then read the data record, which could be erased by _db_dodelete between the calls to _db_readidx and _db_readdat in db_nextrec.

16.2 Assume db_nextrec calls _db_readidx, which reads the key into the index buffer for the process. This process is then stopped by the kernel and another process runs. This other process calls db_delete, and the record being read by the other process is deleted. Both its key and data are rewritten in the two files as all blanks. The first process resumes and calls _db_readdat (from db_nextrec) and reads the all-blank data record. The read lock by db_nextrec allows it to do the read of the index record, followed by the read of the data record, as an atomic operation (with regard to other cooperating processes using the same database).

16.3 With mandatory locking other readers and writers are affected. Other reads and writes are blocked by the kernel until the locks placed by _db_writeidx and _db_writedat are removed.

Chapter 17

17.1 `psif` has to read the first two bytes of the file and compare them to `%!`. If the file is seekable, it can then rewind the file and `exec` either `lprps` or `textps`. If the file is not seekable, it has to put the two bytes that it read back onto the standard input. One way to do this is to create a pipe and `fork` a child. The parent then sets its standard input to be the pipe and `execs` either `textps` or `lprps`. The child writes the two bytes that it read to the pipe, followed by the rest of the file to be printed.

Chapter 18

18.2 Normally `getopt` is called to process only a single argument list. The global variable `optind` is initialized to 1 in the initialized data segment of the `getopt` function. But in our server we call `getopt` to process multiple argument lists—one argument list per client, so we have to reinitialize `optind` before the first call to `getopt` for each client.

18.3 We maintain the file offset of the `Systems` file in the `Client` structure. If the file is modified after we've saved this offset, but before it's used the next time, there's a good chance that the saved offset does not reference the line that it previously pointed to. While our server could detect if this file has been modified (how?), we have no way of repositioning the file offset to where it used to point to. Our only recourse if the file is modified is not to try dialing again for any client whose in-progress dial doesn't work.

18.4 The only time the `client` array can be moved around by `realloc` is when `client_add` is called, which is only after the `select`, not in the loop in which we use `cliptr`.

18.5 The commands sent to the remote system will be messed up. A check could be added to `take_put_args` to test for this.

18.6 A common technique is to require the person who modifies any of the files to tell the server, to let the server reread the files. The `SIGHUP` signal is often used for this.

18.9 You could execute the `stty` command on the remote system and parse its output, but given the wide differences in the output of this command across different Unix systems, this solution would be hard to implement.

Chapter 19

19.1 Both servers, `telnetd` and `rlogind`, run with superuser privileges, so their calls to `chown` and `chmod` succeed.

19.3 Execute

```
pty -n stty -a
```

to prevent the slave's `termios` structure and `winsize` structure from being initialized.

19.5 Unfortunately the F_SETFL command of `fcntl` doesn't allow the read–write status to be changed.

19.6 There are three process groups: (1) the login shell, (2) the `pty` parent and child, and (3) the `cat` process. The first two process groups constitute a session with the login shell as the session leader. The second session contains just the `cat` process. The first process group (the login shell) is a background process group and the other two are foreground process groups.

19.7 First `cat` terminates when it receives the end of file from its line discipline. This causes the pty slave to terminate, which causes the pty master to terminate. This in turn generates an end of file for the `pty` parent that's reading from the pty master. The parent sends SIGTERM to the child so the child terminates next. (The child doesn't catch this signal.) Finally the parent calls `exit(0)` at the end of the `main` function.

The relevant output from Program 8.17 is

```
cat        e =        270, chars =        274, stat =    0:
pty        e =        262, chars =         40, stat =   15: F        X
pty        e =        288, chars =        188, stat =    0:
```

19.8 This can be done with the shell's `echo` command and the `date(1)` command, all in a subshell.

```
#!/bin/sh
( echo "Script started on "  date ;
  pty "${SHELL:-/bin/sh}";
  echo "Script done on "  date  ) | tee typescript
```

19.9 The line discipline above the pty slave has echo enabled so whatever `pty` reads on its standard input and writes to the pty master gets echoed by default. This echoing is done by the line discipline module above the slave even though the program (`ttyname`) never reads the data.

Bibliography

Adobe Systems Inc. 1985. *PostScript Language Tutorial and Cookbook.* Addison-Wesley, Reading, Mass.

> The "blue book."

Adobe Systems Inc. 1986. *PostScript Language Reference Manual.* Addison-Wesley, Reading, Mass.

> The "red book." Appendix D of the 1985 version of this book contained detailed information on communication across a serial line with a PostScript printer. This information was removed from the 1986 version.

Adobe Systems Inc. 1988. *PostScript Language Program Design.* Addison-Wesley, Reading, Mass.

> The "green book." Chapter 12 contains information on writing a print spooler for a PostScript printer.

Aho, A. V., Kernighan, B. W., and Weinberger, P. J. 1988. *The AWK Programming Language.* Addison-Wesley, Reading, Mass.

> A complete book on the awk programming language. The version of awk described in this book is sometimes called "nawk" (for new awk).

Andrade, J. M., Carges, M. T., and Kovach, K. R. 1989. "Building a Transaction Processing System on UNIX Systems," *Proceedings of the 1989 USENIX Transaction Processing Workshop,* pp. 13–22 (May), Pittsburgh, Pa.

> A description of the AT&T Tuxedo Transaction Processing System.

ANSI. 1989. "American National Standard for Information Systems—Programming Language C," X3.159–1989, ANSI (Dec.).

> The official standard for the C language and the standard libraries.

> This standard can be ordered from Global Engineering Documents at +1 800 854 7179 or +1 714 261 1455.

Arnold, J. Q. 1986. "Shared Libraries on UNIX System V," *Proceedings of the 1986 Summer USENIX Conference,* pp. 395–404, Atlanta, Ga.

> Describes the implementation of shared libraries in SVR3.

713

AT&T. 1989. *System V Interface Definition, Third Edition.* Addison-Wesley, Reading, Mass.

> This is a four-volume set that specifies the source code interface and run-time behavior of System V. The third edition corresponds to SVR4. A fifth volume was published in 1991 containing updated versions of commands and functions from volumes 1–4.

AT&T. 1990a. *UNIX Research System Programmer's Manual, Tenth Edition, Volume I.* Saunders College Publishing, Fort Worth, Tex.

> The version of the *Unix Programmer's Manual* for the 10th Edition of Research Unix (V10). This volume contains the traditional Unix manual pages (Sections 1–9).

AT&T. 1990b. *UNIX Research System Papers, Tenth Edition, Volume II.* Saunders College Publishing, Fort Worth, Tex.

> Volume II for the 10th Edition of Research Unix (V10) contains 40 papers describing various aspects of the system.

AT&T. 1990c. *UNIX System V Release 4 BSD/XENIX Compatability Guide.* Prentice-Hall, Englewood Cliffs, N.J.

> Contains manual pages describing the compatibility library.

AT&T. 1990d. *UNIX System V Release 4 Programmer's Guide: STREAMS.* Prentice-Hall, Englewood Cliffs, N.J.

> Describes the STREAMS system in SVR4.

AT&T. 1990e. *UNIX System V/386 Release 4 Programmer's Reference Manual.* Prentice-Hall, Englewood Cliffs, N.J.

> This is the programmer's reference manual for the SVR4 implementation for the Intel 80386 processor. It contains Sections 1 (commands), 2 (system calls), 3 (subroutines), 4 (file formats), and 5 (miscellaneous facilities).

AT&T. 1991. *UNIX System V/386 Release 4 System Administrator's Reference Manual.* Prentice-Hall, Englewood Cliffs, N.J.

> This is the system administrator's reference manual for the SVR4 implementation for the Intel 80386 processor. It contains Sections 1 (commands), 4 (file formats), 5 (miscellaneous facilities), and 7 (special files).

Bach, M. J. 1986. *The Design of the UNIX Operating System.* Prentice-Hall, Englewood Cliffs, N.J.

> A book on the details of the design and implementation of the Unix operating system. Although actual Unix source code is not provided in this text (since it is proprietary to AT&T) many of the algorithms and data structures used by the Unix kernel are presented and discussed. This book describes SVR2.

Bolsky, M. I., and Korn, D. G. 1989. *The KornShell Command and Programming Language.* Prentice-Hall, Englewood Cliffs, N.J.

Chen, D., Barkley, R. E., and Lee, T. P. 1990. "Insuring Improved VM Performance: Some No-Fault Policies," *Proceedings of the 1990 Winter USENIX Conference*, pp. 11–22, Washington, D.C.

> Describes changes made to the virtual memory implementation of SVR4 to improve its performance, especially for `fork` and `exec`.

Comer, D. E. 1979. "The Ubiquitous B-Tree," *ACM Computing Surveys*, vol. 11, no. 2, pp. 121–137 (June).

Date, C. J. 1982. *An Introduction to Database Systems, Volume II.* Addison-Wesley, Reading, Mass.

Fowler, G. S., Korn, D. G., and Vo, K. P. 1989. "An Efficient File Hierarchy Walker," *Proceedings of the 1989 Summer USENIX Conference*, pp. 173–188, Baltimore, Md.

> Describes a new library function to traverse a filesystem hierarchy.

Garfinkel, S., and Spafford, G. 1991. *Practical UNIX Security*. O'Reilly & Associates, Sebastopol, Calif.

> A detailed book on Unix security.

Gingell, R. A., Lee, M., Dang, X. T., and Weeks, M. S. 1987. "Shared Libraries in SunOS," *Proceedings of the 1987 Summer USENIX Conference*, pp. 131–145, Phoenix, Ariz.

Gingell, R. A., Moran, J. P., and Shannon, W. A. 1987. "Virtual Memory Architecture in SunOS," *Proceedings of the 1987 Summer USENIX Conference*, pp. 81–94, Phoenix, Ariz.

> Describes the initial implementation of the mmap function and related issues in the virtual memory design.

Goodheart, B. 1991. *UNIX Curses Explained*. Prentice-Hall, Englewood Cliffs, N.J.

> A complete reference on terminfo and the curses library.

Hume, A. G. 1988. "A Tale of Two Greps," *Softw. Pract. and Exper.*, vol. 18, no. 11, pp. 1063–1072.

IEEE. 1990. "Information Technology—Portable Operating System Interface (POSIX) Part 1: System Application Program Interface (API) [C Language]," 1003.1–1990, IEEE (Dec.).

> This is the first of the POSIX standards, and it defines the C language systems interface standard, based on the Unix operating system. It is often called POSIX.1.

> This standard can be ordered directly from the IEEE: +1 800 678 IEEE, or +1 908 981 1393.

Kernighan, B. W., and Pike, R. 1984. *The UNIX Programming Environment*. Prentice-Hall, Englewood Cliffs, N.J.

> A general reference for additional details on Unix programming. This book covers numerous Unix commands and utilities, such as grep, sed, awk, and the Bourne shell.

Kernighan, B. W., and Ritchie, D. M. 1988. *The C Programming Language, Second Edition*. Prentice-Hall, Englewood Cliffs, N.J.

> A book on the ANSI standard version of the C programming language. Appendix B contains a description of the libraries defined by the ANSI standard.

Kleiman, S. R. 1986. "Vnodes: An Architecture for Multiple File System Types in Sun UNIX," *Proceedings of the 1986 Summer USENIX Conference*, pp. 238–247, Atlanta, Ga.

> A description of the original v-node implementation.

Korn, D. G., and Vo, K. P. 1991. "SFIO: Safe/Fast String/File IO," *Proceedings of the 1991 Summer USENIX Conference*, pp. 235–255, Nashville, Tenn.

> A description of an alternative to the standard I/O library. Available by sending e-mail:
> ```
> echo 'send attgifts/sfio.shar' | mail netlib@research.att.com.
> ```

Krieger, O., Stumm, M., and Unrau, R. 1992. "Exploiting the Advantages of Mapped Files for Stream I/O," *Proceedings of the 1992 Winter USENIX Conference*, pp. 27–42, San Francisco, Calif.

> An alternative to the standard I/O library based on mapped files.

Leffler, S. J., McKusick, M. K., Karels, M. J., and Quarterman, J. S. 1989. *The Design and Implementation of the 4.3BSD UNIX Operating System*. Addison-Wesley, Reading, Mass.

> An entire book on the 4.3BSD Unix system. This book describes the Tahoe release of 4.3BSD.

Libes, D. 1990. "expect: Curing Those Uncontrollable Fits of Interaction," *Proceedings of the 1990 Summer USENIX Conference*, pp. 183–192, Anaheim, Calif.

A description of the expect program and its implementation.

Libes, D. 1991. "expect: Scripts for Controlling Interactive Processes," *Computing Systems*, vol. 4, no. 2, pp. 99–125 (Spring).

This paper presents numerous expect scripts.

Morris, R., and Thompson, K. 1979. "UNIX Password Security," *Communications ACM*, vol. 22, no. 11, pp. 594–597 (Nov.).

A description of the history of the design of the Unix password scheme.

Nemeth, E., Snyder, G., and Seebass, S. 1989. *UNIX System Administration Handbook*. Prentice-Hall, Englewood Cliffs, N.J.

A book with many details on administering a Unix system.

Olander, D. J., McGrath, G. J., and Israel, R. K. 1986. "A Framework for Networking in System V," *Proceedings of the 1986 Summer USENIX Conference*, pp. 38–45, Atlanta, Ga.

This paper describes the original implementation of service interfaces, streams, and TLI for System V.

Plauger, P. J. 1992. *The Standard C Library*. Prentice-Hall, Englewood Cliffs, N.J.

A complete book on the ANSI C library. It contains a complete C implementation of the library.

Presotto, D. L., and Ritchie, D. M. 1990. "Interprocess Communication in the Ninth Edition UNIX System," *Softw. Pract. and Exper.*, vol. 20, no. S1, pp. S1/3-S1/17 (June).

This paper describes the IPC facilities provided by the Ninth Edition of Unix, developed at the Information Sciences Research Division of AT&T Bell Laboratories. The features are built on the stream input–output system and include full-duplex pipes, the ability to pass file descriptors between processes, and unique client connections to servers. A copy of this paper also appears in AT&T [1990b].

Redman, B. E. 1989. "UUCP UNIX-to-UNIX Copy," in *UNIX Networking*, eds. S. G. Kochan and P. H. Wood, pp. 5–48. Howard W. Sams and Company, Indianapolis, Ind.

This chapter contains additional details on Honey DanBer UUCP. It also contains a detailed history of the UUCP programs.

Ritchie, D. M. 1984. "A Stream Input-Output System," *AT&T Bell Laboratories Technical Journal*, vol. 63, no. 8, pp. 1897–1910 (Oct.).

The original paper on Streams.

Seltzer, M., and Olson, M. 1992. "LIBTP: Portable, Modular Transactions for UNIX," *Proceedings of the 1992 Winter USENIX Conference*, pp. 9–25, San Francisco, Calif.

A modification of the db(3) library from 4.3+BSD that implements transactions.

Seltzer, M., and Yigit, O. 1991. "A New Hashing Package for UNIX," *Proceedings of the 1991 Winter USENIX Conference*, pp. 173–184, Dallas, Tex.

A description of the dbm(3) library and various implementations of it, and a newer hashing package.

Stevens, W. R. 1990. *UNIX Network Programming*. Prentice-Hall, Englewood Cliffs, N.J.

A detailed book on network programming under Unix.

Stonebraker, M. R. 1981. "Operating System Support for Database Management," *Communications ACM*, vol. 24, no. 7, pp. 412–418 (July).

Strang, J., Mui, L., and O'Reilly, T. 1991. *termcap & terminfo, Third Edition*. O'Reilly & Associates, Sebastopol, Calif.

> A book on termcap and terminfo.

Thompson, K. 1978. "UNIX Implementation," *Bell Syst. Technical Journal*, vol. 57, no. 6, pp. 1931–1946 (July-Aug.).

> Describes some of the implementation details of Version 7.

Weinberger, P. J. 1982. "Making UNIX Operating Systems Safe for Databases," *Bell Syst. Technical Journal*, vol. 61, no. 9, pp. 2407–2422 (Nov.).

> Describes some problems in implementing databases in early Unix systems.

Williams, T. 1989. "Session Management in System V Release 4," *Proceedings of the 1989 Winter USENIX Conference*, pp. 365–375, San Diego, Calif.

> Describes the session architecture implemented in SVR4, which is part of POSIX.1. This includes process groups, job control, and controlling terminals. Also describes the security concerns of existing approaches.

X/Open. 1989. *X/Open Portability Guide*. Prentice-Hall, Englewood Cliffs, N.J.

> This is a set of seven volumes covering the following areas: commands and utilities (Vol. 1), system interfaces and headers (Vol. 2), supplementary definitions (Vol. 3), programming languages (Vol. 4), data management (Vol. 5), window management (Vol. 6), networking services (Vol. 7).

Index

The function subentries labeled "definition of" point to where the function prototype appears and, when applicable, to the source code for the function. Functions defined in the text that are used in later examples, such as the set_fl function in Program 3.5, are included in this index. The definitions of external functions that are part of the larger examples (Chapters 15–19) are also included in this index, to help in going through these larger examples. Also, significant functions and constants that occur in any of the examples in the text, such as select and poll, are also included in this index. Trivial functions that occur in almost every example, such as close and exit, are not referenced when they occur in examples.

352246 2623